Munsell's Annals of Albany

Volume One
Facsimile Edition of 1850

Don Rittner
With Annotations and Additions

Dedicated to John Wolcott
Historian Extraordinaire

©2021, Don Rittner

All Rights Reserved.

ISBN: 978-0-937666-63-0

New Netherland Press
Schenectady, NY
drittner@aol.com

Introduction

Between 1850 and 1859, Albany, New York printer Joel Munsell published ten volumes of *The Annals of Albany*. Each of these volumes were compendiums of historical information he collected on the history of Albany, New York and combined them, in no apparent order or category, into annual publications for a decade, with occasional edition updates. He collected scraps from newspapers, genealogy, deaths, religion, public and private organizations, maps, illustrations, and included already published pamphlets and other material connected with the history, ancient or modern, of Albany. This collection represents material he collected and published more than 170 years ago. Because of the apparent lack of pagination protocol, a volume can have page numbers jump around, be missing, or incomplete. Often with material already published he left the original page numbers although he included his sequential pagination for the most part. In short, it might get confusing sometimes.

His printing press was at 58 State Street. From 1795 to 1830 this building was the home of John Jay and called Gable Hall. The building was razed in 1902 to make way for the construction of the National Commercial Bank that opened in 1903. The bank building remains today. Munsell's biography was included in Appletons' Cyclopedia of American Biography published between 1887 and 1889:

Munsell's Printing Press, 58 State Street.

"**MUNSELL, Joel**, *printer, b. in Northfield, Mass., 14 April, 1808; d. in Albany, N. Y., 15 Jan., 1880. He established himself as a printer in Albany, N. Y., in 1827, was associate editor of the "Microscope" in 1834, published and edited the "New York Mechanic" in 1841-'3, and subsequently published "The Lady's Magazine," the "Northern Star and Freeman's Advocate," "The Spectator," the "Unionist," the "State Register," the "Guard," the "Typographical Miscellany," "The New York Teacher," the "Morning Express," "Webster's Almanac," "The Daily Statesman," and for three years the "New England Historical and Genealogical Register." He made the history and application of the art of printing a special study, and his collection of works on that subject, the largest in the United States, was in part purchased by the New York state library. Among his services to American historical literature is the "Historical Series" that he projected, edited, and annotated. He was a member of many learned societies, a founder of the Albany institute, and for many years published its proceedings. Mr. Munsell is the author of "Outlines of the History of Printing" (Albany, N. Y., 1839); "Annals of Albany," a contribution to the history of that city (10 vols., 1849-'59); "Every-Day Book of History and Chronology" (New York, 1856);*

"Chronology of Paper and Paper-Making" (Albany, 1857; enlarged ed., 1864 and 1870); and "A Manual of the 1st Lutheran Church of Albany, from 1670 till 1870" (1871). His printing and publishing business is continued by his sons."

The ten volumes contain a wealth of information on the early history of Albany. I am annotating each volume and adding additional information as well as supplemental photographs to celebrate Albany's upcoming 400th anniversary in 2024 from its early start as Fort Orange (1624). For purists, like myself, it is more accurate to be celebrating 410 years since the settlement which grew into present Albany began as Fort Nassau on Castle Island (now Port of Albany) in 1614 and founded by the Dutch under the command of Adriaen Block. Unfortunately, we tend to celebrate in centuries or half centuries.

The addition of photographs are mostly from my previously published Albany books from Arcadia Publishing, Fonthill Media, The History Press, and New Netherland Press. Since photography was not in use when Munsell was publishing these volumes, I tried to supply photos of some of the more landmark buildings and scenes that he describes.

This Volume One Facsimile Edition is from the first printing of 1850. It is printed as he printed it. I have not changed his formatting. Some pages or lines may be slanted but early printing and typesetting was an art back then not science. Albany had a population of 50,763, about half of what it is now. The second edition of Volume One from 1869 of the series has additional information in them. Future volumes will be published as they are done until all ten volumes are completed. When I finish volume ten I will include the missing information from his later editions in an eleventh edition.

My annotations are on the side of each page in smaller font. My additions in this volume are on pages 37, 38, 46, 72, 77, 84, 88, 90, 92, 93, 99, 147, 150, 161, 163, 179, 204, 273, 295, 297, 324, 395, 397, and 397.

Comments and suggestions are always welcome.

Don Rittner, December 2021
drittner@aol.com

Map of Albany in 1847 as frontispiece in the first edition.

THE

ANNALS OF ALBANY.

BY JOEL MUNSELL.

VOL. I.

ALBANY:
J. MUNSELL, 58 STATE STREET.
1850.

PREFACE.

This work was begun as an annual publication, in the year 1849, and the contents of this volume were principally comprised in the *Albany Annual Register* of the years 1849 and 1850. In this edition a part of the ephemeral articles of the first have been omitted, and historical and antiquarian matter substituted. The principal aim of the work was to preserve the memory of the time-honored institutions of the city. The form of a periodical was adopted for the convenience of continuing the publication from time to time as facts should be collected, and in the hope of enlisting others to collect materials. The cooperation of all who may take an interest in such matters is still solicited, in collecting whatever may tend to throw light upon the past, as well as to preserve authentic memorials of the present. Ancestral papers, of an historical, genealogical or statistical character; memoirs of eminent citizens deceased; historical accounts of religious, literary, charitable and benevolent institutions; also of public and private corporations; maps and charts of the city at different periods, or of portions of it; descriptions of antiquities, and rare and curious relics; in short, whatever, connected with the ancient or modern history of Albany, shall tend to illumine the path or enlighten the labors of the future historian, will be duly appreciated. These are the main objects of the work, although other departments have been introduced, in keeping with the original plan, which will be omitted in the future volumes. A synopsis of the events of each year is given, descending sometimes to particulars which may, perhaps, be considered trivial by some readers.

Undoubtedly many omissions will be observed of matters necessary to give completeness to the articles introduced; we shall be glad to receive from those who may notice errors or omissions, the sum of their knowledge, for future use. Above all, we crave a liberal share of patience at the public offices, and of the *oldest inhabitant*, to whom we are already indebted for many favors, and much valuable information. We hope to be instrumental in arresting much that is perishable from entire oblivion, and out of the abundance of material at hand propose to compile a volume annually.

CONTENTS.

Discovery and first voyage up Hudson's River, 1609,	9
Names of settlers in Rensselaerswyck, from 1630 to 1646,	15
Sentence of Willem Juriansen Bakker,	24
Mayors of Albany from 1684 to 1849,	25
Streets, lanes, alleys, &c., 1849,	26
An act for the division and equalization of the wards,	28
Banks, with historical reminiscences,	31
Insurance companies,	34
Clergy, 1848,	35
Practicing attorneys, 1848,	36
Practicing physicians, 1848,	37
Albany charter officers, 1686,	37
Officers of the city of Albany, 1848–9,	38
Officers of companies and societies, 1848–9, 39	45
Custom House,	46
Mohawk and Hudson Rail Road,	46
Income and expenditures of the city, 1842 to 1848,	48
County officers, 1848,	49
Alphabetical list of counties, towns and post-offices,	50
Stage and mail routes in olden time,	56
Principal routes of travel diverging from Albany,	61
Public offices, buildings, &c., 71	226
Albany Academy,	75
Albany Female Academy,	80
State Normal School, 84	297
Houses in Albany, 1786,	85
Reformed Protestant Dutch Church in Albany,	86
Evangelical Lutheran Ebenezer Church,	122
German Evangelical Lutheran Church, 129	293
First Presbyterian Church,	130
Bethel for Watermen,	133
Jewish Synagogues,	134
Universalist Church,	135
Ancient Albany,	137
City of Albany,	138
County of Albany,	142
Albany County Penitentiary,	149
Commission of John Abeel,	152
Lights and shadows of traveling in New York fifty years ago,	153

Contents.

Chronicle of events in Albany, 1847–8,	159
Colony of Rensselaerswyck, from 1614 to 1646,	183
Kiliaen van Rensselaer,	203
Executors of Jeremias van Rensselaer,	204
Arent van Curler,	205
Codirectors of Rensselaerswyck, 1630,	206
Business directory, 1849,	209
Albany County Bible Society,	229
List of freeholders of the city and county of Albany, 1720,	231
Dutch church burials, 1722 to 1757,	235
Family record from Groesbeck Bible,	249
Biographical sketch of Gen. Philip Schuyler,	250
Ancient commerce of Albany,	258
Voyage of an Albany sloop to China,	261
Visit of Peter Kalm to Albany, 1749,	262
Harmanus Bleecker,	276
Vanderheyden Palace,	278
The Wendell House,	280
The Stevenson House,	283
State Street in 1792,	285
A Canadian invasion,	288
A scene of the Revolution in Albany,	289
Births, marriages and deaths, 1848,	295
Civil officers of the city of Albany, 1693,	302
Operation of the cheap postage system in Albany, 1845,	303
Barlow's prediction of the Erie Canal, 1787,	304
Description of Albany in 1823,	305
Distances of county towns from Albany,	313
Dr. Morse's description of Albany, 1789,	314
Albany in 1796,	316
Corporations and associations, 1849,	317
An Albany merchant's stock in 1790,	322
Hudson River,	324
Books in 1772,	325
Closing and opening of the river since 1785,	326
Incidents of a northern winter,	328
Opening and closing of canal, 1824 to 1849,	329
Celebration of the adoption of the constitution, 1788,	330
Cold days sixty years ago,	329
Centennial anniversary,	335
Memoranda of 1784–5,	336
Conditions and prospects of the city in 1789,	338
A Tobacco establishment of 1790,	339
Annals of Albany for 1849,	341
Schedule of real and personal estate, 1847,	367
Bond of the aldermen of Schenectady, 1766,	368
Index	369

ANNALS OF ALBANY.

DISCOVERY AND FIRST VOYAGE UP HUDSON RIVER.

The third Voyage of Master HENRY HUDSON *toward* Noua Zembla, *and at his returne, his passage from* Farre Ilands, *to* New-found Land, *and along to fortie four degrees and ten minutes, and thence to* Cape Cod, *and so to thirtie three degrees; and along the Coast to the Northward, to fortie two degrees and an halfe, and up the Riuere neere to fortie three degrees. Written by* ROBERT IVET, *of* Lime-house.

[Henry Hudson sailed from Amsterdam on the 20th March, 1609, o. s., in the yacht Half-Moon, with a crew of about twenty Dutch and English sailors, on a voyage for the discovery of a north-west passage to India. He encountered ice and storms, which disabled his vessel, and about the middle of July ran into Penobscot bay, on the coast of Maine. From thence he proceeded along the coast southerly till he arrived at Chesapeake bay about the middle of August, when he tacked about and coasted northward until, on the third of September, at three o'clock in the afternoon, he came to three great rivers, and stood for the northernmost. Proceeding leisurely, on the sixth he passed through the Narrows, and was attacked by the Indians, who killed John Coleman one of his men, who was buried at Coleman's point, at Sandy hook. On the ninth the vessel arrived in New York harbor, which they perceived to be a very good one for all winds, and rode all night.

On the twelfth of September, at two o'clock in the afternoon, Hudson weighed anchor, and began the memorable ascent of the great river which perpetuates his name. He proceeded two leagues against the wind, and came to anchor. Twenty-eight canoes full of men, women and children came out from the shore, of whom the mariners were wary. They brought oysters and beans, and had " great tabacco pipes of yellow copper, and pots of earth to dresse their meate in." The remainder of the narrative is copied verbatim from the edition published by the New York Historical Society, *Transactions*, i, 138, et seq]

The thirteenth, faire weather, the wind northerly. At seuen of the clocke in the morning, as the floud came we weighed, and turned foure miles into the Riuer. The tide being done wee anchored. Then there came foure canoes aboord: but we suffered none of them to come into our ship. They brought great store of very good oysters aboord, which wee bought for trifles. In the night I set the variation of the compasse, and found it to be 13 degrees. In the afternoone we weighed, and turned in with the flood two leagues and a halfe further, and anchored all night, and had fiue fathoms soft ozie ground, and had an high point of land, which shewed out to us bearing north by east fiue leagues off vs.

— Hudson was an Englishman working for the Dutch East India Company. A replica of his ship the Half Moon (Halve Maen) was built in Albany, NY in 1989. Due to lack of support in Albany the ship was moved to the Netherlands in 2015.

Hudson's discoveries was followed up by Dutch traders. Adriaen Block's 1613 visit led to a mutiny and his ship The Tyger was burned. He built a small yacht called the Onrust (restless) in 1614 somewhere in New York Bay. A replica of that boat, the first fur trading ship built in America, was built in 2006-2009 in the Schenectady New York area and now serves as a floating museum and classroom in Connecticut.

The fovrteenth, in the morning being very faire weather, the wind south-east, we sayled vp the Riuer twelue leagues, and had fiue fathoms and fiue fathoms and a quarter lesse; and came to a streight between two points, and had eight, nine, and ten fathoms: and it trended north-east by north, one league, and we had twelue, thirteene, and fourteene fathoms. The Riuer is a mile broad: there is very high land on both sides. Then wee went vp north-west, a league and an halfe deepe water. Then north-east by north fiue miles, then north-west by north two leagues, and anchored. The land grew very high and mountainous. The river is full of fish.

The fifteenth, in the morning was misty vntil the Sunne arose: then it cleered. So wee weighed with the wind at south, and ran vp into the Riuer, twentie leagues, passing by high Mountains. Wee had a very good depth, as six, seuen, eight, nine, ten, twelue and thirteen fathoms, and great store of Salmons in the Riuer. This morning our two Sauages got out of a port and swam away. After we were vnder sayle they called to vs in scorne. At night we came to other Mountains, which lie from the Riuers side. There we found very louing people, and very old men: where wee were well vsed. Our Boat went to fish, and caught great store of very good fish.

The sixteenth, faire and very hot weather. In the morning our Boat went againe to fishing, but could catch but few, by reason their Canoes had beene there all night. This morning the people came aboord, and brought vs eares of Indian Corne, and Pompions, and Tabacco: which wee bought for trifles. Wee rode still all day, and filled fresh water; at night wee weighed and went two leagues higher, and had shoald water: so wee anchored till day.

The seuenteenth, faire Sun-shining weather, and very hot. In the morning as soon as the Sun was vp, we set sayle, and run vp six leagues higher, and found shoalds in the middle of the channell, and small Ilands, but seuen fathoms water on both sides. Toward night we borrowed so neere the shoare, that we grounded: so we layed out our small anchor, and heaued off againe. Then we borrowed on the banke in the channell, and came aground againe; while the floud ran we heaued off againe, and anchored all night.

The eighteenth, in the morning was faire weather, and we rode still. In the after-noone our Master's Mate went on land with an old Sauage, a Gouernor of the Countrey; who carried him to his house and made him good cheere.

The nineteenth, was faire and hot weather: at the flood, being neere eleuen of the clocke, wee weighed, and ran higher vp two leagues aboue the shoalds, and had no lesse water than fiue fathoms: we anchored, and rode in eight fathoms. The people of the countrie came flocking aboord, and brought vs Grapes, and Pompions, which we bought for trifles. And many brought vs Beuers skinnes, and Otters skinnes, which wee bought for Beades, Kniues, and Hatchets. So we rode there all night.

The twentieth, in the morning was fare weather. Our Masters Mate with four men more went vp with our Boat to sound the Riuer, and found two leagues aboue vs but two fathoms water, and the channell very narrow; and aboue that place seuen or eight fathoms. Toward night they returned; and we rode still all night.

The one and twentieth was faire weather, and the wind all southerly: we determined yet once more to goe farther vp into the Riuer, to trie what depth and breadth it did beare; but much people resorted aboord, so we went not this day. Our carpenter went on land and made a fore-yard. And our Master and his Mate determined to trie some of the chiefe men of the countrey, whether they had any treacherie in them. So they took them down into the cabbin, and gave them as much wine and aqua vitæ, that they were all merrie; and one of them had his wife with him, which sat so modestly, as any of our countrey women would do in a strange place. In the end one of them was drunke, which had been aboord of our ship all the time that we had been there: and that was strange to them; for they could not tell how to take it. The canoes and folke went all on shoare; but some of them came againe, and brought stropes of Beades: some had six, seven, eight, nine, ten; and gaue him. So he slept all night quietly.

The two and twentieth was faire weather: in the morning our Masters Mate and foure more of the companie went vp with our Boat to sound the river higher vp. The people of the countrey came not aboord till noone: but when they came, and saw the Sauages well, they were glad. So at three of the clocke in the after-noone they came aboord, and brought Tabacco, and more Beades, and gaue them to our Master, and made an Oration, and shewed him all the countrey round about. Then they sent one of their companie on land, who presently returned, and brought a great Platter ful of Venison, dressed by themselues; and they caused him to eat with them: then they made him reuerence, and departed all saue the old man that lay aboord. This night at ten of the clocke, our Boate returned in a showre of raine from sounding of the Riuer; and found it to be at an end for shipping to goe in. For they had beene vp eight or nine leagues, and found but seuen foot water, and unconstant soundings.

The three and twentieth faire weather. At twelue of the clocke wee weighed, and went downe two loagues to a shoald that had two channels, one on the one side, and another on the other, and had little wind, whereby the tide layed vs upon it. So, there wee sate on the ground the space of an houre till the floud came. Then we had a little gale of wind at the west. So wee got our ship into deepe water and rode all night very well.

The four and twentieth was faire weather: the winde at the north-west, wee weighed and went downe the Riuer seuen or eight leagues; and at halfe ebbe wee came on ground on a bank of oze in the middle of the Riuer, and sate there till the floud. Then wee went on land, and gathered good store of chestnuts. At ten of the clocke wee came off into deepe water, and anchored.

The five and twentieth was faire weather, and the wind at south a stiffe gale. We rode still, and went on land to walke on the west side of the Riuer, and found good ground for Corne, and other garden herbs, with great store of goodly oakes, and walnut trees, and chestnut trees, ewe trees, and trees of sweet wood in great abundance, and great store of slate for houses, and other good stones.

The sixe and twentieth was faire weather, and the wind at south a stiffe gale, we rode still. In the morning our carpenter went on land with our Masters Mate, and foure more of our companie to cut wood. This morning, two canoes came vp the Riuer from the place where we first found louing people, and in one of them was the old man that had lyen aboord of vs at the other place. He brought another old man with him, which brought more stropes of beades, and gaue them to our Master, and shewed him all the countrey there about, as though it were at his command. So he made the two old men dine with him, and the old mans wife; for they brought two old women, and two young maidens of the age of sixteene or seuenteene yeeres with them, who behaued themselues very modestly. Our Master gaue one of the old men a Knife, and they gaue him and vs Tabacco. And at one of the clocke they departed down the Riuer, making signes that wee should come down to them; fore wee were within two leagues of the place where they dwelt.

At seuen and twentieth, in the morning was faire weather, but much wind at the north, we weighed and set our fore top-sayle, and our ship would not flat, but ran on the ozie bank at halfe ebbe. Wee layed out anchor to heaue her off, but could not. So we sate from halfe ebbe to halfe floud: then wee set our fore-sayle and mayne top-sayle, and got downe sixe leagues. The old man came aboord and would have had vs anchor, and goe on land to eate with him: but the wind being faire, wee would not yeeld to his request. So hee left vs, being very sorrowful for our departure. At five of the clocke in the afternoone, the wind came to the south-south-west. So wee made a boord or two, and anchored in fourteene fathoms water. Then our Boat went on shoare to fish, right against the ship. Our Masters Mate and Boat-swaine, and three more of the companie went on land to fish, but could not finde a good place. They tooke foure or five and twenty Mullets, Breames, Bases, and Barbils; and returned in an houre. We rode still all night.

The eight and twentieth, being faire weather, as soon as the day was light, we weighed at halfe ebbe, and turned downe two leagues belowe water; for the streame doth runne the last quarter ebbe: then we anchored till high water. At three of the clock in the afternoone we weighed, and turned downe three leagues, vntill it was darke; then wee anchored.

The nine and twentieth was drie close weather: the wind at south, and south by west, wee weighed early in the morning, and turned downe three leagues by a lowe water, and anchored at the lower end of the long Reach; for it is sixe leagues long. Then there came certain Indians in a canoe to vs, but would not come aboord. After dinner there came the canoe with other men, whereof three came aboord vs. They brought Indian wheat, which we bought for trifles. At three of the clocke in the afternoone we weighed, as soone as the ebbe came, and turned downe to the edge of the Mountaines, or the northermost of the Mountaines, and anchored: because the high land hath many points, and a narrow channell, and hath many eddie winds. So we rode quietly all night in seuen fathoms water.

The thirtieth was faire weather, and the wind at south-east a stiffe gale between the Mountaynes. We rode still the afternoone. The people of the countrey came aboord vs, and brought some small skinnes with them, which we bought for kniues and trifles. This a very pleasant place to build a towne on. The road is every neere, and very good for all winds, saue an east-north-east wind. The Mountaynes look as if some metall or minerall were in them. For the trees that grew on them were all blasted, and some of them barren, with few or no trees on them. The people brought a stone aboord like to emery (a stone vsed by glasiers to cut glasse), it would cut iron or steele. Yet being bruised small, and water put to it, it made a colour like blacke lead glistering; it is also good for painters colours. At three of the clocke they departed, and we rode still all night.

The first of October, faire weather, the winde variable betweene the west and the north. In the morning we weighed at seuen of the clocke with the ebbe, and got downe below the Mountaynes, which was seuen leagues. Then it fell calme and the flood was come, and wee anchored at twelue of the clocke. The people of the Mountaynes came aboord vs, wondering at our ship and weapons. We bought some small skinnes of them for trifles. This afternoone, one canoe kept hanging vnder our sterne with one man in it, which we could not keepe from thence, who got vp by our rudder to the cabin window, and stole out my pillow and two shirts, and two bandeleeres. Our Masters Mate shot at him, and strooke him on the brest, and killed him. Whereupon all the rest fled away, some in their canoes, and some leapt out of them into the water. We manned our boat, and got our things againe. Then one of them that swamme got hold of our boat, thinking to ouerthrow it. But our cooke took a sword, and cut off one of his hands, and he was drowned. By this time the ebbe was come, and we weighed and got downe two leagues, by that time it was darke. So we anchored in foure fathomes water, and rode well.

The seconde, faire weather. At break of day wee weighed, the wind being at north-west, and got downe seuen leagues; then the floud was come strong, so we anchored. Then came one of the Sauages that swamme away from vs at our going vp the Riuer with many other, thinking to betray vs. But we perceived their intent, and svffered none of them to enter our ship. Whereupon two canoes full of men, with their bowes and arrowes shot at vs after our sterne: in recompence whereof we discharged sixe muskets, and killed two or three of them. Then aboue an hundred of them came to a point of land to shoot at vs. There I shot a falcon at them, and killed two of them: whereupon the rest fled into the woods. Yet they manned off another canoe with nine or ten men, which came to meet vs. So I shot at it also a falcon, and shot it through and killed one of them. Then our men with their muskets killed three or four more of them. So they went their way; within a while after, wee got downe two leagues beyond that place, and anchored in a bay, cleere from all danger of them on the other side of the Riuer, where we saw a very good piece of ground: and hard by it there was a cliffe, that looked of the colour of a white greene, as though it were either copper, or siluer myne: and I think it to be one of them by the trees that grow vpon it. For they be all burned, and the other places are greene as grasse, it is on that side of the Riuer that is called *Manna-hatta*. There we saw no people to trouble vs: and rode quietly all night; but had much wind and raine.

The third, was very stormie; the wind at east-north-east. In the morning, in a gust of wind and raine, our anchor came home, and we droue on ground, but it was ozie. Then as we were about to haue out an anchor, the wind came to the north-north-west, and droue vs off againe.

Then we shot an anchor, and let it fall in foure fathomes water, and weighed the other. Wee had much wind and raine, with thicke weather, so we rode still all night.

The fourth, was faire weather, and the wind at north-north-west, wee weighed and came out of the Riuer, into which we had runne so farre. Within a while after, wee came out also of *The great mouth of the great Riuer*, that runneth vp to the north-west, borrowing vpon the norther side of the same, thinking to haue deepe water; for wee had sounded a great way with our boat at our first going in, and found seuen, six, and fiue fathomes. So we came out that way, but we were deceiued, for we had but eight foot and an halfe water: and so to three, fiue, three, and two fathomes and an halfe. And then three, foure, fiue, sixe, seuen, eight, nine and ten fathomes. And by twelue of the clocke we were cleere of all the inlet. Then we took in our boat, and set our mayne-sayle and sprit-sayle, and our top-sayles, and steered away east-south-east, and south-east by east, off into the mayne sea: and the land on the souther side of the bay or inlet, did beare at noone west and by south foure leagues from vs.

The fift, was faire weather, and the wind variable between the north and the east. Wee held on our course south-east by east. At noone I obserued and found our height to bee 39 degrees 30 minutes. Our compasse varied sixe degrees to the west.

We continued our course toward England, without seeing any land by the way, all the rest of this moneth of October. And on the seuenth day of Nouember, *stilo nouo*, being Saturday, by the Grace of God, we safely arriued in the Range of Dartmouth, in Deuonshire, in the yeere 1609.

Settlers of Rensselaerswyck from 1630 to 1646. 15

NAMES OF SETTLERS IN RENSSELAERSWYCK.

1630 TO 1646.

Compiled from the books of Monthly Wages and other MSS. See O'Callaghan's Hist. of N. Netherland, i, 433.

1630.

Wolfert Gerritsen, superintendent of farms.
Rutger Hendricksen van Soest, superintendent of the brewery.
Seger Hendricksen van Soest, shepherd and ploughman.
Brandt Peelen van Nieukerke, schepen; had two daughters, Lisbet and Gerritje. The latter married Goosen Gerritsen van Schaick. The father died in 1644. He is mentioned by the Rev. Mr. Megapolensis in his tract on the Maquaa Indians, and by Van der Donck in his Beschryvinge van N. N., as having raised wheat off one field in Rensselaerswyck eleven years in succession. The land was ploughed twelve times in that period; twice the first and once every succeeding year, when the stubble was ploughed and the wheat sown and harrowed under. Van der Donck adds:—"There are many thousand morgens of as good land there as that of which we have spoken." Several descendants of this individual reside in Albany county, where they go by the name of Brandt.
Simon Dircksen Pos, was one of Minuet's council in 1624; died in 1649.
Jan Tyssen, trumpeter, Fort Orange.
Andries Carstenssen, millwright.
Laurens Laurenssen, } sawyers.
Barent Tomassen,
Arendt van Curler, was a magistrate of the colony until the time of his death, and one of the leaders of the settlement at Schenectady, 1641.
Jacob Jansen Stol, succeeded Hendrick Albertzen as ferry-master at Beverwyck.
Mertin Gerrittsen van Bergen, married Neeltje Meynderts; his oldest son was Gerrit; his second, Myndert van Bergen. In the year 1668, he had a lease of Castle Island, called after him, Martin Gerritsen's Island; and in 1690 he lived south of that island, on the west side of the river. He had property in Katskill, Coxsackie, and Albany of which place he was magistrate for a long time.
Claes Arissen.
Roeloff Jansen van Maesterlandt, wife and family; came out as a farmer to the Patroon, at $72 a year. The Rev. Ev. Bogardus, of New Amsterdam, married his widow.
Claes Claessen, his servant. Jacques Spierinck.
Jacob Govertsen. Rayuert Harmensen.
Bastiaen Jansen Krol, Fort Orange.
Albert Andrissen Bradt, de Noorman, married Annetje Barents, by whom he had eight children, viz. Barent; Eva (who m Roeloff Swartwout); Storm; Engeltje (who m. Teunis Slingerland, of Onisquathaw); Gisseltje (who m. Jan van Eechelen); Andries, Jan, and Dirck. The tradition is, that one of the above children was

— Van Curler led 15 families west to found Schenectady in 1661 on the banks of the Mohawk River. Schenectady is a Native American word meaning "Beyond the Pine Barrens," referring to a unique natural ecosystem situated between the Hudson and Mohawk Valleys.

— The Normanskill is named for him. He had the first mill on it.

16   Settlers of Rensselaerswyck from 1630 to 1646.

born on ship-board, on the passage out, in the midst of a heavy storm, in consequence of which he was called Storm van der Zee. Barent Albertsen succeeded his father, in 1672, as a lessee of the water privileges on the Normans Kill, for which he was to pay $150 a year; and Slingerland succeeded, in 1677, as a lessee of the farm which his father had occupied until then on the above stream. Albert de Noorman died 7th June, 1686, and Swartwout, mentioning the occurrence, says:—he was "een van de oudste en eerste inwoonders der colonie Rensselaerswyck." At the time of his decease, he was proprietor of some lots and houses on the island of Manhattans. It was after this man that the creek south of Albany was called the Noormans Kill. Many of his descendants are still met with in and around the latter city.

> The Normanskill was called *Tawasentha* by local Native Americans. Originally controlled by Mohicans and later Mohawks.

1631.

Maryn Adriaensen van Veere. This was the freebooter who afterwards played so prominent a figure in Kieft's time.

Thomas Witsent.

Gerrit Teunissen de Reus, schepen, had a well-stocked farm in Greenbush.

Cornelis Teunissen van Westbroek.

Cornelis Teunissen van Breukelen, Raedts persoon; the descendants of this man now call themselves van Brackelen.

Johan Tiers.

Jasper Ferlyn.

Gerrit Willems Oosterum.

Cornelis Maessen van Buren Maassen (in Gelderland) and Catalyntje Martensen, his wife, came out in the ship Rensselaerswyck. In the passage out was born their first child, Hendrick; had besides him, four other children, viz. Martin, Maas, Steyntje, and Tobias, all of whom were living in the colony in 1662. Steyntje married, 1663, Dirck Wessels, "free merchant here." The father had a farm at Papskenea. He and his wife died in 1648, and were both buried on the same day! (Beyde op eenen dagh zyn begraaven. MS.)

Cornelis Teunissen Bos, bouwknecht to Cornelis Maassen, was commissary at Fort Orange previous to 1662.

1634.

Jan Labbadie, carpenter, native of France, was subsequently commissary to the Patroon, and after that held a like office at Fort Orange, under the company. He married the widow of Mr. Harman van der Bogaert. He came out previous to this year, and was part owner of the Garce.

Robert Hendricksen.   Adriaen Gerritsen.

Lubert Gysbertsen, wheelwright.   Jan Jacobsen.

Hendrick Cornelissen.

Jacob Albertzen Planck, officer, sheriff.   Joris Houten, Fort Orange.

Jan Jansen Dam, or Damen; married Ariaentje Cuvel. He removed subsequently to New Amsterdam, where he was elected one of the Eight Men; amassed considerable wealth, and was one of the owners of the privateer La Garce. In 1649-50 he went to Holland with C.

> The council of Eight Men was an early form of representational democracy in 17th century New Netherland. It replaced the previous Twelve Men and was followed by the Nine Men.

Settlers of Rensselaerswyck from 1630 to 1646.

Dam was replaced on the council by Jan Everts Bout.

van Tienhoven, to defend Stuyvesant against the complaints of Van der Donck and others, and died on his return, 18th June, 1651. He does not seem to have had any children. He had three brothers, Cornelis Jansen, Cuyper; Cornelis Jansen Damen; and Willem Jansen Damen; and two sisters, Neiltje, and Hendrickje. He adopted the son of the last named sister—Jan Cornelius Buys—who assumed his name, having been left 600 Car. guilders. Jan Damen, at his death, willed 400 Car. guilders to the poor of Bunick, province of Utrecht. The inventory of his personal property fills ten folio pages in the records.

1635.

Jan Terssen van Franiker.
Jan Cornelissen, Carpenter.

Juriaen Bylvelt.
Johannes Verbeeck; Raedt Persoon, 1658, 1661.

1636.

He is best known as the founder of the Town of Coeymans. The Coeymans house, which he built around 1690, is still standing and occupied. It is now known as the Araanje Coeymans House. She was the daughter of Barent.

Barent Pieterse Koyemans, alias Barent the Miller, entered the service of the first Patroon, at 30 guilders a year. Three brothers accompanied him to Rensselaerswyck in 1636: viz. David, Jacob, and Arent, who was a lad. It is presumed that they came originally from Utrecht. Barent worked in the Patroon's grist-mill until 1645, in the fall of which year he took charge, with Jan Gerritsen, his partner (who came out with him), of the Patroon's saw-mills, being allowed 150 gl. each a year for board, and three stivers a cut for every plank they sawed. He remained in this employment until 1647, having cut between three and four thousand boards in that time. Previous to 1650, he lived a little south of the 5th or Patroon's creek, and in 1655 took a nineteen years' lease of a farm of maize land at 24 gl. per annum. In 1657 he rented, in company with Cornelis Theunis van Breukelen, for three years, the Upper Mills (as the mills on the Patroon's creek were called, in contradistinction to those on the Norman's kill), which he leased on his own account in 1660 for 13 years. This lease expired in 1673, about which time he purchased by consent of the commissioners at Albany, from the Katskill Indians, a large tract of land, some twelve or fifteen miles south of that city, on the west side of the river. The place had been known, for many years previous, as offering peculiar advantages for the erection of saw-mills, Cryn Cornelissen, and Hans Jansen having erected saw-mills on the creek immediately north of Beeren Island as early as 1651. Coeymans had, no doubt, these advantages in view when he made his purchase, which began at a point on the shore called Sieskasin, opposite the middle of Jan Ryersens island called by the Indians Sapanakock, and ran south to the mouth of Pieter Bronck's kill, as Coxsackie creek was then called. Following up this creek to its head, the line then went west until it struck the head of the waters falling into the Hudson, all the land on which belonged to the Katskill Indians, the waters flowing west to the Schoharie creek being the property of the Mohawks. The line then went northerly to the bounds of Rensselaerswyck, and thence returned to the Hudson River. A patent was obtained for this tract, twelve miles deep and some eight or ten front, from Gov. Lovelace, on 7th April, 1673. But falling as it did within the original bounds of Van Rensselaer's colonie, Coeymans purchased out the Patroon's claims, 22d Oct., 1706, agreeing to pay a quit-ren tof nine shillings a year, and he finally obtained letters patent from Queen Anne, confirming the whole to him and his heirs forever, 6th Aug., 1714. This purchase now constitutes the ancient town of Coeymans, in the county of Albany.—Barent Pietersen had five children—Andreas, Samuel, Peter, Ariantje, and Jannitje. Andreas moved to the Raritans, New Jersey, where he purchased a considerable tract of land, and where some of the Coeymans still reside. Peter married twice; by his first wife he had Mayica, who married Andreas Witbeck; and Elizabeth, the wife of Jacob van Allen. By his second wife, Charlotte Amelia Drawyer, he had Gerritje, who married John Barclay, mayor of Albany; Anna Margaret, who married Peter Ten Eyck, and Charlotte A., who married John Bronck. Mrs. Abraham Verplank of Coeymans is grand-daughter to this Mrs. Bronck. All the descendants of Barent Coeymans, after the first generation in a direct line, were females. Owing to this singular circumstance, the family name is now extinct in this state.

Pieter Cornelissen van Munnichendam, millwright.

Dirck Jansen van Edam, Mauritz Jansen, Arent Andriessen van Frederickstad, Michel Jansen, } van Broeckhuysen.

This Michel brought out his wife and two children. Van Tienhoven says he came out as a "boereknecht," or servant. He amassed a fortune in a few years, in the fur trade, but not being able to agree with the head men of the colonie, he removed, in 1646, to the island of Manhattans. He purchased Eversten Bout's farm in Pavonia, with some stock, for 8,000 gl., and was appointed one of the delegates to Holland in 1649, against the colonial administration, but owing to the unsettled state of his private affairs he could not accept that appointment. It was in a room in this man's house, in New Amsterdam, that Van der Donck wrote his celebrated "Vertoogh," or Remonstrance against the maladministration of affairs in New Netherland.

Jacob Jansen van Amsterdam.

Simon Walings van der Belt; was killed at Pavonia, in 1648, by some savages from the south.

Gysbert Claessen van Amsterdam. Hans Zevenhuyzen.
Cristen Cristyssen Noorman van Vlecburgh and wife. Adriaen Hubertsen.
Rynier Tymanssen van Edam.
Tys Barentsen Schoonmaker van Edam. Thomas Jansen van Bunick.
Cornelis Tomassen, smith, and wife.

Arent Steveniersen, wife and two children; he married, anno 1637, the widow of Cornelius Tomassen, by whom he had two other children.

Johan Latyn van Verdym. Claes Jansen van Nykerk.

Settlers of Rensselaerswyck from 1630 to 1646. 19

Rutger Jacobsen van Schoenderwoerdt; married in New Amsterdam anno 1646, Tryntje Jansen van Briestede (who died at her son's in Rosendal, in 1711). By her he had two daughters and one son. Margaret, one of the daughters, married in 1667, Jan Jansen Bleecker, who came from Meppel, province of Overyssel, to America, in 1658, and was the ancestor of the present highly respectable Bleecker family in this state. Rutger Jacobson was a magistrate in Rensselaerswyck as early as 1648, and continued to fill that office as late as 1662, and perhaps later. He owned a vessel on the river in 1649, in which year he rented, in partnership with Goosen Gerritsen, the Patroon's brewery, at $450 gl. a year, payable in addition one guilder for every ton of beer which they brewed. This duty amounted in the first year to 230 gl., and in the following season they worked up 1,500 schepels of malt. On the 3d of June, 1656, he laid the corner stone of the "new church," in Beverswyck, and we find him subsequently part proprietor of Pachonakelick, called by the Dutch Mohican's, or Long Island, below Bethlehem. He had the character of an upright citizen, and to his credit it must be added, he rose by his honest industry from small beginnings.

Ryckert Rutgerson; was engaged, when he first came out, at 130 gl. per annum for a term of 6 years. In 1648 he took a 6 years' lease of Bethlehem Island, at 300 gl. per annum, besides the tenths. He received three horses, and two or three cows on halves, and the Patroon was to build him a barn and dwelling house, he cutting and drawing the timber, and boarding the carpenters. He was exempt from rent and tithes for the first year. In 1652 he surrendered his lease to Jan Ryersen, after whom this island has since been named.

N. B. The Settlers of 1636 came out in the ship Rensselaerswyck, having sailed from Holland on the 1st October of that year.

1637.

Jan Michaelsen van Edam, tailor, and his boy.
Pieter Nicolaussen van Nordinge.
Teunis Cornelissen van Vechten, succeeded Michel Jansen on his farm in 1646, and lived in 1648 in the south end of Greenbush.
Burger Joris, smith.
Jan Ryersen; the island situate opposite the junction of the towns of Bethlehem and Coeymans, on the Hudson, was called Jan Ryersen's island, in consequence of this man having lived there in 1652.
Abraham Stevensen, surnamed Croaet, a boy.
Cornelis Teunissen van Merkerk.
Goosen Gerritsen van Schaick; married, 1st, Gerritje Brants, daughter of Brant Peelen; 2d, in July, 1657, Annetje Lievens. He was a brewer in the colonie in 1649, in which year he accepted, after a good deal of solicitation, the office of magistrate, or Gerechts persoon. Was afterwards one of the part owners of Nachtenack, the Indian name for the site of the present village of Waterford, Saratoga county.
Willem Juriaensen Bakker, was banished from the colonie, in 1650, at the age of seventy years, in consequence of his reputed misdeeds.

1638.

Jan Dircksen van Amersfoort.
Wybrant Pietersen.
Willem Meynten.
Martin Hendricksen van Hamelward.
Adriaen Berghoorn.
Hendrick Fredricksen.
Gerrit Hendricksen.
Cornelis Leendertsen.
Francis Allertsen, cooper.
Roeloff Cornelissen van Houten.
Volkert Jansen.
Jacob Jansen Nostrandt.
Christoffel Davits; lived in 1650 on a farm at Dominie's Hoeck, now called Van Wie's Point.
Claes Jansen Ruyter. Jacob Flodder, his man.
Gysbert Adriaensen van Bunick; came out in the Key of Calmar.
Teunis Dircksen van Vechten, came out with wife, child, and two servants, in the "Arms of Norway," and had a farm in 1648 at Greenbush, north of that occupied by Teunis Cornelissen van Vechten. He is referred to in 1663 as "an old inhabitant here."

1639.

Jacob Adriaensen van Utrecht. Ryer Stoffelsen.
Cryn Cornelissen; obtained a license in 1651 to erect a sawmill in company with Hans Jansen van Rotterdam, on what is now Coeyman's Creek.
Adam Roelantsen van Hamelward, previously a schoolmaster in New Amsterdam.
Sander Leendertsen Glen; married Catalyn Doncassen. He was one of the Indian traders at Beverswyck, and finally moved to Scotia, near Schenectada, of which tract he obtained a patent from Gov. Nicolls, in 1665. Reference is made probably to this gentleman by the French in their account of the burning of Schenectady, anno 1690, in the following terms: "At daybreak some men were sent to the dwelling of Mr. Sander, who was major of the place at the other side of the river. He was not willing to surrender, and began to put himself on the defensive, with his servants and some Indians. But as it was resolved not to do him any harm, in consequence of the good treatment which the French had formerly experienced at his hands, M. d'Iberville and the great Agniez proceeded thither alone, promised him quarter for himself, his people and property, whereupon he laid down his arms on parole." — Because of his previously good treatment of the French, Glen was not killed during the Schenectady Massacre of 1690 and was able to rescue some of his relatives from becoming hostages after Schenectady was raided and burned. French Indians became restless and suspicious after he tried claiming too many as relatives.
Pieter Jacobson and wife.
Gilles Barentsen.
Cornelis Spierinck.
Johan Poog.
Claes Jansen van Breda.
Class Tyssen.

1640.

Nys Jacobsen. Jannitje Teunissen.
Jan Teunissen, carpenter.
Teunis Jacobsen van Schoenderwordt, brother to Rutger Jacobsen; had 90 gl. a year salary for the first three years, and 100 for the next three. He became a trader in 1651.
Andries Hubertsen Constapel van der Blaes; married Annetje Juriaensen; owned a tile kiln in Beverswyck, and died in 1662.

Settlers of Rensselaerswyck from 1630 to 1646.

Andries de Vos, brother-in-law to Barent Pieterse Coeymans; was Gerechts persoon, or magistrate, in 1648.
Adriaen Teunissen van der Belt.   Jan Creynen.
Jan Jansen van Rotterdam; was killed in the Indian war, 1644.
Jacob Jansen van Campen.   Cornelis Keyne van Houtten.
Jan Cornelissen van Houtten.   Claes Gerritsen,

1641.

Adriaen van der Donck, officer, or Sheriff.
Cornelis Antonissen van Slyck, alias Broer Cornelissen, was the first patentee of Katskill, anno 1646. Van Slyck's Island, opposite Schenectada, was so called after one of his sons, Jacques, to whom it was granted, 13th Nov., 1662, by Director Stuyvesant.
Claes Gysbertsen.   Joris Borrelingen, Engelsman,
Jabob Wolfertsen.   Claes Jansen van Ruth.
Teunis de Metselaer.
Cornelis Cornelissen van Schoonderwoerdt, alias "Vosje."

1642.

Dominie Johannes Megapolensis, Jun.,
  Matheld Willemsen, his wife,
  Hellegond, Dirck, Jan, and Samuel, their children. Samuel M., the last named son, was sent to Harvard College in 1657; spent three years there, and then proceeded to the University of Leyden, where he was licensed, in 1662, as a minister, and obtained the degree of M. D. On his return, he became Collegiate pastor of the church at New Amsterdam, and was appointed by Gov. Stuyvesant one of the commissioners to negotiate with the British the articles relating to the capitulation of the Province.—*Rev. Dr. De Witt.*
Abraham Staes, surgeon.
Evert Pels van Steltyn, brewer, and wife; lived at the Mill Creek, Greenbush.
Cornelis Lambertsen van Doorn.   Joachim Kuttelhuys van Cremyn.
Johan Helms van Baasle.
Juriaen Bestval van Leyderdorp, (near Leyden).
Claes Jansen van Waalwyck.   Paulus Jansen van Gertruydenburgh.
Hans Vos van Baden, court messenger; was sheriff's constable in New Amsterdam in 1661.
Lucas Smith van Ickemsburgh; left the colonie in the spring of 1646, with the character of "een eerlyk ende vroom Jongman"—an honorable and virtuous young man.
Cornelis Crynnesen.
Cornelis Hendricksen van Es, Gerechts persoon or magistrate. His daughter, Elizabeth, married one Banckers. "Cryn Cornelissen declares that, in the spring of 1643, while conveying some of the guests, on the ice, to the wedding of Van Es's daughter, a mare belonging to him, (Gryn), and a stud belonging to Van der Donk, were drowned in the neighborhood of Black, or Horse's point—(omtrent de Swarte, ofte Paerde Hoeck)—for which he understands Van der Donk received 150 guilders ($60) from the wedding party." MS.

The Fort Crailo historic site was built on part of the foundation of his house. He was the first Dutch Reformed minister hired by Van Rensselaer to take care of the settlers of Rensselaerswyck in New Netherland.

— Van der Donck, a lawyer, went on to write the first book and description of New Netherland. Hired by Van Rennselaer to oversee his patroonship lands he was the first to use the term American for settlers and bucked the system. Whereas Van Rensselaer wanted to run a strict regime, Van der Donck would often side with the tenants against the directions of Van Rensselaer. After negotiating peace with the Natives, a war started by the Governor Willem Kieft, he was given the title "jonkheer" or "jonker," the Dutch pronounced it "Yonker." The area he lived in is now called Yonkers. In 1649, Van der Donck was appointed by the then governor general Peter Stuyvesant to be a member of the Council of Nine, a group of advisors and legislators in New Amsterdam. He became at odds with Stuyvesant over running the colony. The conflict ended up in a stand-off and it was decided that the government in Holland would have to resolve the conflict. He won the argument but lost since Holland went to war with England so his efforts were for nothing.

Settlers of Rensselaerswyck from 1630 to 1646.

Cornelis Gerritsen van Schoonderwoerdt.
Wm. Fredericksen van Leyden, free carpenter.
Antonie de Hooges, commis, afterwards Secretary of the Colonie. His daughter, and only child, says Bensen, "married Herman Rutgers, the ancestor of the respectable family of the name among us." De Hooges died, 1658. The well-known promontory in the Highlands was called Anthony's Nose, after him.
Johan Holmes.
Juriaen —— van Sleswyck.
Johan Corstiaenssen, mariner.
Hendrick Albertsen; second time of his coming out. He was the first ferrymaster in Beverwyck; died in 1648 or 1649.
Gertrude Dries van Driesbergen, his wife.   Hendrick Dries, her brother.
Albert Jansen, van Amsterdam.   Jan Jansen Flodder, carpenter.
Geertje Mannix, widow, and two children.   Pieter Wyncoop, commis.
Nicolaus Koorn, sergeant or wachtmeester; succeeded Van der Donck as Sheriff.
Adriaen Cornelissen van Bersingeren.   Arendt Teunissen van Luyten.
Cornelis Segers van Voorhout; succeeded Van der Donck on the farm called Weelysburgh, on Castle island; married Bregje Jacobsen, by whom he had six children; Cornelis, Claes, Seger, Jannitje, Neltje, and Lysbeth. The last named married Francois Boon, without her parents' consent, and was disinherited, having been left by will only £1 Flemish. Seger married Jannitje Teunissen van Vecthen, and was killed, anno 1662, by Andries Hubertsen in a brawl. Many of the Segers family are still residents of the county of Albany. — *Castle Island is now the Port of Albany.*
Jacob Aertsen Wagenaar.
Jan Creyne van Houtten.
Jan Dircksen, Engelsman, van Amersfoort.
Herry de Backer. "I have known a gunner, named Harry de Backer, who killed at one shot from his gun, eleven gray geese out of a large flock."—*Van der Donck.*
Adrian Willemsen; banished for theft in 1644.

1643, 1644, 1645.

Pieter Hertgers van Vee, was one of the commissaries of the court at Fort Orange in 1654: died in Holland, 1670.
Abraham Clock.
Jan Barentsen Wemp, removed subsequently to Schenectady, where he became proprietor of some land. His widow married Sweer Teunissen van Velde. — *Wemp, later known as Wemple, was one of the first settlers of Schenectady with Van Curler. Lived on the West side of Washington Avenue, near what is now the community college.*
Richard Brigham.
Lambert van Valckenburg.
Jacob Jansen Schermerhorn, married Jannitje, daughter of Cornelis Segers. He was a prominent trader in Beverwyck in 1648, when he was arrested, by Stuyvesant, on a charge of selling fire-arms and amunition to the Indians. His books and papers were seized, and

Settlers of Rensselaerswyck from 1630 to 1646.

himself removed a prisoner to Fort Amsterdam, where he was sentenced to banishment for five years, and the confiscation of all his property. By the interference of some leading citizens the first part of the sentence was struck out, but his property was totally lost. These proceedings against Schermerhorn formed, subsequently, a ground of complaint against Stuyvesant to the States General.

Claes Teunissen, alias "Uylenspiegel."

Gysbert Cornelissen van Wesepe; called also Gysbert op de Berg, from the fact of his having lived on a farm called the "Hooge Berg," situate on the east side of the river, a little below Albany, which he rented in 1646 at 300 gl. a year. This farm still retains its original Dutch name, and is now owned by Joachim Staats, Esq. — The Staats house is still standing. In 2018, William Staats who was a descendant and living there died in 2018, perhaps ending four centuries under one family.

1646.

Jan Jansen van Bremen; lived in Bethlehem, and moved, anno 1540, to Katskill.

Harman Mynderts van der Bogaert, arrived in New Netherland, anno 1631, as surgeon of the company's ship the Eendracht; he continued in the company's service to 1633, after which he resided in New Amsterdam until appointed commissary to Fort Orange. He was highly respected, though from all accounts he appears to have been of an irascible temper. An instance is mentioned of his having attempted, in the excitement of a high quarrel, when both appear to have been in a violent passion, to throw the Director-general out of a boat in which they were sailing on the river; he was, it is added, with difficulty prevented from accomplishing his purpose. He occasionally wrote his name Harmanus a Boghardij. He came, I believe, to a violent death in 1649. Carl van Brugge succeeded him as commissary at Fort Orange. — Van der Bogaert drowned in the Hudson River after being pursued by soldiers from Fort Orange. Before that he made a perilous trip on behalf of the Dutch into Native territory to re-establish trading relations that were being advanced by the French. His journal now published as a book gives the earliest insights onto Mohawk practices. His premature death was caused by having sexual relationships with two of his slaves and was caught. Sodomy was punishable by death so he tried to escape (twice) and became trapped under the ice and drowned in the Hudson River near Fort Orange.

Jan van Hoosem.   Hendrick Westercamp.

Jacob Herrick.

Jan Andriessen van Dublin, leased a bouwerie in 1649, described as lying "north of Stoney point, being the north half of the Flatt."

Thomas Higgens.   Jan Willemsen Scuth.

Wolf Nyssen; executed.   Willem Leendertsen, brass-founder.

Peter Bronck's house is now a historic site in Greene Country. — Pieter Bronck; built a tavern in Beverwyck, in 1651, which was then the third at that place; afterwards lived at Coxackie, the creek at which place was called by the Dutch, Peter Bronck's kill.

Tomas Kenningh.   Jacob Jansen van Stoutenburgh.

Jan de Neger; Scherprechter, or hangman to the colonie.

SENTENCE OF WILLEM JURIAENSEN BAKKER.

As the minute in the Gerechts rolle, or court register, of the sentence pronounced against this public disturber will afford some idea of the strictness of the police in those days, we are tempted to translate it.—*O'Callaghan's Hist. of N. Netherland, p. 437.*

"Their worships, the Commissioners and Council of the colonie of Rensselaerswyck, having duly considered and weighed the demand of the Honorable Director, as prosecutor against Willem Juriaensen Bakker, and finding that he was already banished out the colonie by their Worshipful Court, on the 4th February, 1644; and afterward because that he attempted on the Lord's highway with a knife to stab the person of Antonje de Hooges, then commis to the Noble Patroon, whereby he, in as much as in him lay, did commit a murder, for which he, on the 28th August, 1647, was banished from the colonie; and he having by petition prayed for a respite, which was granted to him, he pledged all his goods, and also subjected himself to the banishment of his person, should he happen to insult any person within or without the court, or to do any thing that should be displeasing, or worthy of punishment. Therefore, the Honorable Prosecutor, recapitulating the same, has set forth, to wit, that he, the Delinquent, hath so frightened and shocked a certain woman, [Saertje Cornelis, wife of Thomas Sanderssen Smith,] that according to her complaint, she hath miscarried; Secondly, that he hath unjustly censured some honorable people, among others some of the Worshipful Court here, asserting, as relates to the agreement between him and Jan van Hoesem, that they had written a falsehood; Thirdly, having been quietly spoken to about the purchase of two beasts, he entering the house, called out that he had a knife in his sleeve, and that, if he were meddled with, he should pay the Honorable Prosecutor with it. Besides, being summoned on account of these enormities, he did openly insult the Honorable Prosecutor here, saying, 'I must bury you; I am summoned before the court; I must hang.' Moreover have we been assured by trustworthy persons, that he hath said to certain females who were proceeding to partake of the Lord's Supper, 'Is it a bit of bread you want? Come to my house and I'll give you a whole loaf;' and divers other things. [On being asked his age, 'to the contempt of the court, he said he was about twenty-one, though it is known to us that he is at least seventy years of age.] WHEREFORE, he being a blasphemer, a street-scold, a murderer as far as his intentions are concerned, a defamer, a contemner of law and justice, and a disturber of the public peace, their Worships of the court aforesaid have adjudged and sentenced, as they do hereby sentence and adjudge, that the aforesaid sentence of banishment shall stand fast, and he Willem Juriaensen, is hereby banished out the district and jurisdiction of this colonie, from now henceforth and forever, to leave by the first vessel, and never more to return, on pain of corporal punishment: all with costs of court. Thus sentenced, &c., in College, this 18th July, 1650 to the knowledge of me, "A. DE HOOGES, Secretary.

"27th July, 1650. Resolved, that Willem Juriaensen shall be conveyed on board of Rutger Jacobsen, and then released, Rutger Jacobsen promising to give him a passage in his yacht to the Manhattans."

ALBANY DIRECTORY.
1849.

The following pages, to and including page 74, particularly those containing the names of the officers of societies, routes of travel, and public places, have reference to the year 1848-9.

MAYORS OF THE CITY OF ALBANY.

The following are the names of the mayors of the city of Albany, from 1686 down to 1848, with the terms of service of each:

Peter Schuyler	1686 to 1694	Sybrant G. Van Schaick	1756 to 1761
Johannis Abeel	1694 to 1695	Volkert P. Douw	1761 to 1770
Evert Bancker	1695 to 1696	Abraham C. Cuyler	1770 to 1778
Derick Wessels	1696 to 1698	John Barclay	1778 to 1779
Hendrick Hansen	1698 to 1699	Abraham Ten Broeck	1779 to 1783
Peter Van Brugh	1699 to 1700	John Ja. Beekman	1783 to 1786
Jan Jans Bleecker	1700 to 1701	John Lansing, jr.	1786 to 1790
Johannis Bleecker	1701 to 1702	Abraham Yates, jr.	1790 to 1796
Albert Ryckman	1702 to 1703	Abraham Ten Broeck	1796 to 1799
Johannis Schuyler	1703 to 1706	Phil S Van Rensselaer	1799 to 1814
David Schuyler	1706 to 1707	Elisha Jenkins	1814 to 1819
Evert Bancker	1707 to 1709	Phil. S. Van Rensselaer	1819 to 1821
Johannis Abeel	1709 to 1710	Charles E. Dudley	1821 to 1824
Robert Livingston, jr.	1710 to 1719	Ambrose Spencer	1824 to 1826
Myndert Schuyler	1719 to 1721	James Stevenson	1826 to 1828
Peter Van Brugh	1721 to 1723	Charles E. Dudley	1828 to 1829
Myndert Schuyler	1723 to 1725	Isaiah Townsend	1829 to 1831
Johannis Cuyler	1725 to 1726	Francis Bloodgood	1831 to 1832
Rutger Bleecker	1726 to 1729	John Townsend	1832 to 1833
John De Peyster	1729 to 1731	Francis Bloodgood	1833 to 1834
Hans Hansen	1731 to 1732	Erastus Corning	1834 to 1837
John De Peyster	1732 to 1733	Teunis Van Vechten	1837 to 1838
Edward Holland	1733 to 1741	Jared L. Rathbone	1838 to 1841
John Schuyler	1741 to 1742	Teunis Van Vechten	1841 to 1842
Cornelius Schuyler	1742 to 1746	Barent P. Staats	1842 to 1843
Dirck Ten Broeck	1746 to 1748	Friend Humphrey	1843 to 1845
Jacob C. Ten Eyck	1748 to 1750	John Keyes Paige	1845 to 1846
Robert Sanders	1750 to 1754	William Parmalee	1846 to 1848
Hans Hansen	1754 to 1756	John Taylor	1848 to 1849

Philip S. Van Rensselaer held the office of mayor 17 years—being the longest period that any one person continued in the office.

Jared L. Rathbone was the first mayor elected by the people. Previous to his third term these officers were elected by the Common Council. Of the number seven survive.

STREETS, LANES, ALLEYS, &c.

See appendix for lists of street name changes.

All the streets running west from the river, commence their numbers at the eastern boundary. All those running parallel with the river (except Broadway, North Pearl, Montgomery and Water, which commence their numbers at the southern boundary), commence numbering at the northern boundary. Several of the streets have no buildings upon them.

Academy Park fronts on Eagle and Elk streets and Capitol Park.
Alexander street, from South Pearl to Eagle, 1st south Bassett.
Alms House Square, fronts on Gansevoort, Snipe, Perry and Ferry.
Arch street, from river to Alms House Square, 1st south Ferry.
Bassett street, from river to South Pearl, 2d south Schuyler.
Bleecker street,   "   "   "   1st south Lydius.
Beaver street from Broadway to Eagle, 1st south State.
Bradford street, from Snipe to western boundary, 1st south Schenectady turnpike.
Broadway, from north to south boundary.
Broad street, from Lydius to south boundary, 1st west South Pearl.
Canal Basin, fronts Water, Lawrence, Montgomery and De Witt.
Canal street, from North Pearl to Snipe.
Capitol Park, fronts on Eagle and State, and Academy Park.
Catharine street, from Clinton to Swan.
Centre street, from Lumber to canal basin.
Cherry street, from River to Franklin, 1st south Schuyler.
Church street, from Ferry to Broadway, 1st west Broadway.
Chapel street, from State to Patroon, 1st west North Pearl.
Chestnut street, from Hawk to Lark, 1st south State.
Cortland street, from Delaware turnpike to Alms House Square.
Colonie street, from Water to western boundary.
Columbia street, from river to Eagle, 3d north State.
Clinton Square, fronts on Pearl, Patroon and Orange.
Clinton street, from southern boundary to Arch.
Cross street, from Canal to Orange, 2d west North Pearl.
Dallius street, from southern boundary to Lydius, 1st east Green.
Daniel street, from Beaver to Eagle.
Dean street, from Steuben to Hudson, 1st west Quay.
Delaware Square, fronts on Delaware turnpike, Ferry, Lark, and Lydius.
Delaware street, from Clinton to Eagle.
Dennison street, from Broadway to Liberty.
De Witt street, from canal basin to Broadway.
Diagonal street, from Liberty to junction of Hudson and Union.
Division street, from river to South Pearl, 3d south of State.
Dove street, from northern to southern boundary, 3d west Eagle.
Eagle street, from southern boundary to Canal.

Streets, Lanes, Alleys, &c. 27

Franklin st., from Lydius to southern boundary, 1st east South Pearl.
Fulton street, from Lydius to Plain, 1st west South Pearl.
Gansevoort st., from river to western boundary, southernmost street.
Grand street, from Beaver to Arch.
Hawk street, from northern to southern boundary, 1st west Eagle.
Hamilton street, from river to western boundary, 1st north Lydius.
Hare street, from head of Orange to western boundary.
Herkimer street, from river to South Pearl.
Howard street, from South Pearl to Eagle, 1st south State.
Hudson street, from river to western boundary.
Hudson Square, fronts on Washington, Partridge and Ontario.
High street, from State to Lydius, 2d west Eagle.
Jackson street, from Colonie to Spencer, 1st east Broadway.
James street, from State to Columbia, 1st west   do.
Jay street, from Eagle to Lark, 3d south State.
John street, from river to Franklin, 1st north Ferry.
Jefferson street, from Eagle to Delaware Square, 1st south Lydius.
Knox street, from Elk to southern boundary, 1st west Lark.
Lark street, from southern boundary to Patroon, 4th west Eagle.
Lawrence street, from river to Broadway, 1st north canal basin.
Lewis Alley, from Grand west.
Lumber street, from river to western boundary, 3d south canal basin.
Lydius street, from river to western boundary.
Lancaster street, from Eagle to western boundary, 2d south State.
Lodge street, from Beaver to Columbia, 2d west North Pearl.
Liberty street, from Hudson to Lydius, 1st west Broadway.
Maiden Lane, from river to Eagle, 1st north State.
Mercer street, from Delaware turnpike to Alms House Square.
Montgomery street, from Steuben to northern boundary.
Morris street, from Delaware Square to northern boundary.
Morton street, from Clinton to Dove.
Mulberry street, from river to Franklin, 3d south Lydius.
North Ferry street, from Bath ferry to Broadway.
North Lansing street, from river to Broadway, 2d south canal basin.
North Pearl street, from State to northern boundary.
North Square, fronts on Lark, Canal, Knox and Elk.
Norton street, (late Store Lane,) from Green to South Pearl.
Nucella street, from river to Gansevoort.
Ontario street, northern to southern boundary, 2d west Alms House.
Orange street, from river to Hare, 4th north State.
Park street, from State to Lancaster, 1st west Eagle.
Partridge street, from southern boundary to Schenectady turnpike.
Patroon street, from Broadway to western boundary, 6th north State.
Perry street, beginning at Alms House Square, southern to northern boundary.
Pier, runs from foot of Hamilton, north 4323 feet, and 80 feet broad to the foot of Lawrence street, forming a basin of an area of 32 and 1-10th acres.
Pine street, from Chapel to Eagle, 2d north of State.
Philip street, from Lydius to Hudson, 3d west South Pearl.
Plain street, from South Pearl to Philip, 1st south Hudson.
Pleasant street, from Western to Schenectady turnpike.
Plumb street, from river to Franklin, 1st south Bassett.

Providence street, from Delaware turnpike to Alms House Square.
Quackenbush street, from river to Broadway.
Quail street, from northern to southern boundary, 1st west Alms House.
Quay street, along the dock, from "   " to Orange street.
Rensselaer street, from river to South Pearl, 2d south Ferry.
Robin street, from Alms House Square to Washington, 1st west Snipe.
Rose street, from Hamilton to Lydius, 1st west Green.
Sand street, from Lark to western boundary.
Schuyler street, from river to Clinton, 4th south Ferry.
Second street, from Ten Broeck to western boundary.
South Lansing street, from river to Franklin, 1st south Herkimer.
South Pearl street, from State to Gansevoort.
Spencer street, from river to Broadway, 1st south Lumber.
Spruce street, from Eagle to Lark, 1st north Elk.
State street, from river to western boundary.
Steuben street, from river to Eagle, 2d north State.
Snipe street, beginning at Alms House, to northern boundary.
Swan street, from southern to northern boundary, 2d west Eagle.
Ten Broeck street, from Patroon to Colonie, 1st west North Pearl.
Third street, from Ten Broeck to western boundary.
Union street, from Lydius to Hudson, 2d west Broadway.
Van Tromp street, from Broadway to North Pearl, 1st n. Columbia.
Van Schaack street, from North Pearl to Cross, 1st west Canal.
Van Woert street, from Broadway to western boundary.
Van Zandt street, from South Pearl to Philip, 1st north Lydius.
Vine street, from river to Franklin, south Nucella.
Warren street, from Eagle to Alms House Square, 2d south Ferry.
Washington st., from Academy and Capitol Parks to western boundary.
Washington Square, fronts on State, Knox, Lydius and Willett.
Water street, from northern boundary to Steuben, 1st west Quay.
Westerlo street, from river to Delaware Square, 2d south Lydius.
William street, from Hudson to Howard, 1st west South Pearl.
Wilson street, from Broadway to Ten Broeck, 1st south Lumber.
Willett street, from State to Lydius, 1st west Lark.
Yates street, from Delaware Square to western boundary.

AN ACT

For the Division and Equalization of the Wards of the City of Albany, and for other purposes. Passed March 30th, 1841.

FIRST WARD.—Beginning at a point where the south bounds of the city intersect the west line of Rensselaer street; thence running north along the east bounds of the city to a point opposite the centre of Arch street; thence westerly through the centre of Arch street to the centre of Hallenbake street; thence northerly through the centre of Hallenbake street to the centre of Arch street from the west; thence westerly through the centre of Arch street to the centre of Eagle street; thence southerly through the centre of Eagle street to the south bounds of the city; thence easterly along said south bounds to the place of beginning.

SECOND WARD.—Beginning at the intersection of the centre of Arch street with the east bounds of the city, and running thence northerly along the said bounds of the city to a point opposite the centre of Herkimer street; thence westerly along the centre of Herkimer street to the centre of Pearl street; thence southerly along the centre of Pearl street to the centre of Westerlo street; thence westerly along the centre of Westerlo street to the centre of Hallenbake street; thence northerly along the centre of Hallenbake street to the centre of Westerlo street from the west; thence westerly along the centre of Westerlo street to the centre of Eagle street; thence southerly along the centre of Eagle street to the centre of Arch street; thence easterly along the centre of Arch street to the centre of Hallenbake street; thence southerly along the centre of Hallenbake street to the centre of Arch street from the east; thence easterly along the centre of Arch street to the east bounds of the city and place of beginning.

THIRD WARD.—Beginning at a point in the easterly bounds of the city opposite the centre of Herkimer street, and running thence northerly along said east bounds to a point opposite the centre of Hamilton street; thence westerly along the centre of Hamilton street to the centre of Eagle street; thence southerly along the centre of Eagle street to the centre of Westerlo street; thence easterly along the centre of Westerlo street to the centre of Hallenbake street; thence southerly along the centre of Hallenbake street to the centre of Westerlo street from the east; thence easterly through the centre of Westerlo street to the centre of Pearl street; thence northerly through the centre of Pearl street to the centre of Herkimer street; thence easterly along the centre of Herkimer street to the place of beginning.

FOURTH WARD.—Beginning at a point in the east bounds of the city opposite the centre of Hamilton street, and running thence northerly along said east bounds to a point opposite the centre of State street bridge; thence westerly through the centre of State street bridge and State street to the centre of Eagle street; thence southerly along the centre of Eagle street to the centre of Hamilton street; thence easterly along the centre of Hamilton street to the east bounds of the city and place of beginning.

FIFTH WARD.—Beginning at a point in the east bounds of the city opposite the centre of State street bridge; thence running northerly along said east bounds to a point opposite the centre of Columbia street bridge; thence westerly along the centre of said bridge and of Columbia street to the centre of Pearl street; thence northerly along the centre of Pearl street to the centre of Fox street; thence westerly along the centre of Fox street to the centre of a street thirty-six Ryland feet in width, and leading from Fox to Spruce streets; thence southerly through the centre of said street to the centre of Spruce street; thence easterly through the centre of Spruce street to the centre of Eagle street; thence southerly through the centre of Eagle street to the centre of State street; thence easterly along the centre of State street and of the State street bridge to the east bounds of the city and place of beginning.

SIXTH WARD.—Beginning at a point in the east bounds of the city opposite the centre of the Columbia street bridge, and running thence northerly along said east bounds to a point opposite the centre of Lumber street; thence westerly along the centre of Lumber street to the centre of Ten Broeck street; thence southerly along the centre of Ten Broeck street to the centre of Patroon street; thence easterly along the centre of Patroon street to the centre of Chapel street; thence southerly along the centre of Chapel street to the centre of Canal street; thence easterly along the centre of Canal street to the centre of Pearl street; thence southerly along the centre of Pearl street to the centre of Columbia street; thence easterly along the centre of Columbia street and the Columbia street bridge to the east bounds of the city and place of beginning.

SEVENTH WARD.—Beginning at a point in the east bounds of the city opposite the centre of Lumber street, and running thence northerly along the east bounds of the city until it strikes a point opposite a red cedar post with brick around it, standing on the west bank of the Hudson river, which post is distant twenty-two chains and thirty-six links from the south-east corner of the storehouse of Stephen Van Rensselaer, on a course, north forty degrees and twenty minutes west; thence westerly to the said cedar post; thence north forty-eight degrees west to the west bounds of the late town of Colonie; thence southerly along said west bounds to the centre of Lumber street; thence easterly along the centre of Lumber street to the east bounds of the city and place of beginning.

EIGHTH WARD.—Beginning at the intersection of the centre of Canal and Chapel streets; thence running northerly along the centre of Chapel to the centre of Patroon street; thence westerly along the centre of Patroon street to the centre of Ten Broeck street; thence northerly along the centre of Ten Broeck street to the centre of Lumber street; thence westerly along the centre of Lumber street to the west bounds of the late town of Colonie; thence southerly along said west bounds to the centre of Patroon street; thence easterly along the centre of Patroon street to the centre of Lark street; thence southerly along the centre of Lark street to the centre of Spruce street; thence easterly along the centre of Spruce street to the centre of a street leading from Spruce to Canal streets, of thirty-six Ryland feet in width; thence northerly along the centre of said street to the centre of Canal street; thence easterly along the centre of Canal street to the place of beginning.

NINTH WARD.—Beginning at the intersection of Eagle and State streets, and running thence northerly along the centre of Eagle street to the centre of Spruce street; thence westerly along the centre of Spruce street to the centre of Lark street; thence northerly along the centre of Lark street to the centre of Patroon street; thence westerly along the centre of Patroon street to the west bounds of the late town of Colonie; thence southerly to the south side of Patroon street; thence westerly along the north range of the city to the west bounds thereof; thence southerly along said west bounds to the centre of Lydius street; thence easterly along the centre of Lydius street to the centre of Main Avenue; thence northerly through the centre thereof to the centre of State street; thence easterly along the centre of State street to the place of beginning.

TENTH WARD.—Beginning at the intersection of the centre of Eagle street with the south bounds of the city, and running thence north through the centre of Eagle street to the centre of State street; thence westerly through the centre of State street to the centre of Main avenue; thence southerly through the centre of Main avenue to the centre of Lydius street; thence westerly along the centre of Lydius street to the west bounds of the city; thence southerly along said west bounds to the south bounds of the city; thence easterly along said south bounds to the place of beginning.

BANKS.

The banks are open every day in the year, from ten A. M. to two P. M., except Sundays and holidays. The interest for discount in the banks in this city, is fixed at 7 per centum per annum. Three days of grace are allowed, and the discount taken for the same. Every bill or note offered for discount, must be delivered the day preceding the day of discount. Bills or notes lodged at the banks for collection, when protested for non-payment, the person lodging the same pays the charge of protest. Deposits of money, or notes for collection, must be entered in dealer's book at the time of deposit. No interest allowed on deposits.

BANK OF ALBANY, No. 42 State street: incorporated April 10, 1792; charter expires in 1855; capital, $240,000; shares, $30 each; dividends, May and November; discount day, Thursday. Jacob H. Ten Eyck, president; Jellis Winne, jr., cashier; J. H. Ten Eyck, Teunis Van Vechten, Harmon Pumpelly, Henry Bleecker, Volkert P. Douw, William Walch, Benjamin Tibbitts, David Newland, J. Winne, jr., Andrew D. Lansing, Daniel Cady, directors; E. R. Phelps, teller; N. Bleecker, jr., bookkeeper; John Sill, discount clerk; Charles Lansing and Henry Wilkinson, clerks.

Reminiscences.—A great many projects were on foot in the year 1792. The capitalists were eager for a bank, and a meeting was called on the 3d of February, at Lewis's Tavern, (south side of State street, corner Pearl,) to discuss the subject. There was at this time, it is believed, but one bank in the state, the *Bank of New York*, the stock of which was fifty per cent. above par. It was decided that the interests of the northern part of the state required the location of a bank at Albany. Some one writing for the newspapers, confidently asserted that a hundred thousand dollars would be subscribed in a few hours in the city alone; but it was liberally resolved that the neighboring places should be permitted to share in the honors and emoluments of the enterprise. At a subsequent meeting, the outlines of a plan for the establishment of a bank were presented. The name of the institution to be *The Albany Bank*; the capital, $75,000, to be divided into 500 shares, of $150 each; $15 to be paid on subscribing, and the remainder in three instalments; 13 directors to constitute the board, 9 of whom to be residents of the city. Jeremiah Van Rensselaer, Jacob Vanderheyden, and Barent Bleecker, were to open the books for subscriptions in the week following, and to close them as soon as five hundred shares should be subscribed. Accordingly the committee opened the books on the 17th of February, and the stock was overrun in amount in less than three hours. After the books were closed, offers of 10 per cent. advance were made on the stock, and on Saturday, the day following, it rose to one hundred per cent. cash. Application was immediately made to the legislature for a charter, and as the prospect of its being granted was more or less doubtful during the progress of the bill, the price of the stock rose or fell, creating no little excitement and speculation in this quiet region, where stock *transactions* were quite a novelty. At one time it is said to have stood at $100 premium on a share upon which only $15 had been paid. Stephen Van Rensselaer was elected president. Towards the close of the session the act of incorporation became a law. The first election of directors was held on the 12th of June, at the City Tavern, and resulted as follows: Abraham Ten Broeck, Cornelius Glen, Stephen Van Rensselaer, Jeremiah Van Rensselaer, John Maley, Abraham Van Vechten, Henry Cuyler, John Stevenson, James Caldwell, Jacob Vanderheyden, Goldsbrow Banyar, Daniel Hale, Elkanah Watson. At a meeting of the directors thus chosen, Abraham Ten Broeck was elected president. The bank was opened for deposits on the 16th of July, and began to discount on the 17th. The rate of interest was 6 per cent. In September notice was given that notes of 45 days only would be discounted. The act of incorporation limited the capital stock to $260,000; each share to be 400 Spanish milled dollars, or its equivalent. This did not exhaust the idle capital, and those who were unable to get bank stock, proposed to build an aqueduct. Whether they designed to throw *cold water* on the former project does not appear, but it will be allowed that their scheme promised to furnish an equally useful *circulating medium.*

In 1797 a report was published in the New York papers that the Albany Bank had failed, on account of the great influx of counterfeits of its own bills. The bank had now been in operation five years, and there had not yet been a counterfeit discovered. Its af-

Banks.

fairs appear to have been managed with great prudence and considerable ability; and in proportion to its capital, possessed more specie than any other bank in the country. The current price of its stock was from 45 to 50 per cent. above par. The banking house was originally located in Pearl street, and afterwards removed to the building next to the Mansion House on the south; in February, 1810, it was removed to the north east corner of State and Court streets, the present site of the Exchange; and when the latter building was erected, the bank was removed to No. 42 State street, where it now remains.

NEW YORK STATE BANK, No. 69 State street: incorporated in 1803; charter expires in 1851; capital, $369,000; shares, $28; dividends, 5 per cent, semi-annually, in March and September; discount day, Monday. Rufus H. King, president; J. B. Plumb, cashier; Rufus H. King, G. Y. Lansing, Joel Rathbone, M. T. Reynolds, William Adams, R. Boyd, P. Gansevoort, W. E. Bleecker, W. C. Miller, L. Chapin, J. B. Plumb, A. McIntyre, directors; H. A. Allen, teller; John S. Leake and H. S. Lansing, book-keepers; John H. Van Antwerp, corresponding clerk; William McHarg and John Strother, clerks; Isaac Fondey and James A. Chestney, western department.

Reminiscences.—This bank was incorporated with a capital of $460,000. At a meeting of the directors on the 25th of March, 1803, John Taylor was chosen president, and John W. Yates cashier. It commenced business on Wednesday, Sept. 7; banking hours from 9 to 12, and from 2 to 4. Notes offered for discount were to be drawn payable at the bank, unless the drawer resided in the city of Albany or New York. Discounts were made for 36 days. In December the bank altered its hours of business, opening at 9, and closing at 2. On the 10th of May, 1804, they commenced business in their new banking house, where they have ever since continued. By the act of incorporation, the comptroller, together with John Taylor, Thomas Tillotson, Abraham G. Lansing, Peter Gansevoort, Jr., Elkanah Watson, John R. Bleecker, Francis Bloodgood, John Robinson, Gilbert Stewart, John D. P. Douw, Richard Lush, and Thomas Mather, were constituted the first directors. The business was to be confined to the city of Albany, the rate of interest to be 6 per cent., and the state reserved the right of subscribing 3000 shares.

MECHANICS' AND FARMERS' BANK, corner of Broadway and Exchange street: incorporated in 1811; charter expires in 1853; capital, $442,000; shares, $17; dividends, semi-annually, in May and November; discount days, Tuesdays and Fridays. Thomas W. Olcott, president; Samuel S. Fowler, vice-president; Edward E. Kendrick, cashier; Thos. W. Olcott, Samuel S. Fowler, Friend Humphrey, Henry Newman, James Kidd, Lemuel Steele, Thomas Hillhouse, Hugh Humphrey Harmanus Bleecker, W. W. Forsyth, James B. Jermain, Robert Shepherd, directors; Thomas Olcott, teller; O. M. Beach, second teller; Theodore Olcott, 2d, third teller; Constantine Kowalski, general book-keeper; William McHench, discount clerk; James A. Pratt, entry clerk; Edmund Winne, clerk; John F. Jenkins, notary; John Highland, porter; T. W. Olcott, pension agent; Lemuel Jenkins and Robert Shepherd, accountants.

Reminiscences.—The history of the origin and infancy of this institution, would be quite interesting to the present generation, since there were some phases in banking operations at that remote period, which are unknown now. The capital stock was limited to 600,000 dollars. The first election for directors was held on Monday, June 1, 1812. It seems to have been very generally understood among the stockholders for some time previous, that two federalists should be admitted into the board, the directors named in the law being all democrats; but whose seats should be vacated for their admission, was not so easily agreed upon. The election opened at 10 o'clock, at the Columbian Hotel, in Court street, and was continued to a late hour in the afternoon. It was a warm and animated contest, and finally resulted in the election of the following: Solomon Southwick, president; Benjamin Knower, Elisha Dorr, Isaac Denniston, Benjamin Van Benthuysen, William Fowler, George Merchant, Thomas Lennington, Giles W. Porter, Willard Walker, Walter Wood, Peter Boyd and Isaac Hutton. The two latter were elected in the place of Spencer Stafford and John Bryan. Of that board it is believed there are three or four survivors. At the next annual election Isaac Hutton was elected president, and the direction consisted of Thomas Lennington, Peter Boyd, Benjamin

---

The facade of the State Bank is embedded into the current skyscraper after a couple of different building additions. Original bank designed by Philip Hooker. See my book *Albany Through Time* (Font Hill Media, 2021) for photos of the building evolution.

Banks.

Knower, Russell Forsyth, William Fowler, William Boyd, Elisha Dorr, Walter Weed, Giles W. Porter, Benjamin Van Benthaysen, Charles E. Dudley and Thomas Herring. This bank has ever been conducted with signal ability and success.

COMMERCIAL BANK, No 40 State street: incorporated in 1825; charter expired in 1847, and the institution is now under the general banking law; capital, $300,000; shares, $20; dividends, July and January; discount days, Mondays and Thursdays. John Townsend, president; John L. Schoolcraft, vice-president; James Taylor, cashier; John Townsend, J. L. Schoolcraft, John Gott, James Horner, Augustus James, Giles Sanford, James D. Wasson, Robert H. Pruyn, Andrew White, Anthony M. Strong, Anthony Gould, William C. Durant; John B. Wasson, teller; Frederick S. Pease, book-keeper; George C. Lee, Charles Lansing, James G. Stafford, clerks; John F. Batchelder, discount and Savings Bank clerk.

Reminiscences — On the 20th of October, 1813, John Bogart, George Webster, E. F. Backus, Joseph H. Webb and Vinal Luce gave notice of application to the legislature for a charter to incorporate the Albany Commercial Bank, with a capital of $1,250,000. The banking capital of the state was at this time $20,350 000, exclusive of $810,000 which the state reserved the privilege of subscribing; making an aggregate $21,160,000. Notices of application were now given for eighteen more banks, with an aggregate capital of $15,250,000. Three of these were from Albany, viz.: the Merchants' Bank, Commercial Bank, and North River Bank; in New York, Millers' Bank, Grocers' Bank, Commission Company, Coal Company, Patent Cloth Manufacturing Company, North River Company, Vermont Mining and Smelting Company; also one at Utica, Schenectady, Johnstown, Cooperstown, Auburn, Canandaigua, Geneva and Oxford. No bank, however, was chartered in Albany until 1825, when the Commercial Bank went into operation, having no connection with the one above contemplated. The present bank has at different times lost nearly the whole amount of its capital by peculation, but by extraordinary good management recovered itself again, and enjoys a high reputation for its soundness and the ability of its officers.

CANAL BANK, No. 40 State street: incorporated in 1829; charter expires in 1854; capital, $300,000; shares, $20. This bank failed in July, 1848, the first bank failure in Albany, and its affairs are in the hands of a receiver.

ALBANY CITY BANK, No. 47 State street: incorporated in 1834; charter expires in 1864; capital, $500,000; shares, $100; dividends, April and October; discount days, Tuesdays and Fridays. Erastus Corning, president; Watts Sherman, cashier; Erastus Corning, Ellis Baker, Martin Van Alstyne, Bradford R. Wood, William Seymour, John V. L. Pruyn, John Knower, James M. Cook, Watts Sherman, William Smith, William Humphrey, H. H. Martin, Eli Perry, directors; C. L. Garfield, teller; D. W. C. Rice and John T. Marshall, book-keepers; Isaac Fondey, discount clerk and notary public; Simeon J. Leake, corresponding clerk; T. A. Knower, in western department; Jacob Downing, jr., Dudley Van Vliet, F. Van Vliet and —— Story, clerks.

ALBANY EXCHANGE BANK, No. 3 Exchange Building: certificates filed December 11, 1838, to continue 662 years; capital $311,100, with privilege to increase to $10,000,000; dividends, January and July; discount days, Tuesdays and Fridays. George W. Stanton, president; Noah Lee, cashier; George W. Stanton, Samuel Stevens, James McNaughton, John Taylor, Oliver Steele, John M. Newton, Ichabod L. Judson, Samuel Pruyn, Galen Batchelder, Gaylor Sheldon, L. G. Taylor, William McElroy, F. J. Barnard, directors; Andrew McElroy teller; Joseph M. Lovett, book-keeper; Wm. H. Lee, discount clerk; John Ward, clerk.

ALBANY SAVINGS BANK: incorporated in 1820; being the oldest in the state. Open at the Commercial Bank, No. 40 State street, every day, to receive deposits. It pays an interest of 5 per cent. per annum to depositors, payable half-yearly, on the third Wednesday in January and July. John Townsend, president; Teunis Van Vechten, 1st vice-president; Samuel Stevens, 2d vice-president; John L. Winne, 3d vice-president; William Newton, William McHarg, James Taylor, Rufus H. King, Jacob H. Ten Eyck, Gerrit Y. Lansing, John I. Boyd, Frederick I. Barnard, Benjamin Tibbits, James Stevenson, William E. Bleecker, Robert H. Pruyn, Harmon Pumpelly, James D. Wasson, Friend Humphrey, directors; James Taylor, treasurer; Robert H. Pruyn, secretary. Open during banking hours, from 10 to 2 o'clock.

INSURANCE COMPANIES.

ALBANY INSURANCE COMPANY, No. 56 State street: incorporated March 8, 1811; charter expires 1851; capital, $300,000; shares, $60. Teunis Van Vechten, president; Stephen Groesbeck, secretary; Gerrit Y. Lansing, Rufus H. King, Augustus James, Marcus T. Reynolds, Lewis Benedict, Archibald McIntyre, John Townsend, Wm. C. Miller, Henry Bleecker, Jacob H. Ten Eyck, Herman Pumpelly, John T. Cooper, directors.

The original charter fixed the shares at $100, and limited the number at 500. The directors named in the act of incorporation were, Elisha Jenkins, Philip S. Van Rensselaer, Isaiah Townsend, Dudley Walsh, Henry Guest jr., Charles Z. Platt, Simeon De Witt, Stephen Lush, Chas. D. Cooper, Thomas Gould, John Woodworth, Peter Gansevoort, Christian Miller.

FIREMEN'S INSURANCE COMPANY, corner of State and Green streets; Incorporated in 1831; charter expires 1861; capital, $150,000; shares, $10. James Stevenson, president; Richard Van Rensselaer, secretary; John Taylor, Peter Gansevoort, Thomas McElroy, Hugh Humphrey, George W. Stanton, Lemuel Steele, Egbert Egberts, William Adams, Lansing Pruyn, John M. Newton, Lyman Chapin, Benjamin Tibbits, Stephen Van Rensselaer, Henry Newman, Gerrit V. S. Bleecker, Joel Rathbone, E. P. Prentice, A. E. Brown, Joseph Davis, J. H. Ten Eyck, C. A. De Forest, Andrew White, S. S. Peck, A. Van Vorst, directors.

MUTUAL INSURANCE COMPANY OF THE CITY AND COUNTY OF ALBANY, No. 450 Broadway: incorporated in 1836; charter expires 1856. Erastus Corning, president; Matthew Trotter, secretary; B. P. Staats, Eli Perry, Watts Sherman, Daniel Fry, H. H. Martin, Giles Sanford, John Knower, J. G. Cotrell, Peter Relyea, Ellis Baker, John Van Valkenburgh, Jared A. Post, directors.

MUTUAL BENEFIT LIFE INSURANCE COMPANY, S. Groesbeck, agent, No. 56 State street.

AMERICAN MUTUAL LIFE INSURANCE COMPANY, William C. Miller, agent, No. 56 State street.

NATIONAL LOAN FUND LIFE ASSURANCE SOCIETY OF LONDON, Wm. Lacy, agent, Argus Office.

FIRE INSURANCE COMPANY OF HARTFORD, CT., D. S. Durrie, agent, Albany.

EQUITABLE LIFE INSURANCE, ANNUITY AND TRUST COMPANY, L. Birdseye, agent, No. 59 State street.

CITY FIRE INSURANCE COMPANY OF NEW YORK, P. W. Groot, agent, No. 49 State street.

ÆTNA FIRE INSURANCE COMPANY OF HARTFORD, CT., John F. Jenkins, agent, No. 7 Commercial Buildings.

PROTECTION INSURANCE COMPANY OF HARTFORD, CT., John F. Jenkins, agent, No. 7 Commercial Buildings.

PROTECTION INSURANCE COMPANY OF NEW JERSEY, L. Norton, agent, No. 10 Douw's Buildings.

EAGLE LIFE AND HEALTH INSURANCE COMPANY OF NEW YORK, C. W. Bentley, No. 80 Quay street; Wm. C. Schuyler, No. 10 Douw's Buildings; S. P. Carter, at Wells & Co.'s Express Office, agents.

MUTUAL SAFETY INSURANCE COMPANY OF NEW YORK, J. W. Ford, agent, No. 460 Broadway.

LEXINGTON FIRE AND MARINE INSURANCE COMPANY, Heminway & Dowd, agents, No. 2. Exchange, first floor.

COLUMBUS INSURANCE COMPANY OF NEW YORK, H. C. Southwick, agent, No. 15 Exchange, first floor.

NORTH AMERICAN FIRE INSURANCE COMPANY, S. Groesbeck, agent, No. 56 State street.

CAMDEN FIRE AND MARINE INSURANCE COMPANY OF NEW JERSEY, C. W. Bentley, agent, No. 80 Quay street.

NATIONAL FIRE INSURANCE COMPANY, E. Satterlee, agent, No. 61 State street.

LEXINGTON FIRE AND MARINE INSURANCE COMPANY, agent.

FIRE AND MARINE INSURANCE COMPANY AT SOMERVILLE, Lambert Norton, agent, No. 10 Douw's Buildings.

HOPE MUTUAL LIFE INSURANCE COMPANY OF HARTFORD, CT., Henry R. Gosman, agent, No. 440 Broadway.

NORTH WESTERN INSURANCE COMPANY, J. W. Ford, agent, No. 460 Broadway.

CLERGY.

J. W. Belknap, Arbor Hill Meth.,
S. D. Brown, Washington st. "
J. N. Campbell, 1st Presbyterian,
W. H. Campbell, South Dutch,
W. S. Clapp, Green st. Baptist,
J. Clark, Hudson st. Methodist,
J. J. Conroy, Ct. Joseph's,
B. M. Hall, Garretson Station,
E. A. Huntington, 3d Presbyterian,
D. Kennedy, North Dutch,
W. I. Kip, St. Paul's,
T. A. Kyle, St. Mary's,
M. Lawer, German Methodist,
J. Lowrey, Wesleyan "
B. M. Martin, 4th Presbyterian,
J. McCloskey, bishop, Cathedral,
P. McCloskey, St. John's,
J. Miles, Bethel,
S. F. Morrow, Associate Pres.,
J. Newbourg, Bethel Jacob,
H. N. Pohlman, Evan. Eb. Luth.,
H. Potter, St. Peter's,
Wm. Putnam, St. Mary's,
T. R. Rawson, City Missionary,
L. A. Sandford, Ferry st. Meth.,
F. W. Schmidt, Ger. Evan. Luth.,
E. Selkirk, Trinity,
W. B. Sprague, 2d Presbyterian,
R. Warren, State st. Baptist,
B. T. Welch, North Pearl "
—— Barry, South " "
I. Wise, Synagogue,
I. N. Wyckoff, Middle Dutch.

PRACTICING ATTORNEYS.

Otis Allen,
C. L. Austin,
R. L. G. Bancroft,
D. D. Barnard,
W. Barnes,
L. Benedict, Jr., *Sur'gate*
Lucien Birdseye,
A. Blanchard,
Charles H. Bramhall,
Dudley Burwell,
J. B. Brinsmade, Jr.,
James Brown,
John I. Burton,
Peter Cagger,
J. Callanan, Jr.,
D. Campbell,
William R. Cantine,
William Cassidy,
John Cole,
John A. Collier,
Joseph S. Colt,
A. J. Colvin,
S. Daniels, Jr.,
Amos Dean,
E. F. De Lancey,
E. A. Doolittle,
Isaac Edwards,
James Edwards,
F. S. Edwards,
M. Fairchild,
Wm. W. Frothingham,
Dennis B. Gaffney,
Albert Gallup,
Peter Gansevoort,
F. W. Gibb,
Stephen Groesbeck,
William J. Hadley,
S. H. Hammond, *Dis. Atty*
Nathan Hawley,
Ira Harris,
Hamilton Harris,
John E. Hermans,
S. F. Higgins,
John J. Hill,
Nicholas Hill, Jr.,
Robert J. Hilton,
W. J. D. Hilton,
L. D. Holstein,
Thomas D. James,
Charles M. Jenkins,
B. P. Johnson.
R. L. Joice,
N. G. King,
Hale Kingsley,
James L'Amoreaux,
W. L. Learned,
Charles B. Lansing,
L. J. Lansing,
Jacob Lansing,
E. C. Litchfield,
John A. Livingston,
J. D. Livingston,
H. H. Martin,
H. S. McCall,
W. C. McHarg,
Matthew McMahon,
D. McMartin,
Orlando Meads,
W. D. Morange,
A. Morrell,
John Newland,
Richard H. Northrup,
John Olcott,
J. F. O'Toole,
William S. Paddock,
S. Paddock, Jr.,
Levi H. Palmer,
William Parmelee,
S. H. H. Parsons,
George W. Peckham,
R. W. Peckham,
Calvin Pepper,
Calvin Pepper, Jr.,
John Percy,
John K. Porter,
John V. L. Pruyn,
Robert H. Pruyn,
C. A. Pugsley,
Marcus T. Reynolds,
Julius Rhoades,
A. D. Robinson,
James R. Rose,
James B. Sanders,
M. Sanford,
William C. Schuyler,
George Scoville,
Jacob M. Settle,
S. O. Shepherd,
E. J. Sherman,
Cyrus Stevens,
John C. Spencer,
Samuel Stevens,
Alfred B. Street,
J. B. Sturtevant,
Azor Taber,
Cornelius Ten Broeck,
A. Ten Eyck,
M. Trotter,
John J. Tyler,
T. B. Van Buren,
J. S. Van Rensselaer,
S. D. Van Schaack,
Teunis Van Vechten,
Abraham Van Vechten,
H. C. Van Vorst,
C. C. Wasson,
Robert D. Wasson,
Wm. G. Weed,
Robert H. Wells,
J. I. Werner,
Henry G. Wheaton,
James M. Whelpley,
A. D. L. Whipple,
William D. White,
Jonas Wickes,
John Q. Wilson,
G. L. Wilson,
E. S. Willett,
Bradford R. Wood,
D. Wright, *Recorder*,
Horace Wyman,
T. G. Younglove,
Wm. A. Young.

DENTISTS.

J. C. Austin,
Josephus Brockway, Jr.,
J. Monroe,
Alexander Nelson,
Robert Nelson,
David Newcomb,
N. B. Sherwood,
S. Van Namee,
U. H. Wheeler,
J. S. Wood.

PRACTICING PHYSICIANS.

James H. Armsby,
William Bay,
U. G. Bigelow,
James P. Boyd,
James M. Brown,
—— Carhart.
J. H. Case,
Edward H. Clark,
Mason F. Cogswell,
James Cox,
Dr. Curtis,
H. B. Fay, *Alms House Physician*,
D. E. Fonda,
John O. Flagler,
Samuel H. Freeman,
Edmund E. W. Gale,
Patrick Gannon,
C. C. Griffin,
Otto Heinsius,
John W. Hinkley,
Thomas Hun.
Abel Lyon,
James McNaughton,
Peter McNaughton,
Alexander McNaughton,
Alden March,
Nicholas Markey,
David Martin,
John V. P. Quackenbush,
Barent P. Staats,
Peter P. Staats,
B. A. Sheldon,
Rufus B. Sperry,
John Swinburne,
R. H. Thompson,
John F. Townsend,
John H. Trotter,
Peter Van Buren,
John Van Buren,
Peter Van OLinda,
C. C. Waller,
Peter Wendell,
Herman Wendell,
David Wiltsie,
Joel A. Wing,
William I. Young,
E. D. Jones, ⎫
J. A. Paine, ⎬
Henry D. Paine, ⎬ *Homœopathic*,
Horace M. Paine, ⎬
J. M. Ward, ⎭
Noah S. Dean, ⎫
John Fondey, ⎬
Andrew W. Russell, ⎬ *Botanic*,
William B. Stanton, ⎬
Gerrit Westervelt, ⎭
George Cooke, *Lock Hospital*,
Dr. Lacroix, *Lock Dispensary*.

ALBANY CHARTER OFFICERS.

The original charter of the city of Albany was granted by Gov. Dongan, on the 22d of July, 1686, and the following persons were the first who officiated under the charter.

	Aldermen.	*Assistant Aldermen.*
Peter Schuyler, *Mayor*,	Dirk Wessels,	Joachim Staats,
Isaac Swinton, *Recorder*,	Jan Jans Bleecker,	John Lansing,
Robert Livingston, *Clerk*,	David Schuyler,	Isaac Verplanck,
Jan Bleecker, *Chamberlain*,	Johannis Wendell,	Lawrence Van Ale,
Richard Pretty, *Sheriff*,	Lavinus Van Schaack,	Albert Ruyckman,
James Parker, *Marshal*.	Adrian Garretse.	Melgert Winantse.

These were good substantial Dutch burghers, as their names indicate. The charter has undergone important alterations since that day, and the city councils are filled with the descendants of all nations and tongues upon earth. The succession of mayors from 1686 to 1848, will be found on page 25. The annual election takes place in April, and the following are the present city officers, who hold their places until April, 1849.

OFFICERS OF THE CITY OF ALBANY.

Clerk—L. D. Holstein.
Chamberlain—Christopher W. Bender.
Deputy Chamberlain—H. H. Hickcox.
Attorney—Hooper C. Van Vorst.
Surveyor—George W. Carpenter.
Assistant Surveyor—Samuel McElroy.
Marshal—Nelson Scovel.
Overseer of the Poor—Thomas Kirkpatrick.
Superintendent of the Alms House—John Morgan.
Superintendent of the N. D.—David Benson.
Superintendent of the S. D.—George H. Herbert.
Police Justices—John O. Cole and S. H. H. Parsons.
Deputy Excise Officer—C. W. Bender.
Superintendent of the Markets—Jacob Featherly.
Chief Engineer of the Fire Department—James P. Gould.
Assistant Engineers—P. B. Leddy, J. Parker, S. P. Winne, R. J. Grant, G. W. Burdick.
Alms House Physician—Henry B. Fay.
City Physicians—1st district, James M. Brown; 2d, John Swinburne; 3d, Alexander W. McNaughton; 4th, Alfred Clark; 5th, B. A. Sheldon.
Police Constables—George Brainard, Elisha Mack 3d, Thomas Cowell, Charles Phillips, B. B. Whalen, Robert Nixon.
City Inspectors—1st and 2d wards, John Milliman; 3d and 4th, Wm. Leggat; 5th and 6th, Harmon G. Wynkoop; 7th and 8th, S. V. A. Hilton; 9th and 10th, Richard Bygate.
Captains of the Night Police—John Vandervolgen, Absalom Sharp, Henry Pottenburgh, Levi Ewing, John N. Parker, Walter Coleman.
Assistant Captains—James L. Coley, Nicholas W. Groot, William F. Peacock, Henry Hubbell, Royall Thompson, Joseph Coughtry.
Inspector of Weights and Measures—Paul C. Barney.
Fence Viewers—John Morgan, Barent Sanders.
Receiver of Taxes—H. H. Hickcox, deputy chamberlain.
Supervisors—1st ward, Richard Parr; 2d, Matthew McMahon; 3d, J. Hurdis; 4th, Franklin Townsend; 5th, Wm. White; 6th, Samuel Pruyn; 7th, George W. Welch; 8th, Oliver Wallace; 7th, James A. Tremere; 10th, Adam Van Allen.
Assessors—1st ward, Philip Foy; 2d, Abraham M. Purdy; 3d, James P. Gould; 4th, Cyrus L. Woodruff; 5th, Levi Chapman; 6th, Garret L. Winne; 7th, Josiah Patterson; 8th, Myers Henderer; 9th, Sylvester Rathbone; 10th, Job R. Borden.
Ward Constables—1st ward, John McDonald; 2d, John Kinney; 3d, Daniel Van Buskirk; 4th, Amos Dodge; 5th, John R. Peacock; 6th, Archibald Thompson; 7th, Samuel Winchester; 8th, Francis Bray; 9th, William Pearcey; 10th, S V. R. Brayton.
School Commissioners—Gerrit V. S. Bleecker, John O. Cole, John Simpson, Eli Perry, Henry B. Haswell, John O. Flagler, James Maher; George W. Carpenter, Thomas Mc Elroy.
Justices of the Justices' Court—Abraham Morrell, Conrad A. Ten Eyck, David Russell; David Russell, clerk.
Harbor Master—Thomas Hillson, Jr.
Dock Master—John L. Hyatt.
U. S. Collector of Customs—Albert Gallup.

COMMON COUNCIL.

John Taylor, *Mayor*.
Deodatus Wright, *Recorder*.
1st ward—Wm. L. Osborn,
    Lucien B. Laney.
2d ward—George B. Riggs,
    John W. Harcourt.
3d ward—Charles W. Godard,
    Stephen T. Thorn.
4th ward—George T. Ladue,
    Abram Koonz.
5th ward—Henry Bleecker,
    James McNaughton.
6th ward—J. A. Livingston,
    Charles M. Jenkins.
7th ward—John Benson,
    William Gillespie.
8th ward—P. M. McCall,
    John Harrison.
9th ward—William Cumming,
    Richard H. Thompson.
10th ward—Michael Artcher,
    Daniel E. Bassett.

STANDING COMMITTEES.

Academies and Schools—Thompson, Gillespie, Godard.
Accounts—Bleecker, McCall, Thompson.
Applications to the Legislature—McNaughton, Harcourt, Bleecker.
Alms House—Artcher, McCall, McNaughton.
Board of Health—Mayor, Recorder, McNaughton, Laney, Riggs.
Board of Magistrates—Recorder, Livingston, Jenkins, Osborn, Harrison, Cumming.
City Hall—Mayor, Recorder, Harrison, Benson, Bassett, Artcher.
Engines—Cumming, Harrison, Thorn.
Ferry—Thorn, Riggs, Ladue.
Finance—Jenkins, Laney, Bleecker.
Flagging and Paving, N. D.—Livingston, McCall, Bleecker.
Flagging and Paving, S. D.—Bassett, Laney, Koonz.
Lamps—Koonz, Benson, Jenkins.
Law—Recorder, Osborn, Jenkins.
Levels—Godard, Harcourt, Cumming.
Markets—Ladue, Gillespie, Koonz.
Navigation—Godard, Harcourt, Ladue.
Night Police—Artcher, Osborn, Ladue.
Police—Cumming, Harrison, Koonz.
Streets—Bassett, Riggs, Godard.
Wells and Pumps—Thompson, Gillespie, Thorn.
Land—Livingston, McCall, Bleecker.

ALBANY GALLERY OF FINE ARTS.

The following gentlemen were elected trustees at the annual meeting held on the evening of the 1st of January, viz: John L. Schoolcraft, E. Satterlee, J. McD. McIntyre, Dr. Herman Wendell, Wm. W. Forsyth, Orlando Meads, Dr. David Newcomb, James Kidd, Dr. J. A. Armsby.

ALBANY EXCHANGE COMPANY.

Directors.—John Townsend, John Q. Wilson, James McNaughton, Samuel Stevens, R. H. King, Andrew White, Friend Humphrey.

ALBANY WATER WORKS COMPANY.

The officers and trustees of the Albany Water Works are as follows:

O. Meads, Treasurer.
John Meads, Robert Boyd, Eli Perry, Wm. E. Bleecker, Deodatus Wright, recorder (ex officio), Trustees.

ALBANY HYDRANT COMPANY.

The following are the trustees of this company for the year commencing July, 1848. John Townsend, Erastus Corning, Watts Sherman, James D. Wasson, Rufus W. Peckham, John Taylor, John C. Spencer.

DE WITT CLINTON ENGINE NO. 2.

At an annual meeting of this company, held at their house, Dec. 23, 1848, the following were the officers elected for the ensuing year:

Wm. O'Brien, Foreman.
Wm. Kilbourne, 1st Assistant.
Peter Donelley, 2d Assistant.
James Jones, Clerk.
Richard Waddy, Steward.

EAGLE ENGINE CO. NO. 7.

At a meeting of Eagle Engine No. 7, held December 27th, 1848, the following persons were elected officers for the ensuing year:

Edward Stevens, Foreman.
Julius Tremper, 1st Assistant.
C. M. Beach, 2d Assistant.
L. W. Murray, Clerk.
J. S. Harrison, Steward.
Edmund Stevens, T. A. Johnstone, Delegates to Fire Department.

NEPTUNE ENGINE CO. NO. 10.

At a meeting of Neptune Engine Co. No. 10, held at their house on the evening of December 22, 1848, the following gentlemen were elected officers of said company for the ensuing year:

Archibald Young, Foreman.
Benjamin Turner, 1st Assistant.
Sylvester Lawler, 2d Assistant.
Samuel N. Payn, Clerk.
Jno. Hayden, Steward.
Patrick McLaughlan, Treasurer.

ALBANY AND COHOES RAIL ROAD COMPANY.

The following were elected officers of this company; M. T. Reynolds, John L. Schoolcraft, E. P. Prentice, James Edwards, Theodore Olcott, Archibald McClure, James Kidd, A. White, C. F. Crosby, David Hamilton, Egbert Egberts, Wm. N. Chadwick.

MOHAWK AND HUDSON RAIL ROAD.

The first steam — powered passenger train in the country.

Directors.—John T. Norton, Watts Sherman, Rufus H. King, Gerrit Y. Lansing, Edward C. Delavan, Harmen Pumpelly, H. H. Martin, Augustus James, Isaac Newton.

Office.—Dean street, above Maiden lane.

The New York State Museum in Albany exhibits several Albany fire engines from the 19th century and later.

ABOVE: Albany fire engine and hand pumper.

NEXT PAGE show 19th century Albany fire engines and the Albany Fire Protectives who worked for the Albany Board of Underwriters. Their job was to salvage buildings and contents after a fire.

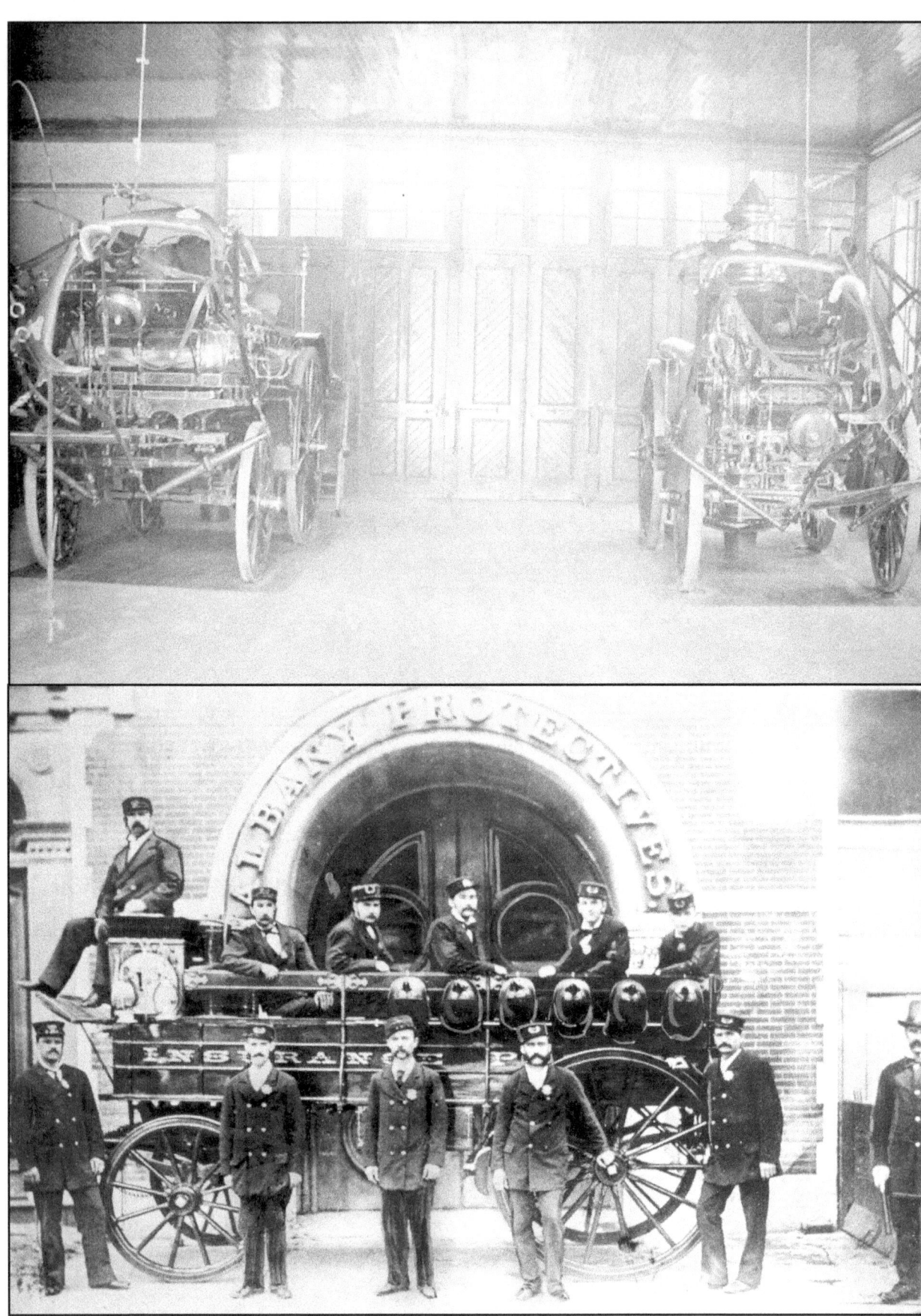

Benevolent Societies, &c.

FIRST GREAT WESTERN TURNPIKE.

Directors.—Gerrit Y. Lansing, Tennis Van Vechten, Gideon Hawley, John V. L. Pruyn, John Townsend, C. Y. Lansing, R. J. Hilton, Henry Bleecker, John T. Cooper, Jacob H. Ten Eyck, Robert H. Pruyn, Wm. C. Miller, Stephen Groesbeck.

— The Great Western Turnpike was the second turnpike in America. It went from Albany to Cherry Valley, a distance of about 60 miles. Chartered in 1799. By 1906 Albany owned the section within city limits. It is now part of Western Avenue and Route 20.

ALBANY AND BETHLEHEM TURNPIKE.

Directors.—Marcus T. Reynolds, Rufus H. King, Philip S. Van Rensselaer, Wm. McHarg, Joel Rathbone, John V. L. Pruyn, Robert Boyd, Ezra P. Prentice, George Dexter.

Organized in—
4. Five
es
Glenmont.
ted at South
l Street in
any and
t up
ning Hill
th to
hlehem
ter, now
ts of
te 9W today.

CHRISTIAN MUTUAL BENEFIT ASSOCIATION.

Officers for the year 1849.

Friend Humphrey, President.
Isaac P. Hand, Edward B. Slason, Vice-Presidents.
Abram Kirk, Corresponding Sec'y.

Thos. W. Valentine, Rec'g Sec'y.
Wm. Tuton, Financial Secretary.
Noah Lee, Treasurer.

Place of meeting, Sons of Temperance Hall, No 7 North Pearl street, on the 1st and 3d Tuesday evenings in each month.

BOARD OF TRADE.

This association of dealers commenced business on the 15th of May, 1848. The following are its officers:

William Chapman, President.
Benj. C. Raymond, 1st Vice-Pres.
Thos. Schuyler, 2d Vice-President.
David H. Carey, Sec'y.

Rufus K. Viele, Treasurer.
Chas. Wright, M. H. Read, O. N. Chapin, T. P. Crook, John Tweedle, Com. of Reference.

HIBERNIAN PROVIDENT SOCIETY.

On the 17th April, 1833, Jas. Halliday, Jas. Maher, Patrick Cassidy, William L. Osborne, Peter C. Doyle, Thomas Gough, Wm. O'Donnell, Michael Cagger, and others, were incorporated under the name of the Hibernian Provident Society, the avowed objects of which were charitable; " to create a fund by a general subscription among the members, which should contribute to their mutual advantage; if, by reason of sickness, they should at any time become destitute of the conveniences of life; and also to organize in one body a numerous class of Irishmen residing in this city, and to concentrate their moral energies, so as to bring fairly before the American people the republican features of their national character; that a number of individuals should combine and reserve a portion of the fruits of their industry, while enjoying health and happiness, for the establishment of a fund for their support, when overtaken by misfortunes or infirmities; especially, that a body of men who have been oppressed in their native land, by a despotic government, and who are influenced by the same associations and sympathies, and are led on by the same devotion in the path of freedom. should associate together for the purpose of vindicating their national character, and of procuring

for themselves, in a proper time, the privileges of American citizens."
The officers of the society for the year 1848, are as follows:

Patrick Grady, President.
John Reynolds, 1st Vice-President.
Joseph Clinton, 2d do.
John Daly, Recording Secretary.

Michael Fives, Corresponding Secretary.
Richard Brown, Treasurer.
Nicholas Markey, Physician.

ST. ANDREW'S SOCIETY.

This society held its 47th anniversary, on the 30th of November last. It was organized on the 10th of October, 1803, and celebrated the nativity of its patron saint on the 30th of November following. At the first election of officers, the following persons were chosen; John Stevenson, president, Geo Ramsey, vice-president; Andrew Brown, 2d vice-president; Rev. John McDonald, chaplain; Dr. Wm. McCelland, physician; William Milroy, treasurer; Archibald McIntyre, secretary; Peter Boyd, assistant secretary; and Daniel Cumming, Peter Sharpe, John Kirk, John Grant, George Pearson, Thomas Barker, Wm. French, John D. Cunningham, managers. It will be perceived that but one of the above is now left among us, but their names will be familiar to the older citizens. The avowed object of the society, was to afford relief to poor and unfortunate Scottish immigrants, without regard to religious or political distinctions; and we are informed that its finances are in a very flourishing condition, and that a large amount is anually dispensed for benevolent purposes. At a meeting held at the City Hotel, on the 9th Dec., 1848, the following were elected officers of the Society for the ensuing year:

James Taylor, President.
Andrew Kirk, 1st Vice President.
D. D. Ramsay, 2d Vice President.
Peter Bullions, Chaplain.
James McNaughton, Physician.
William Gray, Treasurer.

James Dickson, Secretary.
Daniel Campbell, Assistant Sec'y.
Alexander Gray, Peter Smith, Nathan Algie, Hugh Dickson, Geo. Young, Managers.

MECHANICS' BENEFIT SOCIETY.

At the annual election of this Society, held on the 7th Aug., the following persons were elected for the ensuing year:

Eli Abby, President.
W. A. Carr, Wm. Vosburgh, Vice-Presidents.
Jas. A. Buckbee, Treasurer.
R. S. Cushman, Secretary.
S. L. Hodgkins, Assistant Secretary.

J. W. Hinkley, Physician.
S. G. Mink, Alex. Selkirk, L. G. Hoffman, J. P. Wilson, Thos. E. Lee, T. M. Sutliff, J. H. Bowne, Oliver Houlle, Wm. A. F. McNab, Wm. A. Rice, Stewards.

ALBANY SOCIETY OF BROTHERLY LOVE.

This Society of Israelites, was incorporated by act of legislature, May 7, 1844, its avowed objects being charitable and benevolent, to afford relief to its members in case of sickness and infirmity. The persons named in the act of incorporation, were Moses Schloss, Solomon Mark, Isaac Cohen, Lewis Sporborg, and Myer Stern.

— One of Albany's most famous members of the St. Andrew's Society was muralist David Lithgow (1868-1958). He was Albany's most famous turn of the century artist, who was commissioned to paint murals, oil paintings, sculptures, illustrate books, and the historical dioramas and mural for the old New York State Museum in Albany. You can see his work today in the UAlbany campus (14 murals), 10 murals in the Bank of America on State Street (done in 1927), The Washington Avenue Armory, and elsewhere. He came to the US in 1888 with his sister Jessie and settled in Albany, NY. In 1890, he married his wife, Amelia Crounse. He opened an artist studio at 57 North Pearl St., Albany, NY.

Religious Societies, &c.

ALBANY CITY TRACT SOCIETY.

A religious group — that handed out Tracts (religious text), bibles and other religious material.

The annual meeting of the Society, for the election of officers and directors for the ensuing year was held on the 26th Oct., 1848.

Friend Humphrey, President.
Hugh Humphrey, Robert Boyd, R. V. DeWitt, Lem'l Jenkins, Wm. C. Miller, Wm. McElroy, Vice-Presidents.
Erastus H. Pease, Secretary.
Philip Phelps, Treasurer.
Alexander Folsom, Matthew Trotter, Austin H. Wells, T. S. Berry, Geo. B. Hoyt, Walter R. Bush, Wm. N. Strong, G. W. Benjamin, Jeremiah Waterman, James B. Sanders, H. S. McCall, Daniel Campbell, Abram Kirk, Daniel Fry, G. C. Treadwell, T. R. Rawson, William Gibson, Rufus K. Viele, Directors.

ALBANY COUNTY BIBLE SOCIETY.

Officers for 1848.

Rev. Wm. B. Sprague, D. D., President.
Rev. J. N. Campbell, D.D., 1st Vice-President.
Rev. I. N. Wyckoff, D. D., 2d Vice-President.
Philip Phelps, Rec'g Sec'y.
Lemuel Jenkins, Cor'g Sec'y.
William C. Miller, Treasurer.
Rev. Ezra A. Huntington, D. D., Duncan Kennedy, D. D., William H Campbell, D. D., Henry N. Pohlman, D. D., F. W. Schmidt, Andrew Witherspoon, Luman A. Sandford. Thomas Armitage, J. W, Belknap, Messrs. Archibald McIntyre, Rensselaer Westerlo, Nathaniel Davis, Israel Smith, Daniel Fry, Abraham Keyser, George W. Benjamin, Managers.
Rev. Dr. J. N. Campbell, Wm. C. Miller, Nathaniel Davis, Dan'l Fry, Ex. Com.

ALBANY COUNTY MEDICAL SOCIETY.

At an annual meeting of the Albany County Medical Society, held at the City Hall, November 14th, 1848, the following named persons were elected as its officers, viz:

James McNaughton, President.
John Swinburne, Vice President.
B. A. Sheldon, Secretary.
C. C. Walker, Treasurer.
C. C. Griffin, Librarian.
P. McNaughton, Jas. H. Armsby, U. G. Bigelow, J. H. Case, and David R. Burris, County Censors.
Richard H. Tompson, delegate to State Medical Society for 4 years.

ALBANY AND RENSSELAER HORTICULTURAL SOCIETY.

Joel Rathbone, President.
D. Thos. Vail, Herman Wendell, E. P. Prentice, V. P. Douw, Vice-Presidents.
B. P. Johnson, Secretary.
A. E. Brown, Treasurer.

Annual meeting in July.

Amos Briggs, S. E. Warren, J. M. Lovett, Wm. Bruswell, J. McD. McIntyre, James Henry, William Newcomb, James Wilson, A. Osborn.

Military Companies.

ALBANY REPUBLICAN ARTILLERY.

The following persons are the officers for 1848:

CIVIL.
George Fredenrich, President.
Joseph Baker, Vice-President.
Edward Riley, Secretary.
Jacob Fredendall, Treasurer.

MILITARY.
Jacob Fredendall, Captain.

Edward Riley, 1st Lieutenant.
Philip Guardenier, 2d Lieutenant.
Michael Bennett, Orderly Serg't.
Hiram Putnam, Geo. Fredenrich, John Murdon, Sergeants.
Wm. H. Guardenier, Joseph Baker, John Guardenier, Edward Gregory, Corporals.

ALBANY BURGESSES CORPS.

The officers of this company are as follows:

CIVIL.
John F. Schults, President.
Wm. H. Low, Vice-President.
J. C. Cuyler, Secretary.
S. W. Whitney, Assistant Sec'y.
F. H. Keeler, Treasurer.

MILITARY.
Wm. J. Thomas, Captain.
E. J. Lansing, 1st Lieutenant.
E. R. Brower, 2d Lieutenant.
C. Jordan, 3d Lieutenant.

W. K. Whitney, Orderly Sergeant.
J. Whalen, J. Hogan, F. H. Keeler, Sergeants.
James Weed, John Duff, S. Wilkins, R. Henly, Corporals.

STAFF.
Cyrus Stevens, Quarter Master.
H. Van OLinda, Pay Master.
J. F. Schults, Surgeon.
Wm. Davis, Chaplain.

ALBANY EMMET GUARDS.

The following are the officers for 1848-9:

CIVIL.
James W. Morange, President.
Wm. Dwyre, Vice-President.
P. T. Hewett, Secretary.
Mich'l O'Sullivan, Assistant Sec'y.
P. Maher, Treasurer.

MILITARY.
John Osborn, Captain.

N. Hussey, 1st Lieutenant.
P. H. Griffin, 2d Lieutenant.
John Dunden, 3d Lieutenant.
Thos. Kellett, Orderly Sergeant.
P. O'Conner, M. Cassidy, J. McManus, Sergeants.
Wm. Maloy, B. Cooney, J. Feeney, Michael O'Sullivan, Corporals.

ALBANY WASHINGTON RIFLEMEN.

The following are the officers of this company:

CIVIL.
Wm. P. Paff, President.
—— Lochner, Secretary.
Fr. Shadelle, Treasurer.

MILITARY.
Chris. Triger, President.

Wm. P. Paff, 1st Lieutenant.
Hen. Schweitzer, 2d Lieutenant.
J. Huber, Orderly Sergeant.
G. Lochner, Th. Hoffman, Dl. Frederick, Sergeants.
J. Ranseler, Wm. Smite, J. Roshe, J. Bahmer, Corporals.

I. O. OF O. F.

American No. 32, Wednesday evening, at Cooper's Building.
City Degree No. 11, Tuesday evening, Broadway, cor. Steuben.
City Philanthropic No. 5, Friday evening, at Cooper's Building.
Clinton No. 7, Monday evening, corner of Broadway and Steuben.
En-Hakkore Encampment No. 5, meets on the second and fourth Saturdays of each month, at Cooper's Building.
Excelsior Degree No. 15, meets on the first and third Fridays of each month, at Odd Fellow's Hall, corner of Green and Beaver.
Fireman's No. 19, Friday evening, Odd Fellow's Hall, corner of Green and Beaver.
German Colonial No. 16, Monday evening, Odd Fellow's Hall, corner of Green and Beaver.
Herman's Degree No. 31, meets first and third Wednesdays of each month, in Church, near Ferry.
Hope Lodge No. 3, meets Tuesday evening, at Cooper's Building.
Mount Carmel No. 349, Thursday evening, Church, near Ferry.
Mount Hermon No. 38, Monday evening, Church, near Ferry.
New York Encampment No. 1, meets on the first and third Saturdays of each month, at Cooper's Building.
Phœnix No. 41, Tuesday evening, Odd Fellows' Hall, cor. Green and Beaver.
Samaritan No. 93, Monday evening, at Cooper's Building.
Scho-negh-ta-da No. 356, Thursday eve., Broadway, cor. Steuben.
Union No. 8, Thursday evening, at Cooper's Building.

SONS OF TEMPERANCE.

Albany Division No. 24, meets Monday evening, at Hall in State.
Clinton No. 76, Thursday evening, at Commercial Building.
Eagle No. 306, Thursday evening, at No. 3 North Pearl.
Empire Temple No. 33, Friday evening, at Commercial Building.
En Hakkore No. 129, Wednesday evening, at No. 7 North Pearl.
Fort Orange No. 187, Thursday evening, at No. 7 North Pearl.
Tivoli Temple No. 22, Friday evening, at S. of T. Hall, State.
Mutual Alliance No. 130, Monday evening, at No. 7 North Pearl.

MASONIC BODIES.

Mount Vernon Lodge No. 3, corner of Broadway and Steuben.
Master's Lodge,
Temple Chapter No. 5, St. John's Hall, Broadway, cor. Steuben.
Temple Lodge, corner of Broadway and Steuben.
Unitas—Concordia—Fratrum,
Washington Lodge,

CUSTOM HOUSE.

ALBERT GALLUP, DEPUTY COLLECTOR, 407 BROADWAY.

The Custom House was established in 1833, and was thought by some persons to be a proper subject for a little ridicule. In truth the business of conducting it was not very arduous for the first year. There were then but two vessels trading regularly to Boston, namely the schooner Visscher and sloop George Washington, owned by Davis & Centre, whereas now there are above a hundred. Besides, there are several lines of steam propellers trading to different ports, which have come on the river quite recently, of which we believe the Mohawk was the pioneer. There is a line of steam packets between Albany and Hartford, doing a brisk business, and another to Philadelphia. One has recently been established between this city and New London and Norwich. And when it is considered what an enormous quantity of freight is taken overland by the rail road, it is remarkable that the packet business should increase so rapidly. Mr. William Seymour was the first collector, and the first license entered on his book is under the date of July 12, 1833. After this became a port of entry, the government made an appropriation for the improvement of the navigation of the river. It was contemplated to carry a dyke up from a point 25 miles below the head of tide water, at an estimated cost of $860,000, which would effectually relieve the channel of the bars that now obstruct it, and relieve the business men scattered over an immense region of country of the vexations and embarrassments caused in various ways by the daily detention of vessels. The dyke was constructed a part of the distance contemplated, and there abandoned. But it was of great advantage to our commerce, enabling schooners of over 200 tons to reach the city, and steam boats of far greater tonnage make their regular trips at low water. The dyke however is fast going to ruin. A few hundred dollars would have repaired the first breach, but it will now require many thousands, and public attention will probably be effectually aroused to remedy the evil only by some unexpected and overwhelming calamity, arising from the neglect. But a part of the vessels trading to this port are registered here; hence the whole number registered since the first January 1841, does not much exceed 500. The Rochester steam boat is the largest vessel licensed at our port, being nearly 500 tons. The vessel of the largest tonnage that arrives here is the steam boat Isaac Newton, of about 1,300 tons.

MOHAWK AND HUDSON RAIL ROAD.

This was one of the first rail roads constructed in the state. On the 17th April, 1826, Stephen Van Rensselaer, George W. Featherstonehaugh, and others received a charter from the state, for the purpose of constructing a rail road between the Mohawk and Hudson rivers; the capital stock was fixed at $300,000, with permission to increase it to $500,000, or about $31,000 per mile, and the time for completing the road was limited to six years. The work was commenced in 1830, and a double track completed in 1833. It was originally constructed with an inclined plane at each end of the road; the one at Albany a little more than half a mile in length, and both of them having a rise of 1 foot in 18. The road was laid out 15¾ miles in length, 6 of which were at a level, and the rest of it, with the exception of the two inclined planes, had an ascending grade of about 1 foot in 250. The width of the excavations is 36 feet, that of the embankments 26 feet. The deepest excavation is 47 feet, and the highest embankment 44 feet. Greatest altitude 353 feet above tide water at Albany. Stone blocks were placed three feet apart, from centre to centre, laid on broken stone, and cross sleepers of wood rested upon them, 7 inches in diameter and 8 feet long, supporting the timber rails, on which were placed iron bars, three-fifths by two and a half inches, with the upper corners rounded to 1¼ inches width; and the width between the rails 4 feet 9 inches. When the road had been constructed in this manner, it was found to have cost $1,100,000, or upwards of $70,000 per mile, for the double track. The stock sold at one time for 30 per cent premium, but subsequently went down to 25 cents on the dollar, and the road in unskilful hands, was on the point of being abandoned. At this juncture some of our enterprising men took the matter in hand, bought up the stock, and with the assistance of a loan from the city corporation, set about a complete reconstruction of the road. The inclined planes were abandoned, and by a little more circuitous ascent of the rising ground at each terminus, and the use of heavy locomotives, it has become a popular and profitable concern. The company relaid the road with a heavy rail in part in 1843, and fully completed relaying it during the last season. The distance is now about 17 miles. On the 22d Sept., a train of three cars, filled with passengers by invitation, crossed the road from Albany in 30 minutes, and returned in 24 minutes, the speed being at the rate of 1 mile in 1m. 25s., or 42¼ miles an hour.

The following table shows the comparative condition of the company's operations in 1846 and 1847.

	1846	1847
No. passengers,	174,653	229,401
Receipts from passengers,	$92,194	$110,051
" " freight, &c.,	33,641	51,323
	$125,835	$164,374
Repairs and running road,	41,766	60,310
Miles run by passenger trains,	45,357	49,674
" " freight, &c,,	16,515	22,821
Cost of construction to Jan. 1, 1847,		$1,472,966
" " Jan. 1, 1848,		1,473,253

The receipts of the road in 1843 were $60,595; 1844, $89,882; 1845, $98,494. The receipts of 1848 were upwards of $175,000.

The road is fully equipped, as the company own six locomotives, thirty first class passenger cars, twenty-two second class passenger cars, thirty-six freight cars, and thirty-four baggage cars. With good management and economy the company was enabled to resume its dividends in October, 1847, since which it has continued to pay regular dividends, every six months.

A replica of the Mohawk & Hudson Railroad engine and cars was made by the NY Central Railroad. It is now at the Ford Museum in Michigan. Below left is George W. Featherstonhaugh, who first chartered the M&HRR and bottom right is a ticket office in downtown Albany.

City Income and Expenditures.

The amount raised annually by tax, for all purposes connected with the city government, and for the payment of interest on city debt, from 1842 to 1848.

	1842.	1843.	1844.	1845.	1846.	1847.	1848.
City Watch or Night Police,	$16,000.00	$16,000.00	$16,000.00	$16,000.00	$16,000.00	$16,000.00	$19,000.00
Public Lamps,	7,000.00	7,000.00	7,000.00	7,000.00	7,000.00	7,000.00	10,000.00
Common Schools,	7,635.72	7,635.72	7,635.72	7,635.72	8,703.00	9,003.36	9,033.36
Erecting District School Buildings, under act of 1837.	3,700.00	3,250.00	3,100.00	2,950.00	2,800.00	2,650.00	....
For temporary relief of City Poor,	....	....	2,500.00	7,000.00	7,000.00	7,000.00	7,000.00
For interest on City Debt,	10,000.00	10,000.00	30,000.00	33,000.00	35,000.00	32,000.00	47,000.00
For contingent expenses,	20,000.00	20,000.00	20,000.00	20,000.00	20,000.00	20,000.00	40,000.00
For purchase of lot and erection of School House, Arbor Hill, under law of 1848,	....	....	....	....	....	....	7,000.00
On account of City Debt, law 1848,	....	....	....	....	....	....	10,000.00
Improving Streets, &c. law 1848,	....	....	....	....	....	....	22,500.00
	$64,335.72	$63,885.72	$86,235.72	$95,585.72	$96,503.00	$96,653.36	$170,503.36

Payments during each year, from May 1st, 1843 to 1848 inclusive.

	1843.	1844.	1845.	1846.	1847.	1848.
Expense of City Watch or Night Police,	$13,419.07	$16,712.89	$19,801.82	$16,809.42	$16,827.07	$17,249.40
do of Public Lamps,	6,438.81	7,288.40	8,492.36	10,899.49	9,076.85	9,207.30
For temporary relief of City Poor,	6,294.85	6,453.20	3,582.09	3,692.83	8,688.94	11,053.07
For interest on City Debt,	20,534.28	47,447.48	34,898.82	38,649.89	40,181.40	49,923.34
For contingent expenses, in which is included all sums paid for ordinary purposes of city government,	49,814.93	42,902.72	40,424.84	37,249.11	42,792.28	48,636.35

COUNTY OFFICERS.

Counties.	Sheriffs.	Clerks.	Surrogates.
Albany	Oscar Tyler	Lawrence Van Deusen	Lewis Benedict, Jr.
Allegany	Joshua Rathbun	Martin Butts	Wm. G. Angel
Broome	Benj. T. Miller	John C. Moore	E. C. Kattel
Cattaraugus	Alonzo A. Gregory	Francis E. Baillett	Rensselaer Lamb
Cayuga	Joseph P. Swift	Ebenezer B. Cobb	Jacob R. How
Chautauque	Jarvis B. Rice	Matthew P. Bemus	Orton Clark
Chemung	Wm. Skellenger	Green M. Tuthill	J. W. Wisner
Chenango	Wm. Church	Burr B. Andrews	S. M. Purdy
Clinton	Harvey Bromley	Charles H. Jones	Lemuel Stetson
Columbia	Jacob R. Hollenbeck	James Storm	C. B. Dutcher
Cortland	George Ross	Samuel Hotchkiss	Daniel Hawks
Delaware	De Witt C. Thomas	Wm. McLaughry	Edwin More
Dutchess	David N. Seaman	Joseph T. Adriance	John P. H. Tallman
Erie	Timothy A. Hopkins	Moses Bristol	Peter M. Vosburgh
Essex	Norman Page	Edmund T. Williams	H. H. Ross
Franklin	Benjamin W. Clark	Henry S. Brewster	J. R. Flanders
Fulton	Daniel Potter	Stephen Wait	John Wells
Genesee	John Sprague	Samuel C. Holden	H. U. Soper
Greene	Robert Fulton	Isaac Van Schaack	L. Tremain
Hamilton	Robt. G. Ostrander	John C. Holmes	John Dunham
Herkimer	Wm. I. Skinner	Standish Barry	Ezra Graves
Jefferson	Walter Collins	James G. Lynde	L. H. Brown
Kings	Daniel Van Voorhis	John M. Hicks	A. B. Hodges
Lewis	George Shepard	Lucian Clark	Francis Seger
Livingston	Wm. Scott	William H. Whiting	Scott Lord
Madison	Wm. R. Brand	A. Scott Sloan	James W. Nye
Monroe	George Hart	John C. Nash	Moses Sperry
Montgomery	David W. Erwin	Chester S. Brumley	S. Belding, Jr.
New York	John J. V. Westervelt	James Conner	Charles McBean
Niagara	Franklin Spalding	John Van Horn	H. Gardner
Oneida	Lester Barker	Patrick Mahon	O. S. Williams
Onondaga	Joshua C. Cuddeback	Vivus W. Smith	I. T. Minard
Ontario	Phineas Kent	Alex. H. Howell	M. H. Sibley
Orange	Edward L. Welling	Albert S. Benton	B. F. Duryea
Orleans	Austin Day	Herman Goodrich	H. R. Curtis
Oswego	Alvin Lawrence	Jabez H. Gilbert	O. H. Whitney
Otsego	John Brown	Charles McLean	Hiram Kinne
Putnam	Wm. W. Taylor	Reuben D. Barnum	Azor B. Crane
Queens	Isaac Willetts	Abraham D. Snedeker	Henry I. Hagner
Rensselaer	Gilbert Cropsey	Ambrose H. Sheldon	G. T. Blair
Richmond	Jacob M. Guyon	Joshua Mersereau, Jr.	H. B. Metcalf
Rockland	Asbury De Noyelles	Isaac A. Blauvelt	W. F. Fraser
St. Lawrence	Josiah Waid	Martin Thatcher	B. G. Baldwin
Saratoga	Thomas Low	Jas. W. Horton	J. C. Hulbert
Schenectady	John G. Van Voast	Silas H. Marsh	S. W. Jones
Schoharie	Tobias Bouck	Stephen Maham	Demosthenes Lawyer
Seneca	Hugh Chapman	Ebenezer Ingalls	J. K. Richardson
Steuben	Henry Brother	Paul C. Cook	David McMaster
Suffolk	David R. Rose	J. Wickham Case	A. T. Rose
Sullivan	Neal Benson	Matthew Decker, Jr.	A. Dimmick
Tioga	John J. Sackett	Moses Stevens	C. P. Avery
Tompkins	John P. Andrews	Norman Crittenden	Alfred Wells
Ulster	Charles Brodhead	Benj. M. Hasbrouck	Wm. Masten
Warren	James Lawren	Thomas Archibald	E. H. Rosekrans
Washington	Daniel T. Payne	Henry Shipherd	Joseph Boies
Wayne	George W. Barnard	Alex. B. Williams	G. H. Middleton
Westchester	James M. Bates	Munson I. Lockwood	L. C. Platt
Wyoming	Abraham Smith	Abel Webster	W. Riley Smith
Yates	Martin Holmes	Russell R. Fargo	Andrew Oliver

This and some other tables are subject to important changes; they can only be given as they are at the time of printing.

Counties, Towns and Post Offices

ALPHABETICAL LIST of the COUNTIES, TOWNS and POST OFFICES in the State of New York, and the Distances of the County Towns from Albany.

ALBANY COUNTY.
ALBANY City, Hall's Mills, Berne, Helderbergh, Bethlehem, Knowersville, Cedar Hill, Knox, Clarkesville, New Salem, Coeymans, New Scotland, Coeymans Hollow, Preston Hollow, Cohoes, Reidsville, Cooksburgh, Rensselaerville, Dormansville, South Berne, Dunnsville, do. Westerlo, East Berne, Watervliet, Guilderland Centre, Westerlo, Guilderland Centre, West Troy

ALLEGANY CO.
Alfred, Hobbieville, Allen Centre, Hume, Almond, Hunt's Hollow, Amity, Independence, Andover, Little Genesee, ANGELICA 256, Mixville, Belfast, New Hudson, Birdsall, Nile, Black Creek, North Almond, Bolivar, Oakland, Burns, Ossian, Canakadier, Philip's Creek, Caneadea, Philipsville, Centre Almond, Pike, Centre Independence, Portageville, Centreville, Richburgh, Clarksville, Rockville, Cuba, Rushford, Eagle, Scio, East Hill, Short Tract, East Koy, Spring Mills, East Pike, Wellsville, Friendship, West Almond, Genesee, do Clarksville, do Valley, do Genesee, Granger, Whitesville, Grove, Whitneys Valley, Wirt

BROOME COUNTY.
Barker, Osborn Hollow, BINGHAMTON 145, Port Crane, Castle Creek, Sandford, Centre, Shawsville, Chenango, South Windsor, do Forks, Susquehannah, Colesville, Triangle, Conklin, Union, Corbettsville, Union Village, Harpersville, Upper Lisle, Kattelville, Vallonia Sp'gs, Lisle, Vestal, Maine, W. Colesville, Nanticoke, Whitney's Point, New Ohio, Windsor, Ninevah

CATTARAUGUS CO.
Ashford, Machias, Bucktooth, Mansfield, Burton, Napoli, Carrolton, New Albion, Chapelsburgh, North Perrysburgh, Cold Spring, Connewango, Olean, Dayton, Otto, Delavan, Perrysburgh, East Leon, Persia, East Otto, Portville, Elgin, Randolph, ELLICOTTVILLE, 292, Rice, Fairview, Sandusky, Farmersville, Seelyburgh, Franklinville, Sociality, Freedom, South Valley, Great Valley, Ten Mile Sp'g, Hinsdale, Tunungwant Mills, Humphrey, Versailles, Kill Buck, W'st Hinsdale, Leon, Yorkshire, Little Valley

CAYUGA COUNTY.
AUBURN, 172, Niles, Aurelius, Nine Corners, Aurora, North Sterling, Brutus, Owasco, Cato, Poplar Ridge, Cato 4 Corners, Port Byron, Cayuga, Scipio, Conquest, Scipioville, East Genoa, Sempronius, Five Corners, Sennet, Fleming, Sherwood's Corners, Fosterville, Genoa, South Venice, Ira, Springport, Kellogsville, Square, King's Ferry, Sterling, Ledyard, Summer Hill, Levanna, Throopsville, Little Sodus, Union Springs, Locke, Venice, Martville, Victory, Mentz, Weedsport, Montezuma, West Niles, Moravia

CHAUTAUQUE CO.
Arkwright, Clymer, Barcelona, Clymer Centre, Blockville, De Wittville, Busti, Dunkirk, Carroll, Ellery, Cassadaga, Ellicott, Centre Sherman, Ellington, Charlotte, Fluvanna, Chautanque, Fredonia, Cherry Creek, French Creek, Clear Creek, Frewsburgh, Gerry, Hanover, Ripley, Harmony, Salem Cross Roads, Irving, Jamestown, Sheridan, Levant, Sherman, Magnolia, Silver Creek, MAYVILLE 336, Smith's Mills, Mina, Stockton, Nashville, Union Ellery, North Clymer, Van Buren Harbor, Oregon, Panama, Vermont, Poland, Villenovia, Pomfret, Volusia, Portland, Westfield

CHEMUNG COUNTY.
Baldwin, Millport, Beaverdams, Moreland, Big Flats, No. Chemung, Catharines, Post Creek, Catlin, Salubria, Cayuta, Seeley Creek, Chemung, Southport, Dix, Townsend, ELMIRA 198, Van Ettenville, Erin, Veteran, Fairport, Wellsburg, Martin's Hall, West Cayuta

CHENANGO CO.
Bainbridge, New Berlin, do Centre Centre, Columbus, N'th Norwich, Coventry, NORWICH 110, Coventryville, Otselic, East Greene, Oxford, East Guilford, Pharsalia, E. M'Donough, Pitcher, East Pharsalia, do Springs, Genegantslet, Plymouth, German, Preston, Greene, Sherburne, Guilford, Smithville Flats, do Centre, Smyrna, King's Settlement, S. Bainbridge, S. New Berlin, Linklaen, South Otselic, McDonough, W. Bainbridge, Mount Upton, West Linklaen, New Berlin, White's Store

CLINTON COUNTY.
Au Sable, Peasleyville, Beekmantown, Perry's Mills, Black Brook, Peru [162, Cadyville, PLATTSBURGH, Champlain, Redford, Chazy, Rouse's Point, Clinton, Saranac, Clintonville, Schuyler's Falls, Coopersville, Ellenburgh, Union Falls, Farrell Place, West Chazy, Mooers, West Plattsburgh, New Sweden

Counties, Towns and Post Offices

ALPHABETICAL LIST of the COUNTIES, TOWNS and POST OFFICES in the State of New York, and the Distances of the County Towns from Albany.

ALBANY COUNTY.
Albany City, Hall's Mills, Berne, Heldenbergh, Bethlehem, Knowersville, Cedar Hill, Knox, Clarkesville, New Salem, Coeymans, New Scotland, Coeymans Hollow, Preston Hollow, Cohoes, Reidsville, Cooksburgh, Rensselaerville, Dormansville, South Berne, Dunnsville, do. Westerlo, East Berne, Watervliet, Guilderland, Centre, Guilderland Centre, Westerlo, West Troy

ALLEGANY CO.
Alfred, Hobbieville, Allen Centre, Hume, Almond, Hunt's Hollow, Amity, Independence, Andover, Little Genesee, ANGELICA 256, Mixville, Belfast, New Hudson, Birdsall, Nile, Black Creek, North Almond, Bolivar, Oakland, Burns, Ossian, Canakadier, Philip's Creek, Caneadea, Philipsville, Centre Almond, Pike, Centre Independence, Portageville, Centreville, Richburgh, Clarksville, Rockville, Cuba, Rushford, Eagle, Scio, East Hill, Short Tract, East Koy, Spring Mills, East Pike, Wellsville, Friendship, West Almond, Genesee, do Clarksville, do Valley, do Genesee, Granger, Whitesville, Grove, Whitneys Valley, Wirt

BROOME COUNTY.
Barker, Osborn Hollow, BINGHAMTON 145, Port Crane, Castle Creek, Sandford, Centre, Shawsville, Chenango, South Windsor, do Forks, Susquehannah, Colesville, Triangle, Conklin, Union, Corbettsville, Union Village, Harpersville, Upper Lisle, Kattelville, Vallonia Sp'gs, Lisle, Vestal, Maine, W. Colesville, Nanticoke, Whitney's Point, New Ohio, Ninevah, Windsor

CATTARAUGUS CO.
Ashford, Machias, Bucktooth, Mansfield, Burton, Napoli, Carrolton, New Albion, Chapelsburgh, North Perrysburgh, Cold Spring, Connewango, Olean, Dayton, Otto, Delavan, Perrysburgh, East Leon, Persia, East Otto, Portville, Elgin, Randolph, ELLICOTTVILLE, 292, Rice, Sandusky, Fairview, Seelyburgh, Farmersville, Sociality, Franklinville, South Valley, Freedom, Ten Mile Sp'g, Great Valley, Tunungwant Mills, Hinsdale, Humphrey, Versailles, Kill Buck, W'st Hinsdale, Leon, Yorkshire, Little Valley

CAYUGA COUNTY.
AUBURN, 172, Niles, Aurelius, Nine Corners, Aurora, North Sterling, Brutus, Owasco, Cato, Poplar Ridge, Cato 4 Corners, Port Byron, Cayuga, Scipio, Conquest, Scipioville, East Genoa, Sempronius, Five Corners, Sennet, Fleming, Sherwood's Corners, Fosterville, Genoa, South Venice, Ira, Springport, Kellogsville, Square, King's Ferry, Sterling, Ledyard, Summer Hill, Levanna, Throopsville, Little Sodus, Union Springs, Locke, Venice, Martville, Victory, Mentz, Weedsport, Montezuma, West Niles, Moravia

CHAUTAUQUE CO.
Arkwright, Clymer, Barcelona, Clymer Centre, Blockville, De Wittville, Busti, Dunkirk, Carroll, Ellery, Cassadaga, Ellicott, Centre Sherman, Ellington, Charlotte, Fluvanna, Chautauque, Fredonia, Cherry Creek, French Creek, Clear Creek, Frewsburgh, Gerry, Hanover, Ripley, Harmony, Salem Cross Roads, Irving, Jamestown, Sheridan, Levant, Sherman, Magnolia, Silver Creek, MAYVILLE 336, Smith's Mills, Mina, Stockton, Nashville, Union Ellery, North Clymer, Van Buren Harbor, Oregon, Panama, Vermont, Poland, Villenovia, Pomfret, Volusia, Portland, Westfield

CHEMUNG COUNTY.
Baldwin, Millport, Beaverdams, Moreland, Big Flats, No. Chemung, Catharines, Post Creek, Catlin, Salubria, Cayuta, Seeley Creek, Chemung, Southport, Dix, Townsend, ELMIRA 198, Van Ettenville, Erin, Veteran, Fairport, Wellsburg, Martin's Hall, West Cayuta

CHENANGO CO.
Bainbridge, New Berlin, do Centre, Centre, Columbus, N'th Norwich, Coventry, NORWICH 110, Coventryville, Otselic, East Greene, Oxford, East Guilford, Pharsalia, E. M'Donough, Pitcher, East Pharsalia, do Springs, Genegantslet, Plymouth, German, Preston, Greene, Sherburne, Guilford, Smithville Flats, do Centre, Smyrna, King's Settlement, S. Bainbridge, S. New Berlin, Linklaen, South Otselic, McDonough, W. Bainbridge, Mount Upton, West Linklaen, New Berlin, White's Store

CLINTON COUNTY.
Au Sable, Peasleyville, Beekmantown, Perry's Mills, Black Brook, Peru, [162, Cadyville, PLATTSBURGH, Champlain, Redford, Chazy, Rouse's Point, Clinton, Saranac, Clintonville, Schuyler's Falls, Coopersville, Ellenburgh, Union Falls, Farrell Place, West Chazy, Mooers, West Plattsburgh, New Sweden

in the State of New York.

COLUMBIA COUNTY
- Ancram
- Ancram Lead Mines
- Austerlitz
- Canaan
- Canaan Centre
- do 4 Corners
- Chatham
- do Centre
- do 4 Corners
- Claverack
- Clermont
- Copake
- Elizaville
- Flatbrook
- Gallatin
- Gallatinville
- Germantown
- Ghent
- Greenport
- Green River
- Harlemville
- Hillsdale
- Hoffman's Gate
- HUDSON 29
- Kinderhook
- Livingston
- Malden Bridge
- Mellenville
- Moffet's Store
- New Britain
- New Concord
- New Lebanon
- New Lebanon Centre
- New Lebanon Springs
- Niverville
- N'th Chatham
- Smoky Hollow
- Spencertown
- Stockport
- Stuyvesant
- do Falls
- Taghkanic
- Valatie
- W. Taghkanic

CORTLAND CO.
- Blodget's Mills
- Cincinnatus
- Cortlandville
- CORTLAND VILLAGE 140
- Cuyler
- East Homer
- East Solon
- East Virgil
- Freetown
- do Corners
- Hartford
- Homer
- Keeney's Settlement
- Little York
- Marathon
- McGrawsville
- Preble
- Scott
- Solon
- South Cortland
- Truxton
- Union Valley
- Virgil
- Willett

DELAWARE CO.
- Andes
- Arkville
- Barbourville
- Bloomville
- Bovina
- Bovina Centre
- Cabin Hill
- Cannonsville
- Clovesville
- Colchester
- Davenport
- do Centre
- DELHI 77
- Deposit
- East Branch
- East Franklin
- Franklin
- Hamden
- Hancock
- Harpersfield
- Hobart
- Kortright
- Masonville
- Meredith
- Middletown
- Moresville
- New Road
- North Harpersfield
- N'th Kortright
- Pappakunk
- Partridge's Island
- Pepacton
- Roxbury
- Shavertown
- Sidney
- Sidney Centre
- Sidney Plains
- S'th Kortright
- Stamford
- Stratton's Falls
- Tompkins
- Trout Creek
- Walton
- West Davenport
- W. Meredith

DUTCHESS COUNTY.
- Adriance
- Amenia
- Amenia Union
- Arthursburgh
- Attlebury
- Barrytown
- Beekman
- Campbellville
- Channingsville
- Chesnut Ridge
- City
- Clinton Hollow
- Clove
- Crum Elbow
- Dover
- Federal Store
- Fishkill
- do Landing
- do Plains
- Freedom Plains
- Glenham
- Hart's Village
- Hull's Mills
- Hyde Park
- Jackson Corners
- La Grange
- Leedsville
- Lithgow
- Mabbettsville
- Manchester
- Milan [Bridge
- New Hackensack
- N. Hamburgh
- North East
- do Centre
- Pauling
- Peeksville
- Pine Plains
- Pleasant Plains
- do Valley
- PO'KEEPSIE 73
- Poughquag
- Pulver's Corners
- Quaker Hill
- Red Hook
- Rhinebeck
- Rock City
- Salt Point
- Schultzville
- Shenandoah
- South Amenia
- South Dover
- Sprout Creek
- Staatsburgh
- Stanford
- Stanfordville
- Stormville
- Tivoli
- Union Vale
- Up'r Red Hook
- Verbank
- Washington
- do Hollow

ERIE COUNTY.
- Akron
- Alden
- Amherst
- Angola
- Aurora
- Black Rock
- Boston
- Brant
- BUFFALO 325
- Cheektowaga
- Clarence
- Colden
- Collins
- do Centre
- Concord
- East Evans
- E. Hamburgh
- Eden
- Eleysville
- Evans
- Griffin's Mills
- Hamburgh
- Hamburgh on the Lake
- Harris's Hill
- Holland
- Lancaster
- Morton's Corners
- Newstead
- North Boston
- N'th Clarence Reservation
- Sardinia
- South Wales
- Springville
- Tonawanda
- Town Line
- Wales
- Wales Centre
- Water Valley
- Williamsville
- Willink
- Zoar

ESSEX COUNTY.
- AuSable Forks
- Chesterfield
- Crown Point
- ELIZABETHTOWN 126
- Essex
- Jay
- Keene
- Keeseville
- Lewis
- Minerva
- Moriah
- Newcomb
- Port Henry
- Port Kendall
- Port Kent
- St. Armand
- Schroon Lake
- do River
- Split Rock
- Ticonderoga
- Upper Jay
- Wadham's Mills
- West Moriah
- Westport
- Willsborough
- Wilmington
- Woodwardsville

FRANKLIN COUNTY
- Bangor
- Belmont
- Bombay
- Brandon
- Burke
- Chateaugay
- Constable
- Dickinson
- Duane
- East Constable
- F'rt Covington
- Franklin
- Harrietstown
- Hogansburgh
- MALONE 212
- Merrillsville
- Moira
- S'th Dickinson
- W. Constable
- Westville

FULTON COUNTY.
- Bleecker
- Broadalbin
- Brockett's Bridge
- Caroga
- Cranberry Creek
- Ephratah
- Garoga
- Gloversville
- Hoesville
- JOHNSTOWN 45
- Kingsborough
- Lassellsville
- Mayfield
- Mill's Corners
- Newkirk's Mills [ners
- Newton's Corners
- Northampton
- Northville
- Oppenheim
- Osborn's Bridge
- Perth
- Riceville
- Sammonsville
- Union Mills
- Vail's Mills
- West Perth

GENESEE COUNTY.
- Alabama
- Alexander
- BATAVIA 283
- Bergen
- Bethany
- Brookville
- Byron
- Corfu
- Darien
- Darien Centre
- East Bergen
- East Bethany
- E. Pembroke
- Elba
- Le Roy
- Linden
- North Bergen
- Oakfield
- Pavilion
- do Centre
- Pembroke
- Roanoke
- South Byron
- Stafford
- Stone Church
- West Bergen

GREENE COUNTY.
- Acra
- Athens
- Big Hollow
- Bushnellsville
- Cairo
- CATSKILL 34
- Cornwallville
- Coxsackie
- Durham
- East Durham
- East Kill
- E. Lexington
- Gay Head
- Greenville
- Hunter
- Kiskatom
- Leeds
- Lexington
- do Heights
- Medway
- New Baltimore
- Oak Hill
- Palenville
- Prattsville
- Scienceville
- South Cairo
- South Durham
- Tannersville
- Union Society
- West Kill
- W. Lexington
- Windham
- do Centre

HAMILTON CO.
- Arietta
- Benson
- Gilman
- Hope
- Hope Centre
- Lake Pleasant

Long Lake   Sageville
Morehouse   Wells
Morehouseville

HERKIMER CO.
Cedarville   Mohawk
Cold Brook   Newport
Columbia   Newville
Crain's Corners Norway
Danube   Ohio
Dennison's   Ohio City
  Corners   Page's Corners
Devereux   Payne's Cor-
East Schuyler   ners   [low
Eatonville   Payne's Hol-
Fairfield   Pottsville
Frankfort   Russia
Frankfort Hill   Salisbury
Germanflats   do   Centre
HERKIMER 80   Schuyler
Ilion   Stark
Jacksonburgh   Starkville
Jordanville   VanHornsville
Litchfield   Warren
Little Falls   West Schuyler
Manheim   W. Windfield
  do   Centre Wilmot
Middleville   Windfield

JEFFERSON CO.
Adams   North Wilna
Adams Centre   Omar
Alexandria   Orleans
  do   Centre Oxbow
Antwerp   Pamelia
Belville   do 4 Corners
Black River   Perch River
Brownville   Philadelphia
Burr's Mills   Pierrepont
Cape Vincent   Manor
Carthage   Pillar Point
Champion   Plesis   [la
Clayton   Point Peninsu-
Depauville   Redwood
Dexter   Robert's Cor-
East Rodman   Rodman   [ners
Ellisburgh   Rutland
Evans' Mills   Sackett's Har-
Felt's Mills   bor   [ners
Great Bend   Sanford's Cor-
Henderson   Smithville
Hounsfield   South Rutland
Lafargeville   Sterlingville
Le Ray   Stone Mills
Le Raysville   Stowell's Cor-
Limerick   ners
Lorraine   Theresa
Lyme   Three Mile
Mannsville   Bay
Military Road   WATER-
Millen's Bay   TOWN 160
Natural Bridge   Wilna
North Adams   Woodville

KINGS COUNTY.
BROOKLYN 146   Flatlands
Bushwick   Fort Hamilton
East New   Gravesend
  York   New Utrecht
Flatbush   Williamsburg

LEWIS COUNTY.
Brantingham   Lyonsdale
Collinsville   MARTINS-
Constableville   BURGH 142
Copenhagen   Monterey
Croghan   Osceola
Deer River   Pinckney
Denmark   Stow's Square
Diana   Turin
Greig   Watson
Harrisburgh   West Leyden
Houseville   W'st Lowville
Indian River   West Martins-
Leyden   burgh
Lowville   West Turin

LIVINGSTON CO.
Avon   Mivonie
Caledonia   Moscow
Conesus   Mount Morris
Cuylerville   N'th Dansville
Dansville   Nunda
East Avon   Portage
East Spring   Ridge
  Water   River Road
Fowlersville   Forks
GENESEO 238   Scottsburgh
Gibbonsville   South Avon
Greigsville   Sparta
Groveland   Spottswood
  do   Centre South Avon
HemlockLake   Spring Water
Kysorville   Union Corners
Lakeville   West Conesus
Leicester   West Sparta
Lima   York
Livonia

MADISON COUNTY.
Bennett's Cor-   Lenox
  ners   Madison
Bouckville   Morrisville
Bridgeport   Nelson
Brookfield   New Wood-
Canastota   stock
Cazenovia   No. Brookfield
Chittenango   Oneida
Clockville   Oneida Lake
De Ruyter   Oneida Valley
Earlville   Perryville
East Hamilton   Peterboro'
EATON 103   Poolville
Erieville   Pratt's Hollow
Fenner   Siloam
Georgetown   Smithfield
Hamilton   Stockbridge
Lebanon   Sullivan

MONROE COUNTY.
Adams's   Hanford's
  Basin   Landing
Brighton   Henrietta
Brockport   Honeoye Falls
Charlotte   Irondequoit
Churchville   Mendon
Clarkson   Mumford
  do   Centre North Chili
Egypt   O'Connelville
Greece   Parma

Parma Centre   South Chili
Penfield   Spencerport
Perrinton   Sweden
Pittsford   Webster
Riga   West Greece
ROCHESTER   W. Henrietta
Rush   [251 West Webster
Scottsville   Wheatland

MONTGOMERY CO.
Ames   Hagaman's
Amsterdam   Mills
Auriesville   Hallsville
Buel   Minaville
Burtonville   Minden
Canajoharie   Palatine
Charleston   do   Bridge
  do 4 Corners Port Jackson
Cranesville   Root
Flatcreek   St. Johnsville
FONDA 42   Salt Spring-
Fort Hunter   ville
Fort Plain   Spraker's
Freysburg   Basin
Fultonville   Stone Arabia
Glen   Tribes' Hill

NEW YORK.
Haerlem   NEW YORK 145
King's Bridge

NIAGARA COUNTY.
Cambria   Olcott
Chalmers   Orange Port
County Line   Pekin
Hartland   Pendleton
Hickory Cor-   Porter
  ners   Ransomville
Johnson's Cr'k   Reynales'
Lewiston   Basin
LOCKPORT 300   Royalton
Locust Tree   Somerset
Middleport   So Royalton
Mount Cambria   Wheatfield
New Fane   Wilsons
Niagara Falls   Youngstown

ONEIDA COUNTY.
Alder Creek   Kirkland
Amsville   Lairdsville
Augusta   Lee
Ava   Lowell
Babcock Hill   McConnells-
Big Brook   Marcy   [ville
Boonville   Marshall
Bridgewater   New Hartford
Camden   New London
Cassville   N. York Mills
Clinton   North Bay
Deansville   North Gage
Deerfield   N'th Western
Delta   Oneida Castle
Durhamville   Oriskany
East Florence   do   Falls
Florence   Paris
Floyd   [ners Paris Furnace
Greene's Cor-   Pine
Higginsville   Prospect
Hizerville   Remsen
Holland Patent   Rome

in the State of New York.

Sangerfield — Verona
Sauquoit — Vienna
Sconondoa — Walesville
South Trenton — Waterville
Steuben — West Branch
Stokes — West Camden
Taberg — Western
Trenton — Westernville
  do Falls — Westmoreland
UTICA 93 — West Vienna
Vernon — WHITES-
  do Centre — TOWN 96

ONONDAGA CO.

Amber — Manlius Centre
Apulia — Marcellus
Baldwinsville — do Falls
Belle Isle — Marietta
Borodino — Mottville
Brewerton — Navarino
Camillus — Onondaga
Canal — do Hollow
Cardiff — Oran
Cicero — Otisco
Clay — Plainville
Delphi — Plank Road
De Witt — Polkville
Elbridge — Pompey
Euclid — do Centre
Fabius — Salina
Fairmount — Skaneateles
Fayetteville — So. Marcellus
Geddes — So. Onondaga
Hartsville — Spafford
Howlet Hill — do Hollow
Jack's Reef — SYRACUSE 146
Jamesville — Tully
Jordan — Tully Valley
Kirkville — Van Buren
Lafayette — do Centre
Liverpool — Vesper
Lysander — Watervale
Mandana — Wellington
Manlius — Windfall

ONTARIO COUNTY.

Allen's Hill — Naples
Bristol — North Bloom-
Bristol Centre — field
Canadice — Norton's Mills
CANANDAI- — Oak's Corners
  GUA 222 — Orleans
Centrefield — Phelps
Chapinville — Port Gibson
Cheshire — Reed's Cor's
East Bloomfiel — Richmond
Farmington — do Mills
Flintcreek — Rushville
Geneva — Seneca
Gorham — Seneca Castle
Hall's Corners — South Bristol
Honeoye — Victor
Hopewell — West Bloom-
Larned's Cor- — field
  ners — West Farm-
Manchester — ington
  do Centre

ORANGE COUNTY.

Accommoda- — Monroe
  tionville — do Works
Amity — Montgomery
Bloomingrove — Mount Hope
Bullville — Newburgh
Canterbury — New Hampton
Chester — New Milford
Coldenham — New Vernon
Cornwall — New Windsor
Craigsville — Otisville
Crawford — Oxford Depot
Cuddebackvill — Philipsburgh
Deer Park — Port Jervis
Edenville — Ridgebury
Farmingham — St Andrews
Finchville — Salisbury Mills
Florida — Scotchtown
Gaines — Slate Hill
GOSHEN 105 — South Middle-
Hamptonburg — town
Highland Mills — Sugar Loaf
Huguenot — Turners
Kendall — Unionville
Knowlesville — Walding
Little Britain — Walkill
Lyndonville — Warwick,
Medina — Wells' Corner
Middle Hope — West Point
Minisink — West Town

ORLEANS COUNTY.

ALBION 257 — Murray
Barre — North Ridge-
Barre Centre — way
Carlton — Oak Orchard
Clarendon — Ridgeway
East Carlton — Shelby
East Gaines — Shelby Basin
Gaines — South Barre
Hindsburgh — Waterport
Holley — West Carlton
Hulburton, — West Gaines
Kendall — Yates
Millville

OSWEGO COUNTY.

Albion — Palermo
Amboy — Parish
Boyleston — Phœnix
Butterfly — Port Ontario
Central Square — Redfield
Cleveland — Richland
Colosse — Roosevelt
Constantia — Salmon River
Fulton — Sand Bank
Gilbert's Mills — Sandy Creek
Granby — Schroeppel
Greenboro' — Scriba
Hannibal — South Albion
Hastings — do Richland
Hinmansville, — Texas
Hull's Corners — Union Settle-
Kinney's 4 Cor — ment
Mexico — Union Square
New Haven — Vermillion
Orwell — Volney
OSWEGO 167 — West Amboy

West Monroe — West Wil-
Williamstown — hamstown

OTSEGO COUNTY.

Burlington — Otego
  do Flats — Otsdawa
Butternuts — Otsdawa
Cherry Valley — Pittsfield
Colliersville — Plainfield
COOPERSTOWN — Richfield
Decatur [66 — do Springs
East Spring- — Roseboom
  field — Schuyler Lake
East Worces- — South Edmes-
  ter — ton
Edmeston — South Valley
Exeter — do Worces-
Garrattsville — ter
Gilbertsville — Springfield
Hartwick — Unadilla
  do Seminary — do Centre
Laurens — do Forks
Maple Grove — West Burling-
Maryland — ton
Middlefield — West Edmes-
  do Centre — ton
Milford — West Exeter
  do Centre — Westford
Mount Vision — West Laurens
New Lisbon — do Oneonta
Oaksville — Westville
Oneonta — Worcester

PUTNAM COUNTY.

CARMEL 106 — Milltown
Cold Spring — Patterson
Doanesburgh — Philipstown
Farmers' Mills — Putnam Valley
Haviland Hol- — Red Mills
  low — South East
Kent — Towners

QUEENS COUNTY.

Astoria — Jericho
Buckram — Manhasset
College Point — Merrick
East Norwich — Newtown
Farmingdale — North Hemp-
Flushing — stead
Glen Cove — Oyster Bay
Hempstead — South
  do Branch — Oyster Bay
JAMAICA 158 — Rockaway
Jerusalem — Roslyn
  South — Syosset

RENSSELAER CO.

Alps — Grafton
Berlin — Greenbush
Brunswick — Hoag's Corner
Brainard's — Hoosick
  Bridge — Hoosick Falls
Castleton — Junction
Centre Berlin — Lansingburgh
Defriestville — Nassau
Eagle Mills — North Steven-
East Green- — town
  bush — Petersburgh
East Nassau — do 4 Corners
East Sandlake — Pittstown

Poestenkill, South Schodack, Potter Hill, Prospect Hill, South Stevenstown, Raymerton, Sandlake, Tomhannock, Schaghticoke, TROY 6, Schodack, West Sandlak, do Centre, do Stephendo Land'g, town, Stephentown, Wynantskill

RICHMOND CO.
Castleton, Southfield, Northfield, Stapleton, North Shore, Tompkinsville, RICHMOND 158, Westfield, Rossville

ROCKLAND CO.
Clarkstown, Orangetown, Haverstraw, Piermont, Monsey, Ramapo, Nanuet, Rockland Lake, North Haverstraw, Scotland, Nyack, Tappantown, West Hempdo Turnpike, stead

ST. LAWRENCE CO.
Brasher, Morley, Brasher Fall, Morristown, Buck Bridge, Nicholville, CANTON 206, Norfolk, Colton, Oak Point, De Kalb, Ogdensburgh, De Peyster, Oswegatchie, East Pierpont, Parishville, Edwards, Pierpont, Edwardsville, Pitcairn, Flackville, Potsdam, Fine, Rackett River, Fowler, Raymondville, Fullersville, Richville, Gouverneur, Rossie, Hammond, Russell, Helena, Shingle Creek, Hermon, Somerville, Heuvelton, South Canton, Hopkintown, do Edwards, Lawrenceville, do Hammond, Lisbon, Southville, Louisville, Stockholm, Macomb, Waddington, Madrid, West Potsdam, Massena, do Stockholm, Matildaville, Wrightsburgh

SARATOGA COUNTY.
BALLSTON 30, East Line, do Centre, Edgecombe's, Barkersville, Corners, Bemis' Hights, Edinburgh, Blenheim, Fortsville, Burnt Hills, Galway, Charlton, Grangerville, Clifton Park, Greenfield, Corinth, do Centre, Coveville, Hadley, Day, Half-Moon, Dean's Corner, Jonesville, Ketcham Corners, Rexford Flats, Malta, Saratoga, Maltaville, do Springs, Mechanicsvill, Schuylerville, Milton, South Corinth, Moreau, Stillwater, Mt. Pleasant, Visscher Ferry, North Galway, Waterford, Northumberland, West Charlton, Pope's Corners, do Day, Porter's do, do Greenfield, Providence, do Milton, Quaker Spring, Whiteside's Corners, Wilton

SCHENECTADY CO.
Braman's Cor., Mariaville, Duanesburgh, Niskayuna, East Glenville, Princetown, Glenville, Quaker Street, Hoffmans Ferry, Rotterdam [15, SCHENECTADY

SCHOHARIE CO.
Argosville, Gilboa, Barnerville, Hyndsville, Blenheim, Jefferson, Brackabeen, Lawyersville, Broome, Leesville, Byrneville, Livingstonvill, Carlisle, Middleburgh, Central Bridge, Morseville, Charlotteville, North Blenheim, Cobleskill, do Centre, Richmondville, Conesville, SCHOHARIE 32, East Cobleskill, Seward, Esperence, Sharon, Franklinton, do Centre, Fulton, Sloansville, Fultonham, Summit, Gallupville, Waldensville, Gardnersville, Wright

SENECA COUNTY.
Canoga, Seneca Falls, Covert, Sheldrake, Farmer, South Lodi, Fayette, Townsendvill, Junius, Tyre, Lodi, Varick, do Centre, Waterloo, OVID 197, West Fayette, Romulus, do Junius

STEUBEN COUNTY.
Addison, Cohocton, Arkport, Cold Spring Mills, Avoca, BATH 216, Cooper's Plains, Bennett Creek, Corning, Bradford, Cossville, Brimmersville, Dansville, Cameron, Doty's Corner, Campbell, East Cameron, do Creek, do Canisteo, do Town, do Painted Post, Canisteo, Caton, Erwin, Erwin Centre, Pond Settlement, Gibson, Goff's Mills, Prattsburgh, Greenwood, Pultney, Hammond's Mills, Purdey Creek, Hartsville, Rathboneville, Haskenville, Reading, Hornby, do Centre, Hornellsville, Shannon, Howard, South Cameron, Hunter's Land, South Dansville, Jasper, do Hill, Kennedysville, do Pultney, Lindley, Sugar Hill, Lindleytown, Thurston, Mt. Washington, Tobehanna, Mud Creek, Towlesville, North Cohocton, Troupsburgh, North Reading, Tyrone, do Thurston, Urbana, do Urbana, Wayne, Orange, West Addison, Painted Post, do Greenw'd, Patchin's Mills, do Troupsburgh, Peltonville, West Union, Pine Grove, Wheeler, Pineville, Woodhull, Wormleys

SUFFOLK COUNTY.
Amagansett, Miller's Place, Babylon, Moriches, Baiting Hollo', Mount Sinai, Bellport, New Village, Bridghampton, Northport, Brookhaven, Orient, Centreport, Patchogue, Cold Spring Harbor, Port Jefferson, Quogue, Commack, Riverhead, Coram, Sag Harbor, Cutchogue, Sayville, Dix Hills, Setauket, East Hampton, Shelter Island, Fireplace, Smithtown, Flanders, Southampton, Good Ground, Southold, Greenport, Speonk, Hermitage Depot, Stony Brook, Success, Huntington, SUFFOLK 226, Islip, Upper Aquebogue, Jamesport, Manorville, Wading River, Mattituck, West Hills, Middle Island, Yaphank

SULLIVAN COUNTY.
Barryville, Callikoon, Beaverbrook, Fallsburgh, Beaverkill, Forestburgh, Bethel, Fosterdale, Bloomingburg, Gates, Bridgeville, Glen Wild, Burlingham, Grahamsville, Cochecton, Hartwood

in the State of New York.

Hasbrouck, Purvis, Liberty, Rockland, Lumberland, Sandburgh, Monticello, Thompson, Mamakating, Thompsonville, Narrowsburg, West Brookville, Neversink, Parksville, White Lake, Philipsport, Woodbourne, Pond Eddy, Wurtsborough

TIOGA COUNTY.
Apalachin, Nichols, Barton, Owego 167, Berkshire, Richford, Campbell, Shawnee, Candor, Smithsboro', Canfield's Corners, South Owego, Spencer, Factoryville, Tioga, Flemingville, Tioga Centre, Halsey Valley, West Candor, Newark, West Newark, do Valley, Willseyville

TOMPKINS CO.
Burdett, Mecklinburgh, Caroline, Mott's Corners, do Centre, Newfield, Cayutaville, North Hector, Danby, do Newfield, Dryden, do Lansing, East Lansing, Peruville, Enfield, Reynoldsville, do Centre, Searsburgh, Etna, Seneca, Groton, Slaterville, Hector, South Danby, ITHACA 170, do Lansing, Jacksonville, Speedsville, Lake Ridge, Trumansburg, Lansing, Ulysses, Lansingville, Varna, Logan, Waterbury, Ludlowville, West Dryden, McLean, West Groton

ULSTER COUNTY.
Accord, Marbletown, Amesville, Marlborough, Beach Hill, Milton, Bruynswick, Modena, Esopus, Napanock, Glasco, New Hurley, High Falls, New Paltz, Hurley, Landing, KINGSTON 98, New Paltz, Kyserike, Olive, Lackawack, do Bridge, Lake Hill, Pluttekill, Lloyd, River Side, Malden, Rochester

Rondout, The Corner, Rosendale, Tuthill, Saugerties, Ulsterville, Shandaken, Warwarsing, do Centre, West Camp, Shawangunk, do Hurley, Shokan, Woodstock, Southwick

WARREN COUNTY.
Athol, Hyde, Bolton, Johnsburgh, CALDWELL 62, Luzerne, Chester, Pottersville, Chestertown, Queensbury, Glen's Falls, Stony Creek, Hague, The Glen, Horicon, Warrensburg

WASHINGTON CO.
Anaquassook, Hartford, Argyle, Hebron, Bartenville, Jackson, Buskirk's Bridge, Kingsbury, Lake, Cambridge, Low Hampton, Centre Cambridge, Middle Granville, Centre White Creek, North Argyle, do Easton, Comstock's Landing, do Granville, do Greenwich, Dresden, do Hebron, E. Greenwich, North White Creek, Easton, East Salem, Patten's Mills, Fort Ann, Putnam, Fort Edward, Salem, Fort Edward Centre, SANDY HILL 50, Shusan, Fort Miller, South Argyle, Galesville, do Easton, Granville, do Granville, Greenwich, do Hartford, Griswold's Mills, West Hebron, White Creek, Hampton, Whitehall

WAYNE COUNTY.
Alloway, Marion, Arcadia, Newark, Butler, Ontario, Clyde, Palmyra, East Palmyra, Port Glasgow, Fairville, Pultneyville, Galen, Red Creek, Huron, Rose, Locke Berlin, Salmon Creek, LYONS 1×1, Savannah, Macedon, Sodus, do Centre, do Centre, Marengo, do Point

South Butler, West Walworth, South Sodus, Walworth, Williamson, West Butler, Wolcott, Westburgh

WESTCHESTER CO.
BEDFORD 130, Port Chester, Cortland, Poundridge, Cortlandtown, Rye, Cross River, Salem Centre, Croton Falls, Scarsdale, Dobb's Ferry, Shrub Oak, East Chester, Sing Sing, Greenburgh, Somers, Harrison, South Salem, Lewisborough, Tarrytown, Mamoroneck, The Purchase, Moringville, Tuckahoe, Mt. Pleasant, Verplanck, New Castle, Vista, do Rochelle, Westchester, North Castle, West Farms, do Salem, do Somers, Ossinsing, WHITE PLAINS, Peeksville, Whitlockville, Pelham, Yonkers, Pine's Bridge, Yorktown, Plessantville

WYOMING COUNTY.
Attica, Middlebury, Attica Centre, North Java, Bennington, do Sheldon, Castile, do Wethersfield, China, Covington, Orangeville, Cowlesville, Peoria, Dale, Perry, Eagle, do Centre, East China, Pike, do Java, Sheldon, Gainesville, Strykersville, Genesee Falls, Varysburgh, Hermitage, Vernal, Java, WANSAW 303, do Village, Wethersfield, Johnsburgh, do Spring, La Grange, Wyoming

YATES COUNTY.
Barrington, Middlesex, Benton, Milo, do Centre, do Centre, Big Stream Point, North Middlesex, Branchport, Penn Yan, Dundee, Potter, Ferguson Cor, Rock Stream, Italy, South Milo, do Hill, Starkey, do Hollow, West Dresden, Jerusalem, Yatesville

The longest day in Great Britain is 17 hours and 2 minutes. In the United States, it is only 14 hours and 50 minutes. The shortest day in Great Britain is 7 hours and 20 minutes, in the United States it is 9 hours and 10 minutes.

STAGE AND MAIL ROUTES IN OLDEN TIME.

In June, 1785, a company of stage proprietors undertook to make the land passage to New York from Albany, "the most easy and agreeable, as well as the most expeditious," by performing the journey in two days, at 3d. a mile; but in the fall of the year, "for the ease of the passengers," the time of running was changed to three days, and the price raised to 4d. a mile, "agreeably to act of assembly." This was a chartered company, the legislature having in the above year granted to Isaac Van Wyck, Talmage Hall and John Kinney, the exclusive right "to erect, set up, carry on, and drive," stage wagons between Albany and New York, on the east side of the Hudson river, for a term of ten years, and restrained all opposition under a penalty of £200. They were to have at least two covered wagons, each drawn by four able horses, the fare was limited to 4d. a mile, and the trips to be performed once a week, under the penalty of the forfeiture of their charter. At this time the post office at Albany served not only for the adjoining towns, as Schenectady and Greenbush, but also for Orange and Dutchess counties, Cherry Valley, &c., and letters were advertised even for Vermont. By the post office arrangements of January, 1786, the New York mail arrived twice a week, Wednesdays and Saturdays. The post office business at this time could not have been very extensive, there being but two mails in the week, one from New York, and the other from Springfield, which were so unimportant that for several years after the routes were called cross-roads in the government contracts, and terminated at the city. The communication with the neighboring counties and states was kept up by post riders, who met at certain points and interchanged letters and papers, and when the business was not sufficient to support them, subscriptions were raised for the purpose among such citizens as were interested in their continuance..... In 1789 a stage commenced running from Platt's Inn in Lansingburgh, to Lewis's City Tavern, Albany, three times a week, Mondays, Wednesdays, and Fridays. The bill of fare down and back was 4s.; fare one way 3s..... In 1790 a post of this kind left Albany on Monday afternoon, and reached Schenectady the same day; was at Johnstown on Tuesday, at Canajoharie on Wednesday, at Fort Plain on Thursday, at Fort Hunter and Warrensbush on Friday, and arrived at Albany, on its return, Monday forenoon. The post to Vermont left the city on Monday evening, arrived at Pittstown on Tuesday, at Bennington on Wednesday, at Little White Creek and Cambridge on Thursday, at Tomhannic and Schaghticoke on Friday, and at Hoosic on Saturday. This was also the mode, and almost the only means, of circulating newspapers at that day..... It was mentioned at this time (1790), that the trade and commerce of the United States had been greatly benefitted by the regulations at the general post office, whereby the mail was transported five times a week between New York and Philadelphia; and the post master general had signified his intention to make the same arrangements between New York and Baltimore, at the beginning of the next year..... In February, 1790, the legislature granted Ananias Platt the exclusive right of running a stage between Albany and Lansingburgh. Four years later, Mr. Platt, "grateful for public custom," undertook to run his stage twice a day from Lansingburgh to Albany and back. In the winter of 1795 he had increased the number of daily trips to six. In the summer of 1796, the amount of travelling had increased so much as to employ twenty stages daily between Waterford, Lansingburgh, Troy and Albany, averaging more than 150 passengers a day.... In 1791, the post master general was authorized by law to extend the post route from Albany to Bennington, Vt; and the first mail reached that place on the 25th of March, the anniversary of the settlement of the town thirty years before. The printers complained of the careless and irregular manner in which the New York mail was carried. It appears that the contract required the mail to be carried but once a week, though the carriers generally took it twice, and thereby exceeded their contract..... It may be here remarked, that the length of all the post routes in the state, is now, 1848, above 13,000 miles..... In 1792, by the act of congress for extending post roads, and fixing the rates of postage, the mail route from Albany to Bennington was extended through the state of Vermont to the north part of this state on Lake Champlain; and a post road established from Albany through Schenectady to Canajoharie. The rates of postage on newspapers were about the same as they are now, with the exception of the odious three cent appendage. A post was established in the same year from Albany to Whitestown, as a private enterprise, which performed the route once a fortnight. Several gentlemen in the *Genesee country*, established another to meet the one at Whitestown, by which a communication was opened between Albany and the *far west*. The latter post passed through Geneva, Canandarqua, Canawargus and Williamsburgh. Towns were then few and far between. There were but 7 in Saratoga county, 3 in Herkimer, and 4 in Montgomery. Postmaster General Pickering's advertisements for contracts to carry the mails, also proposed to extend the post road west of Albany, "from Connojorharrie to Whitestown, and thence to Kanandarqua." About the same time a private post was established from Niagara to the Genesee river, where it met the one previously mentioned, and interchanged letters and papers. By this means a chain of communication was opened through the whole extent of the state, and the Messrs. Webster in Albany received and forwarded letters gratuitously to every part of the country where there were no mails. Some one proposed this year to establish a line of stages from Albany to Whitestown, a project which the editor of the Gazette says, would have been ridiculed at an earlier day, but which the great intercourse with the western country might justify, and answer a valuable purpose, if the proprietors could succeed in contracting for the mail. In the spring of 1793- Moses Beal "erected a stage," to use his own words, "for the accom, modation of passengers from Albany to Schenectady, Johnstown, and Canajohary, once a week." It left Albany at 6 o'clock on Friday morning, and arrived at Canajoharie the next day. The fare was 3c. a mile. It returned on Tuesday. He proposed to go occasionally as far as Little Falls, if desired! The success of these enterprises emboldened others; and we find that one John Hudson, inn keeper, established a line of stages to run between Albany and Schenectady, three times a week; and John Rodgers, of Ballston, ran a line from that place to connect with it, by which a regular communication was now first established for the convenience of those who visited the springs. The fare was 4s. to Schenectady; those who continued through were charged 3d. a mile. A still bolder scheme was undertaken, to connect the city with the valley of the Connecticut, by a line of stages to Northampton. Arrangements having been made in the fall of the above year, a stage started from each end of the line on Tuesdays and Fridays, in the morning, and met at Pittsfield in the evening, accomplishing the entire route in two days. The proprietors, in their appeal to the public for patronage, remark, that the difficulty of extending a line of stages across the mountains, had always been considered insurmountable, but reflecting that such an establishment would complete the line of an expeditious and sure communication from "Portland, in the province of Maine," through a rich and flourishing country, to Whitestown, in the western part of the state of New York, a distance of upwards of 400 miles, they had determined to make the experiment. The fare was 4c. a mile.... In 1794 the post routes from Albany, or centering in Albany, had increased to five, as follows, preserving the post master general's orthography. 1st. Form Albany to Kinderhook, Hudson, Clermont, Redhook, Rhinebeck, Poughkeepsie, Fishkill, Pickskill and New York, once a week. 2d. From Albany to Lansingburgh, Bennington, Manchester, Rutland, Middleburgh, Vergennes and Burlington, once a week. 3d. From Albany to New Lebanon, Pittsfield, Worthington, Northampton and Brookfield, once a week. 4th. From Albany to Kinderhook, Stockbridge and Springfield, once a week. 5th. From Albany to Schenectady, Johnstown, Canajohary, German Flatts, Whitestown, Old Fort Schuyler, Onondaga, Aurora, Scipio, Geneva and Kanandaigua, once in two weeks. A branch ran from Canajohary through Cherry Valley to Cooperstown, once a week....In January, 1795, Mr. John Hudson ran two stages, one of four horses and the other of two, daily between Albany and Schenectady, and Ananias Platt soon after went upon the same line, making four trips a day. The fare to New York by stage this year, was reduced to 3£ 4s. ($8). It is understood that the price was usually $10. In the following year it was reduced to $6 in the summer; the fare from Albany to Fort Schuyler was $2·50; to Whitestown, $3.....In the same year also (1796), the mails made the transit between Albany and Philadelphia, a distance of about 260 miles, in three days, and from Boston to Philadelphia in four days, from Savannah to Philadelphia in thirteen days..... The post roads diverging from Albany were further increased in 1797, through northern towns. A list of the roads and distances in various directions from Albany, this year, was as follows:

ALBANY TO HARTFORD AND NEW HAVEN.

	Miles.		Miles.
Col. Visscher's and John Staats's Greenbush,	1	Sheffield,	4
McKown's,	4	Canaan,	8
Smith's,	6	Norfolk,	6
John Miller's,	1	Dr. Bidwell's,	4
Kinderhook Plains,	4	Phelps's (Green Woods),	5
Kinderhook Mills,	2	Austin's (New Hartford),	5
Buck's Tavern,	5	Case's (Symsbury),	7
Spencertown,	7	Northington,	4
Green river,	5	West Hartford,	5
Derby's,	5	Hartford,	4
Egremont, foot of Nabletown mountain,	1	Middletown,	15
Cook's,	4	New Haven,	23
Baker's, in Gt. Barrington,	1		138

Stage and Mail Routes.

ALBANY TO NIAGARA.

	Miles.		Miles.
Humphrey's Tavern,	2	Foster's,	5
McKown's,	3	Morehouse's,	6
Douw's,	2	Keeler's or Danforth's,	5
Truax's,	5	Carpenter's,	15
Schenectady,	4	Buck's,	3
Groat's,	12	Goodrich's,	8
John Fonda's,	12	Huggins's,	4
Conally's,	7	Cayuga,	7
Roseboom's Fer. (Can'joharie),	3	Seneca,	3
Hudson's (Indian Castle),	13	Geneva,	11
Aldridge's (German Flatts),	11	Amsden's,	6
Brayton's,	13	Wells's,	8
Old Fort Schuyler,	3	Sanburne's (Canandarqua),	4
Whitestown,	4	Sears's & Peck's,	13
Rome (Fort Stanwix),	12	Genesee river,	14
Whitestown to Laird's Tavern,	9	Indiantown Tonawanda,	40
Oneida Castle,	8	Niagara,	35
Wemp's,	5		
John Denna's,	7		310

Five miles from Albany, — Isaac J. Truax and his son Isaac, Jr., ran taverns and inns along the old King's Highway. They were excavated by the editor in 1973.

ALBANY TO MONTREAL.

	Miles.		Miles.
Flatts,	5	Burlington,	70
Waterford,	7	Sandbar,	14
Half-Moon,	6	John Martin's,	14
Stillwater,	4	Savage's Point,	6
Ensign's,	6	Windmill "	6
Du Mont's Ferry,	8	Isle au Noix,	12
Fort Edward,	12	St. John's,	14
Sandy Hill,	2	Laperara,	18
Fort Ann,	10	Montreal,	9
Skeensborough,	12		
Dr. Smith's,	8		232

ALBANY TO BOSTON.

	Miles.		Miles.
McKown's,	5	Northampton,	13
Strong's,	9	Belchertown,	15
Schermerhorn's,	7	Brookfield,	15
Lebanon Springs,	9	Leicester,	13
Pittsfield,	7	Worcester,	13
Partridgefield,	10	Boston,	44
Worthington,	10		
Chesterfield,	7		177

Note.—From Worcester to Boston the country is almost one continued village, and houses of entertainment in no instance of two or three miles.

ALBANY TO NEW YORK AND PHILADELPHIA.

	Miles.		Miles.
Greenbush,	1	Kinderhook,	4
McKown's,	4	Claverack,	14
Smith's,	6	Livingston's Manor,	7
J. Miller's,	3	Swart's,	15
Kinderhook Plains,	4	Rhinebeck,	9

	Miles.		Miles.
Staatsburgh,	6	Conklin's,	12
Poughkeepsie,	11	Kingsbridge,	12
Fishkill,	14	New York,	15
Nelson's (Highlands),	11	Philadelphia,	95
Peekskill,	9		
Odell's,	10		260

So little improvement was made in regard to speed, that in 1804 a line of stages commenced running between Albany and New York, which occupied three days in the journey, lodging the first night at Rhinebeck, and the next at Peekskill. The avowed object of this line was the ease of the traveller, who was allowed all the time requisite to make the passage agreeable. As far as time was concerned, surely no one could desire to be longer on the road. Fare $8. The steam boats soon after this introduced a new mode of conveying travellers and the mail, with ease and comfort to the passenger, and a considerable increase of speed..... In 1811 a line of stages was formed from Albany to Niagara Falls, which accomplished the journey in three days, at the following rates: from Albany to Utica, $5·50; Utica to Geneva, $5; Geneva to Canandaigua, $5·75; and from thence to Buffalo at 6c. a mile.... In 1814 a line of stages was established by a Mr. Hicks, to run between Albany and Brattleboro', to carry the mail twice a week, but to make the trip between the two places in one day. It was thought the journey to Boston could be performed with greater safety by this route than any other..... In 1818 a line of stages commenced running between Albany and Montreal, on the west side of Lake Champlain, transporting the mail three times a week. By continued gradations, Albany became the centre of a large amount of stage travel, which increased from year to year until about 1830, the dawning of the rail road era. Lines of stages diverged to every point of the compass, and its streets were thronged with vehicles departing and arriving at all hours of the day and night. There were several lines daily to Buffalo, to Montreal, to New York, and to Boston. There was a line to Boston by the way of Charlestown, N. H., one by Brattleboro', Vt., one by Greenfield, Mass., and one by Springfield, Mass., and one by Hartford, Ct. Besides these there were numerous less important lines. The firms of Thorp & Sprague, and Baker & Walbridge, owned an incredible number of stage coaches, which were subsequently laid up on the completion of the rail roads, and other improvements in traveling, and many hundreds of worn out horses went to their rest. The glory of this business has departed; its tired horses and tired men have been superseded by the iron horse, which never tires. Troy is now the seat of staging operations in this region; a few straggling lines take the northern routes over the mountains, and short lines penetrate sections of the country remote from the rail roads. One line still occupies the route, over the Cherry Valley turnpike, terminating at Syracuse; through in 24 hours; fare $2·75, or thereabout. This route accommodates such as halt at by-places, or are a little doubtful of their entire personal safety behind a locomotive. Mr. Joseph Webster, who is the veteran stager of the day, also traverses the Helderberg ridge with a six horse team, to Rensselaerville, and another line leaves the Clinton Hotel, keeping up a communication with Schoharie.

PRINCIPAL ROUTES OF TRAVEL DIVERGING FROM ALBANY.

ALBANY TO TROY.

During the season of navigation there are three modes of conveyance between Albany and Troy, viz.:

1st. By stage which leaves the General Stage Office, No. 436 Broadway, Albany, and the hotels on River street, Troy, half-hourly, from 6 A. M. to 7 P. M. Fare 12½ cents.

2d. By steamboat, hourly, from the foot of State street, Albany, and the Steamboat Landing, River street, Troy. Fare 12½ cents.

3d. By the Troy and Greenbush Rail Road, hourly, from about 6 A. M. to 7 P. M., from the East Albany depot, and the east end of the rail road bridge, Troy. Fare 20 cents.

BETWEEN ALBANY AND BUFFALO.

Between Albany, Niagara Falls and Buffalo, there are several routes and modes of conveyance.

1st. By rail road to Schenectady, thence by rail road or packet boats running on the Erie canal.

2d. By rail road or canal to Rome, thence by stage on plank road and steam boat, via. Oswego.

3d. By rail road, stage or canal to Syracuse, thence by rail road or canal and steam boat, via. Oswego.

4th. By rail road or canal to Rochester, thence by rail road, canal or steam boat.

At Utica, Rome, Syracuse and Rochester, passengers can change from the cars to the packets or line boats, and vice versa, without any inconvenience. There are also many points between Schenectady and Utica where a change may be made.

BY ERIE CANAL AND PACKET BOATS.

During the season of canal navigation, there are two daily lines of packet boats from Schenectady to Buffalo, navigating the Erie canal. Leave Schenectady for Buffalo about 9 A. M. and 9 P. M., or on the arrival of the morning and evening cars from Albany. Fare from Schenectady to Albany, by rail road, 50 cents. Leave Buffalo also about the same hours for Schenectady, arriving morning and evening in time for passengers to proceed without delay by rail road to Albany. At Lockport the packet boats connect with the cars running between Lockport and Niagara Falls, and which connect with cars between Niagara Falls and Buffalo. Travellers who wish a more economical mode than by packet or cars, can travel by line boats, which afford good accommodations at a cheap rate. The usual charge for passage and board being about one and a half cents per mile, or one cent per mile without board. Line boats reach Buffalo from Albany in about seven days. Distance 364 miles.

Routes of Travel.

PACKET BOAT TO BUFFALO.

Stopping Places.	Pl. to Pl	Total.	Stopping Places.	Pl. to Pl.	Total.
Port Schuyler,	6	6	Jordan,	4	190
West Troy,	1	7	Cold Spring,	1	191
Junction Champlain Canal,	2	9	Weedsport,	5	196
Cohoes,	1	10	Centreport,	1	197
Lower Aqueduct,	3	13	Port Byron,	2	199
Willow Springs,	6	19	Montezuma,	6	205
Upper Aqueduct,	7	26	Lockpit,	6	211
Schenectady,	4	30	Clyde,	5	216
Rotterdam,	9	39	Lock Berlin,	5	221
Amsterdam,	8	47	Lyons,	4	225
Schoharie Creek,	5	52	Lockville,	6	231
Smithtown,	2	54	Newark,	1	232
Fultonville,	3	57	Port Gibson,	3	235
Spraker's Basin,	9	66	Palmyra,	5	240
Canajoharie,	3	69	Macedonville,	4	244
Fort Plain,	3	72	Wayneport,	3	247
St. Johnsville,	5	77	Perinton,	2	249
East Canada Creek,	4	81	" Centre,	2	251
Indian Castle,	2	83	Fairport,	1	252
Little Falls,	5	88	Fullam's Basin,	1	253
Herkimer Lower Bridge,	7	95	Bushnell's "	3	256
" Upper "	1	96	Pittsford,	3	259
Frankfort,	5	101	Billinghurst's Basin,	4	263
Utica,	9	110	Rochester,	6	269
York Mills,	3	113	Brockway's,	10	279
Whitesboro,	1	114	Spencer's Basin,	2	281
Oriskany,	3	117	Adams's "	3	284
Rome,	8	125	Cooley's "	3	287
Wood Creek,	2	127	Brockport,	2	289
Hawley's Basin,	2	129	Holley,	5	294
New London,	3	132	Hulberton,	4	298
Higgins's,	4	136	Albion,	6	304
Loomis's,	2	138	Gaines's Basin,	2	306
Oneida Creek,	3	141	Eagle Harbor,	1	307
Canastota,	5	146	Knowlesville,	4	311
New Boston,	4	150	Medina,	4	315
Chittenango,	3	153	Shelby Basin,	3	318
Kirkville,	5	158	Middleport,	3	321
Manlius,	4	162	Reynolds's Basin,	3	324
Lodi,	8	170	Gosport,	2	326
Syracuse,	1	171	Lockport,	7	333
Geddes,	2	173	Pendleton,	7	340
Belisle,	4	177	Tonawanda,	12	352
Camillus,	2	179	Lower Black Rock,	8	360
Canton,	5	184	Black Rock,	1	361
Peru,	2	186	Buffalo,	3	364

Routes of Travel.

BY RAIL ROAD.

Leave Albany for Buffalo and intermediate places about 7 A. M., and 1 and 7 P. M.; running through to Buffalo in about seventeen hours, and connecting at Buffalo with boats running to all ports on the upper lakes. Leave Buffalo for Albany about 8 A. M., and 1 and 5 P. M., connecting with the morning and evening steam boats for New York, and cars for Boston, &c.

Stopping Places.	Pl. to Pl	Total.	Fare.	Stopping Places.	Pl. to Pl	Total.	Fare.
Schenectady,	17	17	·50	Skeneat'les Junction	1	165	
Hoffman's Ferry,	9	26	·75	Sennet,	4	169	
Crane's Village,	4	30	·90	Auburn, 26 miles,	5	174	5·05
Amsterdam,	4	34	1·00	Cayuga Bridge,	11	185	
Tribe's Hill,	5	39	1·15	Seneca Falls,	5	190	
Fonda,	5	44	1·30	Waterloo,	3	193	
Yost's,	6	50	1·45	Gage's,	3	196	
Spraker's,	3	53	1·55	Geneva,	4	200	
Palatine Bridge,	3	56	1·65	Oak's Corners,	5	205	
Fort Plain,	3	59	1·75	Vienna,	3	208	
Palatine,	2	61	1·85	Clifton,	4	212	
St. Johnsville,	3	64	1·90	Shortsville,	4	216	
East Canada Creek,	3	67	2·00	Chapinsville,	3	219	
Little Falls,	7	74	2·20	Canandaigua,	3	222	
Herkimer,	7	81	2·40	Victor,	10	232	
Frankfort,	3	84	2·60	Fisher's,	4	236	
Utica, 94? miles,	11	95	2·75	Railroad Mills,	1	237	
Whitesboro,	4	99		Pittsford,	5	242	
Oriskany,	3	102		Brighton,	5	247	
Rome,	7	109		Rochester, 77 miles,	4	251	7·55
Green's Corners,	5	114		Cold Water,	6	257	
Verona,	4	118		Chili,	4	261	
Oneida,	4	122		Churchville,	4	265	
Wampsville,	3	125		Wardville,	3	268	
Canastota,	3	128		West Bergen,	4	272	
Canasaraga,	3	131		Byron,	4	276	
Chittenango,	2	133		Batavia,	7	283	
Kirkville,	5	138		Alexander,	8	291	
Manlius,	2	140		Attica, 44 miles,	4	295	
De Witt,	5	145		Darien City,	4	299	
Syracuse, 53 miles,	3	148	4·25	Darien Centre,	2	301	
Geddes,	2	150		Alden,	6	307	
Camillus,	6	156		Town Line,	4	11	
High Embankment,	3	159		Lancaster,	6	317	
Half-Way House,	2	161		Cheektawaga,	4	321	
Elbridge,	3	164		Buffalo,	5	326	9·75

At a meeting of the superintendents of the several rail roads forming the line between Albany and Buffalo, in October, 1848, the following schedule was adopted, which went into operation on the 23d of that month.

Routes of Travel.

GOING WEST.

	7 A.M.	2 P.M.	7 P.M.
Leave Albany,	7 A.M.	2 P.M.	7 P.M.
" Schenectady,	8 "	3 "	8 "
" Utica,	12 noon,	8 30 "	12 night,
" Syracuse,	3 P.M.	12 30 A.M.	2 50 A.M.
" Auburn,	4 15 "	2 30 "	3 45 "
" Rochester,	8 30 "	9 "	9 "
Arrive at Buffalo,	12 30 A.M.	1 P.M.	1 P.M.

GOING EAST.

Leave Buffalo,	7 A.M.	2 P.M.	9 P.M.
" Rochester,	11 15 "	7 30 "	1 15 A.M.
" Auburn,	3 20 P.M.	1 15 A.M.	5 30 "
" Syracuse,	5 15 "	3 "	7 15 "
" Utica,	8 15 "	7 "	10 15 "
" Schenectady,	12 15 A.M.	12 30 P.M.	2 15 P.M.
Arrive at Albany,	1 15 "	1 30 "	3 15 "

On the 1st of November, the fares on this line were reduced from $12 to $9·75, as follows:

Albany to Schenectady,	$0·50	Auburn to Rochester,	$2·50
Schenectady to Utica,	2·25	Rochester to Buffalo,	2·25
Utica to Syracuse,	1·50		
Syracuse to Auburn,	·75	Total,	$9.75

It is understood that each train departs within half an hour after its arrival at each of the intermediate places mentioned in the above list.

DISTANCES FROM ALBANY TO NEW YORK,
ON THE HUDSON RIVER.

Overslaugh,	3	New Windsor,	86
Castleton,	8	Cornwall,	88
Schodack Landing,	10	Cold Spring,	91
Coeymans,	12	West Point,	93
New Baltimore,	14	Caldwell's Landing,	101
Kinderhook Landing,	18	Verplanck's Point,	104
Coxsackie,	21	Grassy Point,	106
Hudson,	29	Teller's Point,	110
Catskill,	34	Sing Sing,	112
Bristol, or Malden,	43	Tarrytown,	118
Saugerties,	44	Piermont,	121
Upper Redhook,	45	Dobbs's Ferry,	123
Lower Redhook,	48	Hastings,	125
Rhinebeck,	55	Yonkers,	128
Pelham,	61	Spuyten Duyvel Creek,	132
Hyde Park,	65	Fort Lee, N. J.,	135
Poughkeepsie,	71	Manhattanville,	137
Milton,	75	Bull's Ferry, N. J.,	139
New Hamburgh,	78	New York,	145
Newburgh,	84		

ON THE EAST SIDE OF THE HUDSON RIVER.

Greenbush,	1	Poughkeepsie,	76
Schodack Centre,	10	Fishkill,	89
Kinderhook,	20	Phillipsburgh,	99
Stuyvesant Falls,	25	Peekskill,	108
Hudson,	33	Croton River,	118
Blue Store,	44	Sing Sing,	120
Clermont,	46	Tarrytown,	126
Upper Redhook,	51	Dobbs's Ferry,	132
Lower Redhook,	54	Yonkers,	137
Rhinebeck,	60	King's Bridge,	141
Hyde Park,	70	New York,	154

ON THE WEST SIDE OF THE HUDSON RIVER.

Coeymans,	12	New Hurley,	83
New Baltimore,	14	Shawangunk,	87
Coxsackie,	20	Walden,	90
Athens,	28	Montgomery,	94
Catskill,	34	Goshen,	104
Malden, or Bristol,	43	Chester,	109
Ulster,	46	Monroe,	115
Glasgow,	49	Monroe Works,	121
Kingston,	58	Ramapo,	131
Rosendale,	66	Piermont,	150
New Paltz,	74	New York,	174

ALBANY TO NEW YORK.
BY HOUSATONIC RAIL ROAD AND STEAMBOAT.

Stopping Places.	Pl. to Pl.	Total.	Stopping Places.	Pl. to Pl.	Total.
Greenbush,	1	1	Gaylord's Bridge,	6	92
Schodack,	7	8	New Milford,	6	98
Kinderhook,	8	16	Brookfield,	6	104
Chatham,	7	23	Hawleysville,	6	110
East Chatham,	5	28	Newton,	4	114
Canaan,	5	32	Bottsford's,	4	118
N. Y. State Line,	5	38	Stepney,	5	123
West Stockbridge,	2	40	Bridgeport,	10	133
Van Dusenville,	7	41	Black Rock,	3	136
Great Barrington,	2	49	Norwalk Island,	12	148
Sheffield,	6	55	Greenwich Point,	11	159
Mass. State Line,	7	62	New Rochelle,	11	170
Canaan,	2	64	Throgg's Neck,	8	178
Canaan Falls Village,	3	67	Hell Gate,	8	186
West Cornwall,	7	74	Blackwell's Island,	3	189
Cornwall Bridge,	4	78	New York,	4	193
Kent,	8	86			

DISTANCES FROM NEW YORK TO OREGON.

	Miles.		Miles.
St. Louis, (shortest way, and not by rivers,)	1,033	Fort Bridge,	35
Independence,	266	Kong river,	35
Blue, at Burnett's Trace,	520	Down same to the hills that run on same,	57
Bigg Platte,	25	Down same to the Great Sandusky,	38
Up "	25		
Up the same,	117	Partnith, first waters of the Columbia,	25
Across the North Fork of the same,	31	Fort Hall, on Snake river,	58
Up North Fork to Cedar Grove	18	Partnith again,	11
Up the same to Chimney,	18	Cock Creek,	87
Scott's Bluffs,	20	Solomon Falls,	42
Fort Larima,	38	Crossing Snake river,	27
Big Spring, at the foot of the Black Hills,	8	Boiling Spring,	19
		Down the same to Fort Barse,	40
Keryen North Fork,	30	Burnt River,	41
Crossing of the same,	34	Up the same,	26
Sweet Water,	55	Across to Powder to the Lamepens,	18
Up same to the snow on Rocky Mountains,	60	Grand Round,	15
Main divide of the same,	40	Utile river, over Blue Mount,	43
Waters running to the Pacific Ocean,	2	Dr. Whiteman's,	29
		Walla-walla,	25
Little Sandy,	14	Dallas,	120
Big "	14	Fort Vancouver,	100
Green river,	25	Mouth of the Columbia river,	120
Down the same,	12		
Black Fort of Green river,	22	Total,	3,440

The time occupied in travelling the above overland, is about five months. The voyage by sea round Cape Horn, from six to eight months.

ALBANY TO KEENE.
BY STAGE.

Stopping Places.	Distance	Fare.	Stopping Places.	Distance	Fare.
Arlington,	48	2·25	Grafton	88	3·75
Stratton,	62	2 75	Cambridgeport,	88	4 00
Wardsboro,	66	3·00	Saxon River,	93	4·25
Jamaica,	72	3·50	Bellows Falls,	97	4·50
Townsend,	78	3 75	Walpole,		4·50
Athens,	82	3·75	Keene,		4·50
Second Route.					
Clarendon,		4·00	Chester,		4·75
Shrewsbury,		4 25	Bellows Falls,		5·00
Mount Holley,		4·50	Walpole,		5·00
Cavendish,		4·75	Keene,		5·00

ALBANY TO BOSTON.
BY RAIL ROAD.

Stopping Places.	Pl. to Pl.	Total.	Stopping Places.	Pl. to Pl.	Total.
Schodack,	8	8	North Wilbraham,	6	111
Kinderhook,	7	16	Palmer,	10	117
Chatham,	5	23	Warren,	4	127
East Chatham,	5	28	West Brookfield,	2	131
Canaan,	3	33	South Brookfield,	3	133
Edwards,	2	36	East Brookfield,	2	136
State Line,	3	38	Spencer,	5	138
Richmond,	5	41	Charlton,	4	143
Shaker Village,	3	46	Clapville,	9	147
Pittsfield,	5	49	Worcester,	6	156
Dalton,	3	54	Grafton,	6	162
Hinsdale,	5	57	Westboro,	4	168
Washington,	3	62	Southboro,	4	172
Becket,	9	65	Hopkinton,	3	176
Chester Factory,	7	74	Framingtom,	4	179
Chester Village,	3	81	Natick	4	183
Russell,	8	84	Needham,	4	187
Westfield,	8	92	Newtown,	2	191
West Springfield,	2	100	Angier's Corners,	2	193
Springfield,	6	102	Brighton,	5	195
Wilbraham	3	108	Boston,	0	200

ALBANY TO SARATOGA.
BY RAIL ROAD.

Schenectady, 17; Ballston, 32; Saratoga, 39. Fare through $1·62. Leave Albany about 9 A. M. and 4 P. M. Leave Saratoga about 6 and 11 A. M. During the winter season there is but one train, daily, between Albany and Saratoga.

ALBANY TO BRATTLEBORO', VT.
BY STAGE.

Stopping Places.	Distance	Fare.	Stopping Places.	Distance	Fare.
Hoosick,	28	1.25	Wilmington,	60	3·00
Bennington,	34	1.50	Brattleboro,	75	3·50

ALBANY TO BURLINGTON.
BY STAGE.

Stopping Places.	Distance	Fare.	Stopping Places.	Distance	Fare.
Brandon,	100	5·00	Middlebury,		5·00
Salisbury,			Burlington,	140	7·00
Leicester,					

ALBANY TO HAVERHILL.
BY STAGE.

Stopping Places.	Distance	Fare.	Stopping Places.	Distance	Fare.
Pittsfield	105	5·75	Chelsea,	136	6·00
Bethel,	118	5·50	Montpelier,	155	6·75
Royalton,	122	5·25	Haverhill,	160	7·00

Second Route.

Sherburn,	102	4·75	Hanover,	132	6·25
Woodstock,	108	5·50	Haverhill,	158	7·00
Hartford,	128	5·75			

Leaves Albany Mondays, Wednesdays and Fridays, about 7 A. M., returning on alternate days.

ALBANY TO RUTLAND.
BY STAGE.

Stopping Places.	Distance	Fare.	Stopping Places.	Distance	Fare.
Pittstown,	19	1·00	Granville,	63	3·00
Cambridge,	34	1·25	Poultney,	71	3·50
Salem,	46	1·75	Castleton,	79	3·75
Hebron,	54	2·25	Rutland	90	4·25

ALBANY TO CANADA.

Summer Routes.

During the season of navigation, there are three routes to Canada.

1st. By rail road and the Champlain canal. By this route travellers go by rail road, via. Troy to the Borough, 18 miles; thence by packet boat to Whitehall. The packet usually leaves the Borough about 3 o'clock, P. M., and arrives at Whitehall the following morning, in time for travellers to take the steam boats running to the various ports on Lake Champlain.

2d. By rail road and stage, via. Saratoga Springs. By this route travellers can go from Saratoga, via. Sandy Hill to Whitehall, or through Glen's Falls to Caldwell, and by steam boat 36 miles to the foot of Lake George, thence by stage three miles to Ticonderoga.

3d. By stage, via. Troy on the east side of the Hudson river.

We are indebted for some of the preceding tables to Miller's *Eastern and Western Guide Book*, published by the Merriams of Troy; a useful little work for the traveler, presenting tables of routes on all the great thoroughfares, and other necessary information, for twenty-five cents.

ALBANY TO WHITEHALL.

BY STAGE.

Stopping Places.	Pl. to Pl.	Total.	Stopping Places.	Pl. to Pl.	Total.
Troy,	6	6	Fort Miller,	8	41
Waterford,	5	11	" Edward,	7	48
Mechanicsville,	7	18	Sandy Hill,	2	50
Stillwater,	11	25	Glen's Falls,	3	53
Schuylerville,	4	33	Whitehall,	18	71

BY CHAMPLAIN CANAL.

Stopping Places.	Pl. to Pl.	Total.	Stopping Places.	Pl. to Pl.	Total.
West Troy,	6	6	Fort Miller,	3	40
Junction,	2	8	Moses's Kill,	3	43
Waterford,	3	11	Fort Edward,	5	48
Mechanicsville,	8	19	Glen's Falls Fr.,	2	50
Stillwater Village,	4	23	Dunham's Basin,	1	51
Bleeker's Basin,	2	25	Smith's "	5	56
Wilber's "	2	27	Fort Ann,	4	60
Van Duzen's L.,	5	32	Comstock's L.,	4	64
Schuylerville,	3	40	Whitehall,	8	72
Saratoga Bridge,	2	37			

WHITEHALL TO MONTREAL.
BY LAKE CHAMPLAIN.

Stopping Places.	Pl. to Pl.	Total.	Stopping Places.	Pl. to Pl.	Total.
Benson, Vt.,	13	13	Burlington, Vt.,	14	82
Orwell "	7	20	Port Kent,	10	92
Ticonderoga,	4	24	Plattsburg,	15	107
Shoreham, Vt.,	2	26	Chazy,	16	123
Bridgeport, "	9	35	Rouse's Point,	9	132
Chimney Pt."	6	41	Iseaux Noix C.,	12	144
Port Henry,	2	43	St. Johns, Vt.,	12	156
Westport,	11	54	La Prairie R. R.,	15	171
Fort Cassin,	7	64	Montreal,	9	180
Essex,	7	68			

ALBANY TO MONTREAL.
Winter Route.

Stopping Places.	Distance	Fare.	Stopping Places.	Distance	Fare.
Castleton,	79	3·75	Charlotte,	130	6·75
Sudbury,	91	4·50	Burlington,	140	7·00
Middlebury,	106	5·00	Montreal,	230	14·00
Vergennes	117	5·75			

The time of arrival and departure on all the thoroughfares vary at different seasons of the year, and the fare on all is subject to fluctuation on the packet and stage lines.

A TRIP TO NEW YORK IN '97.

It is mentioned in the papers of 1797, as an instance of remarkable despatch, that Col. William Colbreath, sheriff of Herkimer, left this city on Sunday morning, May 7th, on board a vessel for New York, and returned on Thursday afternoon, 11th, having in a little more than four days, including a day and a half he was in New York, performed a journey of three hundred and thirty miles.

PUBLIC OFFICES, BUILDINGS, &c.

PUBLIC BUILDINGS.

Arsenal, cor. Broadway and Lawrence.
Capitol, head of State street.
Geological Rooms, corner State and Lodge.
Normal School, 119 State street,
State Hall, op. Academy Park.

CITY AND COUNTY.

Albany Academy, fronts Academy Park.
Alms House, Lydius street cont.
City Hall, Eagle street, fronting Washington.
Jail, corner Eagle and Howard.
Medical College, formerly Lancaster School, Eagle street.
Penitentiary, Delaware turnpike.
Powder House, Washington Square.

PARKS AND PLACES.

Academy Park, op. State Hall.
Bull's Head Course, Troy road.
Canal Basin, fronts Water, Lawrence, Montgomery and De Witt.
Capitol Park fronts on Eagle and State street.
Cemeteries, State, above Knox.
Centre Market, corner South Pearl and Howard.
Clinton Park, North Pearl street.
Glass Works Square, corner Broadway and Ferry.
Hay Scales and Yard, corner Plain and Philip
Hudson Street Park, corner Hudson and Liberty.
Little Basin, above first lock.
Lydius Street Park, cor. Eagle and Lydius.
Mineral Spring Garden, 58 Ferry.
National Garden, 770 Broadway.
Newton's Corners, Shaker road.
Rural Cemetery, Troy road.
Steam Boat Landing, Broadway, between Lydius and Hamilton,
Townsend's Park, junction Washington street and turnpike.
Washington Market, foot of Columbia street.

PUBLICATIONS.

Albany Argus, Merch't's Exchange.
Albany Atlas, cor. Broadway and Beaver.
Albany Daily Express, Green near State.
Albany Daily Knickerbocker, Museum Building.
Albany Evening Journal, corner of James and State streets.
Albany Freeholder, 34 Washington.
Albany Patriot, Commerc'l Build'gs.
Albany Spectator, 80 State street.
Albany Switch, Beaver street.
Busy Bee, Arbor Hill.
Christian Palladium, Commercial Buildings.
Cultivator, 10 and 12 Green street.
Horticulturist, 10 and 12 Green st.
Howard's Special Term Reports, 57 Hawk street,
Mechanics' Advocate, Commercial Buildings.
Odd Fellows' Literary Magazine, 11 Cooper's Buildings.

TAVERNS AND REFECTORIES.

Albany and Troy House, 31 Dean.
Albion Hotel, corner of Broadway and Herkimer.
American Hotel, 100 State street.
Beardsley's Hotel, 28 Washington.
Boston Hotel, 15 and 17 Dean.
Boston House, cor. Broadway and Ferry.
Broadway House 505 Broadway.
Bull's Head Tavern, Lydius st.
Carlton House, cor. State and Pearl.
City Hotel, 23 Broadway.
City Hall Coffee House, cor. Eagle and Maiden Lane.
Clinton Hotel, cor. Pearl and Beaver.
Congress Hall, fronts Washington street and Capitol Park.
Cornucopia, cor. State and Green.
Delavan House, fronts Broadway, Steuben and Montgomery.
Eagle Street Hotel, corner Eagle and Daniel.

NYS Geological Hall on Lodge and State Streets in Albany became the first State Museum in the country It currently is the oldest and largest state museum in the US and today is located in the Empire State Mall.

The infamous Cardiff Giant was exhibited here but was proven a fake by NYS Paleontologist James Hall. Mark Twain wrote a humorous account of the hoax called *A Ghost's Tale* in 1870. PT Barnum made a replica but the original has been with the Farmer's Museum in Cooperstown since 1947 and visible to the public.

Public Offices, Buildings, &c.

Eastern Hotel, cor. Broadway and John.
Franklin House, 176 State street.
Hudson Street Temperance House,)e r a r
Lafayette House, 19 Montgomery.
Lumbermen's Exchange Hotel, 192 Water.
Mansion House, Broadway.
Marble Pillar, under Museum.
McCardle's, Beaver street.
Northern Hotel, corner of Broadway and Orange.
Otsego House, 74 Washington.
St. Charles, Hudson street.
Saratoga House, 719 Broadway.
Stanwix Hall, corner of Broadway and Maiden Lane.
Washington Hall, South Pearl.

CHURCHES.

Baptist Church, First, Green street, between Hamilton and Division.
Baptist Church, Second, cor. North Pearl and Maiden Lane.
Baptist Church, Third, State street, opposite the Capitol.
Baptist Church, Fourth, South Pearl, head of Herkimer.
Baptist Church, African, Hamilton, above Pearl.
Bethel, Montgomery street.
Catholic Cathedral, cor. of Lydius and Eagle.
Catholic, St. Mary's, corner Chapel and Pine.
Catholic, St. John's, Ferry street.
Catholic, St. Joseph's, corner North Pearl and Lumber.
Catholic, German, corner Hamilton and Philip.
Dutch Reformed Church, first, cor. Van Schaick and North Pearl.
Dutch Reformed Church, second, Beaver, above Green.
Dutch Reformed Church, third, cor. Ferry and Green.
Episcopal Church, St. Peter's, cor. State and Lodge.
Episcopal Church, St. Paul's, South Pearl, below Beaver.
Episcopal Church, Trinity, Broad, below Lydius.
Episcopal Church, Grace, Spring, above Lark.
Friends' Meeting House, Plain st.
Lutheran Church, corner. Pine and Lodge.
Lutheran Church, German, State near Swan.
Methodist Episcopal Church, first, Hudson, above Grand.
Methodist Episcopal Church, second, North Pearl, above Columbia.
Methodist Episcopal Church, third, corner Ferry and Franklin.
Methodist Episcopal Church, fourth, corner Washington and Swan.
Methodist Episcopal Church, fifth, Swan, between Lumber & Third.
Methodist African Church, State, rear of District School No. 2.
Methodist Epis. Israel Church, Jefferson, above Eagle.
Presbyterian Church, first, corner S. Pearl and Beaver.
Presbyterian Church, sec'd Chapel, above Maiden Lane.
Presbyterian Church, third, North Pearl, opposite Clinton Square.
Presbyterian Church, fourth, Broadway, above Spencer.
Presbyterian Church, Associate, corner Chapel and Canal.
Synagogue, Fulton street.
Synagogue, Rose street.
Unitarian Church, Division street.
Universalist Church, Green, below Hamilton.

MISCELLANEOUS.

Albany Museum, corner State and Broadway.
Apothecaries' Hall, cor. State and North Pearl.
Atlas Buildings, cor. Beaver and Broadway.
Beecker Hall, 531 Broadway.
Blunt's Buildings, cor. South Pearl and State.
Commercial Buildings, cor. Broadway and Hudson.
Cooper's Buildings, cor. State and Green.
Douw's Buildings, corner State and Broadway.

Public Offices, Buildings, &c.

Orphan Asylum, head of Wash. st.
  do.   do.   St. Vincent's, North Pearl near Lumber.
Water Works Reservoir, cor. Eagle and Steuben.

OFFICES, ETC.

Adjutant General's Office, State Hall
Albany Apprentices' Library, 41 Hudson.
Albany and Boston R. R. office, cor. Maiden Lane and Dean.
Albany Burgesses Corps, armory in Exchange Building,
Albany City Bank, 47 State.
Albany Emmet Guards, armory No. 32 Green street.
Albany Institute, Academy Building.
Albany Insurance Co., 56 State.
Albany Republican Artillery, armory in Atlas Buildings.
Albany Savings Bank, 38 State.
Albany and Schenectady R. R. office, Dean street.
Attorney General's Office, State Hall.
Bank of Albany, 42 State.
Bank Department, State Hall.
Baths, Norton street.
Board of Trade, meet in Exchange daily.
Canal Collector's Office, 198 Water.
Canal Department, State Hall.
Chamberlain, City Hall.
City Marshal, City Hall.
City Surveyor, City Hall.
Commercial Bank, 38 State.
Common Council, City Hall.
Comptroller's Office, State Hall.
Clerk Court of Appeals, State Hall.
County Clerk's Office, City Hall.
County Treasurer's Office, cor. Steuben and Broadway.
Court of Appeals, Capitol.
Crier of Courts, 327 State.
Custom House, 407 Broadway.
Deputy Sheriff (Ferguson), cor. Patroon and Hawk.
Exchange Bank, Merchants' Exchange.
Firemen's Insurance Co. cor. Green and State.
Gallery of Fine Arts, No. 528 Broadway.
Gas Co.'s Office, Bleecker Hall.
Gas Company's Works, cor. Grand and Arch.
General Stage Office, under Museum.
Justices' Court, over Centre Market.
Magnetic Telegraph Office, Exchange Building.
Mayor's Office, City Hall.
Mayor's Court, City Hall.
Mechanics' Benefit Society, corner Broadway and State.
Mechanics' and Farmers' Bank, cor. Broadway and Exchange st.
Mutual Insurance Company, 450 Broadway.
National Fire Insurance Co, 61 State
New York State Bank, 69 State.
Pension Office, Mechanics' and Farmers' Bank.
Police Office, over Centre Market.
Post Office, Exchange Building.
Secretary of State, State Hall.
Sexton 1st Baptist Ch. 65 Green.
  do.   1st Dutch, rear church.
  do.   Lutheran, rear church.
  do,   1st Methodist, 146 Lydius.
  do.   2d Methodist, rear church.
  do.   3d Methodist, basement.
  do.   Middle Dutch, 38 Beaver.
  do.   1st. Presbyterian, 48 Beaver.
  do.   4th Pres., 118 North Pearl.
  do.   St. Mary's, 58 Chapel.
  do.   St. Joseph's, 188 N. Pearl.
Sheriff's Office, Jail.
State Agricultural Rooms, cor. State and Lodge.
State Library, Capitol.
Supreme Court Clerk's Office, State Hall.
Superintendent Northern District, City Hall.
Superintendent Southern District, City Hall.
Surveyor General, State Hall.
Surrogate's Office, City Hall.
Under Sheriff, 73 State.
Water Works Co.'s Sec. and Treas., 442 Broadway.
Young Men's Association, Exchange Building.

District and other Schools.

ENGINE HOUSES.

No. 1, 11 Chapel.
    2, 43 do.
    3, Alms House.
    4, 75 Grand.
    5, 236 Washington.
    6, cor. Hawk and Fayette.
    7, 41 Hudson.
    8, (burnt,)
    9, (torn down,)
   10, 10 Wilson.
   11, 106 Arch.
   12, Second st., Arbor Hill.
Hook and Ladder, No. 1, 34 Plain.
  do. do. No. 2, Patroon st.
Tivoli Hose, 32 Plain.
Axe Company, Steuben street.

DISTRICT SCHOOLS.

No. 1, South Pearl, south of Schuyler.
    2, State street, between Hawk and Swan.
    3, Van Tromp street.
    4, Union, near Lydius.
    5, N. Pearl, south of Lumber.
    6, Junction, west of Perry st.
    7, Canal street.
    8, Lydius, west of Grand.
    9, Cor. Ferry and Dallius.
   10, Washington street, east of Lark.

SCHOOLS.

Albany Classical Institute, Eagle, below State.
Albany Female Academy, North Pearl, above Maiden Lane.
Albany Female Seminary, 67 Division.
Albany Medical College, cor. Lancaster and Eagle.
Classical Institute, 7 North Pearl.
Friends' School, 10 Plain.
C. D. Marsh, basement Universalist church.
Miss Allison, basement Universalist church.
Misses Beekman, 56 Westerlo.
Mrs. Brinckerhoff, 112 State.
Misses Cantine, 18 Van Tromp.
Miss Cassidy, 63 Chapel.
Mr. Center, basement 3d Pres. ch.
Miss Collier, Hudson street.
Miss Crane, 125 Hamilton.
Miss Kidd, 73 Division.
Miss Pierce, Franklin House.
Miss Skerritt, 4 High.
Miss Woodbridge, 46 South Pearl.
St. John's, cor. Dallius and Rensselaer.
Wilberforce School, in rear of District School House No. 2, in Chesnut street.

GRAMMAR SCHOOL.

Frederick Beasly, John B. Romeyn, and John M. Bradford, clergymen in Albany, made proposals to the city in 1806, for the establishment of a grammar school, " of such a nature that it might be easily converted into an academy." The first step required by the proposers was a fund of $10,000.

LANCASTER SCHOOL.

In August, 1810, the corporation had under consideration the project of establishing a free school, on the plan of Joseph Lancaster. As yet it is believed there were no public schools in the city. The society of mechanics had a number of years previously erected a building in Chapel street, called Mechanics' Hall, and maintained a school out of their own funds, but it is presumed that its benefits were chiefly confined to the children of mechanics. The building is now occupied as a piano forte manufactory.

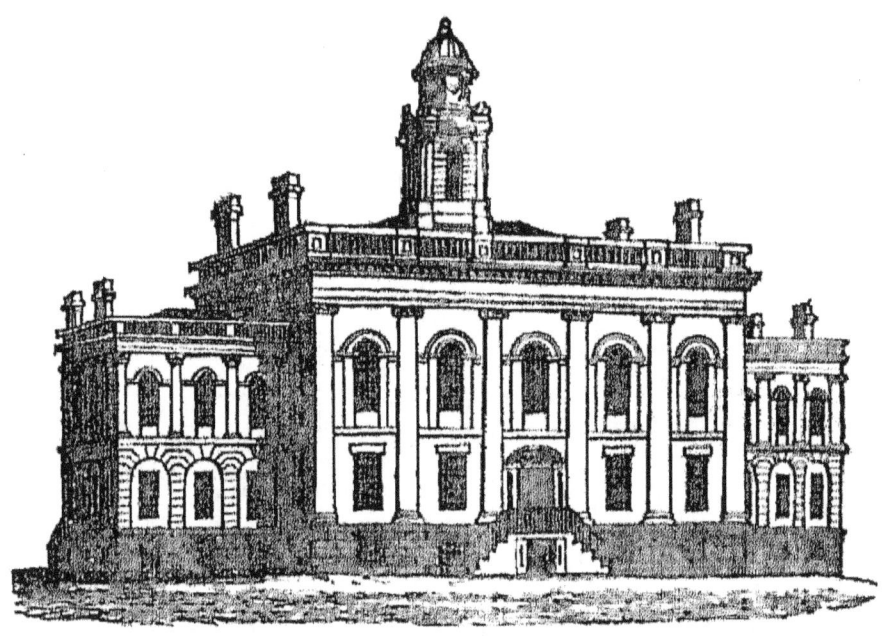

ALBANY ACADEMY.

As early as 1804, a meeting of citizens was held at the City Tavern, on the 18th March, to take into consideration the expediency of instituting an academy. The Lieutenant-Govenor, Mayor, Chancellor, Rev. Eliphalet Nott, Rev. John DeWitt, and Messrs. Henry and Beers, were appointed a committee to report a plan of an institution. The committee's plan was submitted at a subsequent meeting, on the 5th May, and approved. It was proposed to make the academy a reorganization of the city schools, by fusing them all in one. But the project was allowed to slumber until, in January, 1813, the common council made an appropriation for the establishment of a city academy, and a meeting of citizens to confer upon the subject was called at the Capitol, on the 28th of that month. At that meeting Archibald McIntyre was appointed chairman, and a committee of fourteen was chosen to devise a plan of the future institution. The project of a male academy now began to be agitated in good earnest. The board of common council offered the lot in the public square which the Academy now occupies, and also appropriated the amount that should be received from the sale of the lot and materials of the old jail which stood in the rear of the large building now occupied by the State Normal School, and which it was anticipated would produce $12,000. In addition to this it was thought necessary to raise $30,000 by private subscription, to complete the requisite sum for erecting a suitable building and establishing a permanent income.

The institution was incorporated by the Regents of the University, on the 4th of March in the same year, at the instance of the corporation of the city, and appropriate grants were made for its endowment. The trustees named in the charter were Stephen Van Rensselaer, John Lansing, Archibald McIntyre, Smith Thompson, Abraham VanVechten, John

Albany Academy 1907 (top) and 2021 (below). Now used by the Albany City School District. Joseph Henry taught here and invented the electromagnet and electric engine. He went on to become the first secretary of the Smithsonian Institution in DC

V. Henry, Henry Walton, Rev. Messrs. William Neill, John M. Bradford, John McDonald, Timothy Clowes, John McJimpsey, Frederick G. Mayer, Samuel Mervin, and the Mayor and Recorder ex officio.

The building was commenced in 1815. On Saturday, the 29th July, at 4 o'clock in the afternoon, the corner stone was laid by Philip S. Van Rensselaer. The copper plate deposited on this occasion had the following inscription: "Erected for an academy, anno 1815, by the corporation of the city of Albany; Philip S. Van Rensselaer, mayor; John Van Ness Yates, recorder; building committee Philip S. Van Rensselaer, John Brinckerhoff, Chauncey Humphrey, James Warren, and Killian K. Van Rensselaer. Seth Geer architect, H. W. Snyder, sculpt."

The Academy was announced to open on the second Monday (11th) of September, under Rev. Benjamin Allen, of Union College, and Messrs. Neill, Beck and Sedgwick were the committee to receive applications for admission. The courses of instruction were temporarily commenced in the large wooden building on the southeast corner of State and Lodge streets, belonging to Killian K. Van Rensselaer, which was burnt in 1847. The faculty under which the Academy opened, consisted of Rev. Benjamin Allen, principal; Rev. Joseph Shaw, professor of languages; and Moses Chapin, (now Judge Chapin, of Canandaigua) tutor.

The Academy was completed in 1817, and the school opened in it on the 1st September. The courses of instruction have been regularly pursued to the present time, 1848. In August, 1817, the trustees appointed Dr. Theodric Romeyn Beck principal of the institution, which office he resigned at the close of the summer term, in 1848, having occupied with distinguished ability and universal satisfaction, a station which was far from being a sinecure, during the long period of thirty-one years. His resignation was followed by that of the whole faculty, when the trustees, deeming it expedient to reorganize the institution, chose a new set of professors, consisting of the following, with which the fall term commenced:

Rev. WM. H. CAMPBELL, D. D., recently pastor of the Third Ref. Prot. Dutch Church in Albany, Principal and Professor of the Latin and Greek languages.

Dr. T. R. BECK, Lecturer of Physiology and Physical Geography.

GEORGE H. COOK, A. M., of the Rensselaer Institute, Prof. of Mathematics and Natural History.

Rev. JOHN SESSIONS, A. M., of the Sandlake Academy, Prof. of English Language and Logic.

JULIAN MOLINARD, Prof. of the French Language.

JAMES N. CROCKER and WILLIAM J. WRIGHTSON, who had been previously connected with the institution, tutors.

The above compose the present faculty of the Academy, and the number of students is 230.

In 1831, William Caldwell, of the city of Albany, presented $100 to the trustees of the Academy, to be invested in stock, the income of which should be devoted to the purchase of a gold medal, to be given at each annual examination, to the student who shall have made the greatest proficiency in mathematics, and natural philosophy; the student to be of at least three years standing in the Academy, and the medal to be given but once to the same individual. In 1837, Gen. Stephen Van Rensselaer presented $100, in trust, to be appropriated in the same man-

Albany Academy.

ner, as a reward for the greatest proficiency in the Latin and Greek languages, subject to the same reservations, except that the student must be of at least four years standing in the Academy. The late Henry W. Delavan also made a bequest to the Academy, which came into the hands of the trustees in 1839, of $2000, directed to be deposited in the Savings Bank, the income of which is applied to the teaching of such a number of poor boys, in the useful branches of English education, as the income of the fund will allow; no boy enjoying the benefit of the fund more than two years. The names of the students who have obtained the Caldwell medal, are as follows: 1831, William Austin; 1832, no public examination in consequence of the prevalence of the cholera; 1833, Henry Waldron; 1834, Aurelian Conkling; 1835, John Newland; 1836, Henry K. Viele; 1837, George B. Hoyt; 1838, Charles N. Waldron; 1839, Joseph B. Brown; 1840, William J. Gibson; 1841, John J. Olcott; 1842, Philip Phelps; 1843, William Wrightson; 1844, Andrew McElroy; 1845, John K. Croswell; 1846, Francis B. Hall; 1847, Frank Jones; 1848, Jacob C. Koonz. The names of those who have received the Van Rensselaer Medal, are as follows: 1837, Isaac L. K. Miller; 1838, Henry F. Greene; 1839, Charles K. McHarg; 1840, Gilbert L. Wilson; 1841, Philip Phelps; 1842, John C. Bullions; 1843, Oliver Bronson; 1844, Samuel G. Courtney; 1845, William T. Wrightson; 1846, John K. Croswell; 1847, Jacob L. Pearse; 1848, Henry L. Bullions.

The following table comprises a complete list of the trustees since the institution went into operation. The present trustees may be known by the dates that are wanting in the exit column.

Stephen Van Rensselaer	1813 to 1819	James Kent	1819 to 1823
John Lansing	1813 to 1813	William B. Lacey	1819 to 1825
Archibald McIntyre	1813 to 1817	Ebenezer Baldwin	1820 to 1830
Smith Thompson	1813 to 1813	Ph. S. Van Rensselaer	1821 to 1824
Abm. Van Vechten	1813 to 1813	Philip S. Parker	1821 to 1831
John V. Henry	1813 to 1823	Henry R. Weed	1822 to 1831
Henry Walton	1813 to 1815	James Stevenson	1823 to 1826
William Neill	1813 to 1816	John Ludlow	1823 to 1834
John M. Bradford	1813 to 1820	Charles R. Webster	1823 to 1834
John McDonald	1813 to 1821	Isaac Ferris	1825 to 1836
Timothy Clowes	1813 to 1818	Peter Gansevoort	1825
John McJimpsey	1813 to 1815	Alfred Conkling	1826 to 1836
Frederic G. Mayer	1813 to 1818	Isaac Fondey	1826 to 1829
Samuel Merwin	1813 to 1814	James Stevenson	1828
Thedore Sedgwick	1813 to 1823	John T. Norton	1829 to 1834
John Duer	1813 to 1813	Nicholas F. Beck	1829 to 1830
Harmanus Bleecker	1813 to 1822	William B. Sprague	1830
Charles D. Cooper	1813 to 1817	Oliver Kane	1830 to 1834
John Lansing	1815 to 1817	Richard V. DeWitt	1831
William James	1815 to 1832	Archibald Campbell	1831 to 1847
T. Romeyn Beck	1815	Ph. S. Van Rensselaer	1833 to 1841
John Chester	1816 to 1829	James Goold	1834
John W. Yates	1817 to 1828	William C. Miller	1834
Arthur J. Stansbury	1817 to 1821	John N. Campbell	1835
William A. Duer	1817 to 1820	Richard Yates	1835 to 1837
Gideon Hawley	1818 to 1842	Thomas E. Vermilye	1836 to 1839
John Van Schaick	1818 to 1818	Thomas W. Olcott	1836

Albany Academy.

Isaac N. Wyckoff	1837 to 1847
Horatio Potter	1840
Teunis Van Vechten	1841
William H. Campbell	1842
James P. Boyd	1847
Orlando Meads	1847

The mayors and recorders of the city have also been, ex officio, trustees, from 1813 to the present time.

The presiding officers of the board have been as follows:

Hon. Stephen Van Rensselaer, LL. D., senior trustee,	1813 to 1819
Rev. John M. Bradford, D. D., do	1819 to 1826
William James, Esq., do	1826 to 1832
Gideon Hawley, LL. D.,	1834 to 1842
Hon. James Stevenson,	1842 to 1848
Theodric Romeyn Beck, M. D., LL. D., senior trustee,	1848

Those who have acted as clerks of the board are as follows:

Henry Waldron, Esq.,	1813 to 1813
Rev. Timothy Clowes, LL. D.,	1813 to 1816
T. R. Beck, M. D.,	1816 to 1848
Rev. Wm. H. Campbell, D. D.,	1848

The office of principal has fallen but to three persons, as follows:

Rev. Benjamin Allen, LL. D.,	1815 to 1817
T. Romeyn Beck, M. D., LL. D.,	1817 to 1848
Rev. Wm. H. Campbell, D. D.,	1848

The succession of the faculty is as follows:

Professors of Greek and Latin Languages.

Rev. Joseph Shaw	1815 to 1824
Rev. Peter Bullions	1824 to 1848
Rev. Wm. H. Campbell	1848

Prof. Mathematics and Natural Philosophy.

Michal O'Shaunessy	1819 to 1826
Joseph Henry	1826 to 1832
Philip Ten Eyck	1832 to 1848
George H. Cook	1848

Lecturer Physiology and Physical Geography.

T. Romeyn Beck	1848

Prof. English Literature.

Charles Clapp	1835 to 1837
Hugh Blair Jolly	1837 to 1841

Prof. English Language and Logic.

Alex. B. McDoual	1841 to 1842
Philander D. Young	1842 to 1843
John S. Holmes	1843 to 1844
Rev. Samuel Center	1844 to 1848
Rev. John Sessions	1848

Prof. Modern Languages.

J. Molinard	1830 to 1830
M. Leon Cheronnet	1830 to 1831
H. Picard	1831 to 1835
H. L. V. D. Holstein	1835 to 1839
J. Molinard	1839

Lecturer on Chemistry.

Lewis C. Beck	1831 to 1834

Tutors.

Moses Chapin	1815 to 1816
Rev. Isaac Ferris	1816 to 1817
John B. Crocker	1817 to 1817
Michael O'Shaunessy	1817 to 1819
John Thompson	1819 to 1820
Dr. William O'Donnel	1820 to 1829
William Soul	1829 to 1830
Daniel D. T. Leech	1829 to 1831
George W. Carpenter	1831 to 1835
Rev. Sam'l McArthur	1831 to 1833
Griffith W. Griffiths	1831 to 1834
Nathan Hawley	1833 to 1834
Rev. Sam'l McArthur	1834 to 1835
Henry Carpenter	1834 to 1835
Alex. B. McDoual	1835 to 1841
Edward F. Edwards	1835 to 1840
David F. Robertson	1836 to 1838
Samuel S. Smith	1838 to 1847
Austin H. Wells	1840 to 1840
Andrew Shiland	1841 to 1844
Rufus K. Crocker	1844 to 1847
James N. Crocker	1847
William T. Wrightson	1847

The Academy building which was commenced in 1815, and completed in 1817, is constructed of free stone, from near Newark, New Jersey, an excellent and durable building material; and notwithstanding the length of time it has stood, is still one of the most attractive edifices of the city. It is situated on the north-west corner of the public square, on a line with the Capitol. The main building is 70 by 80 feet, and the wings 30 by 45 feet, three stories high, including the basement. It commands a view down Steuben street, having an extensive park in front, surrounded by a substantial iron fence, and planted with ornamental trees. The cost of its erection was about $100,000.

SCHOOL OF 1785.

A school was opened in May by Elihu Goodrich and John Ely. The classical term *academy* had not yet come into use. The Latin and Greek languages were taught, and the most useful branches of mathematics, as well as the *elementaries*. It went on the high pressure principle—*through by daylight*. Hours of study from 6 to 8, 9 to 12, 2 to 5, and 6 to 8. The magisters seem to have been willing to bestow at least time and diligence. Their terms were for Greek and Latin, and mathematics, 20s.; writing and cyphering, 16s.; reading and spelling, 12s. To all which singing "by the latest and most approved method" was added for 12s.

SCHOOL APPROPRIATION.

An act passed the legislature, 7th of April, 1795, appropriating £20,000 annually for the term of five years, for the purpose of encouraging and maintaining schools in the state. The proportion allotted to Albany county was £1,590, or $3975; the law to go into operation on the 7th April. It was a stride towards the free school system.

SABBATH EVENING SCHOOL.

On March 24, 1816, a sabbath evening school was established at Mr. Young's school room, in Washington street, and appears to have been countenanced by the Moral Society. It was attended by 150 children and 50 adults.

SUNDAY SCHOOL.

It was announced that a Sunday Free School would be opened on Sunday, March 21, 1813, at the school room of George Uphold, in Van Tromp street, where several useful branches of English education would be taught from the hours of 6 to 8 in the morning, and 12 to 2 in the afternoon, free of all expense.

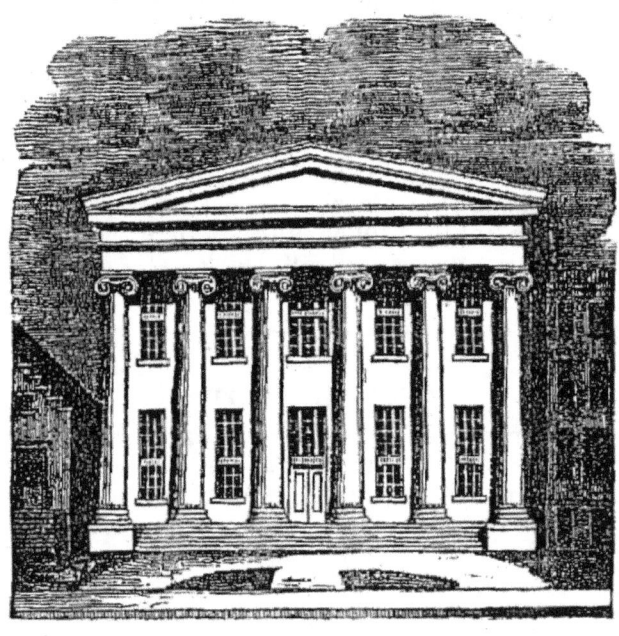

ALBANY FEMALE ACADEMY.

This institution was founded in the year 1814, under the designation of the Union School; a name apparently suggested by the circumstances attending its origin. A number of the most influential citizens, desirous to obtain for their daughters the benefit of a superior education, united for the purpose of securing the services of a competent instructor, rented a suitable building in Montgomery street, and appointed as principal Mr. Horace Goodrich. The original subscription list, which, amid the loss of other documents connected with the early history of the Academy, has been preserved, is as follows:

"We, the undersigned, agree to send to Union School in Montgomery street, under the tuition of Mr. Horace Goodrich, the number of female scholars affixed to our names, for the space of one year, from the first day of May next; and we also agree to pay to Ebenezer Foot twenty-four dollars for each scholar in four equal quarterly payments, the first payment to be on the first day of August next. *Feb.* 24, 1814.

John Ely,	1	T. & J. Russell,	4
Moses Allen,	2	Edward Brown,	1
James Scrymser,	1	G. Stewart,	1
Matthew Gill,	2	Harmanus Ten Eyck,	1
Uriah Marvin,	2	James Kent,	1
Thomas Gould,	1	John V. Henry,	3
Solomon Allen,	1	John Reid,	1
William Fowler,	1	Isaac Hutton,	1
Nicholas Bleecker,	1	Asa H. Center,	1
Abram Van Vechten,	1	[Three names torn away.]	
Benjamin Knower,	1		

It appears from this paper that Mr. Ebenezer Foot was preëminently active in commencing the Academy, and, so far as an individual can claim an honor in which, however, several probably to some extent, participated, he may be regarded as its founder. In a memoir of Mr. Foot, prepared and published at the request of friends, by his brother Samuel A. Foot, of Geneva, we find the following statement, which evidently conveys no more than the truth on this matter. " One act of Mr. Foot's life should not be omitted or forgotten wherever his name is mentioned. The present Female Academy in Albany owes its existence mainly, if not entirely, to him. It is now, and has been for some years, one of the most valuable and useful institutions in the country. It was commenced in February, 1814, under the name of the Union School in Montgomery street. The original subscription paper is now before the writer. It bears date on the 24th day of that month. The subscriptions are payable to Mr. Foot, and it is within the knowledge and recollection of the writer that he started the project and obtained most of the subscriptions. The principal motive of Mr. Foot, no doubt, was to establish a good female school in his neighborhood, to which he might send his daughter. If this was his sole motive, it was a good one. But whatever the motive, whether to qualify his own daughter, or those of his neighbors and friends, for the duties of American ladies, or, more expansive still, to elevate and adorn the female character, and store the female mind with useful knowledge, his name should be kindly remembered by every pupil who has enjoyed or may enjoy the benefits of the institution, and by every friend of female education."

During the first six years and upwards of the existence of Union School, no records were kept of its proceedings, or if kept, they have not been preserved; but no doubt it continued to increase, throughout this period, in numbers and reputation; for, in 1821, an act of incorporation was obtained from the legislature. The board of directors named in the charter, consisted of

James Kent, president,
Gideon Hawley,
Asa H. Center,
John V. Henry,
Teunis Van Vechten,

Peter Boyd,
Rev. John Chester,
Joseph Russell,
William Fowler.

Five of these, it will be seen, were among the original subscribers, and thus had the satisfaction of seeing the enterprise which they began, consolidated and rising into fame.

In the same year, 1821, a more spacious building was reared, still in Montgomery street, the first stone of which was laid on the 26th June; and so rapidly did the school increase, that in 1827 an additional building was required, and erected accordingly. These edifices continued to be occupied by the Academy till 1834, when its celebrity and numbers became so great as to justify and demand the erection of the splendid and commodious edifice where the classes now meet. On the 12th of May, in that year, the new building was opened, when an address was delivered by the president, Rev. John Ludlow. The following persons then constituted the board of trustees and the faculty:

The Female Academy was located on North Pearl Street and was replaced by the Albany Savings Bank which in turn was destroyed by the ugly modern structure that sits in its place.

Albany Female Academy.

TRUSTEES.

Rev. John Ludlow,
Gideon Hawley,
James Clark,
Israel Smith,
Richard M. Meigs,
Edwin Croswell,
Jacob Sutherland,
John T. Norton,
James Vanderpoel,
Ph. S. Van Rensselaer,
Richard V. De Witt,
Thos. W. Olcott,
Ira Harris,

FACULTY.

Alonzo Crittenton, principal.
Henry Hart, professor.
Henri Picard, prof. of French.
Ann Charlotte Lynch, teacher.
Harriet B. Hopkins, "
Charlotte E. Andrews, "
Ann Hickcox, teacher.
Harriet E. Fassett, "
Catharine Pierce, "
Harriet N. Kirk, "
Emma Whitney, "

At the present time the trustees and faculty are as follows:

TRUSTEES.

Greene C. Bronson, President.
Edwin Croswell,
Thomas W. Olcott,
Ira Harris,
Rev. I. N. Wyckoff,
Harmon Pumpelly,
John Q. Wilson,
Rev. W. B. Sprague,
Rev. Duncan Kennedy,
Jas. McNaughton,
Marcus T. Reynolds,
Amasa J. Parker.

FACULTY.

L. Sprague Parsons, Principal.
Chas. Murray Nairne, Professor.
Julien Molinard, Prof. French.
Harriet E. McDoual, teacher.
Mary Pynchon, "
Lucy Jane Fassett, teacher.
Jeannie Miller, "
Emeline Harvey, "
S. A. Bayeux, "
R. Packard, Prof. voc. Music,

besides various professors of the ornamental branches of female education, who do not form part of the regular faculty.

Since the incorporation of the Academy there have been six presidents, as follows:

James Kent, Chancellor of New York, deceased.
Rev. John Chester, pastor of the Second Presbyterian Church, deceased.
Rev. John Ludlow, now provost of the University of Pennsylvania.
Rev. Isaac Ferris, now President Rutger's Institute, New York.
Rev. John N. Campbell, pastor First Presbyterian Church.
Hon. Greene C. Bronson, Judge Supreme Court.

The principals of the Academy since the foundation have been five namely:

Horace Goodrich,
Lebbeus Booth,
Frederick Matthews,
Alonzo Crittenton,
L. Sprague Parsons.

Of these, Messrs. Goodrich and Matthews are dead. Mr. Booth son-in-law of the founder, is resident at Ballston; Mr. Crittenton is principal of the Female Academy at Brooklyn; and Mr. Parsons is now in office.

It will be seen that some of the most distinguished men in the state and country have been, or are, connected with the Albany Female Academy; and if, as is contemplated, a fuller history of the institution than the present sketch, be given to the public, it will also be seen how many American ladies, occupying useful, honorable and high places in society, have received their education at this celebrated school.

This notice would be incomplete if it said nothing of the system and course of instruction pursued in the Academy.

The school consists of six departments, and one of French, which may all be gone through in the space of eight years. Less time, except in extraordinary cases, would be insufficient to do justice to the scheme. The studies of the first or highest department require two years, and one year additional for ancient and modern languages is strongly recommended, and frequently taken. The course is in all respects complete; the system thoroughgoing, judicious and substantial. The writer had no acquaintance with the Academy till within these last two years; but now for upwards of twelve months, he has had the best opportunity daily of observing it, and comparing it with similar institutions, both in this country and in Europe, and it is but due to truth and justice to declare, that the Albany Female Academy is superior to most, and second to none of these, both in the cultivation of mind, and in the maintenance of that cheerfulness of heart, buoyancy of spirit, and unforced love of knowledge, which many have deemed, in the case of females, incompatible with such faithful and severe intellectual discipline as is here practiced. No young lady, unless in the rare instances of incorrigible incapacity, can pass clearly and continuously through the present course of the school, without an accurate knowledge of the ordinary parts of an English education, and a highly respectable acquaintance with literature and science. In regard to those who have talent and diligence enough to graduate, much stronger terms may be employed. It is understood that until lately, the method—of which too many colleges set an example, and which perhaps could not, without difficulty, be departed from in a female Academy—was pursued of granting diplomas to all who had passed over the curriculum, without any very rigid examination as to the extent of their profiting by it. This, the usual plan, has, however, been abandoned in the Albany Female Academy, and a special examination of the strictest and most impartial kind has been instituted, so that now it is certain that no person can receive a diploma unless she fairly and fully proves herself to be all that the diploma affirms she is. Graduation implies not simply attendance during the usual time at school, but also an extensive and accurate knowledge of literature, philosophy, mathematics and natural science, and a diploma from this institution of learning is one of the highest intellectual honors that a lady can obtain. Nor do strictness of discipline, and care in the distribution of honors appear to affect the Academy injuriously, but the reverse, for it never was more flourishing than at the present day. The number of scholars with which the school commenced in 1814, was about 33; at present, and notwithstanding the institution of many seminaries, upon the same model, it exceeds 300, drawn from all parts of the United States.

STATE NORMAL SCHOOL.

This institution was established in 1844, by an act of the legislature, for the instruction and practice of teachers of common schools in the science of education and the art of teaching. An annual appropriation of $10,000 was made for its support, to be paid out of the literature fund. Each county in the state is entitled to send to the school a number of pupils, of either sex, equal to twice the number of members it sends to the assembly, where they have the privilege of remaining until they graduate, defraying all their own expenses, except those of tuition and mileage. Females are not admitted under 16 years of age, nor males under 18. On entering the institution they are required to sign a pledge to devote themselves to the business of teaching district schools. The summer term commences on the first Monday in May, and the winter term on the first Monday in November. The number of graduates during the four years since its organization, is as follows: 1845, 34; 1846, 110; 1847, 110; 1848, 96; total, 350. The number of students during the last term was 146 females, and 147 males; total, 293. Attached to the institution is an experimental school, the object of which is to afford each normal pupil an opportunity of practicing the methods of instruction and discipline inculcated at the school, as well as to ascertain his aptness to teach, and to discharge the various other duties pertaining to the teacher's responsible office. The experimental school has 70 pupils, between the ages of six and sixteen, 35 of whom are free pupils. The edifice now occupied by the school, No. 119 State street, was built by the Mohawk and Hudson Rail Road Company, and used by that corpora-

NORMAL SCHOOL BUILDING
1844-1849

The first building is still in use though it has been renovated.

NORMAL SCHOOL BUILDING
1849-1885

The second Normal School building was purchased in 1885 by the Christian Brothers Academy, a private Catholic college preparatory school for junior and high school boys. In 1939, it left and the building was razed. It is now a parking lot.

tion several years as a depot for the passenger trains, until the termination of the road was changed to Maiden lane. The common council contributes the rent of the building towards the encouragement of the enterprise. In return for which, the free seats in the experimental school are given exclusively to fatherless children residing in the city of Albany. At the last session of the legislature, an appropriation of $15,000 was made for the erection of a new edifice for the purposes of a school, and the city appropriated the lot occupied by Engine House No. 9, corner of Howard and Lodge streets. A spacious and convenient building is in progress of erection, which will be ready for occupation in the summer of 1849. The executive committee having charge of the institution consists of Christopher Morgan, superintendent of common schools, chairman; Gideon Hawley, Samuel Young, Harmanus Bleecker, and William H. Campbell, the latter acting as secretary. The faculty consists of:

Geo. R. Perkins, A. M., Principal and Professor of Mathematics,
Wm. F. Phelps, Permanent Teacher of Experimental School,
Darwin G. Eaton, Teacher of Mathematics, etc.,
Sumner C. Webb, Teacher of Arithmetic, etc.,
Silas T. Bowen, Teacher of Grammar, Mathematics, etc.,
Wm. W. Clark, Teacher of Natural Philosophy and Chemistry,
Truman H. Bowen, Teacher of Vocal Music, etc.,
Elizabeth C. Hance, Teacher of Reading and Geography,
Ann Maria Ostrom, Teacher of Drawing, etc.

The first principal of the institution, was David P. Page, who died in January, 1848, at the early age of 38. He was succeeded by Prof. Geo. R. Perkins, whose reputation as a mathematician is so well known. Under these, and a corps of excellent teachers, the school has attained a lasting reputation in the short space of four years.

HOUSES IN ALBANY IN 1786.

In 1786 the number of houses in Albany was found by actual enumeration to be 550. A statement of the number of houses in the principal cities and towns at this time, will serve to show their relative proportions:

Philadelphia,	4600	Charleston (S. C.),	1540
New York,	3500	Albany,	550
Boston,	2100	New Haven,	400
Baltimore,	1900	Hartford,	300

It will be seen that Albany was the sixth in point of number. The census of Boston was found to be at that time 14,640, exclusive of strangers, which gives seven persons to a house. At this rate Albany would have had 3,850 inhabitants. To carry out the calculation, Philadelphia would have contained 32,200; New York, 24,500; Baltimore, 13,300; Charleston, 10,780. The number of strangers might have increased the estimate one-eighth. The population of these places, however, is known to have differed considerably from the above estimates.

The 1656 Dutch Reformed Church in Albany eventually became too small for its growing congregation, which led to the construction of a new church building in 1715. That structure, depicted in this print, remained standing for nearly one hundred years. The weathercock from the old structure was removed and placed atop the new building. Stylistically, the 1715 church building resembled architecture common to the Dutch province of Zeeland. The building was razed in 1806. Engraved by Henry Snyder. Etching with engraving on laid paper, 0 5/16 H x 10 7/8 W (sheet). George W. Carpenter to AIHA in 1840. Carpenter is listed as a "resident member" of the Albany Institute in 1870. He became a member in 1829. Now in the Albany Institute of History and Art.

REFORMED PROTESTANT DUTCH CHURCH IN ALBANY.

The establishment of this church in Holland is said to have been consummated immediately after the decision of the Synod of Dort, in 1619. The colonists of New Netherland brought with them a strong attachment to the doctrines, worship and government of the church at home, and however deeply interested in secular pursuits, it is known that in very good time they took measures to establish among them the regular ministrations of the gospel. There are no records preserved in the church, by which to ascertain the exact time when it was organized in this part of the colony, though it is claimed by some to have been coeval with the first settlement. Dr. Livingston, a noted preacher in the early part of the present century, says, there were documents in existence which rendered it certain that a considerable church was organized in New York, as early as 1619, and that records were extant, containing the names of members in full communion, dated 1622. At another time, speaking of the Albany settlement, he says, "It is very certain that they had ministers there as early, if not before, any were at New York." Dr. O'Callaghan, on the other hand, asserts that in 1640 no church or clergyman existed yet in Rensselaerswyck, although the colony at New Amsterdam erected a church in 1633; but that in 1642 the Rev. Johannes Megapolensis, "the pious and well learned minister of the congregation of Schoorel and Bergo," came out under the patronage of the patroon, and arrived on the 11th of August. It is ascertained by documents preserved in the Van Rensselaer archives, that the conditions upon which the above named clergyman accepted the call to Rensselaerswyck, were, a free passage, and board for himself and family; an outfit of 300 guilders ($120), and an annual salary of 1100 guilders ($440), 30 schepels (22¼ bushels) of wheat, and 2 firkins of butter, for the first three years; and if the patroon was satisfied with his services, he was to receive an additional sum of 200 guilders ($80) per annum, for another term of three years. The minister's family consisted of himself and wife, and four children. A house for the dominie had been contracted for, but was not erected when he arrived; the carpen-

Van Rensselaer coat of arms, was one of several armorial panels given in 1656 to the First Dutch Reformed Protestant Church of Beverwyck (present-day Albany), New York. The donor of this example was Jan Baptist Van Rensselaer, director of the large estate known as Rensselaerswyck. After the church was demolished in 1805, the window was installed at the head of the staircase in the Van Rensselaer Manor House. Now in the Metropolitan Museum of Art, NYC.

This is one of at least five heraldic windows from the Reformed Protestant Dutch church in Beverwyck (now Albany), erected in 1656. The windows were transferred to a new church in 1715 and returned to donor's descendants when that building was razed in 1806. Rutger Jacobsen Van Schoenderwoert, or Van Woert, paid for this window. He also laid the cornerstone for the 1656 church. Now in the Albany Institute of History and Art.

ter of the colony not being a *reliable* man, if Commissary Van Curler's account of him is correct; but a house constructed entirely of oak was purchased on his arrival, for $120. We are led to infer that the church edifice was, likewise, unprepared for the use of the minister; for the commissary wrote to the patroon that he intended to have one built during the summer, "in the pine grove," 34 feet long by 19 wide; a building previously begun not proving satisfactory for the purpose. The church was clustered in among the other buildings around Fort Orange, which stood near the river between Denniston and Lydius streets, and the church yard was in the rear, on what is now Church street. The furniture of this church consisted of a pulpit ornamented with a canopy, pews for the magistrates and the deacons, and *nine benches for the congregation;* the expense of all which was $32. A new stoop was added to the building in the year 1651, and the church continued to accommodate the faithful till 1656, a period of 13 years from the time of its erection. Mr. Megapolensis retired from the colony in 1649, with the intention of returning to Holland; but he was persuaded to remain at New Amsterdam, where he still resided when that place was surrendered to the English, as did also his brother William, who lent the weight of his influence to prevent the doughty governor, Stuyvesant, from firing upon the enemy. He died in 1670.

In 1652 the Rev. Gideon Schaats (or Schaets) was sent over to supply the pulpit at Albany for three years, under a salary of 800 guilders per annum ($320), which was afterwards increased to 1000, and then to 1300 guilders per annum. He is said to have been 45 years of age when he arrived in the colony, and was accompanied by his two sons and daughter. He is supposed to have died in 1683.

The Rev. Mr Niewenhuysen (or Niewenhuyt) was a colleague of Mr. Schaats as early as 1675. In that year the Rev. Nicholas Van Rensselaer (or Nicholas Ranslaer) arrived here, and set up a claim not only to the pulpit, but also to the manor itself; but failed to obtain either. The Duke of York recommended him to Sir Edmund Andross for a living in one of the churches at New York or Albany. Suspected of being a papist, Mr. Niewenhuysen disputed his right to administer the sacraments, on the ground that he was not approved by the Classis of Amsterdam, to which the Dutch churches here held themselves subordinate. In this controversy the governor took the part of Mr. Van Rensselaer, and summoned Niewenhuysen before him to answer for his conduct;* but he was so grossly maltreated, and so frequently harassed by fruitless and expensive attendances before the council, that the greater part of the people resented the usage he met with; and the magistrates of Albany, in retaliation, imprisoned Mr. Van Rensselaer for "several dubious words" uttered in a sermon. The governor in turn ordered him to be released, and summoned the magistrates to attend him at New York, where warrants were issued to compel them to give security in £5,000 each, to make out good cause for confining the minister. Leisler, who was one of them, refused to comply, and was imprisoned. Sir Edmund, fearful that a great party would rise up against him, was at last compelled to discontinue his ecclesiastical jurisdiction, and refer the controversy to the decision of the consistory of the Dutch church at Albany. It is said that Mr. Van Rensselaer's popularity with the prince grew out of his having predicted, while

* New York Records, vol. iii, p. 54 et seq.

Charles II. was in exile, the day of his restoration; and it is furthermore related that the people of Albany held his prophetic pretensions in high estimation, out of which proceeded many strange tales.

A stone church was erected in 1656, at the intersection of what was then or afterwards called Yonker's and Handelaer's streets, now known as State street and Broadway. The corner stone was laid by Rutger Jacobsen, and the pulpit and bell, promised to be sent over by the Dutch West India Company, arrived in due time, and served the congregation a century and a half.

In 1683, the Rev. Godfredius Dellius arrived, to assist Mr. Schaats in the ministry, who was now about 76 years of age. The Register of Baptisms commences this year, with the name of Mr. Dellius at the head of the page, and has been tolerably well kept ever since. At the time Mr. Dellius arrived in the colony, the church is said to have been very numerous, to which great additions were made by him, especially among the Mohawk Indians. Unhappily he was led into extravagant speculations in land, which involved him in difficulties, and led to his dismissal in 1699, when he returned to Holland. The history of the dominies in New Netherland exhibits a succession of active labors in an unpromising and rather uninviting field; and a series of private woes and difficulties, which drove several of them back to the shores of Europe. The flock was widely extended. Besides the colony of Rensselaerswyck, it embraced the Mohawk Indians, and the settlements on the river. There was a considerable ingathering of neophytes from Kinderhook and more remote places, in all directions.

In 1700, the Rev. ———— Nucella was the officiating minister; and in 1703 the Rev. John Lydius commenced his labors, which terminated in 1709. The pulpit seems to have been vacant two years. The baptismal register has the name of Rev. Gualterus Du Bois, who resided in New York, in 1710; and that of Rev. Petrus Vas, in 1711; neither of whom appear to have been settled pastors.

In 1712 the Rev. Petrus Van Driessen was called, and continued his ministerial labors until his death, which took place about the 1st of February, 1738. In the meantime the church was rebuilt, namely, in 1715, upon the site of the old one, at the confluence of State with Court and Market streets, and a patent or charter procured in 1720. The Rev. Cornelis Van Schie began to officiate as his colleague in 1733; after whose decease, in August, 1744, the Rev. Theodorus Frelinghuysen occupied the pulpit till 1760, when he abruptly left the church and returned to Holland. The story of this ill-fated divine, as told by Mrs. Grant, excites our compassion for a worthy, zealous, and high-minded man. The account of his tragical end is variously told, and may have had a legendary origin.

In the latter part of the year 1760, the Rev. Eilardus Westerlo arrived from Holland, and entered upon the pastoral charge. He became one of the most eminent ministers of the Dutch church in America, and died in 1790, at the early age of 53, in the thirty-first year of his ministry, greatly revered and lamented by his people.

During the occupation of New York by the British, the Rev. Dr. Livingston occasionally assisted Dr. Westerlo, from 1776 to 1779; but when a call was given him in 1780, he declined its acceptance. A disposition was manifested by some of the prominent members of the church, twenty years after, to give him a call to preach to them in the Dutch language; but the trustees reluctantly consented, after several refusals, to grant a salary for the purpose; and when they finally acceded to it, the sum was too small, and the doctor had become too infirm to leave his charge in New York, if he had entertained the wish to do so.

In 1787 the Rev. John Bassett was associated with Dr. Westerlo. The church had now become comparatively wealthy and numerous. In 1798, during his ministry, the congregation having become too large for the dimensions of their ancient church, a new one was completed, in North Pearl street, and services were held weekly in both places. About this time, serious differences arose between Mr. Bassett and his consistory, which led to his withdrawal from the church in 1804. He removed to the Boght, and afterwards to Bushwick, Long Island, where he died in 1820.

The Rev. John B. Johnson became the colleague of Dr. Bassett in 1796, and continued here until 1802, when he withdrew, and removed to Brooklyn. He died at Newtown, Long Island, on the 29th August, 1803. In consequence of impaired health he had withdrawn from the cares of a large congregation, and accepted a call where less exertion was required; but his disease was too deeply rooted, and the change proved ineffectual to his relief. After the death of his wife, who left him in April with three infant children, he rapidly declined. He was distinguished by abilities which marked him for extensive usefulness, and his mind was improved by a liberal education and indefatigable study. He enjoyed great popularity with his people, and during his ministry very gratifying accessions were made to the church. The two ministers preached alternately in the old and new churches.

By the removal of Mr. Bassett in 1804, the church was left without a pastor. At this juncture, a meeting of the *great consistory* was called for the purpose of deliberating upon the concerns of the church, and to decide upon the call of a pastor. This body was composed of the acting board, and the surviving members of all former boards of consistory, and met on the 27th of May, 1805. The following members attended:

John Veeder,
John N. Bleecker,
John B. Bradt,
John H. Wendell,
John D. P. Douw,
—— Pruyn,
Henry Truax,
Douw Fonda,
Gerrit Quackenbush,
Killian J. Winne,
Sol'n Van Rensselaer,
Harmanus P. Schuyler,
Anthony Van Santvoort,
Jacob Ten Eyck,
Leonard Gansevoort,
Gerrit Groesbeeck,

Henry Quackenbush,
Henry Staats,
Isaac Truax,
John Gates,
Gerrit A. Lansing,
Peter Lansing,
Joachim Staats,
James Bleecker,
Elbert Willett,
John J. Bleecker,
John H. Wendell,
Cor's Van Schelluyne,
Philip P. Schuyler,
Cornelius Van Vechten,
William Staats,
Abraham Schuyler,
John P. Quackenboss,

K. K. Van Rensselaer,
Jacob Bleecker, Jr.,
Tennis Ts. Van Vechten,
Harmanus A. Wendell,
Henry Van Woert,
Casparus Pruyn,
Gerardus Lansing,
Jacob J. Lansing,
Cornelius Groesbeeck,
Richard Lush,
Sanders Lansing,
Isaac Bogert,
Jacob Van Loon,
Volkert S. Veeder,
Peter E. Elmendorf,
Abraham Ten Eyck.

In the absence of any pastor, Mr. Peter Dox had presided over the meetings of the board for a long time. They determined to call the Rev. John M. Bradford, under a salary of $1500. He was to be required to preach but once on each sabbath during the first year, and his salary was to be increased $250 in the event of his marriage. The Rev. Mr. Linn, who had been an occasional preacher here several years, was also engaged to preach once on each sabbath. Mr. Bradford was ordained and installed pastor of the church on the 11th of August, 1805.

The project of another new church began to be agitated early in 1799, to be located upon the ancient church yard, where it was subsequently built. In 1805, the ground occupied by the old church at the foot of State street, was sold to the city corporation, for $5,000, and in the spring of the following year it was taken down, and the materials used in the construction of the church on Beaver street. A great deal of interest still attaches to this venerable edifice, and its demolition was viewed with painful emotions by many of the old people, who had been so long accustomed to worship there. It had served the purposes of the congregation nearly a century, and was invested with an unusual religious affection and veneration; the march of improvement has seldom overturned a nobler structure. The site had been selected for the church just a century and a half previous. The one erected in 1643 had before 1656 become inadequate to the accommodation of the community, and it had been determined in the course of the preceding year to erect a new building. To assist this good work the patroon and codirectors subscribed 1000 guilders, or $400, and 1500 guilders were appropriated from the fines imposed by the court at Fort Orange. In the early part of the summer, Rutger Jacobsen, one of the magistrates, laid the corner stone of the sacred edifice, in presence of the authorities, both of the town and colonie, and of the assembled inhabitants. A temporary pulpit was, at first, erected for the use of the minister, but the settlers subscribed twenty-five beavers to purchase a more splendid one in Holland. The chamber at Amsterdam added seventy-five guilders to this sum, for "the beavers were greatly damaged;" and "with a view to inspire the congregation with more ardent zeal," presented them the next year with a bell, " to adorn their newly constructed little church."* A fragment of this bell is still preserved, it is said, in one of the churches, bearing the inscription, " Anno 1601." And when in 1715, the original structure was beginning to decay, and the congregation, becoming too numerous for its dimensions, the foundations of a new one were laid around it, and the walls carried up and enclosed before the first was taken down, so that the customary services were interrupted only three sabbaths. This enlargement was made in the third year of the ministry of the Rev. Petrus Van Driessen; and the ingenuity of the scheme by which so great a work was accomplished without materially interrupting the weekly services, seems to have been a subject of great admiration and universal remark, in all time since. The edifice which had been constructed in this extraordinary manner, was in the Gothic style, and is supposed to be correctly delineated in the accompanying engraving. It occupied almost the entire width of State street, and extended partly across Broadway.

When the church was demolished, very few of the armorial bearings upon its stained windows escaped destruction; still a few relics were preserved. Among these, is one of its small windows; also, the weather-fane, and one of the bags in which the contributions were taken. But above all the

* Hist. N. Neth., ii., 307.

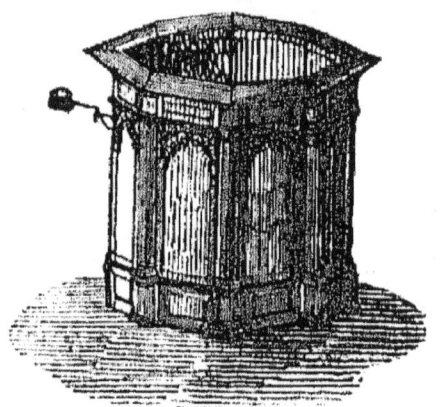 old pulpit is still in existence, and forms a very interesting relic. It was sent over from Holland in 1656, and was continued in the service of the church 150 years. It is constructed of oak, octagonal in form, about four feet high, and three feet in diameter. Although in a dismounted state, and rather off at the hinges, it is otherwise in a very good state of preservation. The accompanying engraving represents it very accurately, as it now stands in the attic of the North Dutch Church. The bracket is seen in front, upon which the dominie placed the hour glass, when he commenced his discourse. This pulpit was occupied by a long line of ministers, whose memory has been so much neglected, that it has been with great difficulty and labor we have traced their names even, and that imperfectly. The following is the best account we are able to give of the succession of the ministry.

1642 to 1649,	Rev.	Johannes Megapolensis.
1652 to 1683,	Rev.	Gideon Schaats.
1675	Rev.	——— Niewenhuysen.
1683 to 1699,	Rev.	Godfredius Dellius.
1699 to ———,	Rev.	——— Nucella.
1703 to 1709,	Rev.	John Lydius.
1710 no pastor,	Rev.	Gualterus Du Bois. (occasional)
1711 do.	Rev.	Petrus Vas. (do.)
1712 to 1738,	Rev.	Petrus Van Driessen.
1733 to 1744,	Rev.	Cornelis Van Sohie.
——— to 1760,	Rev.	Theodorus Frolinghuysen.
1760 to 1790,	Rev.	Eilardus Westerlo.
1776 to 1779,	Rev.	John H. Livingston. (occasional)
1787 to 1804,	Rev.	John Bassett.
1796 to 1802,	Rev.	John B. Johnson.
1805	Rev.	John M. Bradford.

The minutes of the board of consistory were very imperfectly kept previous to the year 1790. The records of the church which we have seen, consist principally of registers of baptisms and marriages, kept often in a very obscure manner, in which the elections of church officers are sometimes interspersed. Soon after the above date, however, a new spirit seems to have animated the board, which was composed of some of the most eminent men of the city. They entered upon the business of erecting a large church, surpassing all others in the city; and among other improvements and regulations which they introduced, they caused the minutes of the board, as far as they had been kept, to be fairly transcribed, and insisted upon their being properly and fully noted. Since then their transactions have been very well preserved.

We have traced the history of this church, one of the oldest in the United States, down to the year 1805, when a new era begins. The church now consists of three congregations, an account of which is deferred to a future time.

The oldest pulpit in America was imported from the Netherlands in 1656, and still serves its original purpose.

APPENDIX.

Call of the Rev. Johannes Megapolensis.—Whereas, by the state of the navigation in the East and West Indies, a door is opened through the special providence of God, also in New Netherland, for the preaching of the gospel of Jesus Christ, for the salvation of men, as good fruits have been already witnessed there, through God's mercy; and whereas the brethren of the Classis of Amsterdam have been notified that Mr. Kiliaen Van Rensselaer hath within the said limits in the North River, as patroon or lord, founded a colony named Renselaerswyck, and would fain have the same provided with a good, honest, and pure preacher; therefore they have observed and fixed their eyes, on the reverend, pious and well-learned Dr. Joannes Megapolensis, junior, a faithful servant of the gospel of the Lord, in the congregation of Schorel and Berg, under the Classis of Alkmaar, whom ye have also called, after they had spoken with the said lord, Mr. Kiliaen Van Rensselaer, in the same manner as they, with his honor's approbation, do hereby call him to be sent to New Netherland, there to preach God's word in the said colony, to administer the holy sacraments of baptism and the Lord's supper; to set an example to the congregation, in a Christian-like manner, by public precept; to ordain elders and deacons according to the form of the holy apostle Paul, 1 Tim., iii., 1; moreover to keep and govern, with the advice and assistance of the same, God's congregation in good discipline and order, all according to God's holy word, and in conformity with the government, confession and catechism of the Netherland churches and the synodal acts of Dordrecht, subscribed by him to this end, with his own hand, and promised in the presence of God, at his ordination, requesting hereby all and every who shall see and read these, to respect our worthy brother as a lawfully called minister, and him to esteem by reason of his office, so that he may perform the duty of the gospel to the advancement of God's holy name and the conversion of many poor blind men. May the Almighty God, who hath called him to this ministry, and instilled this good zeal in his heart, to proclaim Christ to Christians and heathens in such distant lands, strengthen him more and more, in this his undertaking, enrich him with all sorts of spiritual gifts; and bless overflowingly his faithful labors; and when the Chief Shepherd, Christ Jesus, shall appear, present him with the imperishable crown of eternal glory. Amen. Thus given in our classical assembly at Amsterdam, this 22d day of March, 1642. Signed in the name and on behalf of the whole body. Wilhelmus Somerus, loco præsidis; Zloahar Swalmius, scriba classis; Jonas Abeels, elder. Examined and approved by the directors of the West India Company, Chamber of Amsterdam, 6th June 1642 (signed) Charles Looten, Elias de Raet. Mr. Megapolensis embarked in the Houttuyn, and arrived at the colony in August of 1642.—*O'Callaghan's Hist. N. Neth.*, i., 449.

The First Church.—In commissary Van Curler's letter to the patroon, dated June 16, 1643, he says: "As for the church, it is not yet contracted for, nor even begun. I had written last year to your honor, that I had a building almost ready, namely, the covenanted work, which would have been for Dom. Megapolensis; and this house was not agreeable to the taste of Dom. Johannes; in other respects it was altogether suitable for him, so that I have laid it aside. That which I intend to build this summer in the pine grove (*in het greynen bosch*), will be 34 feet long by 19 feet wide. It will be large enough for the first three or four years, to preach in, and can afterwards always serve for the residence of the sexton, or for a school."—*Ibid.*, i., 459.

Note of Hand.—It appears that in 1647, the church was rich enough to loan money to the patroon, as will be seen by the following note of hand to the deaconry: "I, the undersigned, Anthonie de Hooges, have, on the part of the noble patroon of the colonie of Rensselaerswyck, borrowed from the diaconie of the aforesaid place, for the term of one year, to be repaid in cash, at the option of the lenders, with ten per cent interest per annum, the sum of three hundred guilders in seawan, whereof one hundred and twenty is in ordinary seawan, promising thankfully to produce at the aforesaid time, in stated specie aforesaid, to the diaconie of the aforesaid place. In testimony whereof, have I subscribed this acte with mine own hand. Actum R. Wyck, 9th May, 1647."—*Ibid, i.*, 471.

Agreement between Dom. Megapolensis and the Patroon.—The conditions upon which Mr. Megapolensis accepted the call "to administer and promote divine service in the colonie for the term of six successive years, according to previous demission from his classis," were as follows: "Firstly, Dr. Johannes Megapolensis 39 years old, with his wife, Machtelt Willemsen, aged 42 years, besides his children, Hellegond, Derrick, Jan, and Samuel, aged 14, 12, 10 and 8 years, shall furnish and provide themselves with clothing, furniture and other utensils, and these put up in such small and compact parcels, as can be properly stowed away in the ship. In the mean time, as his six years and his salary shall commence so soon as he shall set foot in the aforesaid colonie, the patroon, in addition to free board for them all in the ship, until they reach the colonie, shall over and above make him a present, for future serivce, at once, of three hundred guilders, without deduction. And in case it happen, which the Lord God in his mercy forbid, that he and his family come to fall in the hands of the Dunkirkers, the patroon promises to use all diligence to procure his ransom; to forward him afterwards on his voyage, according as occasion shall again offer, and to cause to be paid him during his detention, for the support of himself and family, forty guilders per month; and also so much here monthly, after he shall have received his liberty and orders, and shall have conveyed him hither, until he embarks. On his arrival, by God's help, in the colonie, the patroon shall cause to be shown to him where he and his shall lodge at first, until a fit dwelling shall be erected for him. So soon as he shall reach the colonie, his hereafter-mentioned salary shall commence, and his board and wages cease, and the patroon be discharged therefrom. Which salary, in order that he and his family shall be able honorably to maintain themselves, and not be necessitated to have recourse to any other means, whether tilling the land, commerce, rearing of cattle, or such like; but by the diligent performance of his duties, for the edifying improvement of the inhabitants and Indians, without being indebted to any person, which he also acknowledges to observe; wherefore the patroon promises to cause to be paid to him for the first three years' salary, meat, drink, and whatever else he may claim in that regard, one thousand, or ten hundred guilders yearly, one half here in this country, the remaining half in proper account there, according as he requires it, in provisions, clothing, and such like, at the ordinary and accustomed prices; and a further yearly addition of thirty schepels of wheat—I say thirty schepels—and two firkins of butter, or in place thereof, sixty guilders in money's worth. Should the patroon be satisfied with his service, he shall give him yearly, the three following years, an increase of two hundred guilders. In case of decease within the aforesaid six years, at which time the salary shall cease, the patroon shall pay to his widow, besides the supplement of the half year in which he shall have entered, a yearly sum of one hundred guilders, until the expiration of the aforesaid six years. He shall, besides, befriend and serve the patroon, in all things wherein he can do so without interfering with or impeding his duties. The aforesaid Johannes Megapolensis having also promised to comport himself in the said colonie as a loyal subject and inhabitant thereof, the above named patroon, on his side, also promises, for him and his successors, to perform and execute what is hereinbefore set forth, and to furnish him with due acte and commission, sealed with the seal of the patroon and the colonie; and in acknowledgment of the truth, without fraud, guile, or deceit, has this writing been signed by both sides. In Amsterdam, this 6th of March, 1642."— *Ibid*, i., 448.

The Rev. Gideon Schaats—the second clergyman in Albany, was born in 1607. He was originally engaged as minister of the colonie of Rensselaerswyck, but in 1657, he was appointed "at the request of the inhabitants of Fort Orange and Beverwyck," minister of the latter place, at a salary of 1200 guilders, "to be collected for the greatest part from the inhabitants." The following is a contract under which he first came to this country: "We, Johan Van Rensselaer, patroon, and codirectors of the Colonie Rensselaerswyck in New Netherland, having seen and examined the actes granted by the venerable Classis of Amsterdam to Dominie Gideon Schaats, so have we invited and accepted the said Gideon Schaats as preacher in our aforesaid colonie, there to perform divine service in quality aforesaid. To use all Christian zeal there to bring up both the heathens and their children in the Christian religion. To teach also the Catechism there, and instruct the people in the holy scriptures, and to pay attention to the office of schoolmaster for old and young. And further to do everything fitting and becoming a public, honest and holy teacher, for the advancement of divine service and church exercise among the young and old. And, in case his reverence should take any of the heathen children there to board and to educate, he shall be indemnified therefor as the commissioners there shall think proper. And he is accepted and engaged for the period of three years, commencing when his reverence shall have arrived thither in the Colonie Rensselaerswick, in the ship the Flower of Gelder, his passage and board being free; and he shall enjoy for his salary, yearly, the sum of eight hundred guilders, which shall be paid to his reverence there through the patroon's and codirectors' commissioners; and in case of prolongation, the salary and allowance shall be increased in such manner as the parties there shall mutually agree upon. And as a donation, and in confirmation of this reciprocal engagement, one hundred guilders are now presented to the dominie. And in addition the sum of three hundred guilders to be deducted from the first earned wages in the colonie, which moneys he doth hereby acknowledge to have received, acquitting thereof the patroon and codirectors. Finally, should the dominie require any money to the amount of one hundred guilders, to be paid yearly here, and to be deducted there, the said payment, on advice from the commissaries there, shall be made here, to the order of the aforesaid dominie. Whereupon, the call, acceptance, and agreement are concluded, each promising on his side, with God's help, to observe and follow the same, which each has promised, and in testimony thereof have both signed this. In Amsterdam, this eighth of May, XVI hundred two and fifty." Was signed Johan Van Rensselaer, Toussaint Mussart, for the codirectors, Gideon Schaats called minister to Rensselaerswick.—*Ibid, ii.*, 567.

Mr. Schaats's Children.—The Rev. Mr. Schaats had three children, two sons and one daughter. Reynier, the oldest, removed to Schenectady, where he was killed, with his son, at the great massacre, Feb. 10, 1690. Bartolomeus, the second, passed over to Holland, 1670, but returned and settled as a silversmith in New York, where he died about 1720, having a son, Reynier, from whom are descended all of the name now in this country. Anneke S., the daughter, married Thomas Davitse Kikebell, of New York. She was by no means a favorite with some of the female portion of her father's congregation, who carried their feelings so far, at one time, as to object to approach the Lord's supper in her company. Her father resented this. Indeed, already female gossip had been caught busy at a tea-party with even the dominie's character; a prosecution for slander ensued, and the parties had to pay heavy damages. Out of this probably arose the ill-will towards the daughter, who was sent by the magistrates to her husband at New York. The dominie in consequence, resigned his charge over the church, after having preached a sermon on 2 Peter, i., 12–15. He was, however, reconciled to his flock, and Anneke returned to her father, by whom she seems to have been much loved."—*Ibid, ii.*, 568.

Dom. Dellius Deposed.—When the Earl of Bellomont arrived as governor of the province, in 1688, Mr. Dellius was despatched in company with Capt. John Schuyler, to Canada, to convey the account of the peace of Ryswick, and to solicit a mutual interchange of prisoners. The dominie allowed his Indian agency to involve him in serious difficulties. The Assembly of 1699 took into consideration sundry extravagant grants of land which had been made by Col. Fletcher to several of his favorites. Among these were two grants to Mr. Dellius, who was accused of having fraudulently obtained the deeds, according to which the patents had been granted. One of these, dated Sept 3, 1696, under the seal of the province, was made by Col. Fletcher for a tract of land " lying upon the east side of the Hudson river, between the nothermost bounds of Saraghtoga and the Rock Rossian," containing about 70 miles in length, and 12 miles broad, subject to a yearly rent of one raccoon skin! Another grant was made to Dominic Dellius, William Pinchon and Evert Banker, dated July 30, 1697, for " a tract on the Mohawk river, 50 miles in length, and two miles on each side of the river, as it runs," subject to an annual rent of one beaver skin for the first seven years, and five yearly forever thereafter. On the 12th May, 1699, the Assembly resolved that, " It having appeared before the house of representatives convened in general assembly, that Mr. Godfrey Dellius has been a principal instrument in deluding the Maquaas Indians, and illegal and surreptitious obtaining of said grants, that he ought to be and is hereby suspended from the exercises of his ministerial function in the city and county of Albany."

Church Records.—The book of baptisms and marriages commenced by Mr. Dellius in 1683, and continued to the present day, has been of great service to many, who from various motives have sought to trace their ancestry, and to others who have resorted to it for the purpose of perfecting papers to obtain pensions; but above all the heirs of Anneke Jantz are there enabled to make out their parentage, and get it established by the certificate of the church master; which having obtained they carefully deposit it in a capacious wallet, with as much satisfaction, apparently, as if they had overcome a great obstacle, and were actually pocketing Trinity church itself. The resort to the books for the above and similar purposes has been so great, that they have become a good deal defaced. In order to the entire preservation of so valuable a record, two large folio volumes have been procured, into which all the names have been copied in a fair and legible hand. Posterity is indebted for this laborious performance to the industry of Dr. John H. Trotter, who, with the zeal and perseverance of a Dutch commentator, has given up his leisure hours for many months, to the arduous task of decyphering and transcribing several hundred pages of Dutch and Indian names, many of them almost unintelligible. The baptisms during the ministry of Dom. Dellius, embracing about sixteen years, were more than 1100. Among these Indian names frequently occur. Under the date of July 11, 1690, are the following:

Suongara (*Little Plank*), aged 40; baptismal name David.
Kowajatense, wife of the above, aged 30; named Rebecca.
Tekaneadaroga aged 22; named Isaac.
Tejonihokarawe (*Open the Door*), aged 30; named Hendrick.
Karanondo (*Uplifter*), aged 50; named Lydia.
Kaadejihendara aged 12; named Seth.
Siouheja (*Lively*), named Rachel.
Skanjodowanne (*Eagle's Beak*), named Manasse.
Sagonorasse (*Fast Binder*), aged 12; named Adam.
Karehodongwas (*the Plucker*), aged 16, wife of Isaac; named Eunice.
Aug. 6, 1690.—Son of Eunice, aged 9 months; named Simon.
Kwaorate, mother of Eunice, aged 60; named Lea.
Karehojenda, aged 30, daughter of Lea; named Alida.
Waniho, aged 40; named Josine.
Daughter of Josine, aged 9; named Jakomine.
Son of Josine, aged 7; named Josua.

The whole number of baptisms on record is about 14,000. The first baptisms under the successor of Mr. Dellius, who was Dom. Nucella, bear date Sept. 3, 1699. In 1701, baptisms seem to have been made of a considerable number of persons belonging to Kinderhook, and in 1707 and 1708, at Esopus, (Kingston). On the 23d and 30th April, 1710, 61 baptisms are entered by Mr. Gualterus DuBois, who left his settlement at New York the previous year. In 1711, the following baptisms were made by Rev. Petrus Vas, who was a settled pastor at Kingston: March

Reformed Protestant Dutch Church.

4th, 14; 11th, 7; Oct. 7th, 16; 12th, 2; 14th, 8; 20th, 3. Also in 1712, by the same, Feb. 10th, 15; 17th, 5. On the 20th April 1712, the first entry is make by Rev. Petrus Van Driessen, of 29 baptisms.

Early Members of the Church.—We are indebted to Mr. S. V. Talcott for the following names of the members of the Reformed Protestant Dutch Church of the city of Albany, "as they were numbered at the end of the year 1683," in the handwriting of Mr. Dellius.

Juriaen Teunis,
Arlaentje Teunis,
Abraham Staats,
Tryntje Staats,
Willem Teller,
Marritje Teller,
Jan Becker,
Mari Becker,
Aarnout Cornelis Vilen,
Gerrigje Vilen,
Andries Teller,
Sophia Teller,
Johannes Provoost,
Cornelis Van Dyck,
Lysbet Van Dyck,
Catryn Rutgirs,
Anaetje Lives (married Goosen Gerritsen Van Scayck, July, 1657),
Jochum Staats,
Lysbet Bancker,
Margeriet Schuyler,
Richart Pritti,
Lysbet Pritti,
Annetje Staats,
Jan Tomes,
Geertruyt Tomes,
Jacob Schermerhoorn (immigrated 1645?),
Janetje Schermerhorn (da. of Cornelis Segers),
Meindert Hermans (Van Den Bogert),
Heleen Hermens (his wife, and da. of Jacob Jans Schermerhorn),
Evert Wendel the Father,
Merritje Wendels,
Johannes Wendell,
Lysbet Wendell (now Schuyler),
Hendrick Cuyler,
Annetje Cuyler,
Henderick Roosenboom,
Gysbertje Roosemboom (du of —— Lansing),
Jan Onderkerck,
Dirck Wesselse Ten Brouck,
Styntje Ten Brouck (da of Cornelis Maasen Van Beuren?),
Marten Krygier,
Jannetje Krygier (da. of —— Hendricks),
Adriaan Gerrits (Papendorp),
Jannetje Gerrits (his wife),

Gerrit Swart,
Antonia Swart,
Wouter Van Den Uythost,
Leendert Phlipsen (Conyn),
Agnietje Leenderts (his wife),
Anna Van der Heyden,
Arien Van Elpendam,
Gerrit Van Esch,
Marietje Van Esch,
Hermen Tomes (Hun?),
Catelyntje Tomes (his wife),
Anna Ketel,
Grietje Gouws (she is dead),
Taakel Dircks,
Marritje Taakels (his wife),
Wynand Gerrits (Van der Poel),
Tryntje Wynands (his wife),
Pieter Loockerman,
Marretje Lookermans,
David Schuyler,
Catelyntje Schuyler,
Peiter Mees Vrooman,
Folikje Vrooman,
Jacob Mees Vrooman,
Lysbeth Vrooman,
Aalbert Ryckman,
Nelletje Ryckman,
Sybrent Van Schayck,
Lysbet Van Schayck (now Corlaar),
Jacob Staats,
Ryckje Staats,
Willem Percker,
Maria Percker,
Robbert Levinchston,
Alida Levinchston (da. of —— Schuyler),
Philip Freest,
Tryntje Freest (da. of —— Kip),
Gerrit Hardenberch,
Joupje Hardenberch,
Abraham Van Tricht,
Lysbeth Van Tricht (now Vanderpoel),
Symen (Jacobs) Schermerhorn,
Wilmje Schermerhorn (now Winnen),
Johannes de Wandelaar,
Sara de Wandelaar (da. of —— Schep-Moes),
Johannes Van Sandt,
Margeriet Van Sandt,
Melchert Wynandts (Vanderpoel),

Arcaantje Wynandts (his wife),
Laurens Van Alen,
Elbertje Van Alen,
Tryntje Rutten (now Roseboom),
Jan Jans Bleecker,
Grietjen Bleecker (da. of —— Van Schoendemund),
Jan Byvang,
Belia Byvang,
Gerrit Lansing,
Elsje Lansing,
Hendrick Lansing,
Lysbet Lansing,
Jan Lansing,
Geertje Lansing,
Jan Nack,
Jan Vinhagel,
Marretje Vinhagel,
Geertje Bout,
Willem Bout,
Luycas Gerrits,
Antje Lucas,
Isaac Verplanck,
Abigail Verplanck (da. of —— Bogert),
Johannes Beeckman,
Machtelt Beeckman (da. of Jacob J. Schermerhorn),
Nicolaas Van Rotterdam,
Lysbet Van Rotterdam,
Harmen Bastiaans (Visscher)
Hester Bastiaans (da. of —— Tierk),
Robbert Sanders (Glen?),
Elsje Sanders (Glen),
Jacob Sanders (Glen),
Caatje Sanders (now Douw),
Nicolaas Rips,
Marie Nicolaas Rips,
Jacob Coenraats,
Geertje Jacobs (his wife),
Johannes Roosenboom,
Margeriet Roosenboom,
Jan Cloet,
Bata Cloet (da. of —— Slightenhast),
Pieter Davids Schuyler,
Alida Schuyler (da. of Slightenhast),
Guysbert Marselis,
Barbar Marselis (his wife, da. of Claas Jacobs Groesbeeck),
Willem Claes Groesbeeck.

Geertruyt Groosbeeck (da. of —— Schuyler),
Johannes Roos,
Cornelia Roos,
Jan Gilbert,
Cornelia Gilbert (da. of —— Van den Bergh),
Evert Wendel (the son),
Lysbeth Wendel (da. of —— Glen),
Cornelis Scherluyn,
Geertruyt Scherluyn (da of Harman B Visscher),
Rachel Rettle,
Jacob Loockerman,
Tryntje Loockerman,
Cantje Loockerman (now Ten Broek),
Jacob Abrahams,
Catelyntje Jacobs (his wife),
Nicolaes Van Elslant,
Aaltje Frans (Pruyn),
Johannes Appel,
Anetje Appel,
Johannes Tomes (Mingaal),
Mari Jans (Mingall, da. of Jan Jans Oothout),
Jacobus Turck,
Cantje Turck (da. of Van Benthuisen),
Levinus Van Schayck,
Margariet Van Schayck,
Henderick Bries,
Marie Bries (now Lokermans),
Reimer Barents,
Bastiaan Harmens (Visscher),
Dirckje Bastiaans (his wife, and da. of Teunis Teunisse de Metsuaier),
Maas Cornelis (Van Buren),
Jacomyn Maas (his wife),
Willem Guysberts (Van den Bergh),
Catryn Willems (his wife),
Cornelis Guysberts (Van den Bergh),
Pieter Winne,
Tanne Winne,
Levinus Winne,
Jan Salomons (Goewey),
Cantje Salomons (his wife, and da. of —— Loockerman)
Barbar Salomons (Goewey),
Dirck Bensing,
Tytje Bensing,
Lysbet Herris (now Kaer),
Huybertje Jeechs,
Pieter Schuyler,
Engeltje Schuyler,
Arent Schuyler,
Maria Van Renselaar,
Ciliaan Van Renselaar,
Anna Van Renselaar,
Teunis (Cornelis) Van der Poel,
Catryn Van der Poel,
Anna Van der Poel,
Hendrick Van Esch,
Annetje Van Esch,
Luycas Pieters (Coeyman),
Ariaantje Lucass [his wife],
Adam Winnen,
Anna Winnen (now Teunisse),
Marten Jans,
Jannetje Martens (his wife, and da. of —— Cornelis),
Marritje Quakelbosch,
Douwe Jelis (died Nov. 27, 1700),
Rebecca Douws (his wife),
Wouter Quakelbosch,
Neeltje Quakelbosch,
Jan (Pieters) Quakelbosch,
Machtelt Quakelbosch (da of Jan Post),
Reinier (Pieters) Quakelbosch,
Lysbit Quackelbosch,
Folekje Brabanders,
Margriet Ketel,
Ysbrant Elders,
Jan de Noorman (the elder),
Marritje Noorman (now Carbith),
Jan (Andries) Douw,
Catryn Douw,
Arien Appel,
Wouter de Rademmacker,
Grietje Wouters (his wife),
Gerrit Reyers,
Annetje Reyers,
Marretje Van Schayck,
Geertje Brickers,
Marretje Zacharias,
Robbert Sickels,
Cornelis Van der Hoeven,
Metje Van der Hoeven,
Merselis Jans,
Annetje Marselis (his wife),
Pieter Bogardus,
Wyntje Bogardus (da. of Cornelis Bosch),
Marten Gerrits (Van Bergen)
Jannetje Martens (his wife; Nieltje Myndert, 2d wife),
Teunis Cornelis (Van Vechten),
Hester-Teunissen (his wife),
Geertje Van der Hoeven,
Jurian Coller,
Lysbeth Coller,
Andries de Sweed (i. e., Andries Alberts Bratt),
Neeltje Andries (da. of Teunis Sway),
Teunis Slingerlandt,
Celia Slingerlant,
Jan Hendricks (Van den Bergh),
Maria Jans,
Jan Van der Hoeven,
Jannetje Ver Wey,
Sara Ketel,
Sela Ketel (now Rachel Van der Heyden),
Antje Cross,
Paulyn Jans,
Wyntje Paulyns (his wife),
Ryck Michiels,
Jannetje Paulyns.
Anna Pieterse (Van Slyck),
Hendrick Maes (Van Beuren),
Lysbeth Hendricks (his wife),
Gerrit Gysberts (Van den Berg),
Teuntje Gerrits (his wife),
Frerick de Drent,
Jannetje Vries (now Salsberry),
Hendrick Marselis,
Barent Pieters (Coeyman),
Jacob Salomons (Goewey),
Lyntje Salomons (his wife),
Geertruyt Rinckhout,
Mattys Hooghteeling,
Maria Hooghteeling,
Jan Jacobs Van Oostrant,
Agniet Van Oostrant,
Philip Leenderts (Conyn),
Wyntje Phlips (his wife, and da. of —— Dirks),
Gerrit Lamberts (Van Vulkenburgh),
Marie Jochems,
Dirck Teunis (Van der Vechten),
Jannetje Direks (rather Van der Vechten),
Gerrit Teunis (Van der Vechten),
Grietje Gerrits (Van der Vechten),
Magdeleen Quakelbosch,
Andries Jans (Witbeek),
Jan Bronck,
Commertje Bronck (da. of Lendert Conyn),
Melchert Abrams (Van Deusen),
Engeltje Abrams (his wife),
Hendrick Abels (Riddenhaas),
Sephia Abels (now Nak),
Johannes (Jans) Oothout,
Hendrick (Jans) Oothout,
Jacobus Jans,
Jannetje Jacobs (his wife),
Mayken Jacobus
Abraham Van Breemen,
Marretje Van Bremen,
Johannes Jans (Witbeek)
Lysbet Jans (Witbeek, da. of Leendert Conyn),
Claes Van Petten,
Jsje Van Petten,

Reformed Protestant Dutch Church.

Cornelis Teunis (Van Vechten),
Annetje Cornelis (his wife),
Marten Cornelis (Van Beuren)
Marretje Martens (his wife),
Cornelia Martens (now Van Deusen),
Angeltje Andries (wife of Andries Jans Witbeck?),
Geertje Gysberts,
Hendrick Ver Wey,
Teunis de Metselaar,
Egbertje Teunis (his wife),
Wilmje Teunis (now Bratt),
Symen Schouten,
Cypien Schouten,
Andries Hans,
Gerretje Andries (his wife, and da. of Teunis Teunisse de Metselaar),
Jsje Hans,
Jacob Van Oostrant,
Mees Hogenboom,
Catryn Hogenboom,
Ariaantje Hoogenboom,
Antoni Van Schayck,
Marietje Van Schayck (da. of —— Van der Poel),
Roeloff Gerrits,
Geertruyt Roelofs (his wife),
Jan Grutters,
Hermen Lievens,
Marretje Hermens (Lieversen),
Jan Van Esch,
Aaltje Van Esch,
Barent Bratt,
Susanna Bratt,
Geurt Hendricks,
Marretje Geurten (his wife),
Andries Carstels,
Harmen Jans Knickelbacker,
Lysbet Harmens (his wife, and da. of —— Bogert),
Wessel Ten Broeck,
Elsje Ten Broeck (now Cuyler),
Lambert Van Valkenborgh,
Alida Vinhagel (now Visscher),
Gysje Vanderheyden (now Geesje Kip),
Cornelia Van der Heyden,
Jan Tysens Hoes (i. e., Goes?)
Styntje Hoes,
Jochum Lamberts (Van Valkenburgh),
Eva Jochum (his wife, da. of —— Vrowman),
Pieter Vosburgh,
Jannetje Pieters (Vosburgh),
Geertruyt Vosburgh,
Mara Jacobs (now Van Vechten),
Jan Martens,
Dirchje Jans (his wife),
Aalbert (Jacobs) Gerdenier,
Marretje Aalberts (his wife),
Jannetje Lamberts (Van Volkenburgh),
Tam Kreeve,
Jannetje Kreeve,
Aaltje Adams,
Teuwis Cool,
Marretje Teuwis (his wife),
Ariaantje Hendriks,
Teuwis Abrams,
Helena Teuwis (his wife),
Samson Bensing,
Tryntje Samsons (his wife a Mathus),
Johannes Bensing,
Mattys Hooghteeling
Nanning Harmens (Visscher)
Cornlis Stephens (Muller),
Hilletje Cornelis (a Lookerman his wife),
Caasper Leenderts (Conyn),
Colette Caspars (Winnen his wife),
Mayken Martens,
Isabella Dellius,
Dorcte Volkens (Douw?),
Catryntje Volkens (Douw),
Maria Schuyler (now Van Dyck),
Mayken Jacobs,
Anerigje Jans,
Philip Wendell,
Bastian Harmans (Visscher),
Rebecca Everts (wife of —— Hanssen),
Hester Bricker (now Slingerland),
Aaltje Arents,
Andries Jans,
Barentje Jans,
Jonas Volkens (Douw),
Chillian Winne,
Thomas Winne,
Barentje Vollewever (surnamed Schaats,
Jacob Teunis Van Schoonderwoeert,
Margriet Van Dam,
Hester Harmens (Visscher),
Willemymtje Nack,
Sara Chyler (now Van Brugge),
Maria Sanders (now Roseboom),
Gerritje Costers (now Roseboom),
Alida Everts (now Oothout),
Paulus Martens Van Benthuysen,
Wouter Pieters Quakelbosch
Pieter Hendricke De Hass,
Pieter Tomes Mingaal,
Helena Byvang,
Rebecca Claes (Groesbeck? now Van Schaak),
Catelyntje Ten Broeck,
Martina Bicker (now Hoogen),
Susanna Wendel,
Benony Van Corlar,
Jan Ratlife,
Antje Van Esch (now Ridder)
Martina Teunis,
Cornelia Ten Broeck,
Susanna Barents,
Sara Sanders (now Greevenrood),
Maria Kateluyne (now Bratt)
Dyrckje Luyckens,
Antje Becker,
Abraham Staats, Jr.,
Elbert Gerrits,
Jan Huyberts,
Johannes Bleycker, Jr.,
Antoni Bries,
Gerrit Lansing, Jr.,
Herbert Jacobs (Van Deusen)
Hendrick Rosenboom, Jr.,
Jan Abeel,
Maria Pareker,
Catryn Villeroy,
Sara Hardenberch,
Annetje Lives,
Abraham Cuyler,
Dirck Barents Bratt,
Solomon Frederick Booch,
Elizabeth Van Gelder,
Symon Van Esch,
Catharina Van Schayck,
Debora Van Dam (wife of Hendrick Hansse),
Margriet Jurries,
Zytje Marselis (wife of Joseph Jansse),
Est de Ridder,
Cornelis Martens,
Jacob Vosbergh,
Isaac Vosberch,
Abraham Jans (Van Alstyne?),
Lambert Jans (Van Alstyne?)
Isaac Jans (Van Alstyne?),
Dorotche Vosburgh,
Teuntje Jans (Van Alstyne? now Winnen,)
Manetje Vosburgh,
Anna Vosburgh,
Geertruy Sickles,
Est Bancker,
Elizabeth Bancker (an Abeel his wife),
David Christiaans,
Abraham Isnacks,
Anna Sickels,
Cornelia Van Male,
Johannes Schuyler,
Margriet Schuyler,
Cornelia Vroman,
Lysbeth Lansing (now Bratt),
Judick Marselis (wife of Lucas Lucasy),

Andries Hans Huyck,
Catryn Andries (a Van Valkenburgh his wife),
Cornelia Tys (Goes?),
Geertruy Jans Witbeek (now wife of Barent Gerritsen),
Marretje Hendericks (now Schermerhorn),
Ariaantje Gerrits,
Lyntje Winne (now Witbeek)
Lysbeth Rosenboom (now Van Deusen),
Johanna Bratt (now Keteluyn),
Henderikje Van Schoonhoven (now Poppi),
Ariaantje Van Schoonhoven,
Frans Pieters Clauw,
Elsje Fransen Clauw,
Adam Dingman,
Geertje Martens,
Geertruy Ten Broeck (now Schuyler),
Anna de Peyster,
Annetje Gerrits,
Eytje Pieters,
Caatje Bleyeker (now Cuyler),
Eva Vinhagel (now Beekman),
Willem Jacobs (Van Deusen)
James Willet,
Maria Wendell,
Abraham Kip,
Henderick Greefradt,
Johannes Pruyn,
Jan Juns Post,
Johannes Bratt,
Huybert Gerrits,
Rut Melcherts,
Cornelis Gerrits,
Anna Sanders,
Maria Van Renssalaer (now Schuyler),
Jacomyntje Vile,
Mayken Oothout (wife of Thomas Harmensen, Jr.?),
Coatje Melcherts (Van der Poel? now Witbeek),
Jannetje Cobus,
Rachel Melcherts (Van der Poel?),
Cornelia Coller,
Catarine Van Alien (now Van der Poel),
Nelletje Quakelbosch,
Francyntje Hendericks,
Geertruy Hoogenboom,
Neeltje Slingerlandt,
Engletje Lives,
Geertruy Jans,
Margriet Brickers,
Susanna Lansing,
Hermen Rutgers,
Cornelia Van Vreedenburch (now Van Yselsteyn),
Hester Davids,
Weyntje Fransen (Clauw?),
Judick (Jans) Van Housen,
Henderick Van Renssalaer,
Joseph Jans,
Jan Fondans,
Marretje Van Petten (now Van Alien),
Catelyntje Van Petten (now Van Vechten),
Margriet Hans (now Visscher),
Henderick Van Dyck,
Abraham Schuyler,
Cornelia Van Olinda,
Arieentje Van der Heyden.
On July 11th, 1690, the following Indians:
Paulus,
Laurens,
Maria.
On October 22d, 1691, the following Indians:
David,
Rebecca,
Lydia.
At the same time the following persons:
Sara Harmens (Visscher),
Marretje Gerrits,
Jannetje Blyker,
Marritje Vanhagel,
Anna Coster,
On March 24th, 1692, the following Indians:
Isak,
Rachel,
Rebecca,
Eunice,
At the same time the following persons:
Meindert Schuyler,
Jacobus Van Dyck,
Johannes Rykman,
Willem Van Alien,
Tammus Noxen,
Luthers Jans (Witbeek),
Andries Douw,
Pieter Lucas Koeyman,
Debora Staats (now Roseboom),
Elsje Rutgers (now Schuyler),
Maria Banker,
Anna Gansevoort,
Christina Ten Broek,
Antje Van der Heyden,
Marietje Pruyn (wife of Elbert Gerretsen),
Rachel Cuyler (now Schuyler),
Tryntje Rykman, now Breese
Marritje Lookerman (now Fonda),
Marritje Bogardus (now Van Vechten),
Grietje Takel,
Barbar Jans (wife of Gerrit Rikse),
Elsje Wendell (now Staats),
Jannetje Oothout (Van Schaack).
September 17th, 1692.
Canastasji (Indian),
Gerrit Rosenboom,
Pieter Verbrugge,
Stephanus Groesbeeck.
December 23d, 1692.
Henderik (Indian).
April 13th, 1693.
Antoni Coster,
Johannes Gerrits (Van Vechten),
Marten Winnen,
Melchert Vanderpoel,
Elizabeth Kreigir,
Tryntje Wendell (now Millington),
Neeltje Schermerhorn (now Ten Eyck),
Elizabeth Ten Broek (now Coster),
Catrine Nack,
Geertruy Van Benthuysen (now Becker),
Maria Van der Poel (of Neoborum),
Cornelis (Indian),
Claus Jans.
October 25th, 1693.
Johannes Harmens (Visscher),
Moeset (Indian),
Maria do.
Sara do.
Jose do.
April 6th, 1604.
Pieter Hogenboom,
Johannes Kip,
Jacobus Van Schoonhoven,
Geertruy Van Schoonhoven,
Jecomintye Van Schoonhoven (now Van Deusen),
Geertje Willems,
Anna Bogardus,
Lydia Ten Broek,
Lysbeth Slingerlandt,
Christine Pruyn,
Catelyntje Schuyler (now Abeel),
Susanna Wendell.
Claartje Brott,
Elsje Hans,
Jannetje Swart (now Van der Zee),
Alida Fondaas (now Van Vechten),
Hester Fondas (wife of John Dircksen),
Lysbeth Jans,
Geertje Quakelbosch (now Groesbeek).

Reformed Protestant Dutch Church.

July 6th, 1694.
Gideon (Indian),
Alida do.

December 26th, 1694.
Meeltje Van Bergen (now Douw),
Dirk Van der Heyden,
David Schuyler,
Margriet (Indian),
Eva do.
Maria do.
Elsje do

January 20th, 1695, of Kinderhook.
Arieentje Barents (wife of Pieter Martens),
Robbert Teuis (Van Deusen).
Johannes Van Allen.

March 21st, 1695.
Thomas Harmens (Hun?),
Hendrick Hans,
Tam Williams,
Agneetje Gansevoort (his wife)
Franz Winne,
Elsje Gansevoort (Winnen),
Claas Sivers,
Albert Rykman,
Gerrit Ryks,
Rachel Winne (of Schenectady),
Hendrik Pruyne,
Tryntje Cornelis (wife of Pieter Waldron),
Sara Foreest,
Claartje Quakelbosch (wife of Dirk Takelsen),
Annetje Hogenboom,
Rachel Slingerlandt,
Maria Wendell,
Dewertje Van Petten,
Anna Van Petten (wife of Claas Siversend,)
Daniel Bratt,
Pieter (Indian),
Joseph do.
Tierk do.
Agniet do.
Lea do.
Susanna do.

December 25th, 1695.
Cornelis Bogardus,
Brant (Indian),
Jacob do.

January 22d, 1696.
Jan Teuwis (Van Deusen),
Marrictje (Van Deusen),
Laurens Claas (Van Schaick)
Catelyntje Teuwis,
Jannetje Jochums (wife of Isaac Jans).

April 9th, 1696.
Myndert Rosenboom,
Abram Lansing,
Catrine Staat (now Schayk),
Saartje Brats (wife of Reynier Mynderts),
Anna Glen (now Wendell),
Maria Salisburry,
Mayken Van Esch (now Wendell),
Margreetje Pels,
Saartje Van Deusen.

June 26th, 1696
Antoni (Indian),
Dorcas do.
Barent do.
Catrine do.

September 18th, 1696.
Johannes (Indian),
Arent do.

April 1st, 1697.
Mayken Van Esch (now Onderkerck),
Annetje Schaats,
Margriet Ryks,
Elizabeth Lansing (now Groesbeck),
Susanne Wendell (now Wyngaard),
Margriet Schuyler (now Livingston),
Catrena Van Schayk (now Quakkenbosch).

December 27th, 1697.
Sara Van Allen,

January 13th, 1698.
Guysbert Scharp,
Hendrik Jans (Witbeck),
Sara Jans (Witbeck),
Marritje Jans (Witbeck),

April 21st, 1698.
Hagar (Indian),
Jacomine do.
Luycas Lucas (Van Hookerke
Solomen Cornels (Van Vechten),
Hasuera Marselis,
Maas Ryks,
Harman Rykman,
Robbert Levingston, Jr.,
Margriet Levingston,
Margriet Van Trigt,
Margriet Blyker,
Margriet Harmens,
Catelina Wendell (now Schuyler),
Neeltje Gerrits,
Dirkje Winne,
Sara Marselis,
Marritje Roelofs (Kidni),
Helena Pruyn,
Lammertje Lokerman (Oothout).

January 8th, 1699, from Kinderhook.
Est Van Allen,
Stephenas Van Allen,
Manuel Van Schaack,
Lysbeth Arnoutse Van Eli.

April 6th, 1699.
Reyer Gerrits,
Jacobus Schuyler,
Andries Nack,
Hendrick Douw,
Jan Jans Van Aarnen,
Wouter Quakelbosch (married Cornelia, da. of Lawrence Bogert),
Matthyse Nak,
Maria Verplank,
Geertje Gerrits (Van den Bergh),
Lysbeth Gansevoort,
Margriet Rykman,
Lysbeth Viele (from Neoborum),
Helena Fonda,
Antje Quakelbosch,
Josina Maas (Van Buren?),
Hillitje Gansevoort,
Maria Quakelbosch,
Neeltje Marinus,
Rachel Douw,
Cornelia Quakelbosch,
Anna Pruyn,
Canastasji (Indian).

September 8th, 1699.
Jonathan Brandhorst.

January 5th, 1700.
Susanna Wendells.

May 8th, 1700.
Claes Fonda,
Daniel Winnen,
Isack Ouderkerck,
Lysbet Wendell,
Mary Ingolsbie,
Rachel Bogardus,
Susanna Trujex.

Patent of Church Pasture.—Thomas Dongan, Captain Generll and Governour in Chief in & over ye Province of New Yorke & Territoryes Depending thereon in America under his most sacred Majesty James ye Second by ye Grace of God King of England Scotland France and Ireland Defender of ye faith &c To all to whom this presents shall come sendeth greeting Whereas by virtue of a certaine Deed of Bargaine & Sale from ye Mayor Aldermen & Commonalty of ye citty of Albany bearing Date yᵉ first day of November in yᵉ third year of his said Majestyus Reigne & in yᵉ year of our Lord one thousand six hundred Eighty & Seaven Godfridus Dellius of yᵉ said Citty Clerk stands seized in his owne Right and to his own use of an Estate of Inheritance in fee simple of & in a certain Piece or Parcell of Land commonly called or known by yᵉ Name of yᵉ Pasture Scituate Lyeing and being to the Southard of yᵉ said Citty nere yᵉ place where yᵉ old Fort stood and extended along Hudsons River till it comes over against yᵉ most Northerly Point of yᵉ Island Commonly Called Martin Garritsons Island haveing to yᵉ East Hudsons River to yᵉ South yᵉ Manor of Rensselaerswyck to yᵉ West yᵉ highway Leading to yᵉ towne yᵉ Pasture late in yᵉ tenure and occupacon of Martin Garrittse & yᵉ Pasture late in yᵉ tenure and occupacon of Caspʳ Jacobs to yᵉ North yᵉ several pastures late in yᵉ tenure & occupacion of Robert Sanders Myndart Harmanse & Evert Wendall & yᵉ several Gardens late in yᵉ tenure & occupacon of Dirick Wessells Killian Van Renslaer & Abraham States together with all and singular yᵉ Profits Commodityes & Apputences whatsoever to the said Pasture Piece or Parcell Land & Premissess or any part or parcell thereof belonging or in any wise Appurtaineing or to or with yᵉ same now or at any time heretofore belonging or used Occupied or Enjoyed as Part or Parcell or Member thereof & whereas yᵉ said Goodfridus Dellius has made his request unto me yᵗ I would on yᵉ behalfe of his Majesty grant & confirm unto him yᵉ said Goodfridus Dellius his Heirs and Assigns yᵉ before menconed Pasture Piece or Parcell of Land & Premisses with yᵉ Appurtences Know yᵉᵉ yᵗ by virtue of my Commission & Authority from his most sacred Majesty & Power in me being and Residing in Consideracon of yᵉ Acquit Rent or Chiefe Rent herein after Reserved and other Good & Lawful Consideratons me thereunto moving I have Given Granted & confirmed and by these presents Do hereby Give Grant & Confirm unto yᵉ said Godfridus Dellius his Heirs & Assigns forever all yᵗ yᵉ before Recited Pasture Piece or Parcell of Land & Premissess with all and every yᵉ Hereditaments and Appurtenances to have and hold all yᵗ yᵉ said Pasture Piece or Parcell of Land & Premissess with all and singular yᵉ Herditaments & Appurtenances to yᵉ said Godfridus Dellius his heirs and Assigns forever to yᵉ only Proper use and behoofe of him yᵉ said Godfridus Dellius his Heirs and Assigns forever to bee holden of his most sacred Majesty his Heirs and Successors in free and Comon Soccage According to yᵉ tenure of East Greenwich in yᵉ county of Kent in his Majestys Realme of England Yielding Rendering and Paying therefore Yearly and every Yeare to his said Majesty his Heirs and Successors forever as a Quitt Rent one shilling Good and Lawfull Mony of this Province att Albany to be paid to such officer or officers as from time to time shall be empowered to Receive the same in Leew & Stead of all Services Dues and Demands whatsoever in testimony whereof I have Signed these Presents with my hand Writing Caused yᵉ same to be recorded in yᵉ Secretary's Office & yᵉ Seale of this his Majestey's Province to be hereunto affixed this thirtieth Day of July in yᵉ fourth yeare of his Maᵗⁱᵉˢ Reigne and in yᵉ Yeare our Lord 1688.

THOMAS DONGAN.

May itt please yoʳ Excy the Attorney Generˡˡ has Perused this Grant & finds nothing therein contained Prejudiciall to his Majestyes Interest
Exxd July yᵉ 30: 1688   W. NICOLLS.

Reformed Protestant Dutch Church. 103

City Records.—Among the records in the City Hall, are three volumes in Dutch, written generally in a good character, embracing about thirty years of the close of the seventeenth century, in which are frequent allusions to church matters, coming under the notice of the council. Some of the city authorities procured the translation of these records a few years ago, but the work was very imperfectly done, in an abridged or mutilated form. Being unable to read the originals, we have copied a few items from the translated volume.

1676. A request of the consistory of Kingston, that Dominie Schaats might come over to administer the Lord's supper and baptism, which was denied because Dominie Schaats was a settled minister, but if they wanted Dominie Rensselaer would agree thereto.....Dominie Van Rensselaer preferred a complaint against Jacob Lesler and Jacob Milborne, for slandering his orthodoxy and ridiculing his preaching and the talents graciously bestowed on him by the Lord &c. &c., requests consequently that it may please the court to give a verdict about this matter as will be most convenient with the truth and justice, and also with the welfare of Christ in the city.....Mandate of his excellency the governor general to the court to do their utmost endeavors to prevent, to smooth and to remove the divers disputes arisen between the pastors and some of the members of the Reformed Dutch Church.....Reconciliation between Dominie Van Rensselaer, Jacob Lesler and Jacob Milborne, also between Dominie Schaats and some members of the consistory, whereby all the former disputes and ecclesiastical discords are thrown in the fire of love.

Feb., 1677. Proclamation was made prohibiting all misdemeanors which have often occurred here on Shrove Tuesday, viz,: riding at a goose, cat, hare and ale, &c., on a penalty of f25 seawan.....Order of the court to prevent and punish severely the shameful violation of the sabbath especially committed by the inhabitants of Kinderhook, and the appointment of Jochem Lambertse deputy sheriff strictly to attend to it.

1678. Captain Philip Schuyler complains about it being refused to Dominie N. Van Rensselaer by the consistory to take his seat in the usual pastor's pew with the elders.....Resolved and ordered that Captain Philip have a suitable seat in the church, behind that of the magistrates.

Feb., 1679. A. Muir requests in the name of the court and consistory of Schenectady, that Dominic Schaats may be sent four Sundays in one year to administer the Lord's supper to said place and community, which request is granted in so far that Dominie Schaats is allowed to go four times in one year to administer the holy sacraments, but not on a Sunday, whereas it would be unjust to let the community be here without preaching.....Appeared before the court Dominie Schaats, the elder and two deacons, who voluntarily offer to take to their charge the rebuilding of the dominie's house, to be in future a suitable dwelling for the pastor, requesting a deed of conveyance.....No person may sell any food or victuals during the time of service on the Lord's day, but after the sermon.....Proclamation by which is expressly cautioned against the violating of the Lord's day as by deplorable experience was found that a great deal of the inhabitants were committing.....Summoned before the court on request of Dominie G. Schaats and the consistory of the Reformed Dutch Church, Ida Barents, to be inquired about the slanderous manner in which some of the members of the Lutheran church, and especially a certain Engeltye, the wife of Solomon Volktie, should have expressed herself in the presence of said Ida Barents, on account of the church and consistory. Appeared before the court Engeltje, to whom the accusation was read, whereupon she prayed and received pardon, on condition of better behavior in future.

1681. Petition of the consistory of the Reformed Dutch Church community, according to the repeated and earnest solicitation of Dominie Schaats, that it would please the court to do their utmost endeavors to obtain them a good orthodox pastor for their church, which is favorably answered by the court, and resolved in consequence to summon several of the principal citizens, in order to know their opinion of the matter.... May. Whereas, Captain Anthony Brockholst has been pleased to give his approbation for the obtainance of a new pastor for the Reformed Dutch Church. It is resolved by the court to collect a sum of money of the community to defray the expenses of his passage hither..... Letter of Captain Brockholst about the sending of Aneke, the daughter of Dominie Schaats with her children to New York to her husband Thos. D. Kikebel, and order of the court to said Aneke to depart thither with the first opportunity..... June. Appointment of two elders and two deacons to collect the contributions of the members of the community for the new appointed pastor..... Resolved that there shall be written to the classis of Amsterdam for the sending of a good orthodox pastor for the Reformed Dutch Church of Albany, who will enjoy a yearly salary of ƒ800 in beaver, and the contribution in behalf of his passage thither, amounts to the sum of ƒ648 beaver, which is deposited with Messrs. J. H. Van Baal, Richard Van Rensselaer and Abel De Wolff, to be used for said purpose..... Dec. The sheriff, ex-officio, claims of Jan Van Loon ƒ800 seawan, for a fine having greatly upbraided and injured Martin Cornelis, who had changed the Roman Catholic religion for the Protestant, and calumniated the Protestant church itself by saying among other things to Marten, that he had turned from God to the devil, on which several witnesses were examined.

May, 1682. Resolution about making a new gallery in the north side of the church, by means of contribution on the community. Contract with an architect to build another gallery in the church..... List of twenty-four persons who are entitled because of their contributions to seats on the new made gallery in the church, as follows: Peter Schuyler Philipse, Arent Schuyler, Philip Schuyler, Jr., Johannes Schuyler, Martin Gerritsen, Johannes Wendell, Johannes Cuyler, Joachim Staats, Levinus Van Schayck, Sybrant Van Schayck, Jacob Lokermans, Robert Livingston, Albert Rykman, Martin Cornelise, Claes Van Petton, Dirk Wessells, Cornelis Teunise, Johannes Janse, Myndert Harmense, Jan Stoffolse Abeel, Anthony Van Schayck, Jacob Janse Flodder, Arnout Cornelise Viele, Evert Banker..... Consented that Robert Livingston may occupy for himself and his posterity, a seat on the new gallery, as a reward for his trouble in getting contributions..... Resolution of the court to write to the commissaries of Schenectady, to get information whether it was true that the sabbath could be so dreadfully violated there by some Frenchmen, and that such should rather be nourished than hindered by the officer, L. Cobes.

Aug., 1683. Citation of the Reformed Dutch Church to inquire how much of them would please to contribute for the salary of the Holland arrived pastor, Dominie Godefrideus Dellius. List of the subscribers amounts to ƒ1200 beaver, or 350 pistareens. Determination about the just beginning of the ministerial year of Dominie Dellius, and some dispositions in the notarial contract made at Amsterdam, the 20th July, 1682, especially on account of the increase of his yearly salary, in case of the death of Dominie Schaats. Information given by Dominie Dellius of his being willing to perform the notarial contract of his duties, but will be pleased in being paid with Dutch money.....Disposition on account of the yearly salary of Dominie Dellius, being finally fixed at the sum of ƒ900 Dutch money, and also a determination of Dominie Dellius to preach to the community of Schenectady once a month..... Resolution of the court to write a letter of thanksgiving to the classis of Amsterdam, on account of their paternal care in sending of the reverend, godly and deep learned Dominie Godefredius Dellius, and also to write a letter of thanks to Richard Van Rensselaer and Abel de Wolff, for their exertions.....Nov. Nomination of four members of the Reformed Dutch Church delivered to the court, to elect two of them to be church wardens.

Act of Incorporation.—George by the Grace of God King of Great Britain, France and Ireland, defender of the faith, &c., to all to whom these presents shall come or may concern, sendeth greeting: Whereas our loving subjects the Rev. Petrus Van Driessen, Johannes Cuyler, Johannes Rooseboom, Henrych Van Rensselaer, William Jacobse Van Deusen, Rutgert Bleecker, Volkert Van Veghten, Myndert Rooseboom and Dirck Tienbroock, the present ministers, elders and deacons of the Reformed Protestant Dutch Church in the city of Albany, in our province of New York, by their humble petition presented to our trusty and well beloved Colonel Peter Schuyler, president of our council for our province of New York, in council have set forth that the inhabitants of Albany, descended of Dutch ancestors, have from the first settlement of this province by Christians, hitherto held, used and enjoyed the free and undisturbed exercise of their religion and worship in the Dutch language, after the manner of the established Reformed Protestant religion in Holland, according to the common rules, institutions and church government of the national synod of Dort, in Holland, in the year of our Lord Christ one thousand six hundred and eighteen, and one thousand six hundred and nineteen. And that the said minister, elders and deacons, and their ancestors and predecessors, at their own charge and expense, erected, built and hitherto maintained a church within the city of Albany aforesaid, and have dedicated the same to the service and worship of Almighty God, situate, lying and being in the high street commonly called Yonkers street, nigh the bridge in the city of Albany, containing in length on the south side thereof seven rod, three foot four inches; on the north side seven rod, three foot one inch, Ryland measure. and in breadth on the east and west ends, sixty-one foot and five inches, wood measure. And are now not only quietly and peaceably seized and possessed of their said church, but are likewise seized of sundry other demesnes to and for their sole and only proper use and behoof of their said church and congregation, that is to say, one certain messuage or tenement and lot of ground in the aforesaid city of Albany commonly called the Dutch minister's house, situate, lying and being in the

Brewer's street, on the east side thereof, in the third ward of the said city, being in front from the southward to the northward five rod ten inches, and behind toward Hudson's river, six rod fifteen inches, Ryland measure, and in length from the said street to the city stockadoes, bounded on the south side by Jan Solomons, and on the north side by that of the late Hans Hendrycks and the widow of David Schuyler. Also one other certain messuage or tenement and lot of ground, situate, lying and being in the city aforesaid commonly called poor house or alms house, in the first ward of the said city, bounded on the south by the high street that leads to the burying place to the north of Rutten kill, and to the east of Harman Rutgers, and to the west by the lot of Garryt Bancker, containing in breadth towards the street that leads to the Lutheran church by the said Rutten kill, six rod one foot and the like breadth in the rear, and in length on the east side, eight rod and two inches, all Ryland measure. Also that certain parcel of land commonly called and known by the name of the pasture, situate, lying, and being to the southward of the city of Albany, near the place where the old fort stood, extending along Hudson's river, till it comes over against the most northerly point of the island commonly called Marten Gerrytsen's island, having to the east Hudson's river, to the south the manor of Rensselaerswyck, to the west the highway that leads to the city aforesaid, the pastures now or late in the tenure and occupation of Martin Gerrytsen, and the pasture now or late in the tenure or occupation of Casper Jacobs, to the north the several pastures late in the tenure and occupation of Robert Saunders, Myndert Harmans and Evert Wendell, and the several gardens late in the occupation of Dirck Wessells, Killian Van Rensselaer and Abraham Staats, together with the old highway from Beaver kill to the end of Schermerhorn's pasture, adjoining to the same on the west side thereof. Also that certain parcel of pasture land situate, lying, and being to the southward of the said city, and to the westward of the before mentioned pasture, near and about the limits of the said city on the manor of Rensselaerswyck, containing in breadth along the wagon way, six and twenty rod, and in length towards the woods, eight and twenty rod, and in breadth towards the woods twenty five rod. And also all that certain garden lot of ground situate, lying, and being in the great pasture, containing in the breadth six rod and five foot, and in length eight rod and two foot, and stretching backwards with another small lot of three rod and two foot in length, and in breadth one rod and two foot Ryland measure; praying that they may by charter or patent under the great seal of the province of New York, be incorporated and made one body politic in fact and name, and that they and their successors forever hereafter, may not only be enabled to use, exercise and enjoy their aforesaid privileges, and the free use and exercise of their said religion and worship in manner aforesaid, by the name and style of the ministers, elders and deacons of the Reformed Protestant Dutch Church, in the city of Albany, with such other liberties and privileges as have been formerly granted to other Reformed Protestant Dutch churches within the province of New York, with variations, additions and commissions, as long usage and experience has taught them to be most agreeable to their well being and circumstances, but also the grant and confirmation of all those their said inheritances and demesns, to hold to them, the said minister, elders and deacons of the Reformed Protestant Dutch Church in the city

Reformed Protestant Dutch Church.

of Albany, and to their successors and assigns for ever. We being willing to encourage and promote the said pious intentions and the free use and exercise of their said reformed protestant religion, to the same congregation and their successors for ever, in the said city of Albany, know ye, that of our especial grace, certain knowledge, and meer motion, we have given, granted, ratified, and confirmed, and do by these presents for us, our heirs and successors for ever, give, grant, ratify and confirm unto all the inhabitants of Albany, so as aforesaid descended of Dutch ancestors, and professing the said reformed protestant religion, and to their successors for ever, the free use and exercise of their worship, doctrine, discipline and church government, according to the canons, rules, institutions and directions of the Reformed Protestant Dutch Church in Holland, instituted and approved by the National Synod of Dort, and that no person nor persons whatsoever in communion of the said Reformed Protestant Dutch Church in Albany aforesaid, or at any time or times hereafter, shall be molested, disquieted, or disturbed in the free use and exercise of their said religion and worship, they behaving themselves peaceably, and not abusing this liberty to licentiousness, profaneness, and the civil injury or outward disturbance of the National Church of England, as by law established, or other reformed protestant churches in the aforesaid city of Albany. And to the end the same liberties and privileges be hereafter for ever supported, maintained, and continued to them and their successors for ever, we of our especial grace, certain knowledge and meer motion, do likewise will and grant for us, our heirs and successors for ever, unto the same Petrus Van Driessen, the present minister of the same congregation at Albany, Johannes Roseboom, Henryck Van Renssalaer, and William Jacobse Van Deusen, the present elders of the same church, and unto Rutgert Bleecker, Volkert Van Veghten, Myndert Roseboom, and Dirk Tienbroock, the present deacons of the same church, and the inhabitants of Albany communicants of the said church, that they be as they are hereby created and made one body corporate and politick in fact and name, by the name of the minister, elders and deacons of the Reformed Protestant Dutch Church in the city of Albany, and that they and their successors for ever, shall and may by that name have perpetual succession, and be able and capable in the law to sue and be sued, plead and be impleaded, answer and be answered unto, defend and be defended, in all and singular suits, quarrels, controversies, differences, strifes, matters and things whatsoever, and in all courts whatsoever, either in law or equity, of what kind sover, as also by the same name, to have, hold, take, receive, be seized of, possess and enjoy to them and their successors for ever their said church, parsonage or minister's dwelling-house, alms-house, and other their demesnes or inheritances, by fee simple, before mentioned, and such other demesnes or inheritances to purchase and acquire to them and their successors and assigns for ever, and by the same name, the same lands, hereditaments and appurtenances, or any part of them (excepting only the same church); to alienate, bargain, sell, grant, demise, sell and to farm-let to any other person, or persons, body corporate and politic, whatsoever at their will and pleasure, in fee simple for life, or lives, or for term of years, as to them shall seem most convenient and profitable, as any other person or persons, body corporate or politic, may or can do, not exceeding the yearly value of three hundred pounds over and above what they now stand seized and possessed, or for the common use and benefit of the same Dutch Church and of all the members of the same congregation. And we do further will and grant that the minister, elders and deacons of the same church, for the time being, for ever hereafter, be the consistory of the same church, and shall and may have, keep and use a common seal to serve for all grants, matters and things, whatsoever belonging to the same corporation, with such device or contrivance thereon as they or their successors for ever shall think fit to appoint, with full power to break, new make and alter the same at their will and discretion ; and the same consistory shall have and enjoy the like powers and privileges as a Dutch consistory in the Reformed Protestant Dutch Church in Holland do, or may or ought to use and enjoy. And we do will and grant that the same Petrus Van Driessen be the first minister of the said church at the time of this our grant, and the same Johannes Cuyler, Johannes Roseboom, Henryck Van Rensselaer and William Jacobse Van Deusen, be the first elders of the said church at the time of this our grant ; and that the same Rutgert Bleecker, Volkert Van Veghten, Myndert Roseboom and Dirk Tienbroock, be the first deacons of the said church at the time of this our grant, to all intents and purposes; and that the said ministers, together with the said four elders and four deacons, or the minister, elders and deacons for the time being, and the major numbers of them whereof the minister for the time being always to be one—be the consistory of the said church, and have and shall have full power and authority, at all time and times for ever hereafter, to act in all their church affairs and business, by majority of voices, in as full and ample manner as if the minister and all the said four elders and four deacons were personally present and did actually and severally give their votes. But in case of the death, absence or removal of their said minister, then, and in any of these cases, the elders and deacons of the same church, for the time being, or the major number of them, whereof the first elder in nomination we will always to be one, and shall preside, shall have, use and exercise all the power and authorities of a consistory to all intents and purposes, and shall manage and order the church affairs in as full and ample manner as if their said minister were alive, present and consenting thereunto, any thing in these presents to the contrary thereof in any wise notwithstanding. And we will and grant that the same elders and deacons continue in their respective offices until the next anniversary election. And the said elders and their successors, for ever hereafter, have and shall have the full power and authority of receiving and paying the moneys given for the maintenance of the minister or ministry of the same church, whether the same arise by legacy, donation or voluntary contributions or collection from the inhabitants or members of the same congregation, and are to keep exact and true accounts to the consistory, when thereunto by them required And that the said deacons and their successors for ever hereafter, have and shall have the sole power and authority of receiving and paying all the moneys collected and offered at the administration of the Holy Sacrament of our Lord's Supper, and in church in the times of divine service of preaching, for the maintenance of the poor, and are to keep and render exact and true accounts thereof to the consistory aforesaid, when thereunto by them required. which election of the same elders and deacons of the same church is to be at Albany on every second Saturday of December, annually, forever, by majority of voices, of the consistory, in the manner following: That is to say, on each second Saturday of December, annually for ever at Albany, shall be chosen two new elders and two new deacons, who, together with the two elders and two deacons last in nomination in this our charter, shall serve for the year ensuing in their respective offices, and for ever thereafter, the two new ones shall be chosen and added to the younger two elders and deacons of the preceding year, so always as to preserve the number of four elders and four deacons of the said church. And moreover we do will and grant unto the said minister, elders and deacons of the Reformed Protestant Dutch Church, in the city of Albany, and to their successors for ever, that on the second Saturday of December next, and on every second Saturday of December annually forever hereafter at Albany, shall be elected and chosen four discreet persons by the majority of voices of the consistory aforesaid, to be kirkmasters of the said church, whose office and charge is and shall be to build and repair the same church and cemetery, parsonage, alms-house, and all other the hereditaments and appurtenances to the said church belonging, and to have the ordering and direction of the pews and seats in the said church, and the breaking of the ground in the cemetery for burying of the dead, and shall have and receive all the rents and revenues of the said church, coming therefrom or from any other of the said church's inheritances; also, the payments of all sum and sums of money laid out and expended, or to be laid out and expended, in such necessary buildings and reparations of all which the said kirkmasters are likewise to keep and surrender exact and true accounts to the said consistory aforesaid, two of which four kirkmasters last nominated, at the next election shall continue in the same office for two years and two new ones yearly for ever hereafter, to be elected and chosen to serve with the two predecessors in like manner as with the elders and deacons aforesaid and not otherwise. And it is our will and desire that the two elders, two deacons and two kirkmasters, who shall be superseded by a new annual election of two others to succeed in their respective places, shall account and deliver up their several respective charges and moneys to their successors respectively, if any thereof be in their hands and possession, respectively in public manner. And we do likewise will and grant that the said kirkmasters shall be under the direction of the said consistory for the time being. And in case there shall not be enough in the hands either of the elders, deacons or kirkmasters, for the performing and finishing of any of their respective charges and trust of their particular respective funds before mentioned, which they be hereby respectively impowered to receive and manage, that then it shall and may be lawful to and for the consistory aforesaid, to order and direct the lending of what sum shall be necessary out of any of the aforesaid funds towards deficiency of any other of the said funds, so that there be no failure of any of the same three several charges or trusts upon any unforseen contingency or emergency. And we do likewise will and grant that in all elections of officers or other acts or orders of the consistory the minister or president of the consistory shall have but one vote. And if it shall happen there be an equal division of the voices or votes, so that the matter, or thing in dispute cannot receive the determination of a majority of voices, that then it shall and may be lawful to determine the same by lot, leaving it to the sole wisdom of God to determine the same as he shall think fit. And we do likewise will and grant that it shall be in the power of the minister of the said church, for the time being, by himself or in case of his death, absence or removal, in the president or first elder who shall preside for the time being, or in the power of the major number of the whole consistory for the time being, to call a meeting of the consistory for the good and service of the said church, and the affairs of the said corporation, whensoever they shall see meet within the said city of Albany; and in case it shall please God that any of the said elders, deacons or kirkmasters, for the time being, shall happen to die, remove, or otherwise be disabled from serving and officiating in their respective offices, within the year for which they are so chosen or appointed to serve; we do will and grant that it shall and may be lawful to the consistory, for the time being, to assemble and meet together at Albany, at any other time of the year than the time of anniversary election, and so often as there shall be occasion to elect and choose other elders, deacons and kirkmasters in their respective rooms and stead, to officiate for the remaining part of the year until the next anniversary election; which person or persons so chosen as aforesaid into any of the aforesaid offices of elders, deacons or kirkmaster, shall have like power and authority to act in their respective offices as if they had been elected and confirmed at the aforesaid time of the anniversary election aforesaid, or as if the same persons so dying, being absent or otherwise disabled, were alive, present and capable to do the same; and we do will and grant unto the said minister, elders and deacons of the Reformed Protestant Dutch Church in the city of Albany, and to their successors for ever, the advowson and patronage of the said church; (that is to say) that after the decease of the aforesaid Petrus Van Driessen, or next and all other avoidances thereof, that it shall and may be lawful to and for the elders and deacons of the aforesaid church or the consistory of the aforesaid church and their successors for ever, to present and call another minister to succeed in the cure of souls in the aforesaid church and congregation of the Reformed Protestant Dutch Church in the city of Albany, provided always such minister, so called or presented by them to the said living, be always a person amenable to the laws of Great Britain and this Province, and pay due obedience and allegiance unto us and our royal heirs and successors, the kings and queens of Great Britain. And that it shall and may be lawful to and for the present minister or incumbent of the said church and his successors, or any of them to have, take, receive and keep for his end and their own use and support, that maintenance that now is or shall be agreed upon between him or them and the said consistory from time to time, and at all times hereafter. And it shall and may be lawful to and for the said elders of the same church, and their successors for ever, to collect and receive the voluntary subscriptions of the inhabitants of Albany, belonging to the said congregation, for and towards the payment of their said minister, or their minister for the time being, and to pay and cause to be paid unto the said minister and his successor, the minister of the said church, for the time being, his yearly stipend or salary, according to agreement, by quarterly even payments thereof, or otherwise, as it shall be agreed upon by and between them, the said minister of the said church and the aforesaid consistory. And we do will and grant that the said deacons of the said church, and their successors for ever, shall and may lawfully and peaceably, from time to time, and at all times hereafter, at the meeting of the said congregation for the public service and worship of Almighty God, to collect and receive the free and voluntary alms and oblations of the members of the said congregation, and the free and voluntary offerings made by the communicants at their receiving of the holy sacrament of the Lord's Supper for the uses aforesaid, and to dispose thereof for the pious and charitable uses aforesaid. And we do will and grant that the kirkmasters aforesaid, and their successors for ever, shall and may from time to time, and at all times hereafter, and so often as it shall be necessary, shall and may demise, grant, and to farm let, of the demesnes of the said church, demisable and grantable to and for the profit and advantage of the said church, and receive and collect the rents and revenues arising therefrom, or otherwise, and apply the same for and towards the buildings and reparations of the said church and parsonage, and other the hereditaments belonging to the said minister, elders and deacons of the Reformed Protestant Dutch Church in the city of Albany, and such other uses as are proper and necessary, provided always that the said elders, deacons and kirkmasters in their separate offices, be always accountable to and under the direction of the consistory of the said church for the time being, and not otherwise. And we do further will and grant that it shall and may be in the power of the consistory of the said church, and their successors for ever, if they shall agree thereupon, and find themselves able and capable of maintaining him at any time or times hereafter, to nominate and call one or more able and sufficient minister, lawfully ordained according to the constitution aforesaid, in all things to assist and officiate in the ministry which doth belong to the sacred office and function of a minister of the gospel in the said church, provided always that there be no preheminency or superiority in that office, and not otherwise. And we do likewise will and grant to the said minister, elders, and deacons of the Reformed Protestant Dutch Church in the city of Albany, and their successors for ever, that it shall and may be lawfull to and for the consistory of the said church, to nominate and appoint a clerk or precentor, schoolmaster, sexton, bellringer, and such and so many other officers and servants of the same church, as they shall think convenient and necessary, and to call them by the same or what other names they shall think fit. And we do will and grant that it shall and may be lawfull to and for the consistory of the said church, and their successors from time to time, and at all times hereafter, to make rules, orders, and ordinances for the better discipline and government of the said church, provided always that such rules, orders, and ordinances shall not be binding, nor effect any other of our reformed protestant subjects within the same city, than the voluntary members of their said congregation, and be no ways repugnant to our laws of Great Britain and of this colony, but agreeable to the articles of faith and worship agreed upon and instituted by the National Synod at Dort, aforesaid. And further of our especial grace, certain knowledge and meer motion, we have given, granted, ratified, and confirmed unto the aforesaid minister, elders, and deacons of the Reformed Protestant Dutch Church, in the city of Albany, and to their successors and assigns for ever, all that their said church and ground whereon it standeth, their said parsonage or minister's dwelling house, with its herditaments and appurtenances thereunto belonging or any ways appertaining, and all the alms house or poor house aforesaid, all that the pasture or pastures, and all other the premises aforesaid, together with all and singular edifices, buildings, gardens, orchards, backsides, wells, ways, hollows, cellars, passages, privileges, liberties, profits, advantages, hereditaments, and appurtenances whatsoever, to all and every of them belonging, or in any ways appertaining. And all that our estate, right, title, interest, properly and demand of, into or out of the same or any part of any of them, and the revertions, remainders, and the yearly rents and profits of the same, saving only the right and title of any other person or persons, body corporate and politick whatsoever, to any of the premises hereby granted, or meant, mentioned, and intended to be hereby granted, or to any of them, to have and to hold, all that their said church and ground parsonage or minister's dwelling house, alms house or poor house, pasture or pastures, and all and singular other the premises with their and every of their heridiatments and appurtenances unto the aforesaid minister, elders and deacons of the Reformed Protestant Dutch Church, in the city of Albany, their successors and assigns for ever, to the sole and only proper use, benefit and behoof of the aforesaid minister, elders and deacons of the Reformed Protestant Dutch Church, in the city of Albany, and their successors and assigns for ever, (save only as before is saved and expressed) to be holden of us, our heirs and successors for ever, free and common soccage as of our manor of East Greenwich, in the county of Kent, within our realm of Great Britain, yielding, rendering and paying therefore, yearly and every year, for ever unto us, our heirs and successors for ever, at our custom house in New York, unto our and their receiver general for the time being, on the feast day of the Annunciation of the Blessed Virgin Mary, commonly called Lady Day, the annual rent of one pepper corn, if the same be lawfully demanded, in lieu and stead of all other rents, services, dues and duties and demands whatsoever, for the same church parsonage, alms house, pastures, and all other the above granted premises, with the heriditaments and appurtenances. And we do hereby will and grant unto the aforesaid minister, elders, and deacons of the Reformed Protestant Dutch Church, in the city of Albany, and to their successors for ever, that these our letters shall be made patent, and that they and the record of them remaining in our secretary's office of our province of New York, shall be good and effectual in the law to all intents and purposes whatsoever, according to the true intent and meaning of them, and shall be construed, reputed, esteemed and adjudged in all cases most favorable for the benefit and behoof of the aforesaid minister, elders and deacons of the Reformed Protestant Dutch Church in the city of Albany and of their successors forever, notwithstanding the not true and well reciting of the premises, or of the limits and bounds of any of them, or any part of them, any law or other restraint, incertainty or imperfection whatsoever to the contrary thereof in any way notwithstanding. In testimony whereof we have caused the great seal of our province of New York to be affixed to these presents, and the same to be entered of record in one of the books of patents in our said secretary's office remaining. Witness our said trusty and well beloved Colonel Peter Schuyler, president of our council at Fort George, the 10th day of August, in the 7th year of our reign, anno domini 1720.

John Henry Lydius.—The council of the province in 1747, brought serious charges against John Henry Lydius, son of the dominie, alleging that he was a person of desperate fortunes; that he had resided several years in Canada, married a woman there of the Romish church, after having abjured the protestant religion, and that his intrigues, together with other popish emissaries, had tended to alienate the friendship of the Indians and perplex the administration.

Rev. Mr. Frelinghuysen.—A regiment came to town about this time, the superior officers of which were younger, more gay, and less amenable to good counsel than those who used to command the troops, which had formerly been placed on this station. They paid their visits at the Flats,* and were received; but not as usual, cordially; neither their manners nor morals being calculated for that meridian. Part of the Royal Americans, or independent companies, had at this time possession of the fort; some of these had families: and they were in general persons of decent morals, and a moderate and judicious way of thinking, who, though they did not court the society of the natives, expressed no contempt for their manners or opinions. The regiment I speak of, on the contrary turned those plain burghers into the highest ridicule, yet used every artifice to get acquainted with them. They wished in short to act the part of very fine gentlemen; and the gay and superficial in those days were but too apt to take for their model the fine gentleman of the detestable old comedies. These dangerously accomplished heroes made their appearance at a time when the English language began to be more generally understood; and when the pretensions of the merchants, commissaries, &c., to the stations they occupied were no longer dubious. Those polished strangers now began to make a part of general society. At this crisis it was that it was found necessary to have recourse to billets. The superior officers had generally been either received at the Flats, or accommodated in a large house which the colonel had in town. The manner in which the hospitality of that family was exercised, the selection which they made of such as were fitted to associate with the young persons who dwelt under their protection, always gave a kind of tone to society, and held out a light to others.

Madame Schuyler's sister was married to the respectable and intelligent magistrate,† who administered justice not only to the town, but to the whole neighborhood. In their house, also, such of the military were

---

* The residence of the Schuylers.

† Cornelius Cuyler, mayor of Albany, who had been a most successful Indian trader in his youth, and had acquired large possessions, and carried on an extensive commercial intercourse with the traders of that day, bringing from Europe quantities of those goods that best suited them, and sending back their peltry in exchange; he was not only wealthy, but hospitable, intelligent, and liberal minded, as appeared by his attachment to the army; which was, in those days, the distinguishing feature of those who in knowledge and candor were beyond others. [It will be seen by reference to the list of mayors of Albany, page 25, that the authoress has committed a mistake in the name of this person. Mrs. Grant returned to England in 1768, when but 13 years of age, and there was no mayor of the name during her residence in America.]

received and entertained, as had the sanction of her sister's approbation. This judicious and equitable person, who in the course of trading in early life upon the lakes, had undergone many of the hardships, and even dangers, which awaited the military in that perilous path of duty, knew well what they had to encounter in the defence of a surly and self-righted race, who were little inclined to show them common indulgence; far less gratitude. He judged equitably between both parties; and while with the most patriotic steadiness he resisted every attempt of the military to seize any thing with a high hand, he set the example himself, and used every art of persuasion to induce his countrymen to every concession that could conduce to the ease and comfort of their protectors. So far at length he succeeded, that when the regiment to which I allude arrived in town, and showed in general an amiable and obliging disposition, they were quartered in different houses; the superior officers being lodged willingly by the most respectable of the inhabitants, such as not having large families, had room to accommodate them. The Colonel and Madame happened, at the time of these arrangements, to be at New York.

In the meanwhile society began to assume a new aspect; of the satellites, which on various pretexts, official and commercial, had followed the army; several had families, and those began to mingle more frequently with the inhabitants, who were as yet too simple to detect the surreptitious tone of lax morals and second-handed manners, which prevailed among many of those who had but very lately climbed up to the stations they held, and in whose houses the European modes and diversions were to be met with; these were not in the best style, yet even in that style they began to be relished by some young persons, with whom the power of novelty prevailed over that of habit; and in a few rare instances, the influence of the young drew the old into a faint consent to these attempted innovations; but with many the resistance was not to be overcome.

In this state of matters, one guardian genius watched over the community with unremitting vigilance. From the original settlement of the place there had been a succession of good quiet clergymen, who came from Holland to take the command of this expatriated colony. These good men found an easy charge, among a people with whom the external duties of religion were settled habits, which no one thought of dispensing with; and where the primitive state of manners, and the constant occupation of the mind in planting and defending a territory where every thing was, as it were, to be new created, was a preservation to the morals. Religion being never branded with the reproach of imputed hypocrisy, or darkened by the frown of austere bigotry, was venerated even by those who were content to glide thoughtless down the stream of time, without seriously considering whither it was conveying them, till sorrow or sickness reminded them of the great purpose for which they were indulged with the privilege of existence.

The dominies, as these people called their ministers, contented themselves with preaching in a sober and moderate strain to the people; and living quietly in the retirement of their families, were little heard of but in the pulpit; and they seemed to consider a studious privacy as one of their chief duties. Dominie Frelinghuysen, however, was not contented with this quietude, which he seemed to consider as tending to languish into indifference. Ardent in his disposition, eloquent in his preaching, animated and zealous in his conversation, and frank and popular in his manners, he thought it his duty to awaken in every breast that slumbering spirit of devotion, which he considered as lulled by security, or drooping in the meridian of prosperity, like tender plants in the blaze of sunshine. These he endeavoured to refresh by daily exhortation, as well as by the exercise of his public duties. Though rigid in some of his notions, his life was spotless, and his concern for his people warm and affectionate; his endeavors to amend and inspire them with happier desires and aims, were considered as the labor of love, and rewarded by the warmest affection, and the most profound veneration; and what to him was of much more value, by a growing solicitude for the attainment of that higher order of excellence which it was his delight to point out to them. But while he thus incessantly "allured to brighter worlds, and led the way," he might perhaps insensibly have acquired a taste of dominion, which might make him unwilling to part with any portion of that most desirable species of power, which subjects to us, not human actions only, but the will which directs them.

The progress which this regiment made in the good graces of his flock, and the gradual assimilation to English manners of a very inferior standard, alarmed and grieved the good man not a little; and the intelligence he received from some of the elders of his church, who had the honor of lodging the more dissipated subalterns, did not administer much comfort to him. By this time the Anglomania was beginning to spread. A sect arose among the young people, who seemed resolved to assume a lighter style of dress and manners, and to borrow their taste in those respects from their new friends. This bade fair soon to undo all the good pastor's labors. The evil was daily growing; and what, alas, could Domine Frelinghuysen do but preach! This he did earnestly, and even angrily, but in vain. Many were exasperated but none reclaimed. The good dominie, however, had those who shared his sorrows and resentments; the elder and wiser heads of families, indeed a great majority of the primitive inhabitants, were stedfast against innovation. The colonel of the rigiment, who was a man of fashion and family, and possessed talents for both good and evil purposes, was young and gay: and being lodged in the house of a very wealthy citizen, who had before, in some degree, affected the newer modes of living, so captivated him with his good breeding and affability, that he was ready to humour any scheme of diversion which the colonel and his associates proposed. Under the auspices of this gallant commander, balls began to be concerted, and a degree of flutter and frivolity to take place, which was as far from elegance as it was from the honest, artless cheerfulness of the meetings usual among them. The good dominie more and more alarmed, not content with preaching, now began to prophesy: but like Cassandra, or to speak as justly, though less poetically, like his whole fraternity, was doomed always to deliver true predictions to those who never heeded them.

Now the very ultimatum of degeneracy, in the opinion of these simple good people, was approaching; for now the officers, encouraged by the success of all their former projects for amusement, resolved to new fashion and enlighten those amiable novices whom their former schemes had attracted within the sphere of their influence; and for this purpose, a private theatre was fitted up, and preparations made for acting a play; except the Schuylers and their adopted family, there was not perhaps one of the natives who understood what was meant by a play. And by this time, the town, once so closely united by intermarriages and numberless other ties, which could not exist in any other state of society, were divided into two factions; one consisting almost entirely of such of the younger class, as having a smattering of New York education, and a little more of dress and vivacity, or perhaps levity, than the rest, were eager to mingle in the society, and adopt the manner of those strangers. It is but just, however, to add, that only a few of the more estimable were included in this number; these, however, they might have been captivated with novelty and plausibility, were too much attached to their older relations to give them pain, by an intimacy with people to whom an impious neglect of duties the most sacred was generally imputed, and whose manner of treating their inferiors, at that distance from the control of higher powers, was often such as to justify the imputation of cruelty, which the severity of military punishments had given rise to. The play, however, was acted in a barn, and pretty well attended, notwithstanding the good dominie's earnest charges to the contrary. It was the Beaux Stratagem; no favorable specimen of the delicacy or morality of the British theatre; and as for the wit it contains, very little of that was level to the comprehension of the novices who were there first initiated into a knowledge of the magic of the scene, yet they "laughed consumedly," as Scrub says, and actually did so, "because they were talking of him." They laughed at Scrub's gestures and appearance, and they laughed very heartily at seeing the gay young ensigns, whom they had been used to dance with, flirting fans, displaying great hoops, and with painted cheeks and colored eye-brows, sailing about in female habiliments. This was a jest palpable and level to every understanding; and it was not only an excellent good one, but lasted a long while; for every time they looked at them when restored to their own habits, they laughed anew at the recollection of their late masquerade.

The fame of these exhibitions went abroad, and opinions were formed of them no way favorable to the actors or to the audience. In this region of reality, where rigid truth was always undisguised, they had not learned to distinguish between fiction and falsehood. It was said that the officers familiar with every vice and every disguise, had not only spent a whole night in telling lies in a counterfeited place, the reality of which had never existed, but that they were themselves a lie, and had degraded manhood, and broke through an express prohibition in scripture, by assuming female habits; that they had not only told lies, but cursed and swore the whole night, and assumed the character of knaves, fools, and robbers, which every good and wise man held in detestation, and no one would put on unless they felt themselves easy in them. Painting their faces, of all other things, seemed most to violate the Albanian ideas of decorum, and was looked upon as the most flagrant abomination. Great and loud was the outcry produced by it. Little skilled in sophistry, and strangers to all the arts "that make the worse appear the better reason," the young auditors could only say "that indeed it was very amusing; made them laugh heartily, and did harm to nobody." So harmless, indeed, and agreeable did this entertainment appear to the new converts of fashion, that the Recruiting Officer was given out for another night, to the great annoyance of Mr. Frelinghuysen, who invoked heaven and earth to witness and avenge this contempt, not only of his authority, but, as he expressed it, of the source from whence it was derived. Such had been the sanctity of this good man's life, and the laborious diligence and awful earnestness with which he inculcated the doctrines he taught, that they had produced a correspondent effect, for the most part, on the lives of his hearers, and led them to regard him as the next thing to an evangelist; accustomed to success in all his undertakings, and to "honor, love, obedience, troops of friends," and all that gratitude and veneration can offer to its most distinguished object, this rebellion against his authority and contempt of his opinion, (once the standard by which every one's judgment was regulated), wounded him very deeply. The abhorrence with which he inspired the parents of the transgressors, among whom were many young men of spirit and intelligence, was the occasion of some family disagreements, a thing formerly scarcely known. Those young people, accustomed to regard their parents with implicit reverence, were unwilling to impute to them unqualified harshness, and therefore removed the blame of a conduct so unusual to their spiritual guide; "and while he thought, good easy man, full surely his greatness was a ripening, nipt his root." Early one Monday morning, after the dominie had, on the preceding day, been peculiarly eloquent on the subject of theatrical amusements, and pernicious innovations, some unknown person left within his door a club, a pair of old shoes, a crust of black bread, and a dollar. The worthy pastor was puzzled to think what this could mean; but had it too soon explained to him. It was an emblematic message, to signify the desire entertained of his departure. The stick was to push him away, the shoes to wear on the road, and the bread and money a provision for his journey. Too conscious, and too fond of popularity, the pastor languished under a sense of imaginary degradation, grew jealous, and thought every one alienated from him, because a few giddy young people were stimulated by momentary resentments to express disapprobation in this vague and dubious manner. Thus, insensibly, do vanity and self-opinion mingle with our highest duties. Had the dominie, satisfied with the testimony of a good conscience, gone on in the exercise of his duty, and been above allowing little personal resentments to mingle with his zeal for what he thought right, he might have felt himself far above an insult of this kind; but he found to his cost, that "a habitation giddy and unsure hath he that buildeth on the fickle heart" of the unsteady, wavering multitude.

Madame now returned to town with the Colonel; and finding this general disorder and division of sentiments with regard to the pastor, as well as to the adoption of new modes, endeavored, with her usual good sense, to moderate and heal. She was always of opinion that the increase of wealth should be accompanied with a proportionate progress in refinement and intelligence; but she had a particular dislike to people's forsaking a respectable plainness of dress and manners for mere imperfect imitation and inelegant finery. Liberal and judicious in her views, she did not altogether approve the austerity of the dominie's opinions, nor the vehemence of his language; and as a Christian, she still less approved his dejection and concern at the neglect or rudeness of a few thoughtless young persons. In vain the Colonel and Madame soothed and cheered him with counsel and kindness; night and day he mused on the imagined insult; nor could the joint efforts of the most respectable inhabitants prevent his heart from being corroded with the sense of imagined unkindness. At length he took the resolution of leaving those people so dear to him, to visit his friends in Holland, promising to return in a short time, whenever his health was restored, and his spirits more composed. A Dutch ship happened about this time to touch at New York, on board of which the dominie embarked; but as the vessel belonging to Holland was not expected to return, and he did not, as he had promised, either write or return in an English ship, his congregation remained for a great while unsupplied, while his silence gave room for the most anxious and painful conjectures; these were not soon removed, for the intercourse with Holland was not frequent or direct. At length, however, the sad reality was but too well ascertained. This victim of lost popularity had appeared silent and melancholy to his shipmates, and walked constantly on deck. At length he suddenly disappeared, leaving it doubtful whether he had fallen overboard by accident, or was prompted by despair to plunge into eternity. If this latter was the case, it must have been the consequence of a temporary fit of insanity; for no man had led a more spotless life, and no man was more beloved by all that were intimately known to him. He was, indeed, before the fatal affront, which made such an undue impression on him, considered as a blessing to the place; and his memory was so beloved, and his fate so regretted, that this, in addition to some other occurrences falling out about the same time, entirely turned the tide of opinion, and rendered the thinking as well as the violent party, more averse to innovations than ever. Had the Albanians been Catholics, they would probably have canonized Mr. Frelinghuysen, whom they considered as a martyr to levity and innovation. He prophesied a great deal; such prophecy as ardent and comprehensive minds have delivered, without any other inspiration but that of the sound, strong intellect, which augurs the future from a comparison with the past, and a rational deduction of probable consequences. The affection that was entertained for his memory, induced people to listen to the most romantic stories of his being landed on an island, and become a hermit; taken up into a ship when floating on the sea, into which he had accidentally fallen, and carried to some remote country, from which he was expected to return, fraught with experience and faith. I remember some of my earliest reveries to have been occupied by the mysterious disappearance of this hard-fated pastor.—*Mrs. Grant's American Lady*, p. 170, et seq.

A rumor, not well authenticated, was common among the people, that he embarked, on his return, in the same vessel with the person appointed to supersede him, and when made acquainted with the fact, very soon disappeared, and was supposed to have thrown himself into the sea.

Rev. Eilardus Westerlo.—This divine was born in the province of Groeningen, Holland, in 1738, and received a thorough university education. It was still a custom with the American churches to send to Holland for ministers to supply their pulpits; and in answer to the requisition of the church at Albany for a pastor, Mr. Westerlo, who was then at the University of Groeningen, was induced to accept the call.

He arrived here in 1760, and entered upon the pastoral charge in October of that year, having been previously installed in Holland. He proved to be a man of great powers of mind, extensive erudition, and became one of the most eminent ministers of the Dutch church in America. He possessed caution and prudence, and great dignity of manners, yet was affable and courteous to all. His pastoral duties were discharged with exemplary fidelity over a field unusually extensive. He took a conspicuous part in severing the church from its dependence upon the mother country, and its reorganization upon the present plan. During the war of the American revolution, he took strong grounds in the cause of the people, and at a most critical time, when Burgoyne was advancing on the city from the north, he animated and inspired the people by having his church open every day for the purpose of prayer and address. He died on the 26th of December, 1790, at a time of life when age had scarcely begun to impair his frame, and was buried in the family vault of Stephen Van Rensselaer, his funeral obsequies being attended by a large concourse from the city and neighborhood. Amid the arduous cares of his ministry, he found time to prepare a Hebrew and a Greek Lexicon, in 2 vols., folio, which remain in manuscript, in the possession of his son, Rensselaer Westerlo, Esq.

Dominie Bassett.—In 1793 Benjamin Lincoln, Timothy Pickering and Beverly Randolph passed through Albany on their mission of peace to the Indians at Niagara. They were accompanied by delegates from the society of Friends, among whom was William Savery, an eminent minister, under whose faithful preaching while in England, Elizabeth Fry was transformed from a gay girl into a steadfast Christian, and a philanthropist of world-wide renown. The commissoners were received with great civility here; Dominie Bassett waited upon them, and introducing himself promised to offer up prayers for the success of their pious design, and added that a thousand or more people would unite with him in his supplications. He seemed to the good Quakers to be a good-natured, tender-spirited man.

Ancient Customs.—The pyramidal roof and belfry of the old church are familiar to the present generation, from the print of it; but where is the remembrancer of its customs? The men sat with hats and muffs during divine service, and in the midst of the dominie's sermon, uprose the deacons and presented to each hearer a small black bag, containing a little bell, borne on the end of a staff, somewhat resembling a shrimp net. In this way the contributions were collected. The tinkle of the bell roused the sleepy and diverted for the moment the busy thoughts of the traders from muskrat and beaver skins. The bags, with their load of coppers and half joes being duly replaced, the dominie resumed the broken thread of his discourse. The Indians are said to have dreaded the coming of a Sunday before they had closed the sale of their peltry, for to their apprehension it seemed that the man in black spoke sharply to the people about the bargains they had been driving, and that the drift of the sermon might be guessed at by the lower prices offered for their skins on Monday. The practice of taking collections for the poor during the sermon was discontinued in 1795.

Antiquities of the Old Stone Church.—In demolishing the old church, care was taken to preserve only a small portion of the armorial bearings

Reformed Protestant Dutch Church.

on the stained glass windows. The late Killian Van Rensselaer, writing to Charles R. Webster, from Washington, in March, 1806, says: "I had no idea the old church would have been so soon demolished. I would have given a great deal to have been in Albany when the windows were attacked, for I would certainly have given $100 for the old family coat of arms. I had directions from Mr. Oliver Wendell in Boston, to obtain the glass containing his family arms at any price, and in case of his death to deposit it in the Cambridge Museum. Pray make some inquiries about the remnant saved, and if possible save it for me, as well as the Van Rensselaer arms. You will find the name at the foot of the glass on which the heraldry appears." One of the old church windows is preserved, a small one, in a shattered condition; also the pulpit and the weathercock, and a bag and pole, with which it was customary to take the contributions, which was done in this wise. The minister paused in the midst of his sermon, when the deacons arose, and taking up these implements, brought them to a perpendicular position against their shoulders. An address was then pronounced from the pulpit upon the collection about to be taken in aid of the poor members of the church, and the ceremony was then accompanied by the singing of the choir. This was designed to give solemnity to the rite. The form of the receptacle concealed the amount of the gift, so that the munificent were not invited by ostentation, nor the needy to deposit their scanty pittance with diffidence. The collection so taken, however, was not unfrequently plentifully mixed with a variety of coin unrecognized by the statute, consisting of any substance that fell into the bag with a chinking sound. The deacons, to rid themselves of this class of contributors, procured a number of shining, open plates, for the purpose; but their chagrin may be imagined, when, on presenting themselves thus equipped before the audience, they found some of the honest burghers expressing their indignation at the innovation, by turning their backs upon them. A little war, wordy but bloodless, ensued; the plates, however, carried the day, and still maintain their place; and the gleanings eleemosynary are sel-

dom mingled with base coin..... The stone step which was placed at the entrance to the porch on the south side, still retains its original position in the street, and points out the precise spot of the vestibule to the ancient sanctuary, and is the identical stone which was impressed by the footsteps of several generations, in passing to their devotions. It may be discerned when the streets are in a tolerable state of cleanliness, on the left of the cross-walk that leads from Douw's Building to the Exchange..... When the church in State street was about to be removed, the trustees of the church at the Boght, where Mr. Bassett then officiated, applied for the old pulpit; but it having been resolved to preserve that relic in the church, they next applied for the pew doors and hinges, which were granted to them..... In July, 1802, Mr. William Groesbeeck, who had been clerk of the church for a great number of years, died, and the desk he had occupied was hung in mourning. He was succeeded by his sons, Cornelius and David, who were the last of the *voorzingers*.

Burial Customs and Ceremonies.—The burial ground for a great number of years was the present site of the Middle Dutch Church, where the bodies are said to have been found lying in some places three or four tiers deep. The dead were removed from under the church in State street to this ground, after it had been selected for a place of burial. When the church was built, the grave stones were laid down upon the graves, and covered over to the depth of three feet, and we are told that it was customary, when the ground was wholly occupied, to add a layer of earth upon the surface, and commence burying over the top of the last tier of coffins. There is now in the possession of Mr. Harmanus Bleecker, a book of burials in this church yard, embracing about 35 years. When the basement of the house occupied by Mr. E. H. Pease was excavated, the boxes were discovered in which the bodies of the revolutionary soldiers, killed or deceased during that war, were buried. These relics have been frequently disturbed by the improvements constantly going on. After the lot was abandoned as a place of burial, the new church yard was located south of the Capitol Park in the vicinity of State street. The graves were many feet above the surface of the lots, as they now are, vast excavations having been made in that part of the city.....The Indian commissioners previously spoken of, are said to have witnessed a burial, and been surprised at the ways of the people. No women attended the body to the grave, as they had been accustomed to see; but after the corpse was borne out, they remained to eat cakes, and drink spiced wine. They retired quietly before the men returned, who resumed the feast and regaled themselves. Spiced wine, and cakes, and pipes were provided, and wine was sent to the friends of the family. The best room in the house was specially appropriated as "the dead room," and was rarely opened but to be aired and cleaned.

Sale of the Pasture.—In 1791 the consistory directed "the ground commonly distinguished as the church pasture," to be laid out into lots. They lay on the "west side of Court street, leading from the ferry to the town." At this time a gate swung across the way a little above Lydius street, and a common road from thence to the ferry lay along the bank of the river through *the pasture*. Although the names of some of the streets in that region have been changed within a few years, several of them still bear the names of the ministers. The area which they intersect was once the property of the church, and when sold produced less than a hundred dollars a lot. These have since been filled in to a considerable extent and rendered valuable. There were comparatively but few lots built upon south of Lydius street, between Pearl and Broadway, so late as twenty years ago, though now teeming with a dense population.

The parsonage, or as it is termed in the charter, the minister's house, which belonged to the congregation, and was occupied by Mr. Westerlo during the last six years of his life, was the building more recently known as the Bleecker House, and was taken down three or four years since, to make room for Bleecker Hall. The first preaching in English was by Mr. Livingston, about 1776; in 1782 Mr. Westerlo began to preach in English, and Mr. Bassett, his colleague, was the first settled English pastor.

EVANGELICAL LUTHERAN EBENEZER CHURCH.

The edifice occupied by this congregation as a place of worship, is pleasantly located on the corner of Pine and Lodge streets. It is constructed of stone, and is said to be a very creditable specimen of architecture, though of rather moderate size. The corner stone was laid on Thursday, Sept. 16, 1816, by the Rev. Mr. Mayer, the pastor, assisted by Philip Hooker, the architect. Its dimensions are 40 by 60 feet, and the expense of its erection was about $25,000. In 1848 it was repaired, and its interior thoroughly renovated, at an expense of upwards of $4,000.

We have not been able to ascertain the precise date of the first establishment of a Lutheran church in Albany. The early immigrants, coming from Holland, were principally Calvinists, with strong predilections for the principles propounded by the Synod of Dort, and embodied under the name of the Reformed Protestant Dutch Church; yet, although the predominating sect, they seem to have found many difficulties in the way of supporting their church, which was often without a pastor. Before 1630, however, the Lutherans had a church here, in spite of the opposition they met with; for they seem to have been the first sect which the dominant party thought necessary to restrain in their mode of worship.* Application had been made at an early date, to the directors in Holland, to allow professors of this creed liberty to elect a pastor, and perform the free exercise of their religion in New Netherland. But these privileges were refused, and orders were sent over " to employ all moderate exertions to lure them to our churches, and to matriculate them in the public reformed religion."† Moderation is of little avail, where conscience interposes scruples. Fathers were compelled, contrary to their principles, to assist at the baptism of their children in the Dutch church, and as well as the sponsors, to declare their belief in the doctrines promulgated by the Synod of Dort. Many who objected to this were imprisoned. In a letter dated March 10, 1656.‡ De Decker alludes to a certain placard drawn up and published by the authorities at Beverwyck, "against the congregation of some Lutherans, which has also been executed against the contraveners and disobedient." The Lutherans also sent over complaints, which led to the censure of Stuyvesant, and the aggrieved were permitted to worship *in their own houses.* This, however, was not enough; they demanded freedom from interrup-

---

* O'Callaghan's History of New Netherland, p. 319-20, vol. 2.
† Albany Records, IV., 130.   ‡ Fort Orange Records.

tion in their worship. The director general avowed his determination to enforce the law against schismatical worship. The Lutherans appealed to him, Oct. 24th, 1656, as follows: "We, the united brethren of the Augsburg Confession here in New Netherland, show with all due reverence how that we have been obedient unto your honor's prohibitions and published placards, unwilling to collect together in any place to worship our God with reading and singing, although we solicited our friends in our fatherland to obtain this privilege; who as our solicitors exerted themselves in our behalf by the noble directors of the West India Company, our patrons; when after their letters to us, containing their entreaties, they obtained that they resolved unanimously and concluded that the doctrine of the unaltered Augsburg Confession might be tolerated in the West Indies and New Netherland, being under their direction, as is the practice in our fatherland under its excellent government; wherefore we address ourselves to your honor, willing to acknowledge your honor, as dutiful and obedient servants, with prayer that you will not any longer interrupt our religious exercises, which we, under God's blessing, are wishing to make, with reading and singing, till as we hope and expect, under God's aid, next spring, a qualified person shall arrive from our fatherland to instruct us, and take care of our souls." Accordingly, in July of the following year, the Rev. Johannes Ernestus Goetwater, a Lutheran minister, arrived with a commission from the consistory at Amsterdam, authorizing him to act as pastor to the Lutheran congregation at the Manhattans. The Dutch ministers, Megapolensis and Drisius, took active measures to procure his instant expulsion, demanding that he should be sent back to Holland in the same ship in which he arrived. Sickness alone prevented the immediate execution of the harsh and unchristian mandate, and he was put *on the limits* of the city for the time being, and finally forced to embark for Holland.* The department at Amsterdam, although desirous of soothing the feelings of the Lutherans, could do little to relieve their grievances, and in the hope of winning them over, ordered some alterations to be made in the formula of baptism, as then practiced in the American orthodox church, to make it less objectionable.

The British dynasty brought with it full permission to the Lutherans to follow their mode of worship. On the 13th of October, 1669, Gov. Lovelace publicly announced that he had "lately received letters from the duke, wherein it is particularly signified unto me, that his royal highness doth approve of the toleration given to the Lutheran church in these parts. I do therefore expect that you live friendly and peaceably with those of that profession, giving them no disturbance in the exercise of their religion, as they shall receive no countenance in, but on the contrary strictly answer any disturbance they shall presume to give unto any of you in your divine worship." It is supposed to have been about this time that the Lutherans erected a church and parsonage in Albany, where the Centre Market now stands. Capt. Abram Staets (or Staas †) obtained a patent of that lot on the 25th of October, 1653, which he sold to the officers of the Lutheran congregation on the 28th of March, 1680. The original deed, having the above date, which we have examined

* O'Callaghan's History of New Netherland, ii., 345, 346.

† He arrived 1642, in the same ship with Dom. Megapolensis, and is believed to be the ancestor of those who take the name of Staats.

with a great deal of interest, is in good ancient Dutch, and was made by Robert Livingston, "Secretary van Albany, Colonie Rensselaerswyck ende Schaenheehtady." It recites that Major Abram Staas, in the presence of Andries Teller and Cornelis Van Dyck, commissaries, conveyed the premises to Albert Bratt, Myndert Frederikse (*A*), Anthony Lispenard and Carsten Frederikse, elders and deacons of the Lutheran congregation. The lot was described as being bounded on the east by the public highway, 12 rods 11 feet; on the south by the first kill and the common road, 21 rods 1 foot; on the west by the little kill, (*cleyn killitie*,) 6 rods 4 feet; and on the north by the old road, belonging to Mr. Pretty, Jacob Sanders, Johannes Wendell, Myndert Harmense, and Hendrick Cuyler, 23 rods 5 feet. Ryland* measure. It also states that the lot was already occupied by a Lutheran church, and a house in which the dominie lived. The consideration money is not stated, but it is distinctly set forth that the *first and last penny were paid*, which certainly puts a very creditable finish to the aspect of the transaction.

It will be seen by reference to the ancient map of the city, on another page, bearing date 1695, that the same spot is marked by a Lutheran church and burying ground, fronting on South Pearl street, and extending from Howard to Beaver street; or rather to the palisades, which formed the southern boundary of the city at that point.

We have not been able to learn anything further of the history of this church, during the lapse of nearly a century; in the meantime a German Reformed congregation seems to have erected a house of worship on Arbor Hill (*C*). Although the Lutherans still had possession of their lot in Pearl street, yet it is recollected by some of the elder citizens, that about the close of the revolution they had no church, but held their meetings for worship in a private house on the corner of Howard and Pearl street, a front room in which was fitted up with seats sufficient to accommodate the few members belonging to the congregation at that time. We believe there are no records extant to account for these things, or giving any information as to the origin or organization of the church. It is found, however, to have been regularly incorporated August 26, 1784, and on the 7th of September following, Rev. Henry Moeller was called. The trustees were J. P. Hildebrand, Charles Newman and Christian Ehring. The condition of the church at this time may be gathered from a letter written by Mr. Moeller in 1818, in which he says: "I wish, brethren, you would call to remembrance the condition of your congregation in 1784 and 1785, when you had no church, and I was your pastor. I traveled in company with an elder, the now deceased Mr. Ehring, to New York, Philadelphia, Schenectady, and adjacent country, and collected, together with the generous donations of the citizens of Albany, and with what the cheerfulness of the poor congregation could afford, the sum of £640, which was esteemed a large collection of money at that time. The honest Mr. John Geyer, now deceased, was treasurer, and the building was paid for soon after it was finished. The congregation had engaged to pay me £100 salary, leaving to me one-third of the time free to attend the Low Dutch congregation at Loonenburgh. But finding that the congregation proved unable to pay me more than £50, besides furnishing me with fire-wood, I remitted

---

* This is the orthography in most of the ancient records. A Rynland or Leyden foot is equal to 12 3-8 inches English measure, and a Dutch or Amsterdam foot, about one inch less than the Rynland.

the rest, and employed myself in vacant congregations, some of them laid in perfect wilderness, till I found my arduous task would waste my strength before the ordinary time of age, I took a call to Pennsylvania. After twelve years you did me the honor to present me a second call. I found the charge easier than before, but my travels to Hellerberg and Beaverdam, which congregations were necessary to make up a necessary living, proved injurious to my health, to which was added the heavy expense of keeping a horse and chaise, and the increase of prices for fire-wood and other necessaries. I left you the second time, and am now comfortably settled for the short rest of my life."

The records of the church to which we have had access, extend no farther back than the 28th of May, 1786, when the communion was administered. The congregation then appears to have had no settled pastor. In the following year the trustees publicly expressed their acknowledgements for the receipt of donations, to the amount of £552 12s. 2d.; more than £214 of which, they say, was obtained in Albany and its vicinity. The total cost of their building was £640 ($1600). About ten years later a complaint was made of hindrances, and that their church was still unfinished.

From the time Mr. Moeller left, in 1785, to 1794, the church was supplied with the word and ordinances by neighboring ministers. Among these were the Rev. Messrs. Schwertfeger, Groetz, and Johann Frederick Ernst, pastor of Loonenburgh (Athens) and Claverack. In June, 1794, Rev. Anthon Theodore Braun became their pastor, and remained till 1800. In 1801 the Rev. Heinrich Moeller again took charge of the congregation, and remained till 1806. In 1807 the Rev. Frederich George Mayer was settled as pastor, and remained until he was removed by death in December, 1843. In July of that year, the Rev. Henry Newman Pohlman, the present efficient pastor, accepted a call from the congregation, and was installed on the 24th of September. Under his ministry the church is gradually increasing in numbers, and there are at present about one hundred members in communion. The services of the church were in German until 1808, when at a meeting of the trustees, elders and deacons, held May 16th at the house of Martin Hebeysen, it was resolved that the sermons, after Whitsunday, should be delivered in English, except one sermon in the forenoon of the last Sunday in each month.

At the close of the last century, an effort was made to procure the location of a Lutheran seminary in Albany. The Rev. John Christopher Hartwick died in 1796, possessed of a large estate, which he left by will for the endowment of an institution for training up young ministers of the gospel, and misionaries to be sent among the Indians, according to the Augustan Confession and the tenets of the Evangelical Lutheran church. The executors named in his will were Jeremiah Van Rensselaer of Albany, and Frederick A. Muhlenberg of Philadelphia, formerly a Lutheran minister of New York, but at this time speaker of the house of representatives in congress. His scheme contemplated the erection of a town on his tract in Otsego county, to be called New Jerusalem, where the theological school should be established, in which "no heathenish author should be read, until when, by divine providence, the revenues should increase, classical learning might be added." The administrators, on looking into the affairs of the testator, found that a large part of the landed estate, about 13,000 acres, including the intended site of the New Jerusalem, was claimed by Judge Cooper, who professed to have purchased it of Mr. Hartwick at $2 per acre, payable at a distant time. Mr. Hartwick had desired to be buried in the Lutheran church of Albany, and his wishes were complied with. A marble tablet bearing his inscription (B) is placed in the floor of the church, in front of the pulpit. It being uncertain that much of anything remained to found the contemplated school, the trustees of the church at Albany desired to have the institution connected with their church, promising to raise $3,000 towards the erection of a suitable building. In fact, they claimed the estate, and deprecated the idea of erecting a college in the wilderness, as a "monument like the pillar of Absalom." They say that the Oneida Indians were provided with a Presbyterian minister forty years before, that "other nations have the same, and now the Indians have sold all their land, which will be inhabited by Christians, so that the whim of a college and a New Jerusalem, may fall away, and it may be better to support with it the congregation of Albany, which, from the time of Gov. Van Tromp, has always been oppressed. We, Lutherans of Albany, are the next heirs of Mr. Hartwick. . . . His own writings will show with what affection we took care of him." At another time, writing to the curators of the estate, the trustees, who at this time were J. Conrad Ruby, Martin Hebeysen and Daniel Pohlman, still complain of the neglect shown to their interests by those having charge of the legacy—"mournfully observing that our poor Ebenezer is entirely forgotten, notwithstanding we appointed in our stead two worthy friends and gentlemen, the most Rev. Dr. Kunze and Mr. Jeremiah Van Rensselaer, our advocates for our distressed Ebenezer. Yet in their twelve resolves, nothing appeared for such a poor flock of Lutheran Christians to support their pious business. We collect about £18 per annum from the members of our church, and no more. Our church is not finished and more like to decay. But we are forgotten, though we know that Hartwick loved us, for he would be with us, even when dead. It is now in your power to support that poor church out of an estate freely granted by the owner." The solicitations of the trustees seem to have been crowned with partial success; for on the 17th of October, 1801, articles of agreement, drawn by Peter E. Elmendorf, were entered into between them and the trustees of the estate, by which all the estate was to be deposited with the trustees of the church, within two years, for the purposes of the seminary, subject to the order of the curators, John C. Kunze and Jeremiah Van Rensselaer. The foundation of an edifice was laid in Park street; but the arrangement seems to have given so much dissatisfaction among the Lutheran churches, as to lead to its abandonment. Accordingly at a meeting of the trustees on the 14th April, 1808, they resolved that since it was found impossible to execute the trust committed to them, they would redeliver the property into the hands of the surviving executor, Jeremiah Van Rensselaer; and two years after the materials used for the foundation were ordered to be sold. The seminary was finally located at Hartwick, in Otsego county, and is now in successful operation, under a special charter, obtained of the legislature in 1816.—(See Session Laws, c. 166.)

In 1816, the city corporation purchased the lot on South Pearl street, which had been in possession of the congregation almost a century and a half, and paid for it $32,000. The boundaries were a little differently described at this day, as follows: "on the east by South Pearl, late

Washington street; on the south by the Rutten kill; on the west by a small run of water called Fort Killitie; and on the north by Howard, late Lutheran street." There was at the time a small market on Howard street, above the church, called Fly market. The common council presented to the congregation the lot which they now occupy on Pine street, on condition of the removal of their dead from the old burying ground on Pearl street. The expense of excavating the lot was $5,000. They have since built a consistory and parsonage on the premises, the former having been consecrated on the 10th of July, 1836; the state having previously, 1832, purchased the westerly and unoccupied part of their lot, for $45,000, upon which the State Hall was erected. With this money the trustees excavated and built upon the property fronting on State, Park and Lancaster streets, which was occupied by them as a cemetery until the common council granted them their present cemetery lot by deed dated Nov. 1, 1803. These old cemetry grounds have been excavated to a great depth to make proper grades for streets and building lots—the cemetries of all the churches having been removed from thence to their present location west of Knox street, on the south side of State, at about the same time.

(*A*) Att a Court of Mayor and Aldermen held for yᵉ Citty of Albany, yᵉ 17th day of August, 1686. Present Peter Schuyler, Jan Jans Bleeker, Johannes Wandel, Dirck Wessells, Adrian Gerritse, Levinus Van Schaik. Hercules, yᵉ negro of Myndert Frederikse being brought before yᵉ Court by warrant of yᵉ Mayʳ to answer yᵉ fellonious taking out of his master's house a small chest wherein some bags of wampum was contained, belonging to yᵉ Poor of yᵉ Lutheran Church, and being examined doth confess yᵉ fact yᵗ upon Thursday night last he came to his master's house, and finding yᵉ window of yᵉ chamber open, went in and stole away yᵉ small chest wherein yᵉ money of yᵉ poor of yᵉ Lutheran Church was kept, and broke yᵉ chest open without yᵉ gate, at yᵉ water side with an axe *Ordered*, yᵗ yᵉ sᵈ Negroe be committed and secured in yᵉ Common Goale till yᵉ next Court of Sessions, when he is to be brought to his tryall.—*Albany Records, iii.*, 4.

(*B*) The following is the inscription on the tomb stone alluded to:

Hier ruhet
Johann C. Hartwick
Prediger der Evangelisch
Lutherischen Kirche
Gebohren in Sax-Gotha
den 6 Januer 1714
Gestorben
den 16 Julius 1796
Seines alters
82 Jahre 6 Monat

Das kurzoesteckte ziel der tage,
  Ist siebenzig, ist aghtzig jahr,
Ein unnbegrif von mueh und plage,
  Auch wennsnoch so kostlich war,
Geflügelt eilt mit uns die zeit,
In eine lange ewigkeit.

(C) The followers of Zwinglius, who differed from the Lutherans in some matters relating to the sacrament,* took the name of German Reformed. In the *Albany Gazette*, printed by the Robertsons in 1772, was published an advertisement of a lottery to be drawn in March of that year, for the benefit of the German Reformed Church, which is the first we hear of them in this place. Lotteries were not an unusual means of raising money even for churches at that day. The spot pointed out as the location of this edifice, is between Orange and Patroon streets, west of Ten Broeck street, where its foundation had an altitude considerably above the present grade of the latter street, overlooking a deep ravine on the south. The object to be attained by the selection of so retired a location, is somewhat difficult to conceive, unless it was to set it " upon a hill that it should not be hid," for it was far out of town at that day. An idea of its remoteness may be had from the circumstance of some one having opened a tavern so far from any landmark, that he described it as "situated on the pleasant road to the German church." A cross-road ran diagonally up the hill from what is now Orange street to Patroon street, both of which were then common roads, and the church stood a little west of the cross-road, with a burying ground in front. It was a wooden edifice, about fifty feet square, with a tower at the north entrance, furnished with a bell. It was provided with an organ, the first one known to have been used in a church in Albany. The only notice we can find respecting it in the public archives, is an act passed March 27, 1794, " for the relief of Paul Hochstrasser and others," as follows: "Whereas it hath been represented that Paul Hochstrasser, John Abbet and John Tillman, having expended large sums of money in erecting a building for the Reformed German congregation in the city of Albany with sundry appurtenances, which sums were never reimbursed by the said congregation through the means of their inability. And whereas also it has been further represented, that the said congregation is dispersed, and the building become useless: Be it enacted by the people of the state of New York represented in Senate and Assembly, That Abraham Hun, Teunis Ts. Van Vechten and John C. Cuyler, be, and hereby are appointed trustees, for the purpose of selling the aforesaid building, with the appurtenances, exclusive of the right of soil; and out of the moneys therefrom arising, to settle with all such persons who may have any demands against the same; and should the moneys therefrom arising not be competent to satisfy the said claims, they shall be and hereby are authorized to pay each claimant a just proportion of the moneys arising from the said premises, according to his, her, or their respective demands." The church appears to have been sold accordingly, and afterwards occupied by the Seceders. It was subsequently taken down, and the frame work is still standing near Lydius street, about two miles out. On the 14th of April, 1803, Paul Hochstrasser and John Ram applied to the consistory of the Reformed Protestant Dutch Church for permission to bury their deceased relatives in the ground belonging to that church, alleging that the grave yard of the German Reformed Church had become almost a public common; that the former wished to take up the remains of his mother, and the latter those of his children, and deposit them elsewhere. When

* Serious disturbances have recently arisen in Prussia, in consequence of an edict of the king, directing the union of these two churches in one.

the pier was built, the lot upon which this church stood was excavated, and the earth used to fill in that work. The bones of the dead buried there were placed in boxes, and left by the road side in a ravine, till some one having occasion to use the boxes, the bones were turned out upon the ground, and afterwards plowed under. It is believed that there is one member of this church still living, who now attends the Lutheran church.

GERMAN EVANGELICAL LUTHERAN CHURCH.

The building occupied by this congregation is situated in State street, above Swan. It was originally built for the use of a Methodist congregation, and purchased of them in 1842, for eighteen hundred dollars.

It will have been seen in our account of the Lutheran Ebenezer Church, that the use of the German language in the services of the sanctuary, virtually ceased in 1808. But the large number of immigrants from Germany rendered it necessary for the pastor of that church to resume its use in 1834. Accordingly from that time a service in that language was held in the evening of the Lord's day, and occasionally during the week. After the erection of the Lecture Room of the Ebenezer Church, on the corner of Lodge and Steuben streets, in 1836, the Germans were regularly supplied with the word and ordinances in their mother tongue, by the Rev. William Moellman, from Hanover, in Germany. And when he accepted a call from Cincinnati, and removed to that city, the services were continued with more or less regularity by the Rev. F. G. Mayer, the pastor of Ebenezer.

In 1841, in consequence of the rapid increase of the German population, and the inconvenience of holding service in two languages, it was deemed expedient to organize a separate congregation, which was done on the 8th of August in that year. Early in 1842, by the effective aid of the mother church, and the kind liberality of the citizens of Albany, they succeeded in purchasing the church above mentioned, which was set apart for the worship of God in the German language, with appropriate solemnities, on the 10th of May. The first pastor of this church was the Rev. George Saul, who remained with them a year and seven months, and then removed to Canajoharie. He was succeeded by the Rev. Edward Meyer, in October, 1842, who, after a ministry of four and a half years, resigned his charge, and removed on the first of May, 1847, to Lockport, Niagara county. While he was their pastor, the congregation, at the cost of $500, purchased a lot for a burial ground on the north side of the Schenectaday turnpike in Washington street, which was consecrated with appropriate solemnities, on the 26th of November, 1846.

On the 26th of September, 1847, the Rev. Frederick William Schmidt, the present efficient pastor, was installed, and entered upon the discharge of his ministerial duties. Under his ministry the church is increasing in members and usefulness. The debts of the congregation are nearly discharged, a balance of three hundred dollars only remaining; and the hope is fondly entertained that a German Evangelical Lutheran Church, so necessary for the spiritual well being of this important part of our population in this city, is firmly established on a sure and solid basis.

FIRST PRESBYTERIAN CHURCH.

The Presbyterian Church in Albany, was formed at the conclusion of the French war, in the year 1763. In October of that year the corporation of the city executed a deed in trust for the congregation, to John Macomb, Daniel Edgar, Samuel Holladay, Robert Henry, Abraham Lyle and John Munro, for the ground on which the first building for public worship was erected by the church. This lot was bounded on the north by Beaver street, on the east by William street, on the south by Hudson street, and on the west by Grand street, including, it is supposed, all the ground now comprised within these boundaries. The house erected on this spot was of wood, of considerable size, with a tall steeple, and fronted to the east. It was occupied by the church till A. D. 1796. From the date of the formation of the church, A. D. 1763, till the commencement of the war of the revolution, the church had two pastors, viz.: Rev. William Hanna, who remained with them two years, and was succeeded by the Rev. Andrew Bay, who continued in the pastoral charge for five years. The only elders known to have been ordained in the church during this time, were Robert R. Henry and Matthew Watson. There are to be found, however, during this period, no sessional records, nor any records of communicants, baptisms, marriages or deaths. On the 12th of July, 1785, a unanimous call was given to the Rev. John McDonald, who was ordained and installed pastor of the church on the 8th of November of the same year, and continued in that office till A. D. 1795. On the first of January, 1786, the church, which had been scattered, and without stated services during the war, was reorganized, and four elders and two deacons were ordained. The first communion after the new organization was held on the third sabbath of April, 1787, when 116 members were admitted. In the spring of 1794, proposals were issued for building a brick church, the materials for which were already procured, as well as the lot, extending on Washington (Pearl) street, from Beaver street to Store lane (Norton street.) The building was completed in 1796, in an elegant style for the day, being altogether the best church edifice in the city, and was opened on the 20th of November of that year. Its dimensions were 64 by 76 feet. In 1831 an addition of 16 feet was made to it on the north end, and the interior remodeled, so as to place it in advance of the other churches again for internal elegance. On the 3d of October, 1798, Eliphalet Nott was installed pastor of the church, where he continued to preach until he was removed to the presidency of Union College, which office he has ever since filled. During the past season a new edifice has been erected for the use of the congregation, on the corner of Hudson and Philip streets. The following is a list of the ministers, elders, and deacons of the church, since its first organization.

MINISTERS.

1763 Rev. William Hanna continued till 1765.

—— Rev. Andrew Bay continued five years.

1785 Rev. J. McDonald continued till 1795.

1795 Rev. David S. Bogart a licentiate from the Dutch classis, New York, supplied the pulpit for about two years.

1798 Rev. Eliphalet Nott continued till September, 1804,

First Presbyterian Church.

1804 Rev. John B. Romeyn continued till October, 1808.
1809 Rev. William Neill continued till August, 1816.
1817 Rev. Arthur Jos. Stansbury continued till June, 1821.
1822 Rev. Henry R. Weed continued till November, 1829.
1830 Rev. John N. Campbell.

TRUSTEES.

With the places of their nativity as far as ascertained.

1785 Robt. Henry; Matthew Watson; Theodorus Van Wyck Graham; Danl McIntire, Scotland; James Boyd, Scotland; John Robison, Scotland; John W. Wendell, Boston; Robt. McClelland; Hunloke Woodruff, Elizabethtown, N. Y.
1787 James Bloodgood; Jas Caldwell, Ireland; Abraham Eights, New York.
1789 Richard Sill; Alex. Chesnut.
1790 Charles R. Webster, Hartford
1791 Enoch Leonard.
1792 John V. Henry, Albany.
1796 Elisha Kane, Dutchess county; Wm. McClelland.
1797 Francis Bloodgood; Geo Pearson.
1799 James Barkley; John Grant, Scotland.
1801 Peter Sharp; John Cuyler.
1802 Gilbert Stewart.
1803 Wm. P. Beers, N. E.; Wm Caldwell, Albany; James Kane, Dutchess co.
1804 Andrew Brown.
1805 Isaac Hutton.
1806 Tho. Mather, Lyme; George Webster, Hartford.
1807 Robert R. Henry, Albany; Elenzer F. Backus, New Haven; John Boardman, Weathersfield; Hugh Boyd, Lansingburgh.
1809 John Woodworth, Schodack.
1810 Charles Z. Platt.
1811 Wm. Boyd, Scotland.
1813 Peter Boyd, Albany.
1816 Isaiah Townsend, Orange co; John Marvin, Lyme.
1820 Wm. James, Ireland; Elisha Dorr, Lyme.
1821 Isaac Hamilton; Wm. McHarg, Albany.
1823 Willard Walker, S. Brookfield.
1824 Wm. Fowler; James King.
1832 Rufus H. King, Ridgefield, Ct.
1833 Robert Gilchrist.
1835 James McNaughton, Scotland.
1836 Levi Philips, Mass.
1838 Andrew E. Brown, Albany.
1840 John Gibson, Albany.
1841 Alden March, Mass.; Benj. Tibbitts.
1845 Isaiah Townsend, Albany; Wm. White, Albany; Wm. Mitchell, Albany.
1846 Danl Fry, Albany.
1847 Robert Boyd, Albany; John D. Hewson, Albany.
1848 Anthony M. Strong, Albany; Wm. C. Durant.

There are now four Presbyterian churches in the city. It is proposed to give an account of the others in future, if the necessary facts can be procured.

DEACONS.

1786 James Boyd, John Folsom.
1794 Peter McHench, James Chestney.
1805 James Hodge, Andrew Hoffman.
1812 Chester Bulkley.
1820 Stephen J. Rider, Green Hall.
1823 Abraham Covert.
1832 Walter R. Morris.
1836 Amos Fassett.
1837 Elihu Russell, William G. Brown.

ELDERS.

- 1786 Matthew Watson, Robert R. Henry, Daniel McIntyre, Peter Sim, John Boyd.
- 1787 Joseph Newland, John Folsom.
- 1790 Donald McLeod, Abraham Eights, Hunloke Woodruff.
- 1794 James Boyd, Isaac Hutton.
- 1805 Elias Willard, Gilbert Stewart, John Boardman.
- 1812 Ananias Platt, Nehemiah B. Bassett.
- 1819 John Woodworth, Theodorus Van Wyck Graham, Timothy Fassett.
- 1820 Peter McHench, Peter Boyd.
- 1823 Green Hall, Stephen J. Rider, Josiah Sherman.
- 1831 Israel Williams.
- 1837 Amos Fassett, Elias Warner.
- 1842 Elihu Russell, Daniel Fry, Frederick S. Pease, Thomas McMullen.

Reminiscences.—At the ordination of Mr. McDonald in 1785, the society gave a public dinner to the three ministers who ordained him, probably to give eclat to the event. The trustees appropriated the seat on the right hand of the main door to the use of the corporation, and the opposite one to the governor; the pew on the right hand of the pulpit to the minister, and that on the left hand to the elders and deacons. The clerk was allowed 3s. for publishing marriages, and 6d. for every person christened. Three pounds ($7.50,) was the price fixed for burying an adult under the church, and 3s. for a person under 14 years of age. It was ordained that "children must behave well;" and courtesy was enjoined towards strangers. It was the sexton's duty to warn persons to attend funerals, and to walk before the corpse, for which he was allowed a fee of 12s. On the 4th of January, 1790, it was resolved "that 1,000 coppers be stamped *church penny*, and placed in the hands of the treasurer, for the purpose of exchanging with the congregation at the rate of twelve for one shilling, in order to add respect to the weekly collections." The Presbyterian burying ground was on Hudson street, above Pearl, and that as well as the church, is spoken of as being on the hill, while the region below is called the plains. On the 17th of May, 1792, Stephen Lush and Leonard Gansevoort, Jun., conveyed to the trustees of the Presbyterian church, "the lot on the plains," in consideration of £110 ($275). The title seems to have been considered doubtful. The corporation lease and release is drawn in consideration of 5s. The lot is thus described in the first mentioned lease: "abutting to the north to the creek or kill called the Fuyck's kill; to the south on the common highway; to the west the hills; and to the east Anthony De Hooge's." The lot was used for a stave yard, through which the kill passed, and still passes, about midway under the church, being arched over as a drain. The entrance into Washington street, as it was then called, from State street, was through a gate, which was taken away some years later, when the street was opened to its present width. On the 15th of July, 1793, the trustees decided that the salary of the preceptor Mr. McFarlan, was inadequate, and voted him £8 ($20) per annum. On the day the church was opened for public service, the Rev. Dr. Smith, president of Union College, preached two sermons. A call had been given to the Rev. David S. Bogert, of the city of New York, to become the pastor of the church, with a salary of $1,000 per annum. At a subsequent day, in order to prevent the passing of vehicles during service, the trustees procured the passage of a law which allowed two chains to be stretched across the street, at each end of the church, which effectually barricaded it to all but foot passengers. The chains were removed about twenty years ago.

UNITED PRESBYTERIAN CHURCH.

Mr. McDonald, who was deposed in 1795, by the Presbytery of Albany, removed to Canada. At a meeting of the Presbytery of Montreal, Sept. 15, 1800, he was restored to the exercise of the ministry, and in the following year laid the foundation of an edifice on the corner of Chapel and Canal (then Fox) streets, and organized a church, under the name of the United Presbyterian Church. It is now known by another title. The materials for its history were not fully obtained in season for this publication.

BETHEL FOR WATERMEN.

The above institution commenced its operations in May, 1843, in the following manner. A few pious persons, who were convinced that boatmen had been too long neglected, resolved to try the experiment of establishing meetings in the city for their benefit. They procured a suitable room in Stanwix Hall, fitted it up for service, and invited Rev. John Miles, a Wesleyan Methodist minister, to labor for and with them. Mr. Miles accepted the invitation, and entered upon the duties of his office by preaching his first bethel sermon on State Street Bridge, Sabbath morning, May 14, 1843, from Proverbs, xi., 30. "He that winneth souls is wise." A board of managers was early formed, consisting of twelve, from different sections of the Christian church. At their first meeting, held to adopt measures to sustain the cause, the following preamble and resolution were offered, and unanimously adopted: "From a conviction that it is our imperative duty to do good unto all men, even to the neglected boatmen, sailors and strangers, (as many such persons are constantly arriving in our city,) we the undersigned think it necessary that something should be done in their behalf; and we agree to form ourselves into a board of managers for the Albany Bethel; to enact laws by which it shall be governed, and to do all we can to have it permanently sustained." The room in Stanwix Hall was kept but one year, as at the close of the same, Clark Durant, Esq., who had shown himself a very warm friend of the undertaking, by contributing liberally towards its support, came forward and purchased the neat and commodious house lately occupied by the Third Presbyterian Church, for which he paid $5000, and has tendered its use gratuitously, so long as it can be sustained as a free bethel. The building, of which the above is a representation, is situated in Montgomery street, between Orange and Columbia streets; its dimensions are 50 by 60 feet. Mr. Miles is still the chaplain, faithful and devoted in the discharge of his duties. The meetings are all public, and the seats all free. The Bethel is entirely free from any sectarian influence, having no organized church, but standing entirely on neutral ground. It is supported by the voluntary subscriptions of those who take an interest in the spiritual and temporal welfare of watermen and the stranger within our gates. There is also a sabbath school connected with it, which was commenced in June, 1844.

JEWISH SYNAGOGUES.

There are two Hebrew congregations in this city. The Bethel Congregation consisted originally of sixteen members, all of them Germans, who came over in 1837, from Europe, and after having been for a short time in New York, they settled in this city in the fall of 1837. Before that time there were very few Israelites residing in Albany. There are now more than 100 members in the congregation. Their place of worship is called synagogue, where they perform their service in the Hebrew language. Their meeting days are every sabbath or Saturday, and besides on thirteen holidays and twenty-seven half-holidays. Their first place of worship was in Bassett street, but on the 2d of September, 1842, they dedicated a new synagogue at No. 76 Herkimer street, formerly a church belonging to the Hibernian Benevolent Society; which cost, after having been altered and repaired, about $3500. There is one minister or rabbi to the congregation, who is elected annually, for the term of one year. Mr. Henry Seehling was the second minister, and held the place about five years, when he was succeeded by the present incumbent, Rabbi Vise Traub, about four years since.

In the spring of the year 1841, three members and eight seat holders quitted the Bethel Congregation and commenced a new society under the title of Beth Jacob, which counts at present about forty members. Their service is the same as the Bethel Congregation. They met at No. 8 Rose street, until some time during 1848 they erected a synagogue in Fulton street, at an expense of $4,500. The officiating minister is Rabbi Jacob Newborgh.

Each congregation has a separate burial ground. There is also a Mutual Benefit Society of Israelites in this city, to which nearly all the members of the Bethel Congregation belong. The object of this society is to support the poor sick, as well as their own members, and to give relief to the families of the poor and the sick, and to see that in case of death the corpse is properly buried.

The Congregation, as well as the Mutual Benefit Society, are supported by monthly contributions and free offerings.

SOCIETY OF FRIENDS.

The Society of Friends in the city of Albany first met for religious worship in different places, where they could obtain suitable rooms, from 1827 to 1833, a considerable part of the time in the Lancasterian School House, in Eagle street, by permission of the common council. In 1835 they became an organized society, and built a meeting house on the south side of Plain street, below Grand. The dimensions of the building are 36 by 42 feet, and 22 feet walls above the basement, and seated so as to accommodate about four hundred persons. It has a large and commodious basement, which is occupied as a school room. The school is under the charge of a member of the society, and numbers about 50 pupils. This edifice was erected by the Society here, with the assistance of the Yearly Meeting of New York, at an expense of $5000. The congregation numbers about 150 persons.

UNIVERSALIST CHURCH.

There was preaching occasionally by Universalist clergymen in this city, for a few years previous to 1829. In the fall of that year the first Universalist meeting house in Albany was erected on Herkimer street, being a temporary wooden building 50 by 27 feet. Subsequently it was elevated for the purpose of forming a basement and $10\frac{1}{2}$ feet added to its depth; it then had cost about $1500. On the 1st of March, 1830, a meeting was held to take into consideration the formation of a Universalist Society, when it was resolved to form one. On the 23d of March, 1830, the first Universalist Society in the city of Albany was organized, when about thirty persons signed the constitution, which contains a confession of Christian faith; the society therefore comprises the church. The Rev. Wm. S. Balch commenced his labors in the latter part of February, 1830, who, in consequence of poor health, removed at the expiration of three months. The Rev. Isaac D. Williamson commenced his labors on the 17th of June, 1830, and resigned the 1st of May, 1837. The brick meeting house in Green street, now occupied by the society, was commenced the 25th of July, 1833, and completed in August, 1834. It is a substantial, neat, and convenient edifice, 80 by 48 feet, constructed in accordance with the Grecian Doric order, and with the lot, cost about $14,000. The Rev. Stephen R. Smith commenced his labors the 18th of September, 1837, and left the society on the 1st of May, 1842; was succeeded by Rev. S. B. Britton, who left the society in April, 1843, after which the Rev. L. B. Mason supplied the desk until the fall of 1845, when he left in consequence of ill health. The society was then without stated preaching until the spring of 1846, when Rev. S. B. Britton returned and remained for one year, after which Rev. R. P. Ambler preached for about eight months; since which there has been no settled pastor until November 1st, 1848, when Rev. W. H. Waggoner was engaged as pastor, and installed on the 20th of December. There is a sunday school attached to the society, consisting of more than one hundred scholars. The library consists of 200 volumes, of very carefully selected books. The congregation numbers about four hundred, and has sixty communicants.

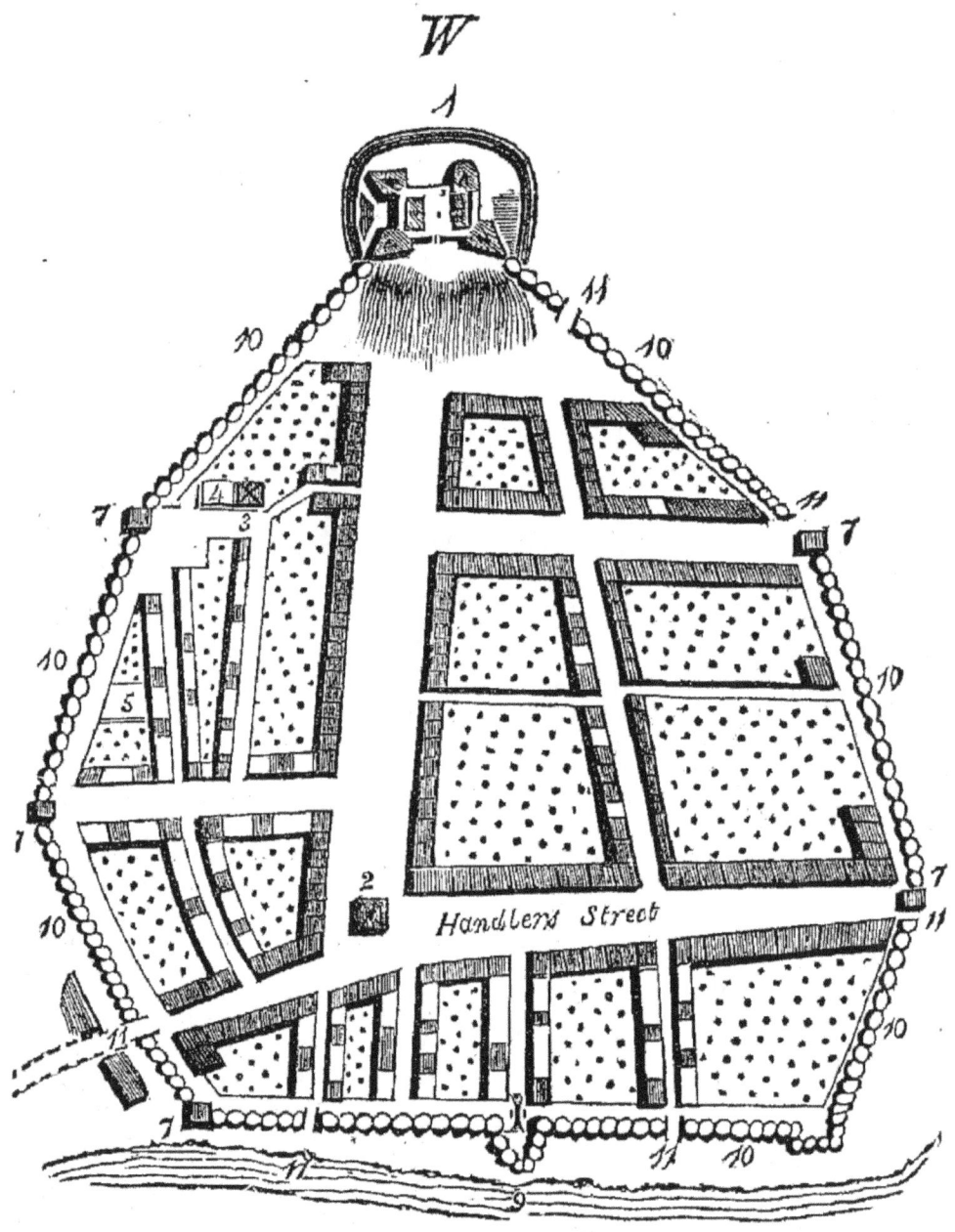

PLAN OF ALBANY, 1695.

1. The Fort.
2. Dutch Calvinist Church. Dr. Dellius pastor.
3. German Lutheran Church.
4. Its burying place.
5. Dutch Calvinist burying place.
7. Blockhouses.
8. Stadt House.
9. A great Gun to clear a gulley.
10. Stockade.
11. City Gates, six in all.

ANCIENT ALBANY.

The denizens of this ancient city know by tradition that it was formerly protected against the incursions of the French and Indians, by palisades, a kind of fortification, consisting of upright posts planted firmly in the ground, and peculiar in the manner of its use to the settlements of this country. Occasionally in making excavations, the relics of these ancient wooden walls are met with, but from the difficulty we have had in gathering authentic oral information about the limits which they described, we are inclined to believe that few if any at this day can give a satisfactory account of them. The accompanying diagram shows the line of these old defences. It is not known whether it was drawn after any accurate survey, but could hardly have been otherwise, from its correspondence with the same portion of the city at the present day. We can see how the curvatures and diagonal lines presented by our streets had their rise in the course of the protecting enclosure, which latter was run to correspond with the declivities on either side of the high ground upon which this part of the city stands, and terminating in a regular fort at Lodge street. It was drawn in 1695, by the Rev. John Miller, a chaplain in the British army, and is unquestionably a true picture of the form and boundaries of the city a century and a half ago—reaching from Hudson to Steuben street on Broadway, and from the river west to Lodge street. A more extended line of palisades was afterwards constructed, bounded by Hamilton street on the south, and crossing Broadway on the north at the house occupied by the late venerable Abraham Van Vechten, a little north of Orange and Van Tromp streets. The north gate was placed there, and was a local name as late as the beginning of the present century, dividing the city of Albany from the Colonie, which was a separate town, until the year 1815, when a portion of it was annexed, and called the fifth ward. It was a century after this draft of the city was made before it began to increase very rapidly in population, since which it has expanded around this nucleus, "as from a stroke of the enchanter's wand."

The following is the description given of Albany in 1695, by the author alluded to :

"As the city of New York is the chief place of strength belonging to this province for its defence against those enemies who come by sea, so Albany is of principal consideration against those who come by land, the French and Indians of Canada. It is distant from New York 150 miles, and lies up Hudson's river on the west side, on the descent of a hill from the west to the eastward. It is in circumference about six furlongs, and hath therein about 200 houses, a fourth part of what there is reckoned to be in New York. The form of it is septangular, and the longest line that which buts upon the river, running from the north to the south. On the west angle is the fort, quadrangular, strongly stockaded and ditched round, having in it twenty one pieces of ordnance mounted. On the north-west side are two blockhouses, and on the south west as many : on the south-east angle stands one blockhouse; in the middle of the line from thence northward is a horned work, and on the north-east angle a mount. The whole city is well stockaded round, and in the several fortifications named are about thirty guns."

Arms of the city of Albany.

CITY OF ALBANY.

Albany enjoys an eligible situation on the west bank of the Hudson river, near the head of tide water. Its latitude is 42° 39′ 3″ north; its longitude 73° 32′ west of Greenwich, and 3° 13′ east of Washington. The city of New York is distant meridionally 135¼ miles; by the road on the west side of the river 145 miles; by the river a little less. The distance of Boston is 164 miles; of Montreal, 230; of Washington, 370. The city appears to great advantage from the river, having a southeastern aspect; rising rapidly from the bank, and presenting its public buildings in bold relief. Its habitations occupy the alluvial valley of the Hudson, about a quarter of a mile in width, and ascend three hills of about 140 feet elevation, separated by deep valleys, through which considerable streams of water formerly ran, known as the Foxen kill, the Rutten kill, and the Beaver kill. The view from either of the heights is picturesque; to the north may be seen the city of Troy and adjacent villages, and in the distance the hills of Vermont. To the east the beautiful extent of country lying beyond the Hudson river; and to the south the Helderbergs, and the Catskill mountains with the river flowing at their base.......Before the arrival of white men, it was known to the Indians in the valley of the Mohawk, by the name of *Schaughnaughtada*, or *Scho-negh-tá-da*, which signified over the plains ; a name which the Dutch applied to an Indian settlement where the city of Schenectady now stands, as being over the plains from Albany.......The first European vessel which is known to have penetrated this region, was the Half Moon, Captain Hendrick Hudson, in Sept., 1609. A boat from that vessel is said to have moored at some point on what is now Broadway. Several Dutch navigators followed during the next three or four years, and erected trading houses at Albany and New York, for the purpose of collecting furs of the Indians. Our city, therefore, is, next to Jamestown, Va., the oldest colony in the Union. One of the early pioneers in this traffic, was Hendrick Chrystance (or Corstiaensen), by

Albany's first seal from 1686.

Albany's seal in 1752.

Present Seal

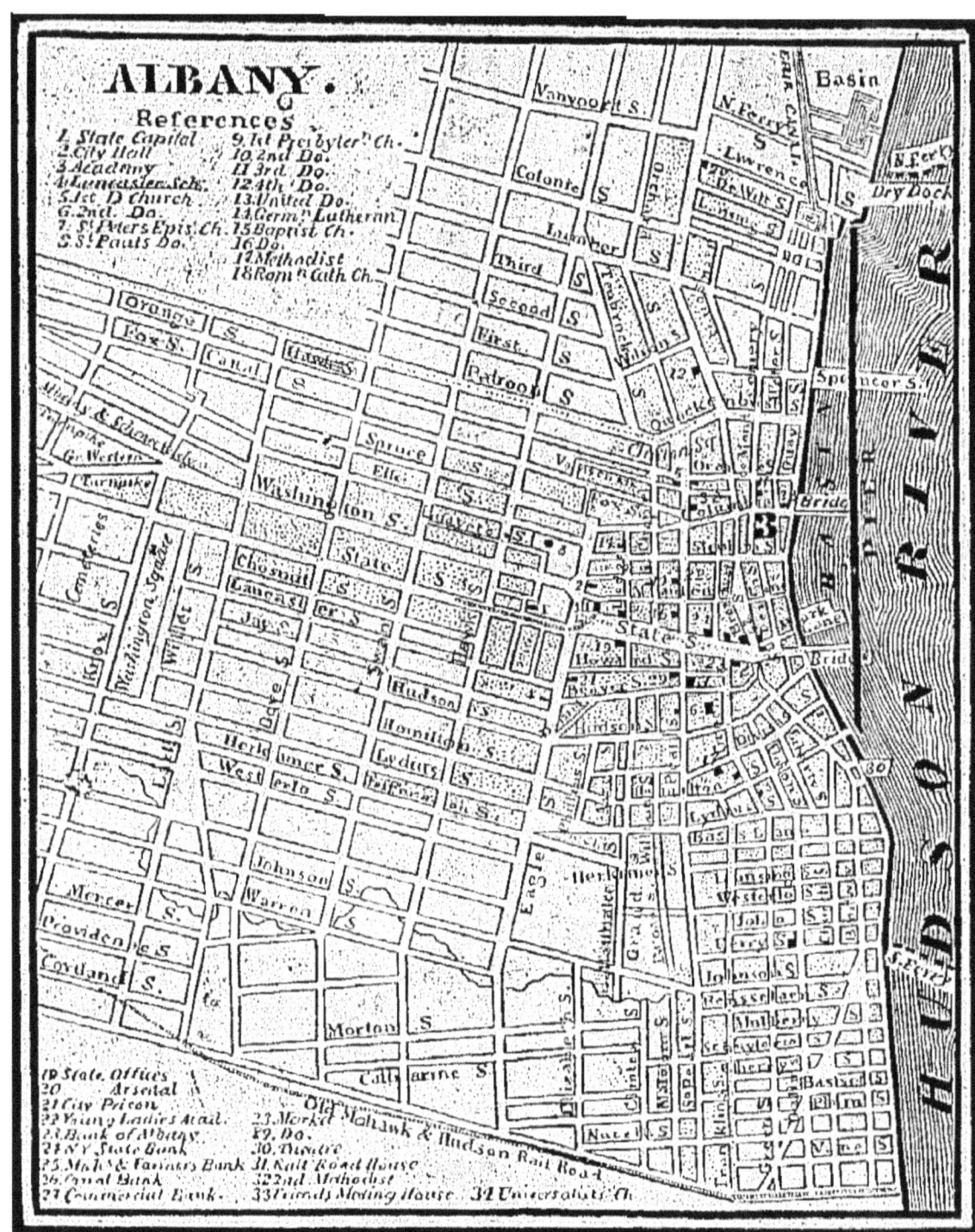

whom a fort was erected in 1614, on the island below the city, known as Marten Gerritsen's or Castle Island, Boyd's island, etc. This island, which contains about 70 acres, will soon be difficult to identify, having been several years ago connected with the main land at the north end by an embankment, and the narrow inlet behind it, is rapidly filling up. That fort appears on the Figurative Map made in 1616, found by Mr. Broadhead in Holland. It was a stockade, 50 feet square, encircled by a ditch 18 feet wide, and was defended by 2 pieces of cannon, and 11 stone guns, and garrisoned by 12 men under Jacob Jacobs Elkens. The trading house within the fort was 36 by 26 feet. When it was carried away by the spring freshet in 1617, a spot was chosen near the outlet of the Norman's kill and a fort erected there. That place was abandoned in 1623, and a new fort built in what is now Broadway, at the new steam boat landing, near the site of the Fort Orange Hotel. The fort mounted eight large cannon, called by the Dutch *stone gestucken*, by which it is understood that they were loaded with stones instead of iron balls. It was named Fort Orange, in honor of the Prince of Orange, who then presided over the Netherlands. This fort was intended to afford convenient accommodations for traffic with the Indians, and to serve as a protection against sudden attacks from them. It was only occupied during the autumn and winter by the traders, who as yet made no attempts at colonization. .....In 1630, the commissary of the Dutch West India Company, purchased of the Indians two tracts on the west side of the river, for Kiliaen Van Rensselaer, a wealthy pearl merchant of Amsterdam. The territory thus acquired included the fort, and the same year a number of colonists sailed from the Texel with their families, provided with farming implements, stock, and all other necessaries, and arrived at the mouth of the river on the 24th of May, after a passage of sixty-four days. On their arrival at Fort Orange, they were provided with humble accommodations in the vicinity. The names of the settlers that arrived this year, are given by Dr. O'Callaghan, in his History of New Netherland, vol. 1, p. 433, as follows: Wolfert Gerritsen, superintendent of farms. Rutger Hendricksen van Soest, superintendent of the brewery. Seger Hendricksen van Soest, shepherd and plowman. Brandt Peelen van Nieukerke, schepen; he died in 1644; his descendants take the name of Brandt. Simon Dircksen Pos. Jan Tyssen, trumpeter, Andries Carstenssen, millwright. Laurens Laurenssen and Barent Tomassen, sawyers. Arendt van Curler, commissary. Jacob Jansen Stol; succeeded Hendrick Albertsen as ferrymaster. Martin Gerrittsen van Bergen; he had a lease of Castle Island, in 1668, which afterwards took his name. Claes Arissen. Roeloff Jansen van Maesterlandt, wife and family; came out as farmer to the patroon at $72 a year. Claes Claessen, his servant. Jacques Spierinck, Jacob Govertsen, Raynert Harmensen, and Bastiaen Jansen Krol. Albert Andriessen Bradt, de Noorman. It was from him that the Norman's kill takes its name, the water privilege of which he leased; as well as a large farm situated on that stream, which fell into the hands of Teunis Slingerland, who married his daughter, Engeltje.......Seven years later (1637) Mr. Van Rensselaer purchased the tract on the opposite side of the river, "for certain quantities of duffels, axes, knives and wampum," and thus became the proprietor of a tract of country 24 miles along the river, and 48 in extent, east and west. Over this extensive tract he possessed all the authority

TOP. A portion of the 1617 Cornelius Hendrickson Map showing Fort Nassau (Nassau) on Castle Island, now part of Albany, NY. BOTTOM. Portion of a 1616 Cornelius Hendrickson map showing the location of Fort Orange and the remains of Fort Nassau on the island.

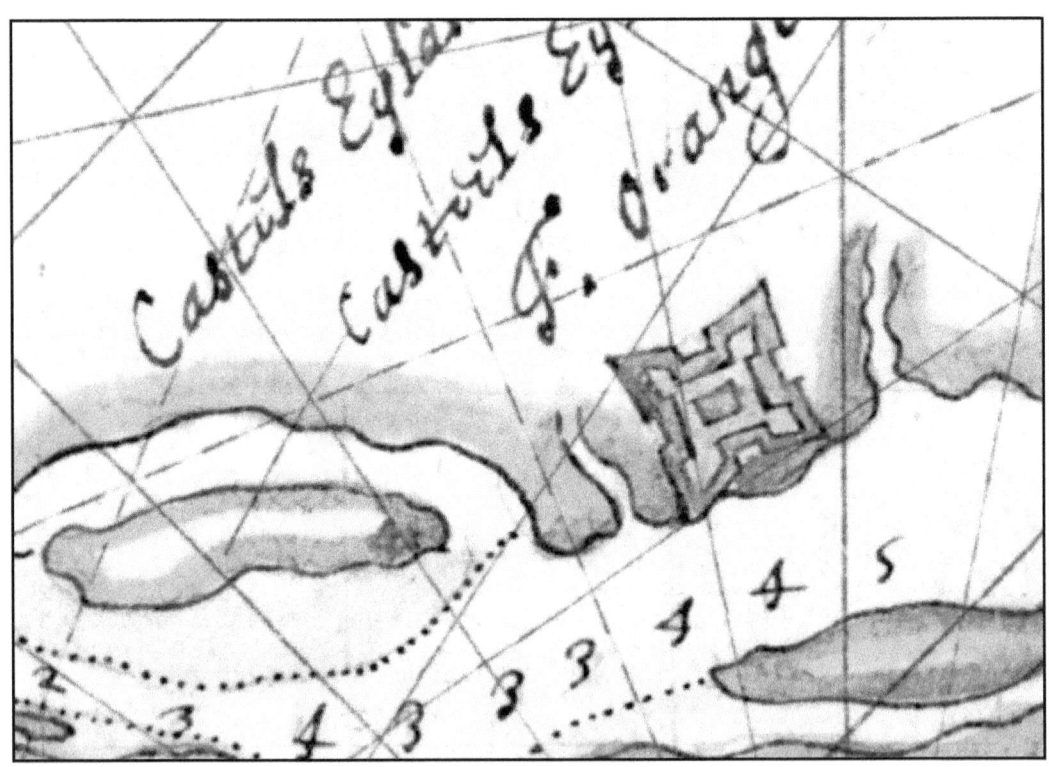

of a sovereign, and made a large outlay for its settlement, giving it the name of Rensselaerswyck. The administration of justice and the management of its financial affairs he committed to the care of a commissary general. Fortunate in the selection of these, his colony prospered much more than that at New Amsterdam, and it was to the good offices of Van Curler, or Corlear, the first commissary, that the colonists at New Amsterdam were indebted more than once, for their preservation from the hands of the Indians.......In 1642 Mr. Van Rensselaer sent over the Rev. Johannes Megapolensis as minister of Rensselaerswyck, at his private expense. It is not certain that he visited the colony himself. He died in 1646, and the estate descended to his son Johannes, then a minor; between whose agent and Gov. Stuyvesant serious difficulties occurred, which it was necessary to refer to the states general of Holland for arbitration.......In 1664 the province came into the possession of the English, when the name of Beverwyck, by which it had been known, was changed to Albany, that being one of the titles of the Duke of York. It had also been equally well known as Williamstadt, Fort Orange, and the Fuyck, which latter signifies the bend in the river. Fort Orange was built in 1623, and Williamstadt in 1647 at the head of State street. The right of soil was confirmed to the patroon by a new patent, but the government was retained in the hands of the colony....In 1686, Gov. Dongan granted a charter to the citizens of Albany. At first a trading station, then a hamlet, next a village, it was now dignified with the title of city. It has finally become the *capital of the state*—the EMPIRE STATE! The charter gave the city an area of one mile in width on the river, and extending in a north-west direction, at the same width, thirteen and a half miles, to the north line of the manor of Rensselaerswyck; containing 7,160 acres. Peter Schuyler, the friend of the Indians, was named the first mayor, and the first common council consisted of the following persons: Peter Schuyler, mayor; Isaac Swinton, recorder; Robert Livingston, town clerk; Dirk Wessels, Jan Jans Bleecker, David Schuyler, Johannes Wendell, Lavinus Van Schaick, Adrian Gerritsen aldermen; Joachim Staats, John Lansingh, Isaac Verplanck, Lawrence Van Ale, Albert Ryckman, Melgert Wynantse, assistant aldermen; Jan Bleecker, chamberlain; Richard Pretty, sheriff; James Parker, marshall.......The Schuyler family, for several generations, exerted a powerful influence over the Indians. In all the treaties with them the city of Albany bore a conspicuous part; and so entirely had they won the confidence of the savages, that from the date of its settlement, it was never invaded by a hostile tribe; although, in 1689, when the citizens refused to submit to the administration of Leisler and Milborne, they yielded allegiance through fear of an Indian invasion. ....During the revolution, the Albany committee nobly sustained their countrymen in the struggle. Burgoyne had boasted, at the commencement of the campaign, that his army should revel upon the spoils of Albany; but he only visited the city as a captive. Sir Henry Clinton twice attempted to invade it, but met with sufficient obstacles to prevent his success.......In 1795 the town of Colonie was annexed, forming the fifth ward. It became the capital of the state in 1807. Since the introduction of steam boats and the completion of the canals, the growth of the city has been rapid, and the lines of rail roads, which connect it with Boston and Buffalo, are giving it a still greater impulse. From its central position, Albany forms a kind of natural entrepot between New York and a vast interior country, comprising the Canadas, part of Ohio, Michigan, Illinois, and even Wisconsin and Iowa, on the one side, and parts of the New England states on the other. Flour and other agricultural products form the principal articles of export. The city has about 120 streets, and is divided into ten wards. Its population, by the last census, was 41,139. Each ward elects two aldermen who, together with the mayor and recorder, form the Common Council........The architecture of the city has undergone a very great change in the last 30 years. Many of the public and private buildings of Albany are now of an elegant and costly character. The Capitol, occupied for legislative purposes, the state courts and the state library; the State Hall, erected for the accommodation of the public officers; the City Hall, occupied for city and county business, and the Albany Academy, all face the public square at the head of State street, and the foot of Washington street. A few rods south of these is the County Jail, and the Medical College, in Eagle street. The Female Academy is a handsome edifice, situated in North Pearl street. The Albany Exchange is situated at the foot of State street. The Orphan Asylum is located one mile west of the City Hall; and the Penitentiary near Lydius street on the Delaware turnpike. These will be more fully described in another place, as well as the churches, and other important buildings.......The trade, commerce and manufactures of Albany are important, and rapidly increasing. Its iron foundries are among the largest in the country. More stoves are manufactured here, than in any other city or town in the Union. It has extensive manufactories of pianofortes, leather, coaches, sleighs, hats, caps and bonnets, the three latter to the amount of nearly a million of dollars a year. In addition to the above, the Albany Nail Works, near Troy, the most extensive establishment of the kind in America, are principally owned in Albany, as also an extensive satinet factory, and flouring mills on the Patroon's creek. The Erie and Champlain canals, which form a junction eight miles above, enter the Hudson at the north end of the city, where a capacious basin has been formed, of more than a mile in length, by means of a pier inclosing a part of what was anciently termed the Fuyck, or bend in the river, of 32 acres area, affording a winter harbor for boats, as well as safe protection to vessels navigating the river or canals, and commodious wharfage. The Mohawk and Hudson rail road, among the first roads built in the country, and connected with the Utica and Schenectady, and Saratoga and Schenectady rail roads, terminates at Albany. The Albany and West Stockbridge rail road connects with the Western rail road at the state line, between Massachusetts and New York, forming a continuous line of rail roads from Albany to Boston. The termination of these rail roads and canals at Albany, renders it the centre of trade and transhipment, and has opened to the enterprise of her merchants and artisans an extent of country unsurpassed in its wealth and resources. In 1832 a company was incorporated with a capital of three millions, to connect Albany with New York by a rail road on the margin of the river, but it was not until 1847 that efficient measures were taken to carry out that great project, when a new charter was granted by the legislature, the stock subscribed, and a portion of the road is already constructed, and will be in operation over a considerable length of it in 1849.

COUNTY OF ALBANY.

Albany county was organized under Gov. Dongan, in 1683, when it comprised the whole of the state north and west of Dutchess and Ulster counties, and part of Vermont. In 1757, the number of taxable inhabitants was 3,800; in 1767, 5,014; and in 1786, after several counties had been set off, 72,360. In 1772 a very large tract was severed and took the name of Montgomery county, out of which a good many counties have since been formed. In the same year Washington county was also set off on the east side of the Hudson. On the 4th of April, 1786, an act passed the legislature, erecting the southeast part of the county of Albany into a new county, by the name of Columbia. In 1788, Clinton county was formed from the northern extremity whose census in 1790 was 1222! and that of Columbia county 27,552, of which 1630 were slaves. The following is a table of the towns which comprised the county of Albany in 1790, and the census of each; the orthography is also preserved.

Towns.	Males.	Females.	Slaves.	Total.
Albany,	1,467	1,467	572	3,506
Water-Vliet,	3,456	3,481	730	7,667
Rensselaerwyck,	3,972	3,504	572	8,048
Stephentown,	3,652	3,362	28	7,042
Schohary,	979	936	154	2,069
Duansburgh,	787	704	4	1,495
Schenectady,	1,979	1,871	467	4,317
Hosack,	1,542	1,455	36	3,033
Halfmoon,	1,818	1,668	121	3,607
Coxsakie,	1,626	1,488	302	3,416
Saratoga,	1,625	1,394	62	3,081
Cattskill,	836	844	308	1,988
Ballston,	3,640	3,117	66	6,823
Schaticook,	786	694	137	1,617
Cambridge,	2,515	2,404	48	4,967
Stillwater,	1,559	1,428	65	3,052
Easton,	1,266	1,179	57	2,502
Pittstown,	1,260	1,134	31	2,425
Freehold,	873	869	6	1,748
Rensselaer-Ville,	1,450	1,316	11	2,777
	37,088	34,315	3,777	75,180

It was ascertained that the county of Ontario at the same time *exceeded three thousand!* In 1791, the legislature divided Albany into three counties, Albany, Rensselaer and Saratoga. By this arrangement, the population of Albany was 28,192, Rensselaer 29,634, and Saratoga 17,463. The rapidly increasing population of the state required the division of the other large counties which had been formed by the dismemberment of Albany; the counties of Tioga, Otsego and Herkimer were cut off from Montgomery, in portions that afterwards admitted of subdivisions. In 1794

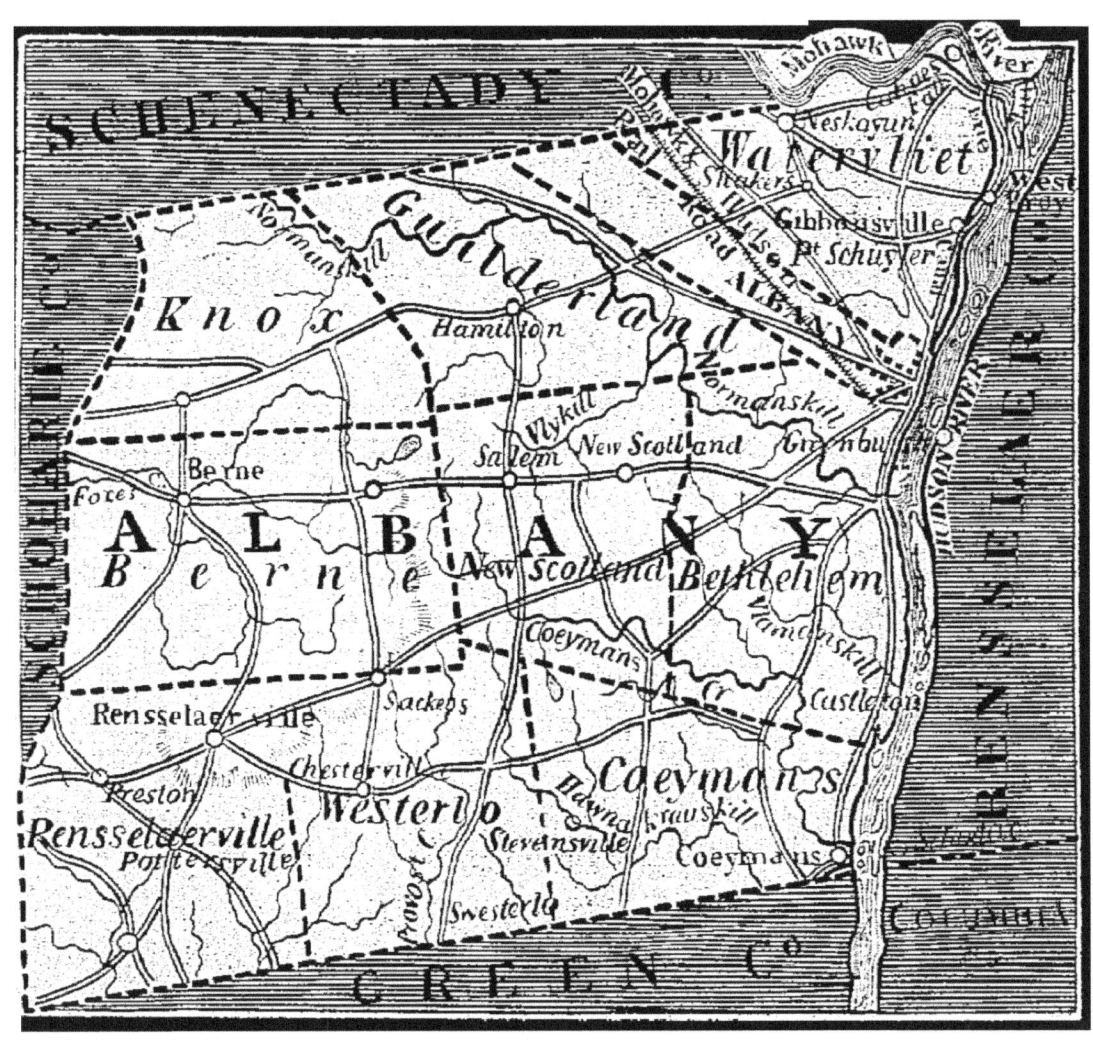

the legislature had in contemplation a design to take another corner from Albany county; but at the adjournment of that body, it remained in the senate, which passed a resolution at its close, that the further consideration of the bill entitled "An act to erect certain lands into a separate county by the name of Delaware," be postponed until the next session. The boundaries of the proposed county described in the bill are curious: "All that part of the counties of Albany, Ulster and Otsego, beginning at the Susquehanna river, at the mouth of the Unadilla, and running from thence along the division line, between the counties of Otsego and Tioga southerly, to the mouth of a brook called Aughquago, which runs into Delaware river near a place called the Cook house; and thence down the said river to a place ten miles below Shohakin, measured along the said river as it runs, and thence northeasterly to the mouth of a creek called the East kill, which runs into the Schoharie kill; and up the middle of the Stony kill to the head thereof, to a hemlock tree marked with the letters W. I. I. W., and thence northwest to the Adiquataygie or Charlotte river; and thence down the middle thereof to the Susquehanna river; and thence down the middle of the same to the place of beginning, shall be and hereby is erected into a separate county by the name of Delaware." This county was not formed until 1797, when it was taken wholly from Otsego and Tioga. The county of Albany then comprised the following towns: Albany, Schenectady, Catskill, Coxsackie, Schoharie, Berne, Coeymans, Bethlehem, Rensselaerville, Watervliet, Duanesburgh, Freehold. The number of electors in the city was 765; in the county, 6087. The following is a list of the taxable inhabitants of the towns in the county of Albany, in July, 1795.

Albany,	806	Bethlehem,	350
Watervliet,	573	Rensselaerville,	495
Coxsackie,	600	Schohary,	507
Catskill,	354	Duanesburgh,	400
Freehold,	524	Berne,	386
Coeymans,	354	Schenectady,	747

In 1809, the corporation of the city of Schenectady applied to the legislature for another division of Albany county, taking the city of Schenectady, the towns of Duanesburgh, and Princetown, and so much of the town of Watervliet as lay beyond the manor line. On a division of the house there were 8 in favor of the new county. This was the final subdivision, leaving the county as it now stands, when it consisted of Albany, Coeymans, Watervliet, Rensselaerville, Berne, Colonie, Bethlehem, and Guilderland. Some of these have been subdivided, and otherwise altered, but the territory is believed to be the same. Its boundaries will be seen on the accompanying map. It consists of the following towns, with the date of their incorporation:

1686	Albany	1795	Berne
1688	Watervliet	1803	Guilderland
1790	Rensselaerville	1815	Westerlo
1791	Coeymans	1822	Knox
1793	Bethlehem	1832	New Scotland

The greatest length of the county is 28 miles; breadth 21; containing an area of about 515 square miles; or 329,110 acres according to the last census. The far greater portion of it belongs to the manor of Rensselaer. The surface is uneven, and in the southwest part hilly and mountainous. The soil in the vicinity of the Hudson is good, and much of it highly cultivated; but in the interior sandy plains occur, most of which were formerly considered mere barrens; they are susceptible of cultivation, however, and under good husbandry are made to yield abundantly. These plains are from ten to eleven miles broad, and stretch from north to south nearly through the whole county. On the Mohawk the land is rugged and sterile. The agricultural productions of the county are oats, corn, rye, buckwheat and barley, principally. Wheat is again becoming more generally cultivated. Potatoes are raised in considerable quantities. The western part is favorable to grazing, and butter is there largely produced. Sheep husbandry is also large and increasing. The Helderberg hills extend through the western part of the county, uniting with the Catskill range on the south. They are from 400 to 500 feet in height and precipitous, but quite uniform, displaying no isolated peaks. They furnish an abundance of fuel consisting principally of hemlock, beech, sugar maple, black birch, bass-wood, and white ash. The swamps afford black ash, and soft maple, with a portion of elm. The eastern sides of the hills abound with sugar-maple, beech, bass-wood and white ash, while the ridges and western aspects, abound with a greater proportion of hemlock. In the eastern part of the county yellow and white pine; black, white and chestnut oak; chestnut, walnut, in the wet lands elm, and hemlock is often found near the streams. The rocks are principally composed of lime and sandstone, abounding in organic remains. The most important mineral productions are bog iron ore, which is found in various places; marl and water limestone is found in Bethlehem, and in the city of Albany is a mineral spring, which evolves carbonic acid, and contains ingredients similar to those found in the celebrated springs at Ballston and Saratoga. There are also several sulphur springs in the county, but none of them have acquired much celebrity. Epsom salts are found at Coeymans Landing, and petroleum in Guilderland. Extensive explorations have been made for coal on both sides of the river, in this region; and although large sums have been expended in the search during a period of full half a century, without any success, and the state geologists have determined that coal can not exist in this locality, there are still found persons anxious to continue the effort to find it. In the limestone of the Helderberg hills are several extensive caverns, in which are found crystals and stalacites of various degrees of beauty and perfection. Calcareous spar and alum also occur in the county.....The county is well watered. The principal rivers and creeks are the Mohawk on the northeast, the Hudson on the east, the Norman's kill, Vlamans kill, Haivnakraus kill, Coeymans creek, Provost creek, Cats kill, and Patroon's creek, &c., running into the Hudson on the east and south, the Foxes' creek and others flowing west; together with several rivulets emanating from durable springs and lakes. Most of these have valuable waterfalls, affording great facilities for manufacturing, and are now made available to a great extent. The Foxen kill and Rutten kill, formerly considerable runs of water flowing through the city of Albany, are now obliterated, and their ancient beds turned into sewers. The Beaver kill, or Buttermilk creek, once a mill stream, affording considerable water power, is also nearly extinguished. The principal waterfall is the Cohoes, having a perpendicular descent of nearly 70 feet, possessing great picturesque beauty, and much resorted to during the summer months by visitors from all parts of the county. The total fall of the Mohawk here is 140 feet, affording power sufficient to propel at least one million of spindles, with all the necessary apparatus.

The statistics of the county, as presented by the last census returns, are as follows:

Towns.	ACRES.		Males.	Females.	Total.	No. of Electors.	Number of School Houses.	Number of Children taught.
	Improved Land.	Total Area.						
City of Albany,	2,387	11,520	20,043	21,096	41,139	7,977	12	6,606
Bethlehem, ...	27,647	36,750	1,750	1,565	3,315	705	14	775
Bern, ...	29,293	43,460	1,868	1,799	3,667	783	22	1,587
Coeymans,....	22,179	29,890	1,505	1,473	2,978	681	14	767
Guilderland, ..	19,581	34,630	1,501	1,494	2,995	682	10	694
Knox, ...	20,042	26,570	1,079	1,082	2,161	500	12	612
New Scotland,.	20,281	36,000	1,687	1,601	3,288	754	15	1,233
Rensselaerville	30,448	41,200	1,821	1,768	3,589	865	16	1,093
Westerlo,.....	28,303	39,420	1,460	1,467	2,927	667	17	1,107
Watervliet, ...	23,181	29,670	5,672	5,537	11,209	2,264	23	1,935
	223,342	329,110	38,386	38,882	77,268	15,878	155	16,410

Towns.	Bap't Churches	Episcopalian.	Presbyterian.	Congregational.	Methodist.	Roman Cath'c.	Dutch Reform'd	Universalist.	Unitarian.	Jews.	Friends.	Grist Mills.	Saw Mills.	Tanneries.	Fulling Mills.	Carding Mills.	Cotton Factor's	Woolen Fac's.
City of Albany,...	5	3	5	1	6	4	3	1	1	1	1	..	1					
Bethlehem,.......	..	..	1	..	2	..	2	..	..	..	..	2	2	1	1	1		
Bern,............	1	..	..	..	3	..	3	2	..	..	1	3	23	3	3	3		
Coeymans,.......	..	..	..	..	3	..	2	..	..	..	..	3	9	2	2	2		
Guilderland,.....	1	..	1	..	..	..	2	..	..	..	..	2	7	2	2	1	..	2
Knox,...........	..	..	..	..	2	..	1	..	..	..	..	2	12	3				
New Scotland,....	..	..	1	..	1	..	4	..	..	..	..	2	9	3				
Rensselaerville,...	2	1	1	..	2	..	..	..	..	..	2	2	14	5	1	1	..	1
Westerlo,........	2	..	..	..	1	..	2	..	1	..	1	3	10	4	3	2	..	1
Watervliet,.......	2	2	2	..	5	1	4	..	..	..	..	7	8	..	1	2	1	5
	13	6	11	1	25	5	23	3	2	1	5	26	95	23	13	12	1	9

1 Medical College	40 lunatics
3 Academies	26,840 neat cattle
2 Female Seminaries	13,939 milch cows
1 Normal School	10,780 horses
160 Inns	66,536 sheep
172 Wholesale stores	32,870 hogs
642 retail do	28,921 acres oats
478 groceries	624,033 bush. do harvested
2 oil mills	15,705 acres rye
15 iron works	163,894 bush. harvested
1 distillery	10,250 acres corn
2 asheries	208,254 bush. do harvested
7 breweries	5,341 acres wheat
46 manufactories	44,149 bush. do harvested
1 paper mill	421 acres flax
1 clover mill	34,984 lbs. raised
3 oil cloth factories	5,762 acres potatoes
9 rope factories	404,594 bush. raised
4558 farmers	173 acres turnips
858 merchants	12,219 bush. raised
203 manufactories	10,973 acres buckwheat
4729 mechanics	183,274 bush. raised
187 attorneys	491 acres beans
88 clergymen	4,487 bush. raised
142 physicians	3,522 acres peas
9 Indians	51,252 bush. raised
26 blind	7,603 acres barley
15 deaf and dumb	120,978 bush. raised

ASSEMBLY DISTRICTS.

The city and county of Albany is divided into four districts, as follows:

1st Dist.—First and second wards of Albany, towns of Bethlehem, Coeymans, Westerlo and Rensselaerville.

2d Dist.—Tenth ward of Albany, towns of Guilderland, New Scotland, Knox and Berne.

3d Dist.—Third, fourth, fifth, sixth and eighth wards of Albany.

4th Dist.—Seventh and ninth wards of Albany, and town of Watervliet.

A REMARKABLE WINTER.

A meteorological table was kept for the month of January, 1802, and published in the Gazette, by which it appears that the lowest range of the thermometer was 10 deg., and the highest 55¼ deg. above zero. The winter was so remarkably mild as to have more the appearance of April; the river was navigable 17 days, so that vessels passed from Albany to New York, and at no time was the ice strong enough for any team to pass on it, and not more than 1¼ inches of snow fell within two miles of the city during the months of December and January.

ALBANY COUNTY PENITENTIARY.

This establishment is located near the junction of Lydius street with the Delaware turnpike, about half a mile distant in a westerly direction from the Capitol. The lands belonging to it include four entire squares, as laid down upon the city map, and contain between ten and twelve acres. The buildings occupy a beautiful and commanding elevation, facing eastward, and present an imposing appearance. As will be seen by the engraving, they comprise a centre building, three stories high besides the basement, 50 feet front and 75 in depth; and two wings, each 100 feet long and 50 feet wide, exclusive of the octagonal towers which flank them. The interior of the south wing forms a spacious hall, 98 feet long, 46 feet wide, and 32 feet high, in the centre of which is a massive block of 96 cells, four tiers in height, with stair cases and surrounding galleries. These cells are each, in the inside, 7 feet by 4, and 7 feet high, supplied with iron bed steads and other necessary furniture. Each cell has a separate and distinct ventilator. The doors are made of round iron bars, which when closed admit nearly as much air and light as when open. The hall is also well ventilated, spacious, light and airy. Besides these, there are 10 larger cells in the octagon towers; making in all 106 cells. This wing is appropriated exclusively to male convicts. In the north wing, occupied by the females, is a block of 40 cells, similar to those just described, with 8 larger ones in the towers, corresponding with those in the southern octagons, making a total of 48 cells. The remainder of this wing is divided into work rooms for the women, and for various other uses. The whole prison contains 154 cells, or dormitories, of which about 144 are used for ordinary purposes. The number, however, can be increased from time to time as occasion may require. The front portion of the central building is appropriated to the residence of the superintendent, his family and the subordinate officers. On the first story, in rear, are the guard chamber, matron's room, &c., &c. In the rear of the second story is the male hospital, a fine apartment 28 by 32 feet; also a female hospital, and a dispensatory connected with both. The third story is handsomely fitted up as a chapel, 36 by 48 feet, furnished with pulpit, seats, &c., in which divine service is regularly held on each sabbath day. A sabbath school has likewise been instituted. The rear part of the basement is devoted to the culinary operations of the prison, most of which are performed by steam; adjoining this is the laundry and bake house. The whole establishment is warmed by hot air furnaces, and furnished with a copious supply of good water; and hot and cold water are distributed wherever necessary.

A brick wall 14 feet high, extending 105 feet beyond the wings, parallel with the front, and running thence 200 feet to the rear, on each side, has been erected. This wall, surmounted by towers, or guard-houses, at the angles, and a sentry walk at top, surrounds the whole prison yard, in the centre of which is a range of work-shops for male convicts, 150 feet long by 28 wide, with cellars of the same size beneath, for the prison stores.

The dimensions of the prison, including the walls and yard, are 460 feet front and rear, and 250 feet deep, covering an area of nearly *three acres*. All the buildings are constructed of brick and stone, and are fire-proof. The bricks were mostly made on the ground, and all the work, usually denominated laborer's work, in and about the premises, from the commencement of the establishment, has been performed by the prisoners. The ground was purchased at the very low price of $3000. The cost of the buildings, exclusive of convict labor, was $35,000. Including interest on that part of the money borrowed for the purpose, and all other contingencies, the total cost is somewhat upwards of $40,000, which by law is directed to be raised in eight equal annual instalments. Three of these instalments have been already added to the county taxes and paid, without enhancing the previous rate of taxation, for the reason, that the former average annual amount of criminal expenses were, by this change of system, sufficiently lessened to defray them; and it is believed that this effect will continue until the whole is paid. The undertaking therefore adds nothing to the public burden; on the contrary it must result in pecuniary gain, for the county acquires this valuable property, (which will always be worth its cost), entirely from the savings made on the former system.

The Penitentiary is principally designed for the confinement, employment and reformation of vagrants and petty criminals, for whom no adequate provision had previously existed. Before its erection, it had been customary to punish these delinquents by simple incarceration in the county jail, where, in utter idleness, corrupted and corrupting each other by indiscriminate intercourse, they remained until the expiration of their sentences, and in most cases, when discharged it was only to return thither in a few days, or weeks at most, to go through the same routine. This course of treatment, so far from having any terrors, or constituting any punishment, had an opposite effect. The jail became a fruitful source of demoralization and vice, while the cost of its maintenance, coupled with the attendant expenses of trials, courts and juries, was annually increasing at an alarming rate. In 1843 the supervisors took the subject into serious consideration. They determined that some measures should be adopted whereby this class of persons might if possible be reclaimed, and at the same time be com-

Albany Penitentiary.

Albany County Penitentiary.

pelled to earn, if not all, at least a part of their subsistence. The necessary legislative authority was obtained in 1844. Messrs. Samuel Pruyn and Barent P. Staats of the city of Albany, and Lewis M. Dayton of the town of Rensselaerville, were appointed commissioners to devise a system of punishment, and a plan for the construction, management and discipline of a penitentiary. In due time the commissioners made their report, which being approved, the ground was purchased, and the buildings commenced in the summer of 1845. The south wing was first erected, and became ready for the reception of male prisoners in April, 1846. During the remainder of that year, and the beginning of the next, the central edifice and north wing were built, and in June, 1847, females were first admitted. The whole number of convicts which have entered the Penitentiary up to the first of November, 1848, is 831, of which number 143 then remained, namely, 101 males, and 42 females.

The county authorities were extremely fortunate in their arrangements. In 1846 Amos Pilsbury, for many years previously the warden of the Connecticut state prison, accepted the office of superintendent or principal keeper of the Penitentiary, for which he was eminently fitted by his long experience and great success in the management of prisons and prisoners. The discipline established is that known by the name of the *silent system*. It contemplates united labor, perfect order, silence and obedience. The physical and mental necessities of the convicts are carefully and fully supplied, and they are constantly, by night as well as by day, under the personal surveillance of the officers. The limits of this article will not admit of a lengthened detail of the precise mode pursued; it is sufficient to say that it has been attended with beneficial effects; several cases of complete and radical reformation have occurred, in which the subjects have returned to a moral and virtuous course of life. Under the experienced government of Mr. Pilsbury, it is said that in the Albany Penitentiary the silent, or as it is sometimes called the Auburn system, is more perfectly and efficiently administered than in any other prison. Besides the superintendent, there are also a deputy-keeper, 4 assistants, 2 guards, or watchmen, a matron, and assistant. The institution is also provided with a chaplain and physician. The whole is under the joint control of the supervisors of the county and the mayor and recorder of the city; who, through a board of three inspectors by them appointed, direct its concerns.

One feature in the management of the Penitentiary should be favorably noticed, as creditable to the good sense of the county government. The institution being purely benevolent and philanthropic in its objects, the supervisors early and wisely determined that no political or partizan considerations should enter into or influence its affairs. On this principle they have acted, and to it in a great measure may the success of the enterprise be attributed. Without enquiring into the particular creed of individuals on political subjects, it is quite sufficient that the persons to whom its direction is confided, are honest, capable, and discharge their duties with fidelity.

The commissioners deserve commendation for the ability with which they have discharged an important trust. Especially to Samuel Pruyn, now and for many years one of our city supervisors, belongs the credit of originating and accomplishing this great philanthropic design. His indefatigable zeal and perseverance, aided by the good counsel of his col-

The Albany Penitentiary closed in 1931. Since 1951, the Veterans Hospital has occupied the site. Below is a postcard of the penitentiary.

leagues, Dr. B. P. Staats and Lewis M. Dayton, has overcome every difficulty and discouragement. The Albany Penitentiary is destined to be the pioneer of a new system of criminal punishment. Already has the county of Erie imitated it, and in the county of Onondaga preparations are making for a similar establishment. If it be a desideratum that the county prisons in the state of New York shall become self-supporting institutions, and at the same time reformatory in morals, there is no hazard in predicting that the example will be extensively followed. The county of Albany has aided materially in hastening a great and important result in political economy. The larger counties will sooner or later adopt the plan, while the smaller ones may unite together and erect district penitentiaries.

COMMISSION OF JOHN ABEEL 1694.

I am indebted to A. Heyer Brown for the following copy of an ancient commission in his possession. John Abeel was the first mayor of Albany who was commissioned in this way, Peter Schuyler, who preceded him, having been named in the charter. In digging for the purpose of laying the foundation of the iron railing which was placed in front of the Middle Dutch Church a few years ago, the workmen exhumed the bones of many persons who had been interred there, among them doubtless those of Mr. Abeel, as his tombstone was thrown out with the others, and was afterwards placed in the pavement of the side walk. This document is written in a very bold old English character; and has the original seal attached, which is a cake of wax about three inches in diameter, and three-fourths of an inch in thickness, stamped with the British arms. In copying it the original orthography has been preserved.

WILLIAM & MARY by the Grace of God of England Scotland France & Ireland King & Queen defenders of the Faith &c To our loving subject John Abeel Esqr Greeting Reposing special trust and confidence in your Loyalty prudence and circumspection We do hereby nominate constitute and appoint you to be Mayor of the city of Albany for one year next ensuing ye fourteenth of October instant wth full power and authority to execute and perform all things whatsoever belonging to said office in as full and ample manner as any former Mayor of the said city hath done or might have lawfully done executed and performed To Hold Exercisse and enjoy the said office of Mayor of the said city with all things thereunto belonging and to have and receive all fees Salarys profitts perquisites benefits advantages priviledges immunities prehemmencys and appurtenances Whatsoever to the said office belonging or in any way appurtaining during the term aforesaid In Testimony whereof we have caused the seal of our province of New York in America to be hereunto affixed Witness Benjamin Fletcher our Capt General and Governor in Chiefe of our Province of New York Province of Pensilvania County of New Castle and the Territorys and Tracts of Land depending thereon in America and Vice Admiral of the same Our Lieut and Commander in chief of the Militia & of all the forces by Sea & Land within our Colony of Connecticut and of all the forts and places of Strength within the same on this fourth day of October in the sixth year of our Reign Anno Dom 1694 DAVID JAMISON P Secry

LIGHTS AND SHADOWS OF TRAVELING IN NEW YORK FIFTY YEARS AGO.

[In 1795, Mr. Isaac Weld Junior, viewing the frightful progress of anarchy in Europe, was desirous of "ascertaining whether in case of future emergency, any part of the United States might be looked forward to as an *eligible place of abode.*" He accordingly made the tour of the United States and Canada, and like a great many others of his genus, found very little to his taste, and nothing to give him the "slightest wish to revisit it." He could not learn that the trees in the wilderness were any where more than seven or eight feet in diameter! nor was there much of any thing on a sufficiently grand scale to meet his anticipations, except the musquitoes which he found at Whitehall. He arrived at New York in the summer of 1796, and gives the following account of his approach to, vexations at, and departure from, Albany.]

Being anxious to proceed on our journey before the season was too far advanced, and also particularly desirous of quitting New York on account of the fevers, which, it was rumored, were increasing very fast, we took our passage for Albany, in one of the sloops trading constantly on the North river, between New York and that place, and embarked on the 2d day of July, about two o'clock in the afternoon. Scarcely a breath of air was stirring at the time; but the tide carried us up at the rate of about two miles and a half an hour. The sky remained all day as serene as possible, and as the water was perfectly smooth, it reflected in a most beautiful manner the images of the various objects on the shore, and of the numerous vessels dispersed along the river at different distances, and which seemed to glide along, as it were, by the power of magic, for the sails all hung down loose and motionless. The sun, setting in all his glory, added fresh beauties to this calm and peaceable scene, and permitted us for the last time to behold the distant spires of New York, illumined by his parting rays. To describe all the grand and beautiful prospects presented to the view on passing this noble river, would be an endless task; all the various effects that can be supposed to arise from a happy combination of wood and water, of hill and dale, are here seen in the greatest perfection. After sunset, a brisk wind sprang up, which carried us on at the rate of six or seven miles an hour, for a considerable part of the night; but for some hours we had to lie at anchor at a place where the navigation of the river was too difficult to proceed in the dark. Our sloop was no more than seventy tons burthen by register; but the accommodations she afforded were most excellent, and far superior to what might be expected on board so small a vessel; the cabin was equally large with that in a common merchant vessel of three hundred tons, built for crossing the ocean. This was owing to the great breadth of her beam, which was no less than twenty-two feet and a half, although her length was only fifty-five feet. All the sloops engaged in this trade, are built nearly on the same construction; short, broad, and very shallow, few of them draw more than five or six feet of water, so that they are only calculated for sailing upon smooth water. The highlands, as they are called, extend along the river on each side for several miles. The breadth of the river is here considerably contracted, and such sudden gusts of wind, commencing from between the mountains, sometimes blow through the narrow passes, that vessels sometimes have their topmasts carried away. The captain of the sloop we were in, said that his mainsail was once blown into tatters in an instant, and a part of it carried on shore. When the sky is lowering, they usually take in sail going along this part of the river.

About four o'clock in the morning of the 4th of July, we reached Albany, the place of our destination, one hundred and sixty miles distant from New York. Albany is a city, and contains about eleven hundred houses; the number however is increasing fast, particularly since the removal of the state government from New York. In the old part of the town the streets are very narrow, and the houses are frightful; they are all built in the old Dutch taste, with the gable end towards the street, and ornamented on the top with large iron weathercocks; but in that part which has been lately erected, the streets are commodious, and many of the houses are handsome. Great pains have been taken to have the streets well paved and lighted. Here are four places for public worship, and an hospital. Albany is in summer time a very disagreeable place; it stands in a low situation, just on the margin of the river, which runs very slow here, and towards the evening often exhales clouds of vapors; immediately behind the town, likewise, is a large sandbank, that prevents a free circulation of air, while at the same time it powerfully reflects the rays of the sun, which shines in full force upon it the whole day. Notwithstanding all this, however, the climate is deemed very salubrious. The inhabitants of this place, a few years ago, were almost entirely of Dutch extraction; but now strangers are flocking to it from all quarters, as there are few places in America more advantageously situated for commerce. The flourishing state of its trade has already been mentioned; it bids fair to rival that of New York in process of time. The fourth of July, the day of our arrival at Albany, was the anniversary of the declaration of American independence, and on our arrival we were told that great preparations were making for its celebration. A drum and trumpet, towards the middle of the day, gave notice of the commencement of the rejoicings, and on walking to a hill about a quarter of a mile from the town, we saw sixty men drawn up, partly militia, partly volunteers, partly infantry, partly cavalry; the latter were clothed in scarlet, and mounted on horses of various descriptions. About three hundred spectators attended. A few rounds were fired from a three pounder, and some volleys of small arms. The firing was finished before one hour was expired, and then the troops returned to town, a party of militia officers in uniform marching in the rear, under the shade of umbrellas, as the day was excessively hot. Having reached town, the whole body immediately dispersed. The volunteers and militia officers afterwards dined together; and so ended the rejoicings of the day; no public ball, no general entertainment was there of any description. A day still fresh in the memory of every American, and which appears so glorious in the annals of their country, would, it might be expected, have called forth more brilliant and more general rejoicings; but the downright phlegmatic people in this neighborhood, intent upon making money, and enjoying the solid advantages of the revolution, are but little disposed to waste their time in what they consider idle demonstrations of joy.

Travel in New York, 1796.

We remained in Albany for a few days, and then set off for Skenesborough, in Lake Champlain, in a carriage hired for the purpose. The hiring of this vehicle was a matter attended with some trouble, and detained us longer in the town than we wished to stay. There were only two carriages to be had in the whole place, and the owners having an understanding with each other, and thinking that we should be forced to give whatever price they asked, positively refused to let us have either of them for less than seventy dollars, equal to fifteen guineas. We on our part as positively refused to comply with a demand which we knew to be exorbitant, and resolved to wait patiently in Albany for some other conveyance, rather than submit to such an imposition. The fellows held out for two days, but at the end of that time, one of them came to tell us we might have his carriage for half the price, and accordingly we took it. Early the next morning we set off, and in about two hours arrived at the small village of Cohoz, close to which is the remarkable fall in the Mohawk river, about ten miles from Albany..... From hence we proceeded along the banks of the Hudson river, through the town of Stillwater, which receives its name from the uncommon stillness of the river opposite to it, and late in the evening reached Saratoga, thirty-five miles from Albany. This place contains about forty houses, and a Dutch Reformed church, but they are so scattered about, that it has not the smallest appearance of a town. In this neighborhood, upon the borders of a marsh, are several very remarkable mineral springs; one of them, in the crater of a rock, of a pyramidical form, about five feet in height, is particularly curious. This rock seems to have been formed by the petrifactions of the water: all the other springs are likewise surrounded with petrifactions of the same kind. The water in the principal spring, except at the beginning of the summer, when it regularly overflows, remains about eight inches below the rim of the crater, and bubbles up as if boiling. The crater is nine inches in diameter. The various properties of the water have not been yet ascertained with any great accuracy; but it is said to be impregnated with a fossil acid and some saline substance; there is also a great portion of fixed air in it. An opportunity is here afforded for making some curious experiments. If animals be put down into the crater, they will be immediately suffocated; but if not kept there too long, they recover again upon being brought into the open air. If a lighted candle be put down, the flame will be extinguished in an instant, and not even the slightest spark left in the wick. If the water immediately taken from the spring be put into a bottle, closely corked, and then shaken, either the cork will be forced out with an explosion, or the bottle will be broken; but if left in an open vessel, it becomes vapid in less than half an hour. The water is very pungent to the taste, and acts as a cathartic on some people, as an emetic on others.

Of the works thrown up at Saratoga by the British and American armies during the war, there are now scarcely any remains. The country round about is well cultivated, and the trenches have been mostly levelled by the plow. We here crossed the Hudson river, and proceeded along its eastern shore as far as Fort Edward, where it is lost to the view, for the road still runs on towards the north, whilst the river takes a sudden bend to the west. Fort Edward was dismantled prior to the late American war; but the opposite armies, during that unhappy contest, were both in the neighborhood. The town of the same name, is at the distance of one or two hundred yards from it, and contains about twenty houses. Thus far we had got on tolerably well; but from hence to Fort Anne, which was also dismantled prior to the late war, the road is most wretched, particularly over a long causeway between the two forts, formed originally for the transporting of cannon, the soil here being extremely moist and heavy. The causeway consists of large trees laid side by side transversely, some of which having decayed, great intervals are left, wherein the wheels of the carriage were sometimes locked so fast, that the horses alone could not possibly extricate them. To have remained in the carriage over this part of the road, would really have been a severe punishment; for although boasted of as being the very best in Albany, it had no sort of springs, and was in fact little better than a common waggon; we therefore alighted, took our guns, and amused ourselves with shooting as we walked along through the woods. The woods here had a much more majestic appearance than any that we had before met with on our way from Philadelphia; this, however, was owing more to the great height than to the thickness of the trees, for I could not see one that appeared more than thirty inches in diameter; indeed, in general, the girt of the trees in the woods of America is very small in proportion to the height, and trifling in comparison of that of the forest trees in Great Britain. The thickest trees I ever saw in the country was that of a sycamore, which grew upon the bank of the Skenandoah river, just at its junction with the Patowmac, in a bed of rich earth, close to the water; yet this tree was no more than about four feet four inches in diameter. On the low lands in Kentucky, and on some of the bottoms in the western territory, it is said that trees are commonly to be met with seven and eight feet in diameter.

Beyond Fort Anne, which is situated at the distance of eight miles from Fort Edward, the roads being better, we once more mounted into our vehicle; but the miserable horses, quite jaded, now made a dead stop; in vain the driver bawled, and stamped, and swore; his whip had been previously worn out some hours, owing to the frequent use he had made of it, and the animals no longer feeling its heavy lash, seemed as determined as the mules of the abbess of Andouilles to go no farther. In this situation we could not help bantering the fellow upon the excellence of his cattle, which he had boasted so much of at setting out, and he was ready to cry with vexation at what we said; but having accidentally mentioned the sum we had paid for the carriage, his passion could no longer be restrained, and it broke forth in all its fury. It appeared that he was the owner of two of the horses, and for the use of them, and for driving the carriage, he was to have had one-half of the hire; but the man whom we had agreed with, and paid at Albany, had given him only ten dollars as his moiety, assuring him, at the same time, that it was exactly the half of what we had given, although in reality it fell short of the sum by seven dollars and a half. Thus cheated by his companion, and left in the lurch by his horses, he vowed vengeance against him on his return; but as protestations of this nature would not bring us any sooner to our journey's end, and as it was necessary that something should be immediately done, if we did not wish to remain all night in the woods, we suggested the idea, in the meantime, of his conducting the foremost horses as postillion, whilst one of our servants should drive the pair next to the wheel. This plan was not started with any degree of seriousness, for we could not have supposed that a tall meagre fellow, upwards of six feet high, and clad in a pair of thin nankeen breeches, would very readily bestride the raw boned back of a horse, covered with the profuse exudations which the intense heat of the weather, and the labor the animal had gone through, necessarily excited. As much tired, however, with our pleasantries as we were of his vehicle, and thinking of nothing, I believe, but how he could best get rid of us, he eagerly embraced the proposal, and accordingly, having furnished himself with a switch from the adjoining thicket, he mounted his harnessed Rosinante. In this style we proceeded; but more than once did our gigantic postillion turn round to bemoan the sorry choice he had made; as often did we urge the necessity of getting out of the woods; he could make no answer; so jogging slowly along, we at last reached the little town of Skenesborough, much to the amusement of every one who beheld our equipage, and much to our own satisfaction; for, owing to the various accidents we had met with, such as traces breaking, bridles slipping off the heads of the horses, and the noble horses themselves sometimes slipping down, &c., &c., we had been no less than five hours travelling the last twelve miles.

Skenesborough stands just above the junction of Wood creek with South river, as it is called in the best maps, but which, by the people in the neighborhood, is considered as a part of Lake Champlain. At present there are only about twelve houses in the place; but if the navigation of Wood creek is ever opened, so as to connect Lake Champlain with the North river, a scheme which has already been seriously thought of, it will, doubtless, soon become a trading town of considerable importance, as all the various productions of the shores of the lake will then be collected there for the New York and Albany markets. Notwithstanding all the disadvantages of a land carriage of forty miles to the North river, a small portion of flour and potash, the staple commodities of the state of New York, is already sent to Skenesborough from different parts of the lake, to be forwarded to Albany. A considerable trade also is carried on through this place, and over Lake Champlain, between New York and Canada. Furs and horses principally are sent from Canada, and in return they get East India goods and various manufactures.

Skenesborough is most dreadfully infested with musquitoes; so many of them attacked us the first night of our sleeping there, that when we arose in the morning our faces and hands were covered all over with large pustules, precisely like those of a person in the smallpox. This happened too, notwithstanding that the people of the house, before we went to bed, had taken all the pains possible to clear the room of them, by fumigating it with the smoke of green wood, and afterwards securing the windows with gauze blinds; and even on the second night, although we destroyed many dozens of them on the walls, after a similar fumigation had been made, yet we suffered nearly as much. These insects were of a much larger size than any I ever saw elsewhere, and their bite was uncommonly venomous. Gen. Washington told me, that he never was so much annoyed by musquitoes in any part of America, as in Skenesborough, *for they used to bite through the thickest boot*

Musquitoes appear to be particularly fond of the fresh blood of Europeans, who always suffer much more the first year of their arrival in America than they do afterwards. The people of the country seem quite to disregard their attacks. Wherever they fix their sting, a little tumor or pustule usually arises, supposed to be occasioned by the fermentation when mixed with the blood, of a small quantity of liquor, which the insect always injects into the wound it makes with its spicula, as may be seen through a microscope, and which it probably does to render the blood more fluid. The disagreeable itching this excites, is most effectually allayed by the application of volatile alkali; or if the part newly stung be scratched, and immediately bathed in cold water, that also affords considerable relief; but after the venom has been lodged for any time, scratching only increases the itching, and it may be attended with great danger. Repeated instances have occurred of people having been laid up for months, and narrowly escaping the loss of a limb, from imprudently rubbing a part which had been bitten for a long time. Great ease is also derived from opening the pustules on the second day with a lancet, and letting out the blood and watery matter.

RUTTEN KILL.

The grading of the great Hudson street ravine, anciently known as the Rutten kill, was nearly completed in 1847, from Hawk to Lark streets, and from near Lydius to State. During a period of about three years, from 50 to 250 persons, and 60 teams, were employed upon the work of grading and filling this extensive area. The ravine, originally 300 feet broad and 50 feet deep, throughout its entire length, received the lofty banks upon its borders, and was raised to a convenient grade, thereby furnishing a large tract for habitation, that had long been waste, or only occupied for brick kilns, and dirty reservoirs, where truant boys fished and bathed. Not less than 600,000 yards of excavation were made in blue clay, and an equal amount of filling was done by one contractor.

MANUFACTURE OF BRICKS.

The number of bricks manufactured in Albany during the last fifteen years, has averaged *sixteen millions* per annum, until the year 1847, when the quantity produced was only half that number in consequence of the reduced price, $2.50 per thousand.

CHRONICLE OF EVENTS IN ALBANY, 1847 AND 1848.

September, 1847.

13. The *Albany Morning Express*, a penny daily paper commenced by Stone & Henly, with a reported sale of 1600 copies of the first number. James Stanley Smith, editor. This constituted the fifth daily paper in the city at this time.......Capt. Abram Van OLinda of the Albany Republican Artillery, killed at the battle of Chapultepec, in Mexico. ......The fall examination of the State Normal School commenced. At the close of the exercises 64 graduates received their diplomas...... The superintendent of the Alms House reported to the Common Council, that the establishment had in charge 404 persons, the majority of them sick.

14. John H. Webb, of the late firm of Webb & Dummer, in this city, died at Hartford, Ct.

15. News received of the battles of Contreras and Cherubusco, which were fought in Mexico on the 18th and 19th of August, in which Lieut. Jacob Griffin of Albany was among the wounded.

16. First frost of the season.......A fire occurred at No. 164 North Pearl street, which destroyed the large carpenter's shop of John Jervis, a two story dwelling house, with several adjoining sheds. The firemen had a quarrel on the occasion.

17. Andrew Hamburgh died, aged 24.

18. Hannah Leavitt died, aged 51; wife of N. K. Leavitt.

19. Rev. John McCloskey installed, by Bishop Hughes, the first bishop of the new diocese of Albany.......Mary Law died, aged 55.

20. Upwards of a hundred vessels in port.

22. Flour $5.75.......William T. Lee, formerly of this city, died at Philadelphia, aged 27.

23. Margaret Nugent died, aged 33; wife of Henry P. Nugent.

24. The Democratic County Convention met; two sets of delegates appeared from one of the wards; failing to effect a compromise, a separation took place, the *Barnburners* choosing Peter Cagger to the state convention proposed to be held at Syracuse, and the *Old Hunkers* choosing Henry Rector. Both parties nominated Conrad A. Ten Eyck for Assembly......Charles C. Vail died, aged 21.;....John Stanwix died, aged 39.......Lydia Platt died, aged 82; widow of the late Ananias Platt.

25. The following steam boats were advertised to leave for New York this day: Hendrik Hudson, Captain Cruttenden; Isaac Newton, Capt. Peck; South America, Capt. Hultse; Columbia, Capt. Tupper; Rip Van Winkle, Capt. Riggs; Alida, Capt. G. D. Tupper; New Jersey, Capt. Hitchcock; all night boats except the Alida.......Martha Tappin died, aged 78.......Wm. J. McDermott died, aged 25; a printer, of New York, formerly of this city.

27. Over 20,000 bushels of corn arrived by canal this day.......The first term of the Court of Appeals held in this city, closed its session, having exhausted the calendar of 40 cases.

29. The Whig County Convention met, and nominated Robert H. Pruyn for Assembly.

30. The amount of flour transported over the Boston and Albany Rail Road since the 1st of January, 352,317 barrels more than the quantity transported in the same space of time last year. Receipts for September, 47,527 barrels.

October, 1847.

1. Catharine Van Benthuysen died, aged 33.
4. Mary M. Dexter died, wife of George Dexter.
5. The district schools of the city held a celebration. The scholars, numbering near 2,000, marched in procession with banners to the park in South Pearl street, below Lydius, known as Kane's Walk, where addresses were delivered and several pieces of music sung. The nine district schools of the city are attended by about 5,000 pupils, usually. ......James Clark died, aged 74; a merchant of good standing and wealth, for many years extensively engaged in the dry goods line, on the corner of Broadway and State street.......Mary A. Davidson died, aged 75.
6. Great meeting at the Capitol of the friends of a general manufacturing law.......Fire in the sheds behind the two story brick row, 182 and 192 North Pearl street; loss about $300.
8. Great meeting of that portion of the democratic party known as the *Barnburners*. There was much rain from above, and indignation from below. John Van Buren recited the wrongs and perils of himself and coadjutors at the recent convention at Syracuse, where they were voted out as irregular delegates. His speech was received with great applause on all sides.
9. During the week ending this day, 16,000 barrels of flour were transported over the rail road to Boston.
10. Abigail Osgood died, aged 28.
13. A convention of *Antirenters* met in the city, and adopted candidates from the tickets of the other parties, of such men as were known to entertain favorable views of their cause.
14. A meeting of the friends of the Wilmot Proviso, for the disposition of the slavery question, convened at the City Hall. Mr. Lewis of Ohio was the principal speaker on the occasion.
15. Mary Osborn died, aged 69; wife of Jeremiah Osborn......Chas. Van Ostrand died in New York, of an enlargement of the heart, aged 37; formerly a compositor in the office of the Albany Argus.
16. Ann Eliza Henderson died at Jersey city; widow of David Henderson, and eldest daughter of Archibald McIntyre of this city.
17. An attempt made to fire the buildings in the rear of McAuley's bakery in Grand street; it was discovered in season to prevent much damage........Mary Mott, formerly of Albany, died at Battle creek, Michigan.
18. The members of the Common Council, and other citizens, took passage in the Hendrik Hudson, to witness the ceremony of laying the corner stone of the Washington Monument, which took place on the 19th. ....Moses Cook died at Syracuse, aged 35; late of this city........ Martin S. Mills died, aged 26.
19. The store of Matthew Jordan entered by burglars, corner of Broadway and Steuben street........Several bakers prosecuted for sell-

ing light bread; the trial adjourned, the bakers contending that the Common Council have no right to regulate the price of bread, or its weight.......A stated session of the United States Circuit Court opened at the City Hall, with a large amount of criminal business on the calendar. Judge Conkling presiding.......A select committee of the House of Assembly reported a bill to tax bachelors and widowers; but the house disagreeing, it was referred to the committee of the whole.......An omnibus commenced running from the Exchange to Newton's Corners on the Shaker road...... Elizabeth Evertsen, widow of Evert Evertsen, aged 88, run over by a horse and cart as she was crossing State street, and so badly injured as to cause her death.

20. The Young Men's Association numbered 1,300 members....... Nicholas Brower died, aged 53.

21. Capt. Frost, a stranger, walking late at night in Quay street, was knocked down by two ruffians, and robbed, and thrown into the Basin; but was rescued, and his life saved.......Richard Schuyler and Robert Allen, concerned in an assault and battery upon Thomas Sampson, captain of a canal boat, with intent to kill, were captured and committed.

23. The trustees of the First Presbyterian Church, having purchased a lot for a new building on the corner of Hudson and Philip streets, contracted with J. R. Hays and Henry Rector for its erection, at $50,000. The foundations were begun...... Flour, $6.50; wheat, $1.40; corn, 71 cents; rye, 86 cents; barley, 80 cents. In consequence of the scarcity of vessels, and the inability of the rail road company to transport flour rapidly enough to meet the eastern demand, freights had advanced materially.

24. A collection taken in St. Joseph's Church for the purpose of raising funds to build a Cathedral in Albany; $4,500 were received....... Peter Bulson died, aged 78.

25. A special committee of the Common Council reported in favor of removing the dead in the Arbor Hill Burying Ground (which are frequently exposed by persons digging there for sand), to a suitable vault in the Albany Rural Cemetery, on the Troy road. No action was taken upon the subject.......The store of R. Reno, in South Pearl street, was entered by burglars, and $5 in cents carried away.

26. A meeting of the elder branch of the democratic party was held at the Capitol in the evening, the younger branch holding a convention at the same time in Herkimer. These events were invested with extraordinary interest.

28. Aurelia McGowan died, aged 40; wife of Minos McGowan...... Dorothy E. Brown died, wife of Stephen A. Brown.

29. Great meeting of the Barnburners at the Capitol; Mr. Wilmot, author of the famous *proviso*, was present, and delivered a long speech. John Van Buren followed, and received great applause for the eloquence, wit and sarcasm of his harrangue.......Genesee wheat $1.45.

30. Margaret Dermody died, aged 52; wife of Patrick Dermody.

31. Robert Lottridge died, aged 77.......Thomas L. Wilson died, aged 26.......The number of deaths at the Alms House for the last three months, 202; the great majority of cases being ship fever, a new epidemic. Permits granted since May 1st, 1200.

November, 1847.

1. Whig rally at the Capitol; said to have been "not very large, but *enthusiastic.*"...... Splendid aurora borealis in the evening...... There were 105 sloops and schooners lying at the Pier, and the Basin was choked with all sorts of craft, making preparation for the close of navigation....... Frances H. Deforest died, aged 17; wife of James P. Deforest.

2. The election resulted, as usual, in the triumph of the whigs.

3. Lucretia Johnson died, aged 68.

4. The weather extremely fine for the season; in the language of the editor of the Troy Budget, "The golden sunshine sleeps on the russet earth as quiet as an infant's slumber!"...... Crawford Livingston died of consumption at the Mansion House in Columbia county. He opened the first express office in this city, known as Pomeroy's Express.

5. The steam tug Commerce left the Pier for New York, with a convoy of 8 tow boats, and 12 lake boats, all heavily laden; and the North America left with 21 lakers in the same condition. This was characterized as a *big haul*. An impetus was given to it by a dreadful scowl in the heavens....... Fire in Tivoli Hollow; a large establishment in which several kinds of manufacturing operations were carried on, was burnt down; loss upwards of $20,000....... Wm. L. Cranston died, aged 26.

7. Townsley's store, 73 Quay street, entered by burglars, who failed to get remunerated for their labor.

9. This day was fixed upon by the Millerites for ending the functions of the Earth; but as on several other days previously appointed for the same catastrophe, the planet continued its accustomed duties, and left the deluded sect in great perplexity....... Sarah Thomas died, aged 58.

10. There had been transported over the rail road to Boston, up to this time, ten months, 455,221 barrels of flour.

11. The number of prisoners in the Penitentiary was 100...... Flour $6·12; wheat $1·38; barley 87c.

13. Catharine Ostrander died at Tully, aged 97; widow of John Ostrander a revolutionary officer and former sheriff of Albany.

17. Warm day for the season...... Charlotte McCauley died, aged 42.

18. Flour $5·87; two-rowed barley 87; rye 92; corn 75c....... John Long died, aged 26.

20. An affray between two engine companies, Nos. 5 and 6; one of No. 5's men had his jaw broken by a blow with a pipe....... An unsuspecting person was lured up Hudson street to the new level, and there robbed of his watch and $150....... Martin White died, aged 64.

21. Elizabeth Baillie died, aged 74.

22. The weather at this time much resembled summer....... Thomas Waters died of apoplexy, aged 65....... Charles Van Loon, pastor of a baptist church in Poughkeepsie, died of apoplexy, aged 28. He was a native of Albany, and a young man of extraordinary talents.

23. Opening lecture before the Young Men's Association by Benjamin F. Butler, and a poem by Epes Sargent.

25. Thanksgiving day; dark and gloomy....... A foot race at the Bull's Head; principal competitors Steeprock and Smoke, two Indians; Smoke won the race by 50 yards, making 10 miles in 1h. 11s.; the track heavy after a rain; 500 spectators supposed to have been present....... Brilliant northern light in the evening.

Chronicle of Events in Albany.

27. A forged draft presented and paid at the Exchange Bank, purporting to have been drawn by Tweddle & Darlington for $1805·25.......Thomas Rock died, aged 31.

28. The thermometer fell to 7° in the morning; the cold was felt severely on account of the suddenness of the change. ....James Alfred Green died, aged 25.......Alfred Goodwin died at Hartford, Ct.; he was of the firm of Goodwin & McKinney, hatters, of Albany.

29. Flour $6·12; no wheat in market; barley 75c.; oats 48c.; among the produce which arrived in the Albany Basin since the morning of the 27th, were 47,000 barrels flour, 52,000 bushels wheat, 20,000 bushels barley, 20,000 bushels oats, 390,000 pounds cheese, and 160,000 pounds butter. The receipts of flour exceeded 20,000 barrels a day about this time.......A slight fall of snow.

30. The mercury in the thermometer went down to zero.......The number of arrests for criminal offences cognizable at the police office during the year ending this day, was 2,859; being about 200 less than the previous year.

December, 1847.

1. The corner stone for a synagogue to accomodate the Jewish congregation of Beth Jacob was laid with appropriate ceremonies, at the corner of Lydius and Fulton streets, by Rabbi Wise.......The amount of tolls at the canal collector's office in this city since the opening of navigation was $358,067·72; do 1846, $263,551·03; showing an increase of 94,517·69, or 35 per cent.......Michael Dwyer robbed Olivette Michal, a catholic priest, of $875, on the Troy Road; and was apprehended a few days after.......Laughlen McPherson died, aged 89. He had resided in the city about twenty years, and was janitor of the Geological Rooms at the time of his death.

4. A rain storm had continued 48 hours, and showed no symptoms of a termination.......John W. H. Canoll died, aged 47.

5. Susan Anderson died, aged 67. She was one of the 18 persons who first united to form a baptist society in this city in the year 1811.

6. The corner stone of the edifice for the use of the First Presbyterian Church was laid without special ceremony, on the corner of Hudson and Philip streets.......T. W. Truax, one of the night police, in attempting to stop a pair of affrighted horses, received a blow which resulted in death.

7. The first popular election of chief engineer of the fire department took place, when James McQuade received 240 votes, and John Niblock 208; majority for the former 32. So great was the contest that absentees were brought from New York and Philadelphia, and only 44 voters were missing.......At a meeting of the Christian Mutual Benefit Society, Lemuel Jenkins was chosen president for the ensuing year.

9. A festival held at the City Hall for the benefit of the Union Mission Sunday School.

10. Rev. Dr. Scoresby of England, lectured before the Young Men's Association, in the Third Presbyterian church, on the Telescopes of Lord Rosse.

12. The river, swollen by the heavy rains of almost two weeks' continuance, overflowed its limits and submerged the Quay and lower part of the city.

13. A man by the name of Burns was drowned in the river at the foot of Hamilton street, by the capsizing of a boat......James Manning died, aged 23; one of the reporters for the *Albany Atlas*.

15. Canal closed.(?) The receipts of some of the principal articles of breadstuffs at Albany and Watervliet were as follows: Flour 3,951,722 barrels; wheat 3,897,576 bushels; corn 6,021,144 bushels. The value of the property received at the above places by canal, was estimated at $72,365,986......Mary Ridgeway died, aged 56.

16. Mr. Parsons, proprietor of the Carlton House, was knocked down and robbed of $138 in the office of that hotel, at 4 o'clock in the morning.......Phoebe Lewis died, aged 75; wife of Col. Henry Lewis.......Store of Mr. Shoemaker in Broadway, robbed by two boys, who were apprehended.

17. Charles D. Townsend died, aged 69. He had been a practitioner of medicine in the city nearly half a century, and acquired considerable eminence in his profession.......Oliver Johnson died at Maderia, whither he had gone for the recovery of his health.

18. First sleighing of any note.......William Roberts died, aged 25. ......James Radliff died, aged 62.......Elizabeth Veazie died, wife of Moses K. Veazie.

19. Catharine Irving died, aged 17.

23. The Middle Dutch Church, which had been closed several months for repairs, was opened, having undergone many improvements and decorations.......The first communication by magnetic telegraph with St. Louis, Missouri.......William Hale died, aged 57.

24. The Columbia steam boat arrived from New York, and was the last boat up this season.

25. Christmas—the day fine, and the sleighing of the best kind....... Fire in the bakery of Stephen Paddock; damage about $300.

26. Heman J. Whelpley died, aged 41; a legal practitioner of extensive business, and an active member of the whig party.......Margaret Delehanty died, aged 53; widow of the late Daniel Delehanty. ......The morning train west (it being Sunday) had but about half a dozen passengers; and the four trains during the day, (two each way) carried but sixty-seven altogether. This state of things was a most powerful argument, undoubtedly, for the suspension of the Sunday trains, which was soon after effected.

30. William I. Winne died, aged 45.

31. The Housatonic train was detained by a dense fog, and did not arrive at the depot in East Albany till 10 o'clock at night.......The trustees of the fire department disbursed $429 to indigent and disabled firemen during the year.

JANUARY, 1848.

1. New Year—the weather scarcely cold enough to require fire....... A steam boat left New York, expecting to reach Albany, but was debarred by the ice.......Lieut. Griffin arrived from the seat of war in Mexico, where he had been twice wounded.......David P. Page, first Principal of the State Normal School, died, aged 38.......James Connolly, while walking on the Quay, was assaulted by a blow, which caused his death.

2. A fire at 2 o'clock in the morning destroyed the frame building at

the head of Van Woert street....... The crockery store of Van Heusen & Charles in State street, robbed.

4. The legislature commenced its session under the new constitution, which limited its duration to 100 days....... The governor's message, consisting of 12,000 words, was telegraphed to New York in 8 hours. It was transmitted to Schenectady by rail road, in 29 minutes, and from thence to Utica in 2 hours 1 minute.

7. River closed.

8. Peter Carmichael died, aged 38...... James Boyd died, aged 38.

11. Thermometer ranged from 15° to 18° below zero.

21. William B. Winne died, aged 90. He was 48 years penny-postman....... The store of T. S. Stillwell broken open and robbed.

22. A pair of horses belonging to a farmer in Nassau, while crossing the river at the Greenbush Ferry, broke through the ice and were drowned.

24. Robert Taylor died, aged 45.

26. The city was refreshed with a shower of rain.

29. Jane K. Wyckoff, wife of Rev. I. N. Wyckoff, died....... Willard Walker died, aged 79; long an intelligent and enterprising merchant.

30. Isaiah Breakey, physician, died, aged 50....... James A. Coulter died, aged 28....... Hugh Riddle, a convict in the Penitentiary, committed suicide.

31. The sabbath schools in the city numbered 33, with 554 teachers, and 2,497 scholars....... Number of criminal arrests in the city during the month, 214....... Alms House expenses for the month, $3,544.

February, 1848.

1. Annual meeting of the New York State Medical Society; Dr. Alex. H. Stevens, president; Dr. Alex. H. Thompson, vice-president; Dr. Peter Van Buren, secretary; Dr. Peter Van OLinda, treasurer.

2. The committee of the whole in the House of Assembly, struck out the enacting clause of the bill to encourage the discovery of coal in the counties of Albany and Rensselaer....... A special meeting of the Common Council, on the resignation of the ward physicians, to devise means of supplying the poor with medical attendance....... Meeting of the Board of Trade to elect its officers; Wm. Chapman, president.

4. Jasper Hallenbake, M. D., died at New Orleans, aged 39; formerly of Albany....... Snow storm commenced on Friday and continued till Saturday evening; the mildness of the weather prevented its accumulation.

6. The store of W. & A. Kerr entered; a bootless depredation.

7. Major-General Quitman arrived in the city from Mexico, and met with an enthusiastic reception; after which he made the tour of the town, escorted by the military.

9. Mayor's Court, Recorder Wright presiding, who announced that there were 16 persons in jail awaiting trial. The civil calendar numbered 12 cases....... Catharine Maher died, aged 25.

10. Elisha C. Porter died, aged 34.

11. A stranger from Poughkeepsie robbed of a watch valued at $170, at a bowling saloon in Washington street.

12. Livingston Ludlow Humphrey died, aged 23.

> The Anti-Rent — Wars, (1839-1846) also known as the Helderberg War was a revolt by settlers who wanted independence from the medieval manor system run by the patroons. The anti-renters dressed up as Indians and attacked (tarred and feathered) sheriffs and others trying to collect the rents. During this time 25,000 people signed anti-rent petitions. In 1844, about thirty Anti-Rent "Indians" approached Elijah Smith of Grafton, who was chopping wood for the patroon. An argument took place and Elijah was shot and killed. The Anti-Rent movement began to lose steam in the 1850s but occasional protests and violence continued into the 1880s.

14. Catharine Van Zandt died, aged 60; widow of John Van Zandt. ......Upwards of 7,000 valentines passed through the post office.

17. The sheriff going out to Bern to sell property taken for rent, was followed by forty men on horseback, blowing horns and insulting him and his posse. No bids being made on the property, he brought away a pair of horses and a wagon.

19. William Jenkinson died, aged 81........Emma Webster died, aged 21; wife of M. L. Webster.......The Directors of the New York and Albany Rail Road decided on adopting the river line of survey, ten to two.

20. The number of convictions for state prison offences in the city during the last ten years, 335. Three persons in that time were convicted of murder, of which number one was hung. The number of petit larceny convictions, 800.

21. Aurora borealis, which assumed such an unusual appearance, as to cause an alarm of fire.

22. The anniversary of Washington's birthday celebrated with great enthusiasm........George W. Hawley died, aged 39........John Carroll died.

23. The store of Samuel W. King on Arbor Hill, robbed of a quantity of goods and money........Elizabeth Davis died, aged 53........Jane Anderson died, aged 29.

24. Announcement of the death of John Quincy Adams........John W. Jackson died, aged 66.

25. William Nordin died, aged 56.

26. Assault upon Mortimer J. Smith, editor of the Castigator, with slung shot, by two men disguised........Amy Roberts died, aged 80.

27. Navigation open as far north as Hudson........The store of David Van Cott, in Lydius street, robbed of $50 worth of cigars.

29. Prof. Agassiz commenced his course of lectures on Natural History at the Albany Female Academy........Fire in Dean street, No. 3; porter house burnt........Lester Bucklin Brown died, aged 22........Jane Frazer died, aged 77; wife of John Frazer........During the month there were 175 cases under medical treatment at the Alms House, of which 7 died.

MARCH, 1848.

1. A fire about 1 o'clock in the morning, at No. 83 Quay street, which communicated with about 20 brick and wooden buildings on the Dock and Broadway, below Hamilton street. Richard Gillespie, a printer, was killed by the falling of a wall, and two persons were burnt in the house where the fire originated. Loss of property estimated at $70,000.

2. Richard Van Zandt died, aged 23.

3. Benjamin Van Benthuysen died, aged 70; Laura A. Bowers died, aged 26; wife of Augustus Bowers.

4. Horace H. Gladding died, aged 20; Miss Buddington, a pupil of the Normal School, died.

5. Richard Rosier died, aged 73; Isabella Orr died, aged 57; wife of Samuel Orr.

6. Joseph Curtiss died, aged 71; Melissa Prime died, aged 34; James H. Brown died, aged 42.

The "Down with the Rent" banner, which may be the only Anti-Rent banner known to survive, belonged to Peter T. Hydorn, a Grafton resident who was a member of the Grafton Anti-Rent Mutual Protection Association. It is hanging in the Grafton Town Hall.

Anti-rent broadside in 1856. Original is at the Albany Institute of History and Art.

7. The house 14 Jay street robbed of the entire clothing of a lodger. ......Circulation of the *Albany Evening Journal*, daily, weekly and semi-weekly, stated to be 14,400.

8. The store of Mr. Hadley on the Dock broken open and robbed of a bad $20 bill.......Stephen Traver died, aged 37.

10. The grand jury presented "the rum and beer shops" of the city and county as a very serious evil, nearly all the business brought before the grand jury originating in these places; that in their opinion the great expenses incurred by the county for Alms House, Penitentiary and Jail expenditures grow out of the riots, robberies, assaults and batteries, and violations of the sabbath that occur or are connected with these places.

11. Thomas W. Harman, attorney, died at Schenectady, formerly a resident in Albany.

12. Alice Adaline Tallman died, aged 44; wife of Jonathan Tallman. ......Ruth Ann Glovenbury died suddenly, suspected to have been murdered........A meteor observed about 11 o'clock in the evening, in the northwest, which burst with an intonation resembling distant thunder.

13. Among the bills reported in the Assembly was one for the removal of the capital to New York; one for the construction of a bridge over the Basin; and one against the construction of a bridge over the Hudson at Albany........Ambrose Spencer died at Lyons, aged 83; he was many years chief justice of the state, and was regarded as one of the most distinguished jurists which the country has produced. He was interred at Albany......Lawrence L. Schuyler died, aged 49........A house in Green street robbed of a box of jewelery valued at $100........Attack upon Mortimer J. Smith, editor of the Castigator, by several persons, one of whom struck him in the face with a slung shot.

14. A meeting of citizens of Watervliet, when several thousand dollars were subscribed towards building a plank road from Albany to the Mohawk river, with a view to its continuance to Saratoga.......The managers of the *Married Sociable* transmitted to the treasurer of the Orphan Asylum $304.50, the avails of their hall given on the 7th in aid of the funds of that institution.......A lad robbed the store of Ford & Grant of $30.

15. Cold day; 3° below 0, at 5 o'clock in the morning........Philip Vanderlip died, aged 54......Odd Fellows' Hall, Cooper's Building, corner Green and State street, dedicated......Broadway Theatre robbed of $91 in specie.

17. St. Patrick's day celebrated with unusual ceremonies at the Catholic churches, and by the Hibernian Provident Society......Thomas Lee died, aged 59.......David B. Beatson, late of Albany, died in New York, aged 40.

18. The funeral of Judge Ambrose Spencer took place from St. Peters church. The procession was one of the most imposing that had been witnessed in many years........Capt. John Cook, of the Artillery, left the city for the army in Mexico, and was escorted to the depot by his company.

19. Chapel of the Penitentiary formally dedicated; sermon by Dr. Wyckoff on the occasion........The stores of Ainsworth & Northrup and Samuel Carey, in State street, robbed; the booty very small.......Rich-

ard Graves died.......Mrs. Elizabeth Foot died, aged 44........Henry Y. Lansing died, aged 29.

20. A farmer from Knox robbed of his pocket book by the ostler of Lockwood's tavern........Capt. B. S. Roberts, of the Mounted Rifles, who was the first to plant the American flag upon the national palace of Mexico, and the first to enter the *halls of the Montezumas*, arrived in Albany and received calls at the Mansion House........Sarah Bay Livingston died at New York; widow of the late Edward Livingston and youngest daughter of the late Chancellor Livingston........Rebecca Elizabeth Mix died, aged 22........John Niblock, walking in the evening in Broadway, was assailed and stabbed in both arms.

21. The steam boat Columbia reached Van Wie's Point, six miles below the city.

22. The ice slipped away quietly, without subjecting us to the usual annoyance of high water, and the steam boat Admiral arrived during the day, and left again in the evening for New York........Charles Quackenboss died of congestion of the brain, aged 33.

23. Sarah Tompkins died, aged 38.

24. The bill authorising the construction of a bridge across the Basin at the foot of State street, of the full width of the street, and another for opening a street on the Pier to the same width, passed the Assembly.

26. The leather factory of C. Hepinstall, in Washington street, robbed of a quantity of leather.

27. The steam boat Isaac Newton, on her way up the Hudson, ran down and sunk a schooner ......The first tow boat fleet of the season arrived from New York, consisting of 17 barges, conveyed by the old Commerce, and laden with spring importations for Albany merchants principally. ......The chamberlain reported that the whole expense of medical service for the poor since May 1, 1847, was $2,832 12......Amount of business done at the Justices' court, for the year ending this day, as follows: whole number of suits 2,400; amount of fees, $3 300; of which $1,189·83 remained uncollected. Each of the members of the court (three justices and one clerk) received $527 56; do. the previous year $738·87.

28. The two sections of the democratic party united in the nomination of Dr. Thomas Hun for Mayor.....The store of F. P. Malburn in Lydius street robbed of $20; that of H. Knowlton in Broadway of 75 cents; and an unsuccessful attempt made to enter that of A. B. Brown. ......Albany and Cohoes Rail Road bill passed the Senate.

29. Nicholas Van Rensselaer, a soldier of the revolution, died, aged 94. He was with Montgomery at the storming of Quebec; was at Ticonderoga, Fort Miller, Fort Ann, and at Bemis's Heights, and was deputed to convey the intelligence of Burgoyne's surrender to the citizens of Albany.......A young man of fashionable appearance arrested for passing counterfeit money.

30. A house in Orange street robbed of a watch by Catharine Tanner.......The whigs nominated John Taylor for mayor.

31. Anna Maria Tyler died, aged 51; wife of Benjamin O. Tyler.

APRIL, 1848.

1. William Caldwell, a retired merchant, died, aged 72. His place of business, in which he succeeded his father, James Caldwell, was at

No. 58 State street. Since his retirement, he resided principally at Caldwell, Lake George, where he had a large estate.......Margaret Jane Bell died, aged 21; daughter of Joseph Bell.

3. Isabella Adeline Peckham, died; wife of Rufus H. Peckham, and daughter of Rev. Wm. B. Lacy.

4. John T. Richards died, aged 23.......Richard Thompson died, aged 45.

5. The dwelling house 21 Green street robbed of a quantity of clothing.

6. A dwelling robbed of $30.......A fire in Chapel street destroyed a carpenter's shop and the candle factory of Josiah Winants.......Hon. Wm. H. Seward delivered an eulogy on the late John Quincy Adams, in the North Dutch Church.......A splendid display of aurora borealis.

7. Fire corner Green and Bleecker streets.......Charles Davis died, aged 26.......Maria Vibbard died, aged 30; wife of Philip G. Vibbard.

8. An attempt to rob William Gibbs, on the Troy road, who defended himself so well as to escape with his life and money.

9. Caroline Schmidt died, wife of Rev. F. W. Schmidt, pastor of the German Lutheran Church.

10. The store of James Taylor, corner of Green and South Lansing streets, robbed of $10 in specie.

11. Charter election, which resulted in the success of the whig candidate for mayor, by 129 majority. The vote stood for Taylor 3115; for Hun 2977......The legislature appropriated $15,000 for the erection of an edifice for the State Normal School—a sum quite inadequate to the purpose.

12. The legislature, having sat out its term of one hundred days, prescribed by the new constitution, adjourned at 2 o'clock in the afternoon, having passed 381 laws.

13. Catharine Douw died, widow of John D. P. Douw.......Mary Ann La Grange died, aged 51.......Gertrude Van Sanford died, aged 67.

14. The new steam tug Baltic, intended for the service of the Albany Tow Boat Company, came up to take her place in the line.......A halibut, captured off St. George's Bank, weighing upwards of 300 lbs., displayed in the Albany fish market.......Meeting of Germans, French and Poles at the National Hotel, to celebrate the establishment of a republic in France, and the rapid progress of republicanism throughout Germany and Europe.

15. The law went into effect prohibiting dogs from running at large without muzzles.......A fire in the vicinity of the Basin above Colonie street, destroyed much property and rendered several families houseless; loss about $12,000. A riot among the firemen.

18. Meeting of the new board of Common Council for organization. The following appointments were made: L. D. Holstein, clerk; H. H. Hickcox, dep. chamberlain; Hooper C. Van Vorst, attorney; George W. Carpenter, surveyor; Samuel McElroy, assistant surveyor; Nelson W. Scovel, marshal; John McBride, overseer of poor; Henry B. Fay, alms-house physician.

19. Cold day; snow fell to a considerable depth, accompanied by a piercing wind from the north.......Mary Jane Wright died, aged 29; wife of Samuel Wright.

20. James Farrell died, aged 78 ......Garrett Middleton died, aged 42.

21. Riot, corner South Pearl and Rensselaer streets; two persons broke into the store of Albert Allen, beat and robbed him, and were arrested therefor.

22. Joseph Graham died, aged 35.......The Armenia, a new steam boat, left New York at 7 o'clock in the morning, made the usual landings, and arrived at the dock at 4 o'clock.......A fire, supposed to have been incendiary, consumed the out houses in the rear of 111 Washington street; 2 horses burnt.

23. Fire on the corner of Dallius and Herkimer streets burnt off the roof.

24. Great fires; commenced on the corner of Westerlo and Church streets, at 4 o'clock in the afternoon, and before it was quelled, destroyed twenty buildings on Church, Westerlo, Dallius and John streets, and among them the Free Missionary Protestant Church. Loss estimated at $30,000. This fire was hardly subdued, before another broke out about 10 o'clock in the evening, near the corner of Green and Beaver streets, which destroyed about twenty more buildings, valued at more than $60,000.......Margaret Yates died; wife of Benjamin Yates.

25. The store of Burrows & Nelligar, corner South Pearl and Plain streets, robbed of $28........William Hamburgh died, aged 20.

26. Chester Moore died of apoplexy, aged 55......Sarah Dodge died, aged 83; widow of Edmond Dodge ......Catharine M. Van Buren died, aged 30; wife of S. G. Van Buren.

27. Elizabeth Whalen died, aged 64; wife of Jeremiah Whalen.

28. Jewish Synagogue, Beth Jacob, in Fulton street, consecrated. ......Great meeting at the Capitol of the friends of progressive liberty, to congratulate on the recent movements in Europe.

29. Jane McNaughton died, wife of Peter McNaughton.......The Carlton House, corner of South Pearl and State street, took fire, and narrowly escaped destruction; loss about $1000.......A two story frame house, corner of Centre and Colonie streets, took fire about 9 o'clock and was partially destroyed.......Ten Eyck's soap and candle factory in Green street took fire about 10 o'clock.......About 1 o'clock the Carlton House was again on fire, but was soon extinguished ......At 11 o'clock in the evening, a fire was discovered in John street, which consumed a shed and stable; a horse was badly burnt.......The coroner and four men going in a wagon to hold an inquest on the body of a man drowned, were precipitated down the embankment of a canal bridge above the Patroon's mansion, and the whole party so severely injured, that another coroner was called to officiate.......A portion of the walls of the Westerlo street church, which was burnt at the late fire, were blown down by the high wind, and buried two boys.

30. A carpenter shop on the Patroon's creek burnt.......The Dundee Warehouse, corner S. Pearl and Division street, set on fire in the basement.......Mary Maher died, aged 60; wife of James Maher....... Sarah Schuyler died, widow of Harmanus P. Schuyler.

MAY, 1848.

1. The Common Council made the annual appointments of watchmen, street-inspectors, &c., and offered a standing reward of $100 for the discovery of any person engaged in setting fire to any building in the city.

2. James Foster died, aged 62.......Elizabeth M. Osbrey died, aged 28; wife of William L. Osbrey.

3. Caroline Smith, accused of stealing a child, having several times escaped the hands of justice, was finally tried and convicted, and sentenced to three years imprisonment at Sing Sing.

4. A fire at 2 o'clock in the morning destroyed two houses and a stable in Denniston street, and burnt three horses. Two robberies were committed at the same time.......Betsey Bently died, aged 80; widow of Capt. Randall Bentley........James Gough died, aged 37.

5. The house corner of Broadway and Lumber streets burnt at 1 o'clock in the morning.......The steam boats Alida and Hendrik Hudson left New York at 7 o'clock in the morning, and arrived at Albany, the former at 2 o'clock 55 minutes, and the latter 15 minutes after, having made but one landing on the way up. The time made by the Alida was as follows: Caldwell 9h. 7m.; West Point, 9h. 34m.; Newburgh, 9h. 55½m.; Poughkeepsie 10h. 40m.; (landed 2½m.); Hyde Park 11h.; Catskill, 12h. 31m.; Athens, 12h. 42m.; Albany, 2h. 55m. The two boats not more than 15m. apart during the whole eight hours, with an ebb tide.

6. Peter Drum died, aged 45.

8. Steam propeller Albany arrived from Hartford, intended for freight and passengers; length 140 feet, burden 240 tons; built in Philadelphia, ...Alfred Wickes died, aged 30.

9. Mrs. Merrifield, wife of Richard Merrifield, died.......Meeting of the friends of Ireland at the City Hall; adopted a constitution, and elected officers, John Tracy in the chair; Robt. Higgins and Matthew Jordan, secretaries; Wm. Hawe, treasurer.

10. Hannah Vosburgh died, aged 82.......George W. Gardner died, aged 35.......Nearly 1000 Swiss emigrants arrived by the morning boats, on their way to Wisconsin.

11. Store of Daniel Brown, corner Broadway and Colonie streets, robbed of $10 cash and other articles.......Abram Pittinger died, aged 47.

12. High water; a rise of 5 feet in 17 hours; docks overflowed....... William Newton of Albany died at Vera Cruz, aged 24.

13. The Albany and Cohoes Rail Road Company elected its officers. ......Two frame houses in Centre street destroyed by fire........Levi S. Hoffman died, aged 45 ......Ann Taylor died, wife of Robert Taylor.

14. Severe frost, which nipt many tender buds.......Edmund Hall, arrested for a robbery committed the night previous.

15. The Board of Trade commenced operations in the rotunda of the Exchange.......The camphene store of S. T. Thorn, in Church street, took fire, which communicated with twenty-five other buildings before it was arrested. A Dutch immigrant lost $1450 in gold, his all.

16. The store of George Dexter, 57 State street, robbed of $25.

17. Two fires occurred, attended with small damage.

18. William A. McKown died, aged 39.

19. An attempt made to fire the buildings between Philip and Grand streets without success.,......Michael Henley died.

20. The office of Joy & Monteath, on the Dock, robbed of $8 in change, and over $300 in counterfeit money which had accumulated during several years business.

23. Hazeltine's store in Washington street robbed of $60; also the store of Joseph Davis in State street robbed of several dollars.

172   *Chronicle of Events in Albany.*

24. The store of Daniel Fry robbed of $25,......William B. Emerson died, aged 36.

29. David Newland's house, 456 Broadway, took fire; damage small.

30. A sportsman's club organized, at a meeting of citizens at the Broadway House; having for its object the observance of the law for the preservation of game.

31. John G. Russ drowned in the basin, in attempting to get on board a canal boat; his wife and children were present at the occurrence...... Business of the Justices' Court for the month of May; suits commenced, 270; amounts received for costs, $194.12; amount outstanding, $115. ......A frost at some places near the city.

JUNE, 1848.

1. Capt. Edward Whitney died, aged 49.......Mary Schuyler died, aged 68; widow of Samuel Schuyler.......Elizabeth Garretson died.

2. Cowell's store on the dock broken open, and robbed of $15....... James C. Mull, stabbed several days previously by an insane man, died of his wounds.

3. Shoe store of William Fossard broken open and robbed of boots and shoes.

4. Matthew Gregory died, aged 91; he was an officer of the revolution, and one of the few survivors of the ancient order of Cincinnati. He came to this city soon after the war, was successful in business, and retired with an ample fortune.

5. The Albany County Court entertained an application for the incorporation of the village of Cohoes, under the act of 1847. The village contains an area of 1¾ square miles, and has a population of 4,200 inhabitants.

6. A barn burnt on Arbor Hill; a battle with paving stones between a crowd of boys, for the honor of drawing a hose cart.

7. The great menagarie of Sands, Lent & Co., entered the city, presenting a pageant of some interest. The huge gilded chariot, drawn by four large elephants, contrasted singularly enough with the Liliputian chariot, drawn by eight Shetland ponies.

12. The store of Mr. Van Heusen, corner of Broadway and Bleecker street, broken open, and a quantity of butter carried off..... The Common Council refused to grant $250 towards defraying the expenses of the Fourth of July Celebration, whereat much wrath and indignation was enkindled.

16. A fire in the charcoal vault of the Delavan House, which was extinguished with small damage.

17. A large building, supposed to be set on fire, situated between North Pearl and Ten Broeck streets, was burnt.......The Pearl Street House burnt.......Andrew Lloyd died, aged 74.......Abby M. Delavan died, aged 47; wife of Edward C. Delavan.

22. Datus E. Frost's provision store, corner of Lydius and Swan streets, destroyed by fire, occasioned by the explosion of a camphene lamp. The firemen had a riot on the corner of State and Pearl streets. The walks and streets were plentifully sprinkled with bricks and stones, on the following morning, and the doors and windows of the houses in the vicinity, presented indellible marks of the force with which the missiles were hurled.

25. An attempt was made to break into the grocery store, corner of North Pearl and Van Schaick streets, but a series of difficulties interposed to render the enterprise unsuccessful.

26. Anna Garrison died, aged 97.

27. A meeting in the park, announced by the blaze of tar and the roar of cannon, to respond to the nomination of Taylor and Fillmore.

29. Anna Matilda Visscher died.

30. James Lightbody died, aged 83.

July, 1848.

1. Elizabeth Campbell died, aged 18.

2. Corner stone of the Catholic Cathedral laid, on the corner of Eagle and Lydius streets, by Bishop Hughes.......Charles Sayles died, aged 70.

4. The national holiday celebrated with its usual accompaniments, but with an unwonted sullenness, on account of what was deemed an overweening parsimony on the part of the Common Council in withholding supplies for ammunition, *ad libitum*......The remains of Capt. Abraham Van OLinda arrived in the morning, from Mexico, and were escorted to the City Hall.

5. Twentieth anniversary of the Albany Female Seminary, under Rev. Mr. Garfield.

7. The funeral honors to the remains of Capt. Van OLinda were performed. The eulogy by Col. John Sharts.......A man killed by an accident, while laying the foundation of the Cathedral, in Lydius street. ......John Summers died.

8. As an instance of commercial despatch quite extraordinary, the steam propeller Mohawk arrived from Hartford in the morning, was unladen, took in about 300 tons of freight, mostly corn, and sailed on her return the same evening.

9. Catharine Staats died, aged 65; wife of William N. Staats....... Bridget English died, wife of Patrick English.

11. Canal Bank closed by order of the comptroller, and a commission issued to investigate its concerns.......Splendid display of aurora borealis in the evening.......Seventh anniversary of the Alumnæ of the Albany Female Academy.

13. The workmen engaged in laying gas pipes in Broadway, above Steuben street, came in contact with the foundation of the ancient mansion of Gen. Ten Broeck, which half a century ago stood across Broadway at that point. At the time it was built it was outside of the city walls or palisades.......The Boston City Guards arrived, as the guests of the Albany Burgesses Corps, by whom they were received and escorted......Enthusiastic meeting of the Friends of Ireland at the Capitol, Hon. Erastus Corning presiding. There was universal sympathy for the cause of Ireland, in view of the expected outbreak in that country, for freedom from British dominion.......The store of Lehrberg & Lederer, in south Broadway, robbed of $1,500 worth of silks.

14. This, it is believed, was the first day of the discontinuance of the Sunday train of cars west.......George S. Brown died, aged 38.

15. Anna T. Gough died, wife of John T. Gough.

16. Garret Hogan died, aged 65. He had filled the offices of county

treasurer, deputy sheriff, and various other places of trust, with great fidelity and zeal for the public interest. He resigned the office of secretary of the Albany County Mutual Insurance Company, on account of ill health, some time before his death, the business of which he had conducted with faithfulness nearly eight years.

17. The steam boat Oswego arrived from New York with a fleet of 5 barges and 24 lake boats in tow, all heavily laden.......Upwards of 300 men engaged in the construction of a new depot to accommodate the increasing trade between this city and Boston. Its dimensions are 750 feet by 133 feet; believed to be the largest building in the United States.

19. Feast of St. Vincent observed at St. Joseph's Church, by the celebration of the pontifical high mass by Bishop McCloskey, and the panegyric of St. Vincent was delivered by Rev. Dr. McCaffrey, of Maryland. ......The Rev. Benj. N. Martin was installed pastor of the Fourth Presbyterian Church. The Rev. E. N. Kirk and the Rev. Mr. Fisher of Cincinnati, former pastors of the church, officiated on the occasion...... Meeting of the *Barnburners* at the Capitol, to respond to the nomination of Martin Van Buren for president; Dr. Barent P. Staats in the chair.

18. Dr. Henry McHarg died, aged 23.......William Long died, aged 62.......Henry R. Gossman died at Cayuga Bridge, aged 28; formerly of Albany......Ann Kilkenny died, aged 29; wife of Francis Kilkenny.

20. John Leonard died, aged 18.

21. An abortive attempt to fire the Tivoli Rail Road Mills, at the upper end of Broadway.......About 700 recruits passed through the city in the morning, destined for the newly acquired territory in Mexico.

24. Sarah Justina Fassett died, aged 23.

25. Company H, 1st Regiment New York Volunteers, Capt. Farnsworth, arrived on board the Hendrik Hudson, and were gallantly received by the several military companies of the city, consisting of the Albany Republican Artillery, Albany Burgesses Corps, Emmet Guards, Van Rensselaer Guards, and Washington Riflemen. Capt. Farnsworth succeeded to the command on the death of Van OLinda. Of the 70 privates who left the city, but 45 returned.

28. Anniversary of the district schools. The pupils assembled in the Capitol Park, to the number of upwards of 2000, and walked in procession to Kane's Walk, corner of South Pearl and Westerlo streets, where appropriate exercises were held.

29. John S. Vandervolgen died.

30. Cornelius Alexander died.......A robber assaulted a lady in the street, who was accompanied by another lady and a gentleman, and wrested from her hand a purse of money and a ring valued at $20, with which he fled and eluded pursuit.

31. A new organ of great power, recently placed in the Middle Dutch Church, was opened for public inspection. It was the largest in the city, and cost $4,000.......A meeting at the Capitol of the friends of Ireland, the mayor in the chair.......Great rain storm at night, which damaged streets and houses. Nearly 3 inches of rain fell, about a week's supply in a rainy season.......The steam boat Oregon, on her trip down the river, came in contact with a sloop, by which several of her berths were stove in, and a young lady in one of them injured.

Chronicle of Events in Albany.

August, 1848.

1. Judge Harris robbed of his pocket book containing $300, at the rail road depot; the robber was immediately arrested.......Jacob Featherly died, aged 45.......Elizabeth Demming died, aged 17.
2. Jeremiah Smith died, aged 88.
3. Mariah Hallenbake died, aged 21; wife of Christopher Hallenbake.
4. The store 58 state street robbed of a large quantity of silks and other articles of dry goods.......The police officers arrested Lewis Van Cord at his house, and found in his possession a large quantity of stolen goods.......Margaret Bryan died, aged 24.......John Glass fell from a tow boat and was drowned.
6. Charlotte Hoard died, aged 84; widow of Jonathan Hoard, a revolutionary soldier.
8. Four military companies arrived from New York as the guests of the Emmet Guards. They were accompanied by Lothian's Band; and having extended their visit to the Watervliet Arsenal, and Troy, returned by the evening boat to New York.
10. Dr. Jonathan Eights died at his residence, corner North Pearl and Columbia streets, aged 75. He practiced his profession in this city nearly half a century, with distinguished skill and success, and was universally esteemed and respected.......William Updike died of paralysis, aged 34.......Mary Jane Van Buren died, aged 22.
12. Thos. Sullivan, a deaf mute, run over by the Troy rail road train and killed.
13. James Aiken died of paralysis, aged 59.
14. A man convicted of stealing a pair of horses from Chauncey Dexter, was sentenced to three years in the state prison.
15. Dr. Morrell made an ascension in a balloon from the Mineral Spring Garden in Ferry street. The ropes were cut about 5 o'clock in the afternoon, and the balloon rose majestically, and took a notherly direction........Thomas Maher, aged 8 years, was drowned in the pond at the head of Canal street, formed by the pent up waters which formerly supplied the Foxen kill. This was the sixth life lost in the pond during two years.
17. The Great Fire. It broke out in a small shed adjoining the Albion Hotel, corner of Broadway and Herkimer streets, said to have been occasioned by a washerwoman's bonnet. The flames spread with great rapidity before a strong south wind, taking in their course both sides of Broadway and Church street, and crossing to the Pier, swept every thing down as far as the cut at the foot of Maiden lane. The large buildings in the vicinity of the Eagle Tavern, presented a temporary barrier to the flames, which having passed, they swept on as far as the corner of Hudson street. The wind then suddenly shifted to the north, and drove the fire in an opposite direction. At night it commenced raining, which rendered the buildings less combustible, and assisted in staying the conflagration. Besides the great number of buildings consumed, vast quantities of every kind of property perished with them. The losses of the insurance companies was full half a million, and the whole loss could not have been much short of three millions of dollars, contained in about 600 houses. The exact area burnt over, including Basin and Pier, was 37 acres, about one-thirtieth of the whole city. It

---

Eights had a son James — who painted early scenes of Albany, now famous among historians for their accuracy, but Eights also was one of the first Americans to visit the Antarctic as a member of the Edmund Fanning "South Sea Fur Company and Exploring Expedition" of 1829.

Albany has seen its share of fires. On November 17, 1793, fire destroyed much of the block of Market Street bounded by State Street, Middle Alley and Maiden Lane. In 1797 several blocks were destroyed in the North end of the city. Just a few months before on April 24, 1848 was a fire that burned 40 buildings. This fire of 1848 burned nearly 600 buildings.

extended 700 feet west from the river on Herkimer street, 350 on Dallius, running northwardly; 900 feet on Union street, continuing in the same direction; 300 feet east on Hudson, and 1600 on Quay street, runing south. This was the most densely populated part of the city....... Robert Harvey died, aged 48.

19. The store of Matthews Brown, corner of Chapel and Canal street robbed of $30.......The firemen had a riot in South Pearl and State streets, as they were returning from a false alarm of fire, and several persons who took no part in the affray were severely injured.

20. The sleeping apartment of Mr. Joseph Parker was robbed of $250 and a gold watch.

21. The Common Council ordained that no wooden building, or building wholly or partially covered with wood, should thereafter be erected in any part of the city of Albany, east of Lark street; and that every eaves trough, cornice and gutter should be made of metal or other incombustible material.

[Margin note: Albany had seen enough fires to finally make this law.]

22. Isaac Brown died at Somerville, N. J., aged 49; formerly a hardware merchant in Albany.

23. Eliza Salisbury died, aged 28; wife of William Salisbury....... Benjamin P. Gregory, formerly of Albany, died at Jersey city, aged 43.

25. Betsey McCarty died, aged 21.

26. Whig meeting called at the Capitol on the receipt of Gen. Taylor's letter, accepting the nomination of the democrats of Charleston, S. C., to run on their ticket with Gen. Butler. Great indignation was expressed at this unexpected turn of things, and the disposition prevailed to throw the General overboard; but it was wisely determined to postpone the act to Monday night.......James Hanley, shot at the riot of the 19th, died of the wound after a week of intense suffering.

27. Perry Tucker died, aged 47.

28. The Common Council decided to improve the burnt district by widening and straightening the streets, and raising the grade of Broadway between Hamilton and Lydius streets........Adjourned indignation meeting of the whigs at the Capitol, convened to digest the Taylor and Butler nomination at Charleston, S. C. It was decided that the alarm of Saturday evening was groundless, and that there was no danger to be apprehended from the circumstance of Gen. Taylor having accepted a democratic nomination.

30. Explosion of a steam boiler at the furnace of Ransom & Co., by which a portion of the roof and wall was blown off, and four of the workmen severely injured.

September, 1848.

1. Col. Robert E. Temple returned to the city from the Mexican campaign.......John Hunt, forger of a check on the Exchange Bank for $1805, in November last, was arrested and committed for trial....... George Eugan died of wounds received by the fall of the draw at the Boston Ferry two weeks before.

2. Mrs. Elizabeth Van Schaack died, aged 42; wife of John Van Schaack.

3. Rev. Elias Vanderlip died, aged 84. He was the patriarch of the Methodist Episcopal Church in this city. He was born at Carl's Neck,

Staten Island, Feb. 10, 1765, and left fatherless at an early age. When the British took New York, he was apprenticed to the shoe-making business. In 1787, he became a convert in the M. E. Church. In 1792, he first began to exhort. In 1796, he settled in Albany and opened a shoe store, but lost all his stock by fire; he was then invited to Niskayuna (now Watervliet) to preach. In 1800, he was ordained a deacon, and his first appointment was to Pittsfield circuit in 1802. In 1804, he was ordained an elder. In 1805, his name was put down for Albany. He preached from 1805 to 1836, when he was obliged by old age to desist. In April last he was laid upon his bed with a broken thigh, from which, with the frosts of years thick upon him, and fearless of death, his immortal spirit winged its flight to a better world.

5. Althia A. Loveland died; a pupil of the Normal School from Franklin, Delaware county.......Mary Relay died, aged 86; widow of Robert Relay.

7. Hon. John C. Spencer, of Albany, delivered the Address before the State Agricultural Society, at its annual fair, in Buffalo.

9. Fire in the building north of the Mansion House, which was burnt out, leaving the walls standing. The jewelary store of Mulford & Wendell, the clothing store of Robert Freeman, the large law library of Samuel Stevens, and the Daguerreotype Rooms of Gavit, besides law offices, work shops and store rooms, were considerably injured before they could be removed, or entirely consumed. Loss about $12,000, mostly insured.......The receipts of the Albany and Boston rail road, for the week ending this day, were $17,000 for passengers alone, being the largest sum received from that source in any one week since the opening of the road.

12. The new steam ferry boat, T. W. Olcott, commenced running at the Albany and Boston Rail Road Ferry........Barney Flinn died, aged 34; a volunteer in the company under Col. Temple.

13. Nomination of Gen. John A. Dix, by the *Barnburner* or *Free Soil* convention at Utica, for the office of governor of the state.......The house of A. McCowan robbed of money and jewelery.

14. Frost; fires necessary in the morning....Annual exhibition of the Albany and Rensselaer Horticultural Society, at the Geological Rooms. ......Meeting of the Clay whigs at the Capitol, when it was resolved to abandon Taylor, and adopt Henry Clay, and attempt to carry his election.......Meeting of the rail road companies at Utica, when it was resolved to reduce the fare between Albany and Buffalo to $9 75, being an average of 3 cents a mile......Elizabeth Wadsworth died, aged 73.

15. Fire in the wooden building, corner of South Pearl and Hamilton street; damage small.......Elizabeth Somers died, aged 48; widow of the late John Somers.

18. The Common Council resolved to extend the area of the steamboat landing south to Lydius street.

19. The members of the city corporation proceeded in a body to Congress Hall to pay their respects to Gen. Worth.......On the opening of the Mayor's court the grand jury came in with thirty indictments without having finished their business. There were 170 criminal cases on the calendar before.......The last remittance from the New York relief committee to the sufferers by the fire in Albany, amounting in the whole to $12,035.......A ship carpenter by the name of Paul, while

engaged at work on a boat, fell into the Basin and was drowned....... Flour $5.75 to $5.87½; wheat $1.30; oats 34 cents.; pork $13. The receipts by canal this day were: flour 6,236 bushels; ashes 47 do; whiskey, &c. 7,600 gallons; corn, 3,296 bushels; barley 2,755; oats 7,246; wheat 4,948; peas and beans 225; clover and grass seed 1,100 lbs.; butter 49,520; cheese 20,262; wool 1,527......Sarah Winne died, aged 80; widow of Kilian I. Winne......Elizabeth Loucks died, aged 63; wife of John H. Loucks.......Esther S. Meech died, aged 20.

20. Henry Z. Whitney died, aged 23.

21. The seventh semi-annual examination of the State Normal School, when 96 pupils graduated.

22. Snow on the neighboring hills.......The heavy iron rail on the Mohawk and Hudson Rail Road being completed, an experimental trip was made with three cars, resting upon india rubber springs, and drawn by the Mohawk locomotive, built by McQueen. The trip was performed in 30 minutes, and the return trip in 24 minutes, being at the rate of 42¼ miles an hour.

23. Dr. Christopher C. Yates died at Parishborough, Nova Scotia; he was originally from Albany, and took a very active and decided part in the controversy on the great question of the origin and treatment of yellow fever.......John W. Lightbody died, aged 26.

25. Robert Sutton and Chauncey Van Lew, two notorious rogues, escaped from jail and eluded pursuit.......William R. Cantine died, aged 49......Thomas Flood died, aged 39.

26. Meeting at the Capitol of the old Hunkers, to ratify the state nominations. R. W. Peckham, Esq., and Mike Walsh were the principal orators, and the consumption of tar was enormous!

27. First heavy frost of the season, which had been unusually cold, with rain 13 days.......Thomas Gale died, aged 28.......Peter H. Hilton died.......Abraham T. Evertsen died, aged 41.......Hannah Ten Eyck died, wife of William Ten Eyck.

28. Convention of Antirenters, who nominated Gen. John A. Dix for governor and George W. Patterson for lieutenant governor.

29. Ellen Ann Graham died, aged 18.

30. Two persons returning from market at night were attacked without provocation, and severely beaten by three ruffians, who escaped detection.......The boarding house 659 Broadway robbed by a young man who got access under pretence of taking board.......David Hemphill died, aged 39.

OCTOBER, 1848.

2. At a meeting of the Common Council, the committee on the reorganization of the Fire Department reported in favor of paying firemen $30 per annum, and appointing a chief engineer, with a salary of $700, to devote his time wholly to the duties appertaining to his office....... Matthew Clerton died, aged 73.

3. The shoe store of Jacob Lansing in Broadway robbed of a quantity of boots.

4. Jane Van Schaack died; widow of the late Nicholas Van Schaack. ......The dwelling house of Elijah Simmons, in Pearl street, robbed of $40.

5. The county convention of whigs nominated John L. Schoolcraft

for congress, and James Kidd for county treasurer.......Sarah Ann Holliday died, aged 33; wife of James Holliday.......Elizabeth Delehant, aged 32; wife of Andrew Delehant.

6. Flour, $5·50 to $5·87; buckwheat, $2·12; wheat, $1·27; corn, 67; barley, 71 to 74.

7. Trotting match on the Troy road for a purse of $200. Jack Rossiter and Lady Moscow were the only competitors; the former won all three heats; time 2·38, 2·39, 2·37. After which Ferguson and McGovern had a two mile foot race for a purse of $30. Ferguson took it in 11.27 minutes.......The grand jury came into court with the following indictments: burglary in the first degree, 3; assault and battery, 6; assault and battery on an officer, 1; grand larceny, 3; obtaining property under false pretences, 1; indecent exposure, 2; passing counterfeit money, 2; robbery, 1; sealed, 10.

8. F. W. Ingmire ordained as a minister of the gospel at the Pearl Street Baptist Church.......A fire destroyed a barn in South Lansing street........William Maternaghan, an auctioneer, long in the employ of J. I. Jones, found drowned in the river below the city......John A. Wilson died, aged 51.

9. Attempt to rob Newton's clothing store.......The steamboat Oswego reached the dock with 36 boats in tow; 13 barges and 23 lakers.

10. The drug and medicine store of Burrows & Nelligar robbed; the only booty was a few pennies.......The Albany Burgesses Corps elected their officers for the ensuing year.

11. Hunt, alias Webb, convicted and sentenced to five years imprisonment, for a forgery on the Exchange Bank.......William K. Amsden died, aged 28.

13. John Gibson assaulted James Galvin with a knife, in Broadway, at 7 o'clock in the evening......Robert Lyle, a native of Scotland, died. ......Catharine Carey died, aged 23.

14. The steam propeller Hartford made her first landing here; intended to run in connection with the Albany, between this city and Hartford; being the third steam packet plying between the two cities. Her capacity about fifty tons greater than the Albany.

15. A fire destroyed the steam saw mill of Clement Warren in Water street, corner of Quackenbush, a large quantity of lumber adjoining, and the fur shop of George C. Treadwell. Loss about $10,000....... Another fire, in the basement of the Baptist Church in South Pearl street, during service; did but little injury.......Riot in the evening at a shanty in the burnt district.

16. Elvenah C. Anderson died, aged 16.......Harriet Booth died, aged 21.......Mrs. Prudence White died, aged 60.

17. Robbery of the house No. 1 Phœnix Place.......Mrs. Ann Bassett died at Penn Yan, aged 86; widow of the Rev. John Bassett, formerly pastor of the Reformed Protestant Dutch Church in Albany....... Mrs. Almira Barnard died, aged 55.

20. James Keeler died at Summit, Wisconsin, aged 76; forty years a resident in Albany.

22. Arthur Quinn died, aged 36.

23. The rail road train from Buffalo, under the new arrangement, came through in 17 hours; the usual time was 24 hours; a gain of nearly one third.......James Butler died, aged 40.

24. Sale of Dutch Church lots on Snipe, Knox, and Sand streets, at $32.50 to $37.50 each......James Frazer died, aged 52.

26. The hall corner of Green and Beaver streets, fitted up for the use of the Independent Order of Odd Fellows, was dedicated with appropriate ceremonies.

27. The iron cover of the great tank belonging to the gas company, in the process of erection in the north part of the city, fell about 2 o'clock, while more than 30 persons were at work upon it, by which one was killed, and others severely injured. The damage sustained by the company was about $1,000.......Giles Fredericks killed by the accident at the gas works......Catharine Foy died, aged 50; wife of Philip Foy.

29. A fire took in the basement of No. 8 Green street, which destroyed the building. Loss $20,000......The stable and slaughter house of James A. Putnam, on Arbor Hill, burnt.......George L. Thomas shot by Jane Elizabeth Britton, in John street......Jane Connick died, aged 72; widow of Andrew Connick.......Elizabeth Scott died, aged 59.

30. Dense fog; the steam boats due in the morning did not arrive till 4 o'clock in the afternoon. The boats which left this city the day before, were overtaken by the morning boats.......George Charles died, aged 81.......Dr. Amos N. Burton died, aged 37.

31. William Duncan Topp died, aged 42.

November, 1848.

1. Mutual agreement of the jewelers to close their stores at 8 o'clock in the evening.......Rev. W. H. Waggoner settled pastor of the Universalist Church.......Trotting match on the Troy road, between Jenny Lind and Mac, which was won by the latter in 2·38.

2. The stables of Judge Gansevoort and Watts Sherman in Washington street set on fire and consumed in the evening.

3. William Annesley died, aged 81.

4. Whig torch-light procession in the evening, during which several outrages and serious accidents occurred........Barn burnt in the rear of 14 Lumber street.

5. Rev. B. T. Welch announced to his congregation, the First Baptist Church, in Pearl street, that he had accepted a call to the Pierpont street church in Brooklyn.

7. Election day; the whig ticket elected by a large majority; on the presidential electors, the vote stood for Taylor 3473; Cass 1833; Van Buren 1376; for congress, J. L. Schoolcraft 3818; C. Bouton 1500; B. R. Wood 1351; for assembly, R. H. Pruyn, 1729; H. Rector 558; Amos Dean 631; Joel A. Wing 1858; Eli Perry 1011; J. R. Van Rensselaer 27; Stewart 727. Connected with the usual balloting, a vote was taken to get the public sentiment on the scheme of supplying the city with water at the public expense. The vote for water was 4405; no water 6; brandy and water strong, 1......By a wonderful achievment of art and science in the telegraph, the result of the elections in Massachusetts and other more remote states was pretty certainly known before 9 o'clock in the evening; and within twenty-four hours after the closing of the polls, it was ascertained almost beyond question that Gen. Zachary Taylor was elected president by a large majority of votes.

10. Cold morning; thermometer indicated 15+0. Some of the ponds in the vicinity frozen over.......A shanty erected on the burnt district took fire and was razed to the ground; during which a man in attempting to push off a sloop from the dock, fell overboard and was drowned. ......Cecilia Williams died in New York; wife of Ezra Williams, and daughter of the late Sebastian Visscher, of Albany.......Jeremiah Wallace died, aged 80.

11. The mayor acknowledged a donation from the Shakers of blankets to the value of several hundred dollars.......A snow storm commenced in the evening.......Jennet White Autey died, aged 48; wife of Alex. Autey.

13. Elizabeth Kelley died, wife of Michael Kelley.

18. Fire in the basement of the Jewish Synagogue in Herkimer st.

19. Fire in the bakery corner Union and Hamilton streets.

20. Snow storm.

21. Monument erected in the cemetery over the grave of Maj. Lewis N. Morris, who fell at the battle of Monterey.

22. Christopher Anthony died, aged 25.

23. Steam boat Belle left this port with 29 boats in tow, and arrived at New York in 42 hours. The tonnage of this fleet was 4500, and its probable value $170,000.......Patrick Morrison died, aged 26.

24. Fire in Broad street destroyed three houses and a stable....... Uriah Marvin died, aged 79.

25. Silas Houghton, an aged and respected citizen died.......Mary Leslie died, aged 53.

26. Joseph S. Clark died, aged 68.......Joseph Blake died, aged 39.

27. The common council at a full meeting passed a new fire law, entirely reorganizing the fire department.......James Hays a news boy, in attempting to jump from the cars fell under the wheels, and was killed. ......The steam boat Belle left the Dock with 39 boats in tow, and arrived in New York in 46 hours. This was by far the largest number of boats ever attempted to be towed by one steam boat on the Hudson river.

28. The Firemen held an indignation meeting at the Capitol, and had a procession with banners in *honor* of the new fire law, which was not framed in consonance with their views and feelings.......Joseph Robinson died, aged 62.......Francis Finnegan died, aged 53.

December, 1848.

3. John Macready robbed the house of P. Maher in Ferry street, while the family were at tea, but was caught in the street by an officer. ......Case of affray and stabbing at the grocery of O'Connell, corner of Green and Lydius streets.

5. Presidential electors of the state of New York met at the Capitol at 4 o'clock afternoon, and having organized, adjourned to the following day, when they cast their votes unanimously for Zachary Taylor for president of the United States.......Wesley Goodwin arrested on the complaint of his wife for brutal usage towards herself and children, for which he was sentenced to the Penitentiary one year.......Alida Visscher died, aged 82; widow of the late Teunis G. Visscher.

6. Horace Pierce died, aged 42.

7. Great competition between the Isaac Newton and Rip Van Winkle steam boats; prices of fare to New York 50 cts. to 0.......Stable burnt on the corner of Dove and Spring streets.

8. Margaret Mayer died, widow of the late Frederick G. Mayer.

9. The canals closed by order of the commissioners, in order to prosecute the enlargement. The weather was still extremely mild, after a week of rain, and no ice had yet formed either in the canal or river. ......Dr. John H. Douglass, an aged and wealthy citizen of Troy, fell and expired in the Capitol, while attending the comptroller's tax sale. ......Beermah B. Herner died, aged 35.

10. Elizabeth Van Bergen died.......Julia Ann Shaw died.

11. Edward Harty died, aged 64.

14. Henry M. Fergusen died, aged 61; Thaddeus Pomeroy died at Clinton, Mich., aged 30, formerly of Albany.

16. Athaliah Serviss died, wife of William Serviss.

17. Charles Roarke died, aged 41.

18. Fire in the area of the Carlton House.......Christiana M. Vandenburgh died, aged 47; wife of John A. Vandenburgh.......The store of James Osborne robbed of a few dollars in change.

20. James Goadby precipitated himself from a third story window upon the street pavement, in a fit of derangement, which caused his death.......Sarah Beuchanan died, aged 65.......James Maroney drowned in the Canal Basin......Rev. W. H. Wagoner installed pastor over the Universalist church.

21 Snow; no steam boat left for New York.......Nancy Lovett died. ......John MacNamara died, aged 30.

22. First sleighing.......Cynthia Webster died at Albion, Orleans county, aged 78; widow of the late Charles R. Webster of Albany.

23. John Thomas, Jr. died......John Timmons, a drayman, killed by a locomotive in attempting to cross the rail road track before the train. ......The cold weather completely closed the river, but the Columbia forced her way up through the ice.

24. Jane D. Thompson died, aged 80........Harriet Bassett died, aged 16.

25. Slight fire in the Delavan House.......David Thomas died.

26. A train arrived from New York by the Housatonic road, which opened on Christmas for the winter travel, promising to make daily trips in eight hours, by daylight.......Fanny Perceval died, aged 50; wife of George Perceval.

27. Rev. Rutger Van Brunt installed pastor over the Third Reformed Protestant Dutch Church in Albany; the former pastor, Dr. William H. Campbell, preached the installation sermon.

28. The river completely shut, no boat having arrived.

29. Jane Ann Boyd died, daughter of the late Peter Boyd.

30. Ceremony of presenting a sword to Gen. Wool took place at the Capitol. The sword, the gift of the state, valued at $1700, was presented by the governor, John Young, and was in approbation of his distinguished services in the war with Mexico.......Seventy freight cars left the depot for New York by the Housatonic road.

31. Trinity church, corner of Herkimer and Franklin streets, purchased by the South Baptist Society, was first used by them for public worship.

THE COLONY OF RENSSELAERSWYCK.

1614 TO 1646.

The Dutch having in 1609 discovered and explored the North river, which has since taken the name of their navigator, Hudson, a number of adventurers followed in this track, who pursued a small trade with the Indians, and made further voyages of discovery along the coast and up the rivers. The most noted of these were Adrian Block, Hendrick Corstiaensen and Cornelius Jacobsen Mey, in the year 1614. We compile from the valuable *History of New Netherland*, by Dr. E. B. O'CALLAGHAN, the following account of the progress of the colony of Rensselaerswyck for a period of thirty-three years.

Intelligence of the discoveries made by Block and his associates having been transmitted to Holland, was received there early in the autumn of 1614. The united company by whom they had been employed, lost no time in taking the steps necessary to secure to themselves the exclusive trade of the countries thus explored, which was guarantied to them by the ordinance of the 27th of March. They sent deputies immediately to the Hague, who laid before the States General a report of their discoveries, as required by law, with a figurative map of the newly explored countries, which now, for the first time, obtained the name of NEW NETHERLAND. A special grant in favor of the interested parties was forthwith accorded by their High Mightinesses, in the following terms:

"The States General of the United Netherlands to all to whom these presents shall come, greeting. WHEREAS Gerrit Jacob Witsen, former burgomaster of the city of Amsterdam, Jones Witsen and Simon Morissen, owners of the ship called the Little Fox, (het vosje,) Captain Jarn de Witt, master; Hans Hongers, Paul Pelgrom, and Lambrecht van Tweenhuysen, owners of the two ships called the Tiger and the Fortune, Captains Adriaen Block and Hendrick Corstiaensen, masters; Arnoudt van Lybergen, Wessel Schenck, Hans Claessen, and Barens Sweetsen, owners of the ship the Nightingale (Nochtegael,) Capt. Thuys Volckertsen, merchant in the city of Amsterdam, master; and Pieter Clementsen Brouwer, Jan Clementsen Kies, and Cornelis Volkertsen, merchants in the city of Hoorn, owners of the ship the Fortune, Capt. Cornelis Jacobsen Mey, master, have united into one company, and have shown to us by their petition, that after great expenses and damages by loss of ships and other perils, during the present year, they, with the above named five ships, have discovered certain new lands situated in America, between New France and Virginia being the sea coasts between 40 and 45 degrees of latitude, and now called NEW NETHERLAND: " And whereas, they further represent that We did, in the month of March, publish, for the promotion and augmentation of commerce, a certain consent and grant, setting forth that whosoever should discover new havens, lands, places, or passages, should be permitted exclusively to visit and navigate the same for four voyages without permitting any other person out of the United Netherlands to visit or frequent such newly discovered places, until the said discoverers shall have performed the four voyages, within the space of time prescribed to them for that purpose, under the penalties therein expressed &c., and request that We should be pleased to accord to them due testimony of the aforesaid grant in the usually prescribed form: Wherefore the premises having been considered, and We, in our Assembly, having communication of the pertinent report of the petitioners relative to the discoveries and finding of the said new countries between the above-named limits and degrees, and also of their adventurers, have consented and granted, and by these presents do consent and grant, to the said petitioners, now united into one company, that they shall be permitted exclusively to visit and navigate the above described lands, situate in America, between New France and Virginia, the seacoasts of which lie between the 40th and the 45th degrees of latitude, and which are now named New Netherland, as is to be seen on the figurative maps by them prepared; and to navigate, or cause to be navigated, the same for four voyages, within the period of three years, to commence from the first day of January, 1615, or sooner, without it being permitted, directly or indirectly, to any one else to sail, to frequent, or navigate, out of the United Netherlands, those newly discovered lands, havens, or places, within the space of three years, as above, on penalty of the confiscation of the vessel and cargo, besides a fine of fifty thousand Netherlands ducats, for the benefit of said discoverers. Provided, however, that by these presents we do not intend to prejudice or diminish any of our former grants and concessions; and it is also our intention that if any disputes or differences should arise from these our concessions, that they shall be decided by ourselves. We therefore, expressly command all governors, justices, officers, magistrates, and inhabitants, of the aforesaid United Netherlands, that they allow said company peacefully and quietly to enjoy the whole benefit of this our grant, and to interpose no difficulties or obstacles to the welfare of the same. Given at the Hague, under our seal, paraph, and the signature of our Secretary, on the 11th day of October, 1614."

Having thus obtained for themselves the exclusive right to visit and trade with the countries in America, lying between the fortieth and forty-fifth degrees of north latitude, of which they strangely claimed to be the first discoverers, so shortly after Hudson's visit, the above named merchants, who now assumed the name and title of The United New Netherland Company, proceeded to make the arrangements necessary to draw from their new possessions the largest returns. On an island situated at the head of the navigation, near the west bank of the Manhattan river, now named De Riviere van den Vorst Mauritius, or Prince Maurice's river, and immediately below the present city of Albany, they caused a trading house to be erected, thirty-six feet long and twenty-six feet wide. Around this was raised a strong stockade, fifty feet square, which was next encircled by a moat eighteen feet wide, the whole being defended by two pieces of cannon and eleven stone guns, mounted on swivels, and garrisoned by ten or twelve men. This post mitted exclusively to visit and navigate the same for four voyages without permitting any other person out of the United Netherlands to visit or frequent such newly discovered places, until the said discoverers shall have performed the four voyages, within the space of time prescribed to them for that purpose, under the penalties therein expressed &c., and request that We should be pleased to accord to them due testimony of the aforesaid grant in the usually prescribed form: Wherefore the premises having been considered, and We, in our Assembly, having communication of the pertinent report of the petitioners relative to the discoveries and finding of the said new countries between the above-named limits and degrees, and also of their adventurers, have consented and granted, and by these presents do consent and grant, to the said petitioners, now united into one company, that they shall be permitted exclusively to visit and navigate the above described lands, situate in America, between New France and Virginia, the seacoasts of which lie between the 40th and the 45th degrees of latitude, and which are now named New Netherland, as is to be seen on the figurative maps by them prepared; and to navigate, or cause to be navigated, the same for four voyages, within the period of three years, to commence from the first day of January, 1615, or sooner, without it being permitted, directly or indirectly, to any one else to sail, to frequent, or navigate, out of the United Netherlands, those newly discovered lands, havens, or places, within the space of three years, as above, on penalty of the confiscation of the vessel and cargo, besides a fine of fifty thousand Netherlands ducats, for the benefit of said discoverers. Provided, however, that by these presents we do not intend to prejudice or diminish any of our former grants and concessions; and it is also our intention that if any disputes or differences should arise from these our concessions, that they shall be decided by ourselves. We therefore, expressly command all governors, justices, officers, magistrates, and inhabitants, of the aforesaid United Netherlands, that they allow said company peacefully and quietly to enjoy the whole benefit of this our grant, and to interpose no difficulties or obstacles to the welfare of the same. Given at the Hague, under our seal, paraph, and the signature of our Secretary, on the 11th day of October, 1614."

Having thus obtained for themselves the exclusive right to visit and trade with the countries in America, lying between the fortieth and forty-fifth degrees of north latitude, of which they strangely claimed to be the first discoverers, so shortly after Hudson's visit, the above named merchants, who now assumed the name and title of The United New Netherland Company, proceeded to make the arrangements necessary to draw from their new possessions the largest returns. On an island situated at the head of the navigation, near the west bank of the Manhattan river, now named De Riviere van den Vorst Mauritius, or Prince Maurice's river, and immediately below the present city of Albany, they caused a trading house to be erected, thirty-six feet long and twenty-six feet wide. Around this was raised a strong stockade, fifty feet square, which was next encircled by a moat eighteen feet wide, the whole being defended by two pieces of cannon and eleven stone guns, mounted on swivels, and garrisoned by ten or twelve men. This post was placed under command of Jacob Jacobz Elkens, who continued here four years in the employ of this association, during which time he was well liked by the natives, with whose language he was thoroughly conversant. Another fort was erected, under the superintendence of Corstiaensen, on an elevated spot on the southern extremity of the island Manhattan, where an insignificant establishment had already existed in 1613, as already stated. Possession was thus taken of the two most important points on the river, to which the powerful Mohawks, the fierce Manhatters, and the various other tribes in the neighborhood, brought their valuable furs to be exchanged for European trinkets and duffels. The post at the mouth of the river was, however, the traders' head-quarters. Hither annually came the ships of the New Netherland Company, and hence was annually exported whatever had been collected from the Indians, after their hunting season, at the neighboring coasts and rivers; from the distant castles of the Five Nations to the hunting grounds of the Minquas. Considerable activity consequently prevailed among the agents and other servants of the company in pushing trade, and exploring the adjoining coasts. Runners scoured the woods, in order to become acquainted with the habits of the Indians, their manner of dealing, and to establish friendly relations with those tribes to which the Dutch were not already known.

The Restless having now thoroughly examined the coasts as far as 38°, and penetrated up the Delaware as far as the Schuylkill, Capt. Hendricksou returned to Holland in the summer of 1616, from his second voyage, for the purpose of laying before the managers of the company the particulars of his explorations. On being presented to the States General, he made a verbal report of his adventures, on the part of his employers, who, at the same time, petitioned their High Mightinesses, setting forth that they had, at considerable expense, discovered and explored certain countries, bays, and three rivers, lying in latitude from 38° to 40°, with a small yacht called the Restless, of about eight lasts burden, commanded by Capt. Cornelis Hendricksen, Jr., of Monnickendam, which yacht the petitioners had built in the aforesaid country. They thereupon demanded, in conformity with the provisions of the ordinance of March, 1614, the exclusive privilege of trading thither.

Skipper Hendricksen's report, it is to be regretted, is both meagre and brief. After the detail of the preceding discoveries, he described the country as well wooded with oak, pine, and hickory, which trees he added, were in some places covered with vines. He stated that he found in those parts male and female deer, turkeys, and patridges, and that the climate was as temperate as that of Holland; that he had traded for seal and sable skins, furs, and other peltries, with the Minquas, from whom he had ransomed three of the company's servants, who had left their employment among the Mohawks and Mohegans, having given, in exchange for them, beads, kettles, and other merchandise.

Whether it was that the States General were dissatisfied with the small amount of information furnished in this report, or that other interests had by this time sprung up, which were anxious to participate in the advantages of the trade to America, or that paramount reasons of public policy influenced their deliberations, their High Mightinesses laid this application on the table, and the exclusive grant to the New Netherland Company expired, by its own limitation, on the 1st of January, 1618, in the spring of which year, the breaking up of the ice, and the accompanying freshet on the River Mauritius, or North river, did so much injury to the company's fort on Castle island, that their servants were obliged to abandon it, and to remove a few miles south, to the banks of the Tawalsontha creek, now called the Norman's kill. Here, on a hill, called by the Indians Tawassgunshee, they erected a new fortification, and concluded with the great confederacy of the Five Nations a formal treaty of alliance and peace.

This celebrated Indian confederation was composed of five tribes, namely the Mohawks, Oneidas, Onondagas, Cayugas, and Senecas, and generally known by the name of the Iroquois. They inhabited the country bounded on the east by the great River Manhattes and Lake Irocoisia, or Champlain; on the west by Lake Erie and the River Niagara; on the north by Lake Ontario and the Great river of Canada; and on the south by the country of the Lenni Lenape, or Delawares. When the Dutch arrived in America, the tribes composing the Five Nations were at war with the Algonquin, or Canada Indians. But the latter having formed an alliance with the French, who some years previous to this date, had commenced the settlement of New France, as Canada was called, derived such powerful aid from the fire-arms of their European allies, that the Iroquois were defeated in almost every rencontre with their ancient enemy. Smarting under the disgrace of these unexpected repulses the Iroquois hailed the establishment among them, now of another European nation familiar with the use of those terrible instruments, which, almost without human invention, scattered death wherever they were directed, and defied the war club and bow and arrow as weapons of attack or defence. Though jealous by nature, and given to suspicion, the Indians exhibited none of these feelings towards the newcomers, whose numbers were too few even to protect themselves or to inflict injury on others. On the contrary, they courted their friendship, for through them they shrewdly calculated on being placed in a condition to cope with the foe, or to obtain that bloody triumph for which they thirsted. Such were the circumstances which now lead to that treaty of alliance, which, as the tradition goes, was concluded on the banks of the Norman's kill, between the Five Nations and the Dutch.

Nothing could surpass the importance the warlike inhabitants of those ancients forests attached to the ratification of this solemn treaty. Each tribe sent its chief as its ambassador to represent it on this occasion. The neigboring tribes—the Lenni Lenape and Mohegans—were invited to attend; and there in the presence of the earth, their common mother—of the sun, which shed its genial heat on all alike—by the murmurs of that romantic stream, whose waters had been made to flow by their common Maker from all time, was the belt of peace held fast by the Dutch and their aboriginal allies, in token of their eternal union. There was the calumet smoked, and the hatchet buried, while the Dutch traders declared that they should forthwith erect a church over the weapon of war, so that it could no more be exhumed without overturning the sacred edifice, and whoever dared do that should incur the resentment of the white men. By this treaty the Dutch secured for themselves the quiet possession of the Indian trade, and the Five Nations obtained the means to assert that ascendancy which they ever after maintained over the other native tribes, and to inspire terror far and near among the other savages of North America.

The West India Company having finally in 1623 concluded its preparatory arrangements, and completed, with the sanction of the States General, the articles of agreement between the managers and the other adventurers, lost no time in commencing operations and forming establishments in New Netherland, which was erected into a province. A fortified post, called Fort Orange, was commenced on the west bank of the river Mauritius, as the North river was called, a few miles north of the redoubt which had been erected in 1618 on Tawalsontha creek, and thirty-six (Dutch) miles from the Island of Manhattans.

In 1629, a charter of privileges and exemptions was passed for the encouragement of patroons to settle colonies, and in the following year several wealthy and influential directors of the Dutch West India company hastened to avail themselves of its advantages. Bastiaen Jansen Krol, commissary, and Dierck Cornelissen Duyster, under-commissary at Fort Orange, having learned that a tract of land called Sannahagog, laying on the west side of the North river, extending from Beeren island, by the Indians called Passapenock, up to the Smackx island, and in breadth two days' journey, was for sale, purchased the same from Paep Sikenekomptas, Nancouttanshal, and Sickoussen, the native proprietors, for Kiliaen van Rensselaer, a pearl-merchant in Amsterdam, and one of the directors of the West India Company. Three months afterwards, Gillis Hoossett purchased, in the presence of Jan Jansen Meyndertsen, Wolfert Gerrittsen, and Jan Tyssen, trumpeter for the same gentleman, from Cottomack, Nawanemit, Abantzene, Sagisguwa, and Kanamoack, the lands lying south and north of Fort Orange, and extending to within a short distance of Moenimines Castle, then situated on what is now called Haver island, at the mouth of the Mohawk; and from Nawanemit, one of the last named chiefs, his grounds, called Semesseeck, stretching on the east side of the river, from opposite Castle island to a point facing Fort Orange, and thence from Pœtanœk, the Mill creek, north to Negagons. These conveyances were subsequently ratified by the respective parties, in the presence of the Director-general and council of New Netherland, who signed an instrument to that effect, "sealed with the seal of New Netherland in red wax," on the same day that the charter of 1629 was proclaimed at Fort Amsterdam. Nearly seven years afterwards—namely, on the 13th April, 1637—an intervening district called Papsickenekaas or Papsskanea as the name is now pronounced, lying also on the east side of the river, and extending from opposite Castle island south to the point opposite Smackx island, and including the adjacent islands and all the lands back into the interior, belonging to the Indian owners, was purchased "for certain quantities of duffels, axes, knives, and wampum," also for Mr. Van Rensselaer, who thus became proprietor of a tract of country twenty-four miles long, and forty-eight miles broad, containing, as is estimated, over seven hundred thousand acres of land, which now compose the counties of Albany, Rensselaer, and part of the county of Columbia,

On the 1st of October 1630, a copartnership was entered into between Kiliaen van Rensselaer, Samuel Godyn, Johannes de Laet, and Samuel Bloemmaert, with whom were association Adam Bissels and Toussaint Moussart, who, by the terms of the contract, were constituted codirectors, of Rensselaerswyck. The common stock of this association was divided into five shares, of which Van Rensselaer held two; De Laet, one; Godyn, one; and Bloemmaert and his associates, one; and the management of the affairs of the colonie was committed to a board consisting of four persons or votes, of which Van Rensselaer represented, or held two; Bloemmaert, or Bissels, one; and De Laet, or Moussart, one. Van Rensselaer was, however not to have any rank or authority in the colonie superior to his associates, except the title of *patroon*, which, with all its feudal honors, was vested in him alone, the partners binding themselves to do fealty and homage for the fief on his demise, in the name, and on the behalf of his son and heirs.

Another association was formed, a few days afterwards, between Godyn, Van Rensselaer, Bloemmaert, De Laet, Mathias van Cuelen, Hendrick Hammel, Johan van Harinckhouck, and Nicolaus van Sitterich, also directors of the West India Company, and Capt. David Pieterssen de Vries, for planting a colonie on the South river. Equalizing all expected advantages, they equipped a ship and yacht for that quarter, where they designed raising tobacco and grain, and prosecuting the whale-fishery, oil bringing then a fair price in Holland. Preparations were also made to expedite farmers and cattle to Rensselaerswyck; and everywhere, at home and abroad, things wore the aspect of prosperity, and " promised fairlie both to the state and undertakers."

The condition of the Dutch settlements on the North river, at this time, is thus alluded to by a contemporary English writer: " This which they have settled in New England upon Hudson's river, with no extraordinary charge or multitude of people, is knowne to subsist in a comfortable manner, and to promise fairlie both to the state and undertakers. The cause is evident: The men whom they carrie, though they be not many, are well chosen, and known to be useful and serviceable; and they second them with seasonable and fit supplies, cherishing them as carefully as their own families, and employ them in profitable labors, that are knowne to be of speciall use to their comfortable subsisting." The Planters' Plea; London, 1630.

The inhabitants of Rensselaerswyck in 1640, who numbered at the time as many traders as individuals, noting the avidity with which the Mohawks sought after fire-arms, willingly paying the English twenty beavers for a musket, and from ten to twelve guilders for a pound of gunpowder, were desirous to share so profitable a trade. They commenced accordingly, to furnish fire-arms to these Indians. The profits which accrued became soon known, and traders from Holland soon introduced large quantities of guns and other munitions of war into the interior. The Mohaws, thus provided with arms for four hundred warriors, swept the country from Canada to the sea-coast, levying tribute on the surrounding terror-stricken tribes.

The charter of 1629 having provided that every colonie should contain, within four years after its establishment, at least fifty persons over fif-

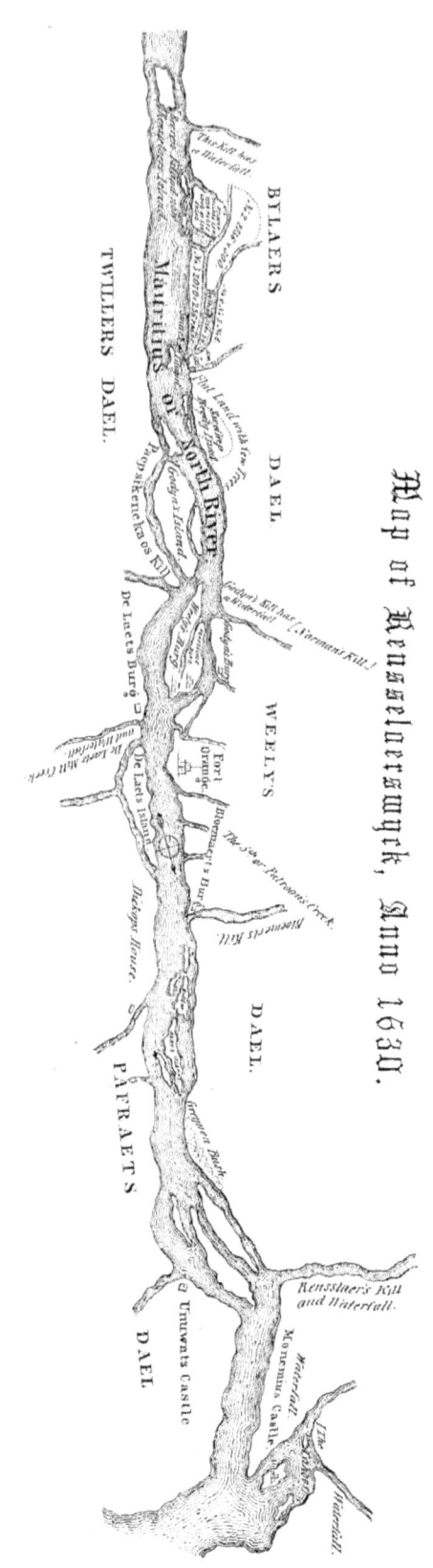

Original Van Rensselaer Map, 1631-32.

teen years of age, one fourth of whom should be located within the first year, the parties interested in the settlement of Rensselaerswyck lost no time in complying with these conditions. Early in the spring of the following year a number of colonists, with their families, and provided with farming implements, stock, and all other necessaries, sailed from the Texel, in the company's ship the Eendracht, Capt. Jan Brouwer, commander, and arrived in safety at the Manhattes, after a passage of sixty-four days. In a short time afterwards they landed at Fort Orange, in the vicinity of which they were furnished with comfortable farm-houses and other dwellings, at the expense of the patroon and his associates. Other settlers followed, with additional stock, each succeeding season, and thus were laid the foundations of those moral, wealthy, and prosperous settlements which we now behold in and around the present city of Albany.

Invested as well by the Roman law, as by the charter, with the chief command and lower jurisdiction, the patroon became empowered to administer civil and criminal justice, in person, or by deputy, within his colonie; to appoint local officers and magistrates; to erect courts, and to take cognizance of all crimes committed within his limits; to keep a gallows, if such were required, for the execution of malefactors, subject however, to the restriction that if such gallows happened, by any accident, to fall, pending an execution, a new one could not be erected, unless for the purpose of hanging another criminal. The right to inflict punishments of minor severity was necessarily included in that which authorized capital convictions, and accordingly we find various instances, throughout the record of the local court, of persons who had, by breaking the law, rendered themselves dangerous to society, or obnoxious to the authorities, having been banished from the colonie, or condemned to corporal chastisement, fine, or imprisonment, according to the grade of their offenses.

In civil cases, all disputes between man and man; whether relating to contract, titles, possessions, or boundaries; injuries to property, person, or character; claims for rents, and all other demands between the patroon and his tenants, were also investigated and decided by these courts; from the judgment of which, in matters affecting life and limb, and in suits where the sum in litigation exceeded twenty dollars, appeals lay to the director-general and council at Fort Amsterdam. But the local authorities, it must be added, were so jealous of this privilege that they obliged the colonists, on settling within their jurisdiction to promise not to appeal from any sentence of the local tribunal.

The laws in force here were, as in other sections of New Netherland, the civil code, the enactments of the States General, the ordinances of the West India Company, and of the director-general and council, when properly published within the colonie, and such rules and regulations as the patroon and his codirectors, or the local authorities might establish and enact.

The government was vested in a general court, which exercised executive, legislative or municipal, and judicial functions, and which was composed of two commissaries, (*gecommitteerden;*) two councillors, styled indiscriminately *raetspersoonen, gerechts-persoonen,* or *raedtsvrienden,* or *schepenen* and who answered to modern justices of the peace.

Adjoined to this court were a colonial secretary, a sheriff, or, *schout fiscaal*, and a *Gerechts-bode*, court messenger, or constable. Each of these received a small compensation, either in the shape of a fixed salary or fees; the commissaries and magistrates, fifty, one hundred, or two hundred guilders annually, according to their standing; the secretary one hundred guilders; and the court messenger one hundred and fifty, with the addition of trifling fees for the transcript and service of papers. The magistrates of the colonie held office for a year, the court appointing their successors from among the other settlers; or continuing those already in office, at the expiration of their term of service, as is deemed proper. The most important functionary attached to this government was, as throughout the other parts of the country, the schout-fiscaal, who, in discharge of his public functions, was bound by instructions received from the patroon and co-directors, similar in tenor to those given to the same officer at the Manhattans. No man in the colonie was to be subject to loss of life or property unless by the sentence of a court composed of five persons, and all who were under accusation were entitled to a speedy and impartial trial. The public prosecutor was particularly enjoined not to receive presents or bribes, nor to be interested in trade or commerce, either directly or indirectly; and in order that he might be attentive to the performance of his duties, and thoroughly independent, he was secured a fixed salary, a free house, and all fines amounting to ten guilders [$4], or under, besides the third part of all forfeitures and amends over that sum, were his perquisites.

Jacob Albertsen Planck was the first sheriff of Rensselaerswyck. Arendt van Curler, who originally came out as assistant commissary, was appointed, soon after his arrival, commissary-general, or superintendent of the colonie, and acted as colonial secretary until 1642, when he was succeeded by Anthony de Hooges. Brant Peelen, Gerrit de Reus, Cornelis Teunissen van Breuckelen, Pieter Cornelissen van Munickendam, and Dirck Janssen were, if not the first, at least among the earliest magistrates of the settlement.

The population of the colonie consisted at this remote period of three classes. Freemen, who emigrated from Holland at their own expense; farmers and farm-servants, who were sent out by the patroon, who judiciously applied his large resources in promoting the early settlement of the country, and in assisting the struggling industry of his people. To accomplish this laudable object, a number of farms were set off, on both sides of the river and adjoining islands, on which he caused dwelling-houses, barns, and stables to be erected. These farms were suitably stocked with cows, horses, or oxen, and occasionally, sheep; and furnished with ploughs, wagons, and other necessary agricultural implements, all which preliminary expenses were defrayed by the proprietor so that the farmer entered on the property unembarrassed by the want of capital, which often tends to impede the progress of settlers in new countries. Some of these farmers were then valued, and an annual rent was fixed, equivalent, in some sort to the interest of the capital expended on their improvement, and payable semi-annually in grain, beavers, and wampum. Other farms were let out on halves, or for the third of their produce; the patroon was entitled, at the same time, to half the increase from the stock, reserved to himself one tenth of the produce of each farm; and in various instances stipulated for a yearly *erkentenis*, or acknowledgment, of a few pounds of butter. The tenant was privileged, however to compound, by the payment of a fixed annual sum for the tenths of the farm, or for his halves or thirds. He was bound, at the same time, to keep the fences, buildings, or farming implements, in repair, and to deliver them up in the same good order in which he had received them, subject in all cases to ordinary wear and tear, but the patroon bore all risks of destruction of the buildings, cattle and other property which might accrue from war, or misunderstanding with the Indians. Wild or unimproved land was usually leased for a term of ten years free of rent or tenths, subject, however, to be improved by the lease, all improvements falling to the patroon on the expiration of the lessee. In addition to the facilities above enumerated, each of the settlers, on leaving Holland, were, like those sent by the West India Company to the Manhattans, generally furnished with clothing and a small sum in cash, the latter to be repaid, at some future occasion, in produce or wampum, with an advance on the principal of fifty per cent. This, however disproportionate it may now seem, can not be considered unreasonable or extravagant, when it is understood that the difference, at the time, between colonial and Holland currency was nearly forty per cent, while between the latter and the value of wampum it was vastly larger. The patroon was bound, at the same time, to supply his colonists with a sufficient number of laborers to assist them in the work of their farms. As compensation for his trouble in engaging these and for his advances in conveying them to America, he was entitled to the sum of sixteen guilders, or six dollars, per annum for each laborer, over and above the yearly wages which the farmer was to allow such servants, and which ranged from forty to one hundred and fifty guilders, and board. This sum provided these servants with necessary clothing, and in the course of time placed at their disposal wherewith to enter on a farm on their own account. It is to be remarked, however, that the first patroon seriously complained that his settlers not only threw altogether on him the payment of these wages, but took large quantities of goods from his store, for which they made no returns whatever, though they were bound to settle at the end of each year, and to hand in an account of the produce of the farm, distinguishing the patroon's tenths, halves, or thirds, the amount paid for wages, and their own expenses, so as to allow him to ascertain what his own profits and losses were at the close of each annual term.

In return for his outlay and trouble, and civil code, which it must be always borne in mind, was the fundamental law of this colonie, vested in the patroon several privileges common to the feudal system. At the close of the harvest, the farmer was bound to hand in a return of the amount of grain which he had for sale, after deducting what was due to the landlord by the lease, and offer to him or his commissary the preemption of such produce. In case he refused to buy it, then the farmer was at liberty to sell the same elsewhere. The like rule obtained in regard to cattle. When these were to be sold, the first offer was also to be made to the patroon, in order, we presume, that he should have an opportunity of retaining the stock within the colonie. Every settler was, likewise, obligated to grind his corn at the patroon's mill, and the latter was equally obligated to erect, and keep such mill in repair, at his own expense, for the accommodation of his colonists. No person could hunt or fish within the limits of the colonie, without license from the patroon, who, on the exchange, sale, and purchase of real estate within the jurisdiction, was entitled to the first offer of such property; or if he declined to resume it, to a certain portion of the purchase money, except such mutation occurred in the natural line of descent. Finally, it was his right, as "lord of the manor," to succeed to the estate and property of all persons who might die intestate within his colonie.

Under the fostering care of its first patroon, and the prudent management of its local magistracy, the colonie of Rensselaerswyck progressively, though slowly, advanced. Portions of its inhabitants occasionally returned to Fatherland, to spread the tidings of their prosperity, and to invite their friends and relatives to join them in their new homes, which from the abundance and cheapness of provisions, deserved truly to be called "a land flowing with milk and honey." A hamlet gradually arose. On account, it is said, of the crescent form of the bank of the river at this point, this hamlet was first called the Fuyck, or Beversfuyck and afterwards Beverswyck, by which name the present city of Albany was legally known until 1664, though it was familiarly called the Fuyck by the Dutch, for many years after the entire country had passed into the hands of other masters.

In order to give greater stability to his settlement, and to become better acquainted with the condition, Mr. Van Rensselaer, it is alleged, visited the colonie in person in 1637. His stay in the country, if he ever did come, was, however, not very long. The demise or resignation of Sheriff Planck now required the appointment of a new officer, and the peculiar position of the settlers, surrounded on all sides by rude and unconverted savages, demanded the guardian supervision and solacing comforts of religion, for as yet neither church nor clergymen existed in Rensselaerswyck. To secure an efficient administration of justice, and to provide a properly qualified clergyman for his people, consequently became a paramount duty.

Adriaen van der Donck, "a free citizen of Breda,"—a lineal descendant of Adriaen van Bergen, part owner of the famous turf-sloop in which a party of Dutch troops were clandestinely introduced in the year 1590, into the castle commanding that city, then in the hands of the Spanish, by which stratagem that stronghold fell into the hands of their High Mightinesses the States General,—and a graduate of the University of Leyden, was selected as the successor of Sheriff Planck. He entered on the performance of his duties, as schout-fiscaal of Rensselaerswyck, in the course of a month or two after his appointment, having, previous to his departure from Holland, taken a lease from the patroon of the west half of Castle island, called Welysburg.

The Rev. Johannes Megapolensis, "the pious and well-learned minister of the congregation of Schoorel and Berge," under the classis of Alknaer, was duly called to disseminate the light of the gospel among the Christians and heathen in the colonie, and regularly commissioned "to preach God's word there; to administer the holy sacraments of baptism and the Lord's supper; to set an example, in a Christian-like manner, by public precept; to ordain elders and deacons; to keep and govern, by and with the advice and assistance of the same, God's congregation in good discipline and order, all according to God's holy word, and in conformity with the government, confession, and catechism of the Netherland churches, and the synodal acts of Dordrecht."

The allowance guarantied to this clergyman was free passage and board for himself, his wife and four children, who accompanied him to New Netherland; an outfit of three hundred guilders, or one hundred and twenty dollars, and an annual stipend, for the first three years, of eleven hundred guilders, ($440,) thirty schepels of wheat, and two firkins of butter, or in place thereof, should he prefer it, sixty guilders in cash. This salary was to be further increased by an addition of two hundred guilders a year, for a second term of three years, if the patroon were satisfied with his services. A pension of one hundred guilders per annum was secured to his wife, in case of his demise within the above term, for and during whatever time might remain unexpired of his engagement.

These preliminaries having been thus arranged, an obstacle was unexpectedly thrown in the way of Mr. Megapolensis's departure by the directors of the West India Company, who claimed the exclusive right to approve of his appointment. To this, however, the feudal lord of Rensselaerswyck demurred; and it was not until after a lapse of several months that a compromise was agreed to, the directors approving of the appointment under protest on the part of Mr. Van Rensselaer, saving his rights as patroon.

The Rev. Mr. Megapolensis and family embarked, together with Abraham Staes, surgeon, Evert Pels, brewer, and a number of other freemen, farmers, and farm-servants, shortly after this, in the ship the Houttuyn, or Woodyard, which was freighted with a quantity of goods for the colonie—between two and three hundred bushels of malt for Mr. Pels—four thousand tiles, and thirty thousand stone for building—besides some vines and madder, the cultivation of which the patroon was desirous of introducing among his people.* On the arrival of Mr. Megapolensis at Rensselaerswyck, a contract was concluded for the erection of a dwelling for himself and family, but the contractor having failed in fulfilling his agreement, a house belonging to Maryn Adriaensen, constructed entirely of oak, was subsequently purchased for his use, for the sum of three hundred guilders, or one hundred and twenty dollars. For the convenience of the settlers at Tuscameatick, (as Greenbush, at the opposite side of the river, was called by the Indians,) a ferry was next established near the foot of the Beaver's kill, (where it still continues

* Mr. Pels erected a brewery in the colonie; Dr. Staes became one of the council in 1643, and was appointed president of the board in 1644, at a salary of 100 florins ($40) per annum. He obtained license to trade in furs, and had also a considerable bouwerie, besides pursuing the practice of his profession. He was the ancestor of the Staats of the present day, the original name having assumed shortly afterwards the termination t now has.

to ply;) and as it was the patroon's intention that the church, the minister's dwelling, the attorney-general's residence, and the houses for the trades-people and mechanics, should be erected in one vicinity, so as to constitute a kerckbuurte, or settlement around the church, orders were transmitted that no persons, (farmers, and tobacco planters excepted) should, for the future, establish themselves, after the expiration of their term of service, elsewhere than in the vicinity of the church, and according to the plan now sent out by the Houttuyn; for, it was justly observed, "if every one resides where he thinks fit, separated far from other settlers, they, should trouble occur, would be unfortunately in danger of their lives, as sorrowful experience hath demonstrated around the Manhattans." A church, thirty-four feet long, and nineteen feet wide—the first in this quarter—was erected in the course of the following year. Though humble in its demensions, when compared with modern edifices of a similar sacred character, it was considered, at this time, sufficiently ample for the accommodation of the faithful, for the next three or four years, after which it might be converted into a schoolhouse or a dwelling for the sexton." A pulpit, ornamented with a canopy, was soon added for the preacher, as well as pews for the magistrates and for the deacons, and "nine benches" for the congregation. The expense of all this necessary furniture amounted to the sum of thirty-two dollars. While providing accommodation for the living the dead were not forgotten. The church-yard lay in the rear, or to the west, of the patroon's trading-house—in what is now very correctly called Church street: and in order "to be safe from the ravages of the Indians," the infant hamlet, living and dead, nestled close under the guns of Fort Orange.

One of the principal aims of the first founders of Rensselaerswyck seems to have been to secure for themselves the valuable trade in furs, the chief mart for which centered at the point where they made their purchase and commenced their settlement. To engross this the more effectually, all foreign and unlicensed traders were rigidly excluded from the colonie. The patroon and his partners were the only privileged importers of European merchandise, the company having, in consequence of the war and other causes, ceased to keep Fort Orange supplied with foreign goods. All settlers were bound under oath not to purchase any peltries from the Indians, on pain of forfeiting their goods and wages, unless duly licensed to carry on such trade, for such a privilege was exclusively vested in the patroon by the sixth article of the charter. The majority of the settlers subsequently obtained such permission; received goods on credit from the patroon's store, and every farmer, as De Vries observes, become a trader. They were, however, obliged to bring in all the furs which they purchased to the patroon's magazine, to be sent over to Holland to him, he retaining, as his share, half the profits. This condition was afterwards modified so far as to allow him to retain only the sixth beaver, and one guilder recognition, or duty, on each of the remaining five-sixths. This system soon produced results which were naturally to be expected. Competition raised the price of peltries nearly one hundred per cent. Prior to 1642 the price of a merchantable beaver, which averaged about an ell square, was six hands, or fathoms, of wampum. In the course of that year the article commanded from seven to seven and a half; but when the traders found that the agents of the patroon, as well as the officers at Fort Orange, did not refuse paying that price, they immediately offered nine; and in the following year advanced the rate to ten fathoms of white wampum for each skin. A joint proclamation was hereupon issued by the authorities of Rensselaerswyck, and those of the Fort, fixing the price of furs at nine fathoms of white, or four and a half of black wampum, and forbidding all persons whatsoever, whether servants of the company or residents in the colonie, from going into the woods to trade in advance with the Indians, on pain of seizure of all their goods. Another proclamation was also issued, prohibiting all traders to come with their sloops within the limits of the colonie under the penalty of forfeiting the same. And on the following court-day a third proclamation followed, for the better securing the monopoly of the import trade to the patroon, by which the inhabitants of the colonie were absolutely forbidden purchasing any goods from the local traders. Orders were given at the same time to Sheriff Van der Donck to enforce these regulation with strictness and severity.

This functionary, between whom and Van Curler, and the other officers of the colonie, considerable jealously and ill feeling already existed, had no desire to render himself unpopular with the colonists. "He should not" he said, "make himself the worst man in the colonie, nor be suspected by the colonists, for his term as officer was but short." He therefore not only refused to enforce these regulations, but when, a few days afterwards, the colonists, contrary to the prohibitions of the court, did purchase duffels and sundry other goods which had been surreptitiously introduced, he connived at their proceedings, and either told the suspected parties to put their goods out of his sight, or neglected entirely to execute his duty, or to make any seizures. Not content with this disobedience of orders, he proceeded, next, secretly to foment feelings of discontent and mutiny among the people, before whom he placed the abovementioned placards in a most odious light, and whom he persuaded into the belief that Van Curler was endeavoring "to steal the bread out of their mouths." His representation had eventually such an effect on the public mind, that a conspiracy was formed against the commissary-general among several of the colonists, who drew up a strong protest against that officer, which, in order that they might remain undiscovered, the ringleaders signed in the form of a "round robin," by affixing to the paper their signatures in "a circle." This done, they next denounced Van Curler in the most vehement terms. Some proposed driving him from the colonie as a rogue; others, more vindictive and turbulent, insisted on taking his life. These threats, fortunately for the character of the settlers, were not followed up by any over act. Van der Donck professed, all the while, an honest desire to second the wishes of the constituted authorities. But when the time for testing his sincerity arrived, he was found wanting in the fulfillment of his promise.

It became apparent now from the ill-feeling which existed between Sheriff van der Donck and the other functionaries in the colonie, and which had already caused in two instances an exchange of blows, that the former could not comfortably prolong his stay in Rensselaerswyck, or hold his office, very agreeably, much longer. He determined, indeed, to return to Holland in the course of the next year, as he was desirous to become a patroon himself, with which view he proceeded, with several colonists, to Katskill, to purchase the lands there from the Indians, for the erection of an independent colonie. But the moment the patroon of Rensselaerswyck received intelligence of this "dishonest," move on the part of "his sworn officer," he immediately forwarded instructions to Van Curler, couched in the following stringent terms:—

"The Patroon of the Colonie of Rensselaerswyck having, on the sixth of this month, given a Commission to Pieter Wyncoop, commis. on board his ship, to purchase for a reasonable price from the natural owners and inhabitants, and from their chiefs, their lands lying about Katskill, in consequence of certain information which he had that Adriaen van der Donck, his sworn officer, dishonestly designed to purchase for him and his, to the prejudice of him, the patroon, his lord and master, the said lands, lying under the shadow of his colonie. Therefore he, by virtue of the sixth and twenty-sixth articles of his *freedoms* and *exemptions*, doth claim that no person shall, against his will, approach within seven or eight miles of him; also that he hath power to enlarge his colonie, on condition of planting a proportionate number of colonists there, which number was, even by this vessel, so increased that he hath already included the same, from Ransselaers-Stein, down to Katskill, remaining on the same side, within his resort. And, further, having obtained certain information that such is, indeed, also true, the commissary-general Arendt van Curler, together with the aforesaid Pieter Wyncoop, are charged not to inquire of the above-named Van der Donck if it be true, (inasmuch as the patroon hath by him sufficient proof thereof,) but him to constrain, should he have done so, to desist, de facto, therefrom, and to cede and to make over to him, the patroon, all whatsoever he hath required, conformably to his oath, having sworn to be true and faithful specially to him, his injury to prevent and his advantages to promote, both which in this matter have not happened; and in case the said purchase be not yet effected, that he, in presence of the commissaries and council of the colonie, do promise, under oath, not to proceed therewith, but to respect him the patroon, and to afford to his (agents) all favor and help, that they may be allowed to make the aforesaid purchase to the best advantage; and should he refuse the one, or the other, to secure his person, inasmuch as he also endeavored, per fas et nefas, (met minne ofte onminne,) to return home in case the patroon should not consent to discharge him; and inasmuch as the lease of his bouwerie, which he hath taken and agreed for in person with the patroon, hath still long to run, which he can not set aside without consent, but shall be bound to keep during that time. And in witness of the truth hath the Patroon subscribed these with his hand, and sealed them with his and the colonie's seal, in Amsterdam, this 10th September, 1643

KILIAEN VAN RENSSELAER,

[Seal] "Patroon of the Colonie of Rensselaerswyck:

"In case Van der Donck should prove obstinate, he shall be degraded from his office, and left on his bouwerie to complete his contracted lease, without allowing him to depart, and his office shall be conferred, provisionally, on Nicolaus Coorn, till further orders, divesting him of all papers appertaining to his charge. But if he will desist, then his office, and his bouwerie, shall he be allowed to hold. Actum as above.

"KILIAEN VAN RENSSELAER,
"in quality as herein above stated."

This order, which had the effect of arresting Van der Donck's intended colonie at Katskill, was conveyed to New Netherland by the patroon's ship, The Arms of Rensselaerswyck, which was dispatched with an assorted invoice of merchandise, consisting of woollen, linen, and cotton goods, ready-made clothing, silks, glass, crockery, leather, fruit, cheese, spices, brandy, gin, wines, cordials, tobacco-pipes, nets, looking glasses, beads, axes, adzes, razors, knives, scissors, bells, nails, spoons, kettles, thimbles, pins, needles, threads, rings, shoes, stockings, gloves, combs, buttons, muskets, pistols, swords, shot, lead, canvas, pitch and tar, candles, stationery, and various other commodities, valued at twelve thousand eight hundred and seventy guilders, to be bartered with the Indians and other inhabitants of the country for tobacco, furs, and other produce. To ensure entire success for this venture, the skipper, supercargo, and pilot of the ship were allowed a direct pecuniary interest in the proceeds of the voyage.

The system of license introduced by the patroon, and the profits which resulted, had already incited a number of private individuals to embark in the fur-trade. As a consequence, this staple was altogether taken out of the hands both of the patroon's and the company's servants, who could purchase scarcely a skin, while private traders exported thousands of peltries. A number of unlicensed traders now resorted to the colonie, who drew the Indians away into "secret trading places," where by means of higher prices, they got possession of the most valuable furs, " not caring whether or not the trade was so injured as to render the patroon unable to meet the expenses of his colonie." Having thus " debauched" the savages, these interlopers succeeded next, by means of "wine and strong drink, which they sold at an usurious rate," in "perverting" many of the colonists, from whom they got, not only peltries, but even large quantities of grain, which the farmers disposed of without either respecting the Patroon's pre-emption right, or paying the tenths, or accounting for the halves or thirds which they were bound by lease to pay.

To arrest these illicit proceedings, the patroon adopted two measures which would, he expected, put a stop to the injuries which his interests were sustaining from the competition that was then exhausting and impoverishing his colonie. One of these was the erection of a fortified post and trading house at Beeren, or Bear's Island, the southern boundary of his estate, which, by commanding the channel of the river, would exclude all vessels, but his own and those of the West India Company, from the upper waters of the Hudson. The other was, to send out a stock of goods sufficient to supply, through his establishments at Beverswyck and Beeren Island, the Mohawks and river Indians, and all the neighboring settlers, with whatsoever they may require in barter for their produce, whether furs or corn. It was with a view to carry out the latter part of this project, that the Arms of Rensselaerswyck now sailed with the above-mentioned valuable cargo.

She arrived at the Manhattans while the war with the Indians was at its height, and at the moment when Kieft was sorely distressed for clothing for the troops which he had enlisted. A requisition was immediately made on Pieter Wyncoop, the supercargo of the ship, for a supply of fifty pairs of shoes to be distributed among the soldiers, payment for which was offered "in silver, beavers, or wampum," at such price as the supercargo might demand. But Wyncoop, perceiving that he could sell these goods to more advantage to the inhabitants than to the director, injudiciously refused to comply with this requisition. A forced levy was the result, and as many soldiers were equipped with shoes from the ship, as "killed five hundred of the enemy." The evil consequence of Wyncoop's refusal did not stop here. The ship was immediately overhauled by authority of the director and council, and a considerable quantity of powder and a number of guns found on board, which were not enumerated in the manifest, and which Wyncoop was charged with intending to sell to the savages. These articles having been made contraband by law, and their introduction forbidden on pain of death, were, together, with the ship, forthwith confiscated.

Wyncoop now too late, perceived the error into which either his instructions or his covetousness had plunged him. In the hope, however, of retriving his loss, he instituted an action against Cornelis Van der Huygens, the Fiscaal at Fort Amsterdam, against whom he protested, in strong terms, for having unloaded his ship, which proceeding he pronounced an insult, a reproach, and a wrong inflicted on the honorable patroon, "the first and oldest patriot of the land," and for which aggression he now demanded redress from the director-general and council. It was much fitter for the fiscal, he added, to discharge and to confiscate such ships as came and traded hither without any commission, and thereby brought contempt on the country and its government, than to affront a patroon who hazarded so much for his colonists and New Netherland. He finally maintained that the powder which he had on board was for the ship's use, and for the defence of Rensselaers Stein, or Castle Rensselaer, as the fortification on Beeren Island was called. This plea profited nothing. The powder was not mentioned in the manifest, and the explanation which was offered was merely used as "a cloak" to cover the real design. "It is far from us," concluded the attorney-general, "to insult the patroon. On the contrary, we are willing to aid him in promoting the welfare of his colonie. But it is you who are endeavoring to frustrate his noble plans, by associating exclusively with private traders, and striving to take them with you to the colonie in direct opposition to the commands of the patroon, who hath sent out his ship to keep free traders from that place. If your conduct is just, free merchants can not be prevented trading thither, and they will be justified in so doing. I deny that any damage whatever has been done. Are you of a contrary opinion? Cite me before any court of justice, whenever you please."

Arendt van Curler, finding that no satisfactory issue was to be expected from this litigation, finally proposed that the ship should be released, and the whole case referred to the Directors in Holland for their decision. As the vessel was suffering considerable injury from detention this proposal was acceded to, "so that the patroon should have no reason to complain;" on the express condition, however, that no goods should be landed from the vessel until permission was obtained from the company, and that such articles as were already seized by the attorney-general should remain confiscated, as they had not been included in the invoice. The vessel sailed soon after for Holland, whether Van Curler also proceeded to give an account of his stewartship.

In the mean time Nicolaus Coorn, "Wacht Meester," or commander in the service of the patroon, had completed his fort on Beeren Island, on which he mounted a number of cannon, sufficient not only for its defence, but for the complete command of the river. A claim to "staple right" was then boldly set up; a toll of five guilders, or two dollars, imposed on every trading-craft passing up or down, which were also obliged to lower their colors in honor of Rensselaers-Stein. And thus a sovereign jurisdiction was asserted over this navigable highway against all persons, save and except the servants of the West India Company.

It was in the summer of 1644, that the yacht the Good Hope, of which Govert Lookermans was master, sailed from Fort Orange for New Amsterdam. Passing Beeren Island, the craft was hailed, and peremptorily ordered "to lower his colors." On being asked for whom, the commander replied, "For the staple right of Rensselaerswyck." But the skipper refused, with an oath, to strike his flag "for any individual save the Prince of Orange and the Lords his masters;" whereupon Coorn fired several shots at the vessel, one of which, says the record, "perforated our princely flag," about a foot above the head of the skipper, "who kept the colors constantly in his hand."

Such an outrage as this could not fail to create excitement in New Amsterdam, when the particulars became known. Philip de Truy, "marshal of New Netherland," summoned Coorn to appear immediately at the Fort to answer for his conduct. The latter pleaded the authority of his patroon. But this was considered no justification. He was condemned in damages, and forbidden to repeat the offence on pain of corporal punishment. He was further required to obtain Van Rensselaer's approval of the sentence, which should be executed on him without fail, if that approval were not forthcoming. This proceeding was followed soon after by a strong protest from attorney-general Van der Huygens, against the establishment on Beeren Island, which was declared to be inconsistent with the privileges granted to patroons and lords of manors. No patroon, it was maintained, could extend this colony, by the fifth article of the charter, more than four miles along one bank, or two miles on both sides of the river, while Beeren Island was more than two miles from the limits of the colonie. The bold attempt to construct a fort there, to command the river, and to debar Fort Orange from free navigation, would, it was added, be ruinous to the company; it was therefore peremptorily ordered that no building whatsoever, much less a fortification, should be constructed beyond the limits of Rensselaerswyck, and Coorn was formerly threatened with further prosecution should he persist in his lawless transactions.

But Nicolaus Coorn, commander of Rensselaers-Stein, was not to be intimidated by the paper bullets of director Kieft's attorney-general. "As the vice commander of the honorable Van Rensselaer, he replied, "I call on you, Cornelis van der Huygens, attorney-general of New Netherland not to presume to oppose and frustrate my designs on Bear's Island; to defraud me in any manner, or to cause me any trouble, as it has been the will of their High Mightinesses, the States General, and the privileged West India Company, to invest any patroon and his heir with the right to extend and fortify his colonie, and make it powerful in every respect. . . If you persist in so doing. . . . . I protest against the act of violence and assault committed by the honorable, Lords majors, which I leave them to settle, while this undertaking has nothing else in view than to prevent the canker of free traders entering his colonie.

In the spirit in which this protest was drafted, were the feudal pretensions of the lord of Rensselaerswyck asserted and maintained, notwithstanding the conviction of Coorn and a warning of Van der Huygens, during the remainder of the patroon's life. The same policy was steadily continued by his executors for several years after his death, which event took place in Amsterdam, in the year 1646.

With the demise of the first patroon terminated, also, Van der Donck's connection with the colonie. He was succeeded in his office of fiscaal by Nicolaus Coorn. He did not, however, quit Rensselaerswyck before experiencing a heavy loss in the destruction of his house on Castle Island by fire, in consequence of which he and his wife temporarily removed to Van Curler's residence, the hospitalities of which were generously offered to him by its proprietor. Differences of opinion now arose between him and Van Curler, as to the party on whom the loss of the house should fall; one maintaining that the property was at the risk of the patroon; the other, of the lessee. A quarrel ensued. Van der Donck gave Van Curler the lie, whereupon the latter ordered him out of his house. Van der Donck removed immediately to Fort Orange, where he remained until the opening of the navigation, when he proceeded to the Manhattans. In the mean time, his claims were referred for adjustment to the proprietors in Holland.

The winter which had just terminated, was remarkably long and severe. The North River closed at Rensselaerswyck, on the 24th November, and remained frozen some four months. A very high freshet, unequaled since 1639, followed, which destroyed a number of horses in their stables; nearly carried away the fort, and inflicted considerable other damage in the colonie. "A certain fish of considerable size, snow-white in color, round in the body, and blowing water out of its head," made at the same time his appearance, stemming the impetuous flood. What it portended, "God the Lord only knew." All the inhabitants were lost in wonder, for "at the same instant that this fish appeared to us, we had the first thunder and lightning this year." The public astonishment had scarcely subsided, when another monster of the deep, estimated at forty feet in length, was seen, of a brown color, having fins on his back, and ejecting water in a like manner, high in the air. Some seafaring people, "who had been to Greenland," now pronounced the strange visiter a whale. Intelligence was shortly after received that it had grounded on an island at the mouth of the Mohawk, and the people turned out in numbers to secure the prize, which was forthwith, subjected to the process of roasting, in order to extract its oil. Though large quantities were obtained, yet so great was the mass of blubber, the river was covered with grease for three weeks afterwards, and the air infected to such a degree with the stench, as the fish lay rotting on the strand, that the smell was perceptibly offensive for two (Dutch) miles to leeward. The whale, which had first ascended the river, stranded, on his return to sea, on an island some forty miles from the mouth of the river, near, which place four others grounded, also, this year.

The greater number of the houses around forts Amsterdam and Orange were, in those days, low-sized wooden buildings, with roofs of reed or straw, and chimneys of wood. Wind or water mills were erected, here and there, to grind corn, or to saw lumber. One of the latter, situate on Nut or Governor's island, was leased in 1639 for five hundred merchantable boards yearly, half oak and half pine. Saw and grist mills were built on several of the creeks in the colonie of Rensselaerswyck, where a *horse mill* was also erected in 1646, of which the following is a Contract, dated Jan. 31. "The mill situate on the fifth kill being, to the great damage of the patroon, and inhabitants of the colonie, [Rensselaerswyck,] for a considerable time out of repair, or unfit to be worked, either by the breaking of the dam, the severity of the winter, or the high water, or otherwise; besides being out of the way, to the prejudice of the inhabitants in going and returning, a contract, after being duly proposed to the court, is therefore, made with Pieter Cornelissen to build a horsemill in the Pine grove, whereby not only the colonie, but also, if so be, the navigators who come hither, may be encouraged to provide themselves with other things. Pieter Cornelisz. shall complete the work for fl. 300, ($120,) I furnishing him fl. 200 in stones, two good horses, the expense of which is to be divided between us, half and half. The standing work, plank, labor, and other expenses, we shall defray in common, bearing, each, equal profit and loss. On the completion of the mill, and on its being ready to go, Pieter Cornelissen shall work one day for himself and the other day for the patroon, and so forth; the patroon paying him one Rix dollar for his day. Should it happen, as we expect, that so great a demand shall arise, so that the mill will not supply all the colonie or strangers, (buytenwoonders,) then P. Cornelisz, is alone authorized and privileged to erect, in company with the patroon, another such mill, on these or such other conditions as are now, or shall hereafter be agreed on. Signed, ANTHONY DE HOOGES, PIETER CORNELISSEN,"—*Rensselaerswyck MSS.*) A mill worked by horses stood, in the course of the last century, as I am informed by an aged citizen, on the lot forming the northeast corner of Hudson and Grand streets, Albany. There was a mill also on the 3d or Rutten kill, in 1646.

A Brewery had been constructed previous to 1637, in the same quarter, by the patroon, with the exclusive right of supplying retail-dealers with beer. But private individuals were allowed the privilege, notwithstanding, to brew whatever quantity of beer they might require for consumption within their own families.*

Rensselaerswyck was the only colonie which remained uninjured by the war. As a consequence its population generally prospered, and sundry farms were taken up. Beaverswyck continued, however, in swadding clothes, for the city which in 1845 holds over forty thousand inhabitants, contained in 1646 no more than ten houses. Several farmers had at an early date begun another settlement south of Beaverswyck, to which they gave the name of Bethlehem. A few bouweries were also cultivated on the east side of the river opposite Fort Orange. Katskill and its fertile bottoms had engaged at an early date the attention of the settlers at Rensselaerswyck, but the pretensions of opposite parties prevented any planting of consequence in that quarter, and Van Slyck, who had received a patent for lands there, had as yet made no commencement. The country between Rensselaerswyck and the Manhattans, on both sides of the river, still remained a wilderness. It is true that the Dutch had built a fort at Esopus, in the year 1614, contemporaneously with the erection of their post on Castle island. This possibly might have been followed by the clearing of some small portions of land in that vicinity, but it is very doubtful whether any such settlements survived the destructive war of 1644-5.

Such was the state of the public affairs when General PETRUS STUYVESANT assumed the government of New Netherland.

*26 Dec. 1646. Whereas their Honors of the Court of this Colonie find that Cornelis Segersz. notwithstanding former placards and prohibitions, has still presumed to meddle with what is not his business—with beer brewing—directly contrary to the grant and authorization given to the brewery of this colonie; Therefore their honors expressly forbid the said Cornelis Segersz, to brew, or cause to be brewed, or otherwise to manufacture any beer, except so much as shall be required by him for his own housekeeping, on pain of forfeiting twenty five Carolus guilders, besides the brewed beer. The said Cornelis Segersz, is further warned that no cloak, or idle excuse shall hereafter avail, but that this ordinance shall be maintained and executed on the spot, without court process, if he shall make any mistake. Let him, therefore, prevent his loss. Actum Rensselaerswyck, 26th October 1646. Pursuant to the resolution of their honors the magistrates of this colonie. A. DE HOOGES.

KILIAEN VAN RENSSELAER,

Merchant of Amsterdam, director of the West India Company, and one of the first patroons of New Netherland, was the thirteenth descendant in a direct line from Henry Wolters van Rensselaer. He married, firstly, Hellegonda van Bylet, by whom he had one son, Johannes who afterwards married his cousin, Elizabeth van Twiller. Kiliaen van Rensselaer married, secondly, in 1627, Anna van Wely, daughter of Joannes van Wely, merchant of Amsterdam, by whom he had four daughters and four sons, namely: 1, Maria; 2, Jeremias (who married Maria, daughter of Oloff Stevensen van Cortland); 3, Hellegonda; 4, Jan Baptiste (who married Susan van Wely); 5, Eleonora; 6, Susan (who married Jan de la Court); 7, Nicolaus (who married Alida Schuyler); 8, Rickert (who married Anna van Beaumont); Kiliaen van Rensselaer's sister (Maria), married Rykert van Twiller, and thus, it is presumed, the relationship originated between Wouter van Twiller, second director-general of New Netherland, and the first patroon of Rensselaerswyck. Of the above children, Maria and Hellegonda died unmarried. Johannes succeeded his father as patroon and Jeremias, Jan Baptiste and Ryckert were, in succession, directors of "the colonie." Nicolaus was a clergyman of the Dutch Reformed Church. On being introduced to Charles II, then in exile at Brussels, he prophesied the restoration of that monarch to the throne of England, which circumstance obtained for him afterwards a cordial reception at the Court of St. James, when he visited London as chaplain to the Dutch embassy. In acknowledgment of the truth of the prediction, the king presented him with a snuff-box, on the lid of which was set his Majesty's miniature. This royal relic is still in the possession of the Van Rensselaer family at Albany.

Mde. Anna van Rensselaer died in Amsterdam on the 12th June, 1670, after a sickness of seven weeks, having survived her husband twenty-four years. Intelligence of her death, communicated by the following letter, was received in this country by her sons, Jeremias and Ryckert, on the 18th Sept. 1670:

"AMSTERDAM, 12th June, 1670.

"Dear Brothers—On the 9th inst. I communicated to you, among other things, per ship Duke of York, Johannes Luyck, skipper, the low condition of our beloved mother, who accompanied me home, sick, from Cralo to Amsterdam, on the first of April. After lying so long, without any strong fever, or any great pain, troubled only with asthma, accompanied by considerable cough and phlegm, and the sprue, she took her departure with great piety from the Church Militant here, to the Church Triumphant above, on the 12th inst, being this day, about one hour after noon, in the presence of all our sisters and brothers who are in this country, and that with a full understanding and trust in the mercy of God, the merits of her and our Saviour Jesus Christ, which, through the grace of the Holy Ghost and belief in the Triune God, so strenghtened her, that all her wishes were to be set free and to be with Christ, who hath taken her so mercifully to himself, that we all, though afflicted children can not be sufficiently thankful to God for so gentle and holy a death. Her body will be committed to the earth in a Christian manner, as in duty bound, on Tuesday next, being the 17th inst. There is no doubt of a stately funeral. May the good God grant her, and us with her, a joyous resurrection at the last day. Amen."—*O'Callaghan's Histr. N. Netherland*, i, 122.

EXECUTORS OF JEREMIAS VAN RENSSELAER.

On the death of Jeremias van Rensselaer, in 1675, the affairs of the colonie of Rensselaerswyck were administered conjointly, during the minority of Kiliaen van Rensselaer (then twelve years old,) by the Rev. Nicolaus van Rensselaer, Mde. Maria van Rensselaer, and Stephanus van Cortlandt. Nicolaus had the directorship of the colonie; Mde. van Rensselaer was the treasurer; and Stephanus van Cortlandt had the charge of the books. Four hundred schepels of wheat were appropriated to defray the yearly expenses of this administration, of which Dom. Nicolaus (who then officiated as second clergyman in Albany,) received one half. The remainder was divided between Mde. van Rensselaer and her brother. Dom. Nicolaus dying in 1679, the chief management of the minor's affairs devolved on his mother and uncle.—*O'Callaghan*.

SENTENCE OF BANISHMENT, 1644.

The following is a translation of a sentence of banishment pronounced on one of the colonists at this early period of its history. "By the President and Council of the Colonie of Rensselaerswyck. Having heard the free confession of Adriaen Willemsen, at present in confinement," to wit:— That he on Saturday last, the 6th of Aug., at the house of the Patroon, where the Commissary-general, Arendt van Curler, resides, climbing in through the window of said house, stole seven beavers, and at noon of the following Monday, eight beavers and one drieling [third of a skin], also that on Saturday aforesaid he had stolen from the cellar of the said house a half [skin] which remained. And having, moreover, examined the demand of the prosecutor against the aforesaid delinquent, observing what appertains thereto; we have hereby ordered and adjudged, and do order and adjudge, that the said delinquent shall be taken to the public place where justice is executed, and there be ignominiously tied to a post for the space of two hours, with some of the stolen property on his head; after which he shall prostrate himself at the feet of the Worshipful Magistrates (de Edele Heeren van den Gerechte,) and beg of God and justice for forgiveness; that he, moreover, shall be henceforward and forever, banished out of this colonie, and never more return thereto. Done in Collegio, this 13th day of August, anno 1644. By order of their worships the President and Council of this Colonie of Rensselaerswyck. ARENDT VAN CURLER."—*O'Callaghan's Hist. N. Netherland*, i, 320.

ARENT VAN CURLER.

Van Curler was — the founder of Schenectady, a village 16 miles to the West on the Mohawk River in 1661. Schenectady was the western most European settlement prior to the American Revolution. Once you left the protected stockade and headed west you were in Indian country. In the winter of 1666 Governor De Courcelle, Governor of New France (Canada) and his party, during an expedition into the Mohawk country, faced starvation and Van Curler supplied them with food. The following year, 1667, he accepted an invitation to visit the French governor in Quebec. He left with several Indians, by way of Lake Champlain. Their small boat overturned in a sudden storm and he drowned in Lake Champlain.

Arent van Curler, was one of those characters who deserve to live in history. His influence among the Indians was unlimited, and in honor of his memory, these tribes addressed all succeeding governors of New York by the name of Corlaer. He possessed feelings of the purest humanity, and actively exerted his influence in rescuing from the savages such Christians as had the misfortune to fall into their hands of whose danger he might receive timely notice. On his marriage with Antonia Slaghboom, the widow of Jonas Bronck, he visited Holland, and on his return moved to the Flatts above Albany, where he had a farm. He was proprietor of a brewery in Beverwyck, in 1661. Being a cousin of the Van Rensselaers, he had considerable influence in the colonie, where he was a magistrate to the time of his decease. He was one of the leaders in the settlement of Schenectady in 1661-2; and on the surrender of New Netherland, was specially sent for by Governor Nicoll, to be consulted on Indian affairs and the interests of the country generally. He was highly respected by the governors of Canada, and the regard entertained for him by M. de Tracy, viceroy of that country, will be best judged of by the following extract of a letter which that high personage addressed him, dated Quebec, 30th April, 1667:—

"If you find it agreeable to come hither this summer, as you have caused me to hope, you will be most welcome, and entertained to the utmost of my ability, as I have a great esteem for you, though I have not a personal acquaintance with you. Believe this truth, and that I am, sir, your affectionate and assured servant. TRACY."

Having accepted this invitation, Mr. Van Curler, prepared for his journey. Gov. Nicoll furnished him with a letter to the viceroy. It bears date May 20th, 1667, and states that "Mons'r Curler hath been importuned by divers of his friends at Quebec to give them a visit, and being ambitious to kiss your hands, he hath entreated my pass and liberty to conduct a young gentleman, M. Fontaine, who unfortunately fell into the barbarous hands of his enemies, and by means of Mons'r Curler obtained his liberty." On the 4th of July following, Jeremias van Rensselaer, writing to Holland, announces, that "our cousin Arendt van Curler proceeds overland to Canada, having obtained leave from our general, and been invited thither by the viceroy, M. de Tracy." In an evil hour he embarked on board a frail canoe to cross Lake Champlain, and having been overtaken by a storm, was drowned, I believe, near Split-Rock. In his death this country experienced a public loss, and the French of Canada a warm and efficient friend.—*O'Callaghan's Hist. N. Netherland, i, 322.*

CODIRECTORS OF RENSSELAERSWYCK, 1630.

The copartnership consisted of Kiliaen van Rensselaer, Samuel Godyn, Johannes de Laet and Samuel Bloemmaert, with whom were associated Adam Bissels and Toussaint Moussart. The contract, and the articles of agreement, are referred to in the judgment of the Court of Holland, dated 14th June, 1650, in re Bloemmaert at al. vs. Van Twiller et al., which judgment was ratified by the States General on the same day. (Hol. Doc. v. 298. Alb. Rec. viii., 72, 73. Rensselaerswyck MSS.) It has been maintained, by some, that there was no partnership interest in the colonie of Rensselaerswyck, and that the claim of Bloemmaert, De Laet, and the other partners was not allowed. But the judgment here referred to shows that such an assertion is contrary to the fact. The suit was decided in favor of Bloemmaert and his associates, and the executors of the first patroon were condemned to account for the rents and profits, and to pay to each of the partners, or their heirs, their just quota. The partnership is, moreover, plainly admitted in the account of the disbursements for the first venture to Rensselaerswyck, anno 1630, wherein the sums advanced by the other codirectors are admitted and acknowledged. Ample evidence of the fact will be further found by reference to the Rensselaerswyck MSS., and to Holland Documents, vi, 303, 304, 306. De Vries also mentions the circumstance. Subsequently, however, Johanna de Laet, widow of Johannes de Hulter, and who married, secondly, Jeremias Ebbing, sold to the Van Rensselaers, in the year 1674, all her right and claim, as heiress of Johannes de Laet, to the colonie of Rensselaerswyck, for the sum of fl. 5,762 10st. or $2,301, which debt was discharged by the transfer to her of certain bouweries and lands which were deemed an equivalent. This lady was proprietor, among other tracts of the Weyland, or pasture, lying between the third and fourth kills, now called, in the map of the city of Albany, Rutten and Fox creeks. On the 20th of April, 1685, Gerrit Bissels and Nicolaus van Beeck (nomine uxorie,) both representing the children and heirs of Adam Bissels and Margt. Reust, entitled to one tenth part; and as attorneys for Abraham Elsevier (husband of Catharina Bloemmaert) and Isbrand Schenk, Constantina Bloemmaert (widow of Isaac Sweers, in his lifetime, vice-admiral in the service of Holland,) and Juffrouw Anna Bloemmaert (widow of Francois Romayn,) children and heirs of Samuel Bloemmaert and Catharine Reust, conjointly entitled to one tenth part of the colonie of Rensselaerswyck, sold, in Amsterdam, to Richard and Kiliaen van Rensselaer, Patroon of said colonie, their respective shares, being two tenths, or one fifth of the whole, for gl. 3,600, payable in three equal yearly parts. Thus all claims on the part of the original partners, to any portion of the colonie, became finally extinguished; and that estate vested altogether and exclusively in the Van Rensselaer family.—*O'Callaghan's Hist. of N. Netherland, i, 127.*

Irregular Pagination

In original book

BUSINESS DIRECTORY FOR 1849.

Artists.
Ames Julius R 3 plain
Hart James M 6 exchange
Heaford & Scattergood 36½ s pearl
Forbes E exchange building

Agricultural Implements.
Emery H L 369 broadway
Thorburn W cor broadway & maiden lane

Apothecaries.
(See *Drugs and Medicines.*)

Architects.
Penchard G 17 douw's building
Rector Henry 83 hudson
Woolet W L 10 steuben

Agency.
Noonan Thomas cor chapel & steuben
Patterson Josiah 63 lawrence
Scovel Ashley 11 douw's building

Auctioneers.
Clark & Jones 73 state
Copp N P 47 washington
Homer W P 72 state
Pillsbury L C under museum
Priest Allendorph & co cor state & green

Bakers.
Andrews F 166 washington
Beals Levi 84 Beaver
Blanchard E 79 church
Graves   green
Hodge John 665 broadway
Honeysett 104 hamilton
Hunter R 36 washington
McCafferty & Holmes 26 n pearl
McEntee John 21 canal
Paddock Stephen 77 s pearl
Peden A washington
Pester William 342 state
Peterson & Clark 807 broadway
Pettingill Michael 89 beaver
Prichard & Packard 186 washington
Putnam C 59 lydius
Turner John 56 hamilton

Barbers.
Andree Augustus 140½ broadway
Bertrand Louis spruce
Bertrand J 1 dean
Chambers John exchange basement
Crannell Mat basement franklin house
Crosby J G 1 maiden lane
De Mun E 450 broadway
Dengel Andrew 208½ broadway
Freeman & Van Vranken 379 broadway
Gardner William 48 hamilton
Garrison Thomas 29 s pearl
Garrison Isaac 3 catharine
Highgate Charles 632 broadway
Johnson Hiram 107 s pearl
L'Arrive John 2 green

Leavitt A J 628 broadway
Lovey D J 170 s pearl
Mitchell Francis cor steuben and chapel
Morgan George 80 s pearl
Norris James J 10 s pearl
Norris Henry B 70 washington
Pope Thomas american hotel
Simons Jacob 27 maiden lane
Stratton & Peterson 708 broadway
Switzer Henry 276 broadway
Tate John A 14t swan
Van Epps F congress hall
Van Vranken F cor hudson and dean
Van Vrankin David 805 broadway
Van Vrankin Robert 2 little basin
Winters J H delavan house

Bedsteads.
Tingley & co tivoli (patroon's creek)
Mayes J

Blacksmiths.
Boyle John 210 s pearl
Caldwell William J 90 green
Conkling J & A 89 green
Haight James O 13 church
O'Brien Matthew 25 washington
Percival George 251 broadway
Percival Gordon canal basin
Shaw Luton 99 green
Whitney James 66 green

Block and Pump-makers.
Brainerd E 23 quay
White F W 2 division

Boarding-houses.
Carter Misses 140 state
Charter Hannah 44 hamilton
Douglas Mrs 26 maiden lane
Fitch Misses 126 state
Fuller Mrs 9 montgomery
Furnald S 29 s pearl
Grant Mrs 2 water
Haskell Mrs 25 columbia
Huyck Miss E 10 rose
Johnson Elizabeth 53 chapel
Kirsinger M 7 howard
Kreuder John 215 broadway
Leggatt William 44 hudson
McNaughton Robert 91 herkimer
Munger Benjamin 6 norton
Rogers Mrs 46 engle
Salisbury Henry 12 s pearl
Seagrave James 13 montgomery
Sherman Rufus M 47 jay
Somerindyck G W 21 hudson
Westfall John S 7 union
Worth William E 11 beaver
Wright Elizabeth 29 westerlo

Bookbinders.
Harrison A L 445 broadway

Hoffman & Bender 71 state
Seymour & Russ 82 state
Steele Charles 388 broadway
Van Benthuysen C 407 broadway
Warner William J 7 n pearl
Weed Parsons and co 67 state

Booksellers and Publishers.
Bender E H 75 state
Durrie D S 388 broadway
Henry James 67 state
Hill Aaron 78 state
Little & co 53 state
Lord Joseph 19 philip
Pease E H & co 82 state

Boot and Shoe Dealers.
Dix J G 404 broadway
Huson D R 164 broadway
Mead & Wait 488 broadway
Mitchell J P 390 broadway
Osborn J 350 broadway
Pittinger   lydius
Prest J & D 816 broadway
Rankin G A 392 broadway
Rankin William 39½ washington
Robinson & Dwight 382 broadway
Snell James 410 broadway
Tripp J 57 washington
Wade & Carroll 430 broadway
Waterman Robert 53 s pearl
Wilcox W M & son 650 broadway
Woolverton G A 356 broadway

Boot and Shoe Makers.
Arnold Seth 207 green
Burton H 34 s pearl
Chapman H E 8 s pearl
Dunham Oscar 56 green
Fossard William 99 state
Laight John 39 green
Low John 116 church
Ramsay D D 547 broadway
Rodgers Sherlock 247 s pearl
Sayles Alexander 90 green
Stone G C 415 broadway
Thompson William 6 canal
Whitney James 39 s pearl
Young & Server 520 broadway

Bowling Alleys.
Cook John 164 state
La Grange John J 21 norton
McNab Peter 46 james
Montross Henry 39 columbia
Palmer & Booge 96 state
Stryker J P cor church and herkimer

Brass-founders.
McElroy William 63 beaver
Maxwell James 94 s pearl
Orr William 64 beaver
Cuyler green

Brewers.
Amsdell William western turnpike
Boyd Robert 61 ferry
Burt Uri cor montgomery and colonie
Dunlop 28 quay

Eggleston Putnam & co 9 dean
Kirk Andrew 904 broadway
McKnight John 95 canal
Taylor and sons 83 green

Brickmakers.
Bassett D E 399 lydius
Goodrich A M 308 lydius
McCall Patrick M 86 Swan

Brokers.
Evertsen Jacob jr 8 exchange
Gough John T 15 merchants' exchange
Groesbeeck brothers 13 exchange building
Hendrickson John 36 state
Hurd J N M 2½ green
Ireland D D 20 green
La Grange Gerrit 455 broadway
Lansing Jacob J 5 james
Payne G R 438 broadway
Pitman R H 398½ broadway
Rice B F 16½ exchange building
Squires Thomas 56 quay
Van Vechten Gerrit W 28 green
Washburn & co basement city bank
Wilson C V lumbermen's exchange

Builders.
(See *Carpenters and Builders.*)

Cabinet-makers.
Alvord E tivoli
Amsden J B 31 n pearl
Arts & Riley 97 state
Clemshire William 17 church
Long W cor lydius and green
McGuire William 116 state
Moseley H T 21 church
Van Loon P 70 green
(See *Furniture warehouses.*)

Cap-makers.
(See *Furs and Caps*, and *Hats, Caps, &c.*)

Carpenters and Builders.
Adams Christopher rear of state
Allanson Peter 1 elm
Boardman William 46 howard
Borden J R 41 jay
Bruce and Clemshire patroon
Cameron W 5 grand
Courtwright E M cor herkimer and church
Cunningham J 90 bleecker
Deforest J J & B S union below hamilton
Hawley Aaron 54 bleecker
Holdridge D F 74 eagle
Jarvis J J cor broadway and spencer
Jones William patroon
Luce Edwin 22 franklin
McGrath Morris 80 arch
Morse Henry lancaster
Morse James A lancaster
Owens James 109 beaver
Sexton & Poinier 49 franklin place
Ward J C 166 lydius

Carpetings.
Corbiere William A 544 broadway
Koonz Abram 43 grand
Van Gaasbeck John 34 green

Carpet Weavers.
Koonz Abram cor grand and hamilton
Ray Anna 297 washington

Carriage-makers.
Caldwell William J 90 green
Chesebro & Elmendorf 19 church
Goold James & co cor ham and division
Lloyd & Jones 80 hamilton
Long & Silsby 234 s pearl
Wemple J D W 53 hamilton

Cartmen.
Appleton William 67 Van Woert
Austin Abraham 275 washington
Baldwin B A hamilton w dove
Becker Hiram 152 orange
Beers Benjamin 2 garden
Bennett James 41 n lansing
Birmingham James 15 rose
Boone William 795 broadway
Booth Thomas 47 fayette
Butler J W 79 church
Cain James orange w swan
Carls John 59 s lansing
Carroll Owen 163 third arbor hill
Chandler Jeremiah 7 dewitt
Cheever C P 10 quackenbush
Clare William 19 orange
Colter Matthew 81 broad
Conner John 45 fayette
Courtney Isaac 8 jay
Crawford Robert 140 green
Crocker Anson 19 orange
Curtin Bart westerlo near elm
Cutler J jr 26 second arbor hill
Cutler Lyman 61 colonie
Ferguson John 143 orange
Finn Michael 36 canal
Finn Patrick 72 canal
Finnigan John 200 lydius
Fitzpatrick Thomas basement exchange
Flandrew John 18 orange
Fowler Charles H 45 van woert
Frost Jacob 49 fayette
Fryer Isaac 410 bowery
Gilvona Thomas canal e swan
Godden William 313 state
Goewey Solomon 912 broadway
Gorman Archibald 99 schuyler
Gormley Patrick 104 jefferson
Grady Patrick 9 westerlo
Griffin Michael 45 n lansing
Grogan Hugh westerlo w swan
Hamilton James 36 n lansing
Hare George 181 spring
Hart Patrick 40 franklin
Haswell John E 266 s pearl
Hatcher William westerlo w swan
Hazard W H 126 n pearl
Herring Thomas 140 s pearl
Hibbard Truman 410 broadway
Hosford Selah swan arb r hill
Hyde Harvey 38 water
Johnson William 206 broadway
Johnson Daniel 119 jefferson
Johnson John M willet
Johnson John 51 bassett
Kennedy Michael canal
Laughlin Felix canal
Lay John 124 third arbor hill
Leach Edward 116 green
Ledwidge Patrick 9 dewitt
Levings J 796 broadway
Long John 65 third arbor hill
Luther John 105 canal
McCormick John 174 broadway
McGrath Morris 32 water
McGuire Hugh cor state and park
McIntyre John 11 ferry
McKown John A 55 grand
McLaughlin William spencer
McWilliams John 45 van zandt
Maher Thomas 72 n lansing
Matthews Andrew 51 lawrence
Maxwell Joseph 40 franklin
Moffit William 76 franklin
Murray Peter cor schuyler and franklin
Murray Dennis 57 canal
Murray Francis john st alley
Murtaugh Michael 21 clinton
Neely Joseph 49 westerlo
Nichols William 126 jefferson
Owens Ira 72 montgomery
Pangburn John 36 spring
Percival J C 105 patroon
Peters Edward 79 canal
Poole John 65 n lansing
Quinlan Michael 107 first
Radliff Jacob 650 broadway
Ramsay John 33 water
Ramsay Philip 221 state
Reed William 216 state
Reed William H 216 state
Reed John S 216 state
Relyea Levi 130 arch
Richards Owen 172 hudson
Rock Charles 64 Rensselaer
Rose Henry 44 spring
Schmertser J A 76 patroon
Seely John 35 lumber
Seymour James 142 lydius
Sharp A M westerlo we swan
Sharp David westerlo we swan
Sheridan Barney cor first and swan
Simons Benjamin 160 spring
Simons George 11 knox
Simons Henry 160 spring
Simons Morris 175 orange
Simons Peter 183 orange
Skinner Charles 213 broad
Smith Jacob 12 orange
Stackpole John B 346 lydius
Stevens Jesse 49 fayette
Stevenson James 17 james
Stewart Adam 47 fayette
Storey Terence 47 van schaick
Taylor Robert 200 green
Thornton Philip 32 jefferson
Tompkins John B 142 jefferson
Truax C V S hamilton w dove
Turner C 21 dewitt

Van Schoonhoven James 65 van woert
Vine Robert 82 washington
Walker S 174 jefferson
Walker E 14 lumber
Walter P 57 rensselaer
Watson Simeon 49 high
Weaver Nicholas 53 dewitt
Whalen William head of canal
Wickham Elias 113 canal
Wickham William 115 canal
Winne Adam 35 jefferson
Wolf Philip 113 canal
Wright S 141 green

Cement, &c.
Warner Jacob 33 broadway
Woodruff Halsey cor plain and grand

Chair-makers.
Bussey John state
McChesney Lucas H 108 state
Parnell W 93½ state
Winne William B 83 state

Chandler.
Dey Ermand John chapel n canal
(See *Soap and Candles*)

China, Glass & Earthen ware.
Fisher Mary 37½ washington
Gregory and co 51 state
Lees Thomas 98 state
McIntosh W S & E C 416 broadway
Van Heusen & Charles 62 state

Clergymen.
Barry J K 2 franklin
Beecher   31 grand
Campbell John N 93 hudson
Campbell William H Albany academy
Clark J 29 plain
Conroy John J 99 colonie
Davenport   grace church
Ferguson   state st
Frazer J 76 ferry
Groube Bartholomew 35 grand
Halloway W W 134 green
Huntington E A 111 n pearl
Jefferies R 18 plain
Kennedy Duncan 55 n pearl
Kip William I 126 state
McClaskey P 51 dallius
McCloskey rev dr 14 lodge
Martin B N delavan
Miles John delaware turnpike
Morrow Samuel F 71 patroon
Noble E 89 third arbor hill
Pepper John 16 high
Pohlman H N 136 washington
Potter Horatio 68 maiden lane
Rawson T R 45 high
Schmidt F W
Selkirk E 68 herkimer
Sessions John Albany academy
Sprague William B 51 washington
Stark D swan and washington
Taggart C M 74 division
Trop Veist 78 arch

Waggoner W H 131 hamilton
Warren C J delavan house
Way P M wesleyan chapel
Wise Isaac 77 ferry
Wyckoff J N 100 lydius

Clocks.
(See *Watches and Jewelry*.)

Clothing Stores.
Allen Hiron W 425 broadway
Baird James 17 s pearl
Bew L 307 broadway
Bulger R 1 exchange building
Cook Thomas cor broadway and hudson
Derby Levi L 373 broadway
Dix Perry 421 broadway
Dorr Elisha 415 broadway
Duncan & Jackson 403 broadway
Duncan H R 483 broadway
Heermans John 417 broadway
Herman Solomon 54 s pearl
Lawton Anthony 424 broadway
Lynch John cor centre and n lansing
Lynch Owen 10 little basin
Mattimore Thomas 23 lawrence
Murray Hugh 401 broadway
Newberg J & S 329 broadway
Newton R N 377 broadway
Parker 459 broadway
Rooney Michael D 399 broadway
Sanders S and co 21 s pearl
Sullivan T 13 little basin
Swift Hugh 55 quay
Tucy Thomas 2 n lansing
White Isaac 331 broadway
Street Richard 409 broadway

Coach-ware and Saddlery.
Steele Roswell 420 broadway
Wright N 444 broadway

Coal dealers.
Belknap McKercher & Campbell   cor spencer and montgomery
Curran H D 205 broadway
Groesbeek J & A 45 columbia
McAuley M cor arch and dallius
Schuyler James cor bassett and franklin
Taylor James 166 broadway
White J G cor hudson and eagle
Wilbur and Townsend 175 broadway

Coffee Factories.
Chase L A and co 9 exchange
Thomas John 10 exchange

Commission Merchants.
Crafts B F 115 pier
Dorr and Englehart 31 quay
Dwight H W 44 quay
French and Stevenson 20 pier
Gilbert Lucien M 33 quay
Hale Sylvester 117 pier
Jones Benjamin P 106 pier
Read and Rawls 113 pier
Root Arthur H 5 hudson
Savage James 121 pier
Van Sickler R M and co 10 maiden lane

Confectioners.

Anderson Mrs 570 broadway
Anderson George 81 state
Bowers David N 916 broadway
Briare B 458 broadway
Burt Edward 10 columbia
Campbell Mrs cor hamilton and green
Clarkson M 98 state
Dennison William 22 s pearl
Fairchild M 66 state
Jewett Miss C 71 n pearl
Latham William G 77 wilson
May Edward 5 n lansing
Winn Mark cor s pearl and herkimer

Coopers.

Byrne John 112 pier
Hawe Matthew 55 dean
Hawe William 74 quay
Parr Richard 94 franklin
Radliff T J 52 philip
Wooley and Harris 120 washington

Coppersmiths.

Griffin P H cor steuben and james
Smith Peter 16 beaver

Counsellors.

Allen Otis 5 douw's building
Austin C L 37 state
Bancroft R L G 445 broadway
Barnard D D 1 academy park
Barnes William 450 broadway
Benedict Lewis jr city hall
Bingham R H 450 broadway
Birdseye Lucien 59 state
Blanchard Anthony 94 state
Bramhall C H 78 state
Briusmude J B douw's building
Brown James 445 broadway
Burton J I 66 state
Burwell Dudley exchange building
Cagger Peter 57 state
Callanan James jr 50 state
Campbell Duncan 60 chapel
Cassidy William atlas office law building
Cole John 513 broadway
Cole John O police office
Collier John A 542 broadway
Colt Joseph S 94 state
Colvin Andrew 106 state
Courtney S G 4 exchange
Cross J R 8 howard
Daniels Spencer 60 state
Dean and Newland commercial building
Deforest Dewitt C 8 exchange building
De Lancey E F 44 state
Denniston Gerrit V 343 state
Dexter James 3 n pearl
Doolittle E A 83 state
Downing George 73 patroon
Edwards F S 1 commercial building
Edwards Isaac 3 n pearl
Edwards James 480 broadway
Ford John W 460 broadway
Forsyth William W 6 state
French James M 3 clinton square
Frisbie John B mansion house
Frothingham W W 513 broadway
Gaffney Dennis B 81 state
Gallup Albert blunt's building
Gansevoort Peter 13 douw's building
Gibb Thomas W 50 state
Groesbeck S A 56 state
Hadley William J 83 state
Hammond L S 450 broadway
Hammond S H 450 broadway
Harris Hamilton 6 exchange building
Harris Ira 6 exchange building
Haswell H B 87 s pearl
Hawley N 21 douw's building
Hawley Gideon 4 exchange building
Higgins Solomon F 75 state
Hill Nicholas 57 state
Hill John J 13 douw's building
Hills A S 22 jay
Hilton R J 78 state
Hilton W J D 51 state
Holstein L D city hall
Howard N jr 57 hawk
James Thomas D 66 state
Jenkins Charles M 44 state
Joice R L commercial building
Kelly W S 94 state
King N G 450 broadway
Kingsley Hale 59 state
L'Amoureux James 8 douw's building
Lansing Jacob 68 state
Lansing C Y 3 douw's buildings
Lansing G Y 513 broadway
Lansing Charles B 513 broadway
Lansing I. I 450 broadway
Learned William L 71 state
Livingston John D 94 state
McHarg William C 61 state
McKown James 44 state
McMahon M 37 state
McMartin Duncan 44 state
Martin H H 152 state
Meads Orlando 489 broadway
Mink Charles W 45 arch
Morange William D 42 james
Morrell A justices' court
Newland John commercial building
Nichols M C G 10 douw's building
Northrop R H 8 douw's building
Nugent H P state hall
Olcott John J 25 n pearl
Paddock William S 71 state
Paige J C Y broadway
Palmer Levi H 7 cooper's building
Parker A J 143 washington
Parmelee William 442 broadway
Parsons S H H police office
Peckham G W 94 state
Peckham R W 94 state
Pepper Calvin 16 high
Pepper Calvin jr 183 hamilton
Percy and Higgins 75 state
Porter John K 57 state
Pruyn J V L 53 state
Pruyn R H 513 broadway

Pugsley C A 442 broadway
Radcliff D V N 703 broadway
Reynolds M T 25 n pearl
Rhoades Julius 8 exchange building
Robertson William D 251 washington
Robinson A D 94 state
Rose James R 75 state
Russell David justices' court
Sanders J B 9 douw's building
Settle Jacob M city hall
Sharp Alexander P 71 state
Shepard S O above m and f bank
Sherman Epaphras J 502½ broadway
Sternbergh Jacob 59 s pearl
Stevens Samuel 480 broadway
Stevens Cyrus 480 broadway
Street A B state library
Sturtevant 3 chapel
Taber Azor 6 commercial building
Ten Broeck C cor s. euben and broadway
Ten Eyck Anthony 53 columbia
Tillinghast J L franklin house
Trotter Matthew cooper's building
Tyler John J blunt's building
Van Buren Thomas B 115 green
Vanderpoel I 5 academy park
Van Epps H V D 7 exchange building
Van Hoovenburgh T S 450 broadway
Van Rensselaer B S 62 chapel
Van Rensselaer J S 2 douw's building
Van Rensselaer Richard cooper's building
Van Schnack S D 25 n pearl
Van Vechten Abraham state hall
Van Vechten Teunis 41 state
Van Vorst Hooper C 6 exchange building
Van Wie Lansing 2 jefferson
Wasson C C 41 state
Weed William G 59 state
Werner John I 59 state
Westerlo Rensselaer 41 n pearl
Wheaton Henry G 83 state
Whelpley J M 75 state
Whipple A D L 81 state
White William D commercial building
Willett E S 79 state
Wilson G L commercial building
Wilson J Q 5 exchange
Wood Bradford R 59 state
Woodhouse D 106 state
Woodworth John 113 state
Worcester Eldad 30 spring
Wright Deodatus 3 n pearl
Wyman H 94 state
Yates Wm cor montgomery and columbia
Yates Henry kane's park
Young William A 4 exchange building
Younglove T G 44 state

Daguerreotypers.
Churchill 54 state
Gavit Daniel E 480 broadway
Mead and brother 2 exchange building
Sisson N E 496 broadway

Dentists.
Austin J C 583 broadway
Brockway J 16 n pearl
Douglass George 77 lydius
Monroe Joshua 17 green
Nelson R and A 22 n pearl
Wheeler U H 18 n pearl
Wood John S cor hudson and s pearl

Distillers.
Clauson H 810 broadway
Tracey and Edson cor mont and colonie
Wilkinson Jacob 27 dean

Dress-makers.
Cameron S 13 park
Cluxton Nancy 65 arch
Davidson M R 56 lafayette
Grew Mrs S 46 s pearl
Hardy Ann 140 jefferson
Holcomb Hannah 41 lark
Kendall Mrs 233 broadway
Lenox Miss 83 beaver
McKee Mrs 43 orange
Moclair Mary 615 broadway
Pardon Maria 23 steuben
Patterson Miss 44 orange
West Miss E 64 chapel
Wilbur D A 38 spring
Wilcox Miss 92 hudson

Drugs, Medicines, &c.
Briggs R B 4 exchange
Burrows and Nellegar 43 s pearl
Burton B 1 delavan house
Byrnes Jonathan 24 s pearl
Dexter George 57 state
Ford & Grant cor washington and hawk
Frothingham C 440 broadway
McClure A and co 74 state
Pierce William H 506 broadway
Pulling H P 70 state
Springsteed & Bullock cor pearl & lydius
Vandenbergh A F cor broadway & hudson
Wharton W A 381 broadway

Dry Goods.
WHOLESALE.
Bleecker George M 408 broadway
King R H and co 49 state
Sheldon and Wood 467 broadway
Smith Carey and Moseley 477 broadway
Strong A M and W N 445 broadway
Woodburn and Dey Ermand 35 state

RETAIL.
Bailey and Ostrom 73 washington
Blatner and co 334 broadway
Boyd S V 428 broadway
Brown William G 490 broadway
Cohn J and I 72 s pearl
Cook Joseph S 530 broadway
Crapo Seth 56 state
Duffey Miss M 408 broadway
Ehrich J and co 2 s pearl
Erwin William H 238 washington
Fryer and McMichael 326 broadway
Gay and Mygatt 486 broadway
Hendrickson Mrs 92½ s pearl
Holmes Henry B 16 s pearl
Humphrey J J 58 state

Business Directory.

Ledderer Abram 43 s pearl
Lehrberg and Lederer 380 broadway
Levi Solomon 52 s pearl
Luke S and H 6 s pearl
McElroy James 696 broadway
McElroy William 646 broadway
Mubbett J G 384 broadway
Mesick Henry T 340 broadway
Minster S 38½ s pearl
Mork Philip 172 s pearl
Mygatt Thomas 486 broadway
Mylet Bartholomew 102 broadway
Newwitter J 40 s pearl
Perry N W 594 broadway
Post J A 474 broadway
Reedstone Isaac 37½ s pearl
Rogers W C 169 s pearl
Sampson Alexander 200 s pearl
Shelline Alfred 81 s pearl
Shrishimer L 142 s pearl
Schloss Moses 341 broadway
Sporborg Joseph 36½ s pearl
Stearns J G 538 broadway
Stilwell William B 80 state
Taylor and Deforest 423 broadway
Van Alen C cor s pearl and hudson
Van Aernem Benjamin 242 washington
Van Gausbeek & Emerson 452 broadway
Van Ness & Brown cor broadw & lumber
Walker Mrs 81 washington
Waterbury R P and co 595 broadway
Waterman J E 63 washington
Watson W H and co 68 state
Wheeler T V L 581 broadway
White George 554 broadway
Wilder N H 57 washington
Wiles Lewis cor s pearl and state
Wiles R P & T H cor hudson and s pearl
Zeh David 40 hawk

Dyers.
Condon James 36 orange
Giffin William 20 norton
Laycock 17 norton
Leddy P B 20 norton
Niblock John 43 hudson

Eating-houses.
Griffin S 6 green
Thompson Mrs 99 state
Wilbur Alvin 80 s pearl

Engravers.
ON WOOD.
Carson Robert H 6 exchange
Pease R H 516 broadway
ON COPPER.
Cooper D M 480 broadway
Gavit and Duthie exchange buildings

Expresses.
Greene and co 14 exchange building
Johnson R L 11 exchange building
Thompson and co 11 exchange building
Wells and co 11 exchange building

Fancy Goods
Shaw Matthew 750 broadway
Spelman B R and R L 494 broadway

Finding Stores.
Covert A 53 dean
Gross S jr 34 hudson
Guest and Laney 43 dean
Holt J and co 45 hudson
Van Schaack John 43 dean

Fire Brick.
Bender M W cor dallius and westerlo
Gott and Palmer cor hudson and hawk

Florists and Nurserymen.
Wilson James near penitentiary
Hall James delaware turnpike

Flour dealers.
Akin E C 73 quay
Artcher Michael 63 quay
Averill and Marshall 38 quay
Barrett and Brown 31 quay
Bement Caleb 9 Hudson
Bennett E B 65 quay
Bentley C W 87 quay
Blatner Henry 21 hamilton
Bowman Peter E 49 quay
Brown Thoms A 31 quay
Carey J and D H 43 quay
Chapman William and son 81 quay
Chipman and Savage 121 pier
Clark A S 46 quay
Cumming Alexander 187 washington
Durant E A 119 pier
Durant Lathrop and co 35 quay
Miller Nathaniel 599 broadway
Patten M and S 39 quay
Ring N and J 63 quay
Snyles J and G M 62 quay
Shepherd and co broadway upper end
Smyth C T 40 quay
Terry O G 120 pier
Tweddle and Darlington 83 quay
Wright and co 116 pier

Fresh Fish.
Parker Joseph north market
Simmons E J centre market

Fruit.
Anderson J H 62 green
Anderson James 25 s pearl
Avery and co 351 and 353 broadway
Childs Daniel 644 broadway
Clark Joseph 68 washington
Fairchild Benjamin 28 second arbor hill
Ford widow 46 green
Hagaman and Cowell 253 broadway
Hawes Isaac L 276 washington
Holland Edward 39 n pearl
Porter F cor hudson and broadway
Robinson Primus 83 state
Shank Robert 51 union
Vanderlip D R cor n pearl and state
Whitecar J 685 broadway

Fur and Caps.
Prentice J H and co 103 water
Treadwell G C and co 449 broadway

Furniture Warehouses.
Harris E A 531 broadway

Howe D 98 state
McKown A F cor s pearl and lydius
Meads John jr 549 broadway
Merrifield and Wooster 49 s pearl
Parsons Harvey 580 broadway
Winne John 15 n pearl

Forwarding Merchants.
Baker H O 103 pier
Brainard B C 29 quay
Brown William cor steuben and water
Carter Joseph I cor quay and hudson
Chamberlain and Olmsted 42 quay
Chapin and co 1 hudson
Chase and co 114 pier
Clark Charles V 96 pier
Clarke W H and co 42 quay
Cuyler C J 66 quay
Evans Louis E 49 quay
Evertsen A 31 quay
Gay George E 102 pier
Godard C W 98 pier
Greene and Mather 66 quay
Hewett H B and co 111 pier
Hovey O S 98 pier
Huber Jacob 211 bowery
Johnson and Curtis 66 quay
Littlejohn Levi S 96 pier
McKissick S 65 quay
Mallory J H and co 1 hudson
Moore George 19 pier
Olmsted D W 42 quay
Patten J W 66 quay
Pease J H and co 1 hudson
Phelps Austin 21 lancaster
Prosser E S cor state and quay
Redfield Charles B 113 pier
Schuyler T 29 quay
Shaw B F 95 pier
Terry O G 120 pier
Travis and co 103 pier
Vandewater W H and co 101 pier
Van Santvoord A 113 pier
Wetmore and Richards 44 quay
Williams H A 44 chapel
Yardley C 79 pier

Gardens.
Mineral Spring 58 ferry
National 772 broadway

Gardeners.
Fitzgerald Patrick 32 canal
Fortune Edward cor lydius and swan
Grady Thomas 82 church
Hermitage William N 58 canal
McDonald Cornelius 57 rensselaer
Maynard John 349 washington
Neely Robert 99 schuyler
Switzer F 167 broad
Turner Isaac 203 lumber

Gas-fitters.
Carroll M J broadway
Munsig and Bormann 623 broadway

Gents' Furnishing Stores.
Baker T S 518 broadway
Lansingh K V R 454 broadway

Globes.
Lancaster C and D 230 lydius
Standish Z 271 washington

Glovers.
Hill Thomas 78 state
Newman Henry 557 broadway

Grocers.
WHOLESALE.
Batcheldor G and E C 18 state
Bulkley and Crapo 50 quay
Cook and Wing 12 state
Crapo William 17 state
Davis William 11 state
Monteith and co 24 dean
Schoolcraft Raymond and co 14 hudson
Stanton G W cor quay and state
Wadley M S and co 347 broadway
Wait and Vernam 359 broadway
Weidman and Shell 10 state
Wilson and Grimwood 7 state
Wilson and Mintroll

RETAIL.
Armitage William M 58 canal
Baillie Charles cor franklin and john
Barker James 45 fayette
Bartholomew C cor hudson and high
Bartley James 65 colonie
Bender William M cor lydius and lark
Bergen Charles 28 quay
Birch G A 45 washington
Blair John S cor pine and chapel
Blake Owen 15 columbia
Blank Thomas cor arch and church
Bortle Richard 272 broadway
Bracken widow 12 clinton
Brammall George C 60 beaver
Brooks Jonathan jr 79 green
Brower Alburtus 404 broadway
Brown Daniel 25 lawrence
Brown Matthew cor chapel and canal
Bulger John 25 quay
Burke John cor hamilton and dove
Burns John 117 pearl
Burton S P 193 broadway
Buss Charles cor hawk and green
Butler Thomas 83 ferry
Bygate Richard 373 lydius
Byrne Michael 214 broadway
Byrne James 120 broadway
Cahill John 150 broadway
Calverly Stubbs 124 broadway
Campbell George 643 broadway
Campbell Hugh 141 broad
Campbell John W 9 ferry
Canan Dennis 13 quay
Carmody Patrick cor franklin & mulberry
Carroll Edward 17 quay
Chamberlain N W 860 broadway
Chandler S T 178 broadway
Chapman Morgan L 36 quay
Clark James 686 broadway
Clark John A 510 broadway
Clark Luke cor maiden lane and lodge
Clarke Michael 9 pine

Business Directory.

Cohn and Rothschild 138 s pearl
Colemay Christopher 53 first arbor hill
Conner James 42 union
Conner Michael 50 colonie
Cook Asher 5 exchange
Corrigan William 160 green
Costigan John 106 orange
Couch John cor washington and snipe
Courtney Joseph cor dallius and john
Cowell and Flaherty 117 quay
Coyle Terence 13 columbia
Cramer Patrick cor rensselaer & franklin
Croister James 126 washington
Cummings George cor division and liberty
Deforest Charles A cor green and hamilton
Deforest Curtis 35 hamilton
Dempsey Patrick 48 van woert
Demsey John cor van zandt and fulton
Dermody Henry cor chapel & van schaick
Diamond William M 76 n pearl
Dickson L J 8 steuben
Dillon John 186 s pearl
Donehue John 40 van schaick
Donnelly F and A 112 quay
Donnelly Thomas 76 orange
Donovan John cor church and mulberry
Dooley Martin 186 s pearl
Dooley Michael 203 water
Dormley Andrew cor quay and john
Dowd John cor lumber and center
Droogan C 3 morton
Dunn Charles 192 broadway
Dunn Philip 351 state
Dunn Philip jr 323 state
Eagan John 99 canal
Eagan Patrick 81 quay
Early Thomas 46 colonie
Eaton S S 82 washington
Eggleston John M 22 quay
Elder George cor orange and chapel
Erwin Robert 27 lumber
Ewing P H cor hudson and daniels
Falke Henry 844 broadway
Falkes George cor clinton and alexander
Farrell James little basin
Feltman John C cor hudson and grand
Finch Orville cor pearl and hudson
Finn Timothy 68 green
Fisher John D cor lydius and lark
Fisher Michael 105 snipe
Fitzsimmons and Smith 15 quay
Flood Mrs cor orange and water
Foley James 52 church
Foot Truman S 311 broadway
Fortune Edward cor lydius and swan
Fox Patrick cor arch and green
Frederick James C 80 washington
Fredenrich Philip centre market
Freest E M P cor water and lawrence
Frisbee Edwin 71 washington
Fryer John 778 broadway
Galipo Nelson cor colonie and centre
Gates Owen T cor state and park
Gaynor Thomas D 34 quay
Gerun Anthony 67 broadway

Gibson Washington 160 broadway
Gould Francis 34 herkimer
Grady Patrick 19 quay
Gratian Patrick 328 washington
Gray James 152 lydius
Griffin R M 201 broadway
Halligan Patrick cor swan and westerlo
Harrison John 71 canal
Hart John 42 second
Hart Owen cor church and green
Hart and Stevens 37 hamilton
Haswell & Ransom cor green & westerlo
Hayes Edward 291 state
Hayes Michael 87 green
Hayes Michael 192 green
Heffernan James cor rensselaer & s pearl
Hennessy Thomas 16 van zandt
Hennessy widow 401 state
Higgins Bernard 29 van woert
Higgins Thomas 21 lawrence
Hill George 61 pier
Hill Henry 45 pier
Hilton S V A 839 broadway
Hiney Jacob 132 arch
Hogeboom P and J 149 broadway
Holler Jacob 189 washington
Houll Oliver third cor swan
Hughes Thomas A cor lark and spring
Hurst William 23 s pearl
Isdell William cor lydius and broad
Jones Thomas 138 broad
Jordan Joseph A 22 clinton
Joynt John 140 s pearl
Kappes John 193 s pearl
Keelin John cor arch and dallius
Kelly Patrick cor arch and broad
Kelly Thomas 40 montgomery
Kennedy Dennis cor first and swan
Kennedy Philip 58 union
Kieley J P cor broad and schuyler
Kiernan William cor eagle and elm
Kiley J P cor arch and broad
Killion Patrick 136 broadway
Kilmer J G 211 green
King S W 46 second arbor hill
Kinney John S foot columbia st bridge
Kirkpatrick Edward centre market
Kirkpatrick Mrs centre market
Lawlor Fanton 261 state
Lawlor Martin cor lumber and water
Lawrence Mary Ann 131 franklin
Lee William 59½ n lansing
Leonard S S cor lydius & delaware turn.
Leonard Thomas 78 franklin
Lightbody Andrew cor church & westerlo
Lochner George 64 washington
Loomis S A cor s pearl and hamilton
Lynch Barnard cor green and schuyler
Lyons 14 quay
Lyons Joseph 53 hawk
McBride J and W 262 washington
McCafferty John 47 lumber
McCarty 369 state
McCaugan 191 broadway
McClelland Joseph 61 eagle

McCole James 9 plain
McEntee James 169 green
McEntee John 21 canal
McEvily Patrick 2 howard
McEvoy John cor green and rensselaer
McGarvey James 22 jackson
McGinn Michael 100 schuyler
McGinnis Patrick 174 montgomery
McGinnity Patrick 56 broad
McGovern John cor arch and dallius
McGran Patrick 77 schuyler
McKenna Barney 134 broadway
McMahon Francis 59 n ferry
McManus James 188 broadway
MacNamara Hugh 227 washington
McNulty Christopher 150 s pearl
MacShane Felix 74 quay
McShea James 225 broadway
Maher Robert 159 broadway
Mallon Thomas w swan
Malone James 78 beaver
Malvy William cor lodge & maiden lane
Martin Boyd cor third and swan
Martin William 352 broadway
Mead Titus cor water and n ferry
Merrifield William eagle near lydius
Miles Joseph cor arch and s pearl
Miller Charles
Mix H and S 235 s pearl
Moakler Michael cor canal and chapel
Monahan John 5 little basin
Moore Jasper 58 green
Moore S B 4 division
Morrow James cor ferry and broadway
Moslain G 150 lark
Mullen John 22 pier
Mulligan P cor jefferson and swan
Murphy Edward 187 s pearl
Murphy Patrick cor schuyler & alexander
Murray Dennis 115 broad
Murray John 8 columbia
Murray John cor westerlo and quay
Murray L 155 orange
Murray Owen cor hamilton and philip
Neff William cor daniel and beaver
Neff & Ford cor broadway and quackenb
Neville Isaac cor water and n lansing
Neville John 8 lydius
Norton Michael 114 canal
Norwood David 81 orange
Nowlan Jeremiah cor philip & van zandt
Oberist Charles 1 columbia
O'Conner John 37 division
O'Flaherty P 160 s pear
O'Hanlon M 15 bleecker
O'Neil M 12 n lansing
Oppenheim G cor franklin and herkimer
Osborn J H and H cor s pearl and lydius
Patree S 174 broad
Pemberton E & J cor n pearl & columbia
Perry Hiram 174 washington
Pester William 312 state
Porter Jeremiah 369 washington
Power D 149 Broadway
Putnam and Shaw foot columbia

Queeny M 199 water
Radfort William F cor ferry and church
Rafferty Charles 13 quay
Ramsay James cor broadway and colonie
Rankin S 108 s pearl
Reardon Timothy 134 broadway
Riley Edward cor swan and second
Robison Mrs 377 state
Rosengarten Joseph 62 s pearl
Rowe Matthew 56 lawrence
Russell Jason 150 washington
Ryan Patrick 133 jefferson
Sayles James 2 william
Sayles James jr cor lumber and water
Scanlon W 5 maiden lane
Schwartz Simson cor green and ferry
Schuyler Cortland and co 870 broadway
Schuyler and Van Antwerp 88 bassett
Scott William B cor swan and second
Serviss John D cor beaver and lodge
Serviss William cor lydius and swan
Shackleton James 19 lawrence
Shaver John 90 washington
Sheridan William cor rensselaer & dallius
Shoory Mrs 89 canal
Shonts John A 210 water
Sickles John A 76 s pearl
Simons John 780 broadway
Simons N E and J C cor lydius and rose
Simpson John 235 s pearl
Slack Granville cor lydius and dove
Slaven Michael cor broadway & schuyler
Smith and Packard cor green and hudson
Smith Barney 17 second
Smith Bernard 269 s pearl
Smith David 8 s pearl
Smith Ezekiel 17 washington
Smith Matthew cor broad and alexander
Spears Ebenezer 68 lawrence
Spencer Spencer 199 washington
Stein Myer 68 westerlo
Sterne Isaac 33 s pearl
Stewart James 23 westerlo
Sutliff E A 29 lancaster
Sutliff George 237 washington
Sutliff T M 741 broadway
Swartz Abram cor arch and broad
Tuggerty Mrs 1 clinton
Tullman Darius 8 n lansing
Turbell G S 65 quay
Thomson Alexander 93 church
Thomson C N 50 philip
Tiernan Owen 121 quay
Triger C 259 washington
Van Aernem J B 11 water
Vanderlip E R cor green and hudson
Van Valkenburgh William 14 n lansing
Van Wormer Peter 237 washington
Van Zandt G D 646 broadway
Veeder and Bates 114 s pearl
Veeder V cor centre and n lansing
Vickers John 259 s pearl
Waddel James 192 n pearl
Waddel Samuel cor n pearl and orange
Wallace Christopher 103 orange

Wallace John 43 rensselaer
Wallace M 713 broadway
Walls Peter cor jefferson and swan
Watts Charles 205 broad
Weeks and Relyea 78 pier
Welch James 57 s pearl
Westheimer Abraham cor Schuyler and s pearl
Whitney James F 200 water
Wilbur Rensselaer cor lydius and dallius
Wilkins H w side little basin
Wilkinson Abraham 45 grand
Williams John H 9 n pearl
Wilson J B cor pine and chapel
Winne J L 734 broadway
Worner J C 291 washington
Wright H 163 broadway
Young George cor pearl and beaver
Young Sidney & co cor lydius and grand
Young S and P 666 broadway

Gunsmiths.
Beebee blunt's building
Churchill O cor green and beaver
Scott W J and R H 9 beaver
Van Valkenburgh S 11 beaver

Hair-work.
Blanchard J W 515 broadway
Stiles Maria 23 hudson

Hardware dealers.
Corning and co 451 broadway
Davidson and Viele 46 state
Fry Daniel 40 state
Humphrey and co 41 state
Miles N B 94 state
Pruyn and Vosburgh 39 state
Warren and Steele 66 state

Hats, Caps and Furs.
Boughton Daniel 411 broadway
Boyd Thomas 537 broadway
Butters Silas 485 broadway
Cotrell J G 48 state
Dickson Hugh 54 state
Frothingham William 444 broadway
Herrick E S 400 broadway
Hills Erastus 60 state
Hussey N 397 broadway
Mayell Alfred 426 broadway
Milwain James 84 state
Robins John S 35½ s pearl
Van Namee and co 402 broadway

Herbs.
Gould James S 413 broadway
McHarg William 22 green

Hides and Leather.
(See *Leather dealers*)

Horticultural Articles.
(See *Seed stores*)

Ice dealers.
Hall and Hawley

Ink.
Rosekrans & Ovens cor exchange & dean
Starr Alexander 666½ broadway

Intelligence Offices.
Boardman D 47½ hudson
Burt John 22½ s pearl

Iron Fence-builders.
Carls J D william
Covert H W cor steuben and water
Starks and Pruyn 48 liberty

Jewelery.
(See *Watches and Jewelry*.)

Junk Shops.
McClelland David 176 broadway
Welch Benjamin 198 s pearl

Justices.
Cole J O police office
Cornell Levi lower end s pearl
Morrell A justices' court
Parsons S H H police office
Sargent Parker justices' court

Lace Goods.
Barclay C 512 broadway
Hindman A G 534 broadway
Leask John 522 broadway

Law Booksellers.
Gould Banks and Gould 104 state
Little and co 53 state

Leather dealers.
Anable and Smith 30 state
Hepinstall G 25 hudson
Holt J and co 45 hudson
Humphrey F cor state and dean
Ruyter John 18 hudson
Seymour Forsyth and co 6 state
Van Schanck John 43 dean
Van Valkenburgh Frost and Ruyter 18 hudson
Watson William and co 59 dean

Liquors, Wines, &c.
Baker James B 7 steuben
Bratt G T cor william and howard
Clauson P J 105 green
Esmay Isaac 28 dean
Fake and Todd 24 state
Foot and Welden 311 broadway
Knowlton Hosea 197 broadway
Maher James 52 state
Malburn Francis 18 lydius
Mascord Edward 27 s pearl
Reid and Cushman 7 dean
Reno Rensselaer 9 s pearl
Boerem Townsend 13 norton

Livery Stables.
Carter Charles 26 steuben
Clemons George rear franklin house
Dexter Chauncey cor hamilton and liberty
Frisby Edward 161 s pearl
Harris George cor maiden lane and james
Reed Benjamin 4 william
Slausson W F 79 maiden lane
Taylor Thomas 114 s pearl
Wallace A F 41 division
Yates H and H 56 montgomery

Locksmiths.
Blackall J & W J cor hamilton and fulton
Lovie Alexander 86 green
Wollensack John 16 van zandt

Looking-glass Manufacturers.
Annesley Lawson 504 broadway
Burton James and co 3 green
Riley George 1 green

Lumber.
Barnard F J and son 220 water
Birdsall William 37 pier
Bloomingdale William H above n ferry
Carroll Arlond 51 pier
Coffee and Brush cor water and spencer
Colburn D K 127 water
Cooley Calvin and co 191 water
Dalton William 13 ten broeck
Dewitt William H 67 pier
Easton Charles P 88 water
Fassett Asa 37 pier
Gay Lusher 32 pier
Goodrich David 43 pier
Griswold, Mattoon and co cor orange and water
Hadlam W cor montgomery and lumber
Higbie Hammonds and co above n ferry
Hunt William H 187 water
Ketchum R V R 127 water
King James B 20 pier
Lord T S 18 pier
Paddock S jr 127 pier
Rathbun Joshua 67 pier
Rogers and Cullender 116 water
Romaine J P 118 water
Ross William H 13 van tromp
Sanford Giles above n ferry
Talcott and Hosmer 61 quay
Tyler Bullock and co 46 water
Van Etter J B 41 pier
Van Valkenburgh B 689 broadway
Vose Franklin upper end pier
Whipple S water n canal lock
Whitlock Robert cor water & quackenbush
Williams C P and co 29 pier
Wilson and Mead above n ferry

Machinists.
Battel Mellen cor orange and water
Dwelle Albert 15 church
Jagger Treadwell and Perry 110 beaver
Lloyd Thomas cor john and quay
Low
Pollard C 160 state
Rodgers John 33 lumber
Townsend F and co cor hawk and elk
Wheeler Melick and co cor union and hamilton

Mahogany.
Meads John jr 549 broadway
Merrifield and Wooster 49 s pearl

Maltsters.
McCulloch W A and co cor dallius and rensselaer
(See *Brewers*.)

Marble Manufacturers.
Dixon John 36 howard cor lodge
Kenny Thomas K 232 state

Masons.
Hays J E 122 green
Page Peter L 6 chesnut
Todd Adam 9 high
Woodruff Cyrus 30 grand

Medicines.
Herrick and co 6 james
Mosher and co 49 washington
Perkins and Gardner 54 beaver

Military Goods.
Meacham R S 84 state
Wright N and co 444 broadway

Milliners.
Adams Mrs 88 hamilton
Allen Mrs Jane 48 orange
Andrus Miss 21 steuben
Anstee Mrs 48 washington
Blanchard J W 515 broadway
Boyd Mrs 31 green
Brayton Misses 47 green
Courter Miss Ann 47 washington
Creswell Mrs 12 s pearl
Davidson Miss 46 hudson
Easton Mrs Betsey 69 n pearl
Ellis Miss S 4 s pearl
Getty Miss 37½ s pearl
Gill Mrs E 69 s pearl
Gilmore L 540 broadway
Gough Mrs 589 broadway
Gracie Mrs 608 broadway
Harris Mrs 45 green
Hempstead Elizabeth 524 broadway
Keeler Mrs C 105 lydius
Kimball Misses 86 washington
Law Miss 83 n pearl
McCormick Mrs 43 orange
McKinney Miss 44 s pearl
Newton Miss 8 n pearl
Purcell Frances 704 broadway
Rawson Mrs E 330 broadway
Roberts Mrs 74 chapel
Singer Miss 50 s pearl
Waterman Miss 20 s pearl
Winants Mrs 37 s pearl
Wooley Mrs 6 s pearl

Morocco.
Colbern Peter cor arch and dallius
Guest and Laney 43 dean

Music Teachers.
Austin Miss Mary 64 westerlo
Cone H R 151 hamilton
Cone Solomon 21 jay
Goold Henry 47 s pearl
Gourley Mrs 117 n pearl
Maeder
Packard Russel 122 washington
Robinson Thomas L 38 n pearl
Shaw O J 703 broadway
and others

Business Directory.

Newspaper Depots.
Cook Peter 464 broadway
Gilbert P L under museum

Newspaper Offices.
Argus exchange building
Atlas law building
Common School Journal 67 state
Cultivator 407 broadway
Dutchman broadway
Express 1 green
Freeholder cor washington and hawk
Journal cor state and james
Knickerbacker museum building
Messenger broadway
Palladium broadway
Spectator broadway
Switch beaver

Notaries.
Fondey Isaac city bank
Jenkins John F 7 commercial building
Lee Noah exchange bank

Nurses.
Barragar Harriet 166 hudson
Birdsall Eliza 83 bleecker
Bishop Elizabeth 31 second arbor hill
Boyd Mrs 25 wilson
Defreest Mrs 19 columbia
Flansburgh Jemima 825 broadway
Godfrey Abbe L 134 n pearl
Lewis Widow Sarah 12 norton
Lisk Sarah 17 washington
Morrison Mary 204 s pearl
Patten Mrs 66 chapel
Sickles Mary 174 n pearl
Tetor Ann 154 orange
Visscher Eliza 71 lumber
Wands Mrs 20 s lansing
Whitney Catharine 70 second
Wiley Lydia 17 franklin
Wood Eliza 25 van woert

Oil-cloth Factories.
Meech H T 5 grand
Russell E and son 501 broadway

Oysters.
Aldrich Adam 36 westerlo
Barnes S S 774 broadway
Burbanks C & G cor broadway and ham-[ilton
Carle James F 84 washington
Cowell R 254 broadway
Cowell and Higby 77 state
Macnamee and Cowell 94 quay
Parker Joseph 606 broadway
Radley William 81 canal
Scott John 48 s pearl
Thomas and Jones 291 broadway
Traber Charles 19 lodge
Van Bramer 113 pier

Painters.
Alden Stephen H 20 beaver
Gladding Freeman 12 william
Gladding G W 93 state
Gladding Joseph 93 state
Gladding T C 49 hawk
Gladding and Morrill 484 broadway
Gregory L R 32 green
Hinkley and Holmes trotter's alley
Hurdis John 9 church
Hutchins S B 10 beaver
Porter Ira 535 broadway
Rogers Stephen 617 broadway
Seaton George E 201 s pearl
Vedder John S 108 lydius

Paints, Oils, and Glass
Davis Joseph and co 78 state
Ford and Grant cor washington and hawk
McClure A and co 74 state
Pulling H P 70 state
Russell E and son 501 broadway
Wharton W A 381 broadway

Paper-hangings.
Harris D jr 8 green
Irwin William 336 broadway
Richardson William 60 s pearl
Steele and co 360 broadway

Paper Warehouses.
Pierce J M 75 washington
Whitney and Bennett 59 state

Passenger Agents.
Morse and Osterhout 6 maiden lane
Morse C L and co 78 quay
Nelligan David cor hamilton and quay
Osborn E 36 quay
Ross John J 145 third
Van Valkenburgh & co cor quay & hodge
Weed Henry 77 lawrence

Pattern-makers.
Gibbs S W 25 green
Clement H 6 james

Physicians.
Adams H 91 state
Armsby J H 609 broadway
Bay William 22 n pearl
Beck T Romeyn 29 elk
Bigelow U G 30 s pearl
Boyd James P cor hudson and grand
Brown James M 97 herkimer
Bucklin Daniel D 618 broadway
Burton R J (thomsonian) 66 chapel
Campbell John 60 chapel
Cogswell Mason F 13 n pearl
Cooke George 3 norton
Cox James cor green and lydius
Cunningham Samuel P 112 church
Dean N S (botanic) 19 norton
Elmendorf P E cherry hill
Emmons Ebenezer 150 hudson
Fay Henry B 5 n pearl
Fonda D E 97 s pearl
Cannon Patrick 690 broadway
Geoghegan William 116 green
Griffin C C 789 broadway
Heinsius Otto cor hudson and union
Herrick Lewis R 6 james
Hinkley John W 33 hudson
Hun Thomas 36 maiden lane
Jones E D (homœopathic) 34 lodge

Kane Hazel 53 washington
La Barte John 105 herkimer
Leseczynski Albert cor broadway & lumb
Levi Joseph 134 s pearl
Lockrow V B 56 beaver
McMurdy R S 24 second arbor hill
McNaughton James 54 n pearl
McNaughton Peter 556 broadway
March Alden 72 hudson
Markey N 74 green
Martin David cor columbia and broadway
Masten William L 118 lydius
Paine Henry D (homœopathic) 70 chapel
Paine John A (homœop.) 563 broadway
Quackenbush J V P 87 n pearl
Rossman J B cor lydius and green
Russell A W (botanic) 88 beaver
Sheldon B A cor state and hawk
Sperry Rufus D 70½ n pearl
Staats B P 53 n pearl
Staats P P 42 lydius
Stanton W B (botanic) 109 s pearl
Swinburne John 66 eagle
Thompson R H 1 washington
Townsend Howard 64 state
Townsend John F 2 academy park
Trotter J H 654 broadway
Van Antwerp (magnetic) william st
Van Buren John 3 washington
Van Buren Peter 115 green
Van Olinda P cor green and hamilton
Wendell Peter 7 academy park
Wendell Herman   "
Westervelt Gerrit (botanic) 71 beaver
Willard S D franklin house
Wiltsie David 31 columbia
Wing Joel A 1 washington
Wood J L cor s pearl and hudson

Pianofortes.
Ballantine and Barhydt 22 union
Boardman and Gray 4 n pearl
Burns Francis P 5 james
Ilsley F I 525 broadway
Mayer and Collier 519 broadway
Meacham R S 84 state
Wood and Gombel 13 n pearl

Plane-makers.
Bensen and Crannell cor state and lodge
Bensen and Munsell 42 howard
Gibson John cor water and spencer

Porter-houses.
Adams John 31 hamilton
Anthony Jacob 7 maiden lane
Basher Joseph 117 arch
Bendal Edward cor arch and broad
Bergeron M 1 division
Briggs W W 28 maiden lane
Buckbee Daniel 6 stanwix hall
Cane Jesse 31 union
Chambers Thomas 79 s pearl
Crannell J W 101 s pearl
Dee Mrs 38 n pearl
Elmendorf John 103 broadway

Farrell Thomas 25 church
Flynn John 3 division
Gabel Nicholas 140 montgomery
Gould James lower end s pearl
House William A 11 maiden lane
Hughes John cor lydius and dallius
Jacobs L C 104 pier
Kranz John 8 rose
Kreuder George 15 montgomery
Lenny William 29 hamilton
Lovell Richard 62 beaver
Luce Walter basement exchange
McCotter Henry 10 columbia
McGowan William 4 beaver
Molloy Joseph 3 dean
Peebles John 14 beaver
Quin Charles 4 howard
Rector John 279 s pearl
Reuter George 153 broadway
Rose J 18 washington
Shallow John 33 hamilton
Van Horn Fredas 167 s pearl
Welch William cor green and mulberry

Portrait Painters.
Gladding T A 41 s pearl
Palmer Sylvanus 22 douw's building
Prime Angustus 496 broadway
Shaver V P 25 van schaick
Taggart J G mansion house
Twitchell A W 593 broadway
Van Zandt T K 75 knox
Wagner M D delavan house
Wilkies T 98 state

Potter's Ware.
Smith David 65 lark
Wallace Oliver 103 orange
Gott and Palmer cor hudson and hawk

Printers.
Andrews E arbor hill
Hastings H J museum building
Kilmer C 6 james
Munsell Joel 58 state
New John 10 beaver
Romaine B F 334 broadway
Stone Henry cor green and state
Van Benthuysen C 407 broadway
Van Dyck H H law building
Weed Parsons and co 67 state

Printers on Copperplate.
Cooper D M 480 broadway
Gavit and Duthie exchange building
Merchant 80 state
Pease R H 516 broadway

Produce.
Appleton William 145 washington
Bedell Daniel 162 washington
Carmichael James 4 exchange
Crauford R B 8 exchange
Grant and Sayles 61 quay
Hallenbeck M I 7 hudson
Hawley Cyrus 192 washington
Higgins Robert 264 washington
Rattoone William 107 washington

Smith Patten and co 39 quay
Wheeler H R 6 exchange
Wing and Byrne 90 quay

Provision dealers.
Avery and co 351 and 353 broadway
Chapman J A and co 3 state
Crook and Palmer 9 state
Cushman and co 20 state
Cushman P C and co 198 hamilton
Goffe W B and J 84 n pearl
Hawkins H D 44 quay
Jones John 675 broadway
Judson Ichabod L 41 quay
Kerr W and J cor s pearl and howard
L'Amoure T E and G 39 washington
Lathrop Dyer 69 washington
Lord Joseph and son 29 washington
McCann Felix 45 quay
McCulloch John 12 exchange
McElroy T cor maiden lane and dean
Merchant L & W 71 quay
Peck S S 8 state
Perry Eli 87 washington
Sanders J B and co 72 quay
Smith Ralph 72 washington
Williams W C 289 washington

Real Estate Agents.
Clark and Jones 73 state
Fellows and Davis 20 green
Fitzpatrick Anthony F 38 steuben
Scovel A douw's building

Refectories.
Acker P basement museum
Adams William cor state and green
Anthony John 96 state
Armstrong William cor arch and s pearl
Battersby James cor patroon and n pearl
Bedell Richard centre market
Bergeron Joseph cor lydius and church
Bradt William 252 broadway
Cassidy Henry 36 water
Charles George H cor green & herkimer
Duff John A 11 montgomery
Franks John 17 hamilton
Galvin John lock number 1
Harris James B douw's building
Hartwell William 580 broadway
Hewson Joseph 196 water
Houck P and J 3 s pearl
Johnson Daniel C 20 lydius
McCardell pier foot state and 15 beaver
McClusky B cor church and s lansing
Maver and Gladding 130 state
Miles James R cor broadway and maiden lane
Moore Andrew 258 s pearl
Reasoner Peter basement exchange
Rice George E cor ferry and broadway
Ruso F and F cor state and pearl
Strain J F basement exchange
Taylor and Leslie 27 hudson
Thayer W B 24 beaver
Wilson J 29 hudson

Saddles, Trunks, & Harness.
Bell James N 473 broadway
Booth Alfred 105 s pearl
Clandenning William 607 broadway
Lloyd and McMicken 342 broadway
McChesney E 545 broadway
Slason E B 375 broadway
Smith William 311 broadway
Traver George 24 washington
Van Vlack William 85 s pearl
Whitney Charles 6 n lansing
Whitney James 10 little basin

Sail-makers.
Disney John 60 quay
Monkley Peter cor hamilton and quay

Sash-makers.
Easterly Thomas 44 elm
Fowler Gilbert C 96 herkimer
Roseboom Charles 94 hudson

Saw-filers.
Anson Levinus 82 ferry
Hermans C J 127 beaver
Topping S 7 norton

Seed Stores.
Emery H L 396 broadway
Thorburn William corner broadway and maiden lane

Sextons.
Blackall James 1st presbyterian 48 beaver
Davison B C near s pearl baptist church
Ensign Guy ferry st methodist church
Litchfield John n methodist church
Pangburn W 36 spring
Pottenbergh H north methodist
Van Bergen P cor van schaick and chapel
Vandenburgh A 38 beaver
Wallace Moses 2 franklin place
Watson Stephen 23 dove
Weaver D L 65 green
Wiley William ferry st methodist
Winne S P 118 n pearl

Skippers.
Austin Jeremiah 92 beaver
Barnard George T 60 n lansing
Buckbee E 27 dewitt
Burns Walter 23 rensselaer
Cassidy George 128 s pearl
Ford Eliakim 120 green
Gillespie Josiah 62 westerlo
Green M R 277 lydius
McEntee Thomas S 100 spring
Mink David 8 ferry
Murray H L 60 westerlo
Page Nicholas 122 n pearl
Sherwood Stephen A 115 church
Silsby Thomas 17 franklin
Winne Gilbert 219 lumber

Soap and Candles.
Hartness John and co 56 jackson
Strain Joseph cor church and herkimer
Taylor and sons 83 green
Ten Eyck M H 70 green

Ten Eyck J H and co 17 s lanting
Wells Agur 177 s pearl

Soda Manufacturers.
Hand and Murtha cor howard and s pearl
Harris John cor broadway and exchange

Stonecutters.
Gray Alexander cor franklin and john
Jones James D 65 herkimer

Stove Dealers.
Baker C A 10 green
Baker Samuel 16 green
Callanan and Wilson 18 green
Clark J H and co 4 green
Coughtry Robert T 33 washington
Gregory E H and co 97 green
Harvey Francis 7 green
Hermance John C 639 broadway
Hoy John 15 green
Learned B P and co 8 maiden lane
McCoy Clark and co 13 green
McLoughlin C 22 hudson
Pasco E L 5 green
Quackenboss Angus 14 state
Ransom S H and co 26 state
Rathbone and co 9 green
Seger Peter 44 washington
Sheur J H 17 green
Tremere & Wands cor beaver and green
Van Wormer and McGarvey 14 green
Vose and co cor maiden lane and dean

Stove-works.
Cobb William 192 washington
Jagger Treadwell and Perry 110 beaver
McCoy Clark and co montgomery
Potts Jesse C cor hamilton and grand
Quackenboss A water
Ransom and co broadway below s ferry
Rathbone and co n ferry
Vose and co cor broadway and bassett

Steam Sawing and Planing.
Gibson John cor water and spencer
Warren Clement cor water & quackenb

Tailors and Drapers.
Booth William 47 high
Carpenter and Kirk 71 state
Chatterson J cor broadway and church
Cook Thomas cor hudson and broadway
Cooney Michael 495 broadway
Davis R C 3 exchange
Duesler Daniel 494½ broadway
Evans Robert 103 s pearl
Freeman Robert 482 broadway
Harvey James M 468 broadway
Howe S B 461 broadway
Kirk Abram 497 broadway
Lee T E and T 471 broadway
Muir William O 52 state
Relyea Peter 446 broadway
Sard Grange 448 broadway
Shamler William 3 stanwix hall
Shepard J G 431 broadway
Shepard S S 313 broadway
Thorn William 13 beaver

Topp William H 546 broadway

Tailoresses.
Arms Mrs 54 division
Claudius Julius 50 church
Reynolds Miss E 73 lumber
Waldron Maria 20 daniels
Wood Emeline 43 orange

Teachers.
Adams E S 59 grand
Anthony C H eagle st
Baldwin A T 119 n pearl
Brinckerhoff Mrs 112 state
Bulkley J W 172 n pearl
Campbell Rev W H albany academy
Cantine Misses 18 van tromp
Crane Mary 125 hamilton
Goeway Magdalen 20 orange
Hall H T 7 n pearl
Heely Emma A orphan asylum
Heely Orissa orphan asylum
Helme Joseph J 140 spring
Hughes William H cor ferry and dallius
Johnson Jeanette R 10 rose
Lord Mrs Sarah L 19 philip
McKaig Andrew 36 grand
Marble Joel 218 state
Matthews N W arbor hill
Merrifield Elizabeth 11 grand
Millard Nehemiah 117 green
Parsons L Sprague female academy
Perkins G R normal school
Purdy Mrs 13 dallius
Reynolds John 350 lydius
Sessions Rev John albany academy
Skerritt Misses 4 high
Steele Samuel 52 westerlo
Ten Eyck P female academy
Trumbull R 157 lydius
Valentine Thomas 182 washington
Wrightson William T
Zelie James 228 state

Teachers of Dancing.
Deuchar Alexander 60 n pearl
Graves A G 80 s pearl
Shaw Eleanor T 128 state

Tin-plate and Sheet-iron Workers.
Austin William cor green and hudson
Bailey Edward 84½ s pearl
Baker Charles 580 broadway
Blakeman E C 92 state
Born Joseph C 90 green
Brooks David washington
Delehanty Michael 26 beaver
Fuller Amasa 638 broadway
Griffin John 716 broadway
McLoughlin C 22 hudson
Sager Peter 44 washington
Van Wormer and McGarvey 14 green
Whalen Thomas 13 church
Whitney and Cluett 18 beaver

Tobacco, Snuff and Cigars.
Brower and Teelin 35 washington
Davis D L cor church and lydius
Gott John 7 james
Greer Alexander 822 broadway
Payn and McNaughton 447 broadway
Ridder T B 78 s pearl
Sprague Horace 54 dean
Van Cott P T 616 broadway

Type & Stereotype-founders.
Munsell J 58 ssate
Van Benthuysen C 407

Umbrellas.
Weaver Daniel L 65 green
Adams G 88 hamilton

Upholsterers.
Blair A and co 36 green
Morange P M 502 broadway

Variety Stores.
Carter George T 446 broadway
Harley Edward cor s pearl and schuyler
Mascord William 620 broadway
Nixon R 16½ s pearl
Pease R H 516 broadway
Reid John 652 broadway
Taylor Mrs 51 s pearl
Van Schanck E 385 broadway

Victuallers.
Putnam Elisha 709 broadway
Putnam James A north market
Safford Peter 21 philip
Stilwell & Collins cor green and division
Swartz George centre market
Todd Dorman and co 580 broadway
Todd Robert 776 broadway

Watches, Jewelry and Plate.
Arms N T 42 s pearl
Carson David 98 state
Carson Thomas 98 state
Crew J T 38 state
Cutler J N 33 beaver
Given A 550 broadway
Hascy Alexander R 33 state
Hascy Nelson 34 state
Hood and Tobey 44 state
Hoyt George B 394 broadway
McHarg Alexander 12 green
Marsh B 405 broadway
Mix James 24 green
Mix Visscher 14½ green
Mulford and Wendell 460 broadway
Rice J T 21 s pearl
Simpson and Beckel 408 broadway
Waterman George 82 state

Wheelwrights.
Mascraft William 23 washington
Spring Hiram 76 church

Wine, Cider and Vinegar.
Latham and Halsier 13 howard
Spanier Louis 801 broadway

Wines, Teas, &c.
Hendrickson M and J 2 hudson

Jordan Matthew 553 broadway
Mitchell William 364 broadway
Satterlee E R and E 61 state

Wood.
Judson Isaac E 78 water
Leonard Jacob 96 willett
Luther J P and G W 26 quay
McAuley Michael cor arch and dallius
Strevel and Zeh 22 quay
Taylor 166 broadway
Wilbur and Townsend 175 broadway

Wooden-ware, &c.
Bicknell B 397 broadway
Williams W H and co 511 broadway

Wool.
Chapin Lyman 44 quay
Knower John 31 hudson
Newman Henry 457 broadway

Miscellaneous.
Artists' materials — James S Gould 413 broadway
Band and fancy boxes — Miss Frances Galpin 43 maiden lane.
Basket maker — Dominick Rossle 338 bowery
Baths — N S Dean 19 norton
Bell founder — Daniel Curtiss 23 church
Bell hanger — J & W J Blackall corner hamilton and fulton
Bird stuffer — P I Roberts 377 state
Bone dealer — R H Thompson 7 clinton
Bonnet and straw goods — Joseph Walker 536 broadway
Bonnet bleacher — M L Cutler 442½ broadway
Brush maker — J B Armour 389 broadway
Camphine — S T Thorn corner broadway and church
Carver — Henry H Farnham 55 colonie
Chemist — Ebenezer Emmons 159 hudson
Civil engineer and surveyor — R V De Witt 56 state
Clothes cleaner — William Ogden, basement exchange
Coach painter — John W Johnson 90 green
Combs and fancy goods — B R & R L Spelman corner broadway and maiden lane
Coroner — Levi Chapman 50 chapel
Corsets — Mrs Cook 36 S Pearl up stairs
Crier — Peter Ben east albany
Die sinkers — Daniel True 26 green
Draughtsman — E Forbes 9 exchange buildings
Dredger &c — S N Payn 698 broadway
Drum maker — George Kilbourn 130 Orange
Fancy box maker — Frederick G Kautsoh 62 green
Feed store — John Dailey 78 church
Fils cutter — Schley and Linsenbolz 21 church
Fire engines — John Rodgers 33 lumber
Fishing tackle — Steele & Warren 66 state

Furnaces and ranges — William Cobb 192 washington
Glue manufacturer — Thomas Coulson 590 bowery
Gold beater — William Barrett 49 hudson
Grate manufactory — Henderson & Weller 584 broadway
Grindstones — Nathan Davis 77 quay
Hay — John Hilton cor herkimer and quay
Hosiery — Mrs Wiley 42 south pearl
Images — Clemente Tozoni 610 broadway
India rubber goods — James McMullen 386 broadway
Iron Foundry — P W Lamb 45 liberty
Linseed oil — Deyermand & Davis 1 broadway
Lithographer — R H Pease 561 broadway
Lumber inspector — John Cornick 29 pier
Nailor — William McClusky 163 spring
Night scavenger — Joseph Dibble 64 clinton
Oculist — G A Knapp 496 broadway
Oil — Wickes & Tillinghast 13 hudson
Optical instruments — Joseph Gall 30 green
Patent agency — R V DeWitt 56 state
Pension agent — L Jenkins mechanics' and farmers' bank
Plumbers — F W Ridgway 115 state
Plumb level — J W Andrews corner hudson and high
Reporter — William G Bishop 111 hudson
Screw dock — Hiram Fanning corner columbia and dock
Shade manufacturer — Gaylord Heath 2 park
Ship chandler — Leonard D Shaw 1 state
Ship stores — Cole and Van Nostrand 61 quay
Silk and worsted trimming — Miss M Van Horn 597 n pearl
Silver-ware manufacture — Godley & Johnson 6 liberty
Silver plate — William Brown 13 church
Silver smith — Hall Hewsen & Brower 10 plain
Stationer — G Cogswell 21 fayette
Slater — James Dickson 65 beaver
Staves and lumber — Talcot & Hosmer, 61 quay
Steam feed mill — Orins Hall broadway
Surgical instruments — Edward Owens 28 beaver
Surveyors — J D Elliott stanwix hall, G W Carpenter city hall, — Ellis cooper's building
Sweep — Charles Gibbons 62 van schaick
Tallow chandler — George W Paige 70 canal
Tea dealers W S & C C Greenwood 598 broadway
Teacher of french — J Molinard 2 park place
Turner — George Jones 52 chapel
Undertaker — George Patterson 52 hudson
Weigher and measurer — Peter Cure 41 philip
Whitesmith — John Lossing 217 washington
Whitewasher — Jacob Wickham 246 lydius
Wood measurer — John J Lagrange hamilton w dove
Worsted store — Mrs Paepke 23 n pearl
Yankee notions — Hezekiah Dickerman 55 washington

PUBLIC PLACES, OFFICES, &c.

Adjutant General's Office, Capitol.
Albany Academy, Academy Park.
Albany Alms-house, south Lydius west Delaware turnpike.
Albany Apprentices' Library, Hudson.
Albany and Boston Railroad Office, Stanwix Hall, cor Maiden lane and Dean.
Albany Bethel, Montgomery.
Albany Burgesses Corps Armory, cor Broadway and Hamilton.
Albany Emmet Guards, 379 Broadway.
Albany Female Academy, N Pearl.
Albany Female Seminary, 67 Division.
Albany Gallery Fine Arts, 528 Broadway.
Albany Insurance Company, 56 State.
Albany Medical College, Eagle between Lancaster and Jay.
Albany Merchants' Exchange, Broadway foot of State.
Albany Mineral Spring, Ferry near S Pearl.
Albany Museum, cor State and Broadway.
Albany Nursery, Western turnpike two miles out.

Public Places, Offices, &c.

Albany Post-office, Merchants' Exchange.
Albany Republican Artillery Armory, 379 Broadway.
Albany Washington Riflemen, 379 Broadway.
Albany Waterworks, Eagle, Columbia and Steuben.
Albion Hotel, cor Herkimer and Broadway.
American Hotel, 100 State.
Apothecaries' Hall, cor State and N Pearl.
Axe Company, 11 Steuben.
Banks.
    Albany City Bank, 47 State.
    Albany Exchange Bank, Exchange Building.
    Albany Savings Bank, 40 State.
    Bank of Albany, 42 State.
    Commercial Bank, 40 State.
    Mechanics' and Farmers' Bank, cor Broadway and Exchange.
    New York State Bank, 69 State.
Baptist Churches.
    First Baptist Church, Green, between Hamilton and Division.
    Second Baptist Church, N Pearl.
    Third Baptist Church, cor State and High.
    Fourth Baptist Church, S Pearl.
    Baptist Church, African, Hamilton, west of Pearl.
Beardsley's Hotel, 28 Washington.
Bergeron's Albany House, cor Lydius and Church.
Bleecker Hall, 531 Broadway.
Blunt's Building, cor State & Pearl.
Boston R. R. Temperance House, 37 Dean.
Boston Hotel, 15 Dean.
Boston Packet Office, 102 Pier.
Broadway House, Johnson's, 256 Broadway.
Broadway House, Mrs. Paris's, 618 Broadway.
Chamberlain's Office, City Hall.
Canal Collector's Office, 198 Water.
Capitol, head of State.
Catholic Churches.
    Cathedral, cor Eagle, Jefferson and Lydius.
    German Catholic Church, cor Philip and Hamilton
    St John's Church, Ferry.
    St Joseph's Church, cor Lumber and N Pearl
    St Mary's Church, cor Pine and Chapel.
Centre Market, S Pearl between Howard and Beaver.
City Hall Coffee House, cor Eagle and Maiden lane
City Hotel, Broadway.
City Hall, Eagle fronting Washington.
City Marshal, City Hall.
City Surveyor, City Hall.
Clinton Hotel, cor South Pearl and Beaver.
Commercial Buildings, cor Hudson and Broadway.
Comptroller's Office, State Hall.
Congress Hall, cor Washington and the Park.
Cooke's News Office, 464 Broadway.
Cooper's Building, cor State and Green.
County Clerk's Office, City Hall.
County Treasurer's Office, corner Broadway & Steuben, up stairs.
Court of Appeals, 2d floor Capitol.
Delavan House, Broadway.
Douw's Buildings, cor Broadway and State.
Dutch Tavern, 41 Liberty.
Eagle St. Hotel, cor Eagle and Daniel.
Eastern Hotel, 144 Broadway.
Emigrant Association Office, foot of Hamilton.
Engine No. 1, 11 Chapel.
    do   No. 2,
    do   No. 3, attached to Almshouse
    do   No. 4, 75 Grand.
    do   No. 5, 236 Washington.
    do   No. 6, cor Hawk & Fayette.
    do   No. 7, 41 Hudson.
    do   No. 8, Broadway.
    do   No. 9,
    do   No. 10, Wilson.

Public Places, Offices, &c.

Engine No. 11,
  do No. 12, Arbor hill.
Episcopal Churches
  Church of the Holy Innocents, cor Colonie and North Pearl.
  Grace Church, Spring.
  St Paul's Church, S Pearl.
  St Peter's Church, cor State and Lodge.
Exchange Coffee House, 270 Broadway.
Exchange Hotel, 25 Maiden lane.
Farmer's Hotel, 42 Washington.
Farmer's Inn, 157 Washington.
Firemen's Insurance Company, Cooper's Building.
Fountain Inn, 926 Broadway.
Franklin House, State.
Fuller's Albany and Troy Express, 464 Broadway.
Gas Light Company's Works, cor Arch and Grand
General Stage Office, under the Museum.
Geological Musem, Old State Hall.
Gilbert's News Office, cor Broadway and State.
Greene & Co.'s Express, Exchange
Hook and Ladder No. 1, 34 Plain.
  do No. 2, Patroon.
Hose Company No. 1, 34 Plain.
Hudson-street Temperance House, 10 and 12 Hudson.
Jail, cor Eagle and Howard.
Jenkinson's Railroad House, 2 and 4 Dean.
Johnson's Northern Express, 11 Exchange.
Justice's Court, over the Centre Market.
Kearney's Hotel, 173 Montgomery.
Labraiche's Hotel, 19 Hamilton.
Lafayette House, 19 Montgomery.
Law Buildings, cor Broadway and Beaver.
Lockwood's Hotel, 65 Washington.
Lumbermen's Exchange, Little Basin.
Lumbermen's Hotel, in Lumbermen's Exchange.
Lutheran Church, corner Pine and Lodge.
Lutheran Church German, State near Swan.
Mansion House, 470 Broadway.
Mechanics' Benefit Society, Douw's Buildings.
Mechanics' and Farmers' Hotel, 38 Hawk
Methodist Episcopal Churches.
  African Methodist Church, State, rear of District School No. 2.
  First Methodist Epis. Church, Hudson, above Pearl.
  Second Methodist Epis. Church, N Pearl.
  Third Methodist Epis. Church, cor Ferry and Franklin.
  Fourth Methodist Epis. Church, cor Washington and Swan.
  Fifth Methodist Epis. Church, Swan, between Lumber and 3d.
  Wesleyan Methodist, N Pearl, above Patroon.
Mineral Spring Garden, 58 Ferry.
Mission Sabbath School, Rensselaer between Green & Franklin.
Mission House School, 140 Spring above Lark.
Mohawk and Hudson Railroad Office, cor Dean and Maiden lane.
Montoney's Public House, 15 Washington.
Mount Vernon Lodge of Freemasons, cor Broadway & Steuben.
Munger's Hotel, cor Lydius and Dove.
National Garden, 772 Broadway.
National Hotel, 266 Broadway.
Northern Hotel, cor Broadway and Orange.
Normal School, cor Chapel and Howard.
North River Hotel, 274 Broadway.
Odd Fellows' Hall, cor Green and Beaver, and Cooper's Building.
Orphan Asylum, head Washington.
Otsego House, 74 Washington.
Penitentiary, Delaware Turnpike.
Pension Office, at Mechanics' and Farmers' Bank.
Phœnix Hotel, opposite Steamboat Landing.

Picture Gallery, 41 S Pearl.
Police Office, over Centre Market.
Presbyterian Churches.
  First Presbyterian Ch., Hudson.
  Second Presbyterian Church, Chapel.
  Third Presbyterian Church, cor Clinton square and N Pearl.
  Fourth Presbyterian Church, Broadway.
  Associate Presbyterian Church, cor Chapel and Canal.
  Reformed Presbyterian Church, 27 Westerlo.
Reformed Prot. Dutch Churches.
  First Ref. Prot. Dutch Church, North Pearl.
  Second Ref. Prot. Dutch Church, Beaver.
  Third Ref. Prot. Dutch Church, South Ferry.
Saratoga House, 719 Broadway.
Second Advent Chapel, Blunt's Buildings.
Secretary of State's Office, State Hall.
Sheriff's Office, Jail.
State Arsenal, Broadway corner Lawrence.
St Charles, Hudson.
Stanwix Hall, cor Broadway and Maiden lane.
State Agricultural Society, Old State Hall.
State Hall, Eagle cor Steuben and Pine.
State House, Eagle street.
Stearn's Inn. 163 S Pearl.
St Vincent's Orphan Asylum, N Pearl.
Supreme Court Clerk's Office, State Hall.
Surrogate's Office, State Hall.
Surveyor General's Office, State Hall.
Synagogue Bethel Jacob, 88 and 90 Fulton.
Synagogue, Herkimer.
Syracuse House, 218 Broadway.
Tallman's Hotel, 128 Water
Telegraph Office, No. 2 Exchange Building.
Telegraphery, O'Reilley's, under Museum.
Temple Lodge, cor Steuben and Broadway.
Unitarian Chapel, Division.
Universalist Church, Green near Hamilton.
United States Hotel, 91 Washington.
Washington Hall, South Pearl.
Washington House, 17 Montgomery.
Wells & Co.'s Express, Exchange.
William Tell House, 91 Church.
Wilson's Hotel, Hudson.

ALBANY COUNTY BIBLE SOCIETY.

This institution seems to have been founded in 1810. The first annual sermon was preached by the Rev. Samuel Blatchford on the 12th Feb 1811, in the North Dutch Church. It was incorporated by act of legislature, passed April 8, 1811 The managers named in the charter were Rev. John M. Bradford, Rev. William Neill, Rev. Samuel Blatchford, Harmanus Bleecker, John Stearns, John H. Wendell, Stephen Van Rensselaer, Philip Van Rensselaer, Rev. Eliphalet Nott, Abraham Van Vechten, John Woodworth, Douw Fonda, Rev. John McJimpsey, Rev. Frederick G. Mayer. On the 6th February, 1814, a sermon was

Albany County Bible Society.

preached by Dr. Nott in the North Dutch Church, in aid of the funds of the society, when a collection of $271 was taken. The society has been in operation nearly 39 years, during which time the following ministers have preached the annual sermon by appointment:

Samuel Blatchford	1811	William B. Sprague	1831
Eliphalet Nott	1812	James R. Wilson	1832
J. M. Bradford	1813	William Lochead	1833
William Neill	1814	J. N. Campbell	1834
Alexander Proudfit	1815	William James	1835
John De Witt	1816	E. N. Kirk	1836
J. M. Bradford	1817	Edwin Holmes	1837
John Chester	1818	Thomas E. Vermilyea	1838
A. J. Stansbury	1819	I. N. Wyckoff	1839
Joseph Shaw	1820	Ezra Huntington	1840
Thomas McAuley	1821	William B. Sprague	1841
Walter Monteath	1822	Edward D. Allen	1842
Henry R. Weed	1823	Noah Levings	1843
John Ludlow	1824	Duncan Kennedy	1844
James Martin	1825	W. H. Campbell	1845
James Christie	1826	Henry N. Pohlman	1846
Isaac Ferris	1827	William B. Sprague	1847
Henry R. Weed	1828	Allen Steele	1848
Mark Tucker	1829	J. N. Campbell	1849
E. D. Griffin	1830		

The Rev. Benjamin N. Martin is appointed to preach the next annual sermon.

The whole number of Bibles circulated since the formation of the society appears, by the last report, to have been 15,147; of Testaments, 20,757. The number of Bibles distributed gratuitously during the year 1848, was 465; Testaments, 680. The number sold during that year was 242 Bibles, 1342 Testaments. The amount of receipts into the treasury during that year was $1,532·77. The whole amount contributed to the American Bible Society by this institution in thirty-eight years, is $15,638·98.

The officers of the Society for 1849 are as follows:

Rev. William B. Sprague, D. D., President.
Rev. John N. Campbell, D. D., First Vice-President.
Rev. I. N. Wyckoff, D. D., Second Vice-President.
Philip Phelps, Rec. Secretary.
Lemuel Jenkins, Cor. Secretary.
William C. Miller, Treasurer.
Rev. Ezra A. Huntington, D. D., Duncan Kennedy, D.D , William H. Campbell, D. D., Henry N. Pohlman, D. D., F. W. Schmidt, Luman A. Sanford, Rutgers Van Brunt, J. Clarke, Benjamin N. Martin, Messrs. Archibald McIntyre, Rensselaer Westerlo, Nathaniel Davis, Israel Smith, Daniel Fry, Abraham Keyser, George W. Benjamin, Managers.
Rev. Dr. J. N. Campbell, William C. Miller, Nathaniel Davis, Daniel Fry, Ex. Committee.

A LIST OF THE FREEHOLDERS OF THE CITY AND COUNTY OF ALBANY. 1720.*

FIRST WARD.

Evert Wendell	Daniell Kelly	Nicolas Winegaert
Jno Dunbar	Johannis Vandenberg	Cornelis Vandyke
Harmanis Wendell	Joseph Vansante	Johannis Lansen
Peter Van Brugh	Joseph Yeats Snor	Luykas Winegaert
Johannis Schuyler	Winant Vanderpoel	Ryert Gerritse
Antoney Van Schaick	John Kidney	Gose Van Schaick
Mindert Schuyler	Mindert Lansen	Barent Egbertsen
Antoney Vanschaick Snor	Obediah Cooper	Bastian Visser
	Johannis Vansante	Antony Bregardes
Robert Livingston Junr	Matthews Flantsburgh	Thomas Wendell
Tho: Williams	Tobias Ryckman	Johannis Tenbroeck
Coonrodt Tennyck	Peter Ryckman	Antoney Coster
Joseph Yates Junr	Wm. Hilton	Danl. Flantsburgh
Jacob Roseboom	Johannis De Garmoe	Johannis Beekman
Jacob Staats	Claes Van Woort	Johannis Wendell Junr
John Rosie	Henry Holland	Antoney Van Schaick Junr
Wm: Hogan	John Collins	
Johannis Van Alen	Hend: Halenbeek	Philip Livingston
Jacob Lansen	Peter Gramoe	Jacob Beekman
Baltis Van Benthusen	Johannis Ratclif	Rev. Thomas Barclay
Harmanis Ryckman	Luykas Hooghkirck	David Grewsbeck
Fred. Mindertsen	Hendrick Outhout	Stephanis Grewsbeck

SECOND WARD.

Johannis Cuyler	Johannis Vinhagen	Philip Wendell
Nicos: Bleeker	Abram Kip	Jan Lansen
Abram: Cuyler	Cornelius Schermerhorn	Gerrit Roseboom
Warner Van Ivera	Hendrick Tennyck	Cornelis Van Scherline
Reyner Mindertsen	Johannis Beekman Snor	Johans: Evertse Wendell
Barent Sanders	Gerrit Lansen	
Wm. Grewsbeck	Issack Kip	Abram: Lansen
Guisbert Marselis	Nanning Visser	Johannis Roseboom
Herbert Jacobsen	Hendrick Roseboom	John Hogan
Arent Pruyn	Mindert Roseboom	Johannis Visser
Johannis Mingaell	Andries Nach	Benj. Egbertsen
Johannis Hansen	Jan: Janse Bleeker	Jonanis Grewsbeck
Seibolet Brigardes	Johannis Bleeker	Claes Funda
David Van Dyke	Cristofell Yeats	Wm. Jacobsen

THIRD WARD.

Isaac Funda	Johannis Hun	Jacob Evertse
Samuell Babington	Phillip Van Vechten	Jno; Solomonse
Gerrit Van Ness	Lenord Gansivoort	Hendrick Hansen
Albert Ryckman	Jan: Everisen	Abram: Schuyler
Cornelis Borghaert	Evert Janse	Derrick Brat

* See Documentary History of New York, vol. I., page 370.

Freeholders in 1720.

Johannis Van Ostrande
Johannis Evertsen
Tunis Egbertsen
Derrick Tenbroeck
David Schuyler
Winant Vandenbergh
Takel Derrickse
Johannis Backer
Thomas Long
John Gerritse
Elbert Gerritse

Issac Borghaert
Cornelis Masse
Jan Masse
Barnt Brat
Jacob Borghaert Junr
Jacob Visser
Jacobus Luykasse Winegaert
Johannis Pruyn
Wessel Tenbroeck
Peter Winne

Jacob Muller
Johannis Muller
Samll: Pruyn
Reuben Ven Vechten
Cornlis Switzs
Guisbert Vandenbergh
Teirck HarminseVisser
Tunis Brat
Peter Walderom
Rutger Bleecker
Harpert Vandeusen

SCHONECTADY.

Jonathan Stevens
William Coppernoll
Claes Franse
Teirck Franse
Yellous Fonda
Adam Vroman
Phillip Schuyler
David Lewis
Mindert Guisling
Peter Quacumbus
Abram: Meebe
Benj. Van Vlack
Marte Powlisse
Harma Van Slyck
Sanders Gelon
Evert Van Eps
Arent Van Petten
John Weemp
Simon Switzs
Jacob Switzs
Mindert Weemp
Arent Brat
Hendrick Vrooman Junr
Harmanis Vedder
Dow Aukus
Johannis Mindertsen
Adam: Smith
Abram Trucax
Rob: Yeats
Abram: Lythall
Assweris Marselis
Abram: Groot
Hendrick Vrooman Snor

Wouter Vroman
Jno. Baptist Van Epps
Derrick Brat
Jan Barentse Wemp
Barent Vroman
Jan Vroman
Gerrit Van Brackell
Arent Danilse
Simon Vroman
Lawrence Chase
Cornils Vander Volgen
Abram De Grave
Daniell Danielse
Cornelis Pootman
Sam: Hagardoring
Guisbert Van Brakell
Volkert Simonse
Jacob Schermerhorn
Jacobus Vandyke
Helmes Vedder
Arnout De Grave
Johannis Teller
Albert Vedder
Derrick Groot
Gerrit Simonse
Yealous Van Vost
Victore Pootman
Jan Delemont
Caleb Beck
Nicholas Schuyler
Johannis Gelen
Jacob Gelen
Jesse De Grave

Carle Hanse Toll
Daniell Toll
William Marrinas
Arent Schermerhorn
Esays Swaert
Johannis Vroman
Andries De Grave
Joseph Clament
John Bumstead
Harma Phillipse
Jereme Thickstone
Jacob Van Olinda
Arent Vedder
Peter Vroman
Daniell Janse
Peter Danielse
Jan Danielse
Jan Meebe
Johannis Peek
Jacobus Peek
Claes Van Petten
Cornelis Van Slyck
Marte Van Slyck
Cornelis Feele
Arnout Brat Junr
Johannis Vedder
Tunis Vander Volgen
Claes Van Petten
Andries Van Petten
Jan Schermerhorn
Wouter Swaert
Arent Pootman

KENDERHOOK AND PART MANNOR OF LIVINGSTON.

Jochim Van Valkenburgh
Isaac Fansborough
Casper Rouse

Peter Van Alen
Lamert Huyck,
Burger Huyck
Johannis Huyck

Derrick Gardineer
Peter Van Slyck
Jno: Gardineer
Evert Wieler

Freeholders in 1720.

Derrick Goes
Peter Fansburgh
Peter Van Buren
Jno: Goes
Mattias Goes
Luykas Van Alen
Jacobus Van Alen
Evert Van Alen
Johannis Vandeusen

Cornelis Schermerhorn
Johannis Van Alen
Gerrit Dingmans
Bart. Van Valkenburgh
Thomas Van Alstine
Coonrodt Burgaert
Stephanis Van Alen
John Burgaert
Abram: Van Alstine

Lawrence Van Schauk
Elias Van Schauk
Jurie Klaime
Guisbert Scherp
Lawrence Scherp
Hendrick Clawe
Lamert Valkenburgh
Melgert Vanderpool
Lenord Conine

THE NORTH PART OF THE MANNOR OF LIVINGSTON.

Robert Livingston Esqr
Peter Colle
Killian Winne
Jan Emmerick Plees
Hans Sihans
Claes Bruise
Jonat: Rees
Coonrodt Ham
Coonrodt Schureman
Johannis Pulver

Bastian Spikerman
Nicolas Smith
Baltis Auspah
Jno: Wm: Simon
Hanse Jurie Prooper
Abram Luyke
Broer Decker
Jurie Decker
Nicolas Witbeck

Johannis Uldrigh
ffitz: Muzigh
Coonrod Kelder
David Hooper
Gabriell Broose
Solomon Schutt
Jacob Stover
Johanis Roseman
Nicos: Styker

CLAVERACK.

Tobias Tenbroeck
Cornelis Mulder
Cornils Esselstine
Jeremias Mulder
Derrick Hogoboom
Cornelis: Huyck
Isaac Vandusen
Jno: Hoose
George Sidnem
Richard Moor
John Hardyck
Hendr: Van Salsbergen
Jacob Van Hoosem

Kasper Van Hoosem
Jan Van Hoosem
Saml Tenbroeck
Peter Hogoboom
Rob: Van Deusen
Casper Conine
Frank Hardyke
Johannis Van Hoosem
John Bout
Wm: Halenbeck
Johannis Coole
John Rees

Wm: Rees
Johannis Scherp
Andries Rees
Ghondia Lamafire
Hendrick Whitbeck
Jurie Fretts
Hendrick Lodowick
Jacob Eswin
Jurie Jan
Cloude Lamatere
Nicos: Vanduse *Cats Kills.*

COXHACKY AND CATS KILLS.

Mindert Schut
Wessell Tenbroeck
Wm: Lefferrese
Helme Janse
Saml Van Vechten
Gerrit Van berghen
Marte Van berghen
Frank Salisbury
Jno Brunk
Minkas Van Schauk

John Albertse
Arent Van Schauk
Michael Collier
Cornelis Van Wormer
Johannis Halenbeek
Casper Halenbeck
Jan Van Loan
Albert Van Loan
Jno: Van Loan Junr

Abram: Provoost
Jacob Halenbeek
Jno: Casperse
Coonrodt Hotlen
Philip Conine
Jno: Vanhoosem
Lenord Brunk
Peter Brunk
Isaac Spoor

CANASTIGONIE.

Jno: Quacumbus
Jno: ffoort
Jacob Pearse
Derrick Brat

Maes Rycksen
Evert Rycksen
Gerrit Rycksen
Nicholas Van Vranken

Lapion Kanfort
Cornelis Christianse
Eldert Timonse
Jno: Quakenboes Junr

Freeholders in 1720.

HALF MOON.

Peter Ouderkerk
Jacob Cluit
John Cluit
Frederick Cluit
Saml: Creeger
Derrick Takelsen
Mattias Boose Snor
Johannis Christianse

Jacobus Van Schoonho-
  ven
Evert Van Ness
Daniell Fort
Corn'ls Vanburen
Conelis Van Ness
Isaac Ouderkerk
Lavinus Harminse

Tunis Harminse
Winant Vandenbergh
Roolif Gerritse
Hendrick Roolifse
Jno: De Voe
Daniell Van Olinda
Eldert Ouderkerk
Cornelis Vandenbergh

SCHAATKOOKE.

Saml Doxie
Curset Fether
Johannis Knickbacker
Derrick Van Vechten

Johannis DeWandelaer
Simon Danielse
Martin Delamon
Lewis Fele

Daniell: Ketlyne
Peter Winne
Adrian Quacumbus
Abram Fort

COLLONEY RENSELAERS WYCK.

Wouter Barheyt
Johannis Valkenburgh
Jno: Barheyt
Isaac Van Alstine
Jacob Schermerhorn
Jacob Schermerhorn Jr
Johns: Ouderkerk
Claes Gardineer
Andries Gardinier
Hend: Valkenburgh
Jacob Valkenburgh
Andries Huyck
Maes Van Buren
Corn'lis Van Vechten
Jonat: Witbeek
Martin Vanburen
Barent Geritse
Jan Witbeck
Jonas Dow
Andries Dow
Folcort Dow
Jno. Van Vechten
Gerrit Lansen
Volcort Van Vechten
Melgert Vandeuse
Rut Vandeuse
Tho: Witbeck
Luykas Witbeck

Solomon Van Vechten
Cap: Hendrick Van
  Renselaer
Philip Foreest
Martin Van Alstine
Albert Roolifse
Marte Van Alstine Junr
Jno: Funda
Derrick Vanderhyden
Gerrit Vandenbergh
Albert Brat
Cornelis Van Alstine
Johns: Wendell
Jan: Van Alstyne
Adrian Oothout
Peter Coyeman
Barent Staats
Andries Coyeman
Samuell Coyeman
Jno: Witbeek
Coonrod Hooghteeling
Storm Backer
Jno: Backer
Hendrick Van Wyen
Wm: Van Alen
Daniell Winne
Gerrit Van Wie

Jan Van Wie
Gerrit Vandenbergh
Hendr: Dow
Albert Singerlant
Evert Banker
Wouter Vanderse
Killian Vanderse
Johannis Appel
Peter Husyele
Derrick Hagodorn
Andries Brat
Storm Brat
Ome Legrange
Johns: Legrange
Johonnis Simonse
Nicos: Grewsbeck
Jno: Oothout
Mindert Marselis
Jacob Lansen
Abram Ouderkerk
Peter Schuyler Esqr
Abram Wendell
William Ketlyne
Frans Pryn
Jaac Falkenburgh
Claes Bovie
Phillip Wendell

Pursnant to an Order of Court of Judicature held for the Province of New York on the Eleventh Day of June 1720, Directed to Gerrit Vanschaick high Sherif of the City and County of Albany; A Returne of the free holders of the said City and County.

    GERRET VANSCHAIJCK Sheriff

Sept 4 Child of Daniel Hussen
     5 Child of Jacobus Schuyler
     5 Wife of Philip Winne
     5 Daughter of Arye Oothout
     7 Child of Adriaan Quackenbos
     7 Child of Robert Sanders
     8 Child of Gysbert Van Brakel
     9 Son of Gerrit Marselis [Jacob]
    10 Jochim, son of Johs Visscher
    10 Gerrit, son of Hendk Gerritse
    10 Child of Sybrant Quackenbos
    10 Jochem, son of Johs Van der Heyden
    11 Two children of Benjamin Bogart
    12 Child of Hendk Bries
    12 Child of Volkert Van den Bergh
    12 Daughter of Neeltie Brat
    13 Gideon Quackenbos
    16 Child of Sybrant Goes VanSchaick
    16 Child of Benjamin Goewey
    17 Daughter of Neeltie Brat
    17 Child of Evert Lansingh
    17 Child of Peter Schuyler
    19 Little son of Evert Wendell
    20 Nicolas Bleecker jr
    20 Annake, daughter of Petrus Bogardus
    20 Catrina, widow of Willem Groesbeck's child
    20 Daughter of Catrina, widow of Martyn Van Aalstyn
    21 Child of Zacharias Baes
    21 Child of John Willems
    21 Child of Evert Lansingh
    23 Child of Dirk Olver
    23 Child of Isaac Hansen
    23 Daughter of Arye Oothout
    25 Child of Robert Wendell
    26 Child of Abraham H Wendell
    26 Child of Cornelis C Van den Bergh
    26 Schieboleth Bogardus
    27 Child of Rebecca, widow of Hendk Brat
    27 Child of Rychart Hansen
    28 Child of Johs Cloet
    28 Child of Rynier Van Hoesen
    30 Two children of Willem Gysbert Van den Bergh
Oct 1 Wife of Isaac de Voe
     2 Child of Johannis Van Wie
     2 Child of Nicholas Cuyler
     3 Daughter of Willem Van d Bergh
     3 Child of Harmen Hun
     3 Little son of Barent V Yeveren
     3 Child of Jacob Bogart jr
    12 Child of Sybrant Goes Van Shaick
    13 Child of James Stenhuys
    20 Wife of Isaac Ouderkerk
    25 Wife of Rutger Bleeker
Nov 17 Maryte Winne
    26 Child of Johannis Lansingh jr
Dec 2 Child of Harme Knickerbacker
     3 Coenradi (Rutesmayor)
    15 Child of John Fryer

    21 Wife of Gerrit Rycksen
    24 Child of Corneles Waldrum
    25 Wife of Pieter Davids Schuyler

1748.
Jan 13 Geritie Rykerson
    14 Little son of Catalyntie Roseboon
    19 James, son of Rolf Schoon
    26 Daughter of Jellis D Garmo
Feb 9 Geestie Kipp
    25 Annate Hilton
    25 Obadyn Cooper's child.
    28 Child of Johs Van Yeveren
Mar 2 Child of Pieter Schuyler
    23 Wife of Isaac Fonda
    29 Daughter of Cornelia Cooper
    31 Child of Gerrit Marselis
Apr 3 Child of Dirck B VanSchoonhoven
     3 Johs Wendel's cosyn (i. e. nephew?)
     9 Wife of James Steinhuys
    17 Wife of Obadya Cooper
    19 Child of Johs Ten Eyck
    21 Wife of Pieter Van Beuren
    24 Marya Gerritse
May 10 Madame Margrita Collans, in the church
    20 Wife of Abraham Vinhagen
    24 Evert Ryckse
    25 Johannis Berreway
    30 Johannis Hansen
Jun 10 Alyda Visscher
July 5 Child of Thomas Seeger
     8 Nicholas Schuyler
    10 Child of Jan Brat
    17 Child of Adam Yates
    20 Pieter Quackenbos
    21 Child of Robert Sanders, near his house
    21 Child of Abraham Lansingh, near his house
    29 Child of Jacob H Ten Eyck
Aug 3 Johs L Whitbeck
     6 Johs G Lansingh
    15 Child of Antony Van der Zee
    16 Wife of Andries [Mahans]
    17 Child of Jacob Egmond
    27 Rachel, daughter of John Whitbeck
    29 Lydia Van Vechte, in the church
    30 Child of Hendk Van Nes
Sept 2 Catie Van Weie
     4 Pieter Ryckman
    11 Wife of Tomas Coeper
    19 Melgert, son of David Groesbeck
    27 Two children of Cornelis Winne, by his house
Oct 2 Gerrit Js Lansingh
     6 Child of Cornelis Sanford
    13 Wife of Volkert N Douw
    24 Child of Cornelis Van Nes
Nov 3 Bregie, sister of Cornelis Clasen
     3 Wife of Tomas Scherp
     6 Child of Johannis V Douw

1749.
Jan 3 Rynier Van Hoesen

Dutch Church Burials.

1726.
- Janry 22 An Englishman's child
- 27 Egbert Brat's child
- Febry 1 Elisabeth Rosie*
- Mch 22 Everie Jacobse Eel's child
- 29 Peter Ryckman's wife
- May 27 Labreyh Redlif's child
- 30 Antony S. Van Schayck's child
- July 12 Gose Van Schayck Jr's child
- Augt 25 Johs Becker's wife
- Septr 3 Johs Becker's child
- 4 Johs Dfreest's child
- 11 Jacob Roseboom's child
- Octr 17 Salomon Goewerk's wife
- 20 Jeremie Pennerton's child
- Novr 1 Arent Pruyn's child
- 2 Tams Pruyn Jrs. child
- 8 Evert Janse was buried in the Lutheren Church

1727.
- Janry 5 Myndert Marselis' child
- 19 Andries Witbeeck Jr. child
- 23 Samuel Pruyn's daughter*
- Mch 6 Evert Wendell's child*
- 12 Gerret Roseboom's daughter*
- 24 Johannes Muller
- May 26 Jacob Van der Heyden's child
- 27 Tobias Ryckman's child
- Jan Maasen's child
- 30 Jan Milten's wife
- 31 Janetie Van Aelstyne
- June 2 Elsie Winne Jr. daughter of Frans Winne
- 10 Rabecka Fonda
- 12 Sara Greveraedt
- July 12 Hendk Ridder's child
- Augt 1 Mattys Flinsburgh's child
- 6 Ephrim Wendell's child
- 10 Jacob Mulder's child
- 12 Thunis Van den Bergh
- 13 Philyp Dforeest
- Sept 3 Hans Hanse's child
- Nicolaes Groesbeek's child
- 4 Tam Flyt's mother-in-law
- 12 Thunis Slingerland's child
- 10 Jacobus Luychnsse
- 16 Evert Janse's child
- 18 Abram Van der Poel's infant
- 25 Barent Barhyt's child
- Octr 2 Catharina Lydius*
- 13 Catlynna wife of Johs G. Lansing
- Frans Pruyn's little child
- Novr 26 Cornelus Cuyler's little child
- Decr 2 Johs Van der Heyden's child

1728.
- Janry 31 Willem Waldrum's little child
- Feb 11 Maria wife of John Everts Ryck Magsilse
- 26 Jan Lansingh*
- Mch 7 Sybrand Quackenbos' child
- 28 Jurian Hogan's child
- May 6 Elsie Winne mother of Pieter
- 27 Cornelus Van Schurhynse
- 29 Pieter son of Pieter Waldrum
- June 27 Leena wife of Herpert Van Deusen
- July 11 Engeltie wife of Melgert Abrahamse
- Augt 4 Jan Maase's little child
- 20 Lowis Schredel's child
- Sept 9 Harmen Van Hoesen's child
- 27 Johs Lansing Jrs child
- Jeramias Schuyler's child
- Octr 5 Pieter Schuyler's child was buried at the flats
- Novr 10 Johs Wendell's little son was buried at the flats
- Decr 7 Philyp Wendall's son John
- 14 Pieter Schuyler's daughter was buried at the flats
- 17 Isaac Wendell's little son was buried at the flats
- 30 Nicolaes Groesbeeck's wife

1729.
- Janry 13 Capt. Johannis Wendell was buried at the flats
- 14 Johs Frest's little child
- Febry 6 Hans Hansen's little child
- 20 Moses
- 26 Isaac Verplank daughter Abigel
- Mch 12 Gerit Ryckse's daughter Alyda
- 29 Aelyda Schuyler
- June 13 Abram Ouderkerk's child
- 21 Johs Bleeker Jr. little son
- Mattys Van den Bergh's child buried at Papsknee
- 24 Willm Grennie's child
- 30 Elizabeth Muller's child
- July 7 Jacob Eghemond's child
- 13 Johs E. Wendell's child
- 16 Direk Ten Broeck's child*
- 23 Anna Witbeeck daughter of Tamas Willms
- 26 Roeslif Kidnie's child
- Augt 13 Johs Schoonmaker's child was buried at Papsknie
- 18 Pieter Winne's little son
- Septr 13 Anna Brat was buried in the church by Rut Van Woert
- Octr 1 Johs Van Zante's child
- 12 Hendrick Benneway
- 22 Roelif Kidney's child
- Novr 24 Johs de Foreest's child
- 28 Christiena Ten Broeck*
- Decr 7 Gosen Van Schayck's child

1730
- Feb 1 Maritie Schermerhorn
- 11 Egbert Barentsen's child
- 14 Douwe Fonda's child
- 15 Harpert Van Deusen's child
- 16 Andries Gardenier's two children
- Mch 7 Adam Van den Bergh's child
- 15 Samuel Cregeer's child
- April 8 Nanningh Vischer
- 9 Jacob Lansingh's child
- 12 Direk Van Scharluyne's child
- May 8 Johannis Schoonmaker was buried at Papsknee
- 22 Joseph Yats
- June 2 Epharim Wendell's child
- 22 Direk Van Schurluyne's wife
- July 13 Huybertie Yaets.

Dutch Church Burials.

Agt	13	Jacob Thunnise Van Woert
	19	Isaac Greveraet's child*
Septr	5	Solomon Goewyck's child
	5	Isaac Greveraet's child*
	8	Thomas Wendell
	10	Elisabeth Lansingh
	16	Marietie Tymese was buried at Nistagayoene
Octr	5	Jeramiah H. Van Renselaer
	13	Jacobus Redlif's child
Nov	4	Jacob Alestyn
	23	Neeltie Van Schayck
Decr	7	Knie Van Rensselaer
	28	Jan Kasperse
		Claes Luyckasse
		Joseph Yates child

1731.

Jan	4	Jan Oothoudt Jrs. child
	5	Alida V. Vechten (wife of Sol'n?)
Feb	5	Ryner Myndertse's son Reynier
	9	Evert Ryckse's son Rychert
	14	Johs Dpeyster's child*
	27	Mr. Ellet's child
Mch	30	Peter Fonda's child
Apl	14	Willem Vischer
	15	Johs. Migael*
May	1	Chatriena Van den Bergh
	6	Thomas Witbeck buried at Papsknee
June	22	Rutger Van Dusen buried at Papsknee
	29	Abraham Kipp
July	1	Nicolaes Van Arlen
	2	Doctr Epharim Wendell was buried at the flats
Augt	5	Mattys Flensburgh's child
	6	Chattrina D Foorest
	19	Abram Van Armen's child
	21	Elbert Gerritse's wife Marytie
	22	Hendrick Ridder's child
June	28	Johs Quackenbos' child
Augt	23	Uldrick Van Franke's child
Sept	4	Hans Hansen's child
	8	Willem Jacobsen VanDeusen
	10	Harmen Van Vechten's child
	28	Jan Salomonse
Oct	14	Gerrit C. Van den Bergh
	22	John Olyfer [Oliver?] Jr.
Nov	2	Willem Redlif's child
	11	William Crennel's child
	14	Willim Redlif's little son
	16	Thunis Vischer's Isaac
	20	Johs. Lansingh's daughter
	21	Hendrick Halenbeek's child
	22	Hans Hansen's daughter
	23	Jacob Egmond's two children
	27	Myndert Marselis' child
	27	Ephraim Wendell's child
	28	David Van Dyck's child
	28	Harpert Van Deusen's daughter
	28	Pieter Ryckman's child
	30	Wynant C. Van de Bergh's child
Dec	7	Meyndert Marselis' daughter
	7	Jer. Pemmerton's little son

	12	Hester Swits' son
	12	Johs. Seger's two little girls
	12	Gerit Van Zanten's child
	14	Jellis de Garmo's child
	15	Harmanus Wendell*
	15	Jacob Masen's child
	16	Johs. Hun's little son
	17	Johs. Schuyler's Jr. little son was buried at the flats
	17	Bettie Danielse' little son
	18	Symon Veeder's little child
	18	Mattys Dgamo's little child
	19	Isaac Greveraet's child*
	20	Thunis Egbertse's child
	21	Abraham Van de Poel's daughter
	23	Johs G. Lansingh's child
	24	Harmen Van Hoesen's little son
	25	David Van der Heyden's child
	25	Pieter Fonda's
	26	Stephanis V. Renselaer's child
	27	Anthony Brat's child
	27	Johs. Vischer's child
	27	David V. Dyck's
	28	Johs Goewyck's child
	30	Dirck Ten Broeck's Anna*
	30	Leendert Gansevoort's two children
	30	Abraham Onderkerk's daughter
	30	Jacob B. Ten Eyck's child
	31	Gerit W. Van den Bergh's child
	31	Magiel Besset's child

1732.

Janry	3	Maria Gerritse's little son*
	3	David Groesbeeck's child
	4	Benjamin Egbertse's daughter
	6	Isaac Bogart's little son*
	6	Hendk. Roseboom's child
	6	Daniel Hogan's child was buried by R. Beeckman
	6	Jan Brouyn
	7	Johs. Hun's daughter
	8	Wouter Barheyt
	8	Jacob Wendell's child was buried at Greenbush
	12	Johs A. Cuyler's child*
	13	Albert Brat was buried at the flats
	14	Johs. Ten Broeck's child was buried at Greenbush
	15	Willem Waldrum's daughter
	16	Isaac Swits' little son
	17	Epharim Bogardus' child
	19	Andries Witbeck Jrs. child
	20	Hendk. Cuyler's little son
	22	Gerit Van Nes' daughter
	23	David Groesbeeck's child
	25	Isaac Swits' daughter
	25	Johs. Ten Broeck's little son was buried at Greenbush
	25	Hendrick Bries's son was buried at Papsknee
	26	Abram Witbeck's child
	26	Dirck Ten Broeck's little son*
	28	Johs Bleeker Jrs. daughter
	28	Gerrit Marselis' child

Dutch Church Burials.

	29 Johs. Ten Broeck's child was buried at Greenbush
	31 Mattewis Van Deusen's child
Feb	1 Gerrit C. Van Den Bergh's child was buried at Papsknee
	6 Hendrick T. Eyck's little son
	20 Nicolaes Bleecker's child
	27 Johs Symonse Veeder's daughter*
Mch	10 Pieter Schuyler's child was buried at the flats
	21 Arieje Oothout's daughter
	27 Johs. Vischer's daughter was buried at Hogebergh
April	6 Johs. J. Beeckman's child
	6 Hendrick Bries' child was buried at Papsknee
	25 Willem Teller's wife Catrina
May	18 Ryckie, wife of Abr. Lansing
	20 Hendrick H. Roseboom's child
	27 Jer. Pemmerton's two children
June	9 Johs Dforiest's child
	14 Johs Dpeyster's child*
July	12 Abraham Lansing Jrs child
Agt	19 A man was buried by Johs Segers by order of the Mayor
Sept	30 Johs Beeckman
Octr	15 Antony Brat's child
Novr	12 Migul Besset's child
	17 Johs. J. Beeckman's child
	24 Jan Janse Bleecker*
Decr	9 Salomon Goewey's child
	11 Freedk Myndertse's wife
	11 Maragrieta Corneel
	21 Johs. Schuyler Jrs child was buried at the flats
	29 Johs. D Forcest's children
	31 Elsje Sanders
	1733
Jan	11 Isaac Bogert's little child
	29 Isaac Bogart's little child
	31 Barent Stuets' daughter was buried at the Hogebergh
Feb	9 Coenraet Becker
	16 Sarah Roseboom was buried daughter of Jacob Roseboom
Mch	3 Maretie Van Alen
	13 Pieter Fonda's child
	21 Gelyn Splank's child
April	6 Coenraet Rechtmayor's wife
	14 Maes Van Buren was buried at Schoodack
	22 Abra Wyngart's wife
May	4 Mallie Leedyus*
June	2 Ephram Wendel's child
July	4 Antony Bogardus' son
Agt	12 Jan Winne
Septr	18 Barent Egbertse's daughter
Octr	25 Rychert Hanse's wife*
	29 Maragrietie Bleecker*
	1734
Jan'y	8 Jannetje Bogert, [wife Jacob C.]
	17 Aeltie Van Nes buried at the Halfmoon
Febry	12 William Redlif
March	4 Hend'k Bunsen's child
	17 Philip Van Vechten's wife
	17 Johs. Dpeyster's child*
	20 Elizabeth Banckers
	20 Ragel Hoogkerke's child
April	11 Catharin Cuyler*
	14 Geertruy Van Scherlnyne
	24 Willemhelmus V. de Bergh's child
May	25 Jacob Egmond
June	23 Johs Van Vechten was buried at Papsknee
July	10 Evert Banker
Agt	10 Dom. Van Schie's child*
	11 Nich Bleecker's Jr. child
	12 Ryck Hanse's child*
	12 Gysbert Roseboom's child
	19 Judick Hoogkerke
	27 Johs Dforeest's child
	28 Jannetje Ciregeer was buried at Niscauna
Sept	1 Johs Seegers child
	1 Ephar. Wendel's daughter Susannah
	2 Jer: Pemmerton's child
	4 Harmen Vechten's child
	5 Benjamin Winne's child
	6 Cornelis Van Dyck's little son
	12 Isaac Swits' child
	13 Volkert V. Den Bergh's child
	15 Claes Fonda's little son
	17 Stephanus Van Renselaer's child
	20 Nicholas Van Schuyck's child
	22 Pieter Schuyler's child was buried at the flats
Oct	8 Jacob T. Eyck's little child
	22 Johs. Ten Broeck's child
Novr	10 Fredk. Myndertse's daughter
	15 Cornelia Van Scharluyn
Decr	5 Gerret B. Van den Bergh's child
	18 David A. Schuyler's little son*
	1735
Febry	5 Maria wife of P. Wendel
	11 Nedt Broon Servant of Jef: [Mrs?] Livingston
	16 Jacob Staats
Mch	5 Ruben Van Vechte
	16 John Stoward
Apl	12 Isaac Van Alsteyn's child
May	Tomas Serp's child
June	9 Direk Brat was buried by Rut Van Wie
July	2 Thunis Frelin's child
Augt	27 Pieter Livingston's child was buried at the flats
Octr	12 Volkert Oothout's child
	27 Cornelis Van Beuren's little son was buried at Papsknee
Novr	3 Hendk. H. Roseboom's child
	12 Catryn Fyn
	16 Johs De Peyster's little child*
	21 Cornelia Quackenbos
	21 Johs Wyngart's child
Decr	3 Zacharias Sixkel's child
	9 Sybrant Van Schayck's child

Dutch Church Burials.

	14 Nicholas Engelspreeker
	20 Elsje Wendell daughter of Philip
	1736.
Jan.	12 Jurryan Hogen's child
	18 Michael Besset's child
	26 Gerrit Lansing
Mch	2 Geertie Ten Eyck
Apl	8 Johs Cloet's child
	10 Daniel Husen's child
May	13 Catharina daughter of Catie Van Schaick
June	23 David Groesbeeck's child
July	5 Willem Hogen's wife
	5 Johs Dforeest's child
	9 Pieter Livington's child was buried at the flats
	20 Gose Van Schaick
Augt	23 Nicholas Bleecker's child
Sept	28 Cornelis C. Van den Bergh's child
Octr	4 Thunis Fiele's child
	5 Marytie Mingael*
	11 Jonas Douw was buried at Greenbush
	25 Willem Waldrum's child
Nov	7 Jacobus Schuyler's child was buried at the hogeberg
	19 Rychart Hansen's little son*
	24 Isaac Wendell's child was buried at the flats
	29 Dominie Van Schie's child*
Decr	2 Thomas Sherp's child
	1737
Jan	12 Albert Ryckman was buried by Egbert Brat
	23 Hans Hansen's little son Pieter
	25 David Groesbeeck's little son
Feb	4 Antony Van Schaick
Mch	22 Robt Dunbar's child
	26 Edward Holland's wife was buried in the English church
Apl	23 Bastiaen Vischer
May	29 Jacob Bogart's daughter
June	5 Johs Scuyler's wife*
July	2 Migal Besset's son
	26 George hipkins [?] was buried in the English church
	27 Gerret J. Lansing's child
Agt	2 Mattys Vander Heyden's child
	3 The sister of Wm Tellers wife
	11 Dirck Ten Broeck's little son*
	18 Jobs. Onderkerk's child
	28 Abram Fonda's child
	29 Johs Dforeest's child
Septr	3 Adam Yates' child
	16 Domine Van Schie's child
	19 Dirck Hun's little daughter
	19 Sybrant Quackenbos' child
Octr	4 Jacobus V. Valkenbergh's child
	10 Neltie daughter of D. Ryckman
Novr	1 Jan Rosie*
	19 Benjamin Brats daughter was buried by [Oliver?]
	29 Wouter Knickerbacker's child

	17 Douwe Fonda's child
	1738
Jan	16 Gerret Van Benthuysen's wife
	18 Killian Winne's child
Feb	3 Dom: Petrus Van Driesen*
	14 Cornelis Clasen was buried in his Orchard
	12 Migael Basset's child
June	5 Coenraet Rechtmayor's child
	6 Gerret Van Benthuisen's child
	9 Mattys Van der Heyden's child
	22 Barent Sanders wife*
	25 Johs Dforeest's child
Augt	25 Elsje Lansing
	25 Hendk Ridder's child
	26 Nicolas Bleecker's child
Sept	17 Hend M. Roseboom's child
	23 Jacobus Kidnie's child
	27 Jan Van Alstyn
Octr	13 Direk Vander Heyden
	17 Neeltie Ryckman was buried by Antony Brat
	17 Hend'k H. Roseboom's child, do
Novr	7 Casparus Van Geveren
Decr	2 Abram Vosbergh's child
	3 John Van Ostrande's child
	12 Jenneke Blyckers
	23 Johs Bleecker*
	26 Gerritie Dracyers*
	31 Jacob B. Ten Eyck's child
	1739
Jan	4 Willem Hogen's child
Feb	2 Teunis Egbertse's child
	2 Dominie Van Schie's child*
Jan	4 Johs Van Schayck's child
Mch	12 Johs Van Vechte Jrs. child
	23 Jacob Beeckman
Apl	7 Dirckie Vischer was buried by Rut Van Woert
May	9 Jacob Glen's daughter*
June	3 Geurt Benneway's child
	8 Mattys Flensburgh
	8 Adriaen Brat's child
July	10 Hannah Flensburgh
	14 Jacobus Redlif's child
	15 Hendrick Oothont
Agt	7 Fredk Vischer's wife
	21 Rychart Hansen's child
	22 Gerret Ja Lansing's child
	22 Johs Wyngart's child
	23 Johs Douw's child
	26 Wouter Knickerbacker's child
	26 Abram Van Deusen's child
Sept	1 Abram Van Deusen's child
	9 Abram Lansingh's servant Johs
	23 David Van der Heyden's son Nanningh
Octr	3 Leendt Gansvoort's dn. Maria
	4 Egbert Bart Egbertse's child
	15 Theunis Egbertse's child
	21 Johs Van Rensselaer's child was buried at Greenbush
	23 Pieter Schuyler's child was buried at the flats

Dutch Church Burials.

	26 Sybrat A. V. Schuick's little da.	June	Abram Van Arnem's daughter
Novr	12 David A. Schuyler's child		28 Johs Schuyler Jrs daughter was buried at the flats
	16 Susanna wife of Johs Symonse*		
	19 Jacob Glen's child*	July	Hendk Halenbeeck's little child was buried by
	27 Thomas Scherp's daughter		
Decr	18 Johs E Wendell		8 Gerrit Benneway
	12 Aeltie Oothout		10 Maria Roseboom
	22 Giertie Lansing*		12 Anna Van Schayck
	21 Gerrit Roseboom		22 Johs Douw's child
	31 Johs Van Schaick's child		24 Johs Schuyler Jrs child was buried at the flats
	1740		
Jan	4 Anthony Van Dyck	Augt	12 Volkert N. Douw's child
	9 Jacobus Groesbeeck's child		15 Robert Lansingh's child Beeckman
	16 Cornelis Van Dyck's two daughters		
			Andries Brat's child
	19 Billy Sixberry	Octr	6 Dirk Hun's child
	20 Harm. B. Vischer's child		15 Goenraet Ten Eyck's daughter Catrina
Feb	12 Freedk Myndertse		
	25 Hendk Ridder's little child	Novr	1 Thomas Willem's son Philip
Apl	1 Anna widow of Billy Sixberry's child [i. e Billy's child]		6 John Schuyler Jur. was buried at the flats
	27 Gerret Brat's wife	Decr	1 Douwe Js Fonda's child
	29 Johs Maselis' child		12 Hans Eversen was buried at the Lutheran Church
May	12 Antony Van Schuick's da. Elsie		
June	6 Gysbert Marselis was buried by Daniel Brat		19 Arienemie Wendell*
			1742
	21 Claes Van Schayck's wife	Jan	6 Melchert A. Van Deusen was buried at Papsknee
	26 Jan Fonda		
July	4 Hendk Renselaer		8 Dirck Martin's wife and child
	12 Pieter Van Brugh*		15 Angeneetie Schot widow her child
	22 Johs Schuyler*		
	22 Adriaan Brat's child	May	6 Obedia Coeper
	23 Isaac Greveraet's child		11 Sara Van Bruga*
Augt	10 Abram Bogart's sister		28 Johs Jacobuse Lansingh's wife
	12 Gerrit Teunisse Van Vechten's child was buried at Papsknee	June	16 Matty Van der Heyden's child
		July	6 Harpert Jacobse Van Deusen*
	21 Johs De Forest's child		7 Jacob Maasen's child
	25 Tyck Swits		8 Maria Van Dyck
Septr	30 Barent Van Beuren's child was buried at Papsknee		15 Johs Van Vechten was buried at Papsknee
	5 Migal Besset's child		3 Jan Brat's child
	19 Jacobus Redlif's child		27 Johs Beeckman's servant
Octr	23 Marie Van Buren was buried near his own house		31 Anna Van Woert
		Agt	5 Johs Van Vechte's child
Novr	3 Gerrit Johs Lansing's child		6 Johs Van Goesen's child
	29 Volkert N. Douw's child		9 Willem Waldrom's child
	1741		12 Jacob H. Ten Eyck's child
Jan	10 Johs Redlif's wife Selia	Sept	Zacharias Haes' child
	27 Gerrit Ja Lansingh's wife		6 Hester Wendell
	29 Harpert Jacobse's son Gerret		19 Gerrit Ja Lansingh's child
Feb	5 Elisabeth daughter of Catie Van Schayck	Oct	9 Johs Van Schayck's child
			15 Kilinen Van Rauselar's child
	5 Luychas Hooghkerk Jrs child		24 Catriena Engelsprucker
	13 Luychas Hooghkeerk's child	Novr	28 Abram Splank
	26 Johs Beeckman		5 Debora Hansen*
Mch	6 Pieter Garmo		7 Dominie Berly was buried in the English church
	9 Mattys Van der Heyden's child		
	13 Luychas Hooghkerk		9 Johs Douw's child
Apl	3 Sara Schuylers was buried near her residence by P. Schuyler	Decr	24 Voyntie wife of Andries Brat
			25 Johs P. Witbeck
	9 Marngrietie daughter of Maria Roseboom		1743
		Jan	7 Maria Gansevoort
	18 Thomas Scherp's son Tomie		27 Wynant Van den Bergh's daughter Volkie
	24 Anna Sixberry daughter of Johs Redlef		
		Feb	13 Philip Wendell

Dutch Church Burials.

Mch	15 Robert Sanders' wife*	May	2 Cornelis Van den Bergh's child
	4 Catharina Van Ness	June	6 James Stievenson's wife*
	9 Antony S. Van Schayck's wife*		3 Johs Douw's child
	9 Pieter Schuyler's child was buried at the flats		17 Jan Cell's child
			19 Isaac Frelen's child
	27 Catlyntie wife of Gerret Van Ness		23 Johs Lansingh's wife
		July	8 Johs Van Yveren's child
	28 Marytie Van Schayck		9 Isaac Halenbeck's child
Apl	19 Antony Van Schayck's daughter Catriena		13 Johs Van Wie's child
			17 Stephanus Groesbeck
	21 Evert Sixberry's child		31 Antony Van der Zee's wife
May	24 Robert Lansing's child	Augt	9 Benjamin Bogart's child
	30 Chatie Salomonse		10 Wouter Groesbeck's child
June	5 Gerrit Van Nes' child		11 Johs Jacobse Eversen
	5 Johs D. Van der Heyden's child		13 Susanna Van den Bergh, wife of Cornelis Clasen
	20 Jacob Schermerhorn Jr was buried at Papsknee		16 Dom: Cornelis Van Schie*
			16 Gerrit W. Van den Bergh's child
July	10 Johs Eversen's child		16 Jacob Van Woert's little son
Agt	4 Gerret Jn Lansingh's wife		24 Harmen Vischer*
	11 Barent Van Ceuren's wife was buried at Papsknee		25 Antony's Van der Zee's child
			26 Tobyas Ryckman's wife
	15 Antony Van Yveren's child		28 Jan Van Arnem's child
	19 Benamen Winne's child		29 Nicolas Bleeker Jr's child
	22 Jacobus Redlif's child		31 Abraham H. Wendell's child
	26 Abram Witbeck's child	Septr	2 Isaac Greveraet's child
	31 Mattys Van der Heyden's two children		15 Bille Bronly's child
			26 Johs Brat's child
Sept	6 Johs Van Zante's wife	Oct	6 Johs Van Aelen's wife
	Antony Van der Zee's child		14 Cornelis Van Alstyn's child
Oct	1 Vullenpie Brat was buried by Rut Van Woert	Novbr	2 John Ouderkerk's children
			5 Pieter Fonda's wife
	9 Wouter Knickerbacker's child	Decr	8 Willem Hogen's ———
	21 Johs H. Wendell		14 Hendk Van Wie's child
	24 Abraham Ouderkerk		23 Hendrick Van Wie's wife
Novbr	1 Robert Sander's child*		23 Pieter Van Aelen's child
	3 Jacob Van Rutze Voert's child		1745.
	13 Gertie, daughter of Coenraet Ten Eyck	Jany	6 Jacob R. Van Woert's child
			22 Harme B Visscher's child
	21 Henderick Gerritz's child		25 Johs Roseboom*
	27 David Groesbeek's child	Febry	5 Johs Oothout
Decr	3 Johs Redlif's daughter		15 Isaac Onderkerk's child
	6 Thomas Coeper's child	Mar	16 Teunis Slingerland's wife
	10 Gerret W. Van den Bergh's child	April	6 Sanna, da. of Pieter Van Woret
	18 Stephanus Van Rensselaer's son		27 Wilhelmus Ryckman's child
	25 Joseph Redlif's child	May	8 Jeremiah Van Rensselaer (the Patroon)
	1744.		
Jan	4 Wouter Groesbeck's child		12 Jacob, son of Abram Lansing
	5 Dirck De Garmo	June	4 Gerret Van Zant's child
	6 Barent Jans Brat		5 Ned Hock's child
	8 Isaac Frelin's little son		18 Hendk Van Hoesen's child
	13 Harmen Gansevort's child Rensselaer		20 Abraham Lansingh
		July	3 Joseph Van Zante's wife
Febry	7 Dortie Halenbeek was buried in the Lutheran grave yard		3 Jacob Wendell's child
			22 Johs Boom, a high Dutchman
	14 Wilhelmus Ryckman's child		23 Gerrit d'Ridder's child
Mar	2 Gerrit Van Schoonhoven's wife, Lutheran	Augt	4 Dirk Wyt's child
			18 Stephanus Van Rensselaer's da.
	3 Antony Van der Zee's child		22 Cristoffell Abeel's child
	4 Harmanus H. Wendell's child		26 Johs Dpeyster's little son*
	7 Johs M. Flinsburgh's child		27 David Groesbeek's daughter
April	17 Antony Bogardus	Septr	1 Catlyntie, da. or wife of Johs Jn Lansing
	20 Gerrit Johs Lansingh's child		
	28 Cornelis Ridder		4 Hendk, son of David A. Schuyler
	30 Pieter Coeyman was buried on Barren Island		

Dutch Church Burials.

    5 Jacob Wendell was buried at Greenbush
    6 Scheeboleth Bogardus's Eph'm
    6 Jeramee Schuyler's daughter was buried at the flats
   10 Isaac Hansen's child
   10 Gerrit Brat's child
   13 Johs De Foreest's little son
Septr 14 Geradus Groesbeck's child*
   16 Johs, son of Isaac Lansingh
   16 John Courtney's child
   17 Hendk Coster*
   19 Sannaka Wendell, da. of Johs Van
   19 Sybrant Gert Van Schaick's da.
   22 Johs Ja Lansigh's child
Octbr 2 Cornelis Cuyler's child*
    5 Mr. Cateris's child was buried in the English church
    5 Abram Js Fonda's child
    6 Gerrn G Lansingh's wife
   20 Johs Donw's little child
   28 Johs Ja: Everson's child
   29 Jacob Hansen's child
Novbr 8 Geertruy Van Vechte was buried in the Patroon's vault
   15 Elizabeth Wendell was buried at the flats.
   17 Barent Staats Jr's son
   21 Walraven Cloet's son
   21 Arent Slingerland's child
   28 Benumen Hitten's child
   30 Asueros Roseboom's wife
Decr 4 Madalena Lansingh
    5 Sander Van Woert's child
   12 Debora Beeckman
   19 Eysabell Staats*
   22 Mattys Van den Bergh
   23 Daniel Winne Jr's child

1716.

Janry 11 David Van Zante's wife
   20 Lammert Kool's child
   21 Jacob Muller's daughter
   26 Johannis Marselis was buried by Daniel Brat
   28 Johs Yates's child
Feb 14 Tomas Coeper's little child
Mar 8 Walloven Cloet's daughter
   20 Gerret Van Wie's wife was buried by his house
April 1 Maria Van Hoesen in the Lutheran church
    1 Son of Jacob Fort
   10 Jacob Van der Heyden
   11 Wife of Harme Van Hoesen at the Lutheran church
   11 Daughter of Jacob Fort
   13 Little son of Jan Van Arnem
   14 Wife of Johannes Cuyler*
   15 Child of Wouter Js Groesbeek
   16 Jacob Glen*
   21 Willem Groesbeck
   23 Harmen Van Vechten
   27 Child of Abram Fort
May 1 Rychart Van Franke

    3 Gysbert Van Alstyn
   12 Martynis C. Van Alstyn
   12 Jacob Van Yveren
   12 Barent Van Yveren
   12 Son of Ryner Van Yveren
   13 Child of Levynis Winne
   15 Johns Rynr Van Yveren
   16 Jacob C Ten Eyck's child
   19 Fredk Ruyter Jr
   26 John Lagrange's wife
   30 Johs Roelfise's daughter
June 1 Philip Ruyter
    1 Michiel Besset's child
    2 Son of Bobbert Wendell
   15 Daughter of Philip Winne
   17 Child of Adam Yates
   19 Wife of Jochem Van der Heyden
   24 Thierk Beeckman
   24 Geertruy, da. of Nich. Groesbeck
   24 Little child of Gerret G. Lansingh
   26 Gerret, son of Johs Rolifsen
   28 Abram Fielie
   29 Theunis Slingerland
   30 Annata, wife of Direk Wyt
   30 Nicolas Js. Groesbeck
July 1 Wife of Jan de Voo
    6 Isaac Van Aelstyn
    8 Child of Thunis Fiele
   10 Child of Abram Gardenier
   13 Hendrick Brat
   16 Child of Willem Ryckman
   23 Child of David Van Zante
   23 Evert Bogardus
   27 Geradus [K]loedt
   27 Jan de Voe
   29 Child of Franciskis Lansing
   29 Deborn, da. of Hendk H. Roseboom
   29 Wife of Lymon Vedder
   31 Child of Evert Sieger
   31 Harme Bogardus
Aug 1 Gerrit Ja Lansingh
    1 Child of Abram Finhagen
    2 Child of Johs Beeckman
    2 Son of Johs Sieger
    3 Elsie, da. of Jacob Lansingh
    5 Daughter of Johs D'Foreest
    5 Wendell, son of Evert Wendell
    6 Wife of Zacharias Sischel
    6 Child of Sylvand Van Schayek
    7 Child of Michael Bessett
    8 Child of Hendk Fonda
    9 Child of Jacobus Wilton
   12 Child of Johs Van Vechte
   12 Daughter of Jesse D'Foreest
   12 Jacob, son of Johs D'Garm
   13 Child of Johs Slingerland
   14 Barent Vrooman
   15 Hendk H Roseboom
   16 Sylfrand H Van Schaick's child
   17 Child of Johs Visscher
   18 Child of Frans Wey Bosle
   21 Child of Egbert B. Egbertse
   21 Ragel Liversen
   22 Johs A. Cuyler's child

Dutch Church Burials.

22 Child of Sybrand H VanSchayck
25 Willem Vander Zee's child
26 Willem Kittell
26 Johs, son of Jacob Van Woert
26 Willem Ouderkerk
26 Child of Sara Fort
28 Wife of Johannes Beeckman
31 Little child of Claes Gardnier's son in law
Sept 4 Wife of Johs Ryckse
    5 Wife of Robt Lansing
    5 Daughter of Samuel Pruyn
    5 Child of Gysbert Mailstyn [i. e. Gysbert M Aelstyn]
    5 Child of Sybrant G VanSchaick
    7 Son of Mattys Bovie
    8 Sander Van Woert
    9 Hendrick Jacobse Beeckman
    9 Wife of Jonatan Witbeck jr. [Machtel]
    9 Child of Abram Van Arnem
   11 Wife of Johs Hansen
   12 Child of Mr Carteris
   15 Child of Hellagont Lewis
   15 Child of Annietie Groesbeck
   15 Child of Robt Livingston
   16 Child of Wynant C V Bergh
   17 Child of Pieter Schuyler
   18 Daughter of Rychert Hitton
   18 Child of Cornelis Martise Aelstyne
   20 Daughter of Saml Criegeer
   21 Little son of Livynis Winne
   21 Elisabeth, daughter of Rut Van Woert
   21 Child of Jonas Oothout
   22 Child of Isaac Switts
   25 Child of Jacob Blecker
   27 Hendk Gansevoort
   28 Daughter of Lysbeth Van Vechten
   30 Johs Ouderkerk
Oct 1 Wife of Olderick Van Franke
    1 Child of Zacharias Sischel
    4 Daughter of David Dforeest
    7 Child of Pieter Missel
    7 Child of Jonatan Witbeck
   11 Johannis Van Scharlayn
   17 Wife of Hugan Frele
   22 Son of Isaac Bogert
   26 Abraham Dox
   27 Johannis A Cuyler
   30 Child of Jacob Ten Eyck
Nov 2 Martie Fonda
    3 Susanna P Wendell
    5 Killiann Winne, a young man (of Pakesie)
    7 John Schuyler jr, in the church
   10 Daughter of Evert Wendell
   13 Child of Hendk Gerrit Van Nes
   14 Sara, daughter of Isaac Greeveract
   16 Jan Cristinense
   23 Gerritie Roseboom, in the church
   23 Wyntie Berrit
   25 Child of Mr Corrie
Dec 3 Child of Luykas Tomase Witbeck

17 Daughter of Adriaen Quackenbos
19 Catreen Bovie
20 Gerrit Van Wie
25 Johs Van Vechten
26 Lowis Schredell
31 Child of Richert M Van Franke
1747.
Jan 7 Child of Christiaan Lagraniel
   16 Child of Barent A Staats
   17 Sammake Schuyler
Feb 1 Child of Pieter Waldrun, near his house
   23 Wife of Johs Van Rensselaer, in the church
Mar 2 Johs Schuyler, in the church
   12 Gerrit Teunisse Van Vechten
   14 Geertruy Groesbeck
   19 Mayeke Ouderkerk, by Pieter Van Woert
Apr 14 Volckie, wife of Wynant V de Bergh
   16   by William Rogers jr
   19 Child of John Donway
May 1 Child of Arent Van Deusen
    9 Symon Daniels
   10 Son of John Whitbeck died and was buried
   25 Wife of Scheeboleth Bogardus
Jun 10 Child of Abraham Yeats
   21 Cornelis Van Dyck
July 1 Patroon Stephen Van Rensselaer, at the mills
    2 Evert Van Nes' wife
    4 Cornelis Swarthout
   14 Jacob Bleecker
   14 Abraham Cuyler, in the church
   16 Child of Wouter Knickerbacker
   18 Little son of Mr Catries, in the English church.
   24 Wife of Meyndert Schuyler, in the church
   31 Margrietie, daughter of Abram Lansing
Aug 4 Child of Jacob Van Benthuisen
    5 Child of V P Douw, in the church
    5 Child of Benjamin Goewey
    9 Jacob Seene
   11 Son of Peter Van Beuren
   12 Jan Van Nes
   13 Child of Abram Ja Lansing
   14 Child of Benjamin Van Vechte
   15 Child of Mattys Van d Heyden
   18 Child of Andries Van Wie
   19 Johs Marselis jr, by Egbert Brat
   19 Little girl of Elisabeth d Wandlaer
   21 Child of Livynis Winne
   24 Child of Dirck Van der Heyden
   26 Child of Abram Lansingh
   27 Child of Wouter N Groesbeck
   29 Catrina, daughter of Elisabeth Wendell
   30 Daughter of Calyntie Van der Bergh
   30 Child of Bastiaen Tymesse

Dutch Church Burials.

Sept 4 Child of Daniel Hussen
5 Child of Jacobus Schuyler
5 Wife of Philip Winne
5 Daughter of Arye Oothout
7 Child of Adriaan Quackenbos
7 Child of Robert Sanders
8 Child of Gysbert Van Brakel
9 Son of Gerrit Marselis [Jacob]
10 Jochim, son of Johs Visscher
10 Gerrit, son of Hendk Gerritse
10 Child of Sybrant Quackenbos
10 Jochem, son of Johs Van der Heyden
11 Two children of Benjamin Bogart
12 Child of Hendk Bries
12 Child of Volkert Van den Bergh
12 Daughter of Neeltie Brat
13 Giedeon Quackenbos
16 Child of Sybrant Goes VanSchaick
16 Child of Benjamin Goewey
17 Daughter of Neeltie Brat
17 Child of Evert Lansingh
17 Child of Peter Schuyler
19 Little son of Evert Wendell
20 Nicolas Bleecker jr
20 Annake, daughter of Petrus Bogardus
20 Catrina, widow of Willem Groesbeck's child
20 Daughter of Catrina, widow of Martyn Van Aalstyn
21 Child of Zacharias Bries
21 Child of John Willems
21 Child of Evert Lansingh
23 Child of Dirk Olver
23 Child of Isaac Hansen
23 Daughter of Arye Oothout
25 Child of Robert Wendell
26 Child of Abraham H Wendell
26 Child of Cornelis C Van den Bergh
26 Schieboleth Bogardus
27 Child of Rebecca, widow of Hendk Brat
27 Child of Rychart Hansen
28 Child of Johs Cloet
28 Child of Rynier Van Hoesen
30 Two children of Willem Gysbert Van den Bergh
Oct 1 Wife of Isaac de Voe
2 Child of Johannis Van Wie
2 Child of Nicholas Cuyler
3 Daughter of Willem Van d Bergh
3 Child of Harmen Hun
3 Little son of Barent V Yeveren
3 Child of Jacob Bogart jr
12 Child of Sybrant Goes Van Shaick
13 Child of James Stenhuys
20 Wife of Isaac Ouderkerk
25 Wife of Rutger Bleecker
Nov 17 Maryte Winne
26 Child of Johannis Lansingh jr
Dec 2 Child of Harme Knickerbacker
3 Coenradt (Ruresmayor)
15 Child of John Fryer

21 Wife of Gerrit Rycksen
24 Child of Corneles Waldrum
25 Wife of Pieter Davids Schuyler

1748.
Jan 13 Geritie Rykerson
14 Little son of Catalyntie Roseboom
19 James, son of Rolf Schoon
26 Daughter of Jellis D Garmo
Feb 9 Geestie Kipp
25 Annatie Hilton
25 Obadyn Cooper's child.
28 Child of Johs Van Yeveren
Mar 2 Child of Pieter Schuyler
23 Wife of Isaac Fonda
29 Daughter of Cornelia Cooper
31 Child of Gerrit Marselis
Apr 3 Child of Dirck B VanSchoonhoven
3 Johs Wendel's cosyn (i. e. nephew?)
9 Wife of James Steinhuys
17 Wife of Obadya Coeper
19 Child of Johs Ten Eyck
21 Wife of Pieter Van Beuren
24 Marya Gerritse
May 10 Madame Margrita Collans, in the church
20 Wife of Abraham Vinhagen
24 Evert Rykse
25 Johannis Berreway
30 Johannis Hansen
Jun 10 Alyda Visscher
July 5 Child of Thomas Seeger
8 Nicholas Schuyler
10 Child of Jan Brat
17 Child of Adam Yates
20 Pieter Quackenbos
21 Child of Robert Sanders, near his house
21 Child of Abraham Lansingh, near his house
29 Child of Jacob H Ten Eyck
Aug 3 Johs L Whitbeck
6 Johs G Lansingh
15 Child of Antony Van der Zee
16 Wife of Andries [Mahans]
17 Child of Jacob Egmond
27 Rachel, daughter of John Whitbeck
29 Lydia Van Vechte, in the church
30 Child of Hendk Van Nes
Sept 2 Catie Van Weie
4 Pieter Ryckman
11 Wife of Tomas Coeper
19 Melgert, son of David Groesbeck
27 Two children of Cornelis Winne, by his house
Oct 2 Gerrit Js Lansingh
6 Child of Cornelis Sanford
13 Wife of Volkert N Douw
24 Child of Cornelis Van Nes
Nov 3 Bregie, sister of Cornelis Clasen
3 Wife of Tomas Scherp
6 Child of Johannis V Douw

1740.
Jan 3 Rynier Van Hoesen

Dutch Church Burials.

- 22 Child of Tomas Coyper
- 26 Tryntie Vrooman
- 26 Jacobus Van Schoonhoven
- 28 Jan Dreth
- Feb 12 Willem Hilten
- 16 Child of Dirk Van Aesdale
- 17 Child of Jacob H Ten Eyck, by his house
- Mar 6 Child of Pieter Lansingh
- 18 Catrina, daughter of Claes Van Woert
- Apr 3 Wife of Jacob R Van Woert
- 7 Ragel Redliff
- 10 Johannis Visscher
- 14 Sara, wife of Robert Lansingh
- 14 The child of Arye Oothout's [daughter]
- 25 Daughter of Johs Janz Lansingh
- Jun 13 Child of Petrus Van Loon
- 14 Child of Robt Livingston
- 16 Wife of Barent Staats jr
- 17 Child of Cornelis C Van der Bergh
- 27 Child of Johs Ten Eyck
- July 1 Child of Robt Lansingh
- 2 Lievynis Lieversen
- 7 Gelyn Splanck
- 20 Child of Jacobus Cleerment
- 31 Child of Mr Kartryt, in English church
- Aug 3 Child of Volkert Van der Bergh
- 11 Child of Bethe Wilsen
- 18 Child of Jacobus Cleement
- 23 Johannis Pruyn
- 31 Benjamin Van Vechte
- 31 Son of Berrit Staats
- Sept 3 Child of Benjamin Hilten
- 17 Pieter Van Aelen
- Oct 2 Debora Roseboom
- 6 of Jacob Lansingh
- 9 Child of Volkert P Douw
- 24 Child of Harme Gansvort
- 29 Gyshert Roseboom
- Nov 4 Child of Jonas Oothout
- 6 Lyntie, wife of Abram Douw
- 14 Child of Killiaen Van Rensselaer
- Dec 3 John, son of Ruben Van Vechte
- 14 Child of Abram Yates
- 25 Annatie, wife of Antony Van d Zee
- 26 Antie de Ridder

1750.

- Jan 3 Wife of Nicolas Cuyler, at the flats
- 10 Wife of Joseph Yeats [Hendrike?]
- Feb 9 Child of John R Bleecker, in the church
- Mar 7 Child of Roelf, servant of Pieter Winne
- 9 Marya Van Deusen
- 21 Child of Harmen B Visscher
- 22 Child of Antony Brat jr
- Apr 7 Bettie Wilson
- 12 Johs Van Allen
- 17 Robert Wendell
- 24 Cornelis Van Vechte
- 29 Son of James Stevenson, in the church
- May 4 Evert Wendell
- 25 Gerrit Ja Lansingh's child
- June 7 Marte Hogan
- 13 [Tunik?] Hoogh
- 22 Luycas Hooghkerk's child
- 26 Child of Pieter D Wandeller
- July 6 Child of Gerrit Van Franke
- 22 Daughter of Hendrick Lansingh
- 25 Child of Jacob Ja Lansing
- Aug 5 Child of Rychart Hansen
- 23 Abigall Splank
- Sep 15 Nicolaes Van Schaick
- 16 Wife of Johs de Peyster, in the church
- 28 Son of Hendrick Halenbeeck
- 30 Johs F Van Yveren's child
- Oct 17 Salomon Van Vechte, [on the other side?]
- 22 Johs Vinhagen, near his house
- Nov 6 Luychas Hooghkerk's wife
- 17 Child of Marte Bockley
- 18 Elbert Gerrits, in the church
- 19 Little daughter of Annake, widow Pieter Van Alen
- 28 Child of Philip Hansen
- Dec 5 Child of David Van der Heyden
- 11 Child of Johs Douw
- 31 Daughter of Adam Yaets

1751.

- Jan 4 Nicolaes Bleecker, in the church
- 7 Dirck Ten Broeck, in the church
- 14 Child of Staets Zantfort
- 30 Anna Kischenar
- Feb 9 Daughter of Gerrit Van Zante
- 9 Child of John Fryer
- 17 Child of Barennardus Harsen
- Mar 10 Child of Pieter M de Garmo
- 15 Child of Pieter D Wandelaer
- 19 Little son of Rychart Hansen
- 21 Wife of Pieter D Wandelier
- 25 Child of Willem Van Buren, at Papskaeo
- 26 Child of Antony Van Yveren
- Apr 3 Child of Willem Van Zante
- 4 Philip Loock, by his house
- 12 Child of Abraham Lansingh
- 16 Little girl of (Volkert P Douw) Catie Cropel
- 21 Child of Evert Seeger
- 25 Wife of Jacobus Groesbeck
- 29 Hendk de Witt's son's child
- May 4 Little son of Gerrit G Van der Bergh
- 18 Hendrick Douw
- 23 Child of Johs M Felensburgh
- June 4 Little child of Johs Ten Eyck
- 10 Child of Tobias Ten Eyck
- 26 Antony Ay Brat's wife
- July 7 Antony Ay Brat's child
- 14 Child of Geradus Groesbeeck
- 19 Child of Tam Smid
- Aug 10 Child of Billy Bromly
- 26 Child of Michael Besset
- Sep 2 Antony Van Zante

Dutch Church Burials.

5 Annetie, wife of Claes Fonda
15 Wife of Adam Yates
Oct 13 Daughter of Sybrant A Van Schaick
30 Wife of John G Roseboom
Nov 3 Children of Hendrick G Van Nes
12 Child of John R Bleecker, in the church
1752.
Jan   Wife of Volker Douw
Feb 5 Barentie Everse
26 Arye Oothout
26 Daughter of Johs Cloett
Mar 6 Wife of Jacob Mausen
9 Wife of Rolif Seeger
10 Jannetje, wife of Johs Gr Lansingh
Apr 16 Wife of Pieter Willems
May 4 Willem Van Scharluyn
Jun 2 Cornelis de Hiller
27 Samuel Pruyn
30 Child of Killiaen Van Rensselaer
July 2 Elsie Cuyler, in the church
7 Child of Roelif, servant of Pieter Winne
10 Child of Johs Ten Eyck
9 Neeltie Beeckman
11 Asweurus Wendell
26 Children of Gerrit Johs Lansingh
28 Barent Staats, at the Hoghbergh
30 Child of Abram Yates
Aug 9 Child of Johs Gansvoort
9 John Waters
17 Willem Van Beuren, at Papsknee
18 Daughter of Margrietie, widow of Nicolas Bleecker
19 Child of Billy Brombely
26 Elisabeth Hooghkerk
Sep 20 Child of Wilhelmus Van den Bergh jr
26 Child of Wouter Knickerbacker
30 Catie Witbeck, at Papsknee
Oct 1 The sister of Gerrit Van der Bergh's wife
3 Wife of Marte D Stiller
5 Willem, son of David Groesbeeck
5 Child of Dirk Olfer
5 Child of Gerndus Lansingh
13 Cornelis Winne, at Bethelem
21 Ryer Gerrits
22 Child of John Johs Lansingh
30 Child of Tomas Seeger
Nov 12 Child of Gerrit Van Franken
13 Child of Jacob Van Schayck
20 Child of Johs Bleecker jr
23 Thomas Willems
Dec 4 Wife of Johs Bleecker
27 Child of Jacob Coeper
29 Child af Antony Gose Van Schayck
29 Child of Antony Egbertie Brat
1753
Jan 23 Coenradt Te Eycke
Feb 6 Antony Coster, in the church
10 Child of Barenhardus Harsen
16 Child of John Jacobse Eversen

23 Hester Van Arenem
Mar 5 Tryntie Waldrum
20 Elsie, daughter of Leendert Gansevoort
25 Child of Jacob Bogart jr
29 Edward Collins, in our church
May 4 Pieter Schuyler's child, at the flats
19 Child of Abram Yates
Jun 16 Child of Pieter Johs Garmo
26 Willem Meeryda
30 Abraham E Wendell
July 8 Child of Harmen Hun
28 Child of Isaac Hanse
Aug 1 Son of Gerrit Van Zante
10 Child of Johs Flensburgh
11 Child of Johs Gansevoort
13 Child of Marte Van Yveren
Sept 2 Volkert Douw
2 Pieter Schuyler jr, at the flats
3 Cornelis Slingerlandt, at Niscatha
6 Wife of John Bertely, by Koeyeman
9 Child of Adriaen Quackenbos
11 Child of Marte Van Yveren
13 Wife of Thomas Seger
17 Sarah Hoogkerk
22 Hendrick Bries, at Papsknee
23 Child of Philip Hansen
29 Child of Abram Coeper
Oct 16 Joseph Janz Van Zante
20 Mr Smit the schoolmaster's child
22 Wife of Benjamin Egbertz
Nov 7 John Roseboom [Doxter]
28 Child of Isaac Fonda
Dec 5 Child of Steven Van Schack
10 Jeramiah Schuyler, at the flats
15 Child of Jacob Van der Heyden, near his house
1754.
Jan 3 Ragel Van der Heyden, at the flats
13 Elisabeth Corlaer, in the church
Feb 5 Rabecca, wife of Pieter Bogart
22 Wife of Johs Van der Heyden
26 Christoffel Yates
Mar 8 Ariaentie, wife of Douw Van Vechten
11 Elisabeth, wife of Jonas Oothout [was a Lansing]
18 A High Dutchman
Apr 25 Geertruy, wife of Ryer Gerritz
25 Daughter of Johs Van Rensellaer
29 Child of Martin Bockeley
May 10
19 Wife of Marte Bockely
Jun 13 Johs D Freest
23 Child of Isaac Freest
Jul 10 Child of Abram Bogart jr
10 Child of Gysbert Fonda, "tavont"
17 Samuel Coeyman
Aug 11 Harme Hun's child
17 Child of Willem Winne
20 Catryn, wife of James Way
23 Child of Wouter Groesbeeck
23 Jan, son of Harm Van Hoesen

Sept 1 Abram Pells
8 Child of Johs M De Garmo
8 Child of Herry Van Dyck
9 Wife of Samuel Cregier
22 Child of Pieter Waldrum
25 Wife of Petrus Hilton
27 Child of Cornelis Groot.
Oct 2 Child of Petrus Hilton
7 Child of Theunis Van Vechte
10 Child of John Davids
11 Wife of Adriaen Brat
17 Cornelia, daughter of Johs Freest
18 Wife of Antony Johs Brat
21 Child of Adriaen Brat
21 Child of Rykert Hansen
21 Child of Capt Hischen Holland
27 Elisabeth Vischer, mother of H Vischer
29 Hendrick Roseboom
Nov 12 Harmanis P Wendell
14 Geertie Groesbeeck
25 Bettie Groesbeeck
26 Child of Gerrit Lansingh
Dec 3 Child of Ben Williams
7 Luyckas J Wyngart, in the church
12 John Daniels
18 Catrina, wife of David Groesbeek jun
18 Wife of Robert Berret
21 Wife of Wynant C Van denBergh
28 Wife of Hendrick Van Nes
1755.
Jan 4 Annatie, wife of Rychert Van Francke
11 Jacob Eversen
14 Abraham Wendell
16 Child of Johs Yates, at Greenbush
22 Wife of Robert Wendell, at the flats
24 Child of Henry Van Dyck
27 Jannetie Gelen, in the church
Feb 5 Hendk Eversen
Mar 6 Eva Beeckman
13 Child of Jacob Johs Van der Heyden
20 Child of Johs Johs Lansingh
22 Wife of Johannis Goewey
28 Abram To's Witbeck's wife, at Papsknee
May 5 A child buried by David Groesbeeek
6 Child of Abram Yates
7 Wife of Isaac Ouderkerk
8 Child of Johs Seeger's youngest daughter
June 4 Jacob Maasen
6 Daughter of Gerrit Van Zante
7 Daughter of Salomon Goewey
11 Child of Dirk Van der Heyden
12 Wife of Johs Fonda, at the patroon's
July 9 Wife of Rutger Van Woert
11 Wife of Abraham Van Arnem (Ja Lansingh do)

19 Child of John Lansingh
21 Child of John Lansingh
22 Child of Pieter Gansvort
23 Child of Robt Berrit
24 Child of Geradus Lansingh
26 Child of Volkert P Douw, in the church
29 Cornelis Bogart
30 Child of David Abeel
Aug 3 Isaac Fryer, in the English church
4 Marte Van Aelstyn, son of Martyn
10 Child of Bennonie
15 (Janna Peisen)
22 Child of Johs Johs Wendell
23 Child of Philip Deforeest
Sept 2
3 Child of Fredk Gerrits
6 Wife of Daniel Haelenbeeck
11 Child of Harm Gansevort
18 Child of Robt Crannel
27
27 Child of Volkert Van den Bergh
Oct 7 Child of Daniel Haelenbeek
8 Mayors Foot, by Pieter Douw
21 Myndert Schuyler, in the church
24 Willem Hilton, a young man
25 Isaac Fort
31 Johs N Schuyler, at the Hoghbergh
Nov 3 Harm Ryckman
4 Child of Jacob Gerritz VanSchayck
12 John Isa Wendell (in) Boston
16 A New-England officer, by John E Wendell
19 Child of Arent Van Deusen
20 Cristina Cuyler, in the church
22 Child of Pieter M de Garmo
24 Pieter Martin
25 Child of Andries Gardinier
Dec 3 Hendriekis M Beeckman
15 Child of Abram Peeck
17 Child of Abram P Bogart
1756
Jan 2 Elisabeth Brat, in the church
6 Douwe Isa Fonda's wife
6 Herry Abeel
21 Appeelonie Merit
21 By Johs Flensburgh, Sirsieman
Feb 2 Gerrit Roelfse
4 Wife of Rynier Meyndertse, by R V Woert
14 Child of Maria Van der Heyden
Mar 4 Child of Jhs Knickerbacker
4 Child of Johs Ja Eversen
6 Child of Abraham Ten Broeck
18 Willem Nicolaes, in the church
20 Lybitie Olinde
20 Child (son) of Waldraven Cloet
21 Child of Abram H Wendell
26 Child of Harme Gansevoort
Apr 6 Wife of Pieter Douw
6 Samuel Ten Broeck
8 Maria, wife of Cornelis Van Dyck
12 Johs, son of Willem Van Zante

May 18 Child of Abram Van Francke
    18 Cornelis Waldrum
    27 Son of John Raely
    30 Wife of Jacob Van Woert
June 8 A son of Spinger
     9 Luycas, son of Luyckas Hoogkerke
    21 Wife of Abram Mynderse
    27 Thunis Van Vechte
Jul 13 John Bries, by Jan Witbeeken
    21 Child of Thunis Van Vechte
    23 Child of Isaac Fonda jr
    31 Child of Jacob Spruger
Aug 2 Johs Halenbeeck, by Abram Yates
     5 Rutger Bleecker, in the church
    10 Child of Johs Ten Eyck
    10 Madame Van Driesen, in the church
    14 Child of Fredk Cloet
    17 Child of Rutger Van den Bergh
    23 Child of Harm J Visscher
    26 Child of Petrus Vosburgh
    26 A   [Abram Van Duse]
    27 Mary Wyngart
    28 Child of John M Beeckman
    28 Child of John Cloet jr
    29 Child of Johs Ja Muller
    29 Jesee Winne
    30 Child of Abram Ja Lansingh
Sept 1 Child of Abram Van den Bergh
     1 Wife of Hendk Mayor
     5 Child of Bastian T Visscher
     5 Child of Antony Flensburgh
     5 Johs Brat Brat
    11 Leindert Van Vechte
    13 Daughter of Oldrick Van Franke
    17 Child of Johs Van Zante jr
    19 John E Wendell
    19 Wife of Harmanus Wendell
    21 Child of Cornelis M Vanden Bergh
    22 A Roeyland man, by John Peys
    25 Child of Andries Gardanier
    27 Jesse D Forest
    27 Johs Arie Oothout
    29 A   by Johs Visscher Harme
Oct 2 A   by Staets Santford
     6 Johs Poc....
     7 Wife of Albartus Maase
    11 Child of Dirk B Van Schoonhoven
    12 Robert Berret
    15 Child of Albartus Maase
    15 Wife of Pieter Maase
    16 Child of Robert Sanders, buried Barent
    17 Jacob Lansingh, by his house
    18 Marin, daughter of Aswerus
    20 Son of Jacobus Schuyler
    21 Pieter S Bogardus
    24 Maria Van Aelstyn
    26 Johs Beeckman
    26 Johs Pierson
    27 Pieter Lorkerman
    29 Wife of Andries Gardinier jun
    30 Child of James Adam
    30 Child of Pieter Maasen

Nov 4 Pieter Goewey
    5 Barent, son of John Bleecker
    7 Child of Martynis Cregier
   18 Willem Bort, patoomau
   18 Child of Johs Ja Eversen
   29 Daughter of Johs Ten Broeck
Dec 6 Hans Hansen
   17 Jan Maasen jr
   20 Henry Douw, at Greenbush
   28 A Highdutchman's wife
   30 Catie Van Schayck
   31 Madame Elisabeth VanRensselaer
        1757.
Jan 6 Wife of Harm Liverse
    7 Willem Cremmel
    7 Little son of Geradus Groesbeeck
    8 Child of a Highdutchman
   10 Son of Edward Willems
   16 Child of Harm Liverse
   19 Johs Redlif
   21 Wife of David Groesbeeck
   22 Son of Edward Willems
   24 Olderick Van Francke
   26 Child of Geradus Groesbeeck
Feb 1 Wife of Pieter Quackenbos
    6 Son of Geradus Groesbeeck
    9 Wife of Johs Knur
   13 Ragel Bogardus
Mar 15 Johs, son of Roelf Seger
    17 Child of the daughter of Johs Wyngart
    31 Child of Johs Coon
May 2 Catrina, wife of Isaac Vosbergh
    3 Elisabeth Koster, in the church
    6 Two children of Volkert Van den Bergh
    9 Child of Abram Bogart
   10 Johannis Bleecker
   15 Wife of Abram H Wendell
   28 Child of Jacob Van Schayck
   30 Wife of Meyndert Marselis
   30 Daughter of Symon Vedder
June 2 Child of Pieter Waldrum
    7 Child of Johs Van Yveren
   17 Wife of Johs Segers jr
   23 Child of Pieter Hilton
   24 Georgie Lombers
   26 Child of David Sprugert
   30 Catrien, daughter of Gysbert Van den Bergh
   28 Child of Frans Lansingh
Jul 11 Son of Dirk Brat VanSchoonhoven Cose
   21 Child of the widow of Jesse Winne
   27 Wife of Jacob Roseboom
   27 A man, by Staats Zantfort
   31 Little son of Isaac D Fonda
Aug 3 Child of Jellis K Winne
    5 Child of Gysbert Marselis
   10 Child of Harm B Visscher
   13 Child of Pieter Messel
   14 Daughter of Dirk B Schoonhoven
   24 Child of Jonas Oothout
   26 Child of Jacob Ja Lansingh

Dutch Church Burials.

27 Gerrit Janz Lansingh
28 Child of Johs M Beeckman
Sept 1 Child of Johs M Flensburgh
2 Wife of Hendk Seeger
2 Child of Antony Van Yveren
5 Child of Jacob Bogart
7 Little girl of Jonas Oothout
12 Child of Abram Freest
13 A Boston captain, by Abram Lansingh
14 Sara Luyknse
15 Child of Dom Freelinghuyse
20 Child of Pieter M D Garmo
29 John Fryer's child
29 Child of Hend Wendel
Oct 7 Child of Pieter Jonas
9 Child of Jacob G Van Schayck
12 Child of Will Van den Bergh jr
12 Child of Antony Van der Zee
14 Child of Michel Bessett
18 Child of Philip D Foreest
20 Child of Cornelis Santford
20 Child of Marte Van Eyvere
22 Child of Johs Knickerbacker
Nov 9 Child of Bastinen Viescher
12 Child of Petrus Vosburgh
14 Hester Swits
21 Barent Sanders, in the church
22 Child of Thunis Van Woert
30 Child of Pieter Waldrum
Dec 1 Child of Johs Van Zante
5 An officer, by Symon Ridder
10 Child of Hendk Gerrits
12 Lena Lansingh
12 Child of Pieter Lansingh
12 Bastiner G   1599 burials.

FAMILY RECORD FROM THE GROESBECK BIBLE:

Now in the Possession of DAVID GROESBECK, *of Albany.*

1724 Nov 8. I, David Groesbeck senior, married Marin Van der Poel, who died January 18, 1757.
1725 Aug 2. My son William was born.   Died Oct 3, 1752.
1726 Dec 24. My daughter Catrina was born.   Died Jan 1, 1732.
1728 Aug 5. My son David was born (m. 1752).   Died Mar 30, 1795.
1730 Apr 30. My daughter Mary was born.   Died Jan 26, 1732.
1732 Apr 13. My son Melleghast was born.   Died Sep 18, 1748.
1734 Feb 23. My son John was born.   Died Jan 23, 1737.
1736 Apr —. My son Abram died (born dead?).
1737 May 8. My daughter Cathryna was born.
1739 Apr 30. My daughter Gertruy was born.   Died Aug 25, 1745.
1741 Jul 12. My son John was born.
1745 Mar 12. My daughter Catelyna was born.   Died Jan 6, 1766.
1766 (1763?) David Groesbeck senior died.

1692 Mar 17. My father (David Groesbeck sen, son of William Claas Groesbeck) was born.
1763 Feb 3. My father died.
1752 Dec 23. I, David Groesbeck jun, married Catrina Vedder.
1753 Jun 17. My son William was born.
1754 Nov 30. My son Cornelis was born.
1754 Dec 15. My wife died.
1765 Sep 28. I married Sara Winne, who was born July 21, 1754 (m. at 11?).
1795 Mar 30. David Groesbeck junior died.
1818 Apr 20. Sarah Winne, his widow, died.

BIOGRAPHICAL SKETCH OF GENERAL PHILIP SCHUYLER.

By the Hon. JAMES KENT.

THE Dutch family of Schuyler stands conspicuous in our colonial annals. Colonel Peter Schuyler was mayor of Albany, and commander of the northern militia in 1690. He was distinguished for his probity and activity in all the various duties of civil and military life. No man understood better the relation of the Colony with the Five Nations of Indians, or had more decided influence with that confederacy. He had frequently chastised the Canadian French for their destructive incursions upon the frontier settlements; and his zeal and energy were rewarded by a seat in the Provincial Council, and the House of Assembly gave their testimony to the British Court of his faithful services and good reputation. It was this same vigilant officer who gave intelligence to the inhabitants of Deerfield, on Connecticut river, of the designs of the French and Indians upon them, some short time before the destruction of that village in 1704. In 1720, as president of the council, he became acting governor of the colony for a short time, previous to the accession of Governor Burnet. His son, Colonel Philip Schuyler, was an active and efficient member of assembly for the city and county of Albany, in 1743. But the Philip Schuyler to whom I particularly allude, and who in a subsequent age shed such signal lustre upon the family name, was born at Albany in the year 1733; and at an early age he began to display his active mind and military spirit. He was a captain in the New-York levies at Fort Edward in 1755, and accompanied the British army in the expedition down Lake George in the summer of 1758. He was with Lord Howe when he fell by the fire of the enemy, on landing at the north end of the lake; and he was appointed (as he himself informed me) to convey the body of that young and lamented nobleman to Albany, where he was buried with appropriate solemnities in the Episcopal Church.

We next find him under the title of Colonel Schuyler, in company with his compatriot George Clinton, in the year 1768, on the floor of the House of Assembly, taking an active share in all their vehement discussions. Neither of them was to be overawed or seduced from a bold and determined defence of the constitutional rights of the colonies, and of an adherence to the letter and spirit of the councils of the union. The struggle in the House of Assembly, between the ministerial and the whig parties, was brought to a crisis in the months of February and March, 1775; and in that memorable contest, Philip Schuyler and George Clinton, together with Nathaniel Woodhull of Long Island, acted distinguished parts. On the motions to give the thanks of the House to the delegates from the colony in the Continental Congress of September, 1774, and to thank the merchants and inhabitants of the colony for their adherence to the non-importation and the association recommended by Congress, those patriots found themselves in the minority; but their courage and resolution gained strength from defeat.

On the third of March, Col. Schuyler moved declaratory resolutions that the act 4 Geo. III. imposing duties for raising a revenue in America, and for the extending the jurisdiction of admiralty courts, and for depriving his majesty's subjects in America of trial by jury, and for holding up an injurious discrimination between the subjects of Great Britain and those of the colonies, were great grievances. The government party seem to have fled the question, and to have left in the House only the scanty number of nine members, and the resolutions were carried by a vote of seven to two; but their opponents immediately rallied, and eleven distinct divisions, on different motions, were afterwards taken in the course of that single day, and entered on the journal, and they related to all the momentous points then in controversy between Great Britain and the United Colonies. It was a sharp and hard-fought contest for fundamental principles; and a more solemn and eventful debate rarely ever happened on the floor of a deliberative assembly. The House consisted on that day of twenty-four members, and the ministerial majority was exactly in the ratio of two to one; and the intrepidity, talents, and services of the three members I have named, and especially of Schuyler and Clinton, were above all praise, and laid the foundation for those lavish marks of honor and confidence which their countrymen were afterwards so eager to bestow.

The resistance of the majority of the House was fairly broken down, and essentially controlled by the efforts of the minority and the energy of public opinion. A series of resolutions, declaratory of American grievances, were passed, and petitions to the King and Parliament adopted, not indeed in all respects such as the leaders of the minority wished (for all their amendments were voted down), but they were nevertheless grounded upon the principles of the American Revolution. They declared that the claims of taxation and absolute sovereignty on the part of the British Parliament, and the extension of admiralty jurisdiction, were grievances and unconstitutional measures; and that the act of Parliament, shutting up the port of Boston, and altering the charter of that colony, also was a grievance.

These were the last proceedings of the General Assembly of the Colony of New-York, which now closed its existence forever. More perilous scenes, and new and brighter paths of glory, were opening upon the vision of those illustrious patriots.

The delegates from this colony to the first Continental Congress in 1774, were not chosen by the General Assembly, but by the suffrages of the people, manifested in some sufficiently authentic shape in the several counties.

The delegates to the second constitutional Congress, which met in May, 1775, were chosen by a provincial congress, which the people of the colony had already created, and which was held in this city in April of that year, and had virtually assumed the powers of government. The names of the delegates from this colony to this second congress, were John Jay, John Alsop, James Duane, Philip Schuyler, George Clinton, Lewis Morris and Robert R. Livingston; and the weight of their talents and character may be inferred from the fact, that Mr. Jay, Mr. Livingston, Mr. Duane and Mr. Schuyler were early placed upon committees charged with the most arduous and responsible duties. We find Washington and Schuyler associated together in the committee appointed on the fourteenth of June, 1775, to prepare rules and regulations for the government of the army. This association of those great men, commenced at such a critical moment, was the beginning of a mutual confidence, respect and admiration, which continued with uninterrupted and unabated vividness during the remainder of their lives. An allusion is made to this friendship in the memoir of a former president of the New-York Historical Society, and the allusion is remarkable for its strength and pathos. After mentioning General Schuyler, he adds, " I have placed thee, my friend, by the side of him who knew thee; thy intelligence to discern, thy zeal to promote thy country's good; and, knowing thee, prized thee. Let this be thy eulogy. I add, and with truth peculiarly thine—content it should be mine to have expressed it."

The Congress of this Colony, during the years 1775 and 1776, had to meet difficulties and dangers almost sufficient to subdue the firmest resolution The population of the Colony was short of 200,000 souls. It had a vast body of disaffected inhabitants within its own bosom. It had numerous tribes of hostile savages on its extended frontier. The bonds of society seemed to have been broken up, and society itself resolved into its primitive elements. There was no civil government, but such as had been introduced by the provincial congress and county committees as temporary expedients. It had an enemy's province in the rear, strengthened by large and well-appointed forces. It had an open and exposed seaport, without any adequate means to defend it. In the summer of 1776, the state was actually invaded, not only upon our Canadian, but upon our Atlantic frontier, by a formidable fleet and army, calculated by the power that sent them to be sufficient to annihilate at once all our infant republics.

In the midst of this appalling storm, the virtue of our people, animated by a host of intrepid patriots, the mention of whose names is enough to kindle enthusiasm in the breast of the present generation, remained glowing, unmoved, and invincible. It would be difficult to find any other people who have been put to a severer test, or, on trial, gave higher proofs of courage and capacity.

On the nineteenth of June, 1775, Philip Schuyler was appointed by Congress the third major general in the armies of the United Colonies; and such was his singular promptitude, that, in eleven days from this appointment, we find him in actual service, corresponding with Congress from a distance on business that required and received immediate attention. In July, 1775, he was placed at the head of a board of commissioners for the northern department, and empowered to employ all the troops in that department at his discretion, subject to the future orders of the commander-in-chief. He was authorised, if he should find it practicable and expedient, to take possession of St. Johns and Montreal; and pursue any other measure in Canada, having a tendency, in his judgment, to promote the peace and security of the United Colonies.

In September, 1775, Gen. Schuyler was acting under positive instructions to enter Canada; and he proceeded, with Generals Montgomery and Wooster under his command, to the Isle au Noix. He had at that time become extremely ill, and he was obliged to leave the command of the expedition to devolve upon Gen. Montgomery. The latter, under his orders, captured the garrisons of Chambly and St. Johns, and pressed forward to Montreal and Quebec. Montreal was entered on the twelfth of November, 1775, by the troops under the immediate orders of Montgomery; and in the same month, a committee from Congress was appointed to confer with General Schuyler, relative to raising troops in Canada for the possession and security of that province. His activity, skill, and zeal shone conspicuously throughout that arduous northern campaign; and his unremitting correspondence received the most prompt and marked consideration.

While the expedition under Montgomery was employed in Canada, Gen. Schuyler was called to exercise his influence and power in another quarter of his military district. On the thirtieth of December, 1775, he was ordered to disarm the disaffected inhabitants of Tryon county, then under the influence of Sir John Johnson; and on the eighteenth of January following, he made a treaty with the disaffected portion of the people in that western part of the state. The Continental Congress were so highly satisfied with his conduct in that delicate and meritorious service, as to declare, by a special resolution, that he had executed his trust with fidelity, prudence and despatch; and they ordered a publication of the narrative of his march in depth of winter into the regions bordering on the middle and upper Mohawk. The duties imposed upon that officer were so various, multiplied and incessant, as to require rapid movements, sufficient to distract and confound an ordinary mind. Thus, on the thirtieth of December, 1775, he was ordered to disarm the tories in Tryon county. On the eighth of January, 1776, he was ordered to have the River St. Lawrence, above and below Quebec, well explored. On the twenty-fifth of January, he was ordered to have the fortress of Ticonderoga repaired and made defensible; and on the seventeenth of February, he was directed to take the command of the forces, and conduct the military operations at the city of New-York. All these cumulative and conflicting orders from Congress were made upon him in the course of six weeks, and they were occasioned by the embarrassments and distresses of the times.

In March, 1776, Congress changed their plan of operation, and directed Gen. Schuyler to establish his head quarters at Albany, and superintend the army destined for Canada. He was instructed to take such orders as he should deem expedient, respecting the very perplexing and all-important subject of the supplies for the troops in Canada; and those orders as to the supplies were repeated in April, and again in May,

1776. The duty of procuring supplies, though less splendid in its effects, is often more effectual to the safety and success of an army than prowess in the field. Gen. Schuyler, by his thorough business habits, his precise attention to details, and by his skill and science in every duty connected with the equipment of an army, was admirably fitted to be at the head of the commissariat; and he gave life and vigor to every branch of the service. His versatile talents, equally adapted to investigation and action, rendered his merits as an officer of transcendent value.

On the fourteenth of June, 1776, he was ordered by Congress to hold a treaty with the Six Nations, and engage them in the interest of the colonies, and to treat with them on the principles and in the decisive manner which he had suggested. His preparations for taking immediate possession of Fort Stanwix, and erecting a fortification there, received the approbation of Congress; and their records afford the most satisfactory evidence that his comprehensive and accurate mind had anticipated and suggested the most essential measures, which he afterward diligently executed throughout the whole northern department. But within three days after the order for the treaty, Congress directed his operations to a different quarter of his command. He was ordered, on the seventeenth of June, to clear Wood creek, and construct a lock upon the creek at Skeensborough (now Whitehall), and to take the level of the waters falling into the Hudson at Fort Edward and into Wood creek. There can be no doubt that those orders were all founded upon his previous suggestions; and they afford demonstrative proof of the views entertained by him, at that early day, of the practicability and importance of canal navigation. He was likewise directed to cause armed vessels to be built, so as to secure the mastery of the waters of the northern lakes. He was to judge of the expediency of a temporary fortification or intrenched camp on the heights opposite Ticonderoga. Capt. Graydon visited Gen. Schuyler early in the summer of 1776, at his head-quarters on Lake George; and he speaks of him, in the very interesting memoirs of his own life, as an officer thoroughly devoted to business, and being at the same time a gentleman of polished, courteous manners. On the first of August following, he was on the upper Mohawk, providing for its defence and security; and again in October we find him on the upper Hudson, and calling upon the Eastern States for their militia.

There can be no doubt that the northern frontier, in the campaign of 1776, was indebted for its extraordinary quiet and security to the ceaseless activity of Gen Schuyler. At the close of that year he was further instructed to build a floating battery on the lake, at the foot of Mount Independence, and also to strengthen the works at Fort Stanwix.

In the midst of such conflicting and harassing services, he had excited much popular jealousy and ill will, arising from the energy of his character and the dignity of his deportment. He was likewise disgusted at what he deemed injustice, in the irregularity of appointing other and junior officers in separate and independent commands within what was considered to be his military district. He accordingly, in October, 1776, tendered to Congress the resignation of his commission; but when Congress came to investigate his services, they found them, says the historian of Washington, far to exceed in value any estimate which had been made of them. They declared that they could not dispense with his services, during the then situation of affairs; and they directed the president of Congress to request him to continue in his command, and they declared their high sense of his services, and their unabated confidence in his attachment to the cause of freedom.

A governor and legislature were chosen in the summer of 1777; and in that trying season, there was not a county in this State, as it then existed, which escaped a visit from the arms of the enemy. To add to the embarrassment of our councils in the extremity of their distress, the inhabitants of the northeast part of the State (now Vermont), which had been represented in the Convention, and just then ingrafted into the Constitution, under the names of the counties of Cumberland and Gloucester, renounced their allegiance, and set up for an independent state. On the thirtieth of June in that year, they were knocking at the door of Congress for a recognition of their independence and an admission into the Union.

The memorable campaign of 1777 was opened by an expedition of the enemy from New-York to Danbury in Connecticut, and the destruction of large quantities of provisions and military means collected and deposited in that town. In the northern quarter, Gen. Burgoyne advanced from Canada through the lakes, with a well-appointed army of 10,000 men; and for a time he dissipated all opposition, and swept every obstacle before him. Gen. Schuyler was still in the command of the whole northern department, and he made every exertion to check the progress of the enemy. He visited in person the different forts, and used the utmost activity in obtaining supplies to enable them to sustain a siege. While at Albany (which was his head-quarters as previously fixed by Congress), busy in accelerating the equipment and march of troops, Ticonderoga being assailed, was suddenly evacuated by Gen. St. Clair. Gen. Schuyler met on the upper Hudson the news of the retreat; and he displayed, says the candid and accurate historian of Washington, the utmost diligence and judgment in that gloomy state of things. He effectually impeded the navigation of Wood creek. He rendered the roads impassable. He removed every kind of provisions and stores beyond the reach of the enemy. He summoned the militia of New-York and New-England to his assistance; and he answered the proclamation of Burgoyne by a counter proclamation, equally addressed to the hopes and fears of the country. Congress, by their resolution of the seventeenth of July, 1777, approved all the acts of Gen. Schuyler in reference to the army at Ticonderoga; but the evacuation of that fortress excited great discontent in the United States, and Gen. Schuyler did not escape his share of the popular clamor, and he was made a victim to appease it. It was deemed expedient to recal the general officers in the northern army, and, in the month of August, he was superseded in the command of that department by the arrival of Gen Gates. The laurels which he was in preparation to win by his judicious and distinguished efforts, and which he would very shortly have attained, were by that removal intercepted from his brow.

Gen. Schuyler felt acutely the discredit of being recalled in the most critical and interesting period of the campaign of 1777, and when the labor and activity of making preparations to repair the disaster of it had been expended by him; and when an opportunity was opening, as he observed, for that resistance and retaliation which might bring glory upon our arms. If error be attributable to the evacuation of Ticonderoga, says the historian of Washington, no portion of it was committed by Gen. Schuyler. But his removal, though unjust and severe as respected himself, was rendered expedient, according to Chief Justice Marshall, as a sacrifice to the prejudices of New-England.

He was present at the capture of Burgoyne, but without any personal command, and the urbanity of his manners, and the chivalric magnanimity of his character, smarting as he was under the extent and severity of his pecuniary losses, was attested by Gen. Burgoyne himself in his speech in 1778 in the British House of Commons. He there declared, that, by his orders, "a very good dwelling-house, exceeding large storehouses, great saw-mills, and other out-buildings, to the value altogether perhaps of 10,000*l*., belonging to Gen. Schuyler, at Saratoga, were destroyed by fire, a few days before the surrender." He said further, that one of the first persons he saw after the convention was signed, was General Schuyler; and when expressing to him his regret at the event which had happened to his property, Gen. Schuyler desired him "to think no more of it, and that the occasion justified it according to the principles and rules of war. He did more," said Burgoyne; "he sent an aid-de-camp to conduct me to Albany, in order, as he expressed it, to procure better quarters than a stranger might be able to find. That gentleman conducted me to a very elegant house, and, to my great surprise, presented me to Mrs. Schuyler and her family. In that house I remained during my whole stay in Albany, with a table with more than twenty covers for me and my friends, and every other possible demonstration of hospitality."

I have several times had the same relation, in substance, from Gen. Schuyler himself; and he said that he remained behind at Saratoga, under the pretext of taking care of the remains of his property, but in reality to avoid giving fresh occasions for calumny and jealousies, by appearing in person with Burgoyne at his own house. It was not until the autumn of 1778, that the conduct of Gen. Schuyler in the campaign of 1777 was submitted to the investigation of a court martial. He was acquitted of every charge with the highest honors, and the sentence was confirmed by Congress. He shortly afterward upon his earnest and repeated solicitations, had leave to retire from the army, and he devoted the remainder of his life to the service of his country in its political councils.

If the military life of Gen. Schuyler was inferior in brilliancy to that of some others of his countrymen, none of them ever surpassed him in fidelity, activity, and devotedness to the service. The characteristic of his measures was utility. They bore the stamp and unerring precision of practical science. There was nothing complicated in his character: it was chaste and severe simplicity; and, take him for all in all, he was one of the wisest and most efficient men, both in military and civil life, that the state or the nation has produced.

He had been elected to Congress in 1777, and he was re-elected in each of the three following years. On his return to Congress, after the termination of his military life, his talents, experience and energy were put in immediate requisition; and in November, 1779, he was appointed to confer with Gen. Washington on the state of the southern department. In 1781, he was in the senate of this State; and wherever he was placed, and whatever might be the business before him, he gave the utmost activity to measures, and left upon them the impression of his prudence and sagacity. In 1789, he was elected to a seat in the first senate of the United States; and when his term of service expired in Congress, he was replaced in the senate of this State. In 1792, he was very active in digesting and bringing to maturity that early and great measure of state policy, the establishment of companies for inland lock navigation. The whole suggestion was the product of his fertile and calculating mind, ever busy in schemes for the public welfare. He was placed at the head of the direction of both of the navigation companies, and his mind was ardently directed for years towards the execution of those liberal plans of internal improvement. In 1796, he urged in his place in the Senate, and afterward published in a pamphlet form, his plan for the improvement of the revenue of this State; and in 1797, his plan was almost literally adopted, and to that we owe the institution of the office of comptroller. In 1797, he was unanimously elected by the two houses of our Legislature, a senator in Congress; and he took leave of the Senate of this State in a liberal and affecting address, which was inserted at large upon their journals.

But the life of this great man was drawing to a close. I formed and cultivated a personal acquaintance with Gen Schuyler while a member of the legislature in 1792, and again in 1796; and from 1799 to his death in the autumn of 1804, I was in habits of constant and friendly intimacy with him, and was honored with the kindest and most grateful attentions. His spirits were cheerful, his conversation most eminently instructive, manners gentle and courteous, and his whole deportment tempered with grace and dignity. His faculties seemed to retain their unimpaired vigor and untiring activity, though he had evidently lost some of his constitutional ardor of temperament and vehemence of feeling. He was sobered by age, chastened by affliction, broken by disease; and yet nothing could surpass the interest excited by the mild radiance of the evening of his days.

GENERAL HAMILTON AT QUARANTINE.

On Monday evening, the 23d September, 1793, the Hon Alexander Hamilton, secretary of the treasury of the United States, and his lady, arrived at Greenbush opposite to this city, from the seat of government. As they were supposed to have been afflicted with the yellow fever then prevalent in Philadelphia, the city physicians, by request, immediately visited them, and on their return published the following certificate:

ALBANY, September 23, 1793.

This is to certify that we have visited Col. Hamilton and his lady, at Greenbush, this evening, and that they are apparently in perfect health; and from every circumstance we do not conceive there can be the least danger of their conveying the infection of the pestilential fever, at present prevalent in Philadelphia, to any of their fellow-citizens. (Signed) Samuel Stringer, W. Mancius, H. Woodruff, W. McClallen, Cornelius Roosa

In consequence of which on Tuesday morning an order was granted by the mayor, that Col. Hamilton and lady be allowed to cross the ferry.

Schuyler Mansion survived the centuries and is now a New York State owned historic site which has seem a boon in tourism since the play on Alexander Hamilton began. Hamilton was married here to Schuyler's daughter.

A portrait of Philip Schuyler. Painted by Jacob H. Lazarus (1822-91) from a miniature painted by John Trumbull. The original painting is on display at the Schuyler Mansion State Historic Site, Albany.

ANCIENT COMMERCE OF ALBANY.

It has been the custom with fancy scribblers, since the triumph of steam, to amuse the public with much *facetiæ* at the expense of the honest *zeevaarderen* who were wont to navigate the Hudson in the last century, till the youngsters of this day have become pretty thoroughly imbued with the idea that the ancient commerce of the river is only worth remembering for the amusement it affords in that way. The real character of the old skippers ought to be rescued from such imputations and their sturdy, honest enterprise placed in its true light. We give below the manifest of the sloop Olive Branch, Captain Abraham Bloodgood, as a sample of what was occasionally done in the way of distant voyages before the Revolution. Capt. Bloodgood is still remembered by some of the older citizens,* as are also most of the consignors, the memory of whom will be singularly enough awakened by this article. The original account of sales of this voyage, from which we copy, is in the possession of Mr. Robert H. Waterman of this city. It affords a very interesting diary of the success of the adventure to Antigua and St. Christopher's with a very curiously assorted cargo of Albany merchandise, consisting of flour, herrings, horses, *one negro man*, and a great variety of the produce of this latitude; in exchange for which he brought back eighty-one pounds of cotton, a much rarer article then than now, some cash, and *much rum*.

Account Sales of the Cargo of the Sloop Olive Branch, in a voyage to the West Indies from New York, commencing Nov. 3d, 1770.

Sold at ANTIGUA, viz:

One ton of Flour, the property of Henry Van Ranslar, weighing Nt. 30C. 1qr. 4lb—sold for 21s. pr. C.—sold to Messrs. Paterson & Hartshorn,	£31 16 02
One ton ditto, the property of John Stevenson weighing, Nt. 30C. 0qr. 10½lb—sold for 21s. 3d. pr. C.—Mr John Lindsay,	32 05 11
Sold one ton ditto, the property of Richard Van Zant, weighing 27C. 0qr. 19lb, for 21s. pr. C.—Paterson and Hartshorn,	29 02 09
One ton ditto the property of Jane Van Howser, weighing 32C. 0qr. 15lb—sold for 21s pr. C.—Patterson and Hartshorn,	34 04 07
One ton ditto the property of Doctr. Samuel Stringer, weighing 31C. 1qr. 14lb.—sold for 21s. 3d. pr. C—Mr. John Lindsay,	33 16 02
One ton ditto, the property of Nicholas Cuyler, weighing 27 C. 2qr. 0lb.—sold for on an average, *a* 21s. 6d pr C.—different people,	29 11 03

* He was the grandfather of Simeon De Witt Bloodgood, late of this city, and resided in the vicinity of the Fort Orange Hotel. He superintended the building of that house for Simeon De Witt, the surveyor-general, while the latter was absent from the city. The original Fort Orange Hotel, it is well known, occupied the site of the old fort of that name, which stood opposite the Steam Boat Landing. The original Fort Orange Hotel fell a victim to the great fire of August, 1848, and a new one has arisen from the ruins.

Ancient Commerce of Albany.

One ton ditto, the property of Peter Silvester, Esqr., 2 barr's, wg 355 Nt. *a* 24s..	4	05	02
1 barr. ditto, sold wg 190lb. Nt *a* 21s............................	2	01	02
13 barr. ditto, wg. 248 Nt. *a* 21s...............................	26	01	05
	£223	04	07

Sales of Fish, viz:

14 barrs. Herring, the property of Col. Philip Schuyler—sold *a* 12s—sold to Bustie Entwitch, Esqr.	8	08	00
1 barr. do—sold Mr Carr,....................................	1	00	00
10 barrs. do., the property of Henry and Robert Lansingh, *a* 12s.—Entwich, Esq..	6	00	00
20 barrs. do., the property of ditto, sold Mr. John Rose, *a* 20s..	20	00	00
3½ barrs ditto, the property of do., sold *a* 20.—Mr. Carr....	3	10	00
	£38	18	00

Sales of Staves, viz:

7050 Nt. Thd. Staves the property of self and comp'y, *a* £8 pr. M..	62	16	00
32 Ducks, sold *a* 33s. pr. doz'n............................	4	08	00
2 Turkeys, *a* 7s...	0	14	00
3 1-2 Bushels of Pense, *a* 9s................................	1	11	06
18 Pine Plank, *a* 2s. 6d.....................................	2	05	00
15 Ditto Boards, *a* 1s. 6d...................................	1	02	06
An Horse Arning..	1	10	00
11 empty water casks, *a* 8s. 3d..............................	4	10	09
10 Caggs Pease sold for Mrs. Lynot.........................	3	00	00
10 ditto do., for do..	2	10	00
2 ditto do., for do,..	0	05	06
2 ditto do., for do..	0	10	00
3 barrs. of Apples sold for Isaac Van Volkenberg, *a* 24s....	3	12	00
2 ditto, do for do. *a* 20s..................................	2	00	00
2 ditto, do. for do. *a* 7s. 6d..............................	0	15	00
20 Geese sold for ditto, *a* 5s..............................	5	00	00
1 ditto sold for do. *a* 4. 6d...............................	0	04	06
2 barrs. Apples, sold for William Salsberry,.................	2	08	00
2 ditto, do. for do. *a* 12s.,...............................	1	04	00
2 ditto, do. for do. *a* 12s.................................	1	04	00
1 ditto do. for do...	1	00	00
30 bunches of Onions, sold for Mr. Alex. Mac Lean, *a* 9d...	1	02	06
2 hhds. ditto, sold for ditto................................	4	09	00
11 Bunches ditto, sold for ditto. *a* 7d.....................	0	06	05
1 Hhd. do. for do. 122 Bunches, *a* 6d.......................	3	01	00
1 Hhd. do. for do. 113 do. *a* 7d............................	3	06	00
150 strings sold at vandue, for do. loose onions	0	13	00
6 empty Hhds. for do. *a* 8s.................................	2	08	00
1 small horse for self and Doctr. Stringer,..................	13	04	00

Sales at St. Christopher's, viz:—

1 Sorrel horse, the property of William Hunn marked P. V. Z.	7	00	00
1 small Mare the property of William Pemberton............	14	00	00

Ancient Commerce of Albany.

1 Bay horse, the property of Francis Vina, marked H. I....	7 00 00
1 Black horse, the property of John Ross, marked I. L. S..	8 00 00
1 Bay horse, the property of Doctor Sam Stringer,.........	13 00 00
1 Sorrel horse the property of Robert Henery..............	17 00 00
1 Dark Bay horse, the property of Henry Glen, marked B. V. B,..	13 10 00
1 Black horse, the property of Mr. Wemp, marked P. M.,..	14 15 00
1 Black horse, the property of Abraham Bloodgood,........	14 00 00
2 horses, the property of Abraham Tenbrook, marked I D. & A. T. B.,..	39 16 00
1 Negroe Man, the property of Mr. Staats,...............	51 00 00
Total,.....................................	£591 01 09

Returns from the WEST INDIAS, viz:

19 Hogsheads Rum for James Bloodgood & Comp'y O. B., containing 2053 gal a 2s 6d............................	256 22 06
Hhd's to contain the above Rum.........................	21 07 06
12 Barr's Limes for do	6 08 00
Cash received at Antigua for freight,...................	15 10 00
9 Hhd's Rum for Sundry Shippers, pr. their several accounts,	145 17 00
81 lb. Cotton, a 6d....................................	2 01 00
	£447 16 00

These ventures to the West Indies seem to have been more common, after the war of the revolution, to Lansingburgh and Hudson, than to Albany, from the fact that the editor of the Albany Gazette, in 1790, marvelled that the citizens of Albany should remain inactive spectators while their neighbors on the north and the south were "participating in all the blessings of this valuable trade." As an instance in the commerce of Lansingburgh, it was announced that the sloop Arabia, Capt. Johnson, which sailed for the West Indies in June, had sailed again in October on her second voyage thither, with a valuable cargo.

On the 12th of April 1791, it was mentioned as a congratulatory event that 40 sail of vessels had arrived at this port in one day, or passed it for Troy and Lansingburgh; that 18 vessels, of which 16 were of from 40 to 80 tons lay at the port of Lansingburgh, and that the sloop Nancy had performed a trip from thence to New York and back in seven days. In November of the same year it was again announced as an extraordinary occurrence, that 42 vessels of from 40 to 100 tons, principally above 70, were at anchor in the port of Albany.

Among other feats of sloop navigation in those days, we are told that Capt. William Van Ingen, of the sloop Cincinnati, sailed from Albany on the 5th December, 1794, and arrived at New York on the 9th; disposed of his cargo, took in a valuable freight, and returned to this port on the 16th. The navigation had then been uninterrupted for nine months, and was still unimpeded by ice.

The examples of speedy voyages which were boasted of in the last century, read a little oddly now, but yet the sloops, under a good wind, were an overmatch for the steamboats for a long time after the latter made their appearance on the river. In the year 1794, one Col. Wm. Colbreath, sheriff of Herkimer, left this city on Sunday morning, on a sloop for New York, and returned on Thursday afternoon, the 11th, having performed the journey in a little more than four days, including a day and a half he was in New York. The feat was perhaps as much a matter of wonder and admiration, as when the steam boat had been so much improved as to make the passage from New York to Albany in 24 hours.

But the most remarkable of all the expeditions from this port, was the

Voyage of an Albany Sloop to China.

In the fall of 1785, the sloop Experiment, 80 tons burden, Capt. Stewart Dean, was fitted out at this port for China. It was very properly considered a hazardous voyage for so small a craft. She was laden with an assorted cargo, for a regular trading expedition, and was the second adventure from the United States to Canton. She left New-York on the 18th December, and was absent eighteen months. Her return trip was made in four months and twelve days, with a cargo consisting principally of teas and nankins. Several pieces of costly damask silk were also brought to order, or for family gifts. One of the heir-looms in the family of a descendant of the mate of the Experiment, residing in Schenectady, is a dress, made of the silk referred to, in the fashion of that day. Capt. Dean also brought home thirteen sets of China ware, to order, for such families as could afford and thought proper to indulge in such luxuries. These articles were so much valued that they have passed from mothers to daughters, down to the present time; and, though much broken and scattered, are objects of curiosity, not only from the associations connected with this singular voyage, but as showing the form and style of China ware sixty years ago. A set which belonged to Capt. Johnson, a revolutionary veteran, whose house stood with its gable to the street, on the corner of South Pearl and Howard streets, where the Centre Market now stands, was divided among his descendants. One set, however, has been preserved nearly complete, and is in the possession of Mrs. Abraham Ten Eyck, in Broadway. These sets being mostly brought to order, had the initials of the owners' names gilded upon each piece.

It was matter of surprise to the natives and Europeans in those seas, to see so small a vessel arrive from a clime so remote from China, and gave them an exalted conception of the enterprise of the citizens of the United States. At some of the ports where the Experiment touched, it is said that she was an object of alarm to the inhabitants, who mistook her for a tender to a fleet of men-of-war. She returned to New-York on Sunday, April 22, 1787, without the loss of a man during the voyage. On her arrival she was visited by at least two-thirds of the citizens, it is said; very few of whom had expected her return.

Capt. Dean made several voyages to China subsequently, when the famous merchant Howqua formed so favorable an opinion of him that he was accustomed to send over a chest of black tea occasionally for the captain, long after the latter had discontinued his voyages. Capt. Dean died in New-work, a few years since, aged 85, at the house of Mr. Roderick Sedgwick.

VISIT OF PETER KALM TO ALBANY, 1749.

The first mention of coleslaw in America (The word Coleslaw comes from the Dutch word kool = cabbage and sla = salad.) was from Swedish botanist Peter Kalm in 1748-49.

He wrote that his landlady Mrs. Visher (Vischer) made *"n unusual salad,"* which *"tasted better than one can imagine, cabbage, cut into long thin strips, dressed with oil (butter) vinegar, salt, and pepper, well mixed to evenly distribute the oil."*

The project of a scientific expedition to our shores, was suggested to the University of Upsala by Linnæus; who desired that the North American provinces should be explored for the purpose of making such observations and collections of seeds and plants, as would improve the husbandry, horticulture, manufactures, arts and sciences of his country. Accordingly Prof. Kalm, a naturalist of one of the Swedish universities, was selected, who left Upsala on the sixteenth of October, 1747; spent six months in England, and arrived at Philadelphia September 26, 1748. He traversed much of the country from Pennsylvania to Canada, and returned to Sweden in 1751, arriving at the place of his destination on the thirteenth of June. He prosecuted his researches with the industry and perseverance of a true friend of science, spending not only the salary and outfit provided by his friends, but so much of his little fortune, that on his return he found himself under the necessity of retrenching, so as to live on a very small pittance. He afterwards resumed his place of professor at Aobo, where, in a small garden of his own, he cultivated and experimented upon many hundred American plants, there being no garden connected with the University. It was in honor of him that the beautiful *Kalmia* received its name, which is still cultivated in European gardens as an ornamental shrub.

Our traveler is more than once rather plain and unreserved in his remarks upon the character and manners of the people of Albany, as they were seen by, or represented to, him. The charge, so often reiterated since his time, of habitual dishonesty in traffic with the Indians, is very bluntly made, although he admits of honorable exceptions to the general rule. We give the old traveler's own version of what he saw and heard, without attempting to smooth any of the asperities of his remarks, which seem to have been made with honesty of purpose, and are much more excusable in him, than in many of the scribblers who have followed in his track. His account is valuable, as representing the condition of the country a century ago.

JUNE the 10th. At noon we left New-York, and sailed up the River Hudson, in a yacht bound for Albany. All this afternoon we saw a whole fleet of little boats returning from New-York, whither they had brought provisions and other goods for sale, which, on account of the extensive commerce of this town, and the great number of its inhabitants, go off very well. About twelve miles from New-York we saw sturgeons (Acipenser sturio), leaping up out of the water, and on the whole passage we met with porpesses in the river. As we proceeded we found the eastern banks of the river very much cultivated; and a number of pretty farms, surrounded with orchards and corn fields, presented themselves to our view. After sailing a little while in the night, we cast our anchor and lay by till the morning, especially as the tide was ebbing with great force.

JUNE the 11th. This morning we continued our voyage up the river, with the tide and a faint breeze. We passed the Highland mountains, which consist of a grey sandstone, and are covered with deciduous trees together with firs and red cedars. The country was unfit for cultivation, being so full of rocks, and accordingly we saw no farms. The wind vanished away about ten o'clock in the morning, and forced us to get forward with our oars, the tide being almost spent. In one place on the western shore we saw a wooden house painted red, and we were told that there was a saw mill further up; but besides this, we did not perceive one farm or any cultivated grounds all this forenoon. We now perceived excessive high and steep mountains on both sides of the river, which echoed back each sound we uttered; yet notwithstanding they were so high and steep, they were covered with small trees. The last of the high western mountains is called Butterhill, after which the country between the mountains grows more spacious: the farms became very numerous, and we had a prospect of many corn-fields between the hills. Whilst we waited for the return of tide and the change of wind, we went on shore. The sassafras-tree (Laurus sassafras) and the chesnut-tree grow here in great abundance. I found the tulip-tree (Liriodendron tulipifera) in some parts of the wood, as likewise the Kalmia latifolia, which was now in full blossom, though the flowers were already withering. Some time after noon the wind arose from southwest, which being a fair wind, we weighed anchor and continued our voyage. We passed by a little neck of land, which projected on the western side in the river, and was called Dance. The name of this place is said to derive its origin from a festival which the Dutch celebrated here in former times, at which they danced and diverted themselves; but once there came a number of Indians, who killed them all. We cast anchor late at night, because the wind ceased and the tide was ebbing. The fireflies passed the river in numbers at night, and sometimes settled upon the rigging.

June the 12th. This morning we proceeded with the tide, but against the wind. The country here in general is low on both sides of the river, consisting of low rocks and stony fields, which, however, are covered with woods. The land is so rocky, stony and poor, that nobody can settle on it or inhabit it, there being no spot fit for a corn field, and for the space of some miles we never perceived one settlement. At eleven o'clock this morning we came to a small island which lies in the middle of the river, and is said to be half way between New-York and Albany. Towards noon it was quite calm, and we went on very slow. Here the land is well cultivated, and full of great corn-fields, especially on the eastern shore. To the west, also, we saw several cultivated places. The Blue mountains are very plainly to be seen here, appearing through the clouds, and towering above all other mountains. The people here make use of a yellow Agaricus, or mushroom, which grows on maple trees, for tinder: that which is found on the red flowering maple (Acer rubrum) is reckoned the best; and the next in goodness is that of the sugar maple (Acer saccharinum), which is sometimes considered equal to the former. At two in the afternoon the wind began to blow from the south, which enabled us to proceed. The country on the eastern side is high, and consists of a well cultivated soil. We had fine cornfields, pretty farms, and good orchards in view. The western shore is likewise somewhat high, but still covered with woods; and we now and then, though seldom, saw one or two little settlements.

June the 13th. The wind favored our voyage during the whole night, so that I had no opportunity of observing the nature of the country,

This morning, at five o'clock, we were but nine English miles from Albany. The country on both sides the river is low, and covered with woods, excepting a few little scattered settlements. Under the high shores of the river are wet meadows covered with sword-grass (Carex), and they formed several little islands. We saw no mountains, and hastened towards Albany. The land on both sides of the river is chiefly low, and more carefully cultivated as we came nearer to Albany. As to the houses which we saw, some were of wood, others of stone. The river is seldom above a musket-shot broad, and in several parts of it are sands, which require great experience for governing the yachts. At eight o'clock in the morning, we arrived at Albany.

All the yachts which ply between Albany and New-York, belong to Albany. They go up and down the River Hudson, as long as it is open and free from ice. They bring from Albany boards or planks, and all sorts of timber, flour, pease, and furs, which they get from the Indians, or which are smuggled from the French. They come home almost empty, and only bring a few merchandises with them, among which rum is the chief. This last is absolutely necessary to the inhabitants of Albany: they cheat the Indians in the fur trade with it; for when the Indians are drunk, they will leave it to the Albanians to fix the price of the furs. The yachts are pretty large, and have a good cabin, in which the passengers can be very commodiously lodged. They are commonly built of red cedar, or of white oak. Frequently the bottom consists of white oak, and the sides of red cedar, because the latter withstands putrefaction much longer than the former. The red cedar is likewise apt to split, when it hits against any thing; and the River Hudson is in many parts full of sands and rocks, against which the keel of the yacht sometimes hits: therefore they choose white oak for the bottom, as being the harder wood, and not splitting so easily; and the bottom being continually under water, is not so much exposed to putrefaction, and holds out longer.

The canoes which the yachts have along with them, are made of a single piece of wood, hollowed out: they are sharp on both ends, frequently three or four fathoms long, and as broad as the thickness of the wood will allow. The people in it do not row sitting, but commonly a fellow stands at each end, with a short oar in his hand, with which he governs and brings the canoe forwards. Those which are made here at Albany, are commonly of the white pine: they can do service for eight or twelve years, especially if they be tarred and painted. At Albany they make them of the white pine, since there is no other wood fit for them: at New-York they are made of the tulip-tree, and in other parts they are made of red or white cedars; but both these trees are so small, in the neighborhood of Albany, that they are unfit for canoes. There are no seats in the canoes; for if they had any, they would be more liable to be overset, as one could not keep the equilibrium so well.

Battoes are another kind of boats, which are much in use at Albany. They are made of boards of white pine. The bottom is flat, that they may row the better in shallow water: they are sharp at both ends, and somewhat higher towards the end than in the middle. They have seats in them, and are rowed as common boats. They are long, yet not all alike; commonly three, and sometimes four fathoms long. The height from the bottom to the top of the board (for the sides stand almost perpendicular) is from twenty inches to two feet, and the breadth in the middle about a yard and six inches. They are chiefly made use of for carrying goods, by means of the rivers, to the Indians; that is, when those rivers are open enough for the battoes to pass through, and when they need not be carried by land a great way. The boats made of the bark of trees break easily by knocking against a stone, and the canoes cannot carry a great cargo, and are easily overset; the battoes are therefore preferable to them both. I saw no boats here like those of Sweden and other parts of Europe.

The frost does frequently a great deal of damage at Albany. There is hardly a month in summer, during which a frost does not happen. The spring comes very late; and in April and May are numerous cold nights, which frequently kill the flowers of trees and kitchen-herbs. It was feared that the blossoms of the apple-trees had been so severely damaged by the frost last May, that next autumn there would be but very few apples. The oak-blossoms are very often killed by the frost in the woods. The autumn here is of long continuance, with warm days and nights. However, the cold nights commonly commence towards the end of September, and are frequent in October. The people are forced to keep their cattle in stables from the middle of November till March or April, and must find them hay during that time.

During summer the wind blows commonly from the south, and brings a great drought along with it. Sometimes it rains a little; and as soon as it has rained, the wind veers to northwest, blowing for several days from that point, and then returning to the south. I have had frequent opportunities of seeing this change of wind happen very exactly, both this year and the following.

JUNE the 15th. The enclosures were made of boards of fir-wood, of which there is abundance in the extensive woods, and many saw-mills to cut into boards.

The several sorts of apple-trees grow very well here, and bear as fine fruit as in any other part of North America. Each farm has a large orchard. They have some apples here which are very large and very palatable: they are sent to New-York, and other places, as a rarity. They make excellent cider, in autumn, in the country round Albany.

All the kinds of cherry-trees, which have been planted here, succeed very well.

Pear-trees do not succeed here. This was complained of in many other parts of North America. But I fear that they do not take sufficient care in the management and planting of them; for I have seen fine pears in several parts of North America.

Peach-trees have often been planted here, and never would succeed well. This was attributed to a worm which lives in the ground, and eats through the root, so that the tree dies. Perhaps the severity of the winter contributes much to it.

They plant no other fruit-trees at Albany, besides these I have mentioned.

They sow as much hemp and flax here, as they want for home consumption.

They sow maize in great abundance: a loose soil is reckoned the best for this purpose, for it will not grow in clay. From half a bushel they reap a hundred bushels. They reckon maize a very good kind of corn, because the shoot recovers after being hurt by the frost. They have had examples here of the shoots dying twice in spring, to the very ground; and yet they shot up again afterwards, and afforded an excellent crop. Maize has likewise the advantage of standing much longer against a drought, than wheat. The larger sort of maize which is commonly sown here, ripens in September.

They sow wheat in the neighborhood of Albany, with great advantage. From one bushel they get twelve sometimes: if the soil be good, they get twenty bushels. If their crop amounts only to ten bushels from one, they think it very trifling. The inhabitants of the country round Albany are Dutch and Germans. The Germans live in several great villages, and sow great quantities of wheat, which is brought to Albany; and from thence they send many yachts laden with flour to New-York. The wheat-flour from Albany is reckoned the best in all North America, except that from Sopus or Kingston, a place between Albany and New-York. All the bread in Albany is made of wheat. At New-York they pay the Albany flour with several shillings more per hundred weight, than that from other places.

Rye is likewise sown here, but not so generally as wheat.

They do not sow much barley here, because they do not reckon the profits very great. Wheat is so plentiful that they make malt of it. In the neighborhood of New-York, I saw great fields sown with barley.

They do not sow more oats than are necessary for their horses.

The Dutch and Germans who live hereabouts, sow pease in great abundance: they succeed very well, and are annually carried to New-York in great quantities. They have been free from insects for a considerable time; but of late years the same beetles which destroy the pease in Pennsylvania, New-Jersey, and the lower parts of the province of New-York, have likewise appeared abundant among the pease here. It is a real loss to this town, and to the other parts of North America, which used to get pease from hence for their own consumption, and that of their sailors. It had been found that if they procured good pease from Albany, and sowed them near Kingston or the lower part of the province of New-York, they succeeded very well the first year, but were so full of worms the second and following years that nobody could or would eat them. Some people put ashes into the pot, among the pease, when they will not boil or soften well; but whether this is wholesome and agreeable to the palate, I do not know.

Potatoes are generally planted. Some people preferred ashes to sand for keeping them in during winter. The Bermuda potatoes (Convolvulus batatas) have likewise been planted here, and succeed pretty well. The greatest difficulty is to keep them during winter; for they generally rot in that season.

The humming bird (Trochilus colubris) comes to this place sometimes, but is rather a scarce bird.

The shingles with which the houses are covered are made of the white pine, which is reckoned as good and as durable, and sometimes better, than the white cedar (Cupressus thyoides). The white pine is found abundant here, in such places where common pines grow in Europe. I have never seen them in the lower parts of the province of New-York, nor in New-Jersey and Pennsylvania. They saw a vast quantity of deal from the white pine on this side of Albany, which are brought down to New-York, and from thence exported.

The woods abound with vines, which likewise grow on the steep banks of the river in surprising quantities. They climbed to the tops of trees on the bank, and bent them by their weight; but where they found no trees, they hung down along the steep shores, and covered them entirely. The grapes are eaten after the frost has attacked them; for they are too sour before: they are not much used any other way.

The vast woods and uninhabited grounds between Albany and Canada contain immense swarms of gnats, which annoy the travelers. To be in some measure secured against these insects, some besmear their face with butter or grease; for the gnats do not like to settle on greasy places. The great heat makes boots very uneasy; but to prevent the gnats from stinging the legs, they wrap some paper round them, under the stockings. Some travelers wear caps which cover the whole face, and have some gauze before the eyes. At night they lie in tents, if they can carry any with them; and make a great fire at the entrance, by the smoke of which the gnats are driven away.

The porpesses seldom go higher up the river Hudson, than the salt water goes; after that, the sturgeons fill their place. It has, however, sometimes happened that porpesses have gone quite up to Albany. There is a report that a whale once came up the river quite to this town.

The fireflies (Lampyris) which are the same that are so common in Pennsylvania during summer, are seen here in abundance every night. They fly up and down in the streets of this town. They come into the houses, if the doors and windows are open.

Several of the Pennsylvanian trees are not to be met with in these woods, viz. Magnolia glauca, the Beaver-tree; Nyssa aquatica, the Tupelo-tree; Liquidambar styraciflua, the Sweet-gum tree; Diospyros virginiana, the Persimon; Liriodendron tulipifera, the Tulip-tree; Juglans nigra, the Black Walnut-tree; Quercus ——, the Swamp Oak; Cercis canadensis, the Salad-tree; Robinia pseudacacia, the Locust-tree; Gleditsia triacanthos, the Honey-locust tree; Annona muricata, the Papaw-tree; Celtis occidentalis, the Nettle-tree; and a number of shrubs, which are never found here. The more northerly situation of the place, the height of the Blue mountains, and the course of the rivers, which flow here southward into the sea, and accordingly carry the seeds of plants from north to south, and not the contrary way, are chiefly the causes that several plants which grow in Pennsylvania can not be found here.

This afternoon I went to see an island which lies in the middle of the river, about a mile below the town. This island is an English mile long, and not above a quarter of a mile broad. It is almost entirely turned into corn fields; and is inhabited by a single planter, who, besides possessing this island, is the owner of two more. Here we saw no woods, except a few trees which were left round the island on the shore, and formed as it were a tall and great hedge. The Red Maple (Acer rubrum) grows in abundance in several places. Its leaves are white or silvery on the under sides, and, when agitated by the wind, they make the tree appear as if it was full of white flowers. The Water-beech (Platanus occidentalis) grows to a great height, and is one of the most shady trees here. The Water-poplar is the most common tree hereabouts, grows exceedingly well on the shores of the river, and is as tall as the tallest of our asps. In summer, it affords the best shade

---

was the reports of whales in the Albany-Troy area that gave a young Herman Melville, living in Lansingburgh at the time, his interest in the subject area. He wrote his first two books, *Typee* (1846) and *Omoo* (1847) while living across from "Whale Island," in his house at 114th St and 1st Ave next to the Hudson River. *Moby Dick* would come a few years later.

for men and cattle against the scorching heat. On the banks of rivers and lakes it is one of the most useful trees, because it holds the soil by its extensive branched roots, and prevents the water from washing it away. The Water-beech and the Elm-tree (Ulmus) serve the same purpose. The wild Prune-trees were plentiful here, and were full of unripe fruit: its wood is not made use of, but its fruit is eaten. Sumach (Rhus glabra) is plentiful here; as also the wild vines, which climb up the trees and creep along the high shores of the river. I was told that the grapes ripen very late, though they were already pretty large. The American Elm tree (Ulmus americana) formed several high hedges. The soil of this island is a rich mould mixed with sand, which is chiefly employed in maize plantations. There were likewise large fields of potatoes. The whole island was leased for one hundred pounds of New-York currency. The person who had taken the lease, again let some greater and some smaller lots of ground to the inhabitants of Albany, for making kitchen-gardens of; and by that means reimbursed himself. Portulack (Portulaca oleracea) grows spontaneously here in great abundance, and looks very well.

JUNE the 20th. The tide in the river Hudson goes about eight or ten English miles above Albany, and consequently runs one hundred and fifty six English miles from the sea. In spring, when the snow melts, there is hardly any flowing near this town; for the great quantity of water which comes from the mountains during that season, occasions a continual ebbing. This likewise happens after heavy rains.

The cold is generally reckoned very severe here. The ice in the river Hudson is commonly three or four feet thick. On the 3d of April, some of the inhabitants crossed the river with six pair of horses. The ice commonly dissolves about the end of March, or beginning of April. Great pieces of ice come down about that time, which sometimes carry with them the houses that stand close to the shore. The water is very high at that time in the river because the ice stops sometimes, and sticks in places where the river is narrow. The water has been often observed to rise three fathom higher than it commonly is in summer. The ground is frozen here in winter to the depth of three, four, or five feet. On the 16th of November the yachts are put up, and about the beginning or middle of April they are in motion again. They are unacquainted with stoves; and their chimneys are so wide that one could drive through them with a cart and horses.

The water of several wells in this town was very cool about this time, but had a kind of acid taste, which was not very agreeable. On a nearer examination, I found an abundance of little insects in it, which were probably Monoculi. Their length was different: some were a geometrical line and an half; others two, and others four lines long. They were very narrow, and of a pale color. The head was blacker and thicker than the other parts of the body, and about the size of a pin's head. The tail was divided into two branches, and each branch terminated in a little black globule. When these insects swim, they proceed in crooked or undulated lines, almost like tadpoles. I poured some of this water into a bowl, and put near a fourth part of rum to it: the monoculi, instead of being affected with it, swam about as briskly as they had done in the water. This shows, that if one makes punch with this water, it must be very strong to kill the monoculi. I think this

Kalm's Visit to Albany in 1749.

> Fortunately, — Albany's water is much more palatable today.

water is not very wholesome for people who are not used to it, though the inhabitants of Albany who drink it every day, say they do not feel the least inconvenience from it. I have been several times obliged to drink water here, in which I have plainly seen monoculi swimming; but I generally felt the next day somewhat like a pea in my throat, or as if I had a swelling there, and this continued for above a week. I felt such swellings this year, both at Albany and in other parts. My servant, Yungstroem, likewise got a great pain in his breast, and a sensation as from a swelling, after drinking water with monoculi in it; but whether these insects occasioned it, or whether it came from some other cause, I can not ascertain. However, I have always endeavored, as much as possible, to do without such water as had monoculi in it. I have found monoculi in very cold water, taken from the deepest wells, in different parts of this country. Perhaps many of our diseases arise from waters of this kind, which we do not sufficiently examine. I have frequently observed abundance of minute insects in water, which has been remarkable for its clearness. Almost each house in Albany has its well, the water of which is applied to common use; but for tea, brewing and washing, they commonly take the water of the river Hudson, which flows close by the town. This water is generally quite muddy, and very warm in summer; and, on that account, it is kept in cellars, in order that the slime may subside, and that the water may cool a little.

We lodged with a gunsmith, who told us that the best charcoals for the forge were made of the Black Pine. The next in goodness, in his opinion, were charcoals made of the Beech-tree. The best and dearest stocks for his muskets were made of the wood of the Wild Cherry-tree; and next to these, he valued those of the Red Maple most. They scarce make use of any other wood for this purpose. The Black Walnut-tree affords excellent wood for stocks; but it does not grow in the neighborhood of Albany.

JUNE the 21st. Next to the town of New-York, Albany is the principal town, or at least the most wealthy, in the province of New-York. It is situated on the declivity of a hill, close to the western shore of the river Hudson, about one hundred and forty-six English miles from New-York. The town extends along the river, which flows here from N.N.E. to S.S.W. The high mountains in the west, above the town, bound the prospect on that side. There are two churches in Albany, an English one and a Dutch one. The Dutch church stands at some distance from the river, on the east side of the market. It is built of stone; and in the middle it has a small steeple, with a bell. It has but one minister, who preaches twice every Sunday. The English church is situated on the hill, at the west end of the market, directly under the fort. It is likewise built of stone, but has no steeple. There was no service at this church at this time, because they had no minister; and all the people understood Dutch, the garrison excepted. The minister of this church has a settled income of one hundred pounds sterling, which he gets from England. The town-hall lies to the southward of the Dutch church, close by the river side. It is a fine building of stone, three stories high. It has a small tower or steeple with a bell, and a gilt ball and vane at the top of it.

The houses in this town are very neat, and partly built with stones covered with shingles of the White Pine. Some are slated with tiles from Holland, because the clay of this neighborhood is not reckoned fit for tiles. Most of the houses are built in the old way, with the gable-end towards the street; a few excepted, which were lately built in the manner now used. A great number of houses were built like those of New-Brunswick, which I have described*; the gable-end being built, towards the street, of bricks, and all the other walls of planks. The outside of the houses is never covered with lime or mortar, nor have I seen it practised in any North-American towns which I have visited; and the walls do not seem to be damaged by the air. The gutters on the roofs reach almost to the middle of the street. This preserves the walls from being damaged by the rain; but is extremely disagreeable in rainy weather for the people in the streets, there being hardly any means of avoiding the water from the gutters. The street-doors are generally in the middle of the houses; and on both sides are seats, on which, during fair weather, the people spend almost the whole day, especially on those which are in the shadow of the houses. In the evening these seats are covered with people of both sexes; but this is rather troublesome, as those who pass by are obliged to greet every body, unless they will shock the politeness of the inhabitants of this town. The streets are broad, and some of them are paved; in some parts they are lined with trees: the long streets are almost parallel to the river, and the others intersect them at right angles. The street which goes between the two churches, is five times broader than the others, and serves as a market place. The streets upon the whole are very dirty, because the people leave their cattle in them during the summer nights. There are two market-places in the town, to which the country people resort twice a week.

The fort lies higher than any other building, on a high steep hill on the west side of the town. It is a great building of stone, surrounded with high and thick walls. Its situation is very bad, as it can only serve to keep off plundering parties, without being able to sustain a siege. There are numerous high hills to the west of the fort, which command it, and from whence one may see all that is done within it. There is commonly an officer and a number of soldiers quartered in it. They say the fort contains a spring of water.

The situation of Albany is very advantageous in regard to trade. The river Hudson, which flows close by it, is from twelve to twenty feet deep. There is not yet any quay made for the better lading of the yachts, because the people feared it would suffer greatly, or be entirely carried away in spring by the ice, which then comes down the river. The vessels which are in use here, may come pretty near the shore in order to be laden, and heavy goods are brought to them upon canoes tied together. Albany carries on a considerable commerce with New-York, chiefly in furs, boards, wheat, flour, pease, several kinds of timber, &c. There is not a place in all the British colonies, the Hudson's Bay settlements excepted, where such quantities of furs and skins are bought of the Indians, as at Albany. Most of the merchants in this town send a

---

* One of the streets is almost entirely inhabited by Dutchmen from Albany, and for that reason they call it Albany street. These Dutch people only keep company among themselves, and seldom or never go amongst the other inhabitants, living as it were quite separate from them.—*Vol. 1. p. 228.*

clerk or agent to Oswego, an English trading town upon the lake Ontario, to which the Indians resort with their furs. I intend to give a more minute account of this place in my journal for the year 1750. The merchants from Albany spend the whole summer at Oswego, and trade with many tribes of Indians who come to them with their goods. Many people have assured me that the Indians are frequently cheated in disposing of their goods, especially when they are in liquor; and that sometimes they do not get one half, or even one tenth of the value of their goods. I have been a witness to several transactions of this kind. The merchants of Albany glory in these tricks, and are highly pleased when they have given a poor Indian a greater portion of brandy than he can bear, and when they can after that get all his goods for mere trifles. The Indians often find, when they are sober again, that they have been cheated: they grumble somewhat, but are soon satisfied when they reflect that they have for once drank as much as they are able, of a liquor which they value beyond any thing else in the whole world; and they are quite insensible to their loss, if they again get a draught of this nectar. Besides this trade at Oswego, a number of Indians come to Albany from several parts, especially from Canada; but from this latter place, they hardly bring any thing but beaver-skins. There is a great penalty in Canada for carrying furs to the English, that trade belonging to the French West India Company; notwithstanding which the French merchants in Canada carry on a considerable smuggling trade. They send their furs, by means of the Indians, to their correspondents at Albany, who purchase it at the price which they have fixed upon with the French merchants. The Indians take in return several kinds of cloth, and other goods, which may be got here at a lower rate than those which are sent to Canada from France.

The greater part of the merchants at Albany have extensive estates in the country, and a great deal of wood. If their estates have a little brook, they do not fail to erect a saw-mill upon it for sawing boards and planks, with which commodity many yachts go during the whole summer to New-York, having scarce any other lading than boards.

Many people at Albany make the wampum of the Indians, which is their ornament and their money, by grinding some kinds of shells and muscles: this is a considerable profit to the inhabitants. I shall speak of this kind of money in the sequel. The extensive trade which the inhabitants of Albany carry on, and their sparing manner of life, in the Dutch way, contribute to the considerable wealth which many of them acquire.

The inhabitants of Albany and its environs are almost all Dutchmen. They speak Dutch, have Dutch preachers, and divine service is performed in that language: their manners are likewise Dutch; their dress is, however, like that of the English. It is well known that the first Europeans who settled in the province of New-York were Dutchmen. During the time that they were the masters of this province, they possessed themselves of New-Sweden*, of which they were jealous. However, the pleasure of possessing this conquered land and their own was but of short duration; for towards the end of 1664, Sir Robert Carre, by order of King Charles the second, went to New-York, then New Amsterdam, and took it. Soon after Col. Nichols went to Albany, which

* New-Jersey and a part of Pennsylvania were formerly comprised under this name.

then bore the name of Fort Orange, and upon taking it, named it Albany, from the Duke of York's Scotch title. The Dutch inhabitants were allowed either to continue where they were, and, under the protection of the English, to enjoy all their former privileges; or to leave the country. The greater part of them chose to stay, and from them the Dutchmen are descended, who now live in the province of New-York, and who possess the greatest and best estates in that province.

The avarice and selfishness of the inhabitants of Albany are very well known throughout all North America, by the English, by the French, and even by the Dutch in the lower part of New-York province. If a Jew, who understands the art of getting forward perfectly well, should settle amongst them, they would not fail to ruin him. For this reason nobody comes to this place without the most pressing necessity; and therefore I was asked, in several places, what induced me to go to it two years one after another. I likewise found that the judgment, which people formed of them, was not without foundation. For though they seldom see any strangers (except those who go from the British colonies to Canada and back again), and one might therefore expect to find victuals and accommodation for travelers cheaper than in places where travelers always resort to; yet I experienced the contrary. I was here obliged to pay for every thing twice, thrice, and four times as dear as in any part of North America which I have passed through. If I wanted their assistance, I was obliged to pay them very well for it; and when I wanted to purchase any thing, or to be helped in some case or other, I could presently see what kind of blood ran in their veins; for they either fixed exorbitant prices for their services, or were very backward to assist me. Such was this people in general. However, there were some amongst them who equaled any in North America, or any where else, in politeness, equity, goodness, and readiness to serve and to oblige; but their number fell far short of that of the former. If I may be allowed to declare my conjectures, the origin of the inhabitants of Albany and its neighborhood seems to me to be as follows: Whilst the Dutch possessed this country, and intended to people it, the government took up a pack of vagabonds, of which they intended to clear the country, and sent them along with a number of other settlers to this province. The vagabonds were sent far from the other colonists, upon the borders towards the Indians and other enemies; and a few honest families were persuaded to go with them, in order to keep them in bounds. I can not any other way account for the difference between the inhabitants of Albany, and the other descendants of so respectable a nation as the Dutch, who are settled in the lower part of New-York province. The latter are civil, obliging, just in the prices, and sincere; and though they are not ceremonious, yet they are well meaning and honest, and their promises are to be relied on.

The behavior of the inhabitants of Albany, during the war between England and France, which was ended with the peace of Aix la Chapelle, has, among several other causes, contributed to make them the object of hatred in all the British colonies, but more especially in New-England. For at the beginning of that war, when the Indians of both parties had received orders to commence hostilities, the French engaged theirs to attack the inhabitants of New-England; which they faithfully executed, killing every body they met with, and carrying off whatever they found. During this time the people of Albany remained neutral, and carried on a great trade with the very Indians who murdered the inhabitants of New-England. The plate, such as silver spoons, bowls, cups, &c., of which the Indians robbed the houses in New-England, was carried to Albany for sale. The people of that town bought up these silver vessels, though the names of the owners were graved on many of them; and encouraged the Indians to get more of them, promising to pay them well, and whatever they would demand. This was afterwards interpreted by the inhabitants of New-England, as if the Albanians encouraged the Indians to kill more of the people, who were in a manner their brothers, and who were subjects of the same crown. Upon the first news of this behavior, which the Indians themselves spread in New-England, the inhabitants of the latter province were greatly incensed, and threatened that the first step they would take in another war would be to burn Albany and the adjacent parts. In the present war it will sufficiently appear how backward the other British provinces in America are in assisting Albany, and the neighboring places, in case of an attack from the French or Indians. The hatred which the English bear against the people at Albany is very great, but that of the Albanians against the English is carried to a ten times higher degree. This hatred has subsisted ever since the time when the English conquered this country, and is not yet extinguished, though they could never have got such advantages under the Dutch government as they have obtained under that of the English; for, in a manner, their privileges are greater than those of Englishmen.

The inhabitants of Albany are much more sparing than the English. The meat which is served up is often insufficient to satisfy the stomach, and the bowl does not circulate so freely as amongst the English. The women are perfectly well acquainted with economy: they rise early, go to sleep very late, and are almost over nice and cleanly in regard to the floor, which is frequently scoured several times in the week. The servants in the town are chiefly negroes. Some of the inhabitants wear their own hair, but it is very short, without a bag or queue, which are looked upon as the characteristics of Frenchmen; and as I wore my hair in a bag the first day I came here from Canada, I was surrounded with children, who called me Frenchman and some of the boldest offered to pull at my French dress.

Their meat, and manner of dressing it, is very different from that of the English. Their breakfast is tea, commonly without milk. About thirty or forty years ago, tea was unknown to them, and they breakfasted either upon bread and butter or bread and milk. They never put sugar into the cup, but take a small bit of it into their mouths whilst they drink. Along with the tea they eat bread and butter, with slices of hung beef. Coffee is not usual here: they breakfast generally about seven. Their dinner is buttermilk and bread, to which they sometimes add sugar and then it is a delicious dish for them; or fresh milk and bread; or boiled or roasted flesh. They sometimes make use of buttermilk instead of fresh milk, to boil a thin kind of porridge with, which tastes very sour, but not disagreeable in hot weather. To each dinner they have a great sallad, prepared with abundance of vinegar and very little or no oil. They frequently eat buttermilk, bread and sallad, one mouthful after another. Their supper is generally bread and butter, and milk and bread   They sometimes eat cheese at breakfast, and at dinner: it is not in slices, but scraped or rasped, so as to resemble coarse flour, which they pretend adds to the good taste of cheese.   They commonly drink very small beer, or pure water.

The governor of New-York often confers at Albany with the Indians of the Five Nations, or the Iroquese (Mohawks, Senekas, Cayugaws, Onondagoes and Onidoes), especially when they intend either to make war upon, or to continue a war against the French. Sometimes their deliberations likewise turn upon their conversion to the christian religion; and it appears by the answer of one of the Indian chiefs, or sachems, to Gov. Hunter, at a conference in this town, that the English do not pay so much attention to a work of so much consequence, as the French do; and that they do not send such able men to instruct the Indians, as they ought to do. For after Gov. Hunter had presented these Indians, by order of Queen Anne, with many clothes and other presents, of which they were fond, he intended to convince them still more of her Majesty's good will and care for them, by adding, " that their good mother, the Queen, had not only generously provided them with fine clothes for their bodies, but likewise intended to adorn their souls, by the preaching of the gospel; and that to this purpose, some ministers should be sent to them to instruct them." The governor had scarce ended, when one of the oldest sachems got up and answered, " that in the name of all the Indians, he thanked their gracious good queen and mother for the fine clothes she had sent them ; but that in regard to the ministers, they had already had some among them (whom he likewise named), who, instead of preaching the holy gospel to them, had taught them to drink to excess, to cheat, and to quarrel among themselves." He then entreated the governor to take from them these preachers, and a number of Europeans who resided amongst them; for before they were come among them, the Indians had been an honest, sober and innocent people, but most of them became rogues now; that they had formerly had the fear of God, but that they hardly believed his existence at present; that if he (the governor) would do them any favor, he should send two or three blacksmiths amongst them, to teach them to forge iron, in which they were unexperienced. The governor could not forbear laughing at this extraordinary speech. I think the words of St. Paul not wholly inapplicable on this occasion: " For the name of God is blasphemed amongst the Gentiles, through you."—Rom. ii. 24.

JUNE the 21st. About five o'clock in the afternoon we left Albany, and proceeded towards Canada. We had two men with us, who were to accompany us to the first French place, which is Fort St. Frederick, or, as the English call it, Crown Point. For this service each of them was to receive five pounds of New-York currency, besides which I was to provide them with victuals. This is the common price here ; and he that does not choose to conform to it, is obliged to travel alone. We were forced to take up with a canoe, as we could get neither battoes nor boats of bark ; and as there was a good road along the west side of the river Hudson, we left the men to row forwards in the canoe, and we went along it on the shore, that we might be better able to examine it and its curiosities with greater accuracy. It is very incommodious to row in these canoes; for one stands at each end, and pushes the boat forwards. They commonly keep close to the shore, that they may be able to reach the ground easily. Thus the rowers are forced to stand upright, whilst they row in a canoe. We kept along the shore all the evening: towards the river it consisted of great hills, and next to the water grew the trees, which I have before mentioned, and which likewise are to be met with on the shores of the isle in the river situate below Albany. The easterly shore of the river is uncultivated, woody and hily; but the western is flat, cultivated, and chiefly turned into corn-fields, which had no drains, though they wanted them in some places. It appeared very plainly here that the river had formerly been broader; for there is a sloping bank on the corn fields, at about thirty yards distance from the river, with which it always runs parallel. From this it sufficiently appears that the rising ground formerly was the shore of the river, and the corn-fields its bed. As a further proof, it may be added that the same shells which abound on the present shore of the river, and are not applied to any use by the inhabitants, lie plentifully scattered on these fields. I cannot say whether this change was occasioned by the diminishing of the water in the river, or by its washing some earth down the river and carrying it to its sides, or by the river's cutting deeper in on the sides.

THE FAR WEST OF 1795.

Actually it was — Schenectady, 16 miles to the west of Albany that was the "far west." It was the most western European settlement in America at the time before the American Revolution.

A treaty of peace and friendship was concluded at Canandaigua, in 1794, between the United States and the Six Nations, by which the danger of depredations upon settlers was removed, and a large and fertile region opened to the surplus population of the New England States. The Genesee Valley immediately became an El Dorado to the people of those states. The want of roads, and better means of conveyance, in many cases, than ox sleds, rendered it a far off country; but the fame of its wheat fields induced multitudes to brave every hardship in subduing the wilderness. The principal avenue to that country lay through the city of Albany, and the tide of emigration in the winter of 1795 was a great phenomenon to its inhabitants. It was estimated that 1200 sleighs, freighted with men, women, children and furniture, passed through the city in three days of the month of February. On the 28th of that month, a citizen undertook to ascertain the amount of a single day's travel, and counted 500 sleighs from sunrise to sunset — those passing in the night not being enumerated.

A RARE BIRD.

The citizens of Albany were entertained, in November 1788, with the extraordinary sight of an "uncommon bird," killed at Saratoga and sent down as a rarity. "The distance from the tip of one wing to the other, when both were extended, was 9 feet 2 inches; the mouth was large enough to contain the head of a boy ten years old, and the throat so capacious as to admit the foot and leg of a man, boot and all." No one could decide what species the stranger belonged to, till, the counsel of Dr. Mitchell of New-York being called in, it was decided to be a pelican—perhaps the only one that ever extended his discoveries to this region.

HARMANUS BLEECKER.

Mr. Bleecker was a descendant of the celebrated Jan Jansen Bleecker, the ancestor, it is believed, of all who bear that name in this State. Jacob Bleecker, the father of Harmanus, was a merchant and a much esteemed citizen. After having received a classical education, Mr. Bleecker entered upon the study of the law in the office of John V. Henry and James Emott, who were eminent counsellors of the day; and was admitted to practice at the bar of this State in 1801, in the 22d year of his age. He entered into partnership with Theodore Sedgwick, late of Stockbridge; which connection endured for many years, and proved honorable and lucrative to both. Mr. Bleecker in particular became known throughout the State as an eminent advocate, and his name is frequently to be found on the pages of the reports of the days when Kent, and Spencer, and Thompson, and Van Ness, were the great luminaries of the science.*

He was also successful in his political career. Having been several years a member of assembly for this county, he was in 1810 elected to Congress, where he served during the stormy period of the last war with Great Britain, and acting with the federal party, was one of those who opposed the war. At various times he was honored with other important trusts, indicative of the high opinion entertained of him. His name is found in the first board of managers of the Albany Bible Society, incorporated in 1811. He was a regent of the University for several years; a commissioner on the part of this state, for settling the boundary between New-York and New-Jersey. Gov. Clinton, to whom he had been actively opposed for many years previous, offered him the post of adjutant general, which he declined, while he appreciated the magnanimity that dictated the proposal. On the accession of Mr. Van Buren to the presidency, Mr. Bleecker was sent to the Hague as the American minister, where he made an impression that will not be effaced in our generation. It was during his residence at the Hague that he married a lady of the country, Miss Sebastiana Cornelia Mentz, with whom he visited Holland once after the close of his mission.

---

* It will be seen, in the following list of students who acquired their profession in his office, that it includes many who have, by their talents and worth, risen to places of eminence and distinction.

Henry D. Sedgwick, Robert Sedgwick, Solomon Southwick, John W. Taylor (Speaker of the House of Representatives, 1825-26). David Rust, Henry Jones, Abraham Holdridge, Cornelius R. D Lansing, Jacob Dox, Peter P. J. Keon, Jacob Sutherland (Judge of old Supreme Court). Henry W. Channing, John Rodman, Thomas D. Higgins, Sterling Goodenow, Isaac Truax, Gideon Hawley, Peter Gansevoort, Henry Starr, David Raymond, Ebenezer Baldwin, William Darling, Abraham Schuyler, Henry H Fuller, John Porter, E. P. Storrs, James Dexter, Gilbert L Thompson, James C. Bloodgood, John D. Crocker, Cornelius Gates, Frederick Matthews, Bargood E Hand, Richard V. De Witt, Frederick Whittlesey (Judge of Supreme Court), N N. Hall, Henry J. Linn, C. V. S. Kane, Metcalf Yates, Hamilton Bogart, John B. Van Schaick, Augustus Beardslee, Henry G. Wheaton, S V. R. Bleecker, W. Duer Henderson, Charles Fenno Hoffman, Bradford R. Wood, David Dudley Field, D A Noble, Philip S. Van Rensselaer, Harvey Hyde, Charles Walsh, S. Cook, P. V. S. Wendover, E T. T. Martin, Israel T. Hatch, Leonard Bement, W. H. Bogart, John B. Luce, Charlemagne Tower, John James Kane, Henry H. Martin, Charles N. Rowley, Cambridge Livingston, John W, Bradford, Francis Randall.

Mr. Bleecker was one of the most cultivated gentlemen in the state. After his return from Holland, he continued the study of literature in all its varied departments, and paid much attention to theology. Though by association, and by family and inherited sympathies, identified with the older times and people of this country, no man entered more zealously into every progress of the times, and rejoiced that for the great multitude of the people the advancing years were, more and more, years of education and comfort and prosperity. A truer republican our country did not possess; and he carried with him in his diplomatic career, and in his residence abroad, the dignity and the simplicity of an American, never ceasing in every proper and courteous way to commend his country and his country's institutions to the respect of the European. He spoke and wrote the Dutch language with perfect purity and elegance; which, united to his engaging manners and irresistible dignity, procured for him, on retiring from his mission at the Hague, an official expression of regret at his departure from the Dutch government, a compliment the more flattering as it is almost without a precedent.

The Hon. Harmanus Bleecker died at his residence on the corner of Chapel and Steuben streets, on the 19th of July, at the age of seventy years. The ancient house in which he was born on the 19th of October, 1779, stood upon the next lot south, and was taken down a few years ago, when he erected the block which now occupies its site. He was possessed of an ample fortune, which enabled him to consult his taste in the occupation of his time during the latter years of his life, a privilege of which he availed himself wisely.

The pedigree of his branch of the family is as follows:

I. JAN JANSEN BLEECKER, a native of Meppel, in the province of Overyssel, Holland, came to New-Amsterdam in 1658, and subsequently settled at Albany. He was one of the first aldermen named in the charter of Albany, 1686; was recorder from 1696 to 1699, and mayor in 1700. Died Nov 21, 1732, aged 91. In 1667 he married Margaret, daughter of Rutger Jacob-en. His children were JOHANNES, Rutger (recorder 1725, mayor 1726 to 1728), Nicholas, Hendrick, Catharine, Jane, Margaret, Rachel.

II. JOHANNES, born 1668; married Anna Koster 1693; succeeded his father as recorder of Albany 1700, and as mayor 1701; member of the general assembly 1701 and 1702; died Dec. 20, 1738, aged 70. His children were, Johannes, Gertrude, Nicholas, Hendrick, Margaretta, Anna, JACOB, Anthony.

III. JACOB, born March 1, 1715; married Margaret Ten Eyck; died 1747, leaving one son, JACOB.

IV. JACOB, born July 22, 1747; married Elizabeth Wendell 1776. He left two sons, Jacob I. (died unmarried), and HARMANUS.

V. HARMANUS, born Oct. 9, 1779; married Sebastiana Cornelia Mentz, daughter of Dirk Mentz and Immetje Keyser of Holland; died, July 19, 1849, without issue.

The armorial ensigns of the family are thus described:

Arms, az., two embattled chevrons or, empaling, arg. a rose branch ppr. *Crest*, a phæon, or.

VANDERHEYDEN PALACE.
Erected, 1725; Demolished, 1833.

Washington Irving, — famous for short stories like *Rip Van Winkle* (1819) and The Legends of Sleepy Hollow (1820), built his Dutch house in Tarrytown, NY using part of the Albany palace. One of the palace's weathervane, a running horse, is still in possession of the historic site. The southern gable is an exact reproduction of the palace.

This venerated edifice was situated in North Pearl street, the second lot below the corner of Maiden lane, on the site now occupied by the Baptist church. It was built in 1725 by Johannes Beekman, a worthy burgher of the day. The bricks were imported from Holland, as were those of many of the houses erected at that time; and it is supposed to have been, at the time of its demolition, one of the best specimens of the ancient Dutch architecture remaining in the state. It was occupied by Mr. Beekman as his family residence until his death in 1756, after which his two daughters continued to reside in it until their marriage, a short time previous to the war of the revolution. The eldest connected herself with a gentleman of the name of Bain, belonging to the English army, and the youngest to Mr John McCrea. The former moving shortly after her marriage to the West Indies, McCrea and his wife continued to occupy the mansion as their place of abode until after the war commenced, when they removed from the city, and the house was rented. It was afterwards occupied by Mr. George Merchant as an academy; and some eminent professional men are still left to relate the interesting events of many happy hours they spent under his tuition. In 1778 the mansion was purchased by Mr. Jacob Vanderheyden, for the consideration of £1158, lawful money of New York ($2895,) and it was from this gentleman that it received the appellation by which it has since been familiarly known, that of the *Vanderheyden Palace*. It continued to be used as an academy until the great fire of 1797, when the dwelling in which Mr. Vanderheyden lived being consumed, he took up his residence in this house, and continued to occupy it till his death, which occurred in 1820. His family remained there but a few years beyond that event, after which the tenants became as various as they were numerous. The site having been selected by the Baptist society for the location of a new church, this venerable edifice, having stood one hundred and eight years, bowed to the spirit of improvement. Its dimensions were 50 feet front by 20 in depth, having a hall and two rooms on a floor. Although it had been somewhat modernized internally, the massive beams and braces projecting into the rooms, the ancient wainscoting, and the iron figures on the gable ends, involuntarily carried the mind back to dwell upon the days of old. It arrested the antiquarian fancy of Washington Irving, and is described by him in the story of Dolph Heyliger, in Bracebridge Hall, as the residence of Heer Antony Vanderheyden. The weatherfane, a horse under great stress of speed, now glitters above the peaked turret of the portal at Sunny Side, Mr. Irving having secured that relic from the hands of the destroyer, to adorn his unique country seat.

Of the gable enders that graced Pearl street in the palmy days of the Vanderheyden Palace, when the street was yet carpeted with verdure, instead of paving stones, but two remain on the same side of the way, another on the corner of Columbia, and one on the corner of State street, about which we shall have occasion to speak hereafter.

VANDERHEYDEN PALACE.

This gable end on Irving's Sunnyside is a reproduction of the original Vanderheyden Palace and the original running horse weathervane can be seen atop.

THE WENDELL HOUSE,

No. 98 State Street: Erected 1716; Demolished 1841.

This ancient edifice stood on the south side of State street, the easterly line being a little over one hundred feet west of the westerly line of South Pearl street. It was built and occupied by Harmanus Wendell, in the year 1716, as was indicated by the iron figures upon its front, after the manner of the day. The figures are barely observable in the woodcut on close inspection; the engraver not having given them sufficient prominence. Mr. Wendell was engaged in the fur trade, and no doubt many a curious and characteristic scene of Dutch and Indian traffic was carried on within its walls. The building was torn down on the sixth day of September, 1841, for the purpose of erecting a four story brick store on its site, by Messrs. John V. L. Pruyn and Henry H. Martin, the present owners of the property. The door and bow windows in the first story, and the steps in front exhibit the lower portion of the building in its original situation, as ascertained from persons who

The Wendell House around 1805 as painted by James Eights around 1850. To the left is the Stevenson House. See page 283.

Albany continued to have many of their Dutch architectural landmarks destroyed in the nineteenth and first half of the twentieth century. This Dutch Gable House at 674 Broadway was destroyed in the 1940s.

occupied it long since. Some years before its demolition, the steps were removed, and the doors and windows lengthened so as to conform to the level of the street; previously to which, a covered passage way had been constructed for the side entrance, with a door in front, which was its situation when it was taken down. The Stevenson House, described on a subsequent page, and razed at the same time, adjoined the lot on the east, with the passage way referred to between. This relic of the olden time had become so dilapidated by its great age, and the walls so impaired by the excavations made around them, as to render its removal necessary. The editor of the *Albany Argus* alluded to the subject at the time, and made the following retrospective observations in connection with the event:

"What changes has it not witnessed in its life of one hundred and twenty-five years! Then, the great and far west, save the French posts at Detroit, Michilimackinac, Chicago and Du Quesne (Pittsburgh), the French settlements at New Orleans and at Natchez, and a few scattered hamlets or posts on the Ohio and Illinois, was inhabited solely by the nations and tribes of Indians, from the Six Nations of our own colony and region, to the more remote Ottawas, Wyandots, Ottagamies, Hurons, Chippewas, &c. Only thirty-five years before, the adventurous La Salle had launched the first vessel on the great lakes, had reached the Mississippi, and traced it to its mouth. It was only a few years after the first great council of all the distinguished chiefs of the various tribes from Quebec to the Mississippi had been convened at Montreal, with barbaric pomp and imposing ceremonial, and the power of New France strengthened by new alliances with the natives. It was fifteen years after the expedition under M. Cadillac had established the post at Detroit. It was only three years after the chiefs of the Ottawas, having been invited to Albany, returned, disaffected to the French, and at once commenced the siege of Detroit. It was nearly half a century before the English conquest of New-France and the Pontiac war, or gigantic confederation of that remarkable chief. The principal seats of the fur trade were Michilimackinac, Montreal and Albany; and the traffic between the two latter places was as active and prosperous as it could be, in the hands of the subjects of rival powers.

"The city (ancient Beverwyck) and the manorial settlement, including Fort Orange, were little else than a fortified village, with the old church at the foot and in the middle of State street, a few stores and trading places in Chapel street (then Barrack street), and scattered residences on the margin of the river and in the vicinity of Fort Orange, afterwards called Court, now Market street. The city charter had then been granted about thirty years; and the appearance of the city is described as being that of a small town, with two principal streets crossing each other, in one of which (State street) were all the public buildings, viz., the townhouse, two churches (English and Dutch), guard-house, market, &c. There were three docks: lower, or king's dock, middle and upper, and vessels were unloaded by the aid of canoes lashed together, on which a platform was built and the goods placed. The population may have numbered 1000: it was 3506 seventy-four years afterwards (in 1790).

"In the progress of improvement, these two buildings are soon to give place to a spacious structure, for stores, public rooms, &c. &c. We confess that we regret the disappearance of these antique remains of the early history of our city. Upon the demolition of the ancient tenement of the fur dealer, which will quickly follow its associate at the corner of North Pearl and Steuben streets*, not more than one of that age will remain in State street, and scarcely another in the city; although a few in North Pearl street and in the Colonie, of *an uncertain age*, but full a century in years, will continue to present their gables to the eyes of the curious. We regret it, because, go where you will in this new country, you see only the impress and handiwork of the present age. Even in places the earliest settled in the country—and where the trace and fashion of its dawn exist if any where—every thing ancient, every thing venerable, every memorial of other times, is swept away, or carefully concealed under modern alterations or thick strata of paint and whitewash; as if it were a sin to recal old things and scenes, or a duty to dwell only among the very latest devices of the architect and the calculator of rents and profits."

MEETING OF UNITED STATES CREDITORS.

On the 30th September, 1782, a meeting of the creditors of the United States, in the state of New York, was held in the City Hall in Albany, Philip Schuyler, chairman; the object of which was to lay their claims before the public, in an address, and to suggest a general convention of deputies from the public creditors of each state, to devise ways and means of payment. Philip Schuyler, Abraham Ten Broeck, Leonard Gansevoort, John N. Bleecker, Robert McClallen, and Lucas Van Veghten were appointed to receive communications and correspond with other committees. Alluding to the successive violations of the public engagements, and a recent and aggravating one, the withholding the interest hitherto paid by bills on France, upon the moneys loaned previous to March 1st, 1778, they observe, "that its weight is most oppressively felt by those whose zeal in the cause, and confidence in their country have been most conspicuous; who in times of danger have demonstrated their concern for the common safety, by voluntary deposits, in some instances of the whole, in others of a large part of their fortunes, in the public funds, and who now, many of them at least, feel themselves reduced from affluence to indigence, from circumstances of ease and plenty to penury and unaffected distress. They can not but add that there are others, not less meritorious, who have experienced perhaps even a worse fate; those who having made subsequent loans, have long since seen the payment of interest cease; and those, who, when the distresses of the army have had no resource but in the patriotism of individuals, have cheerfully parted with the fruits of their industry, scarcely reserving a sufficiency for the subsistence of their own families, without any compensation since, besides the consciousness of having been the benefactors of their country."

* Now occupied by the stately residence of Dr. Barent P. Staats.

THE STEVENSON HOUSE.
Erected 1780; Demolished 1841.

The above engraving will be recognized by many as an old acquaintance. It was a massy and spacious edifice, commenced by the late John Stevenson, Esq., at the time of the breaking out of the American revolution, and finished about 1780, fifteen years after the completion of the present Mansion House of Stephen Van Rensselaer. For nearly half a century it was the mansion of the Stevenson family, and was occupied by Mr. Van Buren during the period he held the office of governor of this state. It was afterwards rented as a hotel, and finally became the *headquarters* or committee rooms of the democratic party of the city, when its walls resounded to the eloquence of Counsellor Gaffney, and other favorite orators of the day. Its architecture was of a style that became popular at a period subsequent to that of the erection of its neighbor; a few specimens of which still remain in different parts of the city.

It was in the adjoining building, on the left, that Mr. James Stevenson commenced the practice of the law, and that Mr. John Lovett had his office. It was in that building also that Mr. Jacob Green, afterwards professor of chemistry in Jefferson College, Philadelphia, for some time kept a bookstore; and it was in this bookstore that Mr. John T. Norton, now a retired merchant, made his debut in Albany, as a clerk.

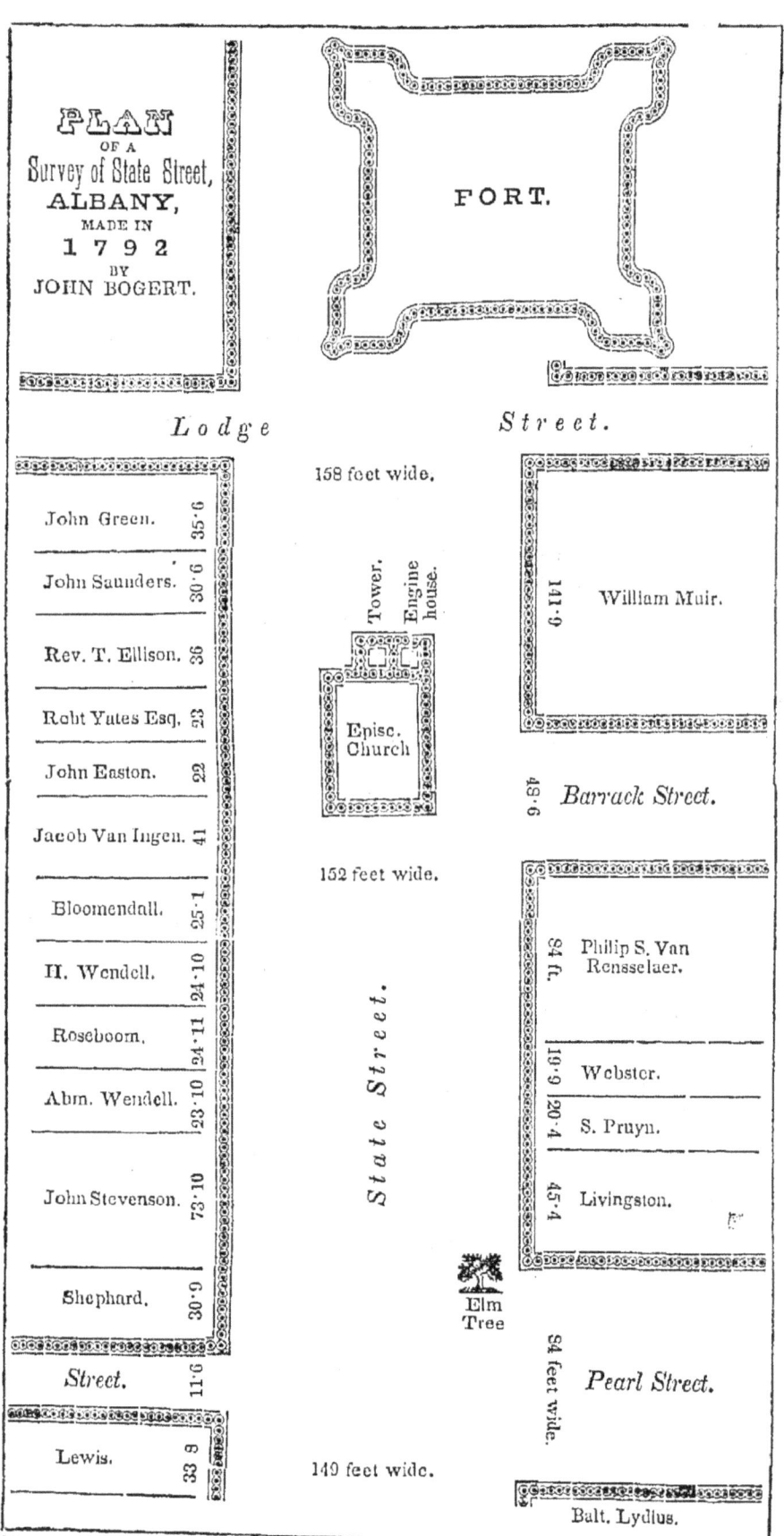

STATE STREET IN 1792.

In connection with the foregoing, a diagram of the section of State street lying between Pearl and Lodge streets, is introduced. The original map appears to have been made from actual survey by John Bogert, in 1792. The dimensions of the lots upon State street, and the name of the owners at that time, are given; together with the location of the Episcopal Church and the Fort, edifices which disappeared half a century ago.

The old English Church, which stood in the centre of State street opposite Barrack, now Chapel street, was erected in 1715. It was alluded to by Kalm thirty-four years afterwards as being built of stone, without a steeple, and standing directly under the Fort. The tower on the west end was a distinct structure, erected after 1750. The bell was cast in England, and is still used in St Peter's Church, bearing this inscription: "St. Peter's Church in Albany, 1751; J. Ogilvie, minister; J. Stevenson, E. Collins, wardens." The Rev. Thomas Ellison was the last rector who officiated in the old church. We hope to have it in our power to present a history of this church in the next volume.

On the northwest corner of the church, and directly in contact with it, stood the City Fire Engine House. The engine kept within it was the only one which the authorities provided for the protection of the city against fire. It is represented to have been a very superior machine, and was one of the only two manufactured by the elder John Mason, a celebrated machinist of Philadelphia — its counterpart was for a long time in possession of the Diligent Fire Company of that city.

As we contemplate the map, and reflect upon the changes which have been wrought upon the owners and occupants of these lots during the last half century, a melancholy yet agreeable interest is awakened. A multitude of thoughts will present themselves to the octogenarian, skilled in antique lore and the traditions of early times, of scenes that will remain unwritten. Beginning at the foot of the map on the south side, the name of Mr. Lewis marks the site of the City Tavern, then, and until the Tontine was opened by Matthew Gregory, the great house of the day. It was removed to open the street, which was a narrow arched passage way at this time, having a gate to protect the entrance into the street below, known as Washington street, now South Pearl. A part or the whole of the Shepard lot was subsequently taken in extending the breadth of the street.

The street in the rear of the lots above Pearl street, is described in a Dutch deed of 1680, given by Dr Abram Staats to the Lutheran Church, as "the old road belonging to Mr. Pretty, Jacob Sanders, Johannes Wendell, Myndert Harmense, and Hendrick Cuyler. Mr. Pretty was the first sheriff under the English charter, and occupied the whole or a part of the large lot afterwards owned by Mr. John Stevenson.

Of the Wendell house we have already spoken. In the rear of it was the printing office of Solomon Southwick, where the *Albany Register* was issued, and the state printing performed, by him, and is still standing.

The house and lot designated as the premises of Mr. Roseboom, were for a time the residence of Thomas Shipboy, another eminent merchant, who died in the year 1798. The old edifice is concealed behind a modern front, but its *zuydelyk* aspect indicates its origin unmistakeably. Mr. Shipboy afterwards occupied the house No. 56 State street, subsequently the store of the late Christian Miller — the strong walls of which have also been carried up so as to present the appearance of a modern structure.

The two next are the site of the American Hotel, belonging to the descendants of the late William James. They were occupied by the great printing and publishing house of the Hosfords, which went down in 1825.

The Van Ingen property is now the residence of Erastus Corning, Esq.

The next belongs to the estate of the late William Gould, who erected a graceful modern edifice, and acquired a handsome fortune upon the premises as a law bookseller.

The house of Judge Yates is still standing, and was occupied by his son, John Van Ness Yates, of distinguished memory, until his death, which occurred a few years ago.

The house occupied by Mr. Ellison is also still standing, looking a little the worse for its age, although it never had much pretension to elegance. It is now the property of Philip Wendell, Esq.; the upper part occupied by him as a dwelling, and the lower part has long been the well known chair factory of L. McChesney.

The late Killian K. Van Rensselaer married a descendant of Mr. John Sanders, of Schenectady, and inherited the lot which bears the name of the latter on the map. Mr. Van Rensselaer erected a large dwelling-house upon the premises, in which he resided till his death a few years ago, since which it has been occupied by Mrs. Brinckerhoff as a ladies' boarding school.

A large wooden building, which was built before the revolution, and we believe for a time used as a tavern, occupied the corner of John Green. In this building the Albany Academy was opened in 1815. It was burnt in 1847; when a substantial brick edifice was erected upon its site, by the heirs of the late Killian K. Van Rensselaer, to whom the property belongs.

The position of the Fort is believed to be very accurately given. The northeast bastion occupied the ground where the Episcopal Church now stands. Its foundations were as high as the top of that church. It was the fourth place selected for a fort, and was first, it appears, enclosed by stockades merely. The diagram here given was made by the Rev. John Miller, a chaplain of the English army, in 1695, when it was surrounded by a ditch. It is purposed at a future day to give a view of the Fort taken at a subsequent period, when it had undergone important improvements, and to prepare as full a history of it as it may be possible to gather at this day.

State Street in 1792.

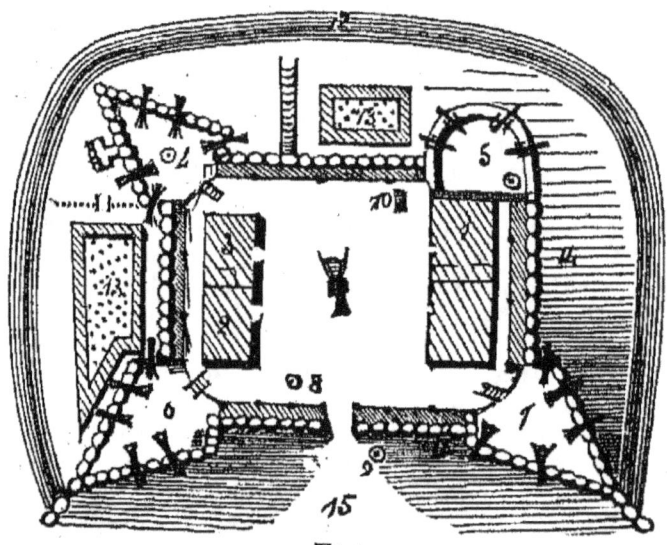

West.

East.

1. Governor of Albany's house.
2. Officers' lodgings.
3. Soldiers' lodgings.
4. Flag-staff mount.
5. Magazine.
6. Dial mount.
7. Town mount.
8. Well.
9. Sentry boxes.
11. Sally port.
12. Ditch fortified with stakes.
13. Gardens.
14. Stockade.
15. Fort gate.

The square in the occupation of William Muir was long since divided up for residences and shops.

The house of the worthy old mayor, Philip S. Van Rensselaer, younger brother of the patroon, is still occupied by his widow.

The next three lots form the well-known Webster Corner. After the memorable fire of 1793, in which the printing office of Mr. Webster was consumed, he took the white house on the Livingston lot, which stands there at this day. The two lots above it were purchased and built upon by himself and brother George, where they resided during their lives. The corner property also came into their hands, and became the theatre of a very extensive printing and publishing business. In the palmy days of the establishment, it was customary twice a week to load with school and other books for the western country, one of those old-fashioned two-story freight-wagons, so common before the opening of the canal. There were no heresies in those days against Webster's Spelling Book.

Intimately associated with the reminiscences of this corner, is the elm tree which throws its rugged arms across the street, and enjoys so extraordinary a degree of popular favor, as to defy the plodding traffickers below, whose signs are obscured by its foliage, to lop a limb or touch a twig. This corner was the property of Philip Livingston, one of the signers of the Declaration of Independence, who was born in Albany in 1716; and the earliest reminiscence we have of the tree, is the circumstance of his having, when a young man, rebuked a sailor, whom he observed preparing his knife to cut it down, then a mere switch. From this datum we may infer that the elm is more than a hundred years old.

The Lydius Corner, opposite, was occupied at the time of the survey by a very eccentric old gentleman, Balthazar Lydius. He died on the 17th November, 1815, aged 78, and was the last male descendant of his family, which was ancient and respectable. The house in which he lived was imported from Holland; bricks, woodwork, tiles, and ornamental irons, with which it was profusely adorned, expressly for the use of the Rev. Gideon Schaets, who arrived in 1652. The materials for the house arrived simultaneously with the old bell and pulpit, 1657. It was supposed to be the oldest brick building in North America at the time of its removal in 1832. The modern Apothecaries Hall was erected by Mr George Dexter upon its site.

A CANADIAN INVASION.

In the year 1687 the French in Canada made preparations to invade the Five Nations under the protection of New York. Information was received at Albany in the fall, of the movements of the enemy, whereupon the following proceedings were had in council. (See *Doc. Hist. N. Y.*, p. 272.)

Council Held at ffort James; ffriday the Ninth of September 1687. Present His Excy the Govern' &c.

Informaçõn being given to his Excy and some of the Members of yᵉ Board that yᵉ ffrench at Canada are providing fifteen hundred pair of Snowshews.

Ordered that yᵉ Mayor and Magistrates of Albany send ordrˢ to the five Nations to bring Down their Wives Children and old men least yᵉ ffrench come uppon them in the Winter and none to stay in the Castles but yᵉ yong men. That they who come be setled some at Cats Kill Levingstons land and along yᵉ River where they can find Conveniency to be neer us to assist them if they should want and that they send Downe with them all yᵉ Indyan Corne that can be spared by yᵉ Young Men who are to stay in yᵉ Castles.

Councill Held at ffort James; Sonday the 11th of Septembr 1687. Present His Excy the Govern' &c.

Letters from Albany giveing account that the people there are in great Consternation thro apprehension that yᵉ ffrench will come down uppon them this Winter.

Resolved that Every tenth man of all yᵉ Militia troupes & Companys within the Province Except those who were out yᵉ last yeare a whaling be Drawn out to go up thither.

Accordingly, forces were sent to Albany, and Gov. Dongan came up himself to assist in sustaining the Indians against their enemies. By the report of Robert Livingston, made to the Council, April 30, 1688, of his disbursements at Albany, for the maintenance of the forces, gifts and presents to the Indians, and relief of French prisoners, from August 11, 1687, to June 1, 1688, amounted to £2067 6s. 4d. It appears that these expenses required a new levy of £2556 4s. to be made upon all the inhabitants and free holders of the province, of which sum the proportion allotted to the city and county of Albany was £240

($570.) The pay of officers and soldiers employed in the service, was as follows:

The Major ten Shillings Cur^tt Money of this Province.

	per diem.		per diem.
The Captn of horse	£0.10.0	The Capt off ffoott	£0.8.0
The Lievt do	0. 7 0	The Lievt	0.4 0
The Cornett	0. 6.0	The Ensigne	0.3.0
The Quartermaster	0. 5.0	The Sergeant	0.1.6
The Corporall	0. 2.0	The Corporall	0.1.0
The Trumpiter	0. 2.0	The Drumbeater	0.1.0
The Troopers	0. 1.6	The rest of the private men	0.0.8

A SCENE OF THE REVOLUTION IN ALBANY.

In the spring of 1778; we went down to Bethlehem and brought home our cattle that had wintered there. As we were driving them slowly back, and as we entered Albany on our return, we met in State street a procession of novel character moving slowly up the hill. We perceived seven persons dressed in white, and soon learned they were of that unfortunate class of disaffected men, who to bad political principles had added crimes against society, which even a state of war would not justify. At Schodack they had distinguished themselves by a series of desperate acts not to be patiently endured by the community, and when they were taken prisoners their fate seemed inevitable. These men had been confined for some time in the city prison, now known as the Old Museum, and had once made their escape, but only to enjoy their liberty for a few hours. Indeed the whole city was under arms when we saw them moving to the fatal spot where they were to suffer. The public indignation was also much excited by their conduct in prison, and the circumstances attending their being brought to suffer the sentence of the law. They were confined in the right hand room of the lower story of the prison. The door of their apartment swung in a place cut out lower than the level of the floor. When the sheriff came to take them out he found the door barricaded. He procured a heavy piece of timber, with which he in vain endeavored to batter down the door, although he was assisted in the operation by some very athletic and willing individuals. During the attempt the voice of the prisoners was heard threatening death to those who persevered in the attempt, with the assertion that they had laid a train of powder to blow up themselves and their assailants. Indeed it was well ascertained that a quantity of powder had passed into their possession, but how, could not be known.

It was afterwards found placed under the floor and arranged to produce the threatened result. The sheriff could not effect his entrance, while a crowd of gazers looked on to see the end of this singular contest. Some one suggested the idea of getting to them through the ceiling, and immediately went to work to effect a passage by cutting a hole through. While this was going on the the prisoners renewed their threats, with vows of vengeance, speedy, awful and certain. The assailants however persevered and as I was informed, and never heard contradicted, procured a fire-engine, and placed it so as to introduce the hose suddenly to the hole in the ceiling, and at a signal inundated the room beneath. This was dexterously performed. The powder and its train were in an instant rendered useless. Still, however to descend was the difficulty, as but one person could do so at a time. The disproportion of physical strength that apparently awaited the first intruder, prevented for some time any further attempt. At last an Irishman, by the name of McDole, who was a merchant, exclaimed, "Give me an Irishman's gun, and I will go first." He was provided instantly with a formidable cudgel, and with this in his hand he descended, and at the same moment in which he struck the floor, he levelled the prisoner near him, and continued to lay about him valiantly until the room was filled with a strong party of citizens who came to his assistance through the hole in the ceiling. After a hard struggle they were secured, and the door which had been barricaded by brick taken from the fire-place was opened

They were almost immediately taken out for execution, and the mob was sufficiently exasperated to have instantly taken their punishment into their own hands. The prisoners seemed to me when moving up the hill to wear an air of great gloom and ill nature. No one appeared to pity them, and their own hopes of being released by some fortunate circumstance, as by the intervention of the enemy, had now vanished for ever.

They arrived in a few minutes at the summit of the hill, near or at the very place now covered with new and elegant edifices, north and east of the Academy, and there upon one gallows of rude construction ended they their miserable lives together.—*Sexagenary.*

TORY EXECUTION PLACE.

From a citizen who witnessed these scenes, we learn that the powder house in the time of the revolution was at a little distance west of the Academy Park. In front of it was a ravine, where the tories were hung and buried. The ravine ran north and south. They were stripped of their coats, hats and shoes, a bandage put over their eyes, in which condition they were executed, and buried in the ravine.

GOVERNOR TRYON IN ALBANY.

The city was honored by a visit from General Tryon, July 20th, 1772, on which occasion a public dinner was given him by the mayor and corporation at Cartwright's tavern; and on the following day he gave an elegant entertainment to the mayor and corporation, the clergy, several gentlemen of the law, and the officers of the militia. On the 24th (Friday) he set out for Schenectady, accompanied by Sir John Johnston, and several gentlemen and ladies, escorted by the Albany troop of cavalry. He was received there by his majesty's justices of the peace, and upwards of 800 of the militia of that township under arms.

FIRST PRESBYTERIAN CHURCH,
Corner of Hudson and Philip streets.

FIRST PRESBYTERIAN CHURCH.

The new edifice, for the accommodation of this large and increasing congregation now worshipping in the church corner of Beaver and South Pearl streets, under the pastoral charge of the Rev. Dr. J. N. Campbell, has been in the course of construction about two years. It is the third house built for the use of this society, the first two having been alluded to at pp. 130 – 132. The engraving opposite, by Mr. R. H. Pease, is a faithful representation of the edifice, which is the noblest specimen of church architecture in the city, as yet completed.

The following are the names of its principal artificers:

H. Rector, Architect.
Joshua R. Hayes, Mason.
Alexander Gray, Stonecutter.
James Dennison & Co., Carpenters.

Boyd & McDonald executed the mastic on the exterior, the plaster, stucco and fresco work of the interior.

The workmanship, throughout, could scarcely be surpassed in elegance and stability.

The entire building occupies an area of about one hundred and twenty by seventy-five feet; and for the convenience of this brief description, the building may be arranged under three general divisions: the tower, occupying the east end; the centre, or main body of the building; and the projection at the west end.

The tower is twenty-six feet square, and one hundred and fifty-six high: its external ornaments consisting of four octagonal turrets — one at each corner, terminating in pinnacles; two belt mouldings; three clock faces; panelled belt; five windows; the entrance doors, and the parapet.

The body of the building is ninety-seven by seventy-five feet, and forty-four feet to the top of the parapets; and relieved externally with eighteen buttresses, four turrets, and perforated for twelve windows.

The projection at the west end is about thirty by seven feet, and contains two angle buttresses, cornice and parapet.

The turrets and buttresses present their usual display of corbels, pediment mouldings, crocketed angles, and terminating finials to their respective pinnacles; the belt and eave cornices are well formed and judiciously arranged; the paneled course is filled with tracery; the clock faces furnished with architrave mouldings, crocketed bands, and terminating finials; the tower windows furnished with corbels, crocketed heads, and finials; and the principal entrance door has recessed jambs, columns, head moulding, tracery, cornice, tudor leaf parapet, side buttresses, and side and center pinnacles. The parapets to the main body of the building, and to the projection at the west end, are plain; that to the tower, open, and somewhat ornamented. The windows have double mullions, transoms, tracery heads, and are glazed with colored and figured glass manufactured for the express purpose. The facing to foundations, the steps, window heads, dressings, and all external ornaments are of cut stone; the other portions masticated to imitate stone.

The principal entrance is into the east side of the tower. The tower contains the inner porch, the screen doors, and the organ and bell lofts; also the apartment designed for the clock. The entrance to the organ, and to the choir gallery, is also through a portion of the tower; and the west side of the tower is perforated and arched, in order to present a full view of the organ. The screen wall, dividing the hall and lobbies from the nave and aisles, is perforated for three doors corresponding with the inner passages along the several ranges of pews, and also for two doors leading to the galleries. Between the front and screen walls is a transverse hall which contains the staircases, all conveniently arranged to give easy access to the different portions of the building. The area west of the screen wall, about seventy-seven by sixty-four feet, is divided by two ranges of columns into nave and side aisles: the columns form the support of the two ranges of galleries, and of the spandrels of the groined ceiling; the centre portion, or nave, terminating at its west end in the recess containing the pulpit, steps, and private entrance; and at the east end, in the organ loft and gallery for the choir.

The main ceiling is formed into three general divisions, corresponding with the nave and side aisles, by groined arches ornamented with ribs, bosses, and the usual display of ornament, and laid off to represent blocks of cut stone masonry, and frescoed: the ribs descend along the different curves of the arches, and rest in a cluster of mouldings upon the ornamented caps of the columns, and upon ornamented corbels along the walls. The ceilings of the galleries, and also those of the porch and hall, are ornamented with spandrels, resting upon corbels, and the angles filled with tracery. In each panel of the galleries, between the columns, are presented five arches resting upon corbels; and from each corbel rises a pinnacle, the arches and pinnacles ornamented with crockets and finials, and terminate below the gallery cornice: the unoccupied spaces are filled with tracery paneling. The gallery for the choir is finished similar to the others, except that the main divisions and angles are formed by projecting octagonal paneling, in form of turrets, and the tracery within the arches perforated quite through.

Within the projection at the west end is formed the recess which terminates the west end of the nave, the floor of the recess forming the area occupied by the pulpit and steps. The recess is ornamented with columns, panels and tracery, and a blank window finishes its center; the window presenting all the variety of mullions, tracery, transom crowned with tudor leaf, usual in ornamental windows. In one side of the recess is a private entrance, with a corresponding blank door at the opposite side, the arches of both finished with crockets and finials. The pulpit is not in a sufficient state of forwardness to admit of a particular description, but will doubtless be in character with the other portions of the building.

The main floor is intended to contain one hundred and fifty-eight pews, and the gallery forty-two. The choir will be of sufficient size to accommodate thirty persons. About twelve hundred persons can be accommodated in pews, gallery and choir, if required. The building is intended to be warmed by means of two furnaces located in the basement.

This church edifice, though entirely divested of the transepts, clerestory, high ceiling, and lofty spires which characterize the cathedral form of church edifices, will be found nevertheless, upon careful inspection, to present, in both general design and in detail, objects worthy the attention of the amateur and lover of the mechanic arts.

Births, Marriages and Deaths in 1848.

The lot on which this edifice is erected is on Hudson street, 150 feet in length, and on Philip street, on which it fronts, about 148 feet in breadth, enclosed by an iron fence of gothic structure. The organ, which is already put up, and is a full organ with three banks of keys, was made by Messrs. Appleton and Warren of Boston. The supposed cost of the whole structure will be nearly seventy thousand dollars.

BIRTHS, MARRIAGES AND DEATHS, 1848.

Abstract made from the returns of marriages, births and deaths, which took place in the city of Albany during the year 1848:—

Marriages.—Whole number of marriages returned, 629; do in which both parties resided in the city, 226; do one of the parties, 298; do both parties resided out of the city, 105; do the parties resided in Massachusetts, 29; Connecticut, 5; Rhode-Island, 2; and other States, 6.

The marriages took place in the several months as follows: January 34, February 38, March 21, April 45, May 57, June 47, July 51, August 61, September 73, October 80, November 63, December 59.

Married in St. John's church, 104; do St. Joseph's, 71; do St. Mary's, 69: total, 244.

Births.—Whole number of births returned, 1325; males 448, females 350, sex not stated 502; males (colored) 9, females do 9, sex not stated do 7; 44 twin children, of which 22 are males and 10 females, and 12 the sex not given.

The births occurred in the several months as follows: January 97, February 70, March 108, April 85, May 92, June 87, July 117, August 120, September 103, October 116, November 98, December 130, unknown 102.

Deaths—The number of deaths returned for 1848 is 1218; males 645, females 488, males (colored) 2, do females 3, sex not stated 80, married 206, unmarried 726, not stated 286, native born 815, foreigners 403.

Deaths in the several months as follows: January 126, February 99, March 121, April 89, May 90, June 72, July 136, August 145, September 104, October 91, November 69, December 76; total, 1218.

Number of those who died under the age of one year is 232; over 1 year and under 5, 319;
over 5 and under 10, 66;
— 10 — 15, 31;
— 15 — 20, 27;
— 20 — 25, 62;
— 25 — 30, 59;
— 30 — 35, 59;
— 35 — 40, 60;
— 40 — 45, 51;
— 45 — 50, 38;
over 50 and under 55, 40;
— 55 — 60, 23;
— 60 — 65, 26;
— 65 — 70, 17;
— 70 — 75, 19;
— 75 — 80, 9;
— 80 — 85, 14;
— 85 — 90, 7;
— 90 — 95, 3;
— 95 — 100, 1;
age not given, 55.

Average age of the persons dying, 20 years and 20 days.

Diseases—151 died of consumption, 59 of diarrhœa, 29 of congestion of the brain, 26 of croup, 24 by accident, 20 of scarlet fever, 21 of teething, 13 of typhus fever, 13 of whooping cough, 252 other diseases, 601 disease not stated.

STATE NORMAL SCHOOL.

STATE NORMAL SCHOOL.

In 1848 the legislature passed an act for the permanent establishment of this school, and appropriated $15,000 for the erection of a suitable building for its purposes, and in the following year an additional appropriation of $10,000 was made for its completion (p. 84, 85 ante). The edifice was finished in July, 1849, and on the 31st day of that month the school was removed into it. It contains, besides the necessary study and recitation rooms, a dwelling for the principal, and is supposed to be amply commodious for all the purposes of the Institution. At the annual exercises of the institution, S. S. Randall, Esq. gave the following account of the origin and progress of the school, in the course of his remarks on the occasion.

For several years prior to 1844, the attention of the friends of common school education in this state had been strongly directed to the inadequacy of the existing agencies for the preparation of duly qualified teachers for our elementary institutions of learning. Liberal endowments had, from time to time, during a long series of years, been bestowed upon the academies in different sections of the state, with a view to the attainment of this object; but the practical inability of these institutions to supply the demand thus made upon them, with all the resources at their command, soon became obvious and undeniable. The establishment of normal schools for this special and exclusive purpose in various portions of Europe where popular education was most flourishing; and in the adjoining state of Massachusetts, long and honorably distinguished for her superior public and private schools—and the manifest tendency of these institutions to elevate and improve the qualifications and character of teachers, had begun to attract the regard of many of our most distinguished statesmen.

On a winter's afternoon, early in the year 1844, in a retired apartment of one of the public buildings in this city, might have been seen, in earnest and prolonged consultation, several eminent individuals whose names and services in the cause of education are now universally acknowledged. The elder of them was a man of striking and venerable appearance—of commanding intellect and benignant mien. By his side sat one in the prime and vigor of manhood, whose mental faculties had long been disciplined in the school of virtuous activity; and in every lineament of whose countenance appeared that resolute determination and moral power, which seldom fails to exert a wide influence upon the opinions and actions of men. The third in the group was a young man of slight frame and pale, thoughtful visage; upon whose delicate and slender form premature debility had palpably set its seal; yet whose opinions seemed to be listened to by his associates, with the utmost deference and regard. The remaining figure was that of a well known scholar and divine, whose potent and beneficent influence had long been felt in every department of the cause of popular education; and whose energy, activity and zeal had already accomplished many salutary and much needed reforms in our system of public instruction. The subject of their consultation was the expediency and practicability of incorporating upon the common school system of this state an efficient instrumentality for the education of teachers. The utility of such a measure and its importance to the present and prospective interests of education, admitted in the minds of these distinguished men, of no doubt. The sole question was whether the public mind was sufficiently prepared for its reception and adoption; whether an innovation so great and striking, and involving as it necessarily must, a heavy and continued expenditure of the public money, might not be strenuously and successfully resisted; and whether a premature and unsuccessful attempt then to carry into execution a measure of such vital importance, might not be attended with a disastrous influence upon the future prospects of the cause of education. These considerations, after being duly weighed, were unanimously set aside by the intrepid spirits then in council; and it was determined that, backed by the strong and decided recommendation of the head of the common school department, immediate measures should be forthwith adopted for the establishment of a STATE NORMAL SCHOOL. The men who thus gave the first decided impetus to the great enterprise, whose gratifying results are now before us, were SAMUEL YOUNG, CALVIN T. HULBURD, FRANCIS DWIGHT and ALONZO POTTER.

Mr. Hulburd, the able and enlightened chairman of the committee on colleges, academies and common schools of the assembly, visited the normal schools of Massachusetts, and after a thorough examination of their merits and practical operations, submitted an elaborate and eloquent report to the house, in favor of the immediate adoption of this principle in our system of public instruction. The bill introduced by him, and sustained in all its stages by his powerful influence and indefatigable exertions, and the cooperation of the most zealous friends of education throughout the state, became a law, and appropriated the sum of $10,000 annually for five successive years, for the purpose of establishing and maintaining a state normal school in this city. The general control of the institution was committed to the regents of the university, by whom an executive committee, consisting of five persons, one of whom was to be the superintendent of common schools, was to be appointed, upon whom the direct management, discipline and course of instruction of the school should devolve.

In pursuance of this provision, the board of regents in June, 1846, appointed a committee, comprising the Hon. SAMUEL YOUNG then superintendent of common schools, the Rev. ALONZO POTTER, Rev. WILLIAM H. CAMPBELL, Hon. GIDEON HAWLEY, and FRANCIS DWIGHT, Esq. This committee forthwith entered upon the execution of their responsible duties; procured on very liberal and favorable terms from the city of Albany the lease for five years of the spacious building in State street recently occupied by the Institution; prescribed the necessary rules and regulations for the instruction, government and discipline of the school, the course of study to be pursued, the apportionment and selection of the pupils, &c., and procured the services of the late lamented and distinguished principal, then of Newburyport, Massachusetts, together with his colleague, the present principal, as teachers. On the 18th day of December, 1844, the school was opened in the presence of a large concourse of citizens and strangers, by an eloquent address from Col.

Young, and by other appropriate and suitable exercises. Twenty-nine pupils, thirteen males and sixteen females, representing fourteen counties only, of both sexes, were in attendance, who after listening to a brief but clear and explicit declaration from Mr. Page, of his objects, views and wishes in the management and direction of the high duties devolved upon him, entered at once upon the course of studies prescribed for the school. Before the close of the first term on the 11th of March, 1844, the number of pupils had increased to 98, comprising about an equal number of each sex, and representing forty of the fifty-nine counties of the state. During this term the musical department of the school was placed under the charge of Prof. Ilsley of this city, and instruction in drawing was imparted by Prof. J. B. Howard.

On the commencement of the second term, on the 9th of April, 1845, 170 pupils were in attendance, comprising a nearly equal proportion of males and females, and representing every county in the state, with a single exception. Of these pupils, about nine-tenths had been previously engaged in teaching during a longer or shorter period. The term closed on the 27th of August with a public examination and other suitable exercises, and thirty-four of the students received the certificate of the executive committee and board of instruction, as in their judgment well qualified in all essential respects, to teach any of the common schools of the state.

On the 15th of October succeeding, the school reopened with 180 pupils, which was increased during the progress of the term to 198, from every county of the state but one. The death of Mr. Dwight, which took place on the 15th of December, and the transfer of the Rev. Dr. Potter to the episcopal diocese of Pennsylvania, created vacancies in the executive committee, which were supplied by the appointment of the Hon. Harmanus Bleecker and the Hon. Samuel Young, the latter gentleman having been succeeded in the office of superintendent of common schools by the Hon. N. S. Benton of Herkimer. The sudden death of Mr. Dwight, who had taken a deep interest in the prosperity and success of the institution, and had given to its minutest details the benefit of his personal supervision and constant attention, cast a deep gloom upon the inmates; and the peculiar circumstances under which it took place were strikingly indicative of the vain and illusory nature of all human expectations. For several weeks previous to his death, Mr. Dwight had manifested much interest in devising appropriate means for the celebration of the anniversary of the opening of the school, on the 18th of December. Alas! how little could he imagine that the long line of normal pupils, with the children of the various public schools of the city, to whom he had been a signal benefactor, and hundreds of his fellow-citizens should, on that day, follow his lifeless remains to their long home!

At the close of the third term, March 18, 1846, a public examination was held which continued during four successive days, and convinced all who felt an interest in the institution, that the work of preparation for the teacher's life was, in all respects, thorough and complete. The diploma of the institution was conferred on 47 graduates.

During this and the preceding term a valuable addition had been made to the board of instruction, by promoting to the charge of several of the principal departments, those graduates of the institution who now so ably and successfully preside over these departments The experimental school, organized at the commencement of the second term, was placed under the general supervision of its present teacher, and has proved an exceedingly valuable auxiliary in the practical preparation of the pupils of the principal school, for the discharge of their duty as teachers.

Two hundred and five pupils were in attendance at the commencement of the fourth term, on the first Monday of May, 1846, of whom 63 received a diploma at its close in September following. During the fifth term, commencing on the 2d of November, 178 pupils only appeared, 46 of whom graduated in March 1847. At the commencement however of the sixth term in May, subsequently, 221 pupils were in attendance, of whom 64 received the diploma of the institution in September; and at the reopening of the school in November, 205 appeared. Up to this period the number of names entered on the register of the school as pupils, including those in attendance at the commencement of the seventh term was 737. Of these 254 had received their diploma as graduates, of which number 222 were actually engaged in teaching in the common schools of the state; and the residue, with few exceptions, in the different academies or private schools. Of those who had left the school without graduating, nearly all were engaged during a longer or shorter period in teaching in the several schools.

And now came that dark and gloomy period when the hitherto brilliant prospects of the institution were overcast with deep clouds of melancholy and despondency—when that noble form and towering intellect which, from the commencement of the great experiment in progress, had assiduously presided over and watched its developement, was suddenly struck down by the relentless hand of the great destroyer—when the bereaved and stricken flock, deprived of their revered and beloved guide, teacher, friend, mournfully assembled in their accustomed halls on that dreary and desolate January day, at the commencement of the year 1848, to pay the last sad obsequies to the remains of their departed principal. In the prime and vigor of his high faculties—in the meridian brightness of his lofty and noble career—in the maturity of his well earned fame as "first among the foremost" of the teachers of America, he passed away from among us, and sought his eternal reward in that better land where the ills and the obstructions of mortality are forever unknown ; where the emancipated spirit, freed from the clogs which here fetter its higher action and retard its noblest development, expands its illimitable energies in the congenial atmosphere of infinite knowledge and infinite love. It is not for me, on the present occasion to pronounce his eulogy, although I knew and loved him well. That has already been done by an abler hand, and it only remains to say that the impress which his masterly and well trained mind left upon this institution, the child of his most sanguine hopes and earnest efforts, and upon the interests of education generally throughout the state, of which he was the indefatigable promoter, has been of the most marked character, and will long consecrate his name and memory.

Since this period the progress of the institution under the auspices of its present enlightened principal, and his devoted corps of assistants has been uniformly onward and upward. At the close of the seventh term 50 pupils were graduated, and the eighth term opened with 208, of whom 46 received their diploma at its close. The ninth term opened on the first day of November last with 175 pupils, and at its close 43 were graduated, and the tenth term which has now just closed, opened with upwards of 200 pupils, of whom 36 are now about to graduate.

During the session of the legislature of '48, a bill was introduced in the senate providing the requisite funds for the erection of a new and suitable building in the city of Albany, for the permanent use of the Normal School, and rendering the annual appropriation for its support permanent. Through the active and unremitted exertions of the present principal this bill became a law, and under its provisions the noble and spacious edifice in which we are now assembled has been erected. A few weeks only have elapsed since the school was transferred to its new location; and notwithstanding the prevalence of a most gloomy and unhealthy season, the attendance of nearly 200 pupils of both sexes, upon the regular exercises of the institution, during the whole of the term now about to close, indicates the firm hold which it possesses upon the affections and regard of its inmates. Through the merciful permission of a superintending power, one only of the pupils of the school has fallen before the devastating pestilence which has swept over our land. And while we bow in humble submission to the stroke which thus solemnly reminded us of our habitual dependence upon Him in whom we "live and move and have our being"—we may, without presumption, offer up our grateful thanksgiving for the preservation of so many lives, thus fearfully exposed to the ravages of the destroyer.

For all substantial purposes, therefore, the Normal School may now be regarded as permanently engrafted upon the settled policy of the state, as a portion of its noble system of public instruction.

The edifice is entirely plain in its finish, and attention has been given to its ventilation. The front on Lodge street is 120, and that upon Howard 78 feet, upon each of which is an entrance; that upon Lodge for the female members of the institution, and the one upon Howard for the male. The building is divided into four stories (with a basement some six feet high), each of which contains a large or principal room for lectures and the general meeting of classes, and several for recitations. Rooms upon the first floor are arranged for the laboratory, the residence of the janitor, and the usual reception room; those upon the second, more expressly for the experimental department; the third, for general lecture and recitation rooms, and the fourth for the opening and closing exercises of the school, and the closing exercises of the term.

This is said to be the largest room in the city, being 46 feet wide by 98 long; and it is suggested as an appropriate one for concerts, lectures, &c. A novel feature in its construction is that it is divested of pillars, or any visible means by which the roof is supported; it being sustained entirely by trussed timbers.

The original draft of the building (which included the residence of the principal in its design, and which is retained in its construction) was intended to be completed in the most approved manner, with all the necessary arrangements and conveniences which belong to an institution of its capacity; but the draft exceeding the appropriation, it was found necessary to make alterations in its entire finish and model; and consequently the entire building, if we except the principal's residence, has undergone considerable change in its structure and finish from the original design. Yet, notwithstanding this necessary reduction, the building and its furniture and fixtures will compare favorably with any similar institution in the state for convenience and adaptation to the wants of its professors and pupils.

The original draft of the building, and from which, in a form much modified, it has been erected, was made by that efficient and scientific architect, Mr. George I. Penchard; the masonry was executed by the competent firm of Orr & Cunningham, and the wood work by the well known establishment of Mr. James Denniston.

CIVIL OFFICERS OF THE CITY OF ALBANY, 1693.

The militia of the county consisted of 359 men, commanded by Major Peter Schuyler, divided into five companies of foot and one of horse.

    Peter Schuyler Esq Mayor
    Dirck Wessels Esq Recorder
    Robt Livingston Esq Town Clerk
    John Apell Esqr Sherriffe

The Aldermen, Collectors, Assessors and Constables elective.

The Mayor's Court hath the Power of the Comón Pleas.

In each County there is a Court of Comón Pleas whereof the first in the Commission of the peace is Judge, and is to be assisted with any two of the three next in the commission of the Peace.

The Mayor and Aldermen are Justices of the Peace and have power to hold Quarter Sessions in the Cittys of N. York & Albany.

Justices of the Peace:—In the County of Albany to joyne the Mayor Recordr and Aldermen in the Quarter Sessions.

Eghbert Theunisse	Nicholas Rispe	
Kilian van Ranslaer Eqrs	Sanders Glenn	Esqrs
Martin Gerritse	Peter Vosbrough	
Dirck Theunisse	Gerryt Theunisse	

The following is a list of the officers of the militia of the county of Albany, in the year 1700, when the regiment numbered 371 men.

Peter Schuyler, Col.,——Lt. Col., Dyrck Wessells, Maj., *Field officers*.

Of a Foot Company in the city of Albany:—Johannes Bleeker, Captain; Johannes Roseboome Leiut.; Abra: Cuyler, Ensigne; *Comn Officers*.

Of another Foote Comn in yo said city:—Albert Rykman, Captain; Wessel ten Broek, Lieut.; Johannes Thomasse, Ensigne.

Of another Foot Compa in the said County:—Martin Cornelise, Captain; Andris Douw, Lieut.; Andris Koyman, Ensign.

Of another Foot Compa in the said County:—Gerrit Teunisse, Captain; Jonas Douw, Jochem Lamerse, Lieuts.; Volckart V. Hoesem, Abra-Hanse, Ensignes.

Of a Foot Compa in yo town of Schenectady:—Johannes Sanderse Glen, Captain; Adam Woman, [Vrooman?] Lieut.; Harman V. Slyke, Ensigne.

Of the Troope of Horse in yo said Regiment:—Kilian Van Renslaer Captain; Johannes Schuyler, Lieut.; Bennone V. Corlaer, Cornet; Anthony Bries, Quartermaster.

OPERATION OF THE CHEAP POSTAGE SYSTEM IN ALBANY.

The returns of the postmaster, Mr James D. Wasson, of the number of letters, newspapers, pamphlets and magazines received at the Post-Office in Albany during the month of October, 1845, were as follows:

```
No. of unpaid and paid letters, at  5 cents,....  34,656
 "      "       "     "        at 10   "    ....   3,804
 "     free letters,..........  at  5   "    ....     162
 "       "         ..........   at 10   "    ....      65
 "     dropped letters,......  at  2   "    ....     730
 "     printed circulars, ...  at  2   "    ....     257
 "     newspapers chargeable and free,......  19,280
 "     pamphlets and magazines,............     410
```

The following is a transcript of the returns for October, 1843, no account having been kept in 1844:

```
No. of letters at   6 cents, ..................   2,127
 "      "       10   "    ..................   3,372
 "      "       12½  "    ..................  10,006
 "      "       18¾  "    ..................   8,182
 "      "       25   "    ..................     864
 "      "       to postmasters, .............   1,597
 "      "       to members of Congress, ......    172
 "     drop letters, ......................   1,629
 "     regular papers, ....................  10,030
 "     free papers, .......................   9,503
 "     irregular papers, ..................   1,752
 "     pamphlets, periodical, ..............     623
 "        "       not periodical, ..........      39
```

The receipts for the month of October during the years 1843, '44 and '45, were as follows, viz:

```
October 1843 ..................... $3,497 76
   "    1844 .....................  2,860 41
   "    1845 .....................  2,225 76
```

The falling off in the receipts of 1844, under the old rates, compared with 1843, was $637·35; and in 1845, under the cheap postage system, compared with 1844, $624·65. But these deficiencies have been far more than realized since, and the system is working well, the business of the office having increased in a very rapid ratio.

BARLOW'S PREDICTION OF THE ERIE CANAL.

The great American poem of Joel Barlow, although a popular book in the last century, is probably unknown to a great many of his countrymen; and few of his admirers, perhaps, ever expected to see the *Vision of Columbus* quoted in after years, to claim the fulfilment of a prediction. The work was published in 1787, when that magnificent project, the Erie Canal, if it had any other place than in the imagination of the poet, was probably regarded only as the visionary chimera of an enthusiast. But the printed scheme of the poet may have awakened the attention of some strong mind to undertake the task of carrying out, what we now behold in successful operation, and which was foreshadowed in these words:

> "He saw, as widely spreads the unchannell'd plain,
> Where inland realms for ages bloom'd in vain,
> *Canals*, long winding, ope a watery flight,
> And distant streams, and seas, and lakes unite.
>
> From fair *Albania*, tow'rd the falling sun,
> Back through the midland lengthening channels run,
> Meet the far lakes, their beauteous towns that lave,
> And *Hudson* joined to broad *Ohio's* wave."

It was thirty years after this was published, that the Erie Canal was commenced, and more than forty before the opening of the Ohio Canal. In 1807, the *Vision of Columbus* was metamorphosed into *The Columbiad*. In the mean time Philip Schuyler and his coadjutors had succeeded in connecting the Hudson with the lakes, by short canals and locks around the falls of the Mohawk, and into Wood creek, which is thus alluded to by the poet:

> "From Mohawk's mouth, far westing with the sun,
> Thro all the midlands recent channels run,
> Tap the redundant lakes, the broad hills brave,
> And Hudson marry with Missouri's wave.
> From dim Superior, whose uncounted sails
> Shade his full seas and bosom all his gales,
> New paths unfolding seek Mackensie's tide,
> And owns and empires rise along their side."

THE OVERSLAUGH.

The legislature passed an act, in April, 1790, for the improvement of the navigation at the Overslaugh, by allowing the proprietors of *Mills* and *Papskni* islands to erect a dam to prevent the passage of the water between them, and throw it into the main channel. This, it was thought, would more effectually benefit the navigation, than the employment of "an unwieldy machine, which at best only affords a temporary relief."

DESCRIPTION OF ALBANY IN 1823.

BY HORATIO GATES SPAFFORD, LL. D.

Albany City, the capital of the state of New York, and of the county of Albany, is situated on the west bank of Hudson river, near the head of tide water, 144 miles north of the city of New York, 30 miles north of Hudson, 6 miles south of Troy, and 15 about southeast from Schenectady. In wealth, population, trade, and resources, it is next in rank to the city of New York, in this state, and takes about the sixth or seventh rank among the principal towns in the United States. The city of Albany, agreeably to the charter, is one mile wide on the river, and extends due northwest to the north line of the manor of Rensselaer, holding its width of one mile, and is about $13\frac{1}{4}$ miles long, the right of soil of which is the absolute property of the corporation in perpetuity. It is bounded northerly by the township of Watervliet, and by the county of Schenectady; southerly by Guilderland and Bethlehem; easterly by the Hudson or the county of Rensselaer: and, with the small exception noticed below, the boundaries have never been altered from the original charter, granted in 1686. The area is about 7160 acres, which also constitutes a township, for all the purposes of civil government. Of this extent, only a small proportion is under populous improvement, or any kind of cultivation, the western part having a sterile clay or sandy soil, principally in wood, while the compact population is immediately on the margin of the Hudson. To the stranger, the situation of Albany is seldom thought pleasing; for the ground is singularly uneven, and there is a peculiar dissonance of taste in the plan of the city, as well as in the style of its architecture. A low alluvial flat extends along the river, and in the rear of this rises the river-hill, abruptly, to near the height of the plain which extends to Schenectady. This flat is from 15 to 100 rods wide; and the hill, which is composed of alternate strata of fine blue clay and silicious sand, though deeply gullied by some small water-courses, rises, within half a mile of the river in the direction of State street, till it gains an elevation of 153 feet; thence, for another half mile, the ascent is about 60; making about 220 feet above the level of the river, in the distance of one mile.

The principal streets of Albany are parallel with the river, except State street, a spacious and central one that extends from the Hudson to the Capitol, being nearly east and west, with several others, less considerable, intersecting the main streets nearly at right angles. South Market, formerly Court street, extends from the Ferry, at the southern extremity of the compact part and near the south bounds of the city to State street, and has a large share of population and business. North Market street opens opposite this, and extends from state street to the northern bounds of the city, and to near the Mansion House of Major General Stephen Van Rensselaer. These streets thus extend through the city nearly parallel with the Hudson, between which there are several other streets, less extensive, as Dock street, Quay street, &c., populous, principally occupied with store-houses, shops, &c. State street, extends from the river in a narrow avenue to the open area at the meeting of North and South Market streets, where it opens to the liberal width of 150 to 170 feet, and extends 1900 feet to the Capitol, with an average ascent of 6¼ feet in 100. The Public Square, an open space of liberal extent, spreads a handsome area on the east side of the Capitol; and from the centre of this, Washington street, spacious and level, extends westward in a right line on a commanding plain, to the junction of the Great Western turnpikes. These streets have been laid out in a style which may be characterized as modern in Albany, being straight and spacious. North Pearl street extends north from State street to the northern extremity of the city, just on the brow of the river-hill, and next west of North Market street: and South Pearl, formerly Washington street, opens on the south side of State street, opposite North Pearl street, extending south to the south bounds of the city, ranging just at the foot of the river-hill. Between this and South Market street, there are several other streets, and a compact population, crowded, on the north towards State street, but thin in the southern part where South Pearl street diverges westward from the river, between which lie the grounds formerly denominated the Pasture, from their being appropriated to grazing. The flats here were originally subject to annual inundation, and though recently raised some feet, are now hardly above high-water mark. North and South Market streets, are the most populous and rich, and do by far the most business. But, through the compact population on each side of State street, other streets extend from the hill to the river, parallel to State street, which are closely built, and contain many very valuable brick houses and stores; these are intersected by others also in opposite directions, a bare enumeration of which would be useless and uninteresting, while it would swell this article far beyond the limits assigned to it.

The position of Albany was first chosen by a commercial people, for a military post, that should extend the trade with the Indians, and give to that trade a better security and character. Here seemed the head of the tide, and sloop navigation; and here the adventurers found a good ship-channel so close in with the shore as to save docking,—and a fertile intervale of low and rich alluvion, where they erected a stockade to guard against surprise by the Indians. This was about 1614.

This establishment was on the bank of the river, in what has since been called the Pasture, immediately above the Steam-Boat Dock. About 1623 it was enlarged, better stockaded, and called Fort Orange, according to the best accounts. A later work was erected on the river-hill, in a more commanding position, but retained the same name, except in a very limited circle, where it was called Williamstadt, till 1664, when the whole country passed into the hands of the English, who gave the present name in compliment to the Duke of York and Albany, then lord proprietor.

The charter of Albany, incorporating "the ancient settlement there as a city," was granted in 1686, a few months previous to that of New York, and Albany has now the oldest charter of any city in the United States.

The plan of this city, the style of its public and private works, with the whole character of its police and municipal regulations, are much improved within the last twenty years. Originally, the inhabitants had to consult present convenience, rather than taste and future elegance,

Albany in 1823.

more congenial too with the Dutch character; though if Yankee, or Anglo-American ostentation, enjoying the ease and luxury of opulence and progressive improvement, reproach with parsimony the ancient character of the inhabitants of Albany, a just discrimination may find the happy medium, perhaps, somewhere between these extremes of national character. A Dutch purse, talk as we may about parsimony, contracted views, want of taste, &c. &c., is yet a very good thing with which to embellish an estate, or a town. The corporation of this city was formerly rich, but it became lavish, if not prodigal, though aiming, perhaps, only at liberality and public spirit, and it is now poor, and involved in debt. Many improvements have been made, but in doing this it is now felt that they have been rather in a style of extravagance, in which the good people have been paying " too dear for their whistle." " Pride was not made for man," or rather, too much of it, any more than for cities, or communities. Property in Albany is very much depreciated in value, by the imposition of taxes, to pay for past follies. But let us look at its public buildings and works.

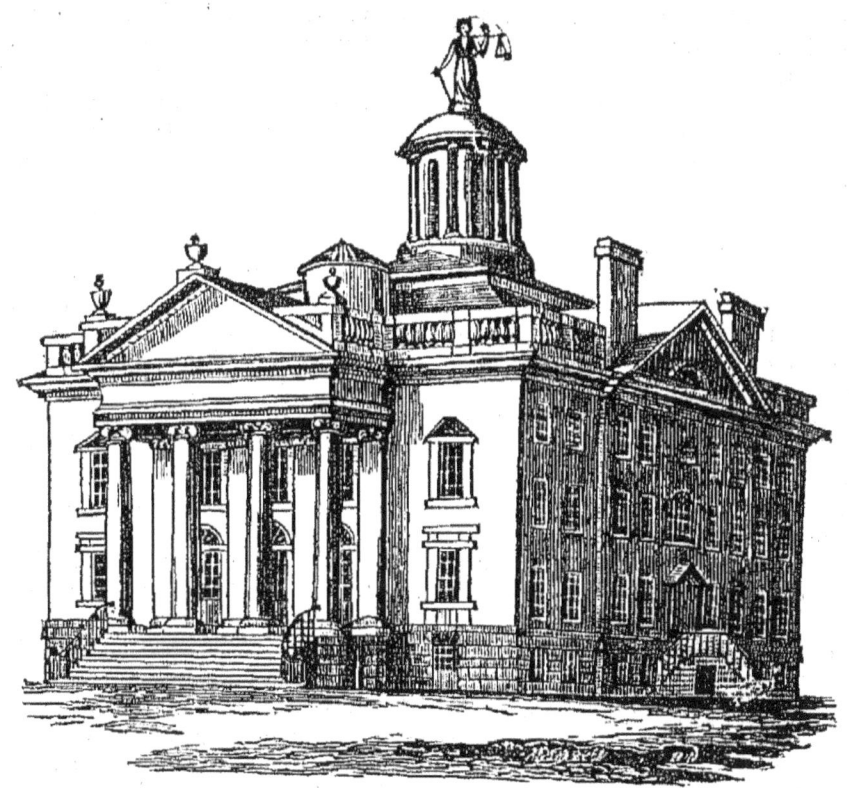

CAPITOL OF THE STATE.

The Capitol, or State House, erected for the use of the legislature, certain officers of state, the higher courts, &c., was in part designed, also, for city offices, and erected in part at the expense of the city. The whole expense exceeds $120,000, $34,000 of which was paid by the

The New York State Capitol building before it was demolished for the current one.

city. This building stands at the head of State street, adjoining the public square, and on an elevation of 130 feet above the level of the Hudson. It is a substantial stone building, faced with freestone taken from the brown sandstone quarries on the Hudson below the Highlands. The east front, facing State street, is 90 feet in length; the north, 115 feet; the walls are 50 feet high, consisting of 2 stories and a basement story of 10 feet. The east front is adorned with a portico of the Ionic order, tetrastile; the columns, 4 in number, are each 3 feet 8 inches in diameter, 33 feet in height exclusive of the entablature which supports an angular pediment, in the tympanum of which is to be placed the Arms of the State. The columns, pilasters, and decorations of the door and windows, are of white or grey marble, from Berkshire county in Massachusetts. The north and south fronts have each a pediment of 65 feet base, and the doors are decorated with columns and angular pediments of freestone. The ascent to the hall at the east or principal front, is by 15 stone steps, 48 feet in length. This hall is 58 feet in length, 40 feet in width, and 16 in height, the ceiling of which is supported by a double row of reeded columns; the doors are finished with pilasters and open pediments; the floor vaulted, and laid with squares of Italian marble, diagonally, chequered with white and grey. From this hall, the first door on the right hand opens to the Common Council Chamber of the corporation of Albany; opposite this, on the left, is a room for the Executive and Council of Revision. On the right, at the west end of the hall, you enter the Assembly Chamber, which is 56 feet long, 50 wide, and 28 in height. The Speaker's seat is in the centre of the longest side, and the seats and table for the members are arranged in front of it, in a semicircular form. It has a gallery opposite the speaker's seat, supported by 8 antique fluted Ionic columns; the frieze, cornice, and ceiling-piece, (18 feet diameter,) are richly ornamented in stucco. From this hall, on the left, you are conducted to the Senate Chamber, 50 feet long, 28 wide, and 28 *feet high*, finished much in the same style as the Assembly-Chamber. In the furniture of these rooms, with that of the Council of Revision, there is a liberal display of public munificence, and the American Eagle assumes an imperial splendor. There are two other rooms on this floor, adjoining those first mentioned, which are occupied as lobbies to accommodate the members of the legislature.

From the west end, in the centre of the hall, you ascend a staircase that turns to the right and left, leading to the Galleries of the Senate and Assembly Chambers, and also to the Supreme Court Room, which is immediately over the hall: its dimensions are 50 feet in length, 40 in breadth, and 22 in height. This room is handsomely ornamented in stucco. An entresole or mezzazine story, on each side of the Court Room, contains four rooms for jurors and the uses of the courts.

The attic story contains a Mayor's Court Room, a room for the Society of Arts, for the State Library, and the State Board of Agriculture. The basement story contains the County Clerk's Office, cellars and vaults for storage, and dwelling rooms for the Marshal of the city. In the Common Council Room, there are portraits of some distinguished Americans,—and before revising this article, I took some pains, without success, to look at, so that I could at least enumerate them. In the Assembly-Chamber, there is an admirable full length portrait of Washington, by Ames, of Albany, and in the Senate Chamber, one of George Clinton, unrivalled in faithfulness, and unexcelled in execution. The walls of these chambers are hung with maps, and I very lately had occasion to regret the difficulty of gaining access to them.

This building is roofed with a double-hip, or pyramidal form, upon the centre of which is erected a circular cupola, 20 feet diameter, covered with a domical roof, supported by 8 insulated columns, of the Ionic order, and contains a small bell for the use of the courts. The centre of the dome sustains a pedestal, on which is placed Themis, facing State street, a carved figure in wood of 11 feet in height, holding a sword in her right hand, and a balance in her left.

The Public Square, on the southwest of which stands the Capitol, has recently been laid out in the style of a Park, surrounded by a handsome fence, levelled, laid out into walks and avenues, and planted with shrubbery, and trees, the latter of very diminutive size. Facing this on the west is Gregory's Row, a handsome range of well-finished brick buildings, extending also around the corner and up the south side of Washington street, on the north side of which there are some good buildings, and extending northward, facing the Academy Park. Washington street avenue, across the Public Square, seems to divide it into two parks, *Capitol Park* and *Academy Park*, separately enclosed, the latter laid out and planted in the same style as the former. On the northwest corner of the Public Square, opposite the Capitol, north of Washington street, stands the Albany Academy, a large and elegant pile of masonry, faced with the red sandstone of Nyac, the same as that used in the Capitol. It is truly an elegant building, in design and execution the most chaste in the city, though in common with every other it is set rather too much in the ground, but makes a good appearance and has a commanding prospect. I have not time to describe it minutely, nor does it comport with my plan to do so. It cost the city $91,802·45, exclusive of the lot on which it is erected, and a donation to the trustees of the old jail, and lots of ground on which it was situated. It is three stories in height, has a front of 90 feet, five teachers, and about 140 students. The State Hall, erected by the state, for the principal public officers, is a plain, substantial edifice, two stories and a basement, situated on the south side of State street, midway between the Capitol and the Banks. This building accommodates the principal offices of state, such as the Secretary's, Comptroller's, Treasurer's, Surveyor-General's, and the Clerk of the Supreme Court's offices. The Jail, probably one of the best constructed in the state, cost the city $40,525·86; and the Lancaster School House, from a very bad policy, $23,918·93: to this may be added as an item, that the corporation contracted a debt of $32,000 for the purchase of a site from the Lutheran Church, for a market. Among the other public buildings, we may notice three banks, and twelve houses for worship, belonging to Presbyterians, Episcopalians Lutherans, Baptists, Methodists, some Independents and Seceders, and Roman Catholics.

The Arsenal, is a large brick edifice, filled with military stores belonging to the state of New York, situated in the north part of the city, late Colonie. The City Powder House, stands on the plain at the Washington Square; and a Powder House, erected in 1811, by the state, at the expense of $3,000, stands on an eminence of the plain, near the three mile-stone. The Alms House is also on the plain, near the Washington Square, the annual expense of which, with the support of the poor, is about $8,000.

There are two Ferries, one to Greenbush village, from the south part, and one to Bath village, from the north part, on the border of Watervliet. From the south or principal ferry, the docks, or quays, extend north along the river, nearly one mile, and the street fronting this is pretty compactly built for the most of that distance. Here are usually seen from 80 to 200 sloops and schooners, with a scene of activity honorable to the character of the place. The usual tides at Albany are from one to three or four feet; but variable according to the wind, and the strength of the current in the Hudson. To this city, the sloop navigation may be said to be pretty good.

There are a great many associations for business purposes, and many literary, charitable, humane, and benevolent societies, which I have not room to notice, and a Chamber of Commerce, Marine Society, &c., &c. There are also an Insurance Company, and a Savings Bank. The Albany Library, is a very respectable one, as is the Apprentices' Library, and its Water Works, for supplying the city with pure and wholesome water, are entitled to particular consideration. Ames's Gallery of Portraits, Mr. Cook's Reading Room, and the Museum of Mr. Towbridge, must not be omitted. The city is well supplied with printing establishments, having one daily, three semi-weekly, and two weekly newspapers, and printing and bookselling business to a great amount. Steamboats run daily between this city and New York, and there are stages in abundance, daily, in all directions, for Albany is a great thoroughfare, and will probably continue such, if nothing more. The Post-Office is well located, in North Market street, a little north of State street, near the two Mansion Houses, hotels, and the Albany, and Mechanics' and Farmers' Banks. There are three Air Furnaces in this city, which make a very great variety and amount of castings; and there are many mechanical establishments, in the different trades, though Albany, in proportion to its wealth and population, is not conspicuous in the extent of its manufactures, having no water-power for hydraulic works. The substitution of steam-power, and the very great importance to such a place, of mills, factories, &c., seem to have been strangely overlooked.

But let us turn our attention to the Canals, and the great Basin, from which so much is anticipated at Albany. The Erie Canal, and the Champlain Canal, having formed a junction in Watervliet, 8¾ miles north of this city, flow on in one channel, which enters the present city of Albany in the fifth ward, late a part of Colonie, three fourths of a mile from the Capitol, where there is a small Basin, and descends to the Hudson in the rear of the State Arsenal, near the north ferry. From this place, a Basin is to be made, extending down stream, on the west side of the river, about 4000 feet in length, to Hodge's dock, in the line of Hamilton street. It will embrace the west part of the river, extending along in front of the city, formed by an outer mole of 80 feet in width, and about 18 in height, on the east side of which there is to be a street of 25 feet in width. The Basin will be from 80 to 300 feet in width, averaging 10 feet water. It is connected with the Canal, at the upper end, by a boat lock, and with the Hudson river at the lower end, by a sloop lock. The works are rapidly progressing, and are intended to be completed in 1824, being more than half finished. Should the Canal continue to terminate here, this Basin will doubtless be of great importance to Albany, but I rather suspect it will ultimately be extended downward to the head of ship navigation.

The town of Colonie, described in the first edition of my Gazetteer, in 1813, has since been consolidated or abolished. the northern part being annexed to Watervliet, and the southern to Albany, forming the fifth Ward, February 25, 1815. But for this, this good old Dutch city would not have had its Canal, which does not come within the limits of its old charter, though the Basin will, and extend almost down to the first position of Fort Orange, noticed above.

There are many companies of firemen, well regulated, and well provided with engines and other means of effective operations. But while a well-timed vigilance guards against the ravages of the fire of the elements, it were well to check the destruction arising from that of the mind. A deplorable defect in the system of public guardianship exists somewhere, and the small groceries and shops that retail ardent and other spirits are so numerous as to call loudly for reform.

The city of Albany is governed by a Mayor, Recorder, 10 Aldermen, and 10 Assistant Aldermen, denominated in the laws, "the Mayor, Aldermen, and Commonalty." The Common Council must consist of 5 aldermen, 5 assistants, and the mayor or recorder, to be competent to the enacting of laws. For the better administration of justice, the city is divided into five wards, each of which elects two aldermen and two assistants, with such other officers as are found necessary to the purposes of government, including, also, the usual town officers, such as supervisors, assessors, &c., each ward being a town, as respects elections, officers, &c. The charter election is held on the last Tuesday in September, and the town election, on the day of general town elections in this state. A large proportion of the houses are of brick, well secured against fire. The whole number of houses and stores is about 2000. There are also a Mechanic Hall, Uranian Hall, and sundry school-houses, in addition to the buildings already enumerated. The shipping, including that annually paying wharfage in this city, amounts to about 400, principally sloops, and an immense amount of business is done, principally with New York, though a good deal with Boston, Philadelphia, &c. The shipment of wheat, annually, is probably to the amount of two to three millions of dollars. Importations, principally from England, are made to a great amount, in the dry goods and hardware business, in which are embarked very great capitals. The Troy Iron and Nail Works, a very extensive concern, is owned in Albany.

The annual expenses of the city, amount to about $45,000. In 1821, the expenditures were $45,614, including $11,168 to commissioners of the city stock; and the receipts for the same year, $49,507, $14,000 of which was for support of poor and night watch, raised by tax. The city debt amounted to $250,342, for the reduction of which, there was a sinking fund of $106,108, $81,000 of which is in city lands. To these notices it may be proper to add, as an evidence of the public spirit in which these burdens have been imposed, that the corporation of Albany, in 1813, publicly offered a reward of $1,000, for the discovery of a mine of fossil coal, if within five miles of the navigable waters of the Hudson river, and of a stratum not less than four feet. The coal to be sure, has not been discovered, but no one will pretend to say it never will be, or that such a discovery would not be of immense importance to the city of Albany, and the public.

Mills' Island, in the Hudson, a very large and valuable one, commencing just below the city, is principally in Bethlehem, partly in Albany. The principal obstructions to the navigation of the Hudson below this city, to a free sloop navigation, are, the bar or bars, or rather the flats, sand-bars, and narrow channels, called the *Overslagh*, or *Overslaugh*, in Bethlehem, three miles below, and Winne's Bar, also in Bethlehem, eight miles. Attempts have been made, and are still making, to remove these, but not with the success desired. Should the dam and sloop lock, below Lansingburgh, prove as beneficial as it is hoped they may, the same means will probably be resorted to here, for the benefit of Albany and Troy. The alluvial matter has been steadily increasing in the Hudson, say from ten or twelve miles below Albany, ever since the first survey of the river, and it is a perfectly rational conjecture, that it will continue to increase, and to multiply the obstructions to navigation.

Albany has a Globe Manufactory, entitled to distinguished notice, and a Lyceum of Natural History, recently established, for which it has a room in the Academy. The actual distance between Albany and New York, by land, is only 144 miles, and perhaps no more measured on the ice, but the sloop channel may still be safely reckoned, as formerly, at 160 miles, or very nearly. This city pays annually $500 towards the support of the *Lancaster School*, which also receives $676 from the school fund, and collects about $250 a year for tuition money. The annual expense of this very excellent school, is about $1400, and the number of scholars 600 to 800. It was founded during the mayoralty, and by the exertions of the late Mayor P. S. Van Rensselaer, a good deed for the people, by a man of good deeds.

Population, in 1820, including the annexation from the late town of Colonie, 12,630: of this number, there were employed in agriculture, 75; in commerce and trade, 468; in manufactures and trades, 909; 238 foreigners not naturalized; 643 free blacks, 109 *slaves*; taxable property, $3,970,070; schools, 1, the Lancaster school receiving all the public moneys, an excellent plan, for populous towns; public moneys received in 1821, $1,401 93, the school being kept twelve months in twelve; number of children therein, in 1821, 685: electors, 2,357; acres of improved land, occupied, 1,515; number of cattle, 654; horses, 653; sheep, 272: yards of cloth made in families, in 1821, 1,023: 1 distillery. Albany has no water-power for hydraulic works.

The first settlement of this city was made by some Hollanders about 1612, and next to Jamestown in Virginia, it is the oldest settlement in the United States. In 1614, a temporary fort was erected. Fort Orange was built about 1623. Albany received its charter in 1686. And it is worthy of remark that this city was enclosed by stockade defence against the Indians about 1745, when there were six block-houses erected, the last of which with the last remaining vestige of that work, was destroyed by fire in the summer of 1812.

Distances of the County Towns from Albany.

Albany is situated in north latitude 42° 39′, and 73° 13′ west longitude, from the Royal Observatory of England. Distances from Albany: to the city of New York, 144 miles; Philadelphia, 234; Washington city, 373; Boston, 171; Hartford, 92; Quebec, 394; Montreal, 247; Buffalo, by Utica, by land, 296; via Cherry-Valley, 282; by the Canal 360; to Detroit, 664.

The eastern section of the Erie Canal was completed, opened for navigation, when boats descended to the Hudson at Albany, and the great festival was held, Oct. 8, 1823. This completes the line of Canal navigation from Albany to Rochester. It was *a great day*, celebrated with great pomp, a grand display of all sorts of pride and ceremonies, attended, probably, by 30,000 people. The Champlain Canal was completed September 10, 1823.

DISTANCES OF THE COUNTY TOWNS FROM ALBANY.

County.	County Seat.	Dist.	County.	County Seat.	Dist
Allegany,	Angelica,	250	Ontario,	Canandaigua,	195
Broome,	Binghamton,	145	Orange,	Goshen.	105
Cattaraugus,	Ellicottville,	262		Newburgh.	84
Cayuga,	Auburn,	169	Orleans,	Albion,	257
Chautauque,	Mayville,	336	Oswego,	Oswego.	167
Chemung,	Elmira,	198		Pulaski.	153
Chenango,	Norwich,	110	Otsego,	Cooperstown,	69
Clinton,	Plattsburgh,	164	Putnam,	Carmel	100
Columbia,	Hudson,	29	Queens,	Hempstead C. H.	172
Cortland,	Cortland,	140	Rensselaer,	Troy,	6
Delaware,	Delhi,	77	Richmond,	Richmond,	161
Dutchess,	Poughkeepsie,	75	Rockland,	New City,	129
Erie,	Buffalo,	284	St. Lawrence,	Canton,	223
Essex,	Elizabethtown,	126	Saratoga,	Ballston Spa,	26
Franklin,	Malone,	212	Schenectady,	Schenectady,	15
Fulton,	Johnstown,	45	Schoharie,	Schoharie,	22
Genesee,	Batavia,	249	Seneca,	Ovid,	189
Greene,	Catskill,	37		Waterloo.	164
Hamilton,	Lake Pleasant,	72	Steuben,	Bath,	216
Herkimer,	Herkimer,	80	Suffolk,	River Head,	235
Jefferson,	Watertown,	164	Sullivan,	Monticello,	110
Kings,	Brooklyn,	149	Tioga,	Owego,	167
Lewis,	Martinsburgh,	134	Tompkins,	Ithaca,	163
Livingston,	Geneseo,	23	Ulster,	Kingston,	55
Madison,	Morrisville,	102	Warren,	Caldwell,	62
Monroe,	Rochester,	211	Washington,	Sandy Hill,	50
Montgomery,	Fonda,	47		Salem.	47
New-York,	New-York,	144	Wayne,	Lyons,	181
Niagara,	Lockport	277	Westchester,	Bedford.	125
Oneida,	Rome,	176		White Plains,	129
	Whitestown,	97	Wyoming,	Warsaw,	251
Onondaga,	Syracuse,	133	Yates,	Penn-Yan,	192

DR. MORSE'S DESCRIPTION OF ALBANY IN 1789.

The following extract from Morse's *American Geography* will serve to correct a very common error in relation to the singular position in which the reverend doctor is said to have placed the citizens of Albany in regard to the streets! It is extracted from the original edition, published in 1789, a copy of which we happen to possess. This edition is now so rare, that it was with great difficulty a copy could be procured, two or three years ago, for the British Museum. It will be seen that the people, as well as the houses, are placed in a true and proper position, as far as their *standing* is concerned, and the doctor's English will be vindicated.

The city of Albany is situated upon the west side of Hudson's river, 160 miles north of the city of New York, in latitude 42°, 36', and is by charter one mile upon the river, and 16 miles back. It contains about 600 houses, built mostly by trading people on the margin of the river. The houses stand chiefly upon Pearl, Market and Water streets, and six other streets or lanes which cross them nearly at right angles. They are built in the old Dutch Gothic stile, with the gable end to the street, which custom the first settlers brought with them from Holland. The gable end is commonly of brick, with the heavy moulded ornament of slanting with notches, like stairs, and an iron horse for a weather cock, on the top. There is one little appendage to their houses, which the people, blind to the inconvenience of it, still continue, and that is the water gutters or spouts which project from every house, rendering it almost dangerous to walk the streets in a rainy day. Their houses are seldom more than one story and an half high, and have but little convenience, and less elegance; but they are kept very neat, being rubbed with a mop almost every day, and scoured every week. The same neatness, however, is not observed in the streets, which are very muddy most of the year, except those which are paved; and these are seldom swept and very rough.

The city of Albany contains about 4000 inhabitants, collected from almost all parts of the northern world. As great a variety of languages are spoken in Albany, as in any town in the United States. Adventurers, in pursuit of wealth, are led here by the advantages for trade which this place affords. Situated on one of the finest rivers in the world, at the head of sloop navigation, surrounded with a rich and extensive back country, and the store-house of the trade to and from Canada, and the Lakes, it must flourish, and the inhabitants cannot but grow rich. Hudson, however, is their rival. Other rivals may spring up.

Albany is said to be an unsociable place. This is naturally to be expected. A heterogeneous collection of people, invested with all their national prejudices, eager in the pursuit of gain, and jealous of a rivalship, can not expect to enjoy the pleasures of social intercourse or the sweets of an intimate and refined friendship.

A gentleman of observation and discernment, who resided some time in Albany has made the following observations, which, though of general application, I beg leave to introduce under this particular head.

To form a just idea of the manners and customs of the inhabitants, we must confine ourselves to the Dutch, who being much the most numerous, give the *tone* to the manners of the place. Two things unite more particularly to render these disagreeable to foreigners; first, a natural prejudice which we all possess in favor of our own, and against the manners of another place or nation: secondly, their close union, like the Jews of old, to prevent the innovation of foreigners, and to keep the balance of interest always in their own hands.

It is an unhappy circumstance when an infant nation adopt the vices, luxuries and manners of an old one; but this was in a great measure the case with the first settlers of Albany, most of whom were immediately from Amsterdam. Their diversions are walking and sitting in mead-houses, and in mixed companies they dance. They know nothing of the little plays and amusements common to small social circles. The gentlemen who are lively and gay, play at cards, billiards, chess, &c., others go to the tavern, mechanically, at 11 o'clock—stay until dinner, and return in the evening. It is not uncommon to see forty or fifty at these places of resort, at the same time; yet they seldom drink to intoxication, unless in company, or on public occasions, when it is thought to be no disgrace.

They seldom admit many spectators to their marriages; but the day after, the groom prepares a cold collation, with punch, wine, &c. to partake of which, he expects all his friends will come, at 11 o'clock without any invitation. A dictator, with absolute power, is then appointed to preside at each table, or in each room, and it seldom happens that any are suffered to leave the house, until the whole circle exhibits a shocking specimen of human depravity.

Their funeral ceremonies are equally singular. None attend them without a previous invitation. At the appointed hour they meet at the neighboring houses or stoops, until the corpse is brought out. Ten or twelve persons are appointed to take the bier all together, and are not relieved. The clerk then desires the gentlemen (for ladies never walk to the grave, nor even attend the funeral, unless of a near relation) to fall into the procession. They go to the grave, and return to the house of mourning in the same order. Here the tables are handsomely set and furnished with cold and spiced wine, tobacco and pipes, and candles, paper, &c. to light them. The conversation turns upon promiscuous subjects, however improper, and unsuitable to the solemnity of the occasion, and the house of mourning is soon converted into a house of feasting.

The best families live extremely well, enjoying all the conveniencies and luxuries of life; but the poor have scarcely the necessaries for subsistence.

The ground covered by this city charter, is of a thin, poor soil. In the river before the city is a beautiful little island, which, were it properly cultivated, would afford a faint resemblance of Paradise.

The well-water in the city is extremely bad, scarcely drinkable by those who are not accustomed to it. Indeed all the water for cooking is brought from the river, and many families use it to drink. The water in the wells, if Kalm was well informed, is unwholsome, being full of little insects, resembling, except in size, those which we frequently see in stagnated rain water.

The public buildings are a Low Dutch church, one for Presbyterians, one for Germans or High Dutch, one for Episcopalians—a hospital and the City Hall.

Dr. Morse's Description of Albany in 1796.

ALBANY IN 1796.

In the edition of 1796, the notice of Albany was somewhat varied, as follows:

Many new houses have lately been built in this city, all in the modern style, the inhabitants are paving the streets in the New York plan, with foot-ways, and making other improvements.

The city of Albany contains about twelve or fourteen hundred houses, and 5000 inhabitants, collected from various parts. As great a variety of languages are spoken in Albany, as in any town in the United States, but the English predominates, and the use of every other is constantly lessening. Adventurers, in pursuit of wealth, are led here by the advantages for trade which this place affords.

Albany is unrivalled in its situation. It stands on the bank of one of the finest rivers in the world, at the head of sloop navigation. It enjoys a salubrious air, as is evinced by the longevity of its inhabitants. It is the natural emporium of the increasing trade of a large extent of country west and north; a country of an excellent soil, abounding in every article for the West India market; plentifully watered with navigable lakes, creeks and rivers; as yet only partially peopled, but settling with almost unexampled rapidity, and capable of affording subsistence and affluence to millions of inhabitants. No part of America affords a more elligible opening for emigrants than this. And when the contemplated locks and canals are completed, and convenient roads opened into every part of the country, all which will, it is expected, be accomplished in a few years, Albany will proably increase and flourish beyond almost every other city or town in the United States. The trade of Albany, indeed, already increases with great rapidity. They sensibly feel the good effects of establishments made immediately after the peace. These effects will multiply when the immense quantities of produce which are now sold to supply the multitudes of new settlers, (who will soon be able to supply themselves) shall be diverted from these channels and sent to Albany.

The well water in the city is extremely bad, scarcely drinkable by those who are not accustomed to it. It oozes through a stiff blue clay, and it imbibes in its passage, the fine particles common to that kind of soil. This discolors it, and when exposed any length of time to the air, it acquires a disagreeable taste. Indeed all the water for cooking is brought from the river, and many families use it to drink. But the inhabitants are about to remedy this inconvenience by constructing water-works, to convey good water into the city.

At Bath, opposite this city, a large, neatly finished, and ingeniously constructed *bathing-house* has lately been erected, divided into four apartments in which the visitants may be accommodated at pleasure, with a warm, cold, or shower bath, only by the turning of a cock.

The public buildings are a Low Dutch church, one for Presbyterians, one for Germans or High Dutch, one for Episcopalians, a hospital, the city hall, a handsome brick goal, and the city hotel.

A bank was established here in 1794.

CORPORATIONS AND ASSOCIATIONS.

Such societies and institutions as have changed their officers since the elections recorded on pages 39 to 42, are inserted again.

ALBANY EXCHANGE BANK.—Since the demise of the late president, a change has taken place in the directory. Election Sept. 4, 1849.

John M. Newton, Ichabod L. Judson, John Taylor, James McNaughton, Samuel Pruyn, Lansing G. Taylor, Chauncey P. Williams, Samuel Stevens, George W. Stanton jr., William McElroy, Oliver Steele, Gaylor Sheldon, Frederick J. Barnard, Thomas L. Greene, Christopher W. Bender.

At a subsequent meeting of the Board of Directors, Samuel Pruyn was reelected president, and I. L. Judson vice-president.

ALBANY CITY BANK.— On the 12th June, the following gentlemen were elected directors of this bank:

Erastus Corning, Peter Wendell*, John Knower, Watts Sherman, Ellis Baker, Bradford R. Wood, William Seymour, J. V. L. Pruyn, William Smith, William Humphrey, Eli Perry, David H. Cary, Henry H. Martin.

Inspectors of the next election—Hiram Perry, John I. Burton, Robert Thompson.

BANK OF ALBANY.— The following gentlemen were elected directors of the bank on the 8th May:

Jacob H. Ten Eyck, Teunis Van Vechten, William Walsh, Andrew D. Lansing, Benjamin Tibbitts, Herman Pumpelly, David Newland, John Van Zandt, Jellis Winne jr.*, Henry Bleecker, James A. Wilson, Duncan McMartin, Daniel Cady.

Inspectors of election — Herman Ten Eyck, Christopher Y. Lansing, Richard Van Rensselaer. E. E. Kendrick, cashier.

COMMERCIAL BANK OF ALBANY.—The directory of this bank consists of the following persons:

John Townsend, John L. Schoolcraft, John Gott, Giles Sanford, James D. Wasson, Robert H. Pruyn, Andrew White, Anthony M. Strong, Anthony Gould, Visscher Ten Eyck, John D. Hewson, Alexander Davidson, John B. James.

Inspectors of the next election — John I. Boyd, John M. Newton, Charles B. Lansing.

MECHANICS' AND FARMERS' BANK.— The following gentlemen were unanimously elected directors of this bank:

Thomas W. Olcott, Samuel S. Fowler, Friend Humphrey, Thomas Hillhouse, Robert Shepherd, Lemuel Steele, Robert Dunlop, James Kidd, William W. Forsyth, James B. Jermain, Hugh Humphrey, Henry A. Newman, William H. Dewitt. The last named is in the place of Harmanus Bleecker*, who, from ill health, declined a reëlection.

* Since deceased.

ALBANY BURGESSES CORPS.— On the 9th October last, the following were elected officers for the ensuing year:

Franklin Townsend, captain; Justus W. Blanchard, first lieutenant; Hale Kingsley, second lieutenant; J. Baldwin, third lieutenant; James Easterly, orderly sergeant; Harvey Tuton, second sergeant; William Burgess, third sergeant; Samuel Wilkins, fourth sergeant.

Staff Officers — L. Benedict jr., quartermaster; W. J. Thomas, paymaster; J. F. Schultz, surgeon; William Davis, chaplain; William H. Low, president; R. S. Handee, vice-president; Jacob C. Cuyler, secretary; Stephen W. Whitney, assistant secretary; John V. S. Visscher, armorer.

ALBANY CITY MISSIONARY SOCIETY. — The following statistics are gathered from the annual report of the agent, Rev. Mr. Rawson, of his operations for the year ending May, 1849:

- 76 visits to the almshouse; reading the scriptures, &c. 133 times in different rooms.
- 35 to sabbath and day schools.
- 102 to the jail.
- 136 to the penitentiary.
- 257 to hotels and porter houses.
- 56 to sick and other families.
- 102 to shops and livery stables.
- 57 bibles and 31 testaments have been distributed.
- 200 copies of Edwards's Sabbath and Temperance Manual.
- 11 funerals attended.

69395 pages of tracts distributed.

And there have been several hopeful conversions, and a number of backsliders reclaimed.

ALBANY COUNTY MEDICAL SOCIETY. — At the annual meeting of the society, held at the City Hall, November 13, the following officers were elected:

James McNaughton, president, John Swinburne, vice-president; Benjamin A. Sheldon, secretary; J. B. Rossman, treasurer; C. C. Griffen, librarian.

Censors — P. McNaughton, J. H. Case, Howard Townsend, N. G. Bigelow and D. R. Burris.

YOUNG MEN'S ASSOCIATION.—The election for officers of this institution took place Feb. 9. The canvass was conducted with much spirit, but in a friendly manner. The whole number of votes taken was 696. This is, with one exception, the largest vote ever taken at an election. The following persons were elected:

William Dey Ermand, president; Rufus G. Beardsley, first vice president; Edward C. C. Batchelder, second vice-president; William B. Sprague, third vice-president; Richard H. Northrop, corresponding secretary; James T. Stevenson, recording secretary; James I. Johnson, treasurer; W. F. Phelps, George C. Lee, James A. Pratt, John N. Cutler, C. D Rathbone, William D. Morange, Joseph A. Wells, A. L. Winne, R. Higgins, L. S. Hammond, managers.

Debating Society—William H. Greene, president; D. W. C. DeForest, first vice-president; James Martin, 2d do.; W. R. Thomas, secretary

Corporations and Associations. 319

ALBANY FIRE DEPARTMENT.—The several fire companies met by their delegates (two from each company), on the 10th January, and elected their officers, viz:

Samuel N. Payne, president; Baltus Prime, vice president; Visscher Ten Eyck, treasurer; Hale Kingsley, secretary; John Morrison, collector. James M. Whyte and Daniel D. T. Charles were chosen trustees for the term of three years.

FIRE POLICE.— The Common Council appointed the following gentlemen to the fire police, under the law of 1849:

John Osborn, captain; Abraham Herrick, Jeremiah Baldwin, Terence Leddy, first ward; William H. Linberger, Richard Dowd, Alexander Waters, second ward; John W. Brasier, John P. Russ, William Van Vleeck, third ward; Augustus Prime, John Jerroloman, fourth ward; James Hart, William Lockerty, fifth ward; John Mills jr., Russel N. Hamlin, R. J. Patten, sixth ward; Edward Scully, Patrick Ledwick, Adrian J. Cox, seventh ward; Theo. Carman, William McLaughlin, Henry Teater, eighth ward; Henry Simmons, ninth ward; George C. Scott, William White, John Stackpole, tenth ward.

ENGINE COMPANY No. 4. — At the annual meeting of this company, Nov. 13, the following officers were elected for the ensuing year:

John B. Stonehouse, foreman; Michael Reardon, assistant foreman; Andrew McFarlane, clerk; Andrew Peterson, steward; Frederick Newdorf, treasurer.

MOUNTAINEER ENGINE COMPANY No. 5.— At the annual meeting of the company, Nov. 13, the following officers were elected:

Charles E. Phelps, foreman; Ariel Lathrop, first assistant foreman; Jacob Rapp, second assistant foreman; William N. Graham, clerk; George B. Wadleigh, treasurer; Gerrit Lansing, steward.

Delegates to the Fire Department — William J. Packard and George B. Wadleigh.

ENGINE COMPANY No. 7. — At the annual meeting of the company, Nov. 13, the following officers were elected for the ensuing year:

J. Tremper, foreman; I. Jones, first assistant foreman; P. Philips, second assistant foreman; H. M. Bundy, clerk; William Kingsbury, treasurer; R. Bygat, steward.

DANIEL D. TOMPKINS ENGINE COMPANY No. 8.—At the annual meeting of this company, Nov. 13, the following officers were elected for the ensuing year:

William T. Johnston, foreman; John McBride, assistant foreman; F. C. Feeney, second assistant foreman; Jerome Terry, clerk; Samuel Templeton, treasurer; Robert Bradwell, steward.

Delegates to the Fire Department — S. Templeton and J. McBride.

JOHN RODGERS'S ENGINE COMPANY No. 12.—At the annual meeting of this company, Nov. 13, the following officers were elected for the year ensuing:

Baltus Prime, foreman; Thomas Kearney, first assistant; George W. Baker, second assistant; James Buchanan, clerk; Thomas O'Hagan, steward; Matthew Morrison, treasurer.

Corporations and Associations.

HIBERNIAN PROVIDENT SOCIETY.—At the annual election of officers of the Hibernian Provident Society, on the 6th March, the following persons were elected:

Patrick Grady, president; James Rogan, first vice-president; John Seary, second vice president; John Daly, recording secretary; John Donohoe, corresponding secretary; Richard Brown, treasurer; John Higgins, John Purcell, Edward Donohoe, Patrick Murray, Patrick Flynn, Thomas Kelly, Michael McCormick, executive committee; Patrick Powers, Joseph Clinton, Henry Dermody, finance committee; Nicholas Markey, physician.

MECHANICS' BENEFIT SOCIETY.—The following officers were elected for the ensuing year, on Monday, August 6th:

W. A. Carr, president; H. E. Brower, first vice-president; S. G. Mink, second vice president; J. A. Buckbee, treasurer; R. S. Cushman, secretary; S. L. Hodgkins, assistant secretary; J. W. Hinckley, physician.

Stewards—Henry F. Near, first ward; Michael Delehanty, second ward; L. G. Hoffman, third ward; Jesse P Wilson, fourth ward; W. A. Rice, fifth ward; John Vosburgh, sixth ward; James W. Parsons, seventh ward; Oliver Houll, eighth ward; Ed. C. Batcheldor, ninth ward; Paul Cushman, tenth ward.

BOARD OF TRADE —At an election of the Board of Trade, held on the sixth February last, the following gentlemen were unanimously elected officers for the ensuing year:

Arthur H. Root, president; David H. Cary, first vice-president; Erastus S. Prosser, second vice-president; James T. Stephenson, secretary; George M Sayles, treasurer; Oliver G. Terry, Samuel Cary, Charles W. Durant, Lewis E. Evans, Lucian M. Gilbert, reference committee.

Inspectors of election — Charles T. Smyth, Horace Averill.

ALBANY EXCHANGE COMPANY.—At an election held January 8th, the following gentlemen were elected directors of this company for the ensuing year:

John Townsend, Samuel Stevens, Friend Humphrey, Rufus H. King, Andrew White, John Q. Wilson, James McNaughton.

ALBANY AND BETHLEHEM TURNPIKE COMPANY.—At an election of this company, the following persons were chosen directors:

M. T. Reynolds, Philip S. Van Rensselaer, William McHarg, Joel Rathbone, John V. L. Pruyn, Robert Boyd, Ezra P. Prentice, George Dexter, Samuel H. Ransom.

Inspectors— John McHarg, Joseph T. Rice jr., Edwin R. Herrick.

ALBANY AND SANDLAKE PLANK ROAD.—At a meeting of the stockholders of this company on the first Sept. 1849, the following persons were elected officers for the ensuing year:

Richard J. Knowlton, Gideon Butts and Samuel R. Fox of the town of Sandlake; Dewitt C. Deforest and James Dearstyne of the town of Greenbush; John V. L. Pruyn, William Smith, Stephen B. Gregory and Archibald McClure of the city of Albany; and John Defreest, Cornelius Dearstyne and Samuel S. Fowler, inspectors of the next election.

Corporations and Associations.

ALBANY AND SCHENECTADY RAILROAD.—At a meeting of the stockholders on the 13th June, the following gentlemen were elected directors:

John T. Norton, Watts Sherman, Rufus H. King, G. Y. Lansing, H. H. Martin, H. Pumpelly, Augustus James and Lyman Chapin of Albany, and Richard H. Winslow of the city of New-York.

At a subsequent meeting, John T. Norton was unanimously elected president, and Watts Sherman vice-president.

ALBANY AND SCHENECTADY TURNPIKE COMPANY.—At an election held January 2, the following gentlemen were elected directors of this company for the ensuing year:

Teunis Van Vechten, Stephen Van Rensselaer, John J. Boyd. David Newland, John Townsend, Benjamin Tibbits, John Constable, Andrew E. Brown. J. H. Ten Eyck.

T. Van Vechten, president; B. Tibbits, secretary.

ALBANY AND WEST-STOCKBRIDGE RAILROAD.—At a meeting of the stockholders, the following gentlemen were elected directors for the ensuing year:

Marcus T. Reynolds, Thomas W. Olcott, Teunis Van Vechten, Friend Humphrey, Lewis Benedict, John V. L. Pruyn, George Dexter, Samuel S. Fowler, William H. Tobey, George Bliss and Addison Gilmore.

FORT-HUNTER AND ALBANY PLANK ROAD COMPANY.—At a meeting of stockholders, held at Blood's Hotel on the 16th August, the following gentlemen were elected directors for the ensuing year, viz:

John Townsend, Robert J. Hilton and James D. Wasson of the city of Albany; Israel R. Green, Silas H. Marsh and James Frost of Duanesburgh; and Peter I. Enders, David Johnson and Samuel C. Jackson of Florida.

GREAT WESTERN TURNPIKE ROAD.—The following persons are directors of the First Company of the Great Western Turnpike Road:

Teunis Van Vechten, Gerrit Y. Lansing, John V. L. Pruyn, John Townsend, Robert J. Hilton, John T. Cooper, Jacob H. Ten Eyck, Robert H. Pruyn, Stephen Groesbeeck, William C. Miller, John L. Schoolcraft, James D. Wasson, Andrew White.

UTICA AND SCHENECTADY RAILROAD.—The following gentlemen were elected directors of the Utica and Schenectady Railroad for the ensuing year:

Erastus Corning, Nicholas Devereux, Nathaniel S. Benton, Alonzo C. Paige, John Townsend, James Hooker, Thomas W. Olcott, Marcus T. Reynolds, Gardner G Howland, J. Phillips Phœnix, E. T. T. Martin, Livingston Spraker, John Ellis.

MUTUAL INSURANCE COMPANY OF THE CITY AND COUNTY OF ALBANY.—The following gentlemen were elected directors of this company for the ensuing year:

Erastus Corning, Friend Humphrey, Barent P Staats, Eli Perry, Watts Sherman, Henry H. Martin, John Knower, Ellis Baker, Joshua G. Cotrell, Daniel Fry, Giles Sanford, Jared A. Post, Artemas Fish.

At a subsequent meeting of the board, Erastus Corning was reëlected president, and Friend Humphrey elected vice-president of the company.

BOARD OF SUPERVISORS.—The Board, during its meeting on the 4th May, 1849, made the following appointments:

Samuel Pruyn, chairman; Jas. M. Whelpley, clerk; Howard Townsend, county physician; Alexander McDonald, doorkeeper.

AN ALBANY MERCHANT'S STOCK IN 1790.

The following is an exact copy of the advertisement of an eminent merchant doing business in this city sixty years ago. It will be seen how many articles of that day have become obsolete, or changed their names.

Robert M'Clallen,

No. 10 State Street, north-west corner of Green Street, Albany,

Has lately imported in the Goliah, Capt. Jones, from London, a large and general assortment of GOODS, suitable for the present season, which he will dispose of, wholesale and retail, at a very low advance, viz:

SUPERFINE, second and coarse cloths with trimmings suitable;
Drab, mix'd and blue Yorkshire Plains;
Black satinetts and lastings;
Green, blue and drab Halfthicks;
Scarlet cloaking with Trimmings;
Mixt, blue and claret twill'd coatings;
Claret, red and mix'd plain do.
2, 2½ and 3 point blankets;
Striped do.
Men's ribb'd and plain white and black worsted hose;
Ditto, striped, silk and cotton do.
Blue, yellow, green, red & white flannels;
Green, red and blue broad baize;
Drab, blue, mixt and green single-folded naps;
Imperial and basket buttons;
Fashionable and common coat and vest buttons;
Velvet and worsted toilonette vest patterns;
Purple and garnet wildbores;
Plain and twill'd olive velvets;
Corduroys and superfine thicksetts;
Durants, Calimancoes and moreens;
Brown, blue and striped camblets;
Irish Linens;
A variety of purple and chintz shawls;
Dark blue and spotted cotton handkerchiefs;
Chintzes and calicoes;
Black fring'd Handkerchiefs;
Men's and boy's castor and felt hats;
Plated shoe and knee buckles;
Common brass and steel do.
Bar lead;
Duck and Pigeon shot;
Gun powder;
London pewter;
Dutch tea-pots;
  With a variety of other articles.
  Also, a constant supply of
  LIQUORS AND GROCERIES;
Swede's iron; Crawley & blister'd steel;
Common rum;
Window glass, 6 by 8, 7 by 9 & 8 by 10.
  Pots and pearl ashes, staves, and other kinds of country produce taken in payment.

Besides those enumerated in this advertisement, other merchants mention the following articles, equally curious for their names:

Tammies,	Black Swanskin,
Persians and Pelongs,	Camlets and Camletees,
Osnabrigs,	Bed bunts,
Women's shammy gloves and mits,	Dowlass and Woolen checks
Cruel of all colors,	Leather breeches,
None-so-pretty do.,	Black everlastings,
Plain and spotted Swanskin,	Silk Damascus and Lorettas,
Faggot trimming,	Ticklenburghs,
Blue sagatha,	Moseens,
Bandanoe, ⎫	Buff and White Royal Rib, excellent
Lungee Romals, ⎪	for Breeches and Jackets,
Culgee, ⎬ Handkerchiefs,	Buff and olive Cotton Denim,
Setetersoy, ⎪	Swandown Counterpanes,
Denmark fancy, ⎪	Drab Forest cloth,
Pullicat silk, ⎪	Printed Velvets.
Croncard muslin, ⎭	

In a lecture delivered some two or three years ago, by the Hon. Mr. Sturges, of Boston, on trade and finances, he referred to the singular changes of the fashions. Nankeens, said he, were once imported in large quantities. As late as 1820 there were one million of dollars worth imported—now there is none. In 1806 Canton crape was first used; in 1810, ten cases were imported—in 1816, there were 21,000 pieces; in 1826 the importations amounted to a million and a half of dollars; and in 1842 the article was not imported! Yet the country has lost nothing by the caprice of fashion, as our country women appear as lovely in ninepenny Lowell calico, as in Canton crape.

Silk was once imported in large quantities from China; a cargo of near a million dollars worth was once landed in this country, and now the whole yearly importations from China amount to less than $100,000. Great changes have also taken place in regard to the pay of our Chinese importations. In 1818, $7,000,000 in specie were carried to China, but now our purchases are paid for in bills of exchange on England, from the proceeds of the opium trade. The fur trade was commenced in 1787, and in 1808 there were fifteen Americans engaged in it, and now it has ceased altogether.

IMPRISONMENT FOR DEBT.

The prisoners confined for debt in the City Hall, which was the jail also, celebrated the 5th July, 1790 (the 4th being Sunday.) There was an allusion to the 15th year of American *independence*, and their *confinement for debt*. Their fifth toast was: "May the time come when no *honest* man shall be confined for debt." The time did arrive, in less than half a century, when not even the *dishonest* man was confined for debt.

HUDSON RIVER.

This river bears the name of one of the early navigators, who united invincible fortitude to unwearied assiduity, and who is identified with its history. "This noble river was first discovered by Henry Hudson, in 1609, while in the employ of the Dutch East India Company. By some it is believed that he sailed up that river as far as the present site of the city of Albany, in a small vessel called the Half Moon; but, it is doubtful if any visions of futurity presented to his mind the present importance and celebrity of this beautiful stream, bearing his own name." It rises from numerous sources in the Adirondack mountain region of Essex and Hamilton counties, west of Lakes George and Champlain. Its principal head branches are the Adirondack river, Boreas river, Indian river, Schroon river and the Sacandaga river; the Hoosick river flows into it from the east in the county of Rensselaer, and the Mohawk empties into it between the counties of Albany and Saratoga; from this point it is navigable to its mouth, a distance of 160 miles. Its whole length is 320 miles; the tide flowing up for about half that distance. On the upper part of this river, justly celebrated for its varied and romantic beauties, are several picturesque falls, of which Baker's Falls and Glen's Falls are the most noted. The region of country where it takes its rise, was but little known until of late. In 1836, the state geologists, under an act to provide for a geological survey of the state of New York, commenced their operations; since then this vast wilderness has been fully explored, new localities discovered, and new names given; thus furnishing a great mass of information in regard to the sources of this river, and the mountain region from whence it takes its rise. Here are mountain peaks of Alpine appearance, containing vast deposits of iron ore and other minerals, well worthy a visit by the scientific admirers of wild and romantic scenery. In the head waters of the Hudson, are to be found trout, and other fish of fine flavor, in great abundance; and in its tide waters are taken annually large quantities of shad, herring, bass, sturgeon and many other kinds of fish. From its mouth to the city of Hudson, a distance of 116 miles, it is navigable for ships of a large burthen, and to Albany and Troy for steam boats of a large class. When we reflect that this important river receives the tributary waters of the great western and northern lakes, by means of the Erie and Champlain canals, and then commingles with the Atlantic ocean, after passing the Highlands, the Palisades, and through the secure and spacious bay of New York, well may we give it the appellation of the NOBLE HUDSON.—*Disturnell's Gazetteer.*

The combined action of the tides, arriving in the Hudson by East river and the Narrows, at different periods, carries the swell upward at the rate of 15 to near 25 miles an hour; and this circumstance clearly evinces a high superiority of oceanic influence in the Hudson. Swift sailing vessels, leaving New York at young flood, have repeatedly run through to Albany with the same flood tide. The time of high water is the same at Pollopell island, at the northern limit of the Highlands, as at New York; at Albany it is 3 hours 30 minutes later, where the common tides are little more than one foot. The passage of this river through the Highlands, without any impediment to its navigation, save that of a crooked though deep, and in some places a narrow channel, is a singular fact in geography, and it affords a pleasing diversity of scenery. The Highlands are about sixteen miles wide, and their hills and mountains present many features of vast sublimity. The water is but seldom salt or brackish at Poughkeepsie, and water casks are often filled below the Highlands. Much has been said about extending sloop navigation upward, on this river, above where nature has placed its limit, and immense sums of money have been expended, to little purpose. Few rivers roll down so much alluvial matter as the Hudson, say between Waterford and the head of ship navigation, and this alluvion increases with the opening of the land adjoining, and the decrease of the waters in the Hudson. While the Battenkill, Hoosac river, and the Mohawk, pour in their alluvion, it will be a very hard matter to make the navigation better than nature has made it. We may remove a sand-bar in one place, at the expense of obstructions in some other place, but all this alluvial matter will rest somewhere. The quantity is increasing and will increase, till a different plan is adopted, which shall carry this alluvion farther down the river. This may be done by throwing in all the water of the Mohawk at Waterford, connecting the islands by piers or moles, so as to make as straight and narrow a channel as may be, and a strong current, to the deep tide waters below.—*Spafford's Gazetteer.*

BOOKS IN 1772.

The literature vended at this day seems to have been confined to a very limited number of books promiscuously arranged in the catalogues of other goods. For instance, JOHN HEUGHAN of Schenectady, advertises "Scotch Snuff, Tobacco, *Bibles, Testaments Spelling Books*, Knives and Forks, *Writing Paper, Ink Powder, Quills*, Razors," &c. JAMES GOURLAY & Co. in Cheapside street, next door to the king's arms, Albany, after a copious enumeration of articles, arrive at "Penknives, Pins, *Bibles, Testaments, Spelling Books*, Green and Bohea Tea, Cotton, Pepper, Chocolate, *Playing Cards,* Shirt Buttons, Curtain Calicoes, *Ink Powder*, Knee Garters," &c. THOMAS BARRY, near the Dutch Church, had "Pins, None-so-pretty of different colors, *Testaments, Spelling Books, Histories*, Black Breeches Patterns," &c.

1785, under the head of dry goods, were advertised by THOMAS BARRY "at his store near the Dutch Church," as just imported from Europe and now opening for sale, Bibles, Testaments, Spelling Books, Primers, and Entick's Pocket Dictionaries, Snuff, Tobacco boxes and fiddle strings, rattinetts and shalloons, best China and love ribbons, &c. &c. At the same time ROBINSON & HALE advertise Bibles with Psalms and Psalm books, Testaments and Spelling Books, Primers and Pocket Dictionaries, Young Men's Companions and Arithmetics, which are enumerated rather fantastically with red China tea pots, and shoemaker's tools.

CLOSING AND OPENING OF THE RIVER SINCE 1785.

From the Annual Report of the Regents of the University.

Winters	River closed or ob. with ice.	River open or free of ice.	Days closed	Remarks.
1785–86		March 23, 1786		Eight times in the last 65 years has the Hudson closed before the 1st December; nine times within the same space the river was open till the first and second weeks in January, and once till 3d February. In the majority of cases the navigation closed between the 7th and 20th December. In fifteen of the sixty-five years, the river remained closed for more than one hundred days, and in 1843, 136 days —the longest on record. The years 1741, 1766, 1780, and 1821 are the only ones in a century in which the river has closed over below Powle's Hook, so as to be crossed on the ice. In 1842 the river opened on the 8th January, and was not closed again during the winter. In the year 1806, it will be seen, the navigation was obstructed only 42 days; and the average during the whole 65 years is less than 90 days.
1789–90	Feb. 3, 1790	March 27, 1790	52	
1790–91	Dec. 8, 1790	March 17, 1791	99	
1791–92	Dec. 8, 1791			
1792–93	Dec. 12, 1792	March 6, 1793	84	
1793–94	Dec. 26, 1793	March 17, 1794	81	
1794–95	Jan. 12, 1794			
1795–96	Jan. 23, 1795			
1796–97	Nov. 28, 1796			
1797–98	Nov. 26, 1797			
1798–99	Nov. 23, 1798			
1799–18	Jan. 6, 1800			
1800–01	Jan. 3, 1801			
1801–02	Feb. 3, 1802			
1802–03	Dec. 16, 1802			
1803–04	Jan. 12, 1804	April 6, 1804	84	
1804–05	Dec. 13, 1804			
1805–06	Jan. 9, 1806	Feb. 20, 1806	42	
1806–07	Dec. 11, 1807	April 8, 1807	121	
1807–08	Jan. 4, 1808	March 10, 1808	65	
1808–09	Dec. 9, 1808			
1809–10	Jan. 19, 1810			
1810–11	Dec. 14, 1810			
1811–12	Dec. 20, 1811			
1812–13	Dec. 21, 1812	March 12, 1813	83	
1813–14	Dec. 22, 1813			
1814–15	Dec. 10, 1814			
1815–16	Dec. 2, 1815			
1816–17	Dec. 16, 1816			
1817–18	Dec. 7, 1817	March 25, 1818	108	
1818–19	Dec. 14, 1818	April 3, 1819	110	
1819–20	Dec. 13, 1819	March 25, 1830	102	
1820–21	Nov. 13, 1820	March 15, 1821	123	
1821–22	Dec. 13, 1821	March 15, 1822	92	
1822–23	Dec. 24, 1822	March 24, 1823	90	
1823–24	Dec. 16, 1823	March 3, 1824	78	
1824–25	Jan. 5, 1825	March 6, 1825	60	
1825–26	Dec. 13, 1825	Feb. 26, 1826	75	
1826–27	Dec. 24, 1826	March 20, 1827	86	
1827–28	Nov. 25, 1827	Feb. 8, 1828	50	about
1828–29	Dec. 23, 1828	April 1, 1829	100	
1829–30	Jan. 11, 1830	March 15, 1830	63	
1830–31	Dec. 23, 1830	March 15, 1831	82	
1831–32	Dec. 5, 1821	March 25, 1832	111	
1832–33	Dec. 21, 1832	March 21, 1833	83	

Closing and Opening of the River.

1833–34	Dec. 13, 1833	Feb. 24, 1834	73
1834–35	Dec. 15, 1834	March 25, 1835	100
1835–36	Nov. 30, 1835	April 4, 1836	125
1836–37	Dec. 7, 1836	March 28, 1837	111
1837–38	Dec. 13, 1837	March 19, 1838	94
1838–39	Nov. 25, 1838	March 21, 1839	116
1839–40	Dec. 18, 1839	Feb. 21, 1840	65
1840–41	Dec. 5, 1840	March 24, 1841	109
1841–42	Dec. 19, 1841	Feb. 4, 1842	47
1842–43	Nov. 29, 1842	April 13, 1843	136
1843–44	Dec. 9, 1843	March 14, 1844	95
1844–45	Dec. 11, 1844	Feb. 24, 1845	74
1845–46	Dec. 4, 1845	March 15, 1846	100
1846–47	Dec. 15, 1846	April 6, 1847	112
1847–48	Dec. 24, 1847	March 22, 1848	89
1848–49	Dec. 27, 1848	March 19, 1849	82

NOTES.—1817–18. This winter was long and intensely cold. On the third of March, 1818, the ice moved in a body downwards for some distance, and there remained stationary. The river was not cleared until March 25th.

1820–21. The river closed on the 13th, opened on the 20th, and finally closed December 1. This was one of the four winters during a century in which the Hudson, between Powles' Hook and New York, was crossed on the ice; the other three being 1740, '41, 1765, '66, and 1779, '80.

Jan. 12, 1824. The river was clear of ice and remained so for several days.

1827–28. The river opened and closed repeatedly during this winter. Dec. 21, it closed a second time.

1830–31. Opened in consequence of heavy rains, and closed again on the 10th January, 1831.

1832–33. Opened again January 3; closed again January 11.

1834–35. March 17. River open opposite to the city. March 18, Steamboat John Jay came to Van Wie's Point; ice at the overslaugh.

1847–48. Dec. 24. River closed. Dec. 31. River opened.

As the river *throughout* to New York, has not always been clear of ice on the days stated above, the time at which the first steamboat passed from New York to Albany or vice versa, is also added for a few years.

1835, March 25.
1836, April 10.
1837, March 31, Robert L. Stevens.
1838, March 19, Utica.
1839, March 25, Swallow.
1840, February 25, Mount Pleasant.
1841, March 26, Utica.

1841, February 6, Telegraph. In consequence of heavy rains, the river opened in front of the city of Albany on the 8th January, and can hardly be said to have closed again during the season. The ice, however, continued piled up some miles below, at and about Barren Island, near Schodack Landing, and thus rendered the channel impassable. Cold weather followed about the middle of February, and again obstructed the navigation. A steamboat arrived on the 1st of March, 1842.

1843, April 13, Utica.
1844, March 18, 11 A. M., Utica.
1845, February 24, steamboat Norwich at 1 A. M., from New York. Left that city on the 22d, at 8 P. M. River full of ice from West Point upwards. Ice opposite Albany, stationary, except a small portion that broke away yesterday opposite Lydius street.
1846, March 18, steamboat Columbia and Oneida arrived.
1847, April 7, steamboat Columbia.
1848, March 22, steamboat Admiral.
1849, March 18, steamboat Columbia.

INCIDENTS OF A NORTHERN WINTER.

From the Albany Argus

1848, January 1. Weather mild and rainy. Lake Champlain clear of ice

January 2. Steamboats Norwich and Columbia arrived from New York.

January 7. Weather cold and fine Thermometer marked 4 degrees above zero. Columbia left for New York at 1 o'clock, last boat.

January 9. Snow 6 to 8 inches deep. Steamboat landed mail at New Baltimore.

January 10. Thermometer marked zero at 7 o'clock, A. M.

January 11. Thermometers at Albany, 17 to 18 below zero. At Amsterdam, 36 below. Rochester, 8 below. Troy, 16 below. New York and Brooklyn, 3 above. Boston, 10 below. Fryburgh, Me., 36 to 39 below. Franconia, N. H., 45 below. The steamboat Columbia, which left New York the night before, was compelled to return after running up the river 30 miles.

January 14 and 15. A general thaw. Weather continued to be warm the rest of the month.

February 1. Four to six inches of snow fell.

February 2. Weather warm again.

February 4. The steamboat Columbia came within two miles of Albany.

February 5. Snow fell to a considerable depth.

February 6. Snowed most of the day. Steamboat came to Coeymans.

February 9. Thermometer at zero. Hudson closed to Newburgh.

February 11. Thermometer at zero.

February 12, Floating ice in New York harbor, for the first time this winter.

February 19. Blue birds seen at Bloomingdale, New York.

February 20. Heavy rain storm from the south.

February 23. Steam ferry boat Boston, crossed to East Albany.

February 24. Weather very cold again; thermometer five degrees above zero.

February 28. River open to Hudson.

March 3. Snow storm all day.

March 9. About a foot of snow fell during the night.

Opening and Closing of the Canal. 329

March 12. Thermometer 10 degrees below zero.
March 15. Thermometer at zero at 7 A. M. At Schenectady seven below.
March 16 and 17. Thermometer at zero.
March 18. Thermometer 23 degrees above zero.
March 21. Steamboat Columbia at Van Wie's Point.
March 22. Ice passed out of the river. Steamboat Admiral arrived at Albany.

OPENING AND CLOSING OF THE CANAL FROM 1824 TO 1849 INCLUSIVE.

The following table shows the days of opening and closing of the canal since 1824:

Year.	Opened.	Closed.	No. days.	Year.	Opened.	Closed.	No. days.
1824..	April 30	Dec. 4	219	1837..	" 20	Dec. 9	234
1825..	" 12	" 5	238	1838..	" 12	Nov. 25	228
1826..	" 20	" 18	213	1839..	" 20	Dec. 16	228
1827..	" 23	" 18	241	1840..	" 20	" 3	227
1828..	Mar. 27	" 20	269	1841..	" 26	Nov. 29	218
1829..	May 2	" 17	230	1842..	" 20	" 23	281
1830..	April 20	" 17	242	1843..	May 1	Dec. 1	214
1831..	" 16	" 1	230	1844..	April 18	Nov. 26	223
1832..	" 25	" 21	241	1845..	" 15	" 29	228
1833..	" 10	" 12	238	1846..	" 16	" 25	224
1834..	" 17	" 12	240	1847..	May 1	Dec. 21	234
1835..	" 15	Nov. 30	230	1848..	" 1	" 9	223
1836..	" 25	" 26	216	1849..	" 1	" 5	219

COLD DAYS SIXTY YEARS AGO.

On the first of February, 1789, the thermometer at noon indicated 18° above zero, and on the following morning at 6 o'clock was 24° below, being 6° colder than had been ever known in the city. This memorandum was taken from the weather book kept at the museum opposite Denniston's tavern in Green street

On the 3d Nov. of the same year a snow storm began at 10 in the morning and continued through the day, the weather being remarkably cold, and having every appearance of the setting in of winter, a circumstance not before recollected by any of the inhabitants.

On the 9th Dec., 1790, the thermometer indicated 10° below 0, and the weather was pronounced colder for the season than had ever been known before in this city.

28*

CELEBRATION OF THE ADOPTION OF THE CONSTITUTION, 1788.

The delegates nominated by the two parties for the convention to decide on the adoption of the federal constitution, were the following:

FEDERAL.	ANTI-FEDERAL.
Abraham Ten Broeck,	Robert Yates,
Jacob Cuyler,	John Lansing, jr.
Francis Nicoll,	Henry Oothoudt,
Jeronemus Hoogland,	Peter Vrooman,
Peter Gansevoort, jr	Israel Thompson,
James Gordon,	Anthony Ten Eyck,
John W. Schermerhorn.	Dirk Swart,

By the returns from the counties of Albany, Montgomery, Washington, Columbia, Dutchess, Ulster, and Orange, 37 anti-federal candidates were elected to the convention for considering the United States Constitution. The counties of New York, Westchester, Kings, and Richmond, gave 19 federal. The counties of Queens sending 9, was divided. The whole number of delegates sent was 67. In New York the vote was decidedly federal; some of the opposite candidates receiving only 30 votes and the highest, which was given for Gov. Clinton, being but 134. The following is the canvass of the votes for the federal delegates, and will show the strength of the electors in that city, at that period.

FEDERAL.		ANTI-FEDERAL.	
John Jay,	2735	Gov. Clinton,	134
Richard Morris,	2716	Col. Willett,	108
John Sloss Hobart,	2713	William Dunning,	102
Alex. Hamilton,	2713	The remainder each about	30
Robt. R. Livingston,	2712		
Isaac Rosevelt,	2701		
James Duane,	2680		
Richard Harrison,	2677		
Nicholas Low.	2651		

The Convention came to a decision on the 26th July 1788, yeas 30, nays 17; by which New York adopted the Constitution, being the 11th on the catalogue.

When the vote was taken in congress 11 states were represented; the two members from Rhode Island were excused from voting, and of the 22 members remaining there was but one dissenting voice, which was that of Mr. Yates, member from New York—the other New York member, Mr. L'Hommedieu, voting in the affirmative.

The city of Albany, not to be behind her sister cities in patriotic display, set apart the 8th of August as a day of public rejoicings, to celebrate the ratification of the constitution of the United States by the Convention of the state of New York. Almost every trade and profession seems to have united in the jubilee, with appropriate emblems, and formed a truly imposing procession, notwithstanding the preponderance of the anti-federal party at the polls. A page of the Gazette of August 28, is occupied with the proceedings, as follows:

Celebration of the Adoption of the Constitution. 331

Account of the rejoicings in the city of Albany, on Friday, August 8, 1788, on celebrating the Ratification of the Constitution for the Government of the United States, by the Convention of the State of New York.

At sunrise, a gun was fired to announce the day.

At 10 o'clock, A. M., 11 guns were fired for the citizens to assemble in the fields near Watervliet.

At 10½ o'clock, one gun for forming the procession.

At 11, the procession was formed, when the whole line on the march saluted the *Constitution*.

Immediately after the salute, the procession moved, in the following order:

The Albany troop of Light Horse, in full uniform, commanded by Captain Gansevoort.

Music.

The CONSTITUTION, neatly engrossed on parchment, suspended on a decorated staff, and borne by Major-General Schuyler, on horseback.

Standard of the United States, carried by Colonel John A. Wendell.

Eleven ancient citizens, each representing a state that had ratified the Constitution, bearing a scroll of parchment, with the name of the state endorsed in capitals.

AXEMEN: ornamented with garlands of laurels.

An elegant plough, guided by Stephen Van Rensselaer, Esq.

SOWERS: John Cuyler, Esq., and Capt. Jacob Lansing.

A neat harrow, guided by Francis Nicoll, Esq.

FARMERS: neatly dressed, with various implements of husbandry.

FARMERS' FLAG: Geen silk—a sheaf of wheat. Motto—*God speed the plough.*

BREWERS: preceded by a dray carrying a butt.

CARPENTERS: preceded by a carriage drawn by two horses, on which was erected a workshop 14 feet by 7; highly decorated. The flag of crimson silk, with a coat of arms. Motto—*We unite.*

GOLD AND SILVERSMITHS: preceded by a carriage bearing a Gold and Silversmith's shop, 12 feet by 7—covered with a canopy supported by pillars 7 feet high. All the implements of art in the shop, and three artists and an apprentice industriously employed. Flag, blue silk with a coat of arms.

BOAT BUILDERS: with their tools decorated.

TINMEN AND PEWTERERS: with implements of their craft ornamented.

BLOCK AND PUMPMAKERS: with their tools ornamented.

BLACKSMITHS: A carriage, drawn by six horses, supporting a blacksmith's shop 14 feet by 8, containing a forge, bellows, and all the apparatus of the trade, one sledge man, two vice men, one clink, all at work; who made and completed during the procession, a set of ploughirons, a set of scythe mountings, two axes, and shoes for three horses, and followed by master workmen. The flag, black silk with coat of arms. Motto—

> With hammer in hand,
> All arts do stand.

CLOCK AND WATCHMAKERS: An apprentice bearing an embellished ht-day time piece.

AIL MAKERS.

BARBERS: handsomely dressed, bearing implements of their craft, decorated. Flag, white silk and coat of arms. Motto—*Honor and Honesty*.

BAKERS: properly dressed, bearing implements of their art, decorated—an escutcheon, a loaf ornamented.

NAILERS: each wearing a clean white apron, preceded by a carriage drawn by four horses, supporting a nailer's shop, 11 by 9—nailers at work. Flag blue silk, coat of arms. Motto—
> With hammer and heart,
> We'll support our part.

CLOTHIERS.

TOBACCONISTS: dressed in white frocks, each carrying a hand of tobacco decorated with ribands.

CARMEN: In proper dress, preceded by a horse and cart carrying a hogshead marked No. 11. Flag white silk, and coat of arms. Motto—*We hope to rest in God*.

SHIP JOINERS AND SHIPWRIGHTS: With implements of their art ornamented.

RIGGERS.

HATTERS: With decorated tools, preceded by a flag, carried by Mr. Solomon Allen. Coat of arms. Motto—*Success to American Manufactures*.

INSPECTORS OF FLOUR.

MILLERS, in proper dress.

WEAVERS: Bearing shuttles decorated. Flag, purple silk, with coat of arms. Motto—*Weave truth with trust*.

PRINTERS: Preceded by apprentices, decorated with blue sashes, carrying volumes of newspapers. A white silk flag carried by Charles R. Webster; in an escutcheon, the Bible, the Constitution, Sept. 1787, Ratification of the State of New York, July 26, 1788. On a wreath a hand holding a composing stick, proper. Motto—*Our freedom is secured*.

Mr. Webster, and Stoddard* and Babcock†, apprentices, decorated with blue sashes, carrying quires of paper, &c.

PAINTERS AND GLAZIERS.

TAILORS: Ornamented with yellow sashes and cockades, wearing green aprons, preceded by Messrs. Henry and Gibson. A flag of green silk, with a coat of arms. Motto—*Concordia parva res crescunt*.

COACH MAKERS: Preceded by a flag of blue silk and coat of arms. Motto—*Post nubila Phœbus*; followed by a carriage drawn by four horses, on which was erected a large workshop, handsomely decorated, with several men at work, who framed a coach and put several wheels together.

TURNERS: properly dressed, preceded by a flag of pink colored silk, with a coat of arms. Motto—

> We turn to serve the common weal,
> And drive the trade with skill and zeal.

MASONS and BRICKLAYERS: In their proper dress, carrying the implements of their trade ornamented. Flag—blue silk with coat of arms.

SADDLERS and HARNESS MAKERS: With implements of their craft. A flag of blue silk with coat of arms. Motto—*Our trust is in God*.

---

* Printer in Hudson. † Printer in Lansingburgh.

Celebration of the Adoption of the Constitution. 333

TANNERS and CURRIERS: Carrying the implements of their branches, decorated. A flag of pink silk, with coat of arms.

BRASS FOUNDERS: Neatly dressed in green aprons and white cockades, carrying implements of the profession, preceded by an air furnace neatly constructed.

COOPERS: Preceded by Benjamin Winne, aged 84 years; on a carriage drawn by 4 horses, a cooper shop, well constructed, ornamented with 11 pillars, each crowned with a cask: several men at work. Flag, carried by Mr. Robert Hewson, of red silk, with coat of arms.

BUTCHERS: In uniform of white frocks and blue sashes, driving 2 beautiful oxen, ornamented with ribbands, preceded by music. Flag—blue silk, with coat of arms. Motto—*May we never want fat cattle.*

CORDWAINERS: A carriage drawn by 2 horses, on which a handsome shop, 12 feet long and 6 wide, was erected. In the shop, Mr. Fredenrich and several journeymen and apprentices at work, dressed in white, with aprons, yellow sashes and cockades. The carriage was preceded by Mr. David Groesbeck and Mr. Anthony Hallenbake, and followed by masters, journeymen and apprentices—Mr. Matthew Fryer carrying a yellow silk flag with a coat of arms.

STATE STANDARD, carried by Major John D. P. Ten Eyck.

GLASS MAKERS: Dressed in green, carrying various tools and implements of their profession—globes, bottles and other specimens of their manufactory.

A BATTEAU: Elegantly painted and decorated; on a carriage drawn by two grey horses, neatly caparisoned, loaded with goods proper for the Indian trade, navigated by a proper number of batteaumen furnished with setting-poles, paddles, &c., which were used with great skill during the procession. Mr. Gerardus Lansingh, in the character of a trader, and an Indian, properly dressed and ornamented, sitting in the stern. During the repast, the batteau made a voyage towards the Mohawk country, and returned with a full cargo of peltry.

CAPTAINS OF VESSELS: Preceded by Capt. Philip Lansing, carrying a flag of blue silk, on which was a sloop without sails. Motto—"*God sends sails.*"

MERCHANTS and TRADERS, with their clerks, preceded by Mr. Jacob Cuyler, carrying a white flag, in an escutcheon, one ship inward and another outward bound—supported by two sheaves of wheat. Motto—*May our exports exceed our imports.*

The CORPORATIONS of the Dutch, Episcopal and Presbyterian Churches, preceded by the Clergy.

Sheriff and his deputies, with white wands.
Constables with their staves.
Grand Jury.
Members of Corporation.
Judges and Justices of Common Pleas.
The Chancellor.
Gentlemen of the Bar, in gowns, followed by their students.
School masters, followed by their scholars.
Surveyor General
Adjutant General, and officers of Militia, in complete uniform.
Physicians and students.
Detachment of Artillery, commanded by Capt. Lieut. *Hale.* Standard blue silk, on which was a field piece, mortar, and burning shell.

The PROCESSION moved with the greatest regularity through Watervlie' Market, (now Broadway) and State street, to the FEDERAL BOWEI which the van reached at half past twelve o'clock, announced by the firing of a gun.

This edifice made an highly elegant appearance. It was erected o: a most advantageous part of the heights west of Fort Frederick; con manding the most extended prospect of any situation near the city; an. when the flags of the respective divisions were displayed on its battle-ments, that of the United States in the centre, that of the State on the right, and the farmers on the left, the *coup p'œil* was extremely pleasing.

The edifice was 154 feet in length and 44 in breadth, and was raised on 4 rows of pillars, 15 feet in height, which were close wreathed with foliage and composed of 11 arches in front.

From the architrave, which was clothed with verdant branches, festoons of foliage were suspended, which crossed the arches; above the centre of which, were white oval medallions, with the name of a ratifying state on each.

When the procession had drawn up in a line, at the rear of the bower, the company marched off, in regular divisions, to the tables, which were plentifully covered with substantial American cheer; handsomely arranged under the direction of Mr. WM. VAN INGEN. And the tables, which were eleven in number, placed across the collonade, in a line with the arches, were by no means sufficient for the company.

After dinner, the following toasts were drank, each honored with the discharge of eleven guns:

1. The United States.
2. The States which ratified the New Constitution.
3. The Convention of this State.
4. The Eleventh Pillar in the Federal edifice.
5. General Washington.
6. The friendly powers of Europe.
7. Agriculture and Commerce.
8. American Manufactures.
9. Inland navigation and the Fur trade restored.
10. The memory of those Heroes who have fallen in defence of American Liberty.
11. Concord and confidence at home, and respectability abroad.
12. May virtue, patriotism and harmony prevail, and discord be banished from all American councils.
13. May the union of the States be perpetual.

A gun was fired, as a signal for again forming the procession, which was done with the utmost regularity and dispatch The route then taken was down State street into Pearl street, and through it, Columbia street, Market street and Court street, into a spacious pasture south of Fort Orange; where the whole formed a semicircle. After 11 guns had been fired from the Fort, answered by three cheers from the whole, the respective divisions marched off at intervals, and as they passed the Fort, received a salute of a single gun, which they returned with three cheers.

JAMES FAIRLIE, Esq., was the Marshal of the procession. His assistants were THOS. L. WITBECK, CASPARUS HEWSON, JOHN CUYLER, Jr., and JOHN BLEECKER.

It may be mentioned, by way of episode, that when the procession reached Green street, a party of anti-federalists, as they were then called, who had collected there, made an assault upon it, and a skirmish ensued. One of the principal actors in the scene was the late Mr. Jonathan Kidney. A cannon had been procured, and heavily charged; and the excitement was so great, that it would undoubtedly have been discharged upon the line of procession, had not Mr. Kidney prevented it by driving the end of a file into the fuse, and breaking it off. The lighthorse made a charge upon the assailants, wo scampered out of the way. The projecting oven of the old Stone House was torn down to furnish missiles. Among the wounded on the occasion was Mr. James Caldwell, who received a brick upon his forehead.

The election of members of Assembly, terminated in the success of the anti-Federal party, and seems to have been the first party struggle growing out of the dissension on the question of the Constitution. The vote of the two parties in the county of Albany, as canvassed by the supervisors, on the 27th May, 1788, stood as follows. John Younglove seems to have had the votes of both.

ANTI-FEDERAL.		FEDERAL.	
John Lansing,	3048	Stephen Van Rensselaer,	1953
Jeremiah Van Rensselaer,	3042	Leonard Gansevoort,	1888
John Duncan,	2990	Richard Sill,	1877
Cornelius Van Dyck,	3033	Hezekiah Van Orden,	1871
John Thompson,	3006	John Knickerbacker,	1868
Henry K. Van Rensselaer,	2911	Isaac Vrooman,	1851
John Younglove,	4807		

CENTENNIAL ANNIVERSARY.

On Saturday, the 22d day of July, 1786, the corporation and citizens of Albany celebrated the Centennial Anniversary of the charter of the city. "At 11 o'clock the corporation convened in the council chamber, at the City Hall, where they were joined by a great number of citizens; when the bells of the several churches began to ring, they marched in procession westward of the city, where a number of toasts were drank, under the discharge of cannon from the Fort."

The order of procession was as follows: 1, The Sheriff; 2, Under Sheriff; 3, Constables; 4, Mayor; 5, Recorder; 6, Aldermen; 7, Assistants; 8, Clerk and Chamberlain; 9, City Marshal; 10, The Ministers, Elders and Deacons of the Dutch, Lutheran, Episcopal, Presbyterian and German Churches; 11, Fire and Engine Companies; 12, Members of the Legislature, Judges, Justices, and Counsellors at Law; 13, Officers of the Army and Militia; 14, Citizens at large. In addition to the above, we are told that "the countenances of the inhabitants bespoke great satisfaction on the occasion."

MEMORANDA OF 1784-5.

In the year 1784, the post-office at Albany served for the adjoining towns not only, as Schenectady and Greenbush, but also for Orange and Dutchess counties, Cherry Valley, Pleasant Valley, &c., and Vermont.

By the post-office arrangements, two years afterwards, the New-York mail arrived twice a week, Wednesdays and Saturdays, at 8 o'clock P. M.; and two hours after its receipt, the down mail was made up and forwarded.

On the 7th of October, the Marquis Lafayette arrived in the city, on his return from Fort Stanwix, where he had been to attend the Indian treaty. On Friday morning he left for Boston, by the way of Hartford, which latter place he reached on the following Monday—a journey which may now be made in about nine hours.

The city ordinance regulating the Ferry rates, was as follows:

For transporting every person across, except a sucking child, 2 coppers.

For every man, ox, horse or cow,		9 pence.
do. live sheep or lamb,		3 do.
do. dead do.		2 do.
do. barrel of rum, sugar, molasses, or other full brl.,		6 do.
do. pail of butter,		1 do.
do. firkin or tub of butter,		2 do.
do. wagon and two horses,		3 shillings.
do. full chest or trunk,		6 pence.
do. empty do.		5 coppers.
do. skipple of wheat or other grain,		1 do.
do. cwt. of lead, pewter or other metal,		4 do.
do. chaise or chair and horse,		15 pence.
do. saddle without a horse,		2 coppers.
do. dozen pair shoes or boots,		2 do.
do. do. steel traps,		6 do.

And all other articles and things not enumerated, in the same proportion to the rates above specified.

These rates were doubled after sunset until sunrise; and it was enjoined upon the ferry master to keep at least two boats and a scow, two of which should be constantly manned by four able hands.

The health of the city during the winter of 1784-5, was so remarkable, that but one burial took place among the congregation of the Dutch church from the 9th December to the 10th March, and that was a small child accidently run over by a sleigh.

On Saturday the 30th April, 1785, the term of the Supreme Court ended, when Petrus and Christian Cooper were convicted of robbery, and Christian Loucks of horse stealing, all of whom received sentence of death therefor. Two convicted of felony were admitted to benefit of clergy, one whipped for petit larceny, and two discharged by proclamation. The Coopers were hung on the 8th June, and died protesting their innocence. Loucks was pardoned a few days before the time set for his execution.

In June, 1785, a company of "stage-wagon" proprietors undertook to make the land passage between New-York and Albany, "the most easy and agreeable, as well as the most *expeditious*," by performing the

Memoranda of 1784-5.

journey in *two days*, at 3d. a mile; but in the fall of the year, "for the ease of passengers," the time of performing the route was altered to three days, and the price raised to 4d. a mile, "agreeable to act of Assembly." This made two trips a week. No one imagined at that time, probably, that the journey would ever be regularly performed in a single day.

Alexander Laverty, "tayler from London," advertises that "payments will be made easy to those who will please employ him." His prices were, for making a coat 14s.; lapelled do, 16s.; lapelled with slash sleeves, 18s; vest and breeches 6s. 9d.

The price of bread in New York, as regulated by the common council, was 1lb. 1½oz. for 4 coppers; 2lb. 5oz. for 8 coppers. Fine flour 24s. per. cwt.

An ordinance was passed by the corporation for the extermination of dogs, all of whom were to be killed in two days, under penalty of £8, which was to be recovered for the benefit of any person prosecuting.

On the 7th Nov. 1785, the Presbytery of New York ordained John McDonald a minister of the gospel, and installed him pastor of the Presbyterian church in Albany. He was the last pastor who officiated in the old wooden edifice then occupied by the first Presbyterian church near the north east corner of Grand and Hudson streets.

The first theatrical performance in Albany was enacted by a company from New York, having gained permission "for one month only," from "his excellency the governor." They occupied the hospital and the first play was *Venice Preserved*, July 3, 1769.

Under date of Dec. 5, 1786, we learn from the *Gazette*, that "a number of carpenters for these somedays have been employed in fitting up with great expedition the Hospital in this city, as a Theatre." It opened on the 14th with *Cross Purposes*, and *Catharine and Petruchio*; between which was a dance, *La Polonaise*, and *An Eulogy on Freemasonry*. Tickets were to be had at Mr. Lewis's tavern, as no money would be taken at the door. Boxes 8s.; Gallery 4s. A vigorous effort was made to discontinue these performances, by a large and respectable part of community, but the common council determined by a vote of 6 to 4, that they had no legal right to prohibit theatrical exhibitions in the city. A whole number of the Gazette is taken up with the controversy, to the exclusion of every other item.

On the 4th April, 1786, an act passed the legislature of the state of New York for erecting the southeast part of the county of Albany into a new county, by the name of Columbia.

At the July term of the Supreme Court, which closed its session on the 5th of July, Caleb Gardner, convicted of passing counterfeit Spanish dollars, received sentence of death. Two weeks afterwards the sheriff advertised that the persons then under sentence of death in the City Hall would be hanged on Friday, the 14th of September, and that any person willing to undertake the execution was desired to apply to the said sheriff.

CONDITION AND PROSPECTS OF THE CITY IN 1789.

A writer in the Gazette of this year gives the following account of its condition, improvements and prospects:

Every thinking man, who takes a retrospective view of this city, and contemplates what it was seven or eight years ago, and what it now is, will be astonished at the improvements in the city, and the increase of commerce, manufactures, &c., since that period. Then some of the principal streets were shamefully neglected, without a pavement sufficient even for a foot passenger to walk on, without annoying himself with filth. We have a prospect, ere another year shall transpire, of seeing the principal streets not only comfortably, but elegantly paved. In addition to which, the wharves have been repaired and enlarged, and the city adorned with several new private buildings, which would not disgrace some of the principal cities in Europe, and would ornament any in America.

At that period a competent English teacher was scarcely to be found. We now have an academy, which flourishes under the direction of Mr. Merchant, a gentleman who has always given such proofs of his abilities, as to render encomium entirely superfluous.

At that period not more than seventy, at the utmost calculation, shops and stores were kept in this city. Now we behold Market and State streets crowded with stores, and rents in those streets unhanced to such a degree as to put houses out of the reach of inconsiderable traders. Nor had we manufactories of any kind, but depended on importation entirely for every manufactured article. Now we see the citizens stimulated by motives of public spirit, daily promoting them. Messrs. Stevenson, Douw & Ten Eyck have erected a nail manufactory, in which nails of every description are manufactured as cheap, and pronounced to be superior to any imported.

Much praise is also due to James Caldwell, of this city, merchant, for his spirited exertions in promoting the manufacture of tobacco of every description, snuff, mustard and chocolate, for which purpose he has, at great expense, erected mills which are ranked among the first in America; and in which every article manufactured is of the best ingredients, and allowed to be of superior quality.

What a glorious prospect lies before us! A thriving city, situated in the heart of a fertile, extensive and growing country, possessing all the advantages of trade that can be desired, united to the power (some trivial inconveniences excepted) of enjoying those of navigation. Such are the blessings which Nature has bestowed on us. And I flatter myself I am not too sanguine, when I indulge the idea, that I shall live to see the day when this city, adorned with every necessary public building, and other improvements, will become the fixed seat of government of the Legislature; shipping of considerable bulk, owned by our own merchants, opening their canvas before our wharves, and wafting the produce of our country to distant quarters of the globe: in short, that the city will wear an aspect as different from what it did seven years ago, as twilight is from noon-day.

A TOBACCO ESTABLISHMENT OF 1790.

It is believed that Mr. JAMES CALDWELL was the first great tobacco manufacturer of this region.

The editor of the Gazette, in the fall of 1790, gave a description of the recently erected tobacco works of this gentleman, prefaced by some laudatory and prophetic remarks on the present and future condition of the city. "While we receive daily accounts of the progress of manufactures in our infant country," he says, "it affords us a singular pleasure to have it in our power to present the flattering prospects we have of vieing in this respect with any other town on the continent. As the peculiar advantages of our situation entitle us to look forward to the period *when a commerce, great beyond calculation, must circulate through this place*, we have equal reasons, from the advances already made, to anticipate the flourishing state of our manufactures." The establishment recently put in operation by Mr. Caldwell is selected as an instance of the enterprise of the day—the site of which was occupied for the same purpose, by his partner and successor Mr. Solomons, until about twenty years ago.

"The buildings belonging to these works extend on a line along the front about 200 feet. That part which contains the machinery of the mills is 42 feet front. One water-wheel of $3\frac{1}{4}$ feet wide with $1\frac{1}{4}$ inches water, by an upright shaft puts in motion the snuff-mill, which consists of 4 mortars, 16 rollers, and a snuff bolt. A mustard mill, with 2 large rollers, 4 mortars and stampers; a charcoal mill, with a run of stones and cocoa-roaster; an engine for cutting smoking tobacco; a machine for cutting tobacco for the snuff-mill; and a large grindstone for the use of the works. It likewise gives motion to an elegant colossal figure of a man, represented in the act of turning a winch, from which all the machinery apparently receives motion.

"The tobacco is pressed and brought to the knife of the cutting machine on a plan entirely new, without manual labor. All these works, together with a kiln for preparing the mustard seed, are on the first and second floors. Any part may be set in motion or stopped without affecting the others. On the third floor is a kiln for tobacco. Both kilns are on a new and improved construction. Here are a number of hands constantly employed in packing snuff and tobacco. The house for drying and curing tobacco adjoins the mill on the west, and is 70 feet in front. The fire-places are constructed with such improvements as not to require one-fourth the wood commonly consumed for the like purposes. The upper part is occupied as a store-room for tobacco. The house on the west contains the tobacco manufactory; on the lower floor of which are nine complete presses, and a room where the tobacco is formed into rolls, in a manner never before discovered, without either pins or thorns—of which invention the merit is solely due to the manufacturer. On the second floor the spinning is done, where 24 hands are constantly employed in the various parts of the business. There is a machine by which one boy can turn for five or six tables, and can stop either, when occasion requires, without interrupting the rest. This last improvement has been often attempted in Europe and America, but has never before been brought to the perfection it is here.

"The water is conveyed to the mills by a trench, and from thence passes off by a subterraneous conduit, over which is the main road; and the water-wheel is so sheltered that neither can be perceived from the inside or outside of the mill. Besides these buildings, there is an elegant and commodious dwelling-house and several out-houses belonging to the manufactory, all disposed in such a manner as to make a beautiful appearance. They are situated about one mile from the centre of the city, and 400 yards west from the mansion-house of Stephen Van Rensselaer, Esq., at the entrance of the delightful valley, through which a never failing stream passes, that turns a number of other mills within sight of each other.

"Mr. Christopher Batterman,[*] a young man, a native of Boston, is the architect, to whose ingenuity the plan of the works, and the various improvements in the execution are to be ascribed—as he was solely entrusted by Mr. Caldwell with the construction of them. He intends to make Albany his residence. The snuff mill is in such high perfection, that by going only nine months in the year, more snuff can be produced, it is said, than is consumed annually in the northern part of America. We may add, without prejudice or vanity, that these works are superior to any thing of the kind in America; and give evidence of an emulation which will in a few years, in all probability, place Albany on a footing with the first cities on the continent."

July 12, 1794.—"The extensive and beautiful works, belonging to Mr. Caldwell, situated about a mile north of this city, were entirely consumed by fire, together with between five and six thousand pounds worth of stock. The whole loss is estimated at upwards of £13,000. The fire broke out between the hours of one and two in the morning of Saturday, in the chocolate mill, but by what means it caught, no one is able to determine. Nothing was saved of all that range, but one small kitchen."

These works were soon rebuilt.

---

[*] He is believed to have been the ancestor of the Battermans residing in Guilderland; having removed to the glass-works after this establishment was completed, where he resided during his life, and left a large and valuable estate.

ANNALS OF ALBANY FOR THE YEAR 1849.

January.

1. Newyear; weather pleasant, and sleighing good...... Hon. Hamilton Fish and George W. Patterson, Governor and Lieut Governor elect, inaugurated at the Capitol....... Michael McKown died of a wound inflicted by William Maxsted, Dec. 9th....... Total commitments to the penitentiary for the year ending December last, 363; to the jail, 1961.

2. Cold day; mercury 2° above zero. An alarm of fire in the evening: an unfinished building slightly damaged........The Governor's message, by means of the magnetic telegraph, was promulgated at the western and southern extremities of the state simultaneously with its being read in the Capitol.

4. A convention of civil engineers met at the common council room in the City Hall, to discuss a proposition for forming themselves into a society........ The refectory of Adams & Welch entered by burglars.

5. Dr. Wing gave notice in the Assembly of a bill for the removal of the Hallenbeck burial ground, corner of S. Pearl and Hamilton streets. ......Benedict Lewis died, aged 66. John Paterson died, aged 76.

6. Peter Courtright died, aged 34.......Mercury in the thermometer sinking rapidly.

7. Warner Daniels junior, formerly of this city, died in New York, aged 31. Mrs. Euphemia, wife of William Chambers, died, aged 31. Mrs. Philo D. Lyon died....... Rev. Orville Dewey, D.D., having accepted an invitation to preach for the Unitarian Society one year, entered upon the duties of his office.......Weather very cold, the mercury little above zero Fahrenheit's scale.

8. Ice on the river one foot in thickness: By means of a temporary bridge on to it at the foot of State street, an uninterrupted and safe communication is formed with East Albany.

9. William Bradley Cole, a printer, from Albany, died at Nassau, Bahama Islands, aged 27....... Nineteen paintings and sixteen Allston and Stewart medals, prizes allotted to the Albany members of the American Art Union, arrived, and were exhibited at Little & Co.'s Bookstore....... Alderman Jenkins reported the following schedule of the state of the City Railroad Sinking Fund, viz: Amount of sinking fund, Jan. 1, 1849, $231,597.38. Loaned on bonds and mortgages on property in the city, $209,617.00; city stock, $20,000.00; cash in bank, $1980.38.

10. The corporation directed application to be made to the legislature for a law to designate the place of landing and departure of steamboats. ......Dr. Fay, the almshouse physician, reported, that during the last three months, 183 inmates required medical treatment, 122 of whom were cured, 15 died, and 46 are still under treatment.......Receipts of the Albany & Boston Railroad Company over those of last year, $6000.

11. Aggregate valuation of the real estate in the city, $8,209,957.00; personal, $2,729,881.00; total, $10,939,838.00. Amount of taxes as-

sessed for city purposes, $172,079.34; for county purposes, $71,463.10; total, $243,542.44. Incorporated companies pay taxes on $2,004,634.86; private individuals, $725,246.98; total, $2,729,881.84....... Meeting of the Society for the relief of the poor, held in the Middle Dutch Church. ......Amount of profits received at St. Vincent's Orphan Fair, held by the Sisters of Charity, $3144.64....... The coldest day yet; mercury ranging from 8 to 12° below zero....... Dorothea, wife of Capt. James Wilson, died, aged 35.

12. Amos Pilsbury reappointed superintendent of the Penitentiary for three years; and William W. Forsyth and Samuel Pruyn of the city, and Gilbert J. Van Zandt of Watervliet, chosen directors for the same term. ...... The death of Rev. Noah Levings, D.D., former pastor of the M. E. C. in Division street, was announced by telegraph....... The store of H. D. Hawkins in Exchange street, and Griffin's eating house in Green street, were entered by burglars.

13. Louisa, wife of W. W. Van Zandt, and daughter of W. Dowd, died, aged 27.......The Albany California Company left New York in the ship Tarolinta....... Telegraph not in operation....... The gunsmith shop of W. I. & R. H. Scott, in Beaver street, was partially injured by fire.

14. Sarah E. Ford died, aged 25....... Change of weather, resulting in a January thaw.......William Hill, a newsboy, fell through the ice, but was rescued alive.

15. Hon. D. D. Barnard delivered an address in the court room at the City Hall, on the Life and Character of the late Chief Justice Ambrose Spencer....... The weather moist throughout the day, and rain at intervals.

16. The streets and sidewalks covered by a thick coating of ice.

17. Cynthia, wife of Brunson A. Baldwin, died, aged 25,......Prof. Emmons delivered an address on Agricultural Science, in the assembly chamber, before the State Agricultural Society. ...... John B. Gough lectured before the State Temperance Convention.......Patrick Coyle, Michael Flood and Peter Halpen were killed by gas escaping from a pipe which they were repairing. Coyle was injured by the rope with which he was lowering himself with intent to relieve the other two.

18. Fire among the wooden tenements on Quay, between Steuben and Columbia streets; several of them burned....... Richard Mochrie, an old inhabitant of the city, found dead in his bed....... Concert for the benefit of the Mission Sabbath School, held in Dr. Campbell's Church, Pearl street.

19. Nathaniel R. Packard died, aged 64... ...A fire broke out in the block known as the Lumbermen's Exchange, at the Little Basin, and consumed a part of it.

20. James McGrath junior died, aged 28.

21. Trinity Church, in Broad street, opened for divine service.

22. Christian Mary St. John died, aged 33.........Alarm of fire caused by the burning of a small frame building near Troy Iron-works.

23. Frederick Fink, a well known artist of this city, died at his father's residence at Littlefalls. Lewis Farnham died, aged 23. ...... Commencement of the Albany Medical College held: number of students about 100, of whom 20 graduated, receiving the degree of M.D. Valedictory address by Dr. Armsby.

24. James McCulloch died. Lawrence Courtright died, aged 38. ....Six large buildings on the south side of Washington street, occupied as dwellings and storehouses, were burnt.

25. Hardware store of Daniel Fry entered by burglars, who obtained about one dollar in silver for their labor........Rev. Dr. Halley, of Troy, delivered a lecture on the "Probability of the planetary and stellar orbs being inhabited," before the Young Men's Association, in the First Presbyterian Church........Mrs. Elizabeth Blake died, aged 24. George McKenzie died, aged 62........Passengers by the Housatonic route, who left New York at 8 A. M., arrived in the city at 5 P. M.

26. Weather quite mild for the season........Mrs. Barbara Hamburgh died, aged 45. Elizabeth McHarg, sister of the late John P. McHarg, died at Bethlehem, aged 76. John C. Ostrander, formerly of Albany, died at Boonville, Missouri, aged 45.

27. William Osborn arrested on a charge of setting fire to a building in Washington street: subsequently convicted.

28. Wells S. Hammond, esquire, of Cherry Valley, son of Hon. Jabez D. Hammond, died suddenly at Stanwix Hall in this city.

30. An alarm of fire occasioned by the bursting of a camphene lamp, corner of South Pearl and Nucella streets.

31. Catherine O'Connor died. Child of Mrs. David Groesbeck died in consequence of falling into hot water.

February, 1849.

1. Catharine, wife of Conrad Van Alen, died........Caucus was held in the assembly chamber at the Capitol: nominated Hon. William H. Seward for U. S. senator, in the place of Hon. John A. Dix.

2. James Sayles's porter-house, in William street, was entered by burglars........William Rennie drowned.

4. Jason Rudes died, aged 74. Prudence, wife of James Kelly, died.

5. Cornelius Lynch died, aged 35.

6. Ship Robert Bowne sailed from New York for California, with twenty miners from Albany on board........The New York State Medical Society met in the Capitol. A. H. Stevens, M. D., of N. York, was reëlected president; and nearly all the other officers, also, were reëlected........Christopher Keeler died, aged 83.

7. Sale of the medical library of the late Dr. Eights.

8. Election of officers of the Young Men's Association for the ensuing year.

9. Isaac Ward, father of J. C. Ward, died.

10. The store of Philip Dunn, in State street, was robbed of about $140: the robbers escaped.

12. Amos S. Fassett, late of this city, died at Vienna, Oneida county. ...... The house of Henry Switzer, 87 Herkimer street, was entered and robbed of several articles of ladies' wearing apparel, &c.

13. The Governor announced to the Legislature the donation of the late Pope Gregory to the State Library, through M. Vattemare and Bishop Hughes, in return for a copy of the Natural History of the State transmitted to him. The donation includes engravings, &c., executed by the best masters.

14. At the suggestion of the Secretary of State, the Legislature took some incipient steps for the publication of the documents illustrative of the early history of the State, collected in England, France and Holland, in 1839....... The winter exhibition of the Albany and Rensselaer Horticultural Society was held at the State Agricultural Rooms, State street.

15. Francis Fiske died....... A pair of oxen from Wyoming county, weighing nearly 5000 pounds, were exhibited and purchased by Mr. D. D. Shaw.

16. Thermometer, at 5¼ A. M., at 11° below zero...... Mrs. Frances Maria, wife of Mr. James R. Whyte, died, aged 53.

18. John Topp died, aged 49. William Kane died, aged 75.

19. Mrs. Sally White died, aged 53. ...... Mr. C. Leach, of Eaton, Madison county, sold, at Warford's cattle exchange, three oxen for Brighton market, weighing over 2200 lbs. each, at $9 per hundred..... Dry goods store of Henry T. Mesick, 68 Washington street, was broken open, and goods to the value of $300 stolen.

20. Jellis Winne junior, cashier of the Bank of Albany, resigned his office on account of ill health.

21. Nathaniel Tarbell, aged about 37, was killed on the Troy road, near the city, by the upsetting of the stage coach of which he was driver.

22. Washington's birthday celebrated. Members of the Legislature, and several Albanians, partook of an annual dinner at Troy....... Mrs. Ann Lydiott died.

23. Mrs. James Teelin of 37 Washington street, with two others, was assaulted in the street, and robbed of a purse containing a small sum of money.

24. Four inches of snow fell during the night....... Mr. Jennings, in Green street, exhibited a hog weighing 949 lbs. dressed.

25. The house near the Railroad Depot, known as Duff's Broadway House, was totally destroyed by fire, the inmates barely escaping. A neighboring house or two was injured.

27. Streets covered with ice and remnants of snow heaps : walking bad. ...... House of Mr. Traver, in Lodge street, robbed of a large quantity of wearing apparel and some silver plate..:..... Thomas Liggins, confined for grand larceny, made an unsuccessful attempt to break jail.

28. The ladies of the Universalist Society held a tea party, for the benefit of the funds of their church.

March, 1849.

1. Dr. Pierce, of Brookline, Mass., the oldest graduate of Harvard College, delivered a discourse in the First Presbyterian Church, on the life and character of John Quincy Adams....... David Schwartz died, aged 73.

2. A valuable silver watch, with 15 or $20 in money, was stolen from the house 67 Van Woert street.

3. C. P. Williams & Co's lumber office, a large quanty of lumber, and several valuable houses adjoining, were destroyed by fire....... Mrs. Leslie, corner of Lumber and Water streets, was safely delivered of *four* children, since dead.

4. Betsey, wife of Samuel Steele, died, aged 60. Mrs. Catharine Hart died, aged 37. Catherine, wife of Adam Stewart, died, aged 30.

5. Inaugural address of President Taylor received by telegraph..... The directors of the Albany Savings Bank reported $707,595·62 as the amount of its deposits, most of which is in sums less than $100....... Ann Alida, wife of Col. De Russy, died at Fortress Munroe, after a short illness, aged about 40. This lovely woman, says a correspondent of the Evening Post, was the daughter of Isaac Denniston, esquire, of Albany, and as amiable as she was lovely. No one acquainted with the society of that city about twenty years since, can have forgotten how much this lady was admired; nor how, with two other ladies, connections of her family, equally beautiful, though of differing styles of beauty, she was a grace that attracted universal homage. It was not often that so much personal elegance could be found in such close affinity. With a refined taste, a love of letters, and a more than ordinary talent, this lady was the "cynosure of every eye." And now that she has passed away from the friends who loved her, and the circle she adorned, we call to mind, with the deepest emotion, those virtues, talents and attractions, which made the morning of life so brilliant; which drew around her in after years the most devoted friends, and now enshrine her memory in hearts where her living image was ever present.

7. Ice in the river said to be yet nearly three feet in thickness....... A. J. Winters, a grocer from Albany, was killed in attempting to get into the cars at Rome, Oneida county.

9. Jacob Featherly died, aged 25. Hannah, wife of Stephen Parsons, died at New-Baltimore, aged 90.

11. James H. Crane died.

12. Christina, wife of Oliver H. Perry, died, aged 28. George H. Scrafford died, aged 37. Thomas Dutson died, aged 63. ...... A canal was cut through the ice to East Albany, for the use of the Boston and Albany ferry boat.

13. Mrs. Sylvester Topping died....... Weather quite spring-like... A baker's sleigh, with two men and other loading, fell through the ice: recovered.

14. Mrs. N. S. Washburn died. Mrs. Margaret Rankin, wife of John Ogden Dey, formerly from Albany, died at Oakwood farm near Cayuga Bridge, aged 47........ A canal cut through the ice, for the use of the Bath ferry boat.

16. Curtis Ware, aged 37, died.

17. Steamer Columbia, Capt. Hulse, arrived about 11 P. M., making her way through the ice; the first boat since the closing of the river in December........High Mass said in St. Mary's Church, in honor of St. Patrick's anniversary........Mrs. Mary Ann McGarvey died, aged 45.

19. Steamer Columbia left, heavily laden with passengers and freight ...... Peter McKenna died, aged 80.

20. James Branion died of consumption, aged 17. Mrs. Ann Groot died in her 60th year.

21. The ice from the Mohawk floated past the city. ...... Steamer Oregon came to the new landing place; her first trip since the closing of navigation....... Sloop Miriam of Albany, Capt. Johnson (a colored man), arrived from New York in 17 hours. ...... Miss N. C. Brainard died. Grace, wife of William Kennedy, died.

22. Steamer Baltic, of Schuyler & Co.'s line, with the Trojan, belonging to Durant, Lathrop & Co., each with several boats in tow, left for New York....... Steamer Isaac Newton arrived, the second boat through....... The Evening Journal entered its twentieth year....... Washington Hunt inaugurated as Comptroller.

23. Martin Van Alstyne, for many years a successful hardware merchant in the city, died, aged 65.......At the meeting held at the City Hall, to take into consideration the frauds of the Canal Bank, Teunis Van Vechten was chairman.

24. John I. Burton, aged 24, died. Michael Daley was found dead in the street, having, in a fit of delirium, sprung from the second story window of his house.

25. A wall in Liberty street, standing since the late fire, was blown down, damaging several adjoining buildings....... Deborah, wife of John Burton, died, aged 66.

26. A bill to establish a hospital in Albany passed the lower house: question still pending in the Senate.......At the request of the supervisors, the Legislature has recently abolished ward assessors, and substituted a board of three individuals....... Mr. John Hermans died in the 29th year of his age. John Van Ness junior died.

27. Mary Bard, wife of R. S. Warren, died, aged 32.......Mr. Saxton lectured on California in the Assembly Chamber.

28. Jonathan Kidney, a soldier of the revolution, and one of the oldest inhabitants of the city, died....... The boats from New York were greatly impeded by a severe wind storm.

29. Rev. Stephen Bush and wife, from this city, as missionaries to Siam, arrived at Batavia, Island of Java, in 98 days.

31. A machine for sewing and stitching was exhibited at the Mansion House....... The finance committee of the Common Council reported that the city debt, on the first of May last, was $877,896 00.

April, 1849.

2. James Masters, of Rochester, had his pocket picked at the Western Railroad Depot.......A barn and stable in Orange street, belonging to Mr. H. Simons, were burned.

3. Hannah Beekman, widow of Peter Douw Beekman, died, aged 83. ...... The Canal Board announced a reduction in the rate of tolls on corn, bloom iron, &c....... A destructive fire occurred, which burned about ten houses on Water and Colonie streets.

4. Henry Williams died, aged 69.......The Common Council appropriated $100 for an alarm bell at the Little Basin.......Mr. Bokee, of the Senate, reported favorably on the bill for the removal of the Hallenbeck burial ground....... The Legislature passed an act in relation to the basin expenses.

5. Mary Ann, wife of Andrew D. Kirk, died....... About 25 houses in North Lansing and Montgomery streets were destroyed by fire...... The grand jury came into court with twenty indictments, four sealed... A prisoner (Bill Barry) made an unsuccessful attempt to break jail.... The ladies of the boatmen who worship at the Bethel presented their pastor, Rev. John Miles, with a rich bedquilt.

6. Mary Ann, wife of Alexander Thompson, died, aged 19.......
—— Easterbrook, from Albany, attempted to shoot his wife, and afterwards himself, at the Howard-street Hotel, New York....... An attempt was made to fire the carpenter shop in Montgomery street, opposite the Bethel....... A woman, name not ascertained, was found dead near the Delaware turnpike: verdict of the jury, intemperance.

7. The city gave the members of the Legislature a complimentary dinner at Congress Hall...... Samuel Gould, a colored fireman on board the Iolas, was killed while repairing the waterwheel.

8. The South Baptist Church, corner of Franklin & Herkimer streets, formerly owned by the Trinity Church, was opened for divine service under the pastoral care of Rev. Mr. Wines....... The scholars under the care of Miss Brainard, at Bethel Jacob, the Jewish synagogue in Fulton street, held an exhibition....... George W. Stanton, president of the Exchange Bank, died, aged 69. Rensselaer Van Schelluyne died, leaving an elder brother the last male descendant of an ancient and wealthy family.

9. The public charity of the city treasury for coal, &c., delivered to the poor, was $3102·87; less by $1816·42 than last year....... Warren Low, at the machine shop of C. Van Benthuysen, was carried up to the ceiling by the belt, and much injured.

10. Edward M. Teall died. Adelaide M., wife of Jason Collier, died. ...... City election, resulting in the choice of the whig candidate for mayor, Friend Humphrey.

12. John R. Black died, aged 78. Eleanor A., wife of Reuben Wilson, died, aged 21....... Several counterfeiters arrested by officer Cowell. Postmaster Wasson, and an agent of the General Post-office identified a young man in Waterford as the robber of the northern mail, who was committed to jail....... House No. 91 Hamilton street was robbed of some wearing apparel....... An alarm of fire, caused by a large conflagration at Troy....... Two horses before a brick wagon near the South Ferry backed off the dock, and were drowned: the driver nearly shared the same fate....... The committee of the Assembly, having in charge the case of Judge Harris with the Canal Bank, exonerated him of any blame.

13. Rachel, widow of the late David P. Winne, died....... A span of horses, belonging to John McEvoy, were killed at Cherry Hill by the caving in of the bank which was being excavated.

15. The carpenter shop of Nathaniel Merrill, in Eagle street, with the house adjoining, was burned down supposed by an incendiary..... Alfred Dorr died, aged 43 Mrs. Rachel Douw Van Schelluyne died.

16. Law establishing a court of special sessions went into operation.

17. The new Common Council met: the mayor was sworn in, and the appointments made nearly as last year....... Catherine, wife of William Francis, found dead in her bed.

18. Uriah St. John died, aged 21. Catherine, wife of James Riley, died, aged 34. Catherine Nichols died.

19. Barent Haynn died, aged 68....... A female infant, wrapped in warm flannels, was found at the door of one of the legal gentlemen, Capitol Park.

20. S. S. Randall, formerly deputy state superintendent of common schools, returned to the city from Virginia....... A meeting was held

to organize the Albany and Schoharie Plank Road Company, Teunis Van Vechten in the chair....... —— Hannegan died.

21. A semi-annual dividend of five per cent. declared on the capital stock of the Mechanics' and Farmers' Bank.

22. Mrs. Irene Pierce died, aged 65. Charles H. Weller died....... An unsuccessful attempt was made by incendiaries to set fire to H. Knapp's store on Quay street.

23. Mary Elizabeth, wife of M. J. Thomas, formerly of Albany, died at St. Augustine.

24. The jewelry store of A. Given, Broadway, was robbed of about $1400 worth of watches...... The Court of Special Sessions was opened by the Recorder and Justice Cole....... A meeting was held by the ladies of Dr. Wyckoff's church, in favor of the Portuguese exiles....... Cornelius Cassidy died, aged 75. Amelia Ward died, aged 20.

25. John Cassidy died, aged 48.

27. John Martin died, aged 60. ...... House No. 277 Lydius street was discovered to have been robbed in the absence of its occupants, of $15 in gold and silver, and several articles of plate.

28. The water was let into the canal its entire length....... A railroad car of a novel construction, from the coach factory of James Gould & Co., was placed on the Champlain and St. Lawrence railroad.

30. Mary A., wife of Mark L. Linn, died. ...... Mayor Humphrey, in compliance with a request by telegraph from New York, caused the arrest of N. G. Klinch for swindling.

May, 1849.

2. Hugh D. Elliot, civil engineer, son of the late Robert Elliot of Albany, died, aged 28, at Junction, Virginia.

3. Thirty prisoners, from the Clinton State Prison, passed through the city to Singsing....... The steamer Isaac Newton brought up over 900 passengers, one of whom, a German boy, was born a few hours previous to landing: the mother was able to assist in unlading the baggage.

4. Steamer Oregon, Captain St. John, arrived at her wharf with 840 passengers.

7. Jane, wife of Geo. T. Clark, formerly of Albany, died in Michigan, aged 34....... General Worth died at San Antonio de Bexar, of cholera. ...... The first meeting of the merchants on change this season took place....... A forged check for $6800, purporting to be drawn by the cashier of the Bank of Troy on the Merchants' Bank in New York, was presented at the Bank of Albany by A. C. Comstock, who accompanied an officer to Troy, where the forger was discovered.

9. A boy about seven years old, son of Michael Forrester, was burnt to death by his clothes taking fire....... Luther Wheeler died, aged 32. David Evans died, aged 42. William Whipple died, aged 40....... Dr. Dill and Mr. Simpson, lately from Ireland, lectured in Dr. Sprague's church on the religious wants of Ireland.

10. Mrs Catherine Angus died, aged 70.

11. Samuel Pruyn was chosen chairman of the board of supervisors; James M. Whelpley, clerk.

12. Friends' Meeting-house, on Plain street, took fire, but was soon extinguished....... Store of Charles Pohlman, 622 Broadway, entered by burglars, and robbed of $200 worth of clothing.

Annals of Albany, 1849.

13. Benjamin Welch died, aged 76. ...... Rev. Dr. Dewey, of the Unitarian Church, preached his farewell sermon to his people.

14. Margaret, wife of Richard Cosgrove, died, aged 28. Abraham and Hiram Pangburn were found dead in a shanty on the island a little below the city: intemperate. ...... John Osborn was appointed, by the Common Council, captain of the fire police.

15. The Albany Daily Messenger, a penny print, by B. F. Romaine, editor, made its appearance. ...... The Express announced Lewis Benedict as the postmaster to succeed Mr. Wasson. ...... Alida Wynkoop, widow of Dr. Jonathan Eights, died, aged 77. John McIntosh died, aged 39.

16. Isaac P. Hand died, aged 46. ...... The ground was broken for the site of the chapel of the Holy Innocents, corner of North Pearl and Colonie streets — Holy Innocents Church was built and is now lying in disrepair, a symbol of demolition by neglect. Its interior had several stained glass windows designed by John Bolton, brother of William Jay Bolton. William was the first American artist to design and manufacture figural stained glass windows.

17. Elizabeth McCluskey died, aged 60.

18. Francis, wife of Cornelius McDonald, died, aged 25. Thomas Murtough died. ...... News reached the city of the wreck of the steamer Empire, on her upward trip.

19. Sarah, wife of Edward Kellogg and daughter of S. Hastings, died. William Marvin, brother of John and Alexander Marvin of this city, died at New-London, Connecticut, aged 74.

21. The materials for a monument to be erected in the Albany Cemetery, over the remains of Judge Spencer, arrived.

22. Ann, wife of Levi H. Palmer, died. Erectus Tubbs died. Aris, wife of Stephen Townsend, died, aged 67. George T. Clark, merchant, of Dewitt county, Michigan, formerly of Albany, died, aged 47.

23. Jabez W. Knowlton died, aged 26. Sarah M. Pugsley died, aged 43. ...... Eight individuals subscribed $18,000 to the stock of the Albany and Cohoes Railway.

24. Over 4000 hogs reported running at large in the streets.

25. The work of placing a sewer nine feet deep in Hamilton street, was completed. ...... A propeller named M. T. Reynolds, intended for the navigation of the canal, appeared in the basin.

26. The office of the weighmaster at the Little Basin robbed of $50.

27. $500 in notes on the Commercial Bank of Albany, with some clothing, were stolen from the house of Mr. Peter R. Clute, 5 Grand st.

28. Ann B., widow of the late Douw B. Slingerland, died, aged 65. ...... Rev. J. B. Davenport, of Syracuse, accepted a call to the rectorship of Grace Church, and commenced his labors.

29. The work of planking the western turnpike commenced above Snipe street. ...... Mrs. Ellen McMillan was found dead in her bed: verdict intemperance.

30. Drug store of A. McClure, State street, broken open, and a small sum of money stolen.

31. Elijah Cobb died, aged 35. Caroline M. Lightbody died, aged 23. ...... Price of flour declined. ...... The clerks of the Post-office presented a silver pitcher to the retiring postmaster, Mr. Wasson.

June, 1849.

1. The new iron bridge, built by F. Townsend & Co. for the Pier Company, at the foot of Hamilton street, was swung over the opening:

time occupied about one minute....... The district school on Arbor Hill was opened with appropriate exercises....... Catherine J. Angus, wife of Charles W. Mink, died, aged 42.

2. Mrs. Grace H. Shattuck died, aged 58.

3. The severe storm cut off telegraphic communication with the west: 15 or 20 poles were blown down.

4. Henry Husthouse, aged 18, died of cholera....... Mercury in the thermometer rose to 89° in the shade.

5. M. Maurice Strakosch, pianist, gave a concert in the Female Academy....... Orcutt & Co.'s furnace, in Hamilton west of Swan street, was burned....... The body of a man was found floating in the basin, near the Columbia street bridge.

6. The mayor, as chairman of the Board of Health, requested physicians, hotel keepers, &c., to report at his office, every day at noon, the cases of cholera occurring in their practice or houses....... The lumber offices of James B. King and B. Van Etten, on the Pier, were entered by robbers.

7. The ceremony at laying the corner stone of the chapel of the Holy Innocents took place under the direction of Rt. Rev. Bishop Whittingham, of the diocese of Maryland....... Robert M. Seymour, formerly of the firm of Seymour, Wood & Co., died in New York, aged 51.

8. Isaac Matson died at the Northern Hotel, of cholera, at 3 A. M.: he was from New-York.

9. Daniel Lafferty, aged 27, was drowned near the Columbia street bridge....... Two cases of cholera reported to the Board of Health: one fatal, an emigrant.

10. John Powers died, aged 50. John Schoonmaker died, aged 54, at his residence, corner of Orange street and Broadway. Conrad A. Ten Eyck, one of the justices of the Justice's Court, died suddenly by the bursting of a bloodvessel.

11. Three cases of cholera reported since the 9th: one death....... Steamer New World made her first trip to Albany from New York: she is intended for a day boat.

12. The Board of Health report only one case of cholera: fatal. Two deaths of those cholera patients reported on the 11th, occurred....... Fourteen state prisoners, from Singsing, passed through the city for Auburn....... Albany Hydrant Company dissolved.

13. One new case of cholera reported: no deaths....... The citizens in the neighborhood of the Arbor Hill burying ground have commenced converting it into a park; the bones to be collected into a mound in the centre....... The body of a man, about 40 years of age, was found in the river at the foot of Bleecker street.

14. The Temperance Pavilion, a large tent erected in North Pearl street by Mr. Van Wagner, the Poughkeepsie Blacksmith, was crowded to excess.

15. Several persons arrested for putting up signs protruding more than eighteen inches from the front of the buildings....... Two cases of cholera reported, both fatal.

16. Three young lads in a sail boat capsized in the river below the city, and Charles Lansing, one of them, drowned....... The jury empannelled to try Osborn for perjury, returned a verdict of guilty of arson in the third degree: sentenced ten years to state prison....... House

107 Lydius street robbed of $12 in money, and several articles wearing apparel...... Two cases of cholera reported: no deaths.

17. Dr. N. A. Jewett died, aged 46....... A stable in the upper part of State street burned down....... George Winne, son of Jellis Winne of Albany, died at St. Paul, Minesota territory.

18. John G. Chifferder, a German youth, found in a pond south of the old railroad....... Mr. Hughes, of Dove street, died by cholera.

19. Daniel W. Talcott died, aged 60. John Ryan died, aged 85. George Smith, aged about 30, was drowned in the canal....... At midday, $21 were stolen from the store of Mr. Mulligan, corner of Swan and Jefferson, and a house in Westerlo street robbed of a gold watch and several other articles of value.

20. Mrs. Elizabeth Lockwood, widow of Jared Lockwood, formerly of Albany, died at Stamford, Connecticut, aged 85....... A stable, and a quantity of wood in Green street, destroyed by fire. ...... One fatal case of cholera reported.

21. Nelson W. Perry died, aged 21 ...... One cholera case reported, fatal....... The body of a man named Welch was found upon a pile of lumber near Bath Ferry....... The mercury rose to 98° in the shade. A man named Richardson, working on one of the canal boats, died suddenly from heat.......Belden B. Batty, of Albany, accidentally shot at San Francisco, and died.

22. Catherine Bleecker died: Mrs. Elizabeth Phillip died, aged 50. James L. Schermerhorn died, aged 34. ...... Several houses in Canal street burnt.

23. Two fatal cases of cholera reported.

24. James R. Roe, and Hannah his wife, died. ...... Two cases of cholera reported; not fatal.

25. Four cases of cholera: none reported fatal.

26. James B. Baker died, aged 44.......A horse, the property of Star Hawley, valued at $150, backed off the pier and was drowned ...... A boatman from Philadelphia, and two residents in Snipe street, died of cholera.

27. One fatal case of cholera reported.

28. Eight cases of cholera; three of which are reported as fatal.

29. Mrs. Boylan, residing in East Albany, died by cholera....... Amey A. Brown, on a visit from Brooklyn, died of cholera.

30. The *Sunday Dutchman*, a new weekly, appeared.......Five cases of cholera; one fatal,...... Capt. Thomas Wiswal died, aged 49...... John Cotner was arrested in Buffalo, for passing counterfeit $5s on the Mechanics' & Farmers' Bank of Albany.......Number cases of cholera for June, 41; deaths, 22.

JULY, 1849.

1. O. G. De Groff, formerly of Albany, died at Cincinnati of cholera, aged 50.

2. Gen. Herrera and family, from Mexico, took lodgings at Congress Hall....... Seven cases of cholera reported, five of which were fatal.

3. Eleven cholera cases reported: four deaths....... The second exhibition of the Albany and Rensselaer Horticultural Society was held in the Agricultural Rooms, State street.

4. National anniversary was celebrated. Three processions: 1st, Regular, consisting of state and city officers, military, fire and boat companies, citizens and strangers; 2d, Independent, carmen, &c.; 3d, Young Men's Association....... Six cases of cholera reported for the last forty-eight hours; one fatal...... L. Z. Harvey died.

5. Mrs. Harriet Stafford, widow of the late Spencer Stafford, died.... At a meeting of the county court, the grand jury, after a few hours absence, came into court, and reported that they had attended to and disposed of all the business before them, and found no bills........ 7443 barrels of flour arrived by canal.

7. Henry Marvin, son of the late Uriah Marvin of this city, died at East Chatham, aged 52. ...... Three cases of cholera reported: no deaths....... The Receiver of the Canal Bank gave notice that 40 cents, the final dividend and full amount of the circulating bills, would be paid on the 16th instant....... Concert by the *Distins*, singers and performers on the Sax Horn. .... Among other produce received by canal, there were 10,478 bbls. flour, 30,945 lbs. butter, and 29,111 lbs. cheese.

7. Eleven cases of cholera reported at noon for the last twenty-four hours, four of which were fatal.

8. J. C. Witt, agent of the Western Railroad Company, died at Sharon Springs: he was a gentleman of great energy of character and excellent reputation....... Conrad Treadwell died.

9. The Mayor reported, that within the last 48 hours, ten cases of cholera had occurred, four of which were fatal....... Parker Sargent appointed justice in the Police Court, in place of Conrad A. Ten Eyck deceased. ...... Annual examination of pupils in the Albany Female Academy commenced. ...... Adam Frazier, formerly of this city, died at Cincinnati.

10. The county board of supervisors met, and were organized under the law giving them legislative powers. ...... Eight cases of cholera reported to the Board of Health, two fatal. ...... Cornelius J. Cuyler died, aged $51\frac{1}{4}$ years. John W. Diamond died, aged 50.

11. Seven cases of cholera, two of which were fatal, and one death of the cases reported yesterday....... Alexander Worden died, aged 39. ...... Alarm of fire from a house in Grand street. ...... Charles I. Wager drowned while bathing near the lower ferry.

12. Sixteen cases of cholera reported for the last 24 hours, three of which were fatal, and one of the seven reported on the 11th since dead. ...... Six houses destroyed by fire in Broad street: rioting among the firemen. ...... Mercury in the thermometer at 9 A. M. was 86°; 96° at 2 P. M.; and at 7 P. M., 93°....... Schooner Stranger, soon after leaving the dock with a full load of corn, was injured by a steamer, and sunk. ...... Thirty-sixth annual examination of the Albany Female Academy concluded....... Frances F., wife of Israel Smith junior, and daughter of Capt. Charles H. Bell, U. S. N., died. Jane, daughter of Michael McCafferty, died, aged 22.

13. Eleven cases of cholera reported to the mayor as chairman of the Board of Health; three fatal. Two of the cases previously reported proved fatal....... Water in the Hudson lower than had been known for many years. ...... At 58 State street, at $4\frac{1}{4}$ A. M., the thermometer stood at over 82°; at 7 A. M. it fell to 71°.......Ellen, wife of Thomas Dunn, died. J. W. Butler died. Arthur Gibbons, son of S. Stafford,

aged 18, died at the American...... Charles Russel, one of a sailing party of five, was drowned by the upsetting of his boat; age 23....... Tobias Morgan, formerly the slave of John D. Vischer, died of cholera, aged 60....... The store of Samuel B. Moore, grocer, in Broadway, was robbed of $200....... The closing exercises consequent on the annual examination of the pupils in the Albany Female Academy were held in the First Presbyterian Church; Rev. Dr. Kennedy delivered a short address to the graduates.

14. Thirteen cases of cholera reported; four fatal. One previously reported terminated fatally..... John Butler, a cartman, died of cholera.

15. Mrs. Elizabeth Nugent died, aged 38.

16. Forty six cases of cholera reported for the last forty-eight hours, ending at noon; thirteen of which were fatal. Three deaths from cases previously reported....... Thomas Monkland died...... Several buildings between Lawrence and North Ferry street, destroyed by fire...... Frances, wife of William Worth died, aged 41. Solomon Hayes, long and favorably known in Albany, died from cholera, aged 64....... A telegraphic despatch from New York announced the death of D. B. Ogden, esquire, so long prominent in the commerce and councils of the state.

17. Seventeen cases of cholera; three fatal. Two cases formerly reported, fatal..... Victor Post died, aged 33. Samuel Vail died, aged 83.

18. Nine cases of cholera in the city and four in the hospital, one of the latter fatal....... The steamer Alida arrived at her wharf in seven hours from New York, running time....... Stephen Squire of Fultonville, Montgomery county, died in this city....... At 10 P. M. the shoe store of Peter R. Cluett took fire, but was extinguished with little damage....... James Sickles died, aged 75.

19. Thirteen cholera cases were reported to the board for the last 24 hours; six fatal. Three of the fatal cases had been before reported.... Harmanus Bleecker, a prominent and well known citizen, universally respected, died in the 70th year of his age. (See p. 276.)..... The steamer New World left New York at 13 minutes after 7 A. M., reaching Poughkeepsie in three hours sailing time and landed her passengers at Albany, 3¼ P. M., making all her landings.

20. Eight cases of cholera reported to the board. Four deaths of those previously reported....... The steamer Alida reached her landing place five minutes before 3 P. M.; making the whole trip in 6 hours 51 minutes sailing time.

21. Thirteen cases of cholera reported; eight in the city and five at the hospital; two fatal. Two deaths also occurred of those previously reported....... Jane widow of the late Arthur Hooper died, aged 76. Elizabeth, wife of Adam Armstrong died, aged 72.

22. Thomas Moss died in the 58th year of his age. Jellis Winne junior died, aged 71....... Lydia, wife of Thomas Carson died, aged 66. ...... The body of John D. Morey, a young man about nineteen years of age, was found in a deep ravine a little north of the city. Death by suicide.

23. Twenty-two cases of cholera reported as having occurred since noon of the 21st; five fatal. One of these, Ira Hinckley from Osterville, Mass., died on board the schooner *Oliver* at the wharf; he was about 19....... Margaret Trotter, widow of the late Gen. Matthew Trotter died, in her 80th year....... Henry Miller, accused of forgery and counterfeiting was arrested and committed; plates of different banks were

found in his possession......Mary, widow of the late Jason Rudes died, aged 72. Roswell Wilson, of the firm of Callanan & Wilson died at Whitewater, Wisconsin.

24. Thirteen cases of cholera were this day reported; two of which were fatal. Two also of the cases reported at a prior day proved fatal.

25. A very large and brilliant halo (corona) appeared round the sun a little before noon......Fourteen cases of cholera reported as having occurred since last report. Three fatal besides one death of a case reported previously......Ann, wife of Benjamin Ward died, aged 63.

26. The board of health reported that seven cases of cholera have been stated to them as having occurred since last report. One fatal and one more death of the 14 yesterday reported......Elizabeth Singer died in the 70th year of her age. Sally Clark died, aged 70. Mary Quinn died, aged 20. Jane, wife of James Morrow died. James Allen died, aged 82. Barney Lyman died of consumption, aged 21 years..... A good southerly wind brought up a large number of sail vessels from the east which in some measure prevented the steamer's intelligence (this day telegraphed) having any tendency to depress the market.

27. Sixteen cases of cholera; five fatal. Four cases previously reported have terminated fatally. Six of the sixteen cases embrace the report of Drs. Martin and Wiltsie for two days ......Bridget McMannus died, aged 55. John B. Smith died, in the 33d year of his age.

28. Eleven cases of cholera; four fatal, within the last 24 hours. One also of a previous report died. —— Lord, an emigrant lately from England died. Mrs. Winaford Allen died, aged 60 Cornelius Higgins died, aged 83¼ years. Abigail Walker died, aged 66.

29. Ann Eliza, wife of Jacob Griffin died......S. H. Shipley from *Baton Rouge* parish, Louisiana, and Mr. Cochrane, both belonging to a party from Mississippi, died in the city of the prevailing epidemic; they were properly cared for........Martin Truesdell, for many years captain of the steam boats Utica and South America, died at Coxsackie, of bronchitis. Having retired from business, he was elected a member of the legislature for the session of 1848.......Margaret, wife of Benjamin Van Aernam of the city, died at Guilderland, aged 47.

30. For the last 48 hours thirty-one cases and twelve deaths by cholera were reported. Two deaths of cases previously reported.....Thirteen buildings and an immense quantity of lumber in Water street were consumed by fire. Its origin not ascertained.....The new building erected at the expense of the state on the corner of Lodge and Howard streets, was taken possession of by the Normal School, and the evacuation of the old building in State street, completed this day.

31. Sixteen new cases of cholera and seven deaths.......A woman and her child were found dead by cholera in Orange street. They died alone, leaving a child 2½ years old the only representative of the family, the father having died of the same disease a few days previous....... The mayor published a respectful request to the citizens to observe the 3d August as a day of fasting and humiliation, agreeably to the recommendation of the President of the United States. that if consistent God would avert from us his judgments.......William Dennison, a native of Ireland died. George M. Mosher died; aged 53.......At 6 o'clock A. M., the thermometer stood at 82deg. at noon it had descended to 72 deg. and 6 P. M. it was below 65 deg.......Rev. Mr. Taggart ordained and installed pastor of the Unitarian church. Rev. Messrs. Dewey and

Pierpont assisted in the exercises......Number of cases requiring medical aid in the Alms House during the month of July, 249, cured 162; died 57; under treatment 37.......Number cases of cholera for July, 343; deaths 125.

AUGUST, 1849.

1. Nine cholera cases, and one of them fatal, were reported. A fatal termination of a case formerly reported was also given in.......Steam boat South America ran down a sloop loaded with coal, which sunk in 20 feet water.......Number of prisoners in the Penitentiary 173; upwards of 50 being females.......Number of paupers in the Alms House 405. Expenses of the last quarter $2,678.

2. Twenty-four cases of cholera, including seven fatal, were reported. Of a former report two proved fatal.......John Moore died of the prevailing epidemic, aged 66.

3. Great national fast—business generally suspended, and the churches well attended.......No meeting of the board of health; five cases reported of cholera, 2 deaths.......David C. Wainwright died, aged 93. Lucius Allen died, aged 41.......New World steam boat accident, by which she was laid up for repairs, requiring an outlay of several thousand dollars.

4. Thirty-one cases of cholera reported for the last 48 hours; 9 fatal, and one fatal of the cases reported before.......A most welcome and refreshing shower moistened the parched earth; it was accompanied with thunder and lightning. A house was struck in Herkimer street, but with little damage.

5. Sabbath—An attempt was made to fire the lumber yard of Messrs. Rogers & Callendar. Another fire was attempted in South Pearl street in the afternoon.......Edward Pacey, a caulker, extensively known, died of cholera, aged 84.

6. Twenty-five cases of cholera, seven of them fatal were reported as having occurred within the last 48 hours. Three of a former report also proved fatal. A strong southerly wind prevailed and brought with it in the afternoon an abundant and seasonable rain.......Ann, wife of William Clemshire died. James Pacey died of cholera, aged 19.

7. Eight cases of cholera, two deaths. Two deaths of cases previously reported. John P. Cassidy died in New York, formerly of Albany.

8. Six cases of cholera; one fatal. One fatal of those reported yesterday.......Jane Mitchell died, aged 15.

9. Eleven cases of cholera; two fatal. One death of those previously reported. Also four deaths not reported on the 6th and 7th........Anna Maria Soulden died.....Fire in North Pearl street, above Maiden lane; damage small.

10. A great deal of rain fell during the night, which was much needed by vegetation......Ten cases of cholera, and one death; also one death of the cases previously reported.......The board of health required the sextons to report all burials, since May 1, under a penalty of $25 for non-compliance.

11. Eleven cases of cholera, one fatal. Three deaths of previous cases. A marked change was now observable in the progress of the disease.......A salmon weighing 12 pounds was caught in the river above Bath, said to be the first known to have been taken in the Hudson. It was served up at the Mansion House.

12. Fire in Orange street; burnt a shed.......Rev. William W. Halloway was installed pastor of the Third Reformed Protestant Church, corner of Ferry and Green streets.

13. Twenty-six cases of cholera; seven fatal, in last 48 hours; and four deaths of cases previously reported......Johannah Durrie, widow of the late Horace Durrie, and daughter of the late Daniel Steele, of this city, died at Aurora, Cayuga county.......The Albany Republican Artillery made a pleasure excursion to Hudson by steam boat.

14. Seven cases of cholera; three fatal within the last 24 hours, with two deaths from cases of a former report.

15. Eleven cases of cholera, two fatal.....Anna, wife of E. Wickes, Jr., died aged 29.

16. Cholera, eleven cases, two fatal; five deaths of previous cases. Mrs. Ralph Pratt died.......Francis McCaler arrested for burglary in entering the house of Mr. Thorn in North Pearl street, and taking therefrom six watches valued at $30.

17. Anniversary of the great fire of 1848......Seven cases of cholera, three fatal, and three deaths of previous cases. Abby, wife of John Townsend, and daughter of the late Ambrose Spencer, died, aged 60..... Alarm of fire proceeding from a gunsmith's shop in Beaver street.

18 Eight cases of cholera, two fatal; two deaths of previous cases. Samuel Gross died, aged 72. Harriet L., wife of John Dixon, died, aged 50. Isabella, wife of Neil McCotter died, aged 54....An agreement was effected between the Albany and Schoharie Plank Road Company, and the Turnpike Company, by which the two roads would be made to intersect, and arrangements made to prosecute the plank road to its completion.

20. Twelve cases of cholera in last forty-eight hours, three fatal; and two fatal of previous cases. Lucretia Shaver died, aged 83.

21. Eight new cases of cholera, three fatal; four cases fatal of those before reported. Nathaniel White died, of cholera, aged 57.......He came to this city from Hartford, Connecticut, in 1808, at the age of 16, and was apprenticed as a bookbinder to the late Mr. Daniel Steele. It is not an uninteresting fact that Mr. White began his apprenticeship in the same establishment with two prominent and highly valued citizens now living, Mr. Lemuel Steele and Mr. Isaac Newton, and one now deceased, the late Mr. O. R. Van Benthuysen. And he has remained in the same establishment, from that day to the present, without interruption, a period of nearly forty-one years, under the successive firms which have conducted it with eminent and deserved success, viz: Messrs. D. Steele, Packard & Van Benthuysen, and C. Van Benthuysen.

22. Seven new cases of cholera were reported; six at the hospital and one in the city—two deaths of those formerly reported. Mr. Leoline Jenkins, son of Lemuel Jenkins, Esq., of this city, died while on a visit to Greeneville, Greene county, N. Y.

23. One case of cholera reported fatal, and three deaths of cases formerly reported. At 9 A. M. Isaac Whitney died, aged 34.......Severe rain most of the day; wind north east.......Owen Tierney died, aged 35. Isaac L. Whitney died, aged 34. Elias Fink, formerly of Albany, died at Danube, Herkimer county, aged 42.

24. Ten new cases of cholera reported; no death. One of a former report proved fatal. At noon Caroline Enz died, aged 18. John Cahill died, aged   ......Canal Receipts—Flour 4244 barrels.; ashes 62 do

Annals of Albany, 1849.

whiskey 24 do.; corn 11,149 bushels; oats 83 do.; wheat 2655 do.; peas 50 do.; butter 10,129 pounds; cheese 17,057; lard 150 do.; Wool 61,054 do; hams and bacon 3588 do.

[margin note: 1832, 1849 and 1866 were known as the Cholera Years in America.]

25. Fifteen cases of cholera reported. Seven of which were fatal. Also two deaths of cases previously reported. Almira, wife of Alexander Nichols, died. Mrs. Hennessy died, aged 60. Elizabeth, wife of Gerrit Yates, died, aged 74.

26. Sabbath—No cholera report; but the interments were numerous. Ann Moran died, aged $19\frac{1}{3}$ years. Mrs. Elizabeth Wagoner died.

27. Seventy-six cases of cholera reported for the last forty eight hours; eleven of which were fatal. Charles Quinn died. Mrs. Rhoda Dean, formerly of Barnard, died at the residence of her son Amos Dean in this city, aged 80. Catherine, daughter of Peter Johnson, died, aged 19. Wife of Robert C. Russell died. Bridget O'Connor died, aged 39. Tivoli flour from new Genesee wheat sold $6.37\frac{1}{4}$; western 5.25 to 5.75; corn 58 cents; wheat 1.25 to $1.31.

28. Twenty cases of cholera reported since yesterday's report; ten fatal. This high proportion of fatal cases is probably rightly ascribed to an indiscreet use of unripe fruits. William McLaughlin died, aged 55......John G. Stewart, a colored barber, known as a man of considerable talent, and as the editor of several papers, was found dead in his chair, by a customer who entered his shop at the Little Basin.

29. The *Jersey Blue*, a three masted steam-propeller, Captain Daniel Van Buskirk, made her first appearance at the dock with a cargo of coal and iron. She is rated at 222 tons, was built at Newark, and made the trip from that city in less than twenty-four hours.

30. Twelve cases cholera; eight fatal. One death of previous cases. ......Michael McAuley died, aged 43. Aaron Williams died, aged 48. Mrs. Amelia Fosket, lately of this city, died at the residence of her son at Blue House, Cobleton District, S. C., aged 62 years.

31. Nineteen cases cholera; seven fatal. Robert H. Burgess died, aged 50. Mary Ann Williams died, aged 54. William Hillman died. ......Total number of cholera cases for August, 345; deaths 150; as otherwise reported 348 cases and 154 deaths.......Fire at 124 Broad street; a two story frame building, brick front, belonging to George Stanwix, which was burnt down, together with the two story frame buildings, Nos. 126 and 128, owned by Alexander Sampson, and occupied by Michael Barnot and Duncan Livingston.......Almshouse physician reported 211 cases for month of August, requiring aid; 122 cured, 52 died, and 37 under treatment.

September, 1849.

1. Six cases cholera; two deaths, and three deaths of previous cases. ......Cornelius D. R. Lansing died, aged 63.......Albany and Sandlake Plank Road Company elected their officers for the ensuing year.

2. Julia L., wife of Dr. John Van Buren died. C. P. Allen died. Robert Malloy died. Thomas Wallace, formerly of this city, died at Detroit, aged 86.

3. Twenty-two new cases, thirteen deaths, for 48 hours last past..... Louisa W., wife of Rev. T. R. Rawson, died. Benjamin Wilson died, aged 83. Neil McCotter died, aged 57. James B. Van Huysen died, aged 49......Burgesses Corps made an excursion to Saratoga Springs.

......A man named Sheridan, a mason, fell from the scaffolding of a building, corner of Patroon and Ten Broeck streets, and was killed; his age 56.

4. Three cases cholera, one death. Three deaths of previous cases. ......Wiliam Sanford, son of Giles Sanford of this city, died at Astoria, N. Y., aged 26.

5. Six cases cholera, four deaths. The physicians were united in the opinion that the disease as an epidemic, had in a great measure left the city; that where it now occurred it was invited by imprudence or by a peculiarly unfavorable locality; wherefore the board determined to discontinue their daily reports.......Eleanor, widow of the late Milo Shaw died, Clara, wife of George H. Cogswell died, aged 21. John C. Brown died, aged 43.

6. The president, Zachary Taylor, arrived from the west, and took the steam boat for New York.....Betsey, wife of Nicholas Brate died, aged 38.......The wholesale grocery store of G. N. Tarbell, on the dock, was entered by a burglar, who made an unsuccessful attempt at the safe, and retired bootless.

7. Ann Eliza, wife of Henry K. Duncan, died at West Point, aged 25. ......The store of G. A. Wolverton entered by burglars.......The office of C. Cooley & Co., lumber dealers, was also broken open.

8. Hon. Henry Clay arrived in the city from Kinderhook, where he had been to visit Mr. Van Buren. He departed in the afternoon for the west.

9. An alarm of fire, caused by the burning of a chimney in Maiden lane.

10. John Slack, aged 66, formerly of Albany, died at Guilderland, of a fall from a hay mow.

11. Frederick A. Fargo, aged 33, was killed by being run over by the train at Rome.......Nancy A., wife of John Henry, formerly of Albany, died in New York, aged 25.......The St. Charles refectory robbed of its sub-treasury by Jeremiah Buckley, who was arrested and confessed the deed.

12. Splendid display of aurora borealis towards midnight.

13. An immense kettle cast at Townsend's Furnace, for the purpose of manufacturing salt at Syracuse. Its dimensions were 9 feet across the brim, 9 feet deep, and 7 feet across the bottom; weight 12 tons.

14. Amey Mott, late of this city, died at Battle Creek, Mich., in the 82d year of her age.

15. At 4 o'clock A. M., Catharine Tracey died.. .....A collection of $800 taken at St. John's Church in Ferry street, in aid of the erection of the Cathedral; making over $5000 collected in that church altogether, for that purpose.

16. A fire was discovered about 9 A. M. in the loft of Tracy & Edson's liquor store, corner of Dean and Exchange streets, and extinguished with little damage.......Jane Madison, wife of Jasper Latham and daughter of the late H. E. G. McLaughlin, esquire, of Chelsea, Vt. died, aged 40. Ann Hardy, daughter of James Freeman died, aged 29¼ years. Timothy Ensign, late of the firm of Ensign & Thayer, in this city, died at Windsor, Con.

18. The Hose Depot, so long a source of contention as to where it should be located, was commenced on the site of the old hay market lots,

corner of Plain and Philip streets.......Mary, wife of George Geary died, aged 50. Sarah, wife of Andrew McKnight died.......Baron Hecker, the German exiled patriot, came up the river in company with some 50 of his countrymen, en route for his farm on the banks of the Mississippi, in Illinois.

19. James Robinson died, aged 60.......The common council held a special meeting to settle the pier question, &c. Mr. O'Reilley was granted permission to erect telegraph posts within the bounds of the city under the supervision of the street committee. The chamberlin ordered to borrow $30,000 to meet the pier settlement.......First trip on the Hudson river rail road with passenger cars from New York to Peekskill.

20. Fire was discovered about $9\frac{1}{4}$ P. M. in some combustible materials in the shoe shop of Cluett & Co., corner of State and Lodge streets; extinguished without damage.......Mr. Ralph Clark, formerly of Albion, Wis., died, aged 25.......The Albany and Rensselaer Horticultural Society's annual exhibition closed to-day.

21. Joseph Hogeboom died, aged $32\frac{1}{2}$ years. Elizabeth, daughter of the late Nathaniel R. Packard died, aged 19.......Peter Cluett charged with and committed for arson in causing the fire last evening, corner of Lodge and State streets.......The city and pier company closed their negotiations and came to terms with regard to the Basin—the city paying the pier company $30,000—the latter to maintain the bridge.

22. An unusually strong south wind prevailed the whole day, accompanied in the evening with rain........" On Saturday evening at seventeen minutes past 11 o'clock, the Sun rode calmly and mildly over the autumnal equinox, and cast his golden anchor on the wintry coast of Autumn. But as yet, the vast ocean of air through which he sails, is glowing and transparent with the memory of the long Summer days that have passed over it, darting their rich beams to its very depths. Even as we write, however, the remembrance fades, like the sky's blanching souvenirs of sunset; and in the gray distance the cold ghosts of Winter glare and wave their frozen wings, which creak on icy hinges—while in the silence of midnight a prophetic voice of wailing and desolation moans fitfully at the casement."—*Tribune.*

23. John Simons died.......A riot caused by some evil disposed persons throwing stones at a canal boat loaded with immigrants, occurred at the Little Basin.......The accidental burning of a bed in house No. 16 Dallius street, caused an alarm of fire.......Ann K. Fitch, formerly of Greenwich, Conn., died.

24. Weather cloudy and cold.......Edward Thomas died, aged 24. ......Premium articles at the late State Fair, of Albany manufacture, were exhibited in Kidd's Buildings.......Joseph Curdy, a laborer, committed suicide by cutting the arteries of both arms with a razor, and died sitting in a chair.

25. The body of John Donahue was found in the river at the foot of Bleecker street—supposed to have been drowned on Saturday night—age 40.

26. The A. R. Artillery annual target excursion—the cup awarded to W. A. Davis for the best shot, and the gold medal to James H. Chadwick, for 2d best.......The first quinquennial meeting of the State Normal graduates was held in the lecture room of the new building..... John Crippin died, aged 28. Patrick Murray died in his 65th year. Hannah B., wife of Amos P. Palmer, died at Newton's Corners.

27. Closing exercises of the Normal School took place to-day....... The spike factory belonging to the Albany Nail Works, near Troy, and owned by Corning, Winslow & Co. of this city, was destroyed by fire, loss $40,000 above insurance.......John York died, aged 26.

28. George W. Worcester, formerly of this city, died at the hospital, New York, aged 30.

29. The travel between this city and Albany, says the Troy Whig, is immense. The cars, which run hourly, carry a large number of passengers; while the stages which run half-hourly, are crammed full nearly every trip. The number of persons going to and coming from Albany daily is probably in the neighborhood of two thousand. This would be equal to 60,833 per calendar month, and 730,000 a year! This estimate does not, we think, fall short of the mark.

October 1849.

1. A rain storm during the whole day refreshed the earth which had sustained a long drouth.......The military encampment appointed to be held this day was postponed one week.......Henry Holmes, died. Casper Walter died.

2. Albany Medical College opened with a lecture by Dr. T. R. Beck. ......Capt. Henry Terbush, of the steam boat A. L. Lawrence killed by the machinery of the boat.......James Carroll died, aged 57.

3. Working Men's State Convention assembled.......The flags of shipping were displayed at half mast on account of the death of Henry Terbush, captain of the steamer A. L. Lawrence.......Henry A. Newman died, aged 23.......Attempt by burglars to enter the house of D. Cox, corner Green and Lydius streets.

4. Severe rain storm. .....The O'Reily Telegraphery reported from Catskill, though fully connected to Newburgh.......Nathan O. Banks, junior, of Putnam county, in going aboard the Isaac Newton walked off the plank and was drowned.

5. Moses Wallace died.......Rain in the morning and at intervals through the day.

6. Rain again this morning. Telegraphery announced at 3 P. M. rain in New York and Buffalo; very rainy in Albany.......The union democrats nominated county officers.

7. Still the rain fell. A strong northerly wind prevailed. The fourth day without sunshine or even at night star light........Patrick O'Brien died, aged 25.

8. Stars were visible at 5 A. M. At 6 rain again commenced, but cleared away at 8 A. M., when the sun for the first time in four days was visible.......George Mossop, a native of Dublin, in connection with the Albany Museum died, aged 35.......T. D. Sprague, editor of the American Literary Magazine of this city, died at Andover, Conn., aged 30.

9. Frost and a thick fog overspread the city. The mail and other New York steamers were accordingly delayed till noon.......The Synod of Albany (O. S) met in the First Presbyterian Church. The 25th regiment of N. Y. Militia, Col. Frisbie, went into encampment for three days.......George H. Welch, of the firm of Adams and Welch died, aged 28.

10. The Albany, Rensselaerville and Schoharie Plank Road Co. was

organized. Lansing Pruyn as president, David H. Cary, treasurer, and Charles M. Jenkins, secretary.......Iron fence around the State Hall grounds completed.

11. A heavy and drenching rain which commenced on the evening of the 10th, continued till midnight.......Mrs. M. A. Record died, aged 44. Peter Wall died, aged 41........*A Multitude of Fishes.*—Mr. T. Carman of this city, in company with another, took on Thursday night at the Troy dam, no less than 7000 fish, of the sucker tribe! They were all towed down in large floating cars, alive and kicking, and were in the market in good order. They were brought down by the freshet which has swollen the river, and in this instance no doubt, the pockets of enterprising and experienced fishermen.

12. Mrs. Rebecca Bolles, wife of Jeremiah Wallace died, aged 30 years.......The water in the river was over the docks in many places.

13. Thomas I. Morgan died, aged 38. Mary E. Hoffman, daughter of the late Levi S Hoffman, aged 14, died. Mrs. Kaesel died.......An alarm of fire from a house in North Ferry street called out some fire companies, but did no other damage.......Specimens of coal exhibited in the city, obtained by boring at Coeymans. Half a million of dollars have been spent in this neighborhood in searching for coal, without any success, and the geologists have decided that there can be none.

14. The house of Edward Thies, in North Ferry street, entered by burglars and robbed of various articles.

15. Stephen C. Keeler died.

16. Elizabeth, widow of the late Robert Lottridge died, aged 65.

17. Plank road on the old Cherry Valley turnpike completed to Guilderland.

18. Anti Rent Convention; said to have been attended with small effect.

19. *Barley Trade of Albany.*—The city of Albany is known far and wide as *the* barley market of the Union. At *this* market, five sixths of the barley received every year at tide-water from the barley growing counties of the west is bought and sold. The trade lasts about two months, and during that time a very brisk business is done. As an evidence of the increasing demand for this article, we would mention that in 1844 the whole quantity of barley received at tide water from the canals did not exceed 820,000 bushels, while the quantity of the *new crop* of the present year which had reached tide-water on the 22d inst., was 650,101 bushels. Of this new crop, 498,000 bushels have been reported as sold here, in the daily reports of the Argus. This is about five-sixths of the whole receipts, and if to this we add the lots which were sold here to arrive and which do not enter into the reports of the daily sales, the proportion of sales to receipts is more than five-sixths. The sales here may be thus classified: Two rowed barley, 252,400 bushels; four rowed, 201,900; mixed, 43,700. Total, 498,000 bushels.

20. Peter Donelly, a member of the Albany Artillery died ......A company of nearly 300 Portuguese refugees under the charge of the American and Foreign Christian Union, arrived from New York in the steam boat, to spend the Sabbath, on their way to Illinois.

21. Christopher Joselyn alias Lillie was killed in South Broadway, near the steam boat landing ....Jane Moore, wife of M. D. Moore, died at East Albany, aged 35. David B. Douglass, LL. D. died at Ge-

neva College, where he was professor of mathematics and natural philosophy; he laid out the grounds of the Albany Rural Cemetery.

22. Griffin's eating house entered by burglars and robbed of money and segars.

23. John Martin died, aged 32.......Great storm of wind and rain with heavy thunder, in the evening, destroying the circus tent and doing other damage.

24. Robert C. Russell died, aged 51.

25. The common council resolved to submit the water question to the people at the ballot box, where they might decide which of the projects for supplying the city they would choose, or decline, to have water...... Mary Elizabeth Norton died, aged 18. Anna Layton died, aged 16, Sartelle Prentice died, aged 83. David Sheridan died, aged 22, Rosanna McDonald died, aged 19.

26. Dense fog, detaining the steam boats from New York till nearly 11 o'clock A. M.

27. Delia Adams, wife of Sherman Croswell died, aged 39. Anna Eliza, wife of William B. Winne died, aged 37.

29. Peter Wendell, M. D., died, aged 64. He was the longest resident practitioner of medicine in the city, and next to Dr. Bay the oldest. Dr. Wendell was a native of this city—born in 1786. He received the best education that the city afforded, and at the usual time entered the office of the late Dr. Wm. McLellan, then one of the principal physicians here During his course of study, he attended two courses of lectures at the University of Pennsylvania. On his return he commenced the practice of medicine. This was in 1807, and we need scarcely add how extensive and lucrative this proved during the long period of 42 years. Dr. Wendell received the honorary degree of doctor of medicine from the University of Pennsylvania some 15 years or more after he had attended it as a student. In 1823, he was chosen by the legislature a regent of the university, of which body he became chancellor in 1842, and to which last office he has since been annually reappointed......... Great storm in the evening. The wind blew a hurricane, and the rain fell in torrents. The streets descending from the hill became rivers, washing down great quantities of stones, clay and sand; the sewers in some instances became clogged, and the turbid streams overflowing the side walks, poured a torrent into the basements. The telegraph wires were blown down in all directions. The Isaac Newton gallantly breasted the storm, and reached her landing place at the usual hour. The tide in the river was higher than had been known for several years......... Statement of the amount of freight started from the depot at East Albany:—10,053½ barrels of flour; 942 barrels of apples; 1,405 boxes of cheese; 75 bales of wool; 1,159 firkins of butter; 958 barrels of beef. Eight trains, with 361 cars, were sent east; the receipts for freight were $5,423.

30. Margaret Matilda, wife of Amasa Bates died, aged 30.

31. Ellen, wife of Smith T. Van Buren, and youngest daughter of the late Wm. James died, aged 27. Mary, wife of John Griffin died, aged 62. Henry Blake died, aged 70.......A slight fall of snow in the morning.......The aggregate of all assessments approved and confirmed during the year to this date was $66,482 50; on account of which there has been received during the same time $36,952 93, leaving a balance of $29,529 51 due the city...... The earnings of the Albany and Schenec-

tady rail road for the month of October were $19,276; same time last year, $14,732; excess in 1849, (equal to 31 per cent.) $4,544. The receipts of this road will reach $183,000 to $185,000 against $175,000 in 1848.

NOVEMBER, 1849.

1. Ice made in the open cisterns of the city for the first time this season, which had thus far been remarkably free from frosts........Mrs. Amanda Emerson died, aged 52.......Michal Querk, an Irish laborer, crushed to death by a canal boat.

2. There are five flouring mills in successful operation in or near this city, four of them are worked by water and one by steam power. They have each four run of stones, and consume annually about 400,000 bushels of wheat. The millers supply themselves in a great measure with grain from the market, and these mills are now turning out a goodly quantity of flour which forms a small addition to our daily supply. Mr. C. N. Bement, has also a small steam mill in Hudson street, for flouring various kinds of grain for family use.

3. Eliza, wife of G. G. Vandenburgh of this city, died at Burdett, Tompkins co., aged 60.

4. A fire on the corner of Broad and Nucella streets consumed two buildings, one of them owned and occupied by Mr. Thomas Fisher, who some time since lost his eye sight at a fire in Green street, since which he had been allowed the privilege of selling coffee and cakes from a wagon in State street for a subsistence. The fire was undoubtedly the work of an incendiary. While the fire was at its height, and Mr. Fisher and his family had escaped from the house, and the excitement somewhat subsided, he made known to several friends that a trunk, which was on the first floor under his bed, contained, besides valuable papers, over $100 in money. Mr. William Bradt, a courageous and daring young man, volunteered to attempt its rescue, and the next moment was in the room. The bed and a portion of the floor was on fire, and the room filled with smoke. The young man secured the trunk, but was so near suffocated as to be unable to regain the street with it, and was drawn from the building with the trunk in his arms, by one of the hooks of a hook and ladder company, completely exhausted. His hands, eyebrows and clothes were much singed. An offer from Mr. Fisher of $100 as a reward for his intrepidity, was promptly declined by him.

5. Fanny, wife of John C. Heermance died, aged 43 ......The street committee of the common council reported in favor of opening Lydius street, from Allan to Magazine street, which would make that street an uninterrupted thoroughfare of thirteen miles in length.

6. Rachel, wife of Peter Putman, died at Canajoharie, aged 40; formerly of Albany.......The evening boat for New York was detained by the fog till 6 o'clock this morning. The boat due this morning from New York did not arrive till 3 o'clock in the afternoon.......Robert H. Pruyn elected to the Assembly by a majority of 292 votes over the democratic competitor, Dr. Barent P. Staats. The entire whig ticket elected in the city.

364   Annals of Albany, 1849.

7. Sarah, wife of Robert Collins died, aged 41.......The following table is an abstract of the official returns of the county vote:

	DEM.		WHIG.	MAJ.
Judiciary—	Jewett 6218	Spencer 5916		302
	Hogeboom 5569	Wright 6766		1197
State—	Lott 5604	W. Hunt 6933		1329
	Randall 5729	Morgan 6859		1130
	Chatfield 6127	Stevens 6244		117
	Welch 5713	A. Hunt 6872		1159
	Campbell 5917	Seymour 6660		743
	Follett 6131	Beach 6444		313
	Clark 6235	Squire 6369		134
Senator—	McEwen 6041	Johnson 6466		425
Sheriff—	Fenner 6059	Beardsley* 6385		326
Clerk—	Blanchard 5909	Lay* 6598		689
Justice—	Daw 5769	McKown* 6612		852
Coroners—	Brower* 6199	Landon* 6362		
	Parker 6030	Winne* 7041		
	Wadsworth 6019	Blaisdell 6018		

*Elected.

8. The following gratifying testimonial of the skill and enterprise of artists, mechanics and horticulturists of Albany and vicinity, was awarded by the American Institute upon articles exhibited at its late fair: Wilson, Thorburn & Geller, Albany, for a very fine assortment of apples—6 Nos. Hovey's Fruit; the same for a fine assortment of pears Downing's Fruit Trees. Robert Selkirk, Bethlehem, Albany county, for the best and largest pumpkins—Bridgman's Gardner's Assistant. H. L. Emery, Albany, corn and seed planter, and drill bearer—silver medal; the same for improved overshot threshing machine and separator—silver medal; the same for best churn—silver medal; the same for the best ox yoke—diploma; the same for the best hay, straw and stalk cutter, curved knives—diploma; also for a dynamometer for testing ploughs—silver medal. Smith & Feltman, best Britannia ware—silver medal. D. Harris, jr., bronze velvet window shades—diploma. D. E. Gavit, for daguerreotypes—diploma. Learned, for superior cooking stove and W. Cobb, hotel range, received medals. Boardman & Gray, Dolce Campana attachment to piano forte—silver medal. Satterlee, cast iron mirror frames highly gilt and burnished—silver medal.

9. After nearly a week of rainy weather the river commenced rising, and the merchants on the dock began to hoist their goods to the second loft........A Drummond light exhibited successfully for the first time in this city, from the top of the Museum.......Canal boat Hartford, belonging to J. H. Mallory & Co. arrived from Buffalo with 875 barrels of flour between decks—the largest quantity ever brought by one boat..... John Gill died, aged 39.

10. Such of the forwarders and flour merchants along the dock and pier as had not secured their stock from the freshet, met with losses by the sudden rise on Friday night. Every thing presented the appearance of a spring freshet, only that the damage was much greater in not being provided against, at a busy season. Much property was carried away by the overflowing of the pier, and vessels even broke from their moorings. The freshet extended as far as Hudson.......Mary Teresa Shallow died, aged 18.

11. The water in the river had fallen two feet since Friday night.... Trinity Church took fire from its furnace in the evening, but was only slightly damaged.......Samuel W. Harned died, aged 59. Mrs. Honourah Conway died, aged 52.

12. Capt. Samuel A. Brooks, died

13. Ann Stewart died, aged 33.......Josiah Murton, a hand on a schooner, fell overboard and was drowned; age 17.......Annual meeting of Albany County Medical Society; address by Dr. James McNaughton on cholera.

14. Mary A., wife of George E. Cady died, aged 37. The Emmet Guards went down to New York to participate in the funeral obsequies of Gen. Worth on the 15th.

15. Philo Colvard died, aged 74. Hannah Margaret, wife of Thomas Jordan, late of Albany, died at Troy, aged 26.......Jacob Smith, a Jew of Albany, was robbed at Dansville, Livingston county, of $4000 worth of jewelry.

16. Thomas McGuire died, aged 34.

17. The rail road took from this city and delivered in Boston, during the week ending this day, 29,300 barrels flour, averaging nearly 5000 barrels a day.

19. Deidamia, widow of the late Timothy Adams, of Barre, Mass., died, aged 74.......Joseph Mayhew, mate of a Rhode Island sloop, fell overboard and was drowned; aged 40.......Very rainy, from New York to Buffalo.

20. Selah Belden died, aged 35.........Canal receipts at Albany: Flour 9,743 brls.; ashes 26 do; beef 284 do; pork 10 do; whiskey, &c. 42 do: corn 15,268 bushels; barley 7.630 do; oats 6,159 do; rye 3,960 do; wheat 2,200 do; potatoes 7 do; butter 11,528 lbs.; wool 27,130 do; hams and bacon 29,370 do.

21. The canal boat Hartford, Capt. Van Alstyne, which left Buffalo on the 10th inst., arrived at this port with 910 barrels flour shipped to J. H. Mallory & Co.......Henry H. Dodge died by the wound of a pin, aged 18.

22. Nearly 300 emigrants came up from New York, among whom were a number of Hungarians.....Burglars entered the stores of L. M. Gilbert and Averill & Marshall on the dock, blasted the safe open, and retired with a few dollars in copper coin and counterfeit bills.

23. Collins W. Simonds died, aged 30.......Canal receipts at Albany, Nov 23: Flour 22,101 barrels; ashes 64 do; beef 1,816 do; whiskey, &c. 202 do; corn 8,750 bushels; barley 13,713 do; oats 7,823 do; wheat 2,010 do; peas 46 do; potatoes 693 do; seed 6,300 lbs; butter 57,950 do; wool 14,954 do; hams and bacon 4,292 do.

24. Barbary Hamburgh died, aged 24.......A laborer by the name of Coughlin, fell from the Cathedral and was killed; his age 35.

25. Mary Brower died, aged 71. Maurice O'Conner died, aged 70. Patrick McNamara died, aged 44. Mrs. Martha Jacobs died, aged 68.

26. Martha Russell, of New Bedford, died, aged 76.......The Water Works Company proposed to supply the city more effectally with water by increasing their capital to $450,000, and forcing water up from the river.......The finance committee of the common council reported that the sum of $168,003 36 be raised by a tax for the support of the city government for the ensuing year. We annex a statement of the amounts necessary to meet the wants for the several departments:

For expenses of night police		$18,000·00
" public lamps		10,000·00
" contingent expenses (ordinary)	$30,000 00	
" expense of fire department	20,000 00	
On account of payment to pier proprietors to obtain their consent to the law relative to expenditures for excavating Albany Basin, &c.	10,000 00	
		60,000·00
To pay interest on city debt		45,500·00
On account of sinking fund		10,000·00
For support of common schools		9,003·36
" alterations and repairs to district school No. 10		500·00
For temporary relief of city poor		5,000·00
For probable balance that will remain unpaid May 1, 1850, on assessments and apportionments for improving streets, &c., approved and confirmed during the year ending November 1, 1849		10,000·00
		$168,00·336

Canal receipts at Albany: Flour 13.503 barrels; ashes 110 do; beef 264 do; whiskey, &c 189 do; corn 6.255 bushels; barley 16,129 do; oats 5.006 do; rye 3.546 do; wheat 8 300 do; peas 125 do; potatoes 2,575 do; seed 19,000 lbs; butter 80,930 do; cheese 68,260 do; wool 12,158 do.

27. Mrs. Elizabeth M. Noyes died......The upper barley lofts of John Taylor, on the dock, gave way and carried every thing with them into the cellar.

28. Canal receipts at Albany: Flour 31.340 barrels; ashes 147 do; beef 2,410 do; pork 77 do; whiskey, &c. 64 do; corn 1,178 bushels; barley, 4.354 do; oats 7060 do; rye 2,000 do; wheat 431 do; peas 340 do; potatoes 1.923 do; seed 45,000 lbs; butter 120,000 do; cheese 199,540 do; wool 35,733 do; hams and bacon 4.526 do.

29. Thanksgiving.......The Albany and New York steam tug *Oswego* arrived at New York having 41 Canal barges and boats in tow, all deeply laden with produce of various kinds, the largest and almost the *last* tow of the season......Philo Redman murdered on the Schenectady turnpike.

30. James Birmingham died, aged 50.......The canal receipts at Albany during the 4th week in Nov. were—Flour 103.743 barrels; ashes 466 do; beef 9459 do; pork 587 do; whiskey, &c 737 do; corn 24.902 bushels; barley 52,906 do; oats 32,458 do; rye 9.716 do; wheat 14.241 do; peas 765 do; potatoes 7.970 do; seeds 147.615 lbs; butter 533,270 do; cheese 610,725 do; lard 137,280 do; wool 121,865 do; hams and bacon 14.146 do.

The net income of L. Van Deusen, Clerk of Albany county, for last year, as reported by him to the board of supervisors, is $5,517!

Albany Real and Personal Estate and Taxes.

SCHEDULE

Of Real and Personal Estate, Taxes, &c. for the City and County of Albany, for the year 1847.

Wards and Towns.	Acres.	Assessed value.	Equalized val. p acre.	Real estate.	Personal estate.	Total.	State and county tax.	City tax.	Wards and towns.	Common schools.	Roads and bridges.	Collectors' warrants.	Per centage.
First Ward,		$357910		$357910	$23500	$357910	$1625 81	$3067 70	$183 50			$4877 01	$1 36
Second Ward,		604285		580785	32500	604285	2744 97	5178 94	210 50			8134 41	1 37
Third Ward,		902356		869856		902356	4098 96	7733 66	279 00			12111 62	1 32
Fourth Ward,		2967488		1798303	1169185	2967458	13479 90	25437 57	239 25			39156 72	1 30
Fifth Ward,		3509802		1761745	1748057	3509802	15943 33	30082 20	220 50			46246 11	1 33
Sixth Ward,		888850		764050	124800	888850	5037 64	7617 08	188 50			11843 22	1 34
Seventh Ward,		423010		415560	7450	423010	1921 53	3625 78	187 25			5734 56	1 35
Eighth Ward,		280245		276345	3900	280245	1273 43	2402 15	196 25			3871 83	1 38
Ninth Ward,		805670		736670	69000	805670	3659 77	6904 28	249 50			18513 55	1 35
Tenth Ward,		647760		608760	39000	647760	2942 46	5395 01	291 00			8628 47	1 36
		11387336		8169984	3217392	11387376	51727 85	97444 43	2245 25	$863 00		154417 53	
Berne,	39,078	313755	$7 00	373546	68105	341651	1551 98		1347 20	357 06	$200 00	2599 18	0 93
Bethlehem,	33,046	617575	18 00	594825	102000	695825	3165 38		1673 05	340 90	250 00	3828 43	0 75½
Coeymans,	31,509	373457	12 00	378108	64777	442885	2011 38		1317 15	314 34	500 00	3329 03	0 90
Guilderland,	33,037	432174	14 00	462518	75212	537730	2442 04		2463 74	316 13	500 00	4910 78	1 16
Knox,	26,020	229393	7 00	182140	64361	246501	1119 73		737 15	228 10	75 00	1856 88	0 82
New-Scotland,	35,608	570377	14 00	499723	101320	601049	2730 24		1653 00	247 05	500 00	4413 24	0 76
Rensselaerville,	37,056	296578	8 50	314976	59861	374937	1703 15		1263 46	378 80		2966 61	1 00
Watervliet,	37,749	1567940	21 00	1329559	161110	1490969	6772 77		5555 03	1183 10		12327 50	0 78½
Westerlo,	35,789	333092	8 50	304206	86542	390748	1774 98		1163 52	308 96	200 00	2938 50	0 88
	305,982	4733636		4339903	783388	5123291	23272 15		17208 30			40450 45	

PETER SETTLE,

Clerk of the Board of Supervisors, Albany County.

BOND OF THE ALDERMEN OF SCHENECTADY, 1766.

The following is printed from the autograph copy, found among the Vrooman papers, of a bond given by the Aldermen and assistants of Schenectady, in 1766, to carry out certain measures in case of their being sworn into office. The orthography and capitalizing of the original is preserved throughout:

Know all men by these Presents, That wee John Sanders Caleb Beck, Abraham Fonda Joseph R. Yattes, John Glen Junr. & Ryer Schermerhorn Esqrs. Ellected aldermen for the Borrough town of Schenectady, and Henry Glen, Nicolas Van Petten, John Visger. Junr. Abm. Wemple, Nicolas DeGraaf, & Andries Truax Gentlemen Ellected Assistants for said Borrough, are Jointly & Severally held & firmly bound unto Isaac Vrooman & John Duncan Esqrs. of said Borrough in the Sum of Five hundred Pounds Current Money of the Province of New York to be paid to the said Isaac Vrooman & John Duncan for which Payment well & truly to bee made wee hereby bind ourselves severaly & Joinly firmly by these Presents sealed with our Seals dated this 5th. day of Decr. 1766, in the Seventh Year of His Majestys Reign

The Condition of this Obligation is Such That if the above Bounden Aldermen & assistants as above, Shall do well & truly Qualify in their respective Ofices as aldermen & assistants for the Borrough of Schenectady within Eight days after the Governor Grants a New or additional Charter for the said Borrough with the Alterations or Amendments to the Present Charter of the following Articles Vizt. That the Boundarys of the Corporation shall be extended according to letters Pattent dated Novr. 6th. 1764, And that the Aldermen shall not be for life, but that they shall be Ellected Yearly or Every three years, as the Governor shall be pleased to Grant, And that none of the Inhabitants of said Borrough shall be Oblig'd to take out a Licence for there Wagons but to use them at there will and Pleasure And that the Children of the Freeholders and free men give a Certain Sum Not Exceeding Six Shillings for there freedome then this Obligation to be Void and of no Effect otherwise to remain in full force.

Sealed and Delivered
  in the presence of us
    Mauhew Lynd
    Alexander Campbell

John Sanders
Caleb Beck
Abraham Fonda
Joseph R. Yates
Jno Glen Jr.
John Glen Jr for Ryer Schermerhorn

Signed Sealed & delivered by Jno. Glen Junr. for Ryer Schermerhorn, in Presence of us
    Alexander Campbell
    Edward Burrowes

Signd Seald & Deliverd in the Presence of us By Andr. Truax
    John Visger
    Alexander Campbell

Henry Glen
Nicolaes Van pellen
John Visger Jr,
Abm Wempel
Aendres Truax
nicolas degraf

INDEX.

Albany, plan of, 136
" ancient, 137
" distance from principal cities, 138
" first visited, 138
" charter granted, 140
" architecture, 141
" county, 142
" " towns in 1790, 142.
" " incorporated, 145
" incorporated, 145
" population 1795, 153
" in 1789, 314
" in 1796, 315
" in 1823, 305
" charter officers, 37
" penitentiary, 149
" bank of, 31
" city bank, 33
" exchange bank, 33
" savings bank, 34
" ins. company, 34
" academy, 75
" " corner stone laid, 76
" female academy, 80
" sloop in 1796, 153
" evening journal circulation, 167
" hort. society, 177
" and boston rail road receipts, 177
" gal. of fine arts, 39
" exchange co. 39
" water works co. 40
" hydrant co. 40
" and cohoes rail road company, 40
" society of brotherly love, 42.
" city tract society, 43
" county bible soc. 43
" " medical society, 43
" and rensselaer horticultural soc. 43
" repub. artillery, 44

Albany burgesses corps, 44
" emmet guards, 44
" washington riflemen, 44
Abeel, johannis, 25, 152
Academy, albany, 75, 286
" female, 80
Adams, J. Q., 166
Agassiz lectures, 166
Agency, 209
Agricultural society, 312
Agricultural implements, 209
Alarm bell, 346
Albertsen, hendrick, 22
Allen, james, 354
Allen, C. P., 357
Alida, speed of, 171
Alida, speedy trip, 353
Alms-house, 159, 161, 165, 166, 319, 341, 356, 357.
Anti-renters, 160, 166, 178
Anti-rent convention, 361
Appeals, first court of, 159
Arbor hill burying ground, 161, 350.
Arbor hill school, 48, 350
Architects, 209
Armorial bearings, 90
Arms of rensselaerswyck, 198
Arnsby, dr., 342
Arsenal, 309
Artillery, 356, 359
Artists, 209
Artists' materials, 225
Artists' premiums, 364
Assault and battery, 161
Associations, &c., 317
Attorneys, 36
Auctioneers, 209
Aurora borealis, 162, 166, 169, 173
Autumn, 265, 359
Avarice of albanians, 272
Bachelor tax, 161
Baker, J. B., 351
Bakers, 209
Bakers prosecuted, 160
Bakker, wm. juriaensen, 19, 24

Balloon ascension, 175
Band and fancy boxes, 225
Banishment, sentence of, 204
Banks, 31
" of albany, 31 317
" N. Y. state, 32
" mech. and farmer's, 32
" commercial, 33
" canal, 33
" albany city, 33
" albany exchange, 33
" savings, 34
Banks, N. O., 360
Baptist society, 163
Barbers, 209
Barley, 266, 361
Barlow's prediction, 304
Barnburners, 159, 160, 161, 174, 177
Barry, bill, 346
Barry, thos., 325
Basin, 310, 346
Basket-maker, 225
Bassett, J., 89, 119
Bath, 316
Bath ferry, 345
Baths, 225
Batteaux, 264
Batterman, C., 340
Batty, B. B., 351
Bay, andrew, 130
Beaver kill, 146
Beavers, price of, 194
Beck, T. R., 76
Bedstead-makers, 209
Beekman, johannes, 278
Beeren island, 198-9
Bell-hanger, 225
Bell, st. peter's, 285
Bell-founder, 225
Belden, selah, 365
Bement, C. N., 363
Benedict, L., p. m., 341
Bern, 145
Beth, jacob, 134, 170
Bethel for watermen, 133
Bethel congregation, 136
Bethel, jacob, 347

Index.

Bethlehem, 145, 202
Bethlehem turnpike company, 320
Beverwyck, 140
Bible society, albany county, 229
Bible, groesbeek, 249
Bird-stuffer, 225
Birmingham, 366
Births, marriages and deaths, 295
Births, quadruple, 349
Blacksmiths, 209
Black, J. R., 347
Blake, H., 362
Bleecker, rutger, 25
Bleecker, harmanus, 190, 276, 299, 353
Block and pump-makers, 209
Bloodgood, capt., 253
Board of trade, 41, 163, 320, 348
Board of supervisors, 322
Boarding houses, 209
Bogart, D. S., 130
Bone dealer, 225
Bonnet and straw goods, 225
Bonnet bleacher, 225
Book-binders, 209
Book-sellers and publishers, 210
Booksellers, 1772, 325
Boston, trade with, 46
Boston rail road, 311, 362, 365
Boston ferry, 345
Boot and shoe dealers, 210
Boot and shoe-makers, 210
Bowne, robert, sailed, 343
Bowling alleys, 210
Boyd's island, 139
Bradford, J. M., 89, 90
Bradt de norman, 139
Bradt, albert andriessen, de noorman, 15
Bradt, wm., 363
Brannon, james, 345
Brass-founders, 210
Breadstuffs received, 164
Bread, 266, 336
Brewery, 202, 205
Brewers, 210
Bricks, manufacture of, 158
Brick-makers, 210
Bridge over basin, 168, 349
" " hudson river
Britton, S. B., 135
Brock, S. A., 365
Brodhead documents, 344
Brokers, 210
Bronck, pieter, 23
Brown, J. C., 358
Brush-maker, 225
Buildings, 72
Builders, 210

Burgoyne, 256
Burgesses corps' excurs., 357
Burgesses corps, 318
Burgess, R. H., 357
Burglaries, 341 to 366
Burials, book of, 121
Burials, 355
Burial customs, 121
Burials, dutch church, 235
Burial ground, hallenbeck, 341, 346
Burnt district, 176
Burton, J. I., 346
Bush, S., 346
Business directory, 208-29
Butler, B. F., lecture, 162
Butler, J. W., 352
Butler, john, 353
Buttermilk creek, 146, 166
Cabinet-makers, 210
Cahill, john, 356
California, lecture on, 336
California company left, 342, 345
Caldwell, james, 330
Caldwell, wm., 76
Caldwell, wm., died, 168
Campbell, rev. W. H., 76
Campbell, J. N., 131
Camphene, 225
Canal bank, 33, 346, 352
Canal bank, 33, closed, 173
Canals, 310, 313
Canal opened, 348
Canal, closing of, 329
Canals, trade and commerce of, 9, closed, 182
Canal tolls, 163
Canal, erie, predicted, 301
Canal receipts, 164, 356, 365, 366
Canal boat, large load, 364, 365
Canadian invasion, 288
Canoes, 264, 274-5
Cap-makers, 210
Capitol, 307
Capital, removal of, 167
Carpenters and builders, 210
Carpetings, 210
Carpet weavers, 211
Carriage-makers, 211
Cartmen, 211
Carver, 225
Carroll, james, 360
Cassidy, C., 348
Cassidy, J. P., 355
Casting, large, 358
Castle island, 186
Catskill, see katskill
Cattle, stabled, 265
Cathedral, 161, 173, 358, 365
Cement, 212
Centennial anniversary, 335
Charter, 307

Charter election, 169
Charter officers, 37
Charity, public, 347
Charity, fire department, 164
Charcoal, 269
Chandler, 212
Chapel holy innocents, 349, 350
Chair-makers, 212
Change, meeting on, 347
Chemist, 225
Cherry valley pl'nk road, 361
Chief engineer elected, 163
China, glass, &c., 212
China, voyage to, 261
China tea sets, 261
Chiliderder, 351
Chimneys, 268
Cholera, 350 to 358
Cholera cases in july, 355
Cholera cases in aug., 357
Christian mutual benefit society, 41, 163
Churches, list of, 72
Churches, 315
Church, first in albany, 86
" stone, 88
" north dutch, 89
" south dutch, 182
" old lot sold, 90
" pulpit, 91
" ministers of, 91
" note of hand, 93
" records, 96
" baptisms, 96
" early members of, 97
" pasture, pat'nt of, 101
" pasture, sale of, 121
" patent, 165
" antiquities, 119
" collections, 120
" stone step, 120
" burial ground, 121
" opened, 165
" lots sold, 180
" lutheran, 122
" united presb., 132
" ger. ref. 124, 128
" ger. ev. lutheran, 129
" universalist, 135
" first presbyter'n, 130
"   " ministers, 130
"   " trustees, 131
"   " deacons, 131
"   " elders, 132
"   " reminis'ces, 132
" trinity, 132
Circus tent destroyed, 362
City bank, 317
City debt, 346, 366
City missionary, 318
City, prospects of, 330
City rail road sinking fund, 341
City taxes, see taxes

Index. 371

City tavern, 285
City finances, 48
City appointments, 169, 170
City and co. buildings, 71
City records, 103
Civil officers, 302
Civil engineer, &c., 225
Clark, ralph, 359
Clark, G. T., 349
Clark, james, died, 160
Clay, H., in Albany, 358
Clergy, list of, 35
Clergymen, 212
Clemshire, wm., 355
Clocks, 212
Closing of canals, 326
Clothing stores, 212
Clothes cleaner, 225
Cluett, P., 359
Coach painter, 225
Coach ware, &c., 212
Coal dealers, 213
Coal, 146, 165, 312, 361
Cobb, E., 349
Co-directors, 206
Cooymans, 145
Coffee factories, 212
Cohoes, 147
Cohoes village charter, 172
Cohoes rail road, 40, 168, 171, 349
Colonie, 140, 311
Colonie, regulations, 191
Cold days, 163, 165, 167, 169, 178, 181, 182, 244, 341, 342
Cole, W. B., 341
Columbia steamer up, 345
Colvard, philo, 365
Cold, 268, 329
Commercial bank, 33, 317
Common council, 59, 311
Common council, new, 347
Commission merchants, 212
Common schools, 366
Commercial despatch, 173
Commerce, ancient, 258, 260, 270
Combs and fancy goods, 226
Convicts, 166
Confectioners, 213
Constitution, adoption of, celebrated, 330
Convention, const., 330
Contribution bag, 90
Conveyances in 1796, 155
Conveyances in 1746, 274
Cook, capt. john, 167
Coopers, 213
Coorn, nicholas, 22, 190, 200
Coppersmiths, 213
Coroner, 225
Coroner, accident to, 170
Corn, large arrival, 159, 161
Corporation, lavish, 307
Corporations, &c., 317

Corsets, 225
Cotter, john, 351
Coughlin, 365
Counterfeiters arrested, 347
Counsellors, 213
Courtright, P., 341
Courtright, L., 343
County officers, 49
County taxes, 342
Counties, list of, 50, 55
County towns, distances, 313
County clerk fees, 366
County medical society, 318
Court, justices', 168, 172
Court, 337, 336
Crane, L. H., 345
Crape, import of, 323
Creditors, U. S., 282
Crier, 225
Crippen, john, 359
Crittenden, alonzo, 82
Criminal calendar, 161, 165, 177, 179
Curdy, J., 359
Curler, arent van, 15
Custom house, 46
Customs, ancient, 119
Cuyler, C. J., 352
Daguerreotypes, 214
Daly, michael, 345
Dam, jan jansen, 16
Daniels, warner, 341
Davenport, J. B., 349
Davis, W. A., 359
Days, length of, 55
Denn, capt., 261
Deals, exported, 266
Deaths, 295, 336
Debt, 48, 346
Debt, imprisonment, 323
De groff, O. G., 351
Delllus, G., 88
" deposed, 95
" salary subs'ed, 104
Delavan, H. W., 77
Democratic nominat'ns, 168, 360
Democratic convention, 159
" meeting, 161
Dentists, 36, 214
Donnlson, wm., 334
Depot, large, 174
De russy, alida, 345
De witt clinton engine company, 40
Dewey, O., 241, 349
Diamond, J. W., 352
Die sinker, 225
Diligent fire engine, 285
Directory, 1849, 25
Distances from albany to various points, 62 to 70, 313
Distillers, 214
Distins, 352

Diseases, 295
Dist. school celebration, 160, 172
Docks, 281
Documents, brodhead, 344
Dodge, H. H., 365
Dogs muzzled, 169
Dog law, 336
Dominie's house, 102, 121
Donnelly, P., 361
Donahue, john, 359
Dorr, alfred, 347
Douglas, D. B., 361
Draughtsman, 225
Dredger, &c., 225
Dress-makers, 214
Drouth, 265
Drugs, medicines, &c., 214
Drum-maker, 225
Drummond light, 364
Dry goods, 214
Dry goods, 1790, 322
Du Bois, G., 88
Durant, clark, 134
Dutch church 86, 269
" burials, 235
" 3d, 356
Dutchmen, 271
Dutchman, sunday, 351
Dutch parsimony, 307
Dyers, 215
Dyke, 46
Eagle engine company, 40
Easterbrook, 347
Eating houses, 215
Economy, 273
Eights, dr. J., 175, 343
Election, city, 347
Election returns, 364
Election, presidential, 180
Elkens, J. J., 139, 185
Ellison, rev. T., 285, 286
Elliott, H., 348
Elm tree, 284, 287
Emerson wm. B., 172
Emmet guards, 365
Emigration, 275
Emmons, E., 342
Empire wrecked, 349
English preaching, first, 121
Eng. first set. pastor, 121
English church, 269, 284-5
Engine companies, 319
Engine house, 74
" affray, 159, 162, 172, 174
Engineers' meeting, 341
Engravings, 215
Ensign, T., 358
Erie canal, prediction, 304
Estates of merchants, 271
Evans, david, 348
Evangelical luth. church, 122
Evening journal, 346
Exchange bank, 33, 317
Exchange co., albany, 39

Exchange company, 320
Execution place, tory, 290
Expenditures, city, 48
Expenses, 48, 311
Experiment. sloop, 261
Expresses. 215
Express albany morn'g, 159
Express routes, 12
Family rec. groesbeck, 247
Fancy goods, 215
Fancy box-maker, 225
Fargo F., 358
Far west, 275
Farnham, lewis, 342
Fashions, 323
Fassett, amos. 343
Fast, national, 355
Fay, dr., 341
Featherly. J. 345
Federalists, 330
Feed store, 225
Female academy, 352, 353
Ferries, 310, 336
Ferry-master, first, 22
Figurative map, 139
File cutters, 225
Finding stores, 215
Fink, fred. 342
Fink, elias, 356
Fine for calumny, 104
Fires, 159, 160, 162, 164, 166,
  168, 170, 171, 172, 173, 174,
  175, 177, 179, 180, 181, 182,
  341, 342, 343, 344, 346, 347,
  348, 350, 351, 352, 353, 356
Fire engines, 225, 285, 311
Fire law, new, 181
Fire department, 319
Fire departm't charities, 164
  " reorganized, 178, 181
Fire police, 319, 349
Fire, anniversary of, 356
Firemen's insurance co., 34
Fire brick, 215
First great west. turnpike, 41
First pres. church, 293
Fisk, francis, 344
Fish, hamilton, inaug. 341
Fisher, 361
Fisher, T. D. 363
Fishing tackle, 225
Flour, 159, 161, 162, 163, 178
Flour, large transport, 160
Flour arrival, 352, 356, 357, 362, 364, 365, 366
Flour dealers, 215
Flouring mills, 363
Florists and nurserymen, 215
Fog, 362
Foot race, 162, 179
Foot, ebenezer, 80
Forgery, 163, 171, 176, 348
Fort, 270, 284, 286, 287, 312
Fort on beeren island, 198-9

Fort hunter plank road, 321
Fort orange, 85, 187
Fort at albany, 139, 184
Foreigners' meeting, 169
Forwarding merchants, 215
Fourth july, 1796, 154
Fourth july, 172, 173, 352
Foundling, 347
Foxen kill, 146, 175
Frasier, adam, 352
Freeholders in 1720, 231
Frelinghuysen, 88, 113
Fresh fish, 215
Freshet, 163, 200
Friends society, 135
Frost, first, 159
Frost, 171, 172, 178
Frost, effects of, 265, 360
Fruit, 215
Fruits described, 265
Funeral ceremonies, 315
Fund, R. R. sinking, 341
Fur trade, 194, 197
Fur and caps, 215
Furniture ware-houses, 215
Furnaces and ranges, 226
Fuyck, 132, 140, 192
Gallery of fine arts, 39
Gallery built in church, 104
Gallup, albert, 46
Gardens, 216
Gardeners, 216
Gas-fitters, 216
Gas, death by, 342
Gas tank, accident, 180
Genesee valley, 275
Gent's furnishing stores, 216
German immigrants, 359
German language, 125, 129
Ger. ref'ed church, 124, 128
  " ev. luth. church, 129
Gerritsen, martin van bergen, 16
Gill, john, 364
Glen, sander leendertsen, 20
Globes, 216
Glovers, 216
Glue manufacturer, 226
Gootwater, ernestus, 123
Gold-beater, 226
Goodrich, horace, 80
Gough, J. B., 342
Gould, wm., 286
Grace church, 349
Grates, 267
Grains, 266, 360
Grate manufactory, 226
Grammar school, 74
Great fires, 170, 175
Great consistory, 89
Greatwestern turnpike road, 321, 349
Gregory, matthew, 285
Gregory, M., died, 172
Griffin, J. H., 159, 164

Grindstones, 226
Groesbeck, record, 240
Grocers, 216
Gross, samuel, 356
Ground frozen, 268
Guilderland, 145
Gun-smiths, 216
Gutter-spouts, 270, 314
Halibut, large, 169
Hallenbeck burial ground, 341, 346
Halo, 354
Halley, lecture, 343
Halloway, rev. wm., 356
Hamilton, gen., 257
Hammond, wells S., 343
Hanna, rev. W., 130
Hand, isaac P., 249
Hangman, 337
Hardware dealers, 219
Harris, judge, 347
Harned, S. W., 365
Harvey, L. Z., 352
Hartwick, J. C., 125, 127
  " seminary, 126
Harman, thos. W., died, 167
Hatred of albanians, 272-3
Hats, caps and furs, 219
Hayun, barent, 347
Hays, solomon, 353
Hay, 226
Health of city, 336
Hecker, baron, 359
Helderbergs, 146
Hendrick hudson, speed, 171
Herbs, 219
Hermans, john, 346
Herera, gen., 351
Hertgers, pieter, 22
Hibernian prov. society, 41, 320
High water, 163, 171, 268, 361, 364
High mass, 345
Higgins, C., 354
Hides and leather, 219
Hillman, wm., 357
Hochstrasser, paul, 128
Hogeboom, P., 359
Hogs, large, 344
Hogs, running at large, 349
Hogan, garret, died, 173
Holmes, H., 360
Holy innocents, chapel, 349, 350
Hooges, antonie de, 22
Horticultural articles, 219
  " premiums, 364
  " society, 344, 351, 359
Horses killed, 347
Horses drowned, 347, 351
Hosiery, 226
Hospitality, want of, 272
Hospital, 346

Hose depot, 358
Housatonic trains, 164, 343
Houses in albany, 1786, 85
Houses, 201, 269, 270, 311, 314, 316
Hot day, 350, 351, 352
Hudson river, 270, 324
Hudson river sloop, 153
Hudson river rail road, 359
Hudson, henry, sailed from amsterdam, 9
" in N.Y. harbor, 9
Hughes, 351
Humphrey, F., 347, 348
Hungarian emigrants, 365
Hun, thos., 168, 169
Husthouse, H., 350
Hydrant company, 40
Hydrant company dissolved, 350
Ice, 168, 341, 345, 363
Ice left, 168
Ice dealers, 219
Images, 226
Imprisonment for debt, 323
Income, city, 49, 172
Incorporated companies, taxes on, 342
Indian baptisms, 96
Indian treaty, first, 186
Indians cheated, 264, 271
Indian conferences, 274
India rubber goods, 226
Inhabitants, 266, 271, 314
Ink, 219
Insects in water, 268
Installation, 174, 182
Insurance companies, 34
Intelligence offices, 219
I. O. O. F., 45
Iolas, fireman, killed, 347
Ireland, 348
Ireland meeting, 171, 173, 174
Iron fence builders, 219
Iron foundery, 226
Island, 267, 312
Jacobsen, rutger, 19
Jail, 309, 316
Jansen, michel, 18
January thaw, 342
Jenkins, L., 356
Jersey blue propeller, 357
Jewish synagogues, 134
Jewelry, 219
Jowett, N. A., 351
Johnson, capt., 261
Joscelyn, C., 361
Journal, albany even'ng, 167
Junk shops, 219
Jury, grand, 352
Justices, 219
Justices' court, 163
Kalm, peter, 262
Kane, wm., 344
Katskill, 196, 202

Keeler, C., 343
Keeler, S., 361
Kennedy, dr., 353
Kidney, john, 346
Knowlton, J. W., 349
Knox incorporated, 145
Koeymans, barent pieterse, 17
Koorn, nicholaus, 22
" see coorn
Labbadie, jan., 16
Lace goods, 219
Lafayette, 335
Lafferty, D., 350
Lamps, 48, 366
Lancaster school, 74, 309, 312
Lansing, C. D. R., 357
Last day, 162
Law booksellers, 219
Leather dealers, 219
Lee, thos., 167
Legal restrictions, 189
Legislature, dinner to, 347
Legislature, 165
" adjourned, 169
Levings, N., 342
Lewis's tavern, 285
Lewis, B., 341
Liberty meeting, 170
Lightning, 355
Lights and shadows of traveling, 153
Linn, dr., 90
Linseed oil, 226
Liquors, wines, &c., 219
Lithographer, 226
Little basin, alarm bell, 346
Livery stables, 219
Living, 273, 315
Livingston, crawford, 162
Livingston, J. H., 86, 88, 89
Lock-smiths, 220
Looking-glass manf., 220
Low, warren, 347
Ludlow, rev. john, 81
Lumber, 220
Lumber inspector, 226
Lutheran church, 122
Lutherans persecuted, 122
" tolerated, 123
" first minister, 123
" first church in albany, 123
" cost of church, 125
" poor chest stolen, 127
Lyceum, nat. history, 312
Lydius street, 363
Lydius, B., 288
Lydius house, 288
Lydius, J., 88
" john henry, 113
Lyman, B., 354
Lynch, C., 343
Machinists, 220
Mackintosh, john, 349

Mahogany, 220
Mails in olden times, 56
Mail delayed, 360
Matze, 266
Malloy, R., 357
Malsters, 220
Manufacturers, 359
Manufacturing law, 160
Manners, 314
Marble manufactures, 220
Market, cattle, 309
Market, 178
Market lot, 309
Marriages, 295
Martin, J., 348
Martin, john, 362
Martin, rev. B., installed, 164
Martin gerritsen's island, 139
Marvin, wm., 349
Marvin, henry, 352
Mason, L. B., 135
Masons, 220
Masonic, 45
Mass, high, 345
Matson, J., 350
Mayors of albany, 25
Mayer, F. G., 122, 125
M'anley, M., 357
M'caler, 356
M'clellan, R., 322
M'closky, J., installed, 159
M'cotter, N., 357
M'culloch, james, 343
M'donald, john, 130, 337
M'grath, james, jr., 342
M'guire, thomas, 365
M'kenna, peter, 345
M'kenzie, george, 343
M'kown, michael, 341
M'laughlin, wm., 357
M'namara, 365
M'naughton, james, 365
M'pherson, lachlan, died, 163
Meals, 273
Mechanics' benefit soc., 42, 320
Mech. and farmers' bank, 32, 317, 318
Mechanics' school, 74
Mechanics, premiums, 364
Medical society, state, 165, 343
Med. society, albany co., 365
Medical college, 342, 360
Medicines, 220
Megapolensis, J., 21, 86, 192
" call of, 92
" agreem't with patroon, 93
Menagerie, 172
Merchants, 271
Merchants' stock, 1790, 322
Merchant, george, 278
Message, 165, 341
Messenger, albany, 319

Meteor, 167
Military, 44
Military visit, 173
Military encampment, 360
Military goods, 220
Militia officers 1790, 302
Mills' island, 267, 312
Miller, henry, 353
Miles, john, 133, 346
Mills, 201
Milliners, 220
Ministers dutch church, 91
Ministers presb. church, 130
Ministers declined, 274
Minutes of consistory, 91
Minerals, 146
Miss. sabbath school, 342
Mochrie, michael, 342
Mohawk ice, 345
Mohawk and hudson railroad, 40, 46, 141, 178, 321
Monkland, thomas, 353
Moore, john, 355
Morey, john D. 353
Morgan, thomas I, 361
Morgan, tobias, 353
Morrocco, 220
Morris, L. N. 181
Morton, J. 365
Mosher, G. M. 354
Mossop, G. 360
Moss, thomas, 353
Murphy, P. 350
Murtough, T. 349
Music teachers, 220
Musquitoes, 157
Mutual ins. company, 34, 321
Myndert, harman, 23
Nailor, 226
Nails, manufacture of, 330
Nail works burnt, 360
Navigation improved, 46
Navigation closed, 164
Neill, wm. 131
Neptune engine company, 40
New york state bank, 32
New scotland, 145
New netherland, first so called, 183
New world, 350, 355
New world, speed of, 353
Newton, Isaac, steam boat, 346, 348, 360
Newton's cor's omnibus, 161
Newman, H. A. 360
Newspaper depots, 221
Newspaper offices, 71, 221, 310
Nieuwenhuysen, 87
Night scavenger, 226
Noorman, albert andriessen de, 15, 139
Normal school, 84, 159, 169, 178, 297, 354, 359, 360
Northern winter, 328

Nott, eliphalet, 130
Notaries, 221
Nucella, 88
Nurses, 25, 221
O'brien, P. 366
O'conner, 365
Oculist, 226
Odd fellows' hall, 180
Officers, 302
Officers of the city, 38
Offices, &c. 73
Ogden, D. B. 353
Oil-cloth factories, 221
Oil, 226
Olive branch, 258
Old bunkers, 159, 178
Omnibus, newton's corners, 161
Opening of canals, 329
Optical instruments, 226
O'reilly, 359, 360
Oregon, 345, 348
Organ, first in albany, 128
Orphan fair, 342
Orphan asylum, 167
Osborne arrested, 343, 350
Osborn, john, 349
Ostrander, J. C. 343
Overslaugh, 304, 312
Oxen, large, 344
Oysters, 221
Pacey, edward, 355
Packard, N. R. 342
Page, D. P. 164
Page, david L. 85
Painters, 221
Paints, oils and glass, 221
Palisades, 137
Pangburns, 349
Paper hangings, 221
Paper warehouse, 221
Parks, 309
Parsimony, dutch, 307
Parsons, L. sprague, 82
Passage agents, 221
Pasture of dutch church, 101, 121
Pastor, petition for, 104
Patent of dutch church, 115
Patent of ch'h pasture, 101
Patern makers, 221
Patent agency, 226
Patterson, G. W. inaug. 341
Patterson, john, 341
Paving streets, 316
Peas, 266
Peelen, brandt, 15
Pelican, 275
Penitentiary, 149, 162, 167, 341, 342, 353
Pension agent, 226
Periodicals, 37
Personal estate, 342
Physicians, 37, 221
Piano fortes, 222

Pier question, 359
Pierce, dr. 344
Pilsbury, amos, 342
Plan of albany, 136
Plane makers, 222
Plank road, 167, 356, 360, 361
Planck, sheriff, 192
Plan of albany, 306
Plan of state street, 234
Platt, lydia, died, 159
Platt, ananias, 56
Plumbers, 226
Plumb level, 226
Pohlman, H. N. 125
Police, night, 48, 266
Pontifical high mass, 174
Poor, 48, 315, 342, 347, 355, 366
Poor, medical attendance, 165
Population, 312, 314
Porpesses, 267
Portrait painters, 222
Portuguese exiles, 347, 361
Porter houses, 222
Post offices, list of, 50
Post routes, 1848, 57
Post roads, 1797, 58
Postage, cheap system, 303
Post office, 335
Post, victor, 353
Potatoes, 266
Potter's ware, 222
Powder house, 309
Powers, john, 350
Preaching in english, 121, 125, 129
Presbyterian ch., first, 293
Presbyterian church, 130
" united, 132
" new, 161
" corner stone, 163
Premium articles, 359
Prentice, sartelle, 362
Pretty, sheriff, 285
Printers, 222
Printers on copper, 222
Printing establishments, 310
Printing office, southwick's, 285
Print. office, hosford's, 286
Print. office, webster's, 287
Prisoners, 348, 350
Produce, 222
Produce, large arrival, 163
Property depreciated, 307
Provision dealers, 223
Pruyn, R. H. 363
Pruyn, samuel, 342, 348
Public buildings, 71, 315, 316
Public places, offices, &c. 226
Public square, 309
Publications, 71

Index. 375

Pulpit, ancient, 91, 193
Punishments, 189
Quarantine, 257
Querk, M. 363
Quick trip of a sloop, 345
Quitman, gen. 165
Rail road to new york, 166
" albany and cohoes, 168, 171
" depot, 174
" speed, 178, 179
" mohawk and hudson, 46
" speed, do. 47
" boston, 341
" housatonic, 343
" car, novel, 348
Rain, 355, 356, 359, 360, 361, 362, 365
Rain storm, 174
Randall, S. S. 347
Rare bird, 275.
Real and personal est. 367
Real estate agents, 223
Real estate, 311
Recruits for mexico, 174
Redman, philo. 365
Refectories, 223
Ref. prot. dutch church, 86
Relief of fire sufferers, 177
Rensselaers-stein, 198-9
Rensselaerville, 145
Rensselaerwyck, settlers, 15
" colony of, 183
" purchased, 187
" codirectors, 206
" vested in van rensselaer family, 206
Rensselaerville pk. road, 360
Rennie, wm. 343
Reporter, 226
Revolutionary scene, 289
Revolutionary soldiers, 121
Reynolds, propeller, 349
Riot, 170, 352
Rivers, 146
River opened, 168
River closed, 165
River, hudson, 324
River low, 352
River, clos. and opening, 326
Robbery, 160, 161, 162, 163, 164, 165, 167, 168, 169, 170, 171, 172, 173, 175, 178, 179, 181
Roberts, capt. B. S. 168
Robinson, james, 359
Roe, J. R. 351
Romeyn, J. B. 131
Routes of travel from albany, 59
Rudes, jason, 343
Rum shops presented, 167
Russell, C. 353
Russell, R. C. 362

Rutgerson, ryckert, 19
Rutten kill, 146, 158
Ryan, john, 351
Rye, 266
Sabbath evening school, 79
Sabbath violations, 103
Sabbath in Schenectady, 104
Sabbath school mission, 342
Saddles, trunks and harness, 52, 223
Sail boat capsized, 350
Sail makers, 223
Salaries of officers, 190
Salmon, 355
Salt kettle, large, 358
Salutations, 270
Sandlake plank road, 320
Sanders, john, 284, 368
Sanford, wm. 358
Sargent, parker, 352
Sash makers, 223
Savings bank, 345
Saw filers, 223
Sax-horn performance, 352
Schaats, G. 87, 103
" agreement to preach, 84
" children, 95
" anneke, 164
Schenectady rail road, 321, 362
Schenectady turnpike company, 321
Schenectady aldermen, 321, 368
Schenectady children, freedom of, 368
Schermerhorn, jacob jansen, 22
Schermerhorn, J. L. 351
Schmidt, F. W. 129, 169
Schoharie plank road, 346, 356, 360
Schools, 74
School of 1785, 79
School appropriation, 79, 169
Schools, common, 48
School buildings, 48
School, union, 80
Schooner sunk, 352
Schoonmaker, john, 350
Schuyler, peter, mayor, 25, 37
Schuyler, philip, 250, 282
Schuylers, influence of, 140
Scoresby, 163
Scrafford, G. H. 315
Screw dock, 226
Seeders, 128
Seed stores, 223
Segers, cornelius, 22
Sentences, 336, 337
Servants, 191, 273
Settlers arrived, 189
Settlement, first, 312

Settlers, first, 315, 15
Seward nominated, 343
Sewer, hamilton street, 349
Sewing machine, 346
Sextons, 223, 355
Seymour, wm. 46
Seymour, R. 350
Shade manufacturer, 226
Sharts, john, eulogy, 173
Shaker donation, 181
Sheriff insulted, 166
Sheridan, D. 362
Shingles, 266
Ship stores, 226
Shipping, 311
Shipboy, thos. 286
Ship fever, 161
Ship chandler, 226
Shrove tuesday, 103
Sickles, james, 353
Signs, complaint, 350
Silk and worsted trimming, 226
Silver plater, 226
Silver smith, 226
Silver ware manufacture, 226
Simonds, C. W. 365
Simons, john, 359
Sisters of charity, 342
Skippers, 223
Slack, 358
Slater, 226
Slander case, 103
Sleighing, 164
Sloop of 1796, 153
Sloops, north river, 153, 310
Sloop, speed, 260, 345
Sloop sunk, 355
Sloop voyages, 260, 261
Smith, S. R. 135
Smith, G. 351
Smith, J. B. 354
Smith, jacob, 365
Smith, M. J., attacked, 167
Smith, caroline, 171
Snow, 165, 178, 181, 344
Snow, first, 362
Soap and candles, 223
Societies, 42
Soda manufacturers, 224
Soil, 315
Sons of temperance, 45
South america, steam boat, 355
South baptist church, 347
Southwick's printing office, 285
Southwick, solomon, 276
Special sessions, 347
Speedy voyages, 260, 345
Spencer, ambrose, 342, 349
Spencer, ambrose, died, 167
Sportsmans club formed, 172
Sprague, T. D. 360
Squire, S. 353

Staats, B. P. 363
Staats, abraham, 21, 123
St. andrew's society, 42
Statistics of county, 147
Stages in olden time, 66
State buildings, 71
State medical society, 165
State hall, 369
State hall fence, 361
State library donation, 343
State normal school, 297
  do   origin, 298
State street, 270
State street, plan of, 284
State prisoners, 166
Stationer, 226
Stafford, A. G. 352
Stansbury, A. J. 131
Staunton, G. W. 347
Standing committees, 39
Staves and lumber, 226
Steam boat, first up, 345
Steam boat landings, 177,341
Steam boat passengers, 343
  do delayed, 360, 362, 363
Steam boat speed, 170, 171, 353
Steam boat, 159
    " competition, 182
Steam propeller, 357
Steam propeller albany, 171
Steam propel. mohawk, 173
Steam propeller hartford, 179
Steam tug baltic, 169
Steam packets, 46
Steam feed mill, 226
Steam sawing and planing, 224
Steam boiler explosion, 176
Stevenson house, 283
Stewart, J. G. 357
St. john, M. 347
St. john's church, 358
Stone cutters, 224
Storm of wind, 316
Storm, 350
Stores, number of, 330
Stove dealers, 224
Stove works, 224
St. peter's church, 285
St. patrick, 345
St. patrick's, 169
Strakosh, 350
Streets, improvement of, 48
Streets, lanes and alleys, 26
Streams, 146
St. Vincent, festival, 174
Suckers, 361
Sunday dutchman, 351
Sunday school, 79, 163, 165
Sunday trains, 164
Sunday trade prohibited, 103
Supervisors, board of, 322
Supervisors, legislators, 352

Surgical instruments, 226
Surveyors, 226
Sweep, 226
Swiss emigrants, 171
Synagogues, 134, 163, 170
Synagogue, 347
Synod of albany, 360
Taggart, rev. mr. 354
Tailors and drapers, 224
Tailors' prices, 36
Tailoresses, 224
Tallow chandlers, 226
Talcott, D. W. 351
Tarbell, N. 344
Tarolinta, 342
Taxes, 341, 342, 362, 366, 365, 367
Taylor, john, 169
Taylor, zach., in albany, 358
Taylor, gen. Z. elected, 180
Teachers, 224
Teachers of dancing, 224
Teachers, scarcity, 330
Teacher of french, 226
Tea dealers, 226
Teall, E. M. 347
Telegraph, 164, 165, 180, 341, 345, 350, 359, 360
Temple, col., returned, 176
Ten broeck mansion, 173
Ten eyck, C. A. 350
Terbush, 360
Theatre performances, 337
Thermometer, 328, 341, 344, 350, 351, 352, 354
Thomas, E. 359
Thompson, richard, 169
Tide, 268, 310
Tierney, O. 356
Tin, plate and sheet iron workers, 224
Tobacco, snuff and segars, 225
Tobacco establishment, 239
Tolls, 163
Tolls, canal, reduced, 346
Topp, john, 344
Tory execution place, 290
Tow, large, 366
Town hall, 269
Towns, list of, 50
    " incorporated, 145
    " population 1790, 142
Townsend, mrs. john, 356
Townsend's furnace, 358
Townsend, dr. C. D., died, 164
Tow boat haul, 162, 168, 174, 179, 181
Tract society, 43
Trade and commerce of canals, 9
Traveling routes, 61
Treaty, norman's kill, 186
Treadwell, C. 352

Trinity church, 342, 347, 365
Trip to new york 1797, 70
Trotting match, 179, 180
Trotter, mrs. 353
Troy road travel, 360
Truesdell, martin, 354
Tryon, gov., in albany, 290
Tubbs, creotus, 349
Turner, 226
Turnpike companies, 41
Type and stereotype founders, 225
Umbrellas, 225
Undertakers, 226
Universalist church, 138
Unitarian soc. 341, 349, 354
United states creditors, 282
Upholsterers, 225
Utica and schenectady R. R. 321
Valentines, 156
Van alstyne, M. 346
Van benthuysen, O. R. 356
Van brunt, R., installed, 182
Van curler, 195, 205
Vander donck, 21, 192, 195
Van driessen, 88
Vanderlip, elias, died, 176
Vanderheyden palace, 278
Van deusen, L. 366
Van es C. H. 21
Van housen, J. B. 357
Van loon, charles, died, 162
Van ness, john, 346
Van olinda, capt. killed, 159, 173
Van rensselaer medal, 76
    " manor purchase, 139
    " N. 87, 103
    " nicholas, 168, 204
    " anna, 203
    " jeremias, 204
    " kilinen, 203
    " S., 76
    " phillip S., 287
    " kilian, 139
    " K. K., 286
Van schaick, gooson, gerrittson, 19
Van schee, C. 88
Van schelluyne, R. 347
——— Mrs. R. D. 347
Van Wagoner, 350
Variety stores, 225
Vas, petrus, 88
Vessels in port, 159, 162
Vessels, numb. in port, 260
Victuallers, 225
Vincent st., festival of, 174
Vines, 267
Volunteers returned from mexico, 174
Voorzingers, 121
Vote, county, 364
Voyages, speedy, 260

Wager, C. J. 352
Wagoner, W. H. 135, 182
Wainwright, D. C. 355
Walker, Willard, died, 165
Walter, C. 360
Wallace, T. 357
Wallace, M. 360
Wall, P. 361
Wampum, 271
Ward assessors, abol. 346
Ward, isaac, 343
Ward boundaries, 29
Ware, curtis, 345
Washington monument. 160
" birthday, 166
Wasson, 349
Watch, 48
Watches, jewelry and plate, 225
Water question, 362, 365
Water works com. 40, 365
Water vote, 180
Watervliet incorporated, 145
Weather fine, 162
Weather, 342, 343, 345, 359
Webster corner, 287
Webb J. H. died, 159
Weed, H. R. 131
Weigher and measurers, 226
Well water, 268, 315, 316
Welch, B. 349
Welch, 351
Welch, B. T. 180
Weld's travels, 153

Wemp, jan barentsen, 22
Wendell house, 280
Wendell, peter, 362
Wesepe, gysbert cornelissen, 23
Westerlo incorporated, 145
Westerlo, E. 88, 118
West india ventures, 260
Western plank road, 319
Whales, 200
Whelpley, H. J. died, 161
Wheat, 357
Wheel-wrights, 225
Wheeler, luther, 348
Whig convention, 159, 178
Whig majority, 169
Whig meeting, 162, 173, 176, 177
Whig torchlight procession, 180
Whig ticket elected, 363
Whipple, wm. 348
White-smith, 226
White, nathaniel, 356
White-washer, 226
Whitney, isaac, 356
Widower tax, 161
Wilmot proviso, 160
Wilson, B. 357
Wilson, roswell, 354
Williams, henry, 346
Williams, A. 357
Williamson, J. D. 135
Williamstadt, 140

Willemsen banished, 204
Willer, charles H. 348
Wine, cider and vinegar, 225
Wines, teas, &c. 225
Wines, 347
Winter, northern, 328
Winter, remarkable, 148
Winter, severe, 200
Winters, A. J. 315
Winne, george, 351
Winne, jellis, jr. 344, 353
Winne, wm B. died, 165
Wiswal, thomas, 351
Witt, J. C., 352
Wooden ware, &c., 225
Wood measurer, 226
Wood buildings prohibited, 176
Wool, gen. 182
Worth, general, 177, 348, 365
Wool, 225
Worcester, G. W. 360
Wordon, alexander, 352
Working men's conv. 360
Worsted store, 226
W. stockbridge R. R. 321
Wyckoff, jane K. died, 165
Wyncoop, pieter, 196-9
Yachts, albany, 264
Yankee notions, 226
Yates, john van ness, 286
York, J. 360
Young mens' association, 161, 318, 343

Additional appendix follows

TABLE No. 6.

CHANGES IN NAMES OF STREETS IN ALBANY.

The following Table has been prepared in the Office of the City Engineer. It is Arranged Alphabetically by Present Street Names. The Date of the Change is Given wherever it is Known with Certainty.

Present name.	Former name.
Albany street (changed February 13, 1871)	Albany avenue.
Arch	Beaver lane.
Arch	Johnson.
Ash Grove place (Trinity place to Grand, changed April 19 and May 4, 1869)	Westerlo.
Bleecker (former name in use as late as 1831)	Bass street or lane.
Broad (former name still in use in 1831)	Malcolm, Schuyler farm.
Broadway (south of State street)	South Market.
Broadway (north of Clinton avenue)	Street leading to ye mills (1763).
Broadway (north of Clinton avenue)	Road to the mill.
Broadway	Handalaer's (traders).
Broadway (State to Gansevoort)	Court.
Broadway (north of State)	Brewer's.
Broadway (north of State)	Cow.
Broadway	Market.
Broadway (Columbia to Clinton avenue)	Watervliet.
Broadway (north of State)	North Market.
Broadway (changed February 13, 1871)	Troy road.
Canal (changed from Howe to Fox, September 11, 1790)	Howe.
Canal	Fox.
Capitol park	Capitol square.
Central avenue	Albany and Schenectady turnpike.
Central avenue	Schenectady turnpike.
Central avenue (changed July 15, 1867)	Bowery
Chapel	Barrack or barack.
Charles (changed March 19, 1877)	Johnson alley.
Chestnut	Chesnut.
Clinton avenue (changed May 4, 1863)	Patroon.
Clinton street	Church.
Columbia	New.
Columbia (west of North Pearl)	Oak.
Columbia place (north of Columbia, unofficial)	Eagle.
Congress, Capitol place to Swan (changed August 6, 1860)	Spring.
Dallius street, Madison avenue to Hudson avenue (changed February 15, 1904)	Union.
Daniel	Beaver.
Daniel	Wendell.
Daniel	Daniels.
Dean	Water.
Dean (changed November 6, 1826, Steuben to Hudson)	Dock.
Delaware avenue	Delaware turnpike.
Division	Bone lane.
Dove (changed September 11, 1790)	Warren.
Dudley avenue (west of North Pearl street)	North Ferry.
Eagle (changed September 11, 1790)	Duke.
Elberon place	New.
Elk (changed September 11, 1790)	Queen.
Elk (shown on Dutch church map from Clinton avenue to Lark street as)	Spruce.
Elm (changed to Otter, September 11, 1790)	Pitt.
Elm and Westerlo	Otter, formerly Pitt.
Elm	Westerlo
Emmet (changed to Laughlin, February 13, 1871)	Broadway avenue.
Emmet, formerly Broadway avenue (changed September 22, 1879)	Laughlin.
Exchange	Mark lane.
Fourth avenue (changed January 20, 1873)	Nucella or Neucella.
Franklin (changed March 30, 1828)	Vreelenghuysen or Frelinghuysen.
Fulton	William.

TABLE No. 6—(Continued).

Present name.	Former name.
Gansevoort	South.
Garfield place, Colby street to Watervliet avenue (changed September 23, 1901)	Second.
Genesee (changed February 13, 1871)	Watervliet avenue.
Grand	Hallenbeck, Halenbake or Hollenbake.
Grant avenue (changed September 10, 1903)	Grant.
Green	Vandreisen.
Green	Greene.
Hamilton	New.
Hamilton, from Broadway east	Kilby lane.
Hawk (changed September 11, 1790)	Hawke.
Herkimer	Van Schee.
High	South High.
Howard	Luther or Lutheran.
Howard (Pearl to Lodge)	Nail or Nail alley.
Hudson avenue (changed March 4, 1872)	Hudson, formerly Buffaloe.
Hudson avenue (east of Broadway)	Spanish.
Hudson avenue (changed September 11, 1790, to Buffaloe)	Quiter.
Hudson avenue (changed from Quiter, September 11, 1790)	Buffaloe.
James	Middle lane or Middle alley
Jefferson	Herkimer or Herkemer.
John (changed about 1822)	Sturgeon lane.
Judson	Second.
Kenmore place (north side from North Pearl to Chapel, unofficial)	Columbia.
Knox	Swallow, formerly Gage.
Knox (north of Clinton avenue)	First.
Knox (changed to Swallow, September 11, 1790, and Swallow changed to Knox, July 17, 1869)	Gage.
La Fayette (changed to Fayette, April 25, 1825)	Sand.
La Fayette	Fayette.
Lancaster (changed to Tiger, September 11, 1790)	Predeaux.
Lancaster, formerly Predeaux	Tiger, Tigar or Tyger.
Lake avenue	Pidgeon.
Lake avenue (south of Western avenue, changed October 2, 1882)	Perry.
Lark (changed September 11, 1790)	Johnson.
Leonard place (Delaware avenue to Lark, unofficial)	Warren.
Lexington avenue (changed September 4, 1876)	Snipe, formerly Schenectade.
Lexington avenue (changed to Snipe, September 11, 1790)	Schenectade.
Liberty	Cow lane.
Livingston avenue (changed April 21, 1879)	Lumber.
McPherson terrace (west of Judson, unofficial)	Clinton avenue.
Madison avenue (changed to Wolf, September 11, 1790)	Wolfe.
Madison avenue (changed May 20, 1867)	Lydius, formerly Wolf.
Madison place, Eagle to Philip (changed July 1, 1867)	Madison avenue.
Maiden lane	Rom (rum).
Mohawk (changed February 13, 1871)	Hudson River avenue.
Monroe	Van Schaaick.
Montgomery, Quackenbush to Livingston avenue (changed January 22, 1827)	Marsh.
Mosher street (changed November 12, 1900)	Rose.
Mulberry	Spruce lane.
Myrtle avenue	Mink.
Myrtle avenue	West Ferry.
Myrtle avenue	Ferry.
Northern boulevard, State street to Livingston avenue (changed April 2, 1909)	Knox.
North Pearl	Orchard.
North Pearl street, North Albany (changed February 13, 1871)	North Pearl avenue.
North Pearl (from Columbia north to Pleasant street)	Pearl.
Norton	Church lane.
Norton	Store lane.
Ontario	Sparrow.
Ontario (north of Clinton avenue)	Fourth.
*Orange (changed to Hare, September 11, 1790)	Wall.
*Orange (formerly Wall)	Hare.

*Minutes of the Common Council, 1878, page 70, letter from Horatio Seymour relative to proposed change of name.

DEPARTMENT OF PUBLIC WORKS.

TABLE No. 6—(Concluded).

Present name.	Former name.
Park avenue (changed to Mink, September 11, 1790)....	Monckton.
Park avenue..	Johnson.
Park (former name in use as late as 1845)...............	Capitol.
Park View terrace (between Lexington avenue and Robin street, unofficial)....................................	Madison avenue.
Plum...	Plumb.
Pruyn (changed to Denniston, June 16, 1834)............	Embargo alley.
Pruyn (changed from Embargo alley, June 16, 1834)....	Denniston.
Quail..	Turkey.
Quail (north of Clinton avenue)..............................	Third.
Quay...	Water, formerly Dock.
Robin (changed to Duck, September 11, 1790)...........	Schoharie.
Robin (formerly Schoharie)....................................	Duck.
Second avenue (changed January 20, 1873)...............	Whitehall road or avenue.
Second..	Elizabeth.
Seneca (changed April 18, 1892).............................	Ontario or Ontario square.
Sherman (changed February 15, 1869).....................	Sand.
Sheridan avenue (changed May 21, 1900)..................	Canal.
South Ferry..	Ferry.
South Lansing...	Lansing.
South Lansing...	Herring lane.
South Pearl...	Cow lane.
South Pearl...	Washington.
South Pearl (from Gansevoort street to Prentice's line, June 18, 1877)..	Albany and Bethlehem turnpike.
South Pearl (from Gansevoort street to Prentice's line, changed June 18, 1877)..................................	Bethlehem turnpike.
State..	Youker's (gentlemen's).
State (changed to Deer, September 11, 1790)............	Prince.
State (still in use 1814, formerly Prince)..................	Deer.
Steamboat square..	The Watering Place.
Steuben...	Stuben.
Swan (changed September 11, 1790).......................	Boscawen.
Swinton (accepted and changed March 1, 1897).........	Maple.
Ten Broeck place, Ten Broeck to Swan (changed September 18, 1876)...	Third.
Ten Broeck (changed July, 1831)............................	High.
Third avenue (changed January 20, 1873).................	Van Vechten.
Third..	John.
Trinity place (changed from Broad, October 20, 1862)..	Davidson.
Trinity place (changed October 20, 1862, to Davidson, and June 11, 1869)..	Broad.
Union..	Grass lane.
Washington avenue (changed to Lion, September 11, 1790)...	King.
Washington avenue (former name King)..................	Lion.
Washington avenue (former name still used in 1815)...	Washington.
Water..	Quay.
Water (Orange to Columbia in 1803).......................	River or Dock.
West (changed June 1, 1868).................................	De Witt.
Westerlo..	Kane.
Westerlo..	Elm.
Westerlo..	Pitt.
Western avenue (changed June 27, 1865)..................	Great Western turnpike.
Van Woert (west of Broadway)...............................	Lawrence.

www.ingramcontent.com/pod-product-compliance
Lightning Source LLC
Chambersburg PA
CBHW081344230426
43667CB00017B/2714